Far Distant Ships

Far Distant Ships

An Official Account of
Canadian Naval Operations
in World War II

JOSEPH SCHULL

Published in 1991 by Stoddart Publishing Co. Limited
895 Don Mills Road, 400-2 Park Centre, Toronto, Canada M3C 1W3

Republished by arrangement with Helen Gougeon Schull and with permission of the Minister of National Defence.

First Published in 1950 by Authority of the Minister of National Defence
King's Printer
Ottawa

Published in hardcover by Stoddart Publishing Co. Limited in 1987

www.stoddartpub.com

To order Stoddart books please contact General Distribution Services
Tel. (416) 213-1919   Fax (416) 213-1917
Email cservice@genpub.com

10 9 8 7 6 5 4 3 2

National Library of Canada Cataloguing in Publication Data
Schull, Joseph, 1910-1980.
Far distant ships: an official account of Canadian naval operations in World War II
Includes indexes.
ISBN 0-7737-6267-1
1. World War, 1939-1945-Naval operations, Canadian.
I. Title.
D779.C2S27 2001   940.54'5971   C2001-901685-9

U.S. Cataloging in Publication Data
Available from the Library of Congress

Cover Illustration: David Craig
Cover Design: Brant Cowie/ArtPlus Limited

THE CANADA COUNCIL   LE CONSEIL DES ARTS
FOR THE ARTS   DU CANADA
SINCE 1957   DEPUIS 1957

*We acknowledge for their financial support of our
publishing program the Canada Council, the Ontario Arts
Council, and the Government of Canada through the
Book Publishing Industry Development Program (BPIDP).*

Printed and bound in Canada

In the writing of this volume the author has been given full access to relevant official documents in possession of the Department of National Defence; but the inferences drawn and the opinions expressed are those of the author himself, and the Department is in no way responsible for his reading or presentation of the facts as stated.

The Far Distant Ships

*"Those far distant, storm-beaten ships upon
which the Grand Army never looked, stood
between it and the dominion of the world."*
—*ALFRED THAYER MAHAN.*

Mahan was writing of the army of Napoleon and the
ships of Nelson. Yet his words apply unchanged to the war
which began a hundred and thirty-four years after Trafalgar.
When Hitler at the summit of his power looked westward
from a conquered Europe, the long line of the Atlantic convoy and the grey menace of the Home Fleet rose, invisible
and implacable, the barrier he was never to surmount.

Sea power made the conquest of the British Isles an
essential for the mastery of Europe and a key to world rule.
And sea power made that conquest an impossibility. Dingy,
unseen tankers brought in oil for the Spitfires and Hurricanes
over seas held open by the Royal Navy. Cargoes of food and
supplies, rifles and cannon for the beaten armies returning
from Dunkirk, came in by sea. Thereafter sea power—of the
United States and Canada and of other nations as well as
Britain, sea power moving both on wings and keels—made
possible the gathering of mighty resources for the offensive.
Sea power bridged the gulf between the old world and the
new; linked farms and mines and factories, laboratories and
blast furnaces and training camps, with the battlefronts. Sea
power was the means of translating strength into accomplish-
ment; the ability to mobilize and concentrate and thrust at
the chosen time and at the vital point.

This book deals with the Canadian contribution to
Allied sea power. On the Atlantic, throughout the longest and
most crucial struggle of the war, Canada's navy grew to be a
major factor. In almost every other naval campaign her ships

or men were represented; playing frequently an obscure, sometimes a brilliant part. Their work was a share—and no more than a share — of the national effort. The men of the merchant ships wrote an epic which will not be forgotten while the nation remembers its past; and men toiling ashore performed daily impossibilities. The story of our airmen and of our soldiers has already been told, in part. This book is written in comradely remembrance of them all. It may serve to demonstrate, however inadequately, the importance to this nation of the war at sea; to show how near to our lives and interests were "those far distant, storm-beaten ships."

CONTENTS

CHAPTER FOUR

CHAPTER FIVE

CHAPTER SIX

CHAPTER TEN

CHAPTER ELEVEN

ILLUSTRATIONS

MAPS AND DIAGRAMS

Maps by

FAIRBAIRN ART STUDIOS, OTTAWA

NOTE

This summary of Canadian naval operations in the Second World War was commissioned by the Minister of National Defence. For its preparation all records of the naval service have been made available to the writer, as well as much preliminary work done by officers of the Naval Historical Section under the direction of Doctor Gilbert N. Tucker.

Sources include the logs and reports of proceedings of individual ships, the monthly reports on anti-submarine warfare issued by the Admiralty and the Canadian navy, and the official battle summaries compiled by the Admiralty on the larger campaigns and actions. Officers and men who took part in some of the incidents described have also been consulted. "The Fuehrer Conferences," a compilation made by the Admiralty since the war's end of minutes taken at Hitler's meetings with his naval staff, has given useful information on German plans and general naval policy.

The chapters dealing with the Neptune operation and the sections on the landings in North Africa, Sicily, Italy and Southern France are based on the reports compiled by Lieutenant James George from orders, signals, records of proceedings and from interviews with hundreds of officers and men. From an equally exhaustive report prepared by Lieutenant Elizabeth MacLean, W.R.C.N.S., much of the account of the Battle of the Atlantic has been written. Lieutenants Thomas Dale, Freeman Tovell and John Richardson have supplied other material; and free use has also been made of the accounts contributed anonymously to naval publications by men who took part in some of the actions described.

The manuscript has been generally reviewed by officers of the naval service; but the revisions suggested by them have dealt with points of detail or questions of fact. No restrictions have been placed either on the selection of material or on the interpretation of events. It is perhaps hardly necessary to add that none of these officers, nor the historical section, nor the naval service can be held responsible for the use made of the material supplied; and that the errors, omissions and general shortcomings of the work are my own.

JOSEPH SCHULL.

CHAPTER ONE

Eve of Battle

In the closing days of August 1939 the Chief of the Naval Staff was instructed to provide for the seaward defence of Canada, in view of "a state of apprehended war." His duties, as outlined in the directive, were:

(A) The defence of Canadian sea-borne trade: to be effected by the provision of forces placed in positions from which they can counter threatened attacks upon shipping; and the provision of auxiliary minesweeping and anti-submarine vessels in Canadian waters.

(B) Co-operation with the Army and Air Force in defence of the coasts.

It must have seemed a formidable assignment. The half-continent he was charged to defend fronted broadly upon two oceans and was accessible with difficulty from a third. Inward to its very vitals ran a deep-gashed seaway which would bear with wide impartiality the ships of enemy or friend. About a fifth of the wealth flowing in the nation's veins was fed to it by ocean freighters moving, vital and vulnerable, everywhere on "the indivisible sea."

Canada's naval forces consisted of six fairly modern destroyers, five small minesweepers and two training vessels, of which one was a sailing ship. There was a naval base at Esquimalt, reasonably well fitted out by peacetime standards; and another at Halifax, on the immediately threatened coast, which was in less satisfactory condition. Personnel consisted of 145 officers and 1,674 men, most of them thoroughly trained and seasoned by periods of service in the Royal Navy. On the retired list subject to recall were nine officers.

Our lake, river and ocean trade provided a small reserve of merchant seamen, whose officers could navigate and handle a ship with any man, but to whom gunnery, signals and every technique of naval war were unattempted

1

mysteries. Centred around twenty-one Divisions in the larger cities was the Royal Canadian Naval Volunteer Reserve—a body of amateur enthusiasts whose training for the most part had consisted of two or three annual fortnights in naval ships. In British Columbia there was the recently formed Fishermen's Reserve, made up of small-boat men, whose knowledge of coastal waters was valuable, but whose determined independent of outlook made them difficult naval material. It was also known that there were in Canada, scattered among many localities and engaged in every variety of occupation, a number of retired officers, petty officers and men of the Royal Navy. The value of this hidden asset was to be a most comforting discovery in the near future, but for the moment it figured in no calculations. Altogether, including permanent force and reserves, the navy had a paper strength of 366 officers and 3,477 men.

Its operations were directed from a suite of three dingy offices in one of Ottawa's older public buildings. Sitting desk-to-desk in these airless cabins by the Rideau were the ten members of the recently expanded Naval Staff.

Rear Admiral Percy W. Nelles, Chief of the Naval Staff, had been one of Canada's first group of six naval cadets. He had received his preliminary training in *Canada,* a fisheries protection vessel at Halifax; and had gone from there to *H.M.S. Dreadnought* for experience with the Royal Navy. He had served in British ships during the first World War and later had commanded destroyers and a cruiser. He had held his existing appointment since 1934 and had been promoted from Commodore to Rear Admiral in 1938.

Of his staff, two men, supervising finance and the procurement of supplies, were civilians. A third, who formed the only direct link with the Admiralty, was the Royal Navy officer loaned in accordance with established practice to act as Director of Naval Intelligence. The others were Canadian permanent force officers, career men, seasoned and indoctrinated by considerable periods of service in the Royal Navy. They were all comparatively junior; none of them could lay claim to wide administrative experience; and they were reluctantly ashore. Four were destined to return briefly to seagoing commands. One would go down with his ship in mid-Atlantic. For the most part, however, not only they but some of the other officers now in command of ships would have to relinquish the first ambition of a seaman in favour of the demands for organization and direction from Canada, Newfoundland and the United Kingdom.

They were to be faced with responsibilities which might well have daunted them, had the pattern of future events been unrolled at that time. The one obvious and specific qualification which all shared at the moment was that they were available. Another, which was to become apparent as time went on, was the ability to improvise under stress. They had, perhaps, a certain breadth of outlook where naval affairs were concerned because their experience had been deliberately varied. It might also be claimed that "exigencies of the service" had given them some peculiar advantages for the present task. Canadian naval officers were forced to cultivate a certain resourcefulness and ingenuity because they had always to make do with less than was required.

The history of their service was a brief one; politics-bedevilled in places, always overshadowed by financial stringencies, but not entirely lacking in colour. Mainly, perhaps, it reflected the attitude of a country growing to nationhood, claiming nationhood, but curiously reluctant to face the responsibilities which history and geography were thrusting upon it.

During the forty years following Confederation, Canada had no navy and did not wish to think of one. We were building railroads, opening up the hinterlands of the country, developing infant industries. The seas about us were broad and protective and Britannia ruled them.

There had been one hint, in 1880, of an awareness of naval needs. A dispatch from the Governor General to the Colonial Secretary had suggested that Canada "would not be averse to instituting a ship for training purposes if the Imperial Government would provide the ship." To the restrained enthusiasm of this proposal the Admiralty had responded with appropriate generosity. *Charybdis,* an ancient steam corvette, was at that time limping homeward from the China Station. The Canadian Government could have her.

When *Charybdis* arrived in the United Kingdom it was discovered that her boilers were worn out. Canada paid for their replacement. The ship was then coaxed and coddled across the Atlantic by a redoubtable Captain Scott, R.N., retired. Upon arrival in Saint John, *Charybdis* broke loose from her moorings in a gale and damaged much of the shipping in harbour. She had hardly been secured, and the clamour of aggrieved shipowners had not died down, when two Saint John citizens, attempting to come on board, fell through the rotting wood of her gangplank and were drowned. It was sufficient naval experience for the Canadian Government of that time. The wreck was towed from Saint John and turned over to unwelcoming authorities of the Royal Navy. *Charybdis* became a gruesome memory, a political Flying Dutchman which heaved over the horizon when any naval proposal was advanced during the next thirty years.

By 1909, however, the clatter of shipyards in Kiel and Wilhelmshaven began to drown out the cries of "Charybdis" when discussion turned to the sea. There was developing in Germany an actual threat to British supremacy, and the unthinkable had now to be thought of. What would happen if the Imperial Navy ever ceased to control the seaways to all the markets of the world?

The answer to that question held so many ominous possibilities that in 1909 Parliament passed a resolution stating that the Canadian Government would "cordially approve of any necessary expenditure designed to promote the speedy organization of a Canadian naval service in co-operation with and in close relation to the Imperial Navy." The resolution was followed in 1910 by a bill which provided for the establishment of a Naval Service, a Naval Board and

4

a Naval College. A programme was introduced calling for the construction of five cruisers and six destroyers. The ships were to be built in Canada, if possible, and in time of crisis might be placed at the disposal of the British Government.

Royal assent was given to the Naval Service Act on May 4, 1910, and on that day the Canadian Navy came into existence. A year later by command of the King it was designated the Royal Canadian Navy. Rear-Admiral C. E. (later Sir Charles) Kingsmill, a Canadian who had had a long career with the Royal Navy, became Director of Naval Service. The Royal Naval College of Canada was founded at Halifax in 1911. Canadian builders were invited to submit tenders for the construction of the new ships, and in the meantime two old cruisers, *Niobe* and *Rainbow*, were purchased from the British Government.

That was for many years the peak of our naval effort; and it was a peak which remained for the most part visionary. Parliament had passed the naval resolution of 1909 and the Naval Service Act of 1910 with a rare show of unanimity, and in doing so had reflected the general uneasiness of the country over our naval impotence. Now, however, the atmosphere was changed. Parliament and the nation were divided, and not entirely along party lines, over the form our defence measures should take.

The growing urgency of the need was recognized, but a powerful body of opinion favoured contributions to the Imperial Navy for the building of dreadnoughts rather than a Canadian building programme. The proposals stirred up deep problems of Dominion-Imperial relations; and the result of much debate and many negotiations was no ships. The tenders for building the five cruisers and six destroyers grew yellow in the pigeonholes of the impecunious Naval Service; *Niobe* and *Rainbow* were allowed to become inactive; the personnel of the navy reached and remained at a grand total of 336 officers and men.

Yet there was vitality even in that tiny nucleus. When war broke out in 1914, *Niobe* and *Rainbow* went back into

5

service and did useful patrol work. Under command of Captain Walter Hose—later to become the second Chief of the Naval Staff—a fleet of trawlers and small craft carried out minesweeping and anti-submarine operations in coastal waters. A flair for spectacular negotiation, unusual in the ordinary conduct of Canadian affairs, was evidenced when the Premier of British Columbia purchased with no authority and with provincial funds two submarines which were building in Seattle for the Chilean Government. The submarines were moved secretly by night out of Seattle harbour, sailed to a point off Esquimalt and there turned over by the builders to a retired submarine officer of the Royal Navy, who arrived in a launch, bearing the certified cheque of the Province of British Columbia for $1,500,000.

In all of Canada at that time there were discovered only two men who had ever served in submarines. One was the officer who had taken possession of the boats, Lieutenant-Commander Bertram Jones, R.N., retired. The other, Lieutenant Adrian Keyes, R.N., retired, was turned up a day or so later, quite accidentally, by the Chief of the Naval Staff himself, who was in the happy but harried predicament of any unexpectant father suddenly presented with twins.

Amazingly enough, the submarine transaction proved in the event thoroughly sound. Volunteer crews were recruited immediately and trained by the two officers through memorable days and nights. Torpedoes were obtained, the boats were taken to sea, submerged and brought to the surface with what soon became uneventful efficiency. They patrolled the west coast for nearly three years and although their warlike qualities were not put to the test, the atmosphere of security they provided was well worth the cost.

During the war the personnel of the navy reached a total of six thousand officers and men. Seventeen hundred Canadian reservists went on service with the Royal Navy; 598 Probationary Flight officers were enrolled in the Royal Naval Air Service and 43 Surgeon-Lieutenants went from Canada to British ships.

After the war the navy was demobilized with enthusiastic haste. By 1922 it was back to a total of 366 officers and men. The Royal Naval College was closed. Pay was poor and there was no pension system. Prospects seemed bleak indeed.

Even in the leanest years, however, the idea that Canada should have a navy was pretty generally accepted. Between 1920 and 1922 the cruiser *Aurora*, two destroyers and two submarines—all gifts of the Royal Navy—were kept in commission. *Aurora* and the submarines were sold in 1922; but when the destroyers *Patrician* and *Patriot* reached the end of useful service in 1928 they were replaced by *Champlain* and *Vancouver*. Two more destroyers, *Saguenay* and *Skeena*, were acquired from the United Kingdom in 1931, the first two men-of-war built specifically for the Canadian navy; and in 1937 *Fraser* and *St. Laurent* arrived. Meanwhile *Vancouver* and *Champlain*, as well as four minesweepers, which had been in service since 1922, were paid off and four new minesweepers and a small training ship were built in Canada. *Ottawa* and *Restigouche* were acquired in 1938. By August 1939, in addition to the sweepers and lesser craft, the naval force consisted of six destroyers, *Saguenay*, *Skeena*, *Fraser*, *St. Laurent*, *Ottawa* and *Restigouche*, each displacing about 1500 tons.

The German navy—the force with which we had now entered into "a state of apprehended war"—consisted of two 45,000-ton battleships, superior to any vessel afloat, but believed about a year from completion; a large aircraft carrier also uncompleted; two 26,000-ton battleships; three 10,000-ton "pocket battleships" whose deadliness far exceeded their displacement; eight cruisers, twenty-two destroyers, twenty-six merchant vessels which were being converted to armed merchant cruisers, and some fifty-seven submarines whose number was increasing by about two per month.

This peacetime rate of U-boat construction was soon to be increased many-fold. Of the submarines in commission, it was quite possible that some had already taken up wartime dispositions in the Atlantic. The mighty *Bismarck* and *Tirpitz* were still safe in the fitting-out yards; but of the other battleships, pocket battleships and cruisers, some might be at large, prepared for a swoop on our shipping or coastal cities. Any one of the larger ships could have blown the Canadian navy out of the water. In the unlikely event that our entire force could have been brought to bear on one of the cruisers we might have come off victorious; but the victory would have put our navy in dock to lick its wounds for a fatally long time.

Between our coasts and the force of this overpowering enemy was interposed the even more overpowering shield of the Royal Navy. It had always been there. We had grown to nationhood in the shadow of it; and had come to accept it and forget it almost as a fact of geography. There was, however, one disquieting consideration.

The protecting shield was neither immovable nor ubiquitous. It was at times porous. It was a barrier constantly in motion, moving on many keels; sometimes gapping open to close upon an enemy after he had shot his bolt. The Royal Navy would eventually trap and strangle any large German assault and probably any single ship; but it had never been able to eliminate the possibility of a swift raid even on the coast of Britain. A heavy German ship might slip around or between the far-flung squadrons, spend a fruitful hour off Halifax and depart, leaving our destroyers on the bottom and our base a smoking ruin. The same possibility existed for Sydney and Saint John; to a lesser degree for Esquimalt and Vancouver; it could not be entirely ruled out of consideration for Quebec. The security of our coasts and seaports was a qualified and approximate thing.

Coastal shipping was exposed to a more serious threat. Submarines would certainly put out into the Atlantic, and in all probability would wait for no declaration of war to do so. They carried up to twenty-one torpedoes and many of them were equipped to lay mines. If Canadian waters were chosen as a zone of operations, local traffic would suffer heavy loss and crippling dislocation exactly at the time when expanding requirements of war put the greatest demands upon it.

In the face of all these possibilities certain immediate measures could be taken and were, in fact, already under way. Army and Air Force detachments had placed our primitive shore and air defences on a war footing. In co-operation with them, the navy had made preparations for harbour defence. Entrances would require protection by booms and anti-submarine nets; minefields and under-water torpedo tubes were a necessity. Provision had to be made for the examination of all incoming vessels. Detection, warning and signal facilities had to be greatly expanded. All this had been sketched out and, so far as possible, set in place or in motion. Mainly, the work was a re-assessment of requirements which had long been known and long unfilled. Most of our harbour defences would be represented for months to come by signals, letters and telegrams urgently requesting materials which did not exist.

For minesweeping and anti-submarine work in coastal waters a number of small craft—vessels of the Royal Canadian Mounted Police and government departments, craft of the Fishermen's Reserve and a few privately owned yachts—had been earmarked. They were now requisitioned and their fitting out commenced with what war equipment was available. Proceedings of doubtful international legality—strongly reminiscent of the submarine deal of the earlier war—were entered into with citizens of the United States. Eventually these would bring us fifteen large yachts for "private" use, the mainstay of a patrol force of some seventy vessels. At the moment, however, such a force was scarcely an embryo.

The destroyers were based two on Halifax and four on Esquimalt, a disposition which testified to faith in the Royal Navy and to uneasiness about Japan's intentions. Of the minesweepers, three were in the west and two in the east.

Such was the coastal defence of the country, in being or envisaged, as the harvests yellowed in Poland and the

Labour Day week-end approached. It was, of course, entirely inadequate and would be so for months to come. It was even less than that. It was almost irrelevant. Enemy naval forces might inflict death and devastation on our seaward fringes, but this in the hard lexicon of war must be defined only as a harassing nuisance. Where we were most seriously vulnerable we were least able to protect ourselves.

Sixty-three per cent of our export trade and thirty-nine per cent of our import trade was moved by sea. Our cargoes went out to the ports of Europe, Asia, Africa, South America, Australia and the Far East, and other cargoes returned. Sixty-three million tons of ocean shipping entered or cleared from our ports annually. The millstream of ocean trade revolved the wheels of harvesting machines in Saskatchewan, factories in Ontario and Quebec, sawmills in British Columbia. The eastern maritime provinces depended on it most heavily of all. It sent the long strings of freight cars rolling westward and eastward on our railways. It was the base of our vaunted "standard of living;" the cornucopia from which had come the modern homes and the modern roads and the modern automobiles, the libraries and schools and universities and hospitals, the social services, the health services and everything that made life richer, easier and happier as frontier settlements grew to modern cities, thriving towns and farmsteads prospering on a world-wide demand for their products. All these things—our economic security, our modern well-being, our future hopes—depended on the uninterrupted flow of sea-borne trade; on cargo in the holds of dingy freighters ploughing the seven oceans. It was vital; and, so far as Canadian naval resources were concerned, it was dreadfully vulnerable.

There was more than that to be considered. Our physical security, even our qualified and approximate security, existed only so long as the Royal Navy was supreme. The French navy, preoccupied with the Mediterranean quite as much as the Atlantic, would be a dangerous and hampering threat to German ships, but not a primary defence for us.

The United States was a neutral and in any case had her main naval problem in the Pacific. The Royal Navy was the only bulwark upon which we could depend.

The Royal Navy meant more than ships. It meant bases, without which the ships could not operate. It meant ship-yards, repairing, replacing, adding to the navy's strength. It meant the whole vast, centuries-old, shore-based organization behind the ships. Let Britain go down and all this would be lost; not merely lost, but much of it transferred to German hands. The ships—such of them as remained—would be hungry and helpless orphans to whom we could offer no sustenance. The United States dwelt beside us, a sleeping giant; its power unmobilized, its purposes ill-defined. It might wake too late; and without it we should face, empty-handed, an Atlantic highway by which our enemy might come when he would.

Britain had to stand. Britain had to be kept alive and powerful. It was a consideration as vital to a farmer in Manitoba as to a stevedore in Southampton. And sea-borne trade, of tremendous value and importance to Canada, was the very life-blood of Britain.

It pulsed outward and inward from all the ports of the world; and it was watched over with a care worthy of its importance. Trade, in peacetime, flowed along a thousand veins chosen by individuals and dictated by considerations of profit. Ship movements were reported by Lloyd's and information regarding them was available to anyone. Supervision, while the seas of the world lay open and the guns were silent, had the aspect of casual routine; but war would see a swift transformation. The give and take of commerce would become the all-demanding need of a sea-girt island fighting for its existence. The veins of peacetime trade would be gathered into a few great arteries through which, if Britain were to stand, the life-giving flood must pass in safety.

The transformation had got quietly under way about the time of Munich. Rear-Admiral Sir Eldon Manisty, who

11

had been the Admiralty's Manager of Convoys in the first world war, and whose knowledge of trade matters was probably unequalled anywhere, set off without fanfare on a tour of the world. His leisurely junketings carried him along the great routes of trade and detained him for prolonged periods at the key centres. Shortly after his return to London, those centres began to receive detailed and comprehensive instructions, concerned with the routing, reporting and control of merchant shipping in a time of emergency. The instructions were, in total, a handbook of war; a blueprint for merging the routine supervision of peacetime into the immensely greater and more rigorous process of trade control. By the summer of 1939 the contents of the handbook had been digested.

Of all the control centres about the world, Ottawa was, at this juncture, the most important. Ottawa Intelligence Centre included within its purview the whole of North America and a large section of the embracing seas. American and Canadian cargoes, the resources upon which British war power so greatly depended, must be mobilized in that area and shipped from its ports across the route of greatest peril, the North Atlantic.

The Director of Naval Intelligence in Ottawa was, by established custom, a Royal Navy officer on loan from the Admiralty. A new Director arrived to take up his appointment in the course of normal service routine on a sweltering July morning of 1939. Thereafter came other appointments which were not of a routine nature and were not publicized. At widely separated points in North America, preoccupied men in civilian dress, generally middle-aged and with a well-shaved, outdoor look about them, stepped from trains or liners and proceeded with tranquil directness to offices looking down upon a waterfront. They had hardly had time to establish themselves behind their desks when the head of a department known as Naval Distributing Authority arrived from Ottawa to present them with codes and publications which could be transmitted only by hand.

War Organization of Trade

The pace speeded up as August waned. Two retired captains of the Royal Navy who were living in Canada, and two brothers, one a retired captain and one a retired commander of the Canadian navy, opened cryptic telegrams which summoned them to Ottawa by the first plane. On arrival they received a half-hour lecture on totally unfamiliar duties, much of it unheard because of the plane deafness ringing in their ears; and entrained for the ports of Halifax, Sydney, Saint John and Quebec. They went, as naval officers were going at that time even from omniscient Admiralty, burdened with secret books, blankly ignorant of what confronted them and profanely dismayed by the lack of every facility.

They were immediately in communication with Ottawa and with the officers who had preceded them to other points in the Ottawa area. Telegrams, telephone calls, letters of instruction and warning messages began to pour in upon them. Time was narrowing; little of it now remained for the work of organization. Within a few days orders to "commence war reporting" were to go out from Ottawa; and the men hastily assembled in offices along the eastern seaboard of North America would have to carry them out.

The machine now being thrown together was the skeleton of the North American trade control system. It was to be vastly expanded in the future; its work was to be supplemented by many great civilian agencies. Many of its functions would eventually be transferred to the United States and merged into the greater effort of the United Nations, but it was the machine of which Sir Eldon Manisty was to say four years later:

Naval Service Headquarters [Ottawa] has been the basis of the organization and has been the source from which the whole mechanism derived its impetus. This mechanism seems to have worked so smoothly that it has been accepted as being almost automatic.

Four years had smoothed away Sir Eldon's recollections of earlier trials. In the dog days of 1939 the machine was by no means automatic. It was cranky and creaky and untried. But its essential parts were in place.

13

On August 26 an Admiralty telegram arrived in Ottawa and in each of the other Intelligence Centres about the world. It contained the single word, "FUNNEL". With the dispatch of that message all British merchant ships passed from the control of their owners into the control of the Admiralty. The same transfer took place in Canada on the same day. No Canadian-registered ship and no merchant ship in a Canadian port could sail without the authority of the Royal Canadian Navy. The "FUNNEL" telegram was followed immediately by a plain language broadcast from the Admiralty to all British ships:

Admiralty has assumed control of the sailing and routeing of British merchant ships. Organization for official wireless messages is now in force.

The lights were going out again. This was the last general shipping message which the Admiralty would broadcast in plain language for nearly six years. Great Britain had a week, Canada two weeks, of official peace remaining, but war had fastened on the ships of trade.

Throughout the Ottawa area naval control officers assumed their function. The task immediately facing them was enormous and was to grow beyond anything they dared imagine. Trade control was in effect; the veins of peacetime shipping were to be gathered into the arteries of war. Every British merchant vessel passing through North American waters—ships from Australia, the Far East and the West Indies, ships from South America—above all the ships from North American ports—would have to be gathered in from the wide face of the sea, assembled in selected groups, bunkered, stored, provided with codes and orders. Vessels of every speed and type and cargo capacity would have to be formed into orderly fleets, sailed at precise times and by dictated routes with the precision of a crack railway. Each movement through North American waters would have to be linked with every other movement in those waters and around the world, for the stream of trade was a continuous, interdependent thing. The absolute necessity for secrecy would be a harrowing complication; and the whole would have to conform to the iron-bound schedules of naval operations.

The wheels began to turn, stiffly at first but effectually, emitting everywhere the high, staccato whine of wireless signals. Ships preparing to sail were stopped in harbour. Vessels at sea received peremptory diversion orders sending them to unintended ports by unaccustomed routes. Halifax stirred once again with the grim vitality of a key port in a warring world. Ships put in, their schedules interrupted, their masters angry and anxious, demanding explanations which were not forthcoming. Irritable confusion, inexplicable bustle and uncongenial secrecy were the order of the day.

Trade was mobilizing; the merchant ships were gathering. The next essential of the convoy system remained to be provided.

Early on the afternoon of August 31, the destroyers *Fraser* and *St. Laurent,* participating in a civic celebration at Vancouver, called a sudden halt to proceedings. Their guests were ushered ashore with peremptory naval courtesy, gangplanks were hauled in and within two hours the ships were steaming at twenty-five knots for the Panama Canal. Beneath the festive decks of early afternoon, fuel tanks and storerooms had been well supplied. The destroyers' orders were now to "ship warheads and be in all respects ready for action." They were steaming southward from San Pedro as Neville Chamberlain informed the House of Commons that the last of many notes had gone unanswered, and George Lansbury, the lover of peace, rose to declare that, "the cause that I and a handful of friends represent is . . . apparently going down to ruin." Their logs for September 10, the day which marked the Dominion's entry into war, bear the notation, "Course and speeds as required for transit of the canal;" and five days later they arrived in Halifax.

Of the Halifax-based destroyers, *Saguenay* had already a week of anti-submarine patrols behind her and *Skeena* was off on a dash to Bermuda carrying the Commander-in-Chief

America and West Indies Station with his staff. The new arrivals found the port thronged with a motley collection of shipping; heard masters and owners bewailing costly diversions and loss to cargoes. Ships' painting parties were busy defiling clean white sides with the dun grey of war. Merchant officers gloomed profanely over pamphlets of convoy instructions and signal publications more terrible to them than U-boats. Ancient guns from scanty stores were being mounted on after-decks stiffened for the unaccustomed weight; a few machine guns and submachine guns were being issued. Captains, accustomed to the wide freedom of the seas, were proclaiming the impossibility and the absurdity of sailing their cranky freighters nose-to-tail like helpless cows.

And beneath all the grumbling was a surly acceptance of everything that had to be done. Sea-borne trade—trade as we know it in peacetime—had ceased to exist. It went by the same name because it had occured to no one to coin a better; but it was a different thing. Ships would move no longer by the shortest route to dispose of their cargoes to the best advantage. Men would no longer order and receive what they desired and could pay for. The comparatively kindly operations of demand and supply, profit and loss, had given way to something even more fundamental. Sea-borne trade had become a matter of survival; a weapon to be wielded from the highest stategic quarters in response to the brutal imperatives of war.

The first group of ships had been assembled with rough efficiency and in a surprisingly short time. Others would gather in greater numbers; they were gathering now at ports down the American seaboard and around the world. Halifax would see them readied and sailed with ever-increasing precision by a constantly expanding organization. The remaining question, the question that would hover over all our destinies for the next six years, was starkly simple. Could the ships be got across the Atlantic?

On September 16, one day after *St. Laurent* arrived from Vancouver, she moved outward through the Halifax approaches in company with her sister, *Saguenay*. Between the destroyers, waddling eastward with a certain untidy gallantry, were the eighteen merchant ships of Convoy HX-1—Halifax to the United Kingdom.

Awaiting them in the open sea were the British cruisers *Berwick* and *York*, and beyond lay the sleety gloom of the Atlantic. The business of war had begun; and it was perhaps as well that the unaccustomed difficulties of convoy prevented too much speculation on the days ahead.

CHAPTER TWO

The First Year

The battle upon which the ships of Canada were now embarked was to continue for sixty-eight months; on, above and beneath the surface of ten million square miles of sea. It was to range with varying intensity and with swaying fortunes from the waters of the old world to the waters of the new, from far within the Arctic Circle to far south of the Cape of Good Hope; and it was never to yield an absolute, clear-cut victory.

The morale of the German U-boat fleet, the principal adversary in this struggle for the Atlantic, remained high to the end. The signal for surrender, when given at last, was an order from a bomb-battered shelter on land, reluctantly obeyed. It came at a moment when allied dominance on the convoy routes, securely established for two years, was again threatened. In the last twenty-four hours of the war, two merchant vessels and a naval ship were sunk by submarines of a new type and with tactics which the allied navies were ill prepared to meet. Revolutionary German craft which might have defeated the latest anti-submarine weapons were on the slipways; fanatically devoted crews were attacking with unabated determination. Only victory on land prevented another phase of allied reverses at sea. Yet it was the hard-won control of the Atlantic, securely held through the crucial years, which made that victory possible.

The dimensions of the coming struggle were not fully apparent in those mid-September days of 1939. Even less apparent was the future scope of Canadian participation. The first escort voyage of *St. Laurent* and *Saguenay* set a pattern which all Canadian ships were to follow with unvarying monotony and no spice of battle for many months. Destroyers were ships of small "endurance." Their fuel capacity permitted a direct Atlantic passage at economical speed, but not the ceaseless zigzagging and the far-ranging protective sweeps which were necessary for a convoy voyage. Until May of 1940 the work of the Canadians would be confined to local escort, shepherding convoys from the focal areas of the coast to the high seas where they would be taken over by more powerful ships. On September 17 in midafternoon, 353 sea miles to the eastward of Halifax, *St. Laurent* and *Saguenay* parted company with the convoy and its escorting cruisers and turned back to base. At dusk they passed *Fraser*, outward bound with HXF-1, the first "fast" convoy, consisting of unarmed merchant ships capable of making over fifteen knots.

Skeena was to take her turn with convoy HX-2 on September 23; *Ottawa* and *Restigouche* were soon to come around from the west coast to join the cycle. A new acquisition, the destroyer *Assiniboine*, formerly *H.M.S. Kempenfelt*, arrived in Halifax from the United Kingdom on November 17 and was on convoy duty the next day.

By that time both shore and sea duties had entered upon a seemingly endless process of expansion. Two convoys a week were sailing from Halifax, each requiring local destroyer escort. Anti-submarine patrols had to be maintained off the congested port and in the waters through which scores of ships were daily approaching. There was in addition the necessity of reinforcing the British West Indies Squadron, which had been depleted by the use of its cruisers for ocean escort work; and Canadian destroyers served in relays in the Jamaica area.

Another responsibility which lay outside the province of the escorts but heavily upon the navy's Trade Division was the routeing of "independent" ships. Only the United Kingdom convoys had as yet been organized. Ships departing for other ports had to be given routes and sailing orders and reported onward to other Intelligence areas. For incoming ships a system of approach routes had to be devised. A submarine lying off the port would have a submerged speed of only two to eight knots and upon sighting a vessel it would have to manoeuvre itself into position for attack. By bringing ships into Halifax on a series of varying courses approaching fanwise there was a good chance that the majority of them would pass well away from a possible enemy. It was hardly adequate protection; but it was the best available.

The character and first main theatre of the naval war had been fairly well marked out even before it officially began. The sweeping of enemy trade from the seas—traditional and imperial function of British sea power—had been largely anticipated by the enemy. At a pre-arranged signal, nearly coinciding with the Admiralty's FUNNEL telegram, German merchantmen had abandoned their voyages and dashed for neutral ports. The work of sealing them in or of intercepting them if they attempted a break-out was a comparatively minor preoccupation of the Royal Navy. Its principal concern was the maintenance of the flow of British and Allied trade, which was threatened immediately in the north and south Atlantic by German surface ships, and in the approaches to the United Kingdom by submarines.

The pocket battleship *Deutschland* had left for its war station off the bulge of Brazil during the last week of August. The *Graf Spee* was waiting in Denmark Strait to enter the Atlantic by this northern gateway. Both were accompanied by supply ships and could operate for months over tremendous areas of sea. Their orders were to threaten merchant shipping always, destroy it when they could, and keep out of the way of British battle squadrons. All of this the Admiralty knew or suspected, and flag officers looked forward grimly to months of weary hunting with large forces of ships before these elusive enemies could be chased home or brought to bay.

Twenty-one U-boats had left their German bases at about the same time as the pocket battleships, and had taken up positions off the British Isles. Their patrol line curved in a great crescent from the north of Ireland to a position off the coast of Portugal. All ships approaching or leaving the United Kingdom would have to run this gauntlet; and there were hundreds of them still sailing independently after the main ocean convoys had been organized. British and allied freighters had no doubt of the risk they ran. The hazards confronting passenger liners and neutrals were, for a time, somewhat more equivocal.

Several German declarations, although they forbade ships carrying non-combatant passengers and the freighters of neutral nations to enter British waters, had nevertheless exempted them from sinking without warning. Nor were the declarations as empty as they appeared to a disillusioned world. Hitler, at least in the beginning, meant them to be adhered to. He foresaw that even the shreds of his reputation might prove useful to him among the neutral nations; and he feared above all things the premature entry of the United States into the war. The torpedoing of the passenger liner *Athenia*, on September 3, had been the blunder of an "overexcited" U-boat captain, and flatly against orders. Raeder, the Commander-in-Chief of the German Navy, and Doenitz, his Admiral Commanding U-boats, had received the news with consternation. When the U-boat returned to base the captain had been severely reprimanded. The boat's log had been falsified, the crew sworn to secrecy; and after that there had still remained the unpleasant necessity of bearing the news to Hitler.

The Fuehrer had greeted it with one of his earlier and milder rages; on this occasion not without cause. Few in the world outside the Nazi camp, and few enough within it, believed that the sinking was anything but deliberate. It was taken as a declaration of "unrestricted submarine warfare," a phrase which German propaganda recoiled from for many months. It hardened opinion in all the neutral nations; and particularly in the United States it gave new depth to a hostile groundswell which could already be felt. Above all, it drove the allies to supreme efforts in convoy organization and shipbuilding. Had Germany's intentions at sea remained obscure, there might have been hesitation, particularly in Canada, as to the manner in which resources required

21

for air, land and sea should be distributed. The prospect of savage U-boat warfare, even though it was based on a preliminary misconception, resulted in an unheard-of shipbuilding effort which bore fruit a year later at a time when the darkest of forebodings were all too grimly realized.

The U-boat captain who sank *Athenia,* therefore, struck a heavy blow at the Nazi cause on the first day of war. Yet he was not to be without confederates, among whom Doenitz and Raeder stand high. "Blunders" similar to the *Athenia* incident occurred with growing frequency during the weeks that followed; and called down gentler rebukes when the captains returned to base. Raeder and Doenitz, though they attempted to carry out Hitler's orders, were never impressed by his concern for neutral opinion. They were very sure that they were in for an all-or-nothing war; and their policy was to push the Fuehrer as rapidly as possible toward the abandonment of all restrictions. The young men at sea behind the periscopes were even farther along the road than their indulgent admirals; and neutral merchantmen very soon learned that their best chance of safety lay in convoy.

By the end of September forty ships totalling 150,000 gross tons had been sunk by mine or torpedo in the approaches to the British Isles. The loss was accepted as inevitable during a period of organization; and by October the British escort forces seemed to be gaining the upper hand. Yet they were strained to the limit to provide inward and outward protection through a submarine zone which extended only some four hundred miles westward from Land's End. Beyond that area the ships of outward-bound convoys had to disperse and sail independently. They enjoyed for the remainder of their voyages a precarious immunity which would vanish as soon as the U-boats reached farther west. For the moment, however, submarines were not the principal danger on the main Atlantic; nor were the dispersed ships, outward bound and frequently in ballast, the likeliest targets. The greater threat was posed by the heavy German surface ships; and for them the most inviting prizes would be the inward bound convoys laden with cargo. The nightmare of the pocket battleship lay heavy enough on every ship that plied the Atlantic; and heaviest of all, perhaps, on the convoys sailing from Canada.

Battleships were the only answer to such a threat; and battleships were provided. *Revenge* and *Resolution* became familiar shapes looming in the mists off Halifax or towering above her jetties. *Barham* and *Malaya* followed, supplemented by cruisers and armed merchant cruisers. Their work lay on the high seas; their orders were to take convoys eastward to a point within range of British local escorts; and frequently they made the complete voyage from Canadian to British ports. On the western side Canadian destroyers provided the local escort, running out to the mid-Atlantic fringes with the convoys, turning them over to the larger ships, turning back for a few hours in harbour before they were required for the next stint of escort or patrol.

Each voyage on local escort meant from two and a half to three days at sea. Frequently destroyers were called upon to make two voyages a week. Anti-submarine patrols had to be carried out, damaged ships had to be assisted to harbour, and every form of vigilance maintained against attacks which did not come but were possible at any time. The sea miles and the hours of sea time mounted on the logs of the destroyers and left their mark on the faces of the ships' companies. Yet no Canadian ship, by the end of 1939, could boast of an enemy vessel sighted or a depth charge dropped in good, murderous earnest. In the endless conversations which helped to pass the endless hours of zigzagging across familiar waters by the side of drab merchantmen, heavy-lidded sailors complained, as their fathers had done before them, that the war would be over before they got into it.

Such forebodings were not shared in higher naval circles ashore. By January of 1940 Raeder was pleading with Hitler for permission to send two mine-laying submarines into the Halifax approaches. The Fuehrer refused at the time because of the danger of sinking American ships and precipitating the entry of the United States into the war. He considered the proposal attractive, however, and set it aside for later consideration. Canadian staff officers, with no knowledge of these westward-looking debates, were nevertheless sure that the immunity of North American waters would not long continue. Submerged in paper work, envious of their seagoing brothers, they fought their way through a multitude of conflicting demands, groping for the main outlines of the struggle which faced them. The movement of trade was under way, ocean convoys were sailing on schedule, and "feeder" convoys were being organized. The sea transport of troops began with cc voy TC-1, which sailed on December 10 carrying 7,400 men of the First Canadian Division. At noon on that day *Ottawa, Restigouche, Fraser* and *St. Laurent* led the liners, *Aquitania, Empress of Britain, Duchess of Bedford, Monarch of Bermuda* and *Empress of Australia* out of the Halifax approaches and turned them over to a powerful British covering force for the voyage to the United Kingdom. From that time until the United States entered the war, the organization and local escort of troop convoys remained an additional commitment of the Canadian navy.

The resources of the naval service were still hugely inadequate, but they were increasing. Bases were being staffed and supplied; a few of the needs of manning, training and equipment were being met. Multiplying responsibilities were gradually being sorted out and divided among newcomers. The entire organization was expanding with tumultuous haste as tendrils of additional requirements shot out from the main stem.

A department for the "defensive equipment of merchant ships," instantly known as DEMS, was set up. It doled out what small supplies of weapons and ammunition there were, installed guns, trained naval ratings and merchant seamen to handle them, and added its demands for more armament to the multitude of requirements which would not be adequately met for months and years. Wireless facilities for communication with ships at sea were expanded out of all

Convoy conference at Halifax. Members, captains and naval officers studying orders before the sailing of a convoy.

The
NORTH ATLANTIC
SEPTEMBER 1939 to MAY 1940

RADIUS OF
LOCAL
ESCORT

CONVO

ESCORT BY BATTLESHIPS CRU

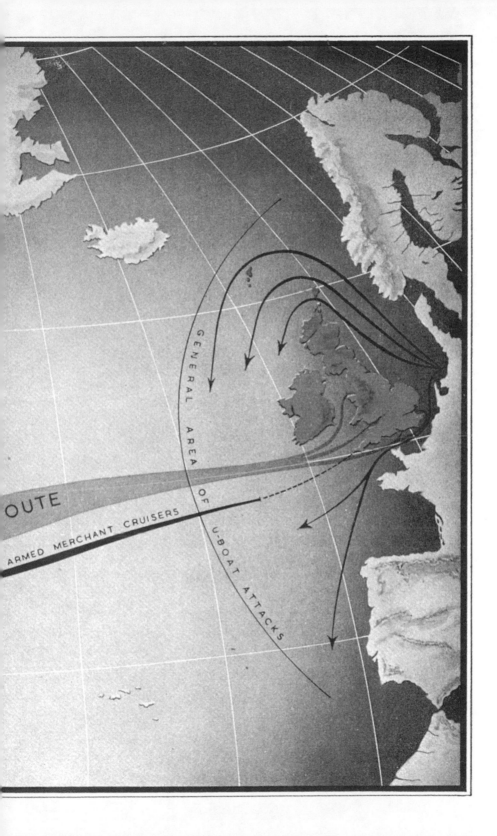

OUTE

ARMED MERCHANT CRUISERS

GENERAL AREA OF U-BOAT ATTACKS

recognition, to handle a signal traffic which for one station in one month totalled 180,000 cypher groups. Small ships for the coastal patrols were found, equipped, armed and finally got to sea. Zones along both coasts were organized for the control of navigational warnings, and a communications system was set up by which lights in any area could be extinguished on the approach of an enemy ship. Coastal defences were being organized; anti-submarine booms, nets and warning devices were being built and set in place. Halifax was reasonably well defended by the end of November, but the supplementary ports were still in a state of comparative nakedness, and everywhere the need of more facilities for handling the growing multitude of ships was a clamorous urgency.

For every operation and every plan men were a primary requirement. All reserves had been called up and all Royal Canadian Naval Volunteer Reserve divisions enrolled to their full complement in the first days of war; yet the vicious circle of shortages operated against recruiting as against everything else. Volunteers there were in plenty, but volunteers were of little use without men to train them; and the shortage of trained men was the most serious of all. Every ship at sea required not only a larger wartime complement but a long series of attentions from a shore-based administrative service. To detach experienced men for use as training officers, either from ships or from responsible positions ashore, was a grievous operation but it had to be performed.

The Royal Navy was training some of our first recruits in England; but its facilities were in a state of strain comparable to our own, and had to be supplemented. A Canadian officers' training establishment was commissioned as *H.M.C.S. Stone Frigate,* a part of the Royal Military College at Kingston, and later transferred to *H.M.C.S. Royal Roads* at Esquimalt. King's College, Halifax, was to be a still later addition. A naval training plan for university students was eventually to be introduced to operate in conjunction with the R.C.N.V.R. divisions. Divisions were also called upon from the first to give basic training to naval ratings; after which the youngsters who had learned boat drill on a green lawn, tied a few knots, discovered that walls were bulkheads and that going down the steps of a drafty old barracks was going ashore, proceeded to depots at Halifax and Esquimalt for "advanced" training within sight of the sea and occasionally upon it.

The transition from a prairie wheatfield to the deck of a sea-going ship had sometimes to be made within a period of ninety days. Years had to be telescoped into months. The entire training system was under-staffed, ludicrously ill equipped, and would soon be called upon to meet undreamed-of requirements under every stress of war. Yet it was to pass into the service some eighty thousand men whose performance would reflect not unfavourably upon both the machine and the quality of its material.

Overriding every other requirement was the need of ships. Three vessels at once attracted the naval eye: the liners *Prince Robert* and *Prince David,* owned by Canadian National Steamships, and the former *Prince Henry,* which had been sold to Clarke Steamships. They were small luxury liners, each of 6,000 tons, 385 feet in length, with a maximum speed of 22 knots and an endurance of 3,600 miles. Their conversion into armed merchant cruisers would be a sizeable task; and the Admiralty looked askance on them at first because of their comparatively limited range. It was soon apparent, however, that such objections would have to be set aside. The ships were acquired by the navy in November and the work of stripping off their upper decks for replacement by a light cruiser superstructure was begun. A year later they were to be commissioned as the largest ships of the 1941 navy and were to give convincing demonstration of their usefulness.

A greater decision regarding ships had already been made, and was to affect the entire course of the Atlantic battle. It was recognized in Ottawa as in Whitehall that the essential struggle would be between the convoy and the

26

submarine. The chain of ships linking North America with Europe was long and vulnerable and might be attacked anywhere along its length. It was under attack now in the approaches to the British Isles; it might shortly be assailed in mid-Atlantic or in Canadian waters. Escort ships—hundreds of them—would be required all along the convoy routes; and there were no hundreds of escort ships available.

There was, however, an idea which had emerged as a blueprint and a prototype before the war began. Its source was the whaling ship. Whales, it had been observed some thirty years before, had characteristics in common with the submarine. They surfaced quickly and made off at high speed. When they dived they turned very quickly under water and pursuit required a highly manoeuvreable vessel. They frequented stormy and inhospitable waters and the ships of the hunters had to be seaworthy. Moreover, whaling ships had to be comparatively cheap and simple to build.

Mr. William Reed, of Smith's Dock Company, at South Bank on the Tees, had had a long experience with whaling ships in many waters. Out of this experience he had designed and built a few small patrol vessels for the Admiralty during the first World War. As a second war loomed upon the horizon he had been called on again, and had designed a somewhat larger ship which came to be known as the "patrol vessel, whaler type." By July of 1939 one or two ships had been built to the design and were being tried out.

The plans for this "patrol vessel, whaler type" reached Canadian naval headquarters three days after war was declared. In another three days an urgent signal was on its way to the Admiralty suggesting that some of the vessels might be built in Canada.

The suggestion, even as first made, was ambitious enough for a country which had never built a warship larger than a small minesweeper. The requirements of the future were not unveiled in their imposing fullness. The patrol vessels, if they could be built, were envisioned as a force only

27

for protection of the western terminals of the convoy routes, the approaches to the coast and the waters of the Gulf of St. Lawrence. Neither in Ottawa nor in Whitehall could anyone foresee the situation as it would develop in June 1940. But it was foreseen that the need of ships would be a continuing and incalculable thing and that the resources of Britain, even supplemented by those which the United States could make available, might not be sufficient. Canada, too, must contribute. An unprecedented national effort was called for; and the idea grew that these little vessels, still untried and still on paper, were the ships which Canada could build and man.

Somewhere along the chain of debate and decision over the patrol vessels they acquired the tradition-laden name of "Corvette." It was a name they were to wear bravely and a tradition they were to enrich so greatly that it is easy to forget the terrifying proportions of the gamble they involved. There was only the vaguest idea at the moment of where or how the ships were to be built. There had been no time to assess the potentialities of Canadian shipyards; and in any case the results of such a survey would have been discouraging. Yards were lacking, workmen were lacking, many of the necessary trades and skills were non-existent. Materials were in short supply around the world. What was required was practically a revolution in Canadian industry.

Assuming that that could be accomplished—and it was a large assumption—there was a second question. Nobody knew for certain what the corvettes could do. No conclusive verdict could be passed on the one or two which the British had in operation. If the corvette-building programme proved a fiasco, if the ships were not successful against submarines, or if enough of them could not be built in time, the effects of the failure would be incalculable. A great segment of our manpower and our industry, a year of our precious time would have been lost; thrown away in what was certain to be dubbed a hare-brained experiment. The planned and necessary addition to the strength of the Royal Navy could not be given. The chain of the Atlantic convoys might be disrupted. British ships might have to be recalled from the Mediterranean and other parts of the world, leaving great gaps in our defences. It would be a naval catastrophe with world-wide repercussions.

The decision to make the gamble was taken, although the size of the issues turning upon it would not be fully revealed for two years. Canadian shipyards were to build, and the navy was to man, sixty-four corvettes, and, in addition to the corvettes, ten Bangor minesweepers. This programme, large as it seemed, was to be hugely expanded in the future. It was perhaps the first of the great projects linking the services with industry in the total effort of total war. Canadians were going to build the shipyards, find the materials, train the workmen, master the innumerable skills necessary for building a fleet of warships. They were going to find and train the men to fight the ships. And the only reason for believing the job could be done was that it had to be done.

By February 1940 the building of the corvettes and minesweepers was under way. The work of refitting the Prince ships was also proceeding. The navy entered upon a calamitous year of warfare with seven overworked destroyers which had not yet seen battle, its shore organization a seething, half-formed mass, and a ship-building programme about which many doubts were entertained.

There was beginning to fall over the crucial waters far to the east an oppressive lull. So far the battle in the approaches to the British Isles had not gone too badly. British dominance of other seas was unshaken; and the defeat of the *Graf Spee* in December by three cruisers had shown that the pocket battleship was not so tough a customer as had been feared. Merchant ship casualties were serious but had been more than replaced by new construction. The magnetic mine had been mastered. Above all "asdic" had come into its own.

The word itself was a naval hybrid, assembled from the initial letters of the Allied Submarine Detecting Investigation Committee, a group of British, French and American experts formed in 1917 to study methods of locating submarines under water. The committee had disbanded at the conclusion of the first World War, but the Royal Navy had continued its work intensively and very secretly.

The basic principle of the asdic method was as old as the days when ship captains off a rocky shore made an estimate of their position by shouting and timing the return of the echo. For the shout asdic substituted a supersonic beam transmitted under water by means of an alternating electric current applied to quartz crystals which contracted and expanded under its influence. The beam of sound went out through the water and upon contact with objects of a certain consistency returned an echo—the famous "ping." Both the outgoing beam and the returning echo were rendered audible to the human ear and transmitted to the headphones of an operator.

While many underwater objects—large schools of fish, certain rock formations, even certain tide and water conditions—returned echoes, it was possible for a trained operator to distinguish among them the authentic "ping" of the beam against a metallic hull. He had other evidence to assist him: "doppler," the change of pitch in the echo as the hull moved away or approached; "hydrophone effect," which was the sound of propellers. Supplementary instruments, constituting actually a second and third asdic set, enabled him to calculate the U-boat's range, bearing, depth, course and speed.

This gear for underwater groping, whose name at least is familiar to everyone today, was a high-level secret in 1939. No piece of naval equipment was more rigorously guarded or less likely to be talked about than the curious egg-shaped dome of the asdic housing projecting from the ship's bottom. Officers trained in the complicated technique of asdic were a strictly limited *corps d'élite* in the Royal Navy before the war, and in the Canadian navy only two officers had taken the complete course.

The measures of secrecy justified themselves when the war began. Asdic detection, followed as it was by the shattering impact of 300-pound depth charges, was a most unpleasant surprise for German U-boats. They had no device and very little in the way of formal tactics with which to meet it; and within two months it had forced them to confine themselves to night attacks when they would have a reasonable chance of escaping on the surface. The survivors of many sunken U-boats gave testimony to the dread of those uncanny fingers of sound groping beneath the surface and to the despair with which they heard the spaced, inexorable, high-pitched tapping of the beam against their hulls.

Asdic had done much to neutralize the advantage which the Germans had expected from their improved submarines and the highly trained crews with which they began the war. The fighting had gone along on about an equal basis, and seemed in February to be turning in favour of the Allies. The Admiralty did not flatter itself, however, that any successes had occurred to justify the slackening of U-boat activity which began late in February, became more noticeable in March and settled to a dead calm in early April.

The submarines had actually been withdrawn for the Scandinavian campaign; and the calm was shattered on April 9 by the invasion of Denmark and Norway. On April 11, while the nerves of the world were still jangling from that shock, Winston Churchill, First Lord of the Admiralty, told a shaken House of Commons that, "the very recklessness with which Hitler and his advisers have cast the interests of the German Navy upon the wild waters . . . makes me feel that these audacious, costly operations may be only the prelude to far larger events." Six weeks later the German armies were plunging triumphantly through France, with Holland and Belgium prostrate behind them. On May 23, British destroyers fought a point-blank action with German tanks entering Boulogne; and when the destroyers withdrew with the remnants of the beaten garrison the swastika waved where Napoleon had stood and begged for the hours of sea mastery which would give him the world.

The First Year

In Halifax, on the afternoon of the 24th, the Canadian destroyers *Restigouche, Skeena* and *St. Laurent* were preparing to go to sea on an unscheduled voyage. Leaves had been cancelled, libertymen summoned back to their ships and all prospect of an Empire Day celebration ruined with truly naval efficiency. The mood on board *St. Laurent* was particularly black, as she had been recalled from one convoy and was under orders for sea again before a man could step ashore. The mess deck "buzz," discredited and discouraged by nine months of unvarying monotony, gave promise only of another local convoy run. If there was any bright feature of the day it must have been the mild spring weather which had enabled the men to relieve their crowded mess decks by sending heavy clothes and miscellaneous cold weather gear ashore.

With early evening came the familiar "cable party fall in" and the equally familiar call for sea dutymen to muster. The destroyers nosed their way out of harbour while men on watch speculated without much curiosity over the fact that there appeared to be no convoy in evidence.

The explanation came several hours later. There was to be no convoy this time and no turning back to Halifax after twenty-four hours. The lambie coats left in Halifax would not be seen by their owners for a considerable time. An urgent cable from the United Kingdom had arrived in Ottawa the day before. Invasion was an imminent possibility and every ship which Canada could send was required in British waters.

Restigouche, Skeena and *St. Laurent* were on their way. *Assiniboine* and *Ottawa* were in refit at Halifax and would not be operational until about the middle of June. *Saguenay* could not make the crossing as she was also badly in need of refit. *Fraser,* en route to Bermuda, had been ordered to continue her voyage, refuel at Bermuda and proceed directly to the United Kingdom.

The first wartime passage of the three destroyers was uneventful but scarcely monotonous. By day and by night the men went through intensive air raid and anti-submarine exercises. The commanding officer of *Restigouche* saw the efficiency of his ship increase rapidly during the voyage and suggested that the improvement "was no doubt accelerated by the realization of the ship's company that we were rapidly approaching an extremely active war zone."

It may well have been so. While still a day's steaming from the United Kingdom the ships were ordered to a position off Ushant on an abortive submarine hunt; and when they finally secured at Plymouth on June 1 the evacuation of Dunkirk was at its height. The First Lord of the Admiralty found time for cordial words to the newcomers:

> The presence of units of the Royal Canadian Navy in our midst inspires us all to a still harder effort. Confident both of your skill and of your valour we wish you good luck in the fierce and exacting toil which lies before you.

Fraser, from Bermuda, followed her sisters into Plymouth on June 3; and after a week spent in replacing one of each ship's torpedo mountings with high-angle guns, the destroyers became part of the great force engaged in fending off U-boats and E-boats and in salvaging the melancholy remnants of defeat.

German infantry and armour were sweeping along the western coast of France, driving into the sea the broken fragments of British and French divisions. Here and there, at isolated bays and harbours, a few battalions of soldiers might be rescued by ship; a few hundreds out of the hundreds of thousands of refugees might be saved. Parties of engineers from England might be landed ahead of the advancing enemy to conduct vitally important demolitions. In this work the Canadian destroyers joined with many British ships.

Restigouche and *St. Laurent*, at sea on June 9, saw from thirty miles distant the flames of Le Havre rising six hundred feet into the night sky. On June 11 they were off St. Valéry en Caux in the neighborhood of Dieppe, assisting the British destroyer *Broke* to embark wounded. Part of the British 51st Division was holding a six-mile line in the vicinity but reported itself "in no immediate need of evacuation." *St. Laurent* moved a little way up the coast to Veules and took on board forty French troops. She returned to the neighborhood of St. Valèry an hour or so later to find *Restigouche* and the British destroyer still standing by for evacuation.

At about eight o'clock in the morning five or six salvoes splashed into the water a hundred yards from *St. Laurent* and *Restigouche.* A German battery had taken up position on the cliffs behind the town and there was no longer any possibility of embarking troops. The three destroyers engaged the battery, although they were unable to observe the fall of their shells behind the three hundred foot cliff. When they broke off after a desultory action, Canadian ships had exchanged their first fire with the German enemy.

On June 21, the day of France's humiliation at Compiègne, *Fraser* was sent to St. Jean de Luz, far down the west coast on the Franco-Spanish frontier. The little town was one of the last remaining exit points for refugees from France; and thousands of Polish troops who had fought with the French army were also retreating there for evacuation.

The Canadian destroyer, in company with British ships, arrived off St. Jean de Luz on the evening of the 22nd. She was immediately ordered to carry out an anti-submarine patrol; and the night was further enlivened by the work of shepherding in a stream of vessels arriving for the evacuation. At dawn she was ordered northward for a rendezvous with the British cruiser *Galatea.*

From *Galatea* she received two secret hand messages, one for Sir Ronald Campbell, the British Ambassador to France, and the other addressed to Admiral Darlan. Orders from *Galatea* were to proceed at full speed for Arachon, where Sir Ronald was believed to be. He was to be handed his dispatch and was to be asked to arrange for transmission of the other message to Admiral Darlan.

Toward noon as *Fraser* was approaching Arachon, she was hailed by a sardine boat, tossing wretchedly in the midst of a driving rain. On board the boat were the British Ambassador, the Canadian Minister to France, Lieutenant-Colonel George P. Vanier, the South African Minister and several members of their respective staffs. All of these had remained at their posts up to and a little beyond the point of safety; and there was now no possibility of getting a message to Darlan. *Fraser* embarked the party, swung round again, made another rendezvous with *Galatea* for the transfer of her passengers, and returned to St. Jean de Luz.

Here *Restigouche* and several British destroyers joined her toward evening. The melancholy tumult of evacuation was now fully under way. Boatloads of defeated soldiers and destitute civilians were streaming out from the jetties to the liners, tramp steamers, trawlers and pleasure craft which jostled each other in the rough waters of the harbour. Destroyers threaded a dangerous way among the thronging ships, marshalling the loaded vessels into groups for escort to England, while other destroyers zigzagged outside on anti-submarine patrol.

The dreary process went on for some forty-eight hours; and was about completed toward noon of the 25th. Sixteen thousand soldiers and thousands of civilians had made their escape. German forces were now known to be approaching the port overland from the north; and *Fraser* and *Restigouche* entered the harbour to speed up the last of the departing ships and take off their own evacuation parties. They had just got their men on board when a tank and an armoured car towing a field gun appeared on the brow of the hill above the town. Although the guns appeared to be French, they were brought to bear on the ships; and the meaning of the threat was clear. The terms of the armistice signed at Compiègne had come into effect and were to be enforced. *Fraser* and *Restigouche,* now under the orders of the British cruiser *Calcutta,* stood out to sea.

The three ships proceeded in company toward Bordeaux, where enemy vessels had been reported. Nothing was sighted off the Gironde, however; and after a brief patrol *Calcutta* gave the order for a return to the United Kingdom.

It was now about ten o'clock in the evening with a fresh breeze, a moderate swell and visibility of about one and a half miles. *Fraser* was off the starboard bow of *Calcutta*, a mile and a half distant. *Restigouche* was on the cruiser's port quarter, a mile and a half to the left of her and slightly astern. The ships were travelling at high speed, with the possibility of attack by submarine or from the air at any time. They had been in continuous action for nearly a week, carrying on rescue work and embarking troops and refugees under threat of submarine attack, air attack and every harassment of a general evacuation. *Fraser's* commanding officer had had one night's sleep in the preceding ten and there is little likelihood that the captain of *Calcutta* had had more.

As the ships steamed on, just visible to each other in the darkness, *Calcutta* signalled for "single line ahead," and *Fraser* altered course to comply. Her commanding officer's intention was to turn inward toward *Calcutta*, run back down to starboard of her and come into station astern. On the cruiser's bridge, however, when the dim silhouette of *Fraser* was seen altering to port ahead, the assumption was made that she intended to come across *Calcutta's* bows and pass down her port side. At the speed the ships were making the destroyer would have had little room to cross in front; and *Calcutta's* captain therefore ordered a sharp turn to starboard; at the same time giving the order for one blast to be sounded on the siren.

The turn to starboard by the cruiser and the turn to port by the destroyer put the two ships on courses converging with fatal rapidity. *Calcutta's* signal blast for a starboard turn was *Fraser's* first warning of approaching disaster; and nothing could now be done to avert it. The vessels were swinging under helm and moving together at a combined speed of thirty-four knots. Engines were put astern and wheels reversed but no order could take effect in time. The ships covered the last two hundred yards intervening between them in less than eleven seconds and *Calcutta*, still swinging to starboard, sheared her way through the forward part of *Fraser*. The destroyer's forepart broke clean off and floated away bottom up. Her entire bridge, with the captain and bridge personnel, was lifted onto *Calcutta's* bow and remained there, swaying and groaning above the cruiser's forecastle.

Restigouche was in station about fifteen hundred yards astern of *Calcutta*. With the crash of the impact she raced up alongside *Fraser* and worked herself inward toward the afterpart of the broken ship. Rocking in a heavy swell which threatened to dash her against the jagged mass of steel, *Restigouche* brought her stern around to touch the stern of *Fraser*. While the hulls of the two ships ground perilously together, sixty of *Fraser's* crew, including one stretcher case, were safely transferred. For the men already in the water *Restigouche* and *Calcutta* lowered their boats, dropped carley floats and let down scramble-nets along their sides.

Fraser's bow had floated away, carrying the cries of its marooned occupants into the darkness. *Restigouche* coming up from astern, had at first mistaken it for a half-submerged wreck. When she identified it for what it was she endeavoured to work alongside, but just as she was approaching the bow capsized. The men clinging to the guard-rails were thrown into the water and had to be picked up by the ships' boats. Altogether, in spite of darkness and a rising swell, 16 officers and 134 men were rescued. Forty-seven Canadian and nineteen British sailors were lost.

The after portion of *Fraser* could not be salvaged with the enemy so near and British ports so far distant. Neither could it be sunk by torpedo for fear the explosion would bring air attack from the German-held coast. A scuttling party was put on board; and after a search for injured men and the removal of confidential books, flooding valves were opened and the remainder of the ship went down at a few minutes past midnight.

The First Year

The loss of *Fraser*, heavy blow though it was for the navy and for the homes of forty-seven Canadians, was a minor incident of those disastrous days; one of the casualties which were as certain to occur under conditions of prolonged and incessant strain as under direct shellfire. Nor could it be lingered upon. The island was girding for invasion; the first bombs were beginning to fall on the ports; and the full extent of the "colossal military disaster" which had overtaken the Allied cause was now apparent.

The British Isles were encompassed by a mighty crescent of air and naval bases extending from Narvik to Bordeaux. Planes from those bases were already raining bombs on British seaports and on ships in the Channel. Submarines from Bergen and Trondheim were active in northern British waters. In a matter of weeks or months U-boat flotillas would be based on the French Biscay ports. They would no longer have to make the dangerous passage from Germany through the English Channel or around the north of Scotland. They would put forth directly into the Atlantic from Brest, Lorient, St. Nazaire, La Rochelle, Bordeaux, their voyage shortened, their range of operations extended by six hundred to a thousand miles. Not only was Britain threatened with invasion by a triumphant army twenty miles across the water, but the lines of sea-borne supply on which she depended for strength and very life were threatened as they had never been threatened before.

Skeena, Restigouche and *St. Laurent* now turned with scores of British ships to a desperate battle for the convoy routes through the southwestern approaches. U-boats were beginning to arrive in greater numbers; the *Luftwaffe* was everywhere over the Channel and far out to sea. The great ports of the south and east were under constant attack; in their scanty hours of harbour time between U-boat hunts and the rescue of survivors from sunken vessels, Canadian destroyers landed parties to assist in combatting air raids.

All the ships, British and Canadian, were fighting a forlorn holding action which had to be abandoned. Late in

38

June Convoy HX-52, nearing Plymouth from the west, was turned round off the Lizard and sent up through the Irish Sea. By early July the hard necessity of revising the whole supply system of the United Kingdom was conceded. The ports of the south and east were out of action so far as convoys were concerned. There remained only the Mersey and the Clyde. Cargoes must be landed in the west and north, broken up and shuttled about the island over bombed railways and through the "bomb alleys" of the local convoys. Precious days of sea time must be lost for the great ocean convoys by sending them upward through the Northwestern approaches; and with the retreat of the convoys must follow the escort forces. *Skeena, Restigouche* and *St. Laurent* went northward with British destroyers to operate from Liverpool, Greenock, Rosyth and later Londonderry.

German submarines were already reaching farther west; but they had made no appearance as yet within the range of our Halifax-based destroyers. The local escort work of *Ottawa* and *Saguenay* was unvaryingly monotonous. *Assiniboine*, returning from the Caribbean in April 1940, had brought back a single lively memory.

She had been on patrol in West Indian waters one rough March day when the British cruiser *Dunedin*, near the coast of the Dominican Republic, had signalled her to come and lend a hand. *Dunedin* had intercepted *Hannover*, a German merchantman which had been attempting a dash for home. As soon as she was stopped, *Hannover* had set herself on fire; and *Dunedin* was now running alongside her, fighting the blaze. *Assiniboine* arrived upon a scene which, according to *Dunedin's* captain, "looked like the last act of a Drury Lane melodrama." The merchantman, her engines knocked out of commission and her steering gear smashed, was lurching about the sea, belching fire from fore and after hatches into a rising wind. *Dunedin*, dodging wildly to maintain her perilous position alongside, was adding clouds of steam to the effect as water from her hoses billowed along the red-hot decks. Some of *Hannover's* crew had made off

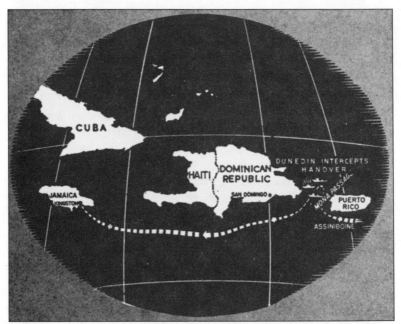

HANNOVER INTERCEPTED MARCH 8, 1940

in the ship's boat and *Dunedin* had had no time to pursue them. The German captain and chief officer, however, were still on their bridge under the baleful eye of a seaman with fixed bayonet. Looking very handsome at the gaff of the main-mast was the White Ensign, flying above the swastika.

Assiniboine wasted little time in admiring the view. The prize was drifting rapidly toward the three-mile limit of the Dominican Republic and if it got into neutral waters all the work would go for nothing. Coming alongside *Hannover*, *Assiniboine* got a line on board and towed her seaward. Then, changing places with *Dunedin,* she played her hoses into the merchantman while the cruiser towed.

For four days and nights, in the face of freshening winds and rising seas, the two ships and their captive struggled along in this way with clouds of steam and smoke rising from the cargo in *Hannover's* holds. The sides of the merchantman were higher than the cruiser's deck and rose some thirteen feet out of the water above *Assiniboine*. All the German's gear had been so effectively sabotaged that there was no possibility of steering her and she yawed wildly, threatening to crush the eggshell sides of the destroyer with every lurch. Neither *Dunedin* nor *Assiniboine*, however, intended to give up their prize and by dawn of the fifth day they were off Jamaica. The complications of salvage had been added to by an unusually convinced Nazi who had jumped overboard from *Dunedin* and set out swimming strongly, apparently for the Fatherland. Since he ignored the life preservers thrown to him, *Assiniboine* lowered a boat; and the remainder of the incident is recorded in her log:

> 1410—Proceeded at 20 knots to pick up man overboard from H.M.S. *Dunedin*.
> 1425—Sighted man swimming strongly.
> 1426—Lowered whaler.
> 1430—Whaler picked up man who requested coxswain to shoot him. Coxswain regretted that he had no gun.

A little later, when the prisoner was safely on board the Canadian destroyer, *Dunedin* signalled:

> Man has persecution mania and has been trying this for days. You had better watch out. Heil Hitler!

Assiniboine replied:

> Have three lifebuoys, two white, one red, and one German who wants to be shot. German is in spud locker, as we are out of spuds.

The diversion over with, the question remained as to how the unmanageable *Hannover* was to be got into Kingston harbour without tugs. Finally, to the consternation of the harbour master, *Dunedin* secured herself to the German's port side, *Assiniboine* took similar action on his starboard side and between them the two ships edged their lurching prisoner into harbour at six knots. *Hannover* was a most useful prize, destined to sail again as *Empire Audacity*, and the whole salvage operation was described by Commander-in-Chief, America and West Indies Station, as "a feat of seamanship of which officers and men in both ships can be justly proud."

The First Year

In June, the little converted light ship *Bras D'Or*, soon to be lost with all hands, made technical capture of the Italian merchantman *Capo Noli* as she was trying to escape from the Gulf of St. Lawrence on the eve of Italy's declaration of war. The incident served to lighten the general monotony of naval life on the near side of the Atlantic; but operations in the western hemisphere, however real their difficulties, had still an unreal quality. The men in *Assiniboine*, *Ottawa* and *Saguenay* heard fretfully of the doings of their sister ships in Britain. *Restigouche*, by August, was preparing to sail for Halifax and a long-postponed refit. The home-based destroyers were eager to replace her and to emulate her record. It was a satisfactory one for the first Canadian ship to return from British waters. Since the beginning of the war she had steamed 26,181 miles, and fought off a score of air and submarine attacks. She bore the scars of shell fragments from German field guns; and she had acted as senior officer of escort for 242 merchant vessels, none of which had been lost to the enemy.

CHAPTER THREE

State of Siege

O*ttawa* was the destroyer chosen to relieve the returning *Restigouche;* and she sailed for the Clyde on August 16, 1940. Saguenay followed her just two months later. By early November both the newcomers had joined *Skeena, St. Laurent* and scores of British ships in the battle for the northwestern approaches.

"Rule Britannia," if anyone found time to play it during the autumn of 1940, must have sounded queerly ironic in those bleak northern waters. The United Kingdom was encompassed by an overpowering enemy and was undergoing such an assault from the air as men had never known before. Sixteen thousand of her people were dead, twenty thousand wounded from mass raids which seemed to be battering her cities and seaports into powder; and the slender channels of reinforcement by sea which were her only hope appeared in imminent danger of strangulation. It was a situation which Adolf Hitler had foreseen months before, compassionately. Coming before the Reichstag on July 19, master of Europe, with his one remaining enemy gripped fast on three sides and overshadowed by three thousand aircraft, he had been able to "see no reason why this war must go on."

The amazing islanders had replied next day with a shower of bombs on every German objective within reach of their few planes. Then, as the autumn wore along, they had produced other reasons more weighty than this defiant nose-thumbing. Their Spitfires and Hurricanes had effectively ruled out the possibility of paralysing and blinding them from the air. Their beaten army, curiously unimpressed by its experience in France, had not only readied itself for defence but had reached abroad again to face the Italians in Libya. Khaki in the regulation too-large and too-small sizes had begun to replace the armlets of the home guard. The ancestral pikes honed up in July had been exchanged for rifles sent in from the United States and Canada or made in home arsenals. There were guns emplaced behind the barbed wire on the beaches, and unpleasant arrangements by which curtains of blazing oil would cover the waters of the likelier landing places.

The resources in planes, cannon, shells, tanks, trained men and every necessity of war were still shockingly inadequate; and still, fortunately, vastly overrated by German Intelligence. Nevertheless, the planners of Operation Sea Lion, which was to have been the invasion of England, may not have been altogether unwise when they decided late in September to postpone their project and devote themselves to methods of siege. They controlled neither the air above the island nor the sea about it. The threatened shores had now a sinister and uninviting appearance; and behind them, amid all the carnage of the air raids, there was a roaring of factories and a purposeful, undismayed clamour of building and making.

Much of the fleet had been disposed against invasion throughout the summer and autumn; but there had been no abdication from other seas. While thousands of trawlers and small craft cleared home waters of the innumerable mines sown by E-boats, planes and submarines, larger ships had been spared to clamp a blockade onto the whole of Europe and make it effective. Wherever German surface raiders threatened the far-flung network of trade—in the Indian Ocean, in the waters of Australia, in the south and middle Atlantic—British ships went doggedly after them. A few cruisers, one or two carriers and some of the older, slower battleships had sought out and taken the measure of the Italian navy in the Mediterranean. There had been no shrinking from losses, no abatement of effort, no willingness to give ground. Total war and almost total disaster had found the British buoyant, defiant and resourceful on land and as crafty and truculent as ever at sea.

STATE OF SIEGE
Eastern Atlantic and British Waters
JUNE 1940 - JUNE 1941

ICELAND

NORTH ATLANTIC OCEAN

TRONDHEIM

BERGEN

NORTH SEA

LONDONDERRY

GREENOCK
ROSYTH
BELFAST

BARROW-IN-FURNESS
LIVERPOOL
MERSEY R.

IRISH SEA

KIEL
Elbe R.
CUXHAVEN
WILHELMSHAVEN

BRISTOL CHANNEL
LAND'S END
LIZARD HD.
PLYMOUTH

THAMES R.

DUNKIRK
BOULOGNE

USHANT
ST. VALERY EN CAUX
BREST

DIEPPE
LE HAVRE

LORIENT

ST. NAZAIRE

LA ROCHELLE

BORDEAUX

BAYONNE
ST. JEAN DE LUZ

GERMAN U-BOAT BASES

GENERAL U-BOAT ROUTES

State of Siege

Their situation still wavered between the critical and the desperate; and had only been held in that perilous equilibrium by mighty efforts. The essential vulnerability of their home island remained unaltered. The lanes of sea supply fed into the north Atlantic from every ocean and narrowed to a few close-grouped channels as they approached the United Kingdom. It was here, upon this unavoidably congested area, that the attacks of planes and U-boats were centred; and the problem of defence had grown more difficult with every day since June. Arriving and departing convoys, barred from the southern approaches, had to make their way through the misty seas northward of Ireland and westward of Scotland. British escort forces, everywhere insufficient, fought to hold sea lanes beset from south of Iceland to the Mull of Kintyre by long-range planes and swarming U-boats.

Some three submarines were coming into action for every one sunk, and they were attacking by new methods which proved ruinously effective. They no longer lay in wait submerged where a convoy might give them the slip by an evasive turn. They rode surfaced and awash during the day, paralleling a convoy's course at binocular range, hardly visible with their conning towers just above water. At night they came in from the side of the darkest horizon to launch their torpedoes and make off at high speed on the surface. The "wolf-pack" group tactics were developing; while aircraft patrolling thousands of miles of sea not only made devastating attacks themselves but homed the U-boats onto convoys and made it practically impossible for ships to sail undetected.

The area of battle, already vast, was expanding inexorably westward, beyond the range of short-legged escorts based on the British Isles. Merchant ship losses were far outstripping new construction; and among those afloat the overloaded, over-worked, over-aged veterans which formed so large a part of the freighter tonnage were staggering under the strain. The number of stragglers who fell out of the columns and limped on alone as defenceless targets was continually increasing. The herded, harried convoys ploughed inward and outward on regular sailing schedules, but with great gaps torn in their ranks by the attackers. During a year of war on all seas 471 ships totalling 2,000,000 tons had been lost to submarines, and as many more to mines, aircraft and surface ships. The priceless tonnage was bleeding away in spite of the work of escorts required everywhere at once, almost incessantly at sea, summoned from convoy to convoy and from new disaster to new attack.

Skeena and *St. Laurent* had had a full share of the trials and frustrations of the battle before their sister ships arrived. During the late summer and early autumn they had joined with British ships in many attacks on submarines and suspected submarines; and brushes with German planes had become routine. Like most of the escorts, however, they had found definite kills hard to come by. Far more common was the work of recovering seamen for the allied cause. *Skeena's* list of rescues included sixty-four men from S.S. *Manipur*, torpedoed north of Scotland on July 17, and twenty more from S.S. *Thornlea* on September 2. When the armed merchant cruiser *Cheshire* was torpedoed west of Ireland on October 14, *Skeena* took on board 220 men and escorted the damaged ship in tow to Belfast. Four days later she gave passage home to six exhausted, oil-soaked survivors from S.S. *Bruse*.

For *St. Laurent*, the first and largest incident of the summer had had its grimly ironic side. On the morning of July 2 she had been inbound for the United Kingdom when she was ordered to a position where the liner, *Arandora Star*, had been torpedoed by a German submarine. She arrived on the scene seven hours later to find 861 German and Italian civilians floundering in the water, clinging to pieces of wreckage, or cramming a half-dozen lifeboats which were scattered miles apart along the horizon. *Arandora Star's* passenger list, except for a few armed guards, had been made up entirely of enemy nationals, arrested in England and bound for internment in Canada.

St. *Laurent* steamed slowly into the oily desolation of sea, and lowered her boats. Then as her whalers pulled away and began their laborious cruise among the hundreds of bobbing heads, the destroyer manoeuvred herself alongside the men clinging to rafts and the larger pieces of wreckage. Most of these were in the late stages of exhaustion and could do little to help themselves. St. *Laurent's* crew had to go over the side after them. For hour after hour Canadian sailors floundered in the water or balanced precariously on crates and pieces of timber as they passed lines about limp bodies whose weight was nearly doubled by the fuel oil and salt water in which they had been immersed. Lying frequently with engines stopped and with no protection from U-boat attacks, the destroyer waited while this work went on among the large groups of survivors, while her own boats cruised about the area, and while *Arandora Star's* boats made their way to her side. She turned back for port at last with all in the water accounted for, and with every bunk and hammock and every square inch of space above or below decks crammed with enemy aliens.

It was one of the largest individual rescues of the war; and the appreciation of the Italian Government was eventually conveyed to St. *Laurent* by way of the Brazilian Embassy. Nevertheless, the Canadians undoubtedly viewed the operation, during its progress, with mixed feelings. The sailors could not know and probably would not have been impressed by the fact that the bedraggled specimens they were hauling from the water included some of the noted chefs and maîtres d'hôtel of London. Nor would the pilots of Coastal Command, which was represented at the scene. A lone British Sunderland had dropped down for a look while the rescue was in progress, and St. *Laurent* had signalled conversationally, "Most of these people are Germans and Italians."

"How bloody funny," had been the pilot's comment, as he wheeled away.

In September the Canadian navy acquired a new ship whose life was tragically brief. Immediately after the loss of

Fraser negotiations had begun with the Admiralty for the purchase of a replacement; and on September 6 the former *H.M.S. Diana* was recommissioned as the Canadian destroyer *Margaree*. She was refitted at the Albert Docks, London, by workers who carried on through the heaviest of the September air raids, and was damaged herself by splinters and fire bombs on the night of September 17. Coming safely through this difficult rebirth as a Canadian ship, she proceeded to Londonderry and sailed from that port on October 20 as escort for a small convoy of five ships.

She was two days at sea on a rough, squally night when disaster occurred. Up to midnight she had been riding out well ahead of the convoy; but as visibility became poorer she reduced speed in order to keep in sight of the merchant ships. About one o'clock a blinding rain squall blew up and continued for twenty-five minutes. As it lifted, *Port Fairy*, the leading merchant ship in the port column, discovered *Margaree* just ahead of her and dangerously close on her starboard bow.

Port Fairy stopped her engines, then went to full astern; but just as she did so *Margaree* made a turn to port, rode across the merchantman's course, and before *Port Fairy's* full astern order could take effect her bow had crashed into *Margaree* just at the bridge and cut the destroyer in half. The fore part drifted clear, turned over and sank within one minute.

Lurching in the rainy darkness and the high sea, *Port Fairy* threw out calcium flares for the men in the water and put herself alongside the after part of *Margaree*. Thirty of the destroyer's men managed to cross over to her deck. Then a heavy swell lifted the two ships simultaneously, ground their sides together and flung them apart. Three men were left marooned on *Margaree's* quarter deck as the ships separated, but they let down a raft and managed to stay afloat in the heaving sea until *Port Fairy* could work herself around to pick them up.

State of Siege

Not a man on the bridge or in the fore part of the destroyer was saved. The commanding officer and 141 of the ship's company were lost; and the cause of the disaster was never fully determined. All that was known was that *Margaree*, at reduced speed, had been falling back in relation to the convoy. The squally, uncertain visibilty had prevented full observation of her movements; and there was no one to tell exactly what had occurred on her bridge during the last seconds before the impact. Such disasters had occurred before in convoy and were to occur again. The risk of them was a calculated risk, accepted under the overriding necessity of sailing large groups of ships in close company through every variety of weather. Radar, just emerging from its swaddling clothes, was greatly to reduce the danger; but it would never be completely eliminated at sea.

As *Ottawa* and *Saguenay* settled into the routine of the northern escort forces their work took on the familiar pattern of their sister ships. After an abortive submarine hunt, the rescue of fifty-five survivors, and an indecisive battle with a lone aircraft, *Ottawa* was summoned to the aid of the merchant ship *Melrose Abbey* on November 5. Southwest of Ireland, the freighter was being shelled by an Italian submarine, one of several new arrivals in the Atlantic by courtesy of Mussolini. *Ottawa* arrived on the scene with the British destroyer *Harvester* at about the same time that *Jervis Bay*, far to the west of them, was steaming into the guns of the *Admiral Scheer*.

As the destroyers hove in sight the Italian dived; and it required five hours of careful search to gain asdic contact with him. Sustained depth charge attacks, continued for several hours more, at last brought oil seeping to the surface. When the contact faded out the destroyers departed, certain of their kill; too certain as they were later to discover.

The attack, like every other attack on a submarine throughout the war, came under review by an Admiralty assessment committee; and the verdict passed in this case, after a study of all reports and charts of the action, was "U-boat probably damaged." Like many similar reports it had a damping effect on the officers and men of supposedly victorious ships, but wider experience was to justify the official caution. Submarines were far harder to kill and submarine hunting was a more complicated technique than many ships at first realized. Long study, months and years of work by scientists, and hard experience at sea would still be required before allied anti-submarine forces were fully proficient.

St. Laurent began a spell of work more arduous than usual on December 1. She was about three hundred and fifty miles west of Ireland with a convoy when a signal arrived ordering her to detach at once and steam to a point fifty miles farther west. Here two convoys, one inward bound and one outward bound, had been passing just after dark when they were attacked by four U-boats. By the time *St. Laurent*, struggling through high winds, heavy seas and fitful snowstorms, arrived on the scene ten ships had been sunk and the armed merchant cruiser *Forfar* was crawling away, a torpedoed cripple.

St. Laurent was first ordered to escort *Forfar* to harbour; a congenial task in its way since *Forfar* was the former Canadian Pacific steamship *Montrose*. About midnight, however, she was called away from *Forfar* to the assistance of a merchant ship far astern which had just been attacked. En route to the new position word came that another salvo of five torpedoes had sent *Forfar* to the bottom; and *St. Laurent* turned again in response to this call. Shortly before dawn she came upon still another sinking ship, the motor vessel *Conch;* and took on board fifty-three of its survivors.

She was just resuming course toward *Forfar's* last reported position when a U-boat appeared a mile away on her starboard bow, diving. *St. Laurent* bore down on the widening swirl where the U-boat had disappeared, passed over the position and gained asdic contact. As the wavering pencil moved across the face of her asdic plot, showing the progress of the enemy making off beneath the surface, *St. Laurent* proceeded deliberately, careful not to endanger her chance of a kill by over-hasty attack. The British destroyer *Viscount*, a senior ship, appeared on the horizon and *St. Laurent* waited until she came up and obtained a confirming echo. Then, with the unseen target firmly held by one or other of the asdic beams, the two ships began the uncanny dance of death which is a deliberate depth charge attack.

Viscount, establishing her contact, steamed slowly along the wavering course followed by the submarine beneath, stalking it at a distance of some twelve hundred yards. *St. Laurent*, running in approximately at right angles to *Viscount's* course and broadside on to the submarine, came directly over her quarry's position. A word of command from the bridge was echoed by a series of orders rapped out on the quarterdeck; then there came a rattle of heavy cannisters rolling along steel rails and two splashes in the water astern. The light bark of the port and starboard "throwers" followed; and four more depth charges hurtled into the air to drop in the water, two on each side and about sixty-five yards out from the ship. Two more charges rolled from the stern rails as the destroyer passed on; then two more. A few seconds later there came a series of muffled explosions from the depths, fountains of water mushroomed in the sea behind the ship and her whole frame shuddered to the impact. *St. Laurent* had "laid her eggs"; a roughly diamond-shaped pattern of ten depth charges, falling in pairs at spaced intervals. One charge of each pair was "heavy", set to explode beneath the submarine; the other "light" to explode above.

With her charges away, the Canadian ship came round to take over *Viscount's* role as stalker astern of the submarine. *Viscount* moved in from the side as *St. Laurent* had done, to repeat the attack process. As *Viscount's* pattern exploded, *St. Laurent* took over again; and the relentless hammering continued for three hours, guided back and forth above the squirming enemy by the incessant "pinging" of the asdic beam. After eighty charges had gone down, carrying twelve tons of explosive, diesel oil began coming to the surface. A little later the contact faded out. The two captains were certain that the U-boat had been sunk in deep water; and later the Admiralty's assessment committee was sufficiently convinced to credit them with a "probably sunk."

From the scene of this action *St. Laurent* went on without delay to the position of *Forfar's* sinking, where she managed to pick up three officers and seventeen men. She set course for Greenock, but was almost immediately ordered fifty miles eastward to the assistance of *Loch Ranza,* another merchantman which had just been torpedoed. Her arrival alongside *Loch Ranza* marked the beginning of a three-day battle through the foulest North Atlantic weather, with the damaged ship crawling at five knots and several times threatening to founder. Battered by towering seas and hidden from time to time in sudden snowstorms, *Loch Ranza* laboured on while *St. Laurent,* held to a dangerous crawl, screened her against further U-boat attack and remained at day-and-night readiness to take off the crew if the ship's bulkheads should give way. The two vessels arrived at Greenock together and *St. Laurent,* after some hundred hours of incessant action, prepared to unload her survivors and give her men a rest.

At about the same time *Saguenay* was limping into a more southerly port, the first Canadian naval casualty from torpedo attack. The destroyer had been proceeding in escort of a convoy during the small hours of the morning of December 1 and about four o'clock was in a position three hundred miles west of Ireland. Travelling at twelve knots in her night station on the port quarter, she was zigzagging and periodically making a wide sweep across the rear of the entire convoy. At five minutes to four a flare shot up from the dark sea, astern and a mile or so to port. It had been fired by a U-boat, still unseen, which was moving in to attack the rear of the convoy. *Saguenay* increased her speed and made for the position from which the flare had risen. A moment later the submarine was sighted half a mile distant. Almost simultaneously, a torpedo struck the destroyer forward on the port side, and "B" gun in the afterpart of the ship opened fire on the German.

By the time two rounds had been fired the submarine had dived; and all *Saguenay's* attention was required to look after herself. The seamen's mess decks where the torpedo had struck were so fiercely ablaze that the entire fore part of the ship had to be cleared. Soon smoke and flame funnelling up through the bridge structure compelled evacuation of the bridge itself. Inflammable materials in the paint shop forward of the mess decks added to the flames. Salt water, pouring through the jagged gash in the ship's side, ignited calcium flares which fed their choking fumes into the general inferno.

A fire party which attempted to make headway against the blaze was beaten back. There was nothing for it but to flood the forward magazine; and as this was done the entire fore part of the ship, for some sixty feet back from the bow, began to bend toward the water. Cables and miscellaneous heavy gear rattled overside and then, as a great section of the smashed hull broke off and sank, the blazing forecastle, relieved of the dead weight, began to lift again.

No order had been given to stop engines; and engineers and stokers, still at their posts, kept the ship moving ahead at about two knots. Flames, breaking out with renewed vigour, still swept the bridge section; and the ship had to be conned from the emergency steering position at the after end. An attempt to go astern was made and immediately abandoned when terrific vibration told of a bent shaft. *Saguenay* had snapped like a whip with the impact of the torpedo, buckling the frames along ten feet of her after part and throwing one propeller shaft out of alignment.

The British destroyer *Highlander*, senior ship of the escort, arrived within an hour or so to find *Saguenay* again limping slowly ahead. Five officers and eighty-five men were transferred to *Highlander* to reduce casualties in case of another torpedo attack; and throughout the night and most of the next day a skeleton crew continued to fight the fires.

In the early evening tugs arrived to take the smouldering ship in tow; but *Saguenay* was now working her speed up toward six knots and considered that she was doing as well by herself as she could in tow. Suggesting that at least one of the tugs might be more urgently required elsewhere, she continued under her own power with one tug standing by; and noon of the next day found her rounding the north of Ireland with all fires out and her steering gear back in operation. Her destination was Barrow-in-Furness, across the Irish Sea from the Isle of Man; and just as she was approaching the port she completed her tale of misfortune by setting off an enemy acoustic ground mine. With further damage to her stern and her last remaining fuel stores contaminated by salt water, she finally had to accept a tow, and reached harbour on the evening of December 5. Twenty-one of her men had been killed.

Among the eighteen injured was Clifford E. McNaught, a seaman who had been in the fore-part of the ship when the torpedo struck. He had volunteered immediately to help the depleted crews of the after guns and had worked with them, manhandling ammunition, until a sudden glare of flame revealed his condition to the officer in charge. Horribly burned about the face and hands in the original explosion, McNaught had continued for the best part of an hour to pass up heavy shells, with each touch of the ice-cold steel further mangling his shredded fingers.

Highlander signalled that, "the fine seamanship displayed by Commander Miles and his officers and ship's company in getting their ship into harbour is deserving of the highest praise." The Admiralty concurred; adding also that the speed with which *Saguenay's* gun had gone into action had forced the submarine under and prevented it from attacking the convoy.

Saguenay would now be out of action for several months. Her crippling, together with the loss of *Margaree*, had reduced the strength of the Canadian Navy by approximately twenty-five per cent; and small though the losses were in comparison to the total losses among British escort forces, they could be ill sustained. Submarine attacks and the necessity to counter them were moving steadily outward into mid-Atlantic. Iceland was being developed as a base for British escort forces and aircraft of Coastal Command. It would be an invaluable relay point; without it short range ships based on the British Isles could not give protection to convoys even as far as mid-Atlantic. But it was beginning to seem likely that escort to mid-Atlantic would not be sufficient; and it was glaringly obvious that even for the present system there were not enough ships.

Most welcome, therefore, were the fifty American destroyers, given in exchange for bases leased in the western hemisphere, which began to arrive in December. The ships were over-age reserve vessels of the United States Navy, built in 1919-20 and paid off after the first World War. Of the fifty, the Canadian navy was to receive seven, six of which were named for Canadian rivers: *Annapolis, Columbia, Niagara, St. Clair, St. Croix* and *St. Francis.* The seventh saw service with the Royal Navy before coming to Canada and retained the name under which the British had commissioned her, *Hamilton.*

As the ships arrived in Canadian ports en route to England, the crews who went on board were struck first of all by the generosity with which the Americans had stored them. Particularly impressed were the British seamen. Every square inch of storage space was crammed with a variety of provisions which were now only a memory in England. Accommodations and fittings were also of a nature unknown to the spartan "juicers." There were bunks in the mess decks instead of hammocks; there were typewriters, radios, coffee-making machines.

There were also compensating defects which became apparent at sea. The ships had been emergency vessels laid down during the closing year of the first World War. They had been built in haste, with only the requirements of an earlier and less technical war in view. They were not sufficiently manoeuvreable against U-boats; and their sea-keeping qualities left much to be desired. They had a narrow beam and shallow draft which made them difficult to handle in rough weather; and their progress through heavy seas was a bitterly bad-tempered fight which wracked their own frames and the frames of their ships' companies. Their messdeck bunks, for all the pleasant appearance they offered in harbour, made exorbitant demands on the men's crowded living space. Their steering gear was flimsy and cranky; and they were to remain to the end of their not inglorious careers seagoing purgatories of which those who sailed in them still speak with mingled horror and affection.

They were, with all their faults, a saving transfusion of strength. *Niagara, St. Clair* and *St. Croix* set out from Halifax for the United Kingdom in December, and fought their way eastward in the teeth of a ten-day gale. Only *Niagara* and *St. Clair* arrived. *St. Croix*, continually losing steam through insufficient suction on fuel lines, had to make a dangerous turn-about in mid-ocean and put back into St. John's, Newfoundland. The two remaining ships had no knowledge of her fate because their wireless transmission was on a wavelength which did not permit of inter-ship communication. Signals from one ship had to be transmitted to Halifax and re-broadcast to the ship for which they were intended. The roundabout, uncertain method practically put the ships out of touch with each other; and their passage in every other way was sufficiently difficult. Their rolling in the worst of the weather reached a maximum of fifty degrees. Nevertheless, when they arrived in the Clyde, bristling with defects for repair by the overworked shipyards, their captains found kind words as well as profane for them. A man who wanted to be at sea in those days couldn't be too particular about his ship.

There were now six Canadian destroyers in British waters, and with the last days of January came four more: *Assiniboine, Restigouche, Columbia* and *St. Francis*. The arrival of the latter group brought also the first extension of Canadian operational command. Commodore L. W. Murray, who had been Deputy Chief of the Naval Staff, crossed as senior officer of the group of four destroyers; and as Commodore Commanding Canadian Ships and Establishments in the United Kingdom began a long and intimate association with the Battle of the Atlantic.

The reinforcements which new building and the addition of the American destroyers provided for British escort forces might have seemed large; but they were soon to be dwarfed by a mounting scale of attack. After a winter diminuendo the dark symphony of destruction rose in crashing chords. During the last week of February 1941, 150,700 tons of merchant shipping were sunk. In the first two weeks of March, 245,000 tons went down; and the scale of losses continued into April and May. Three and four ships and their cargoes were being lost daily, farther and farther afield; and the ratio of replacement showed still a ruinous decline. "Wherever British ships cruise," said Hitler, "we shall set against them our submarines until the hour of decision." The hour of decision, it might have seemed, was approaching with mathematical inexorability.

In Canada the last months of 1940 saw the passage down the St. Lawrence of fourteen small, half equipped, sketchily manned steel warships. They were the first Canadian corvettes, the unsampled fruits of a building programme well in arrears but in process of being carried out. The little vessels, 190 feet in length, 33 in beam, with a speed of 16 knots and a planned armament of one four-inch gun, two machine guns, and a stock of depth charges, could hardly have been impressive to a big-ship man. They were designed for a maximum complement of 92 men, which would have to be increased almost immediately. Their armament was to grow, the number of their anti-submarine devices would be multiplied by gadgets yet undreamed of; and for all this equipment and for the men to operate it, room would have to be found or made. The corvettes would never be handsome ships and they would never be comfortable ships. Yet the captains who took them over, most of them former merchant navy officers, had already conceived a grumbling affection for them. With all their limitations, they performed under the knowledgeable hand of a seaman with something of the spirit of a thoroughbred. They felt seaworthy; and they were to prove so.

The long series of minor miracles which had brought them into being was reflected in the ridged brows of ship-yard executives, naval construction engineers and many late-toiling technicians. On the slipways of the east coast, the Great Lakes and the west coast, the frames of other corvettes were taking shape under the increasing skill of a growing army of workmen. Improved designs were already in the blueprint stage. The ship-building experiment was showing signs of working out. The passage of the fourteen corvettes, some of them weaving down the river with an ice-breaker crashing through the thickening ice ahead of them, was an event and a foreshadowing. The nation, with no evidence as yet of what the ships would be worth, had at least demonstrated that she could produce them.

Of the Prince ships, one was already in commission and had not been idle. *Prince Robert,* originally intended for patrol along the west coast, had gone into operation in September with changed plans and under conditions of considerable excitement. As she was nearing completion there had been growing concern both in the Admiralty and in Canadian naval headquarters over German merchantmen in neutral ports to the south. The Chief of the Naval Staff had noted that "there have been signs of restlessness amongst the German ships laid up in ports of western North and South America. Several have moved and actually proceeded to sea in the past few months." There was always a possibility that these ships might slip out and run for Germany or, worse still, be fitted out as raiders. It was decided in the early days of September that *Prince Robert* would go as reinforcement for British blockading ships, too thinly spread there as everywhere; and the immediate object of her attention was to be the nine-thousand ton freighter *Weser.*

Weser was lying in Manzanillo, Mexico, and was known to be making preparations for sea. *Prince Robert* in

Esquimalt, also preparing for her maiden voyage as a warship, still required stores, a shakedown cruise and a certain amount of training. *Weser's* increasing restlessness, however, began to be the subject of urgent messages to Ottawa and Esquimalt; and *Prince Robert's* preparations were drastically expedited. With what stores she already had she put out for a gunnery shoot on the afternoon of September 11, and at dawn on the 12th sailed for Manzanillo "in a very unready state," to quote her commanding officer.

She arrived off the port to learn that *Weser* had not yet sailed, although evidently intending to do so. *Prince Robert* stood to sea again and patrolled off the port for a week, keeping herself out of sight during the day and closing in to binocular range at night.

After dark on September 25, she had taken up her usual in-shore patrol station when she sighted a merchant ship coming out of Manzanillo Bay. It was *Weser* and she had not sighted *Prince Robert*. She was just clear of the harbour breakwater, however, and there was every possibility that if she did sight the Canadian ship she would put back to safety. To the south of the harbour mouth there was a lighthouse with high land behind. *Prince Robert* ran as close inshore as she dared and crawled along by the lighthouse and the high land so that her silhouette in the darkness might be obscured as much as possible. The manoeuvre was successful. *Weser* continued on her course. The German master said afterward that he had first taken *Prince Robert* for an island and later, perceiving her to be in motion, had decided that she was a Mexican gunboat. He continued seaward and within a few minutes *Prince Robert* had cut him off from land.

There was still the matter of stalking the quarry until he was comfortably outside the three-mile limit. *Weser's* silhouette moved steadily ahead and the dark shape of *Prince Robert* loomed a mile astern, clinging in the German's wake while her ship's company watched silently from action stations. At length the waters of neutrality gave way to the high seas, the unleashed warship churned up alongside the mer-

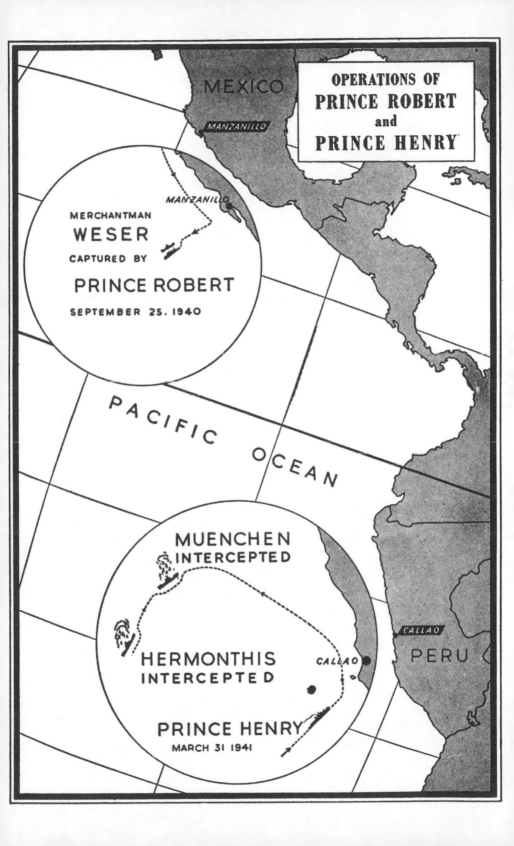

OPERATIONS OF
PRINCE ROBERT
and
PRINCE HENRY

MEXICO

MANZANILLO

MERCHANTMAN
WESER
CAPTURED BY
PRINCE ROBERT
SEPTEMBER 25. 1940

MANZANILLO

PACIFIC

OCEAN

MUENCHEN
INTERCEPTED

HERMONTHIS
INTERCEPTED

CALLAO

PERU

CALLAO

PRINCE HENRY
MARCH 31 1941

chantman's port quarter and her searchlight cut a blinding swath through the darkness. *Weser* came to a startled stop at a shouted order and within minutes a party from *Prince Robert* was on board.

There was little trouble from the German crew. All preparations for scuttling had been made in case of capture; but the Canadian ship had pounced too quickly for any of the plans to be carried out. *Weser* returned to Esquimalt with the White Ensign flying above the swastika on her ensign staff, the first important Canadian prize of the war. She was re-named *Vancouver Island* and made several trans-Atlantic crossings until a German torpedo brought her career to an end.

Prince Robert returned to the Caribbean, and later began a series of Antipodean escort cruises which brought Australian and New Zealand airmen to Canada for training. She was also escort for the *Awatea* with Canadian troops to Hong Kong; and cleared Honolulu for home three days before the Japanese attack on Pearl Harbor. By the time she arrived in Esquimalt from that voyage her two sister ships had been in commission for nearly a year and one of them had had adventures resembling her own.

Prince Henry was commissioned in December 1940 and in February of 1941 was operating under orders of the British cruiser *Diomede* off Callao, Peru. There were four German merchant ships in the port and two of them, *Hermonthis* and *Muenchen,* gave evidence of an intention to sail.

For several weeks *Diomede* and *Prince Henry* maintained a tiresome and unrewarding vigil in the area. On March 16 *Diomede* was called away; and *Prince Henry*, after eight more days of patrolling, entered the harbour of neutral Callao to gain what information she could. The German ships, it appeared, were fuelled for a breakaway and had been wired for firing and demolition to prevent capture. They had a speed of eleven knots and the likelihood was that they would try to run on diverging courses in the general direction of Japan.

Interception of "Hermonthis and "Muenchen"

The commanding officer of *Prince Henry* decided to put to sea and disappear, hoping the Germans would believe he had departed on other errands. He remained well off the port for some ten days, cruising in a wide arc, but at last the expected signal reached him. *Hermonthis* and *Muenchen* had sailed at seven-thirty on the evening of March 31, when *Prince Henry* was sixty miles south of Callao, distant by some three hours steaming at maximum speed. The intentions of the enemy ships, as well as their course and speed, would have to be guessed correctly if they were to be intercepted.

After eight hours of anxious search, *Muenchen* was sighted northward of Callao and fifteen miles from *Prince Henry*. The German appeared to have sighted the Canadian simultaneously, for he altered course to the northward, then came around to the west as *Prince Henry* turned in pursuit Forty minutes later, at seven in the morning, *Prince Henry* drew to within 12,000 yards of the German ship and flashed the international signal, "Stop instantly or I will open fire." *Muenchen* continued on her course and *Prince Henry* sent a shell across her bows. The immediate answer was a cloud of smoke from the superstructure of the merchantman; and the crew could be seen climbing into boats which were immediately lowered and pulled away. By the time *Prince Henry* drew alongside *Muenchen* the ship was a mass of flame and almost hidden by dense clouds of smoke. There was obviously no possibility of salvage.

The other German, *Hermonthis,* was still at large, however, and *Prince Henry* swung off to the southward at full speed in search of him. Four and a half hours later he appeared, low on the horizon to the southeast. He was almost instantly seen to be on fire and lowering boats. *Prince Henry* ran for him, and as she drew alongside lowered her cutter with a boarding party to round up one of the German boats. The combined crew of Germans and Canadians then boarded *Hermonthis.*

The ship was heavily on fire, but there seemed at first some possibility of saving her. An engine room party made its way below and closed the sea-cocks to prevent sinking. *Prince Henry* secured herself to the weather side of *Hermonthis,* and brought her hoses into play. An upper deck party on board the German tried to fight the fires raging in the holds, but for this *Hermonthis'* hoses were necessary and they could not be used since the generators were submerged and there was no pressure on the pumps. For four hours the Canadians fought a losing battle. A heavy sea was pounding *Prince Henry* against the German's listing sides, and ten hoses which she had run across were broken as the ships careened together and lurched apart.

At length it was obvious that the ship could not be saved. The boarding party and the German prisoners who had been impressed into service were withdrawn and *Prince Henry* went in search of the Germans in the other two boats. When these were recovered, she sank the flaming *Hermonthis* with gunfire and retraced her course to perform a similar service for *Muenchen.* This work, however, had been carried out by the Peruvian cruiser *Almirante Grau,* which had also picked up the crew. *Prince Henry* withdrew with her prisoners, and later resumed patrol duties in the Pacific and Caribbean, on which she was relieved from time to time by *Prince David.* There was to be no major excitement for either of the ships, however, until the commencement of American operations in the Aleutians.

Of the fourteen corvettes completed by the end of 1940 two had been sailed unarmed and not yet fully equipped to Britain. Eight more were to follow in January and February but none were to remain there long. The Atlantic battle was spreading westward. Throughout the spring it had raged with mounting intensity and not without success for the ships in British waters. March saw the end of three of the great U-boat aces who had led and inspired the whole German effort. Prien, who had sunk the *Royal Oak,* went to the bottom with all his crew; Schepke was crushed on his conning tower by the charging bow of the destroyer *Vanoc;* Kretschmer was captured. The terrible *Bismarck* was sunk in

May, removing a gnawing anxiety from the whole Atlantic. But there were other surface ships and other daring U-boat captains; too many of them. During June, 590,000 tons of merchant shipping were sunk. Most ominous sign of all, eleven of the ships lost went down in an area which extended to within 800 miles of Halifax. The U-boats were probing for a weaker link in the chain of sea supply, and they were finding it on the western side of the Atlantic.

Such a threat could not be countered by ships based only on the British Isles and on Iceland. The escort system had to expand and carry westward with the attack; and for such an expansion a new base was required. Halifax was a possibility; but five hundred miles nearer the United Kingdom, reaching far out into the Atlantic from the shores of the new world, was a likelier place. It was St. John's, capital of Newfoundland and a port of call for British ships since the days of Cabot. If mid-ocean escort east and west were possible at all it would be most nearly possible from St. John's, and what arrangements could be made must be made without delay.

The Canadian navy was asked and agreed to operate an escort force based on St. John's. The responsibility would entail the use of every Canadian escort ship and as many more ships as the British could spare. It would require a great deal more than that; but later needs would have to be determined by experience. In the meantime, Canadian ships in British waters sailed westward again and with them came the officer under whom they were to operate. On June 13, 1941, Commodore L. W. Murray arrived in St. John's from the United Kingdom to take the appointment of Commodore Commanding Newfoundland Force.

CHAPTER FOUR

The Western Atlantic

THE war was now entering upon what Churchill called, "one of the great climacterics." On June 22, 1941, nine days after the establishment of the Newfoundland Escort Force, Hitler invaded Russia; and the might of the *Wehrmacht* wheeled away from the shores that menaced Britain. The threat of immediate invasion passed; the sun of temporary immunity shone bleakly above a cloud of vast and ambiguous warfare on the continent.

Yet within that cloud were other and darker implications for the beleaguered island, for Canada, and even for the United States, whose cause was now glaringly and inextricably linked with theirs. The collapse of Russia would enable Hitler to turn westward, across the Channel and across the Atlantic, with all the resources of Asia at his command. Even if Russia did not collapse, if Germany were held to an exhausted stalemate by land, there could be no victory and no hope of final peace without an attack fed by sea and mounted from the beach-head of the British Isles. Whether for ultimate defence against a ten-fold mightier Germany, or for sea-borne assault from the west, the resources of the friendly world must be turned into munitions of war and stock-piled in the United Kingdom.

The resources potentially available were more than sufficient; but between the promise of the future and the need of the present lay a perilous gap of space and time. It could be bridged only by ships—all the ships now available and hundreds more. Vast quantities of supplies were every day laden and afloat, moving toward the United Kingdom. Many ships of many convoys were arriving at British ports each week and the tonnage of cargo unloaded was enormous. Yet a great proportion represented the food and staple necessaries which the island required to live by even in peacetime. Only the margin above that minimal daily necessity represented the power to wage war—munitions of every kind, cannon, airplanes, guns, tanks and, above all, aviation gasoline and fuel oil.

The margin must be increased steadily and rapidly. If it were even slightly reduced a vicious circle of evils would be created. If oil stocks fell below the point of safety the operation of ships and planes would have to be curtailed. If planes and ships could not operate to full capacity the attacks by sea could not be effectively met and more tonnage would be lost, creating further shortages which would again reduce operations. The demands of the war, continually increasing, must be met by a corresponding increase of the inward flow of cargo; yet upon that flow the U-boat warfare imposed a steady, sickening drain.

Three merchant ships were going down for every one replaced by the combined ship-building resources of the United Kingdom and the United States. Eight submarines were coming into operation for every one sunk. U-boats swarmed in the Mediterranean. They were off Gibraltar, off the Cape Verde Islands at the bulge of Africa, off Capetown far to the south. The slender channels of reinforcement were being pinched and pierced everywhere along their length. And in the Atlantic, where their severance would be a mortal blow, the thrust was turning with redoubled strength toward a new and vulnerable zone.

The movement of U-boats in force into the western Atlantic made end-to-end escort for the convoys a necessity. The fifteen-hundred mile gap between the end of local escort from Canada and the beginning of local escort from Iceland or from British bases would have to be covered by new forces. Battleships, even if they could still be spared, were no longer appropriate to the new situation. With *Bismarck* and *Graf Spee* sunk and *Scharnhorst, Gneisenau* and *Prinz Eugen* locked up in Brest, the danger from German surface ships was greatly diminished. The need was for many small ships; and because of the limited range of such vessels, they would have to be operated in relays from base to base across the Atlantic.

St. John's, Newfoundland, thus became the key to the western defence system. By its position alone it bridged nearly a quarter of the gap between the Canadian seaboard and Iceland. The first lap of the convoy journey would now be a five-hundred mile voyage from Halifax to a point off Newfoundland. At that point the local escorts would break off and put into St. John's to refuel for their homeward journey to Halifax. Mid-ocean escorts, putting out from St. John's, would take over the convoys from their local escort and shepherd them to the Iceland area; turn them over there to British escorts, refuel in Iceland and return to St. John's with westward-bound convoys. Only with such a system and such a relay point would it be possible for the short-legged destroyers and smaller escort ships to operate across the western Atlantic.

St. John's had a long history as a minor British naval station; and had been a centre of considerable activity since the beginning of the war. Clustering about a small oval harbour sheltered behind the craggy cliffs of the Avalon Peninsula, it had almost every disadvantage except that of geography. It looked out upon the great shallows of the Grand Banks, two hundred miles to the southeast, where the Labrador Current and the Gulf Stream met to breed some of the worst weather in the world. It was small and undeveloped, and it was remote from any industrial centre. Everything required for the construction of a large naval base would have to come from outside the island. Communications were inadequate; skilled labour was scarce; docking facilities, billeting facilities, fuel and fuel storage were all lacking. Everything would have to be brought, everything would have to be built, in the midst of the battle to keep the convoys sailing.

Newfoundland Command, as now constituted, was an extension of the convoy-and-escort system, and was under the general authority of Commander-in-Chief, Western Approaches, the British admiral based in Liverpool to direct the whole Atlantic battle. Nevertheless, Commodore Commanding Newfoundland Force exercised complete autonomy within his zone of operations; and—in addition to Canadian ships—British, French, Norwegian, Polish, Belgian and Dutch ships would be allotted to him. His authority extended to the base of St. John's, to all local escorts operating from the base and to convoys and their escorts while in Newfoundland waters. Canadian naval responsibility was thus greatly increased. Our ships, which had been distributed among British escort forces, were to be assembled as the main component of a separate force under Canadian command; and that force was to be entrusted with a distinct and vital function. Canada had taken over in her own right a sector of the widening Atlantic battle area.

Trade and the convoys, about which all plans revolved, had brought extensive developments on the Canadian side during twenty-two months of war. Port facilities, though they still lagged behind the continually increasing demands made upon them, had grown out of all recognition. The training of DEMS men and the arming of merchant vessels for their own defence had gone urgently forward; and most ships sailing in convoy were now provided with guns and with naval gunners or navy-trained crews to man them. The general problems of convoy organization, the avoidance of delay and the best use of available tonnage, were matters of never-ending concern and were dealt with by a vastly expanded system of control.

There was the closest co-operation between the navy and civilian controllers of shipping and transport. Ship movements and cargo allotments had to be integrated on both sides of the Atlantic and around the world; and integrated again with war plans springing from the councils of Britain. Merchant ship movements, in convoy and out of convoy, were scheduled weeks and months ahead to insure that every precious bottom would be used to the best advantage. A ship's arrival for loading was co-ordinated with the arrival of trainloads of war supplies at a seaport and with the set dates for convoy assembly. Loading and assembly, again, were based on the requirement schedules of the United Kingdom. Each convoy as it moved to sea, a ragged agglomeration of weather-worn, rust-stained freighters, was in reality a cross-section of England's varied needs; a calendar from which the planning and progress of many vital operations might be deduced.

The cargo carried by individual ships dictated their station in the convoy columns, for certain equipment might be required at a particular port at a set time. Ships had to be arranged in accordance with the ports they were bound for and the points along the inner approach routes to the United Kingdom at which they would break off. Troop movements and transport plans in England were keyed to the arrival of trucks and locomotives by certain ships. Food schedules were based on the grain, flour, cheese, bacon, sugar and the multitudinous varieties of tinned, dried, sacked and condensed foods which other ships would bring. Factories timed their schedules to the arrival of iron and steel; defence and attack waited on cargoes of tanks, planes, guns and ammunition. Building programmes went forward as lumber arrived; and every operation of this mechanics' war depended on the timely and sufficient delivery of oil. The process of sea-borne supply from North America, still a principal responsibility of the Canadian navy and its Trade Division, was a huge and delicately geared mechanism revolving at the centre of the whole war effort.

It was a process which, for all its impressive ramifications, depended ultimately on the merchant seamen. Week after week the merchant captains, many of them speaking little English and all of them looking in their matter-of-fact street clothes like tired, small business men, assembled at the convoy conferences, voiced their complaints to the naval officers presiding, cracked their sardonic jokes, and departed to sail their ships. Accustomed to an easygoing spaciousness of sea, they had now to manoeuvre in crowded ranks, without lights, wireless or navigational aids, and with collision and disaster the price of a moment's carelessness. They were burdened down with a multitude of sailing orders and regulations entombed in dismal mimeographed volumes. They were required to master the new and unwelcome art of station-keeping in convoy. Their ships' engines, many of them dating from and before the turn of the century, must be nursed and spoonfed to avoid making smoke and betraying a convoy's presence to a U-boat. Bilges could not be pumped for fear of leaving trails of oil; garbage could not be heaved over the side. In the dark hours a pinpoint of light showing through an uncovered scuttle was likely to be doused by the machine gun bullets of an escort. There were complaints enough to be voiced, questions enough to be asked at each convoy conference; yet, week by week, in a series unbroken to the end of the war, the convoys sailed.

The merchant crews—men of every nationality and of none, thousands of them with homes in occupied Europe and kinfolk they never expected to see again—went about their jobs, grumbling casually. Theirs was an occupation noted in peacetime for its hardness and monotony, yearned for only because of the sense of freedom which it gave a man. Now, to hardship and monotony was added the prospect of death by freezing water or flaming oil, unrelieved by uniforms, recognition or the shoreside amenities provided for the naval crews. And freedom was gone; for behind the merchant service, as behind every service, stood the shadow of compulsion. The ships had to be sailed and these men had to sail them. They were another "few" of whom the many demanded much and to whom much was owed. With each voyage the odds against their ships, and against the men who would be left in the churning water above the wreckage, seemed to grow longer. Still, voyage after voyage, men who had seen a dozen ships go down about them, men who had been torpedoed once, twice, three times, sailed and sailed again. There were outbursts under the strain of it, just as there were in every service; but these were the rarest of exceptions in a record of glum, silent, wonderful endurance.

Already, urgent steps were being taken by the navy to improve conditions for the merchant crews in harbour and at sea. The problems were approached with a large measure of sympathy and intelligence. Canadian solutions proved so successful that many of their features were adopted by both the United Kingdom and the United States; and it was well that this was so. There were to be times in the months and years ahead when crews on the decks of waiting freighters and captains at the tables of a convoy conference would look at each other, wondering if a single faltering word might lead to a general refusal of the odds against them. The word was never spoken. "The morale of the merchant seamen"— drab official phrase though it was—stood for the rock on which the convoy system was securely based.

Ships gathering for the outward voyage assembled now at Sydney as well as Halifax. The main transatlantic convoy had been split into two sections. Slow ships, capable only of speeds between six and nine knots, were sailed from Sydney as SC convoys. Ships doing between nine and fifteen knots sailed from Halifax in the HX convoys, while many ships of fifteen knots or better were sailed and routed independently. Still largely undefended behind these main outward streams was the network of tributaries which fed into it, from American ports, from other Canadian ports, from Newfoundland and the iron mines of Wabana and from the ports of the St. Lawrence.

It now remained to be seen whether this vital trade and the new defences organized to buttress it could withstand the coming attack. The assault was to be a formidable one, aimed with skill and determination at the western mid-ocean zone where the convoys, rounding the shoulder of Newfoundland, turned northward for the long climb into the high latitudes of Iceland. Twenty-five submarines were operating in the northwest Atlantic during June; and of these the greater number were concentrated to the south and east of Newfoundland.

Here, across the routes of the convoys, they were disposed in lines of patrol; each group operating like a great rake whose handle was firmly held by the command post at Lorient on the Biscay coast. Individual U-boats were separated by intervals of about thirty miles and rarely communicated with each other. First sighting reports went to Lorient; Lorient made the tactical dispositions while the shadowing U-boat continued sometimes for days to send reports on the position, course and speed of the convoy. Only when a group had made rendezvous at a selected point along the route would it be homed in for the attack. The principle was to operate always in concentrated strength.

The U-boats themselves were of two types; 500-ton boats with a cruising range of 11,000 miles and 700-tonners with a range of 15,000 miles. Even the smaller boats were capable of remaining at sea for as long as three months. They carried up to 21 torpedoes which could be fired from an extreme range of 15,300 yards to drive in upon a convoy at a speed of 40 knots. A U-boat could fire her torpedoes from the surface or from a depth as great as 200 feet; and she could attain speeds of 16 knots on the surface and as much as 9 knots submerged.

A group of U-boats in co-ordinated night attack, coming in on the surface from many directions, was difficult to detect and intercept; and even when one was sighted it was by no means easy to destroy. A crash dive took a U-boat to periscope depth, about 20 feet below the surface, in a little over 30 seconds. Within another minute, driving forward and downward at a speed of about 8 knots, twisting away on a sharp alteration of course, it would be 120 feet below and some 700 feet distant from the swirl which marked its dive.

Even when located and attacked, a U-boat's capacity to withstand punishment was immense. Within the light outer casing which gave the boat its rakish, graceful lines was enclosed a second hull, the cylindrical "pressure hull" of very tough steel. Vital parts were enclosed within the pressure hull, and were protected by its toughness against tremendous blows. A 300-lb. depth charge, to be lethal, must be exploded within 21 feet. Damage to the outer hull frequently resulted in exciting "evidence" for an attacking ship, but caused the boat itself only minor inconvenience. The oil which often seeped convincingly to the surface after an attack was sometimes deliberately released; and in other cases indicated merely that reserve fuel tanks built into the space between the outer casing and the pressure hull had been ruptured. There were U-boats which had been blown to the surface and lifted clear out of the water by depth charges, and yet made their escape and returned to base. With such powerful and durable weapons, and with fanatic confidence in them, the U-boat fleet had moved into the western Atlantic.

Among the ships gathering to the Newfoundland Command were many who knew this enemy well. The Canadian and British destroyers were now veterans with long months of service in the western approaches. Some of the British corvettes had already more than a year of warfare behind them; and seven of the Canadian corvettes had tasted battle on the other side. But there were also on the way, from the great lakes, from the shipyards along the St. Lawrence and from the west coast by way of the Panama, many new ships and many verdant men. The corvette-building programme was gaining on its schedule and new orders were being placed. The demand was for all the ships that could be built; and for the manpower to operate them.

There were now some nineteen thousand men in all branches of the naval service; in the destroyers, in the Prince ships, in the corvettes already afloat, in the yachts and patrol craft operating in coastal waters, in the bases and the shore establishments and the training depots, and on loan to the Royal Navy. Twelve thousand of them looked back less than a year to the day of their enrolment. Nearly seventy per cent of them had come from Ontario, Quebec and the prairie provinces—the inland areas. They were all volunteers, and their state of health gave little cause for alarm. Not ten per cent of the men who presented themselves to naval examination boards throughout the war were found physically defective. But they were youngsters; the vast majority of them from inland had never seen salt water; and the training system, hastily expanding to keep up with the influx of recruits, had no time for anything but the rudiments of instruction.

Sea training was an impossibility without ships; and ships could not be spared from operations. The fighting ships themselves became the hard training ground for new-comers, lowering their own efficiency in the process. Experienced crews in the destroyers had to be broken up, parcelled out meagrely among many ships, while their places were filled by untrained men. The corvettes went into operation with sometimes not more than half a dozen officers and ratings who had ever been to sea. As they set out on the first voyage, often with most of their crews green and staggering from seasickness, they might have afforded grave cause for doubt as to the effectiveness of the force with which we were entering upon a great naval campaign.

There could be no break in the continuity of the convoys, no time for leisurely organization of the new force. Some destroyers and corvettes were already in St. John's when the Commodore Commanding Newfoundland arrived. More were on the way. Organization into escort groups must progress as the force was built up. An HX convoy from Halifax was already at sea on June 13; and its local escort must be relieved at West Ocean Meeting Point. On June 14 the first group of ships of the Newfoundland Escort Force sailed to meet the convoy at that point.

Foggy weather, unorganized ship-to-shore communications, and breakdowns among over-worked destroyers combined to make the first voyage a nightmare of futility. Rendezvous positions given the ships were inaccurate and arrived late. When the convoy was located, mechanical defects forced two of the destroyers to return almost immediately. The fact that the HX convoy had been combined with an SC convoy made so large a body of ships that protection was inadequate in any case. On this occasion no U-boats were encountered; but the initial difficulties of organization had been demonstrated. A week later, in a double action which took place over some seven hundred miles of sea, they were to be sharply underlined.

Convoy HX 133 sailed from Halifax on June 21; and the Canadian destroyer, *Ottawa,* with a group of one British and three Canadian corvettes, sailed from St. John's to meet it and take it eastward. At about the same time three Canadian and two British corvettes sailed from Iceland to meet westbound convoy OB 336 and proceed with it toward St. John's. Of this latter group the Canadian corvette *Wetaskiwin* was senior ship. *Wetaskiwin* and her group, on arrival at the rendezvous position for OB 336, found that the convoy was not there, and began what was to be a four-day search along its probable track.

Meanwhile convoy HX 133, now proceeding south of Greenland, was being shadowed by U-boats; and during the dark hours of June 23 a ship was torpedoed. The rest of the night was ominously quiet, but by the afternoon of the next day it was known that several U-boats were in contact.

Commander-in-Chief Western Approaches now signalled *Wetaskiwin* to detach two corvettes from her group to go to the support of *Ottawa's* escort group with convoy HX 133. *Wetaskiwin* complied, discovering at the same time that she did not hold the cypher for many of the signalled reports which were reaching her. The search for the missing convoy OB 336 went on, its difficulties greatly enhanced by the impossibility of decoding some of the signals received.

At eleven o'clock on the night of the 24th the threatened attack on HX 133 developed. A ship was torpedoed, and immediately after the explosion a U-boat surfaced astern of the convoy. *Ottawa* and one of the corvettes gave chase briefly, but had to return within an hour as another explosion gave warning of renewed attack.

They had hardly got back in station when three more torpedoes drove simultaneously into three more ships. *Ottawa* swept off to starboard in the direction from which the attack had come; and got an Asdic contact. As she dropped one pattern of charges and prepared for another attack, two corvettes turned in her wake and the wash of their propellers ruined her contact. After that piece of bad luck and bad management *Ottawa* rejoined the convoy, instructing the corvettes to continue the search for the U-boat. The signal was incompletely received and the corvettes broke off the hunt. *Ottawa* could send no orders to them by radio telephone because they did not carry the equipment. They were slow in reading her signals by lamp; and their own lamps were so low-powered as to be visible only at close range.

Meanwhile, Commander-in-Chief Western Approaches, receiving *Ottawa's* signalled reports, ordered *Wetaskiwin* and her two other corvettes to abandon the search for OB 336 and proceed to the assistance of HX 133. Hard on the heels of this order came a signal to *Westaskiwin* from OB 336. That convoy, too, was under attack; and from the tenor of the two signals received almost simultaneously, *Wetaskiwin's* commanding officer was convinced that C.-in-C. W.A. did not know about it.

He was immediately faced with the most difficult decision a captain has to make at sea. The convoy for which he was searching was under attack and had no escort at all. HX 133 had its own escort group; and the two corvettes he had sent to its assistance would soon be arriving. On the basis of all this information, which he did not feel was held by C.-in-C. W.A., he decided to proceed contrary to orders and join Convoy OB 336. This he did, coming up with his convoy at dawn the next day to find that it had lost two ships. His action was later endorsed both by C.-in-C. W.A. and by Commodore Commanding Newfoundland.

The Western Atlantic

Although neither convoy was attacked again, HX 133 had lost five ships, OB 336 had lost two and the difficulties of escort had been greatly increased by incorrect distribution of codes and cyphers, faulty wireless communication, poor signalling work and poor signalling equipment. Chronic and persistent shortages in factories ashore were taking their toll at sea; as were inexperience and lack of training. Signalmen, youngsters who had attained a precarious proficiency in classrooms or on barracks lawns a month or so before, were finding the task of reading Morse from rocking bridges in rain and fog and across heaving miles of sleety sea a little beyond them. No one could expect it to be otherwise, and no one could hope that the war would wait while short-comings were made good.

July, however, did bring one of the periodic lulls in the Atlantic. The northward routeing of convoys, which took them through the almost continual daylight of Greenland summer, made U-boat attack more difficult. Long range planes from Canada and Iceland were beginning to spread their welcome wings over part of the western Atlantic. Still more important, the prospect of effective assistance from the United States Navy began to brighten along the horizon.

On July 7, 1941, President Roosevelt announced that United States warships would protect American shipping en route to Iceland and other strategic outposts. By August plans were being made to include at least one American ship in each convoy and thus insure the assistance of the United States Navy. By September 15 the President's "shoot on sight" order directed against the U-boats had been issued, and co-operation between American ships and ships of the Newfoundland Escort Force, had become an actuality.

Another factor which may have had an effect was the curiously exaggerated respect which the Germans imme-diately conceived for the corvette. It was a respect which they retained, and later on with sufficient reason. U-boats, although faster than corvettes and possessed of almost equal gunpower, never willingly attempted to fight it out on the surface; and their opinion of the ship is perhaps indicated by a press message which emanated from Zurich on August 29, 1941:

> The British Admiralty has introduced new warships, and although our submarines show improvement it must be acknowledged that the worries of our U-boats have greatly increased. Here we cannot reckon on a Blitzkrieg. Many U-boat commanders boil with rage at being unable to attack owing to increased protection by corvettes and merchant cruisers which force them into cover.

Whatever the German opinion and whatever the reason for the lull, the brief summer respite was welcome as the force increased, as group organization and training continued and the new ships ploughed inward and outward on the Iceland run under the wing of the veteran destroyers. They had much to learn and little time in which to master it; and with the first days of September came full employment for all the talents of one group.

Convoy SC-42 sailed from Sydney on August 30, carrying well over half a million tons of supplies for the United Kingdom. At west ocean meeting point it was taken over by a Newfoundland escort group which consisted of the destroyer *Skeena* and the corvettes *Orillia, Kenogami* and *Alberni.* The course was north and east, up into the high latitudes, around Cape Farewell and the tip of Greenland. For seven days the convoy ploughed on uneventfully, the destroyer and the three corvettes ranged about the sixty-four ships they had to protect, spread out over some twenty-five square miles of sea.

On the seventh day heavy German signal traffic made it obvious that U-boats were gathering in strength. The convoy swung due north, running dangerously near to the Greenland coast, in an attempt to throw off the shadowers; but at dusk there came the familiar dull roar of an explosion. The merchant ship, *Muneric,* her belly blown out by a torpedo, sank like a stone.

Kenogami, stationed on the port side, swept back in the gathering darkness along the track of the torpedo. Off her starboard bow the wake of another torpedo churned through

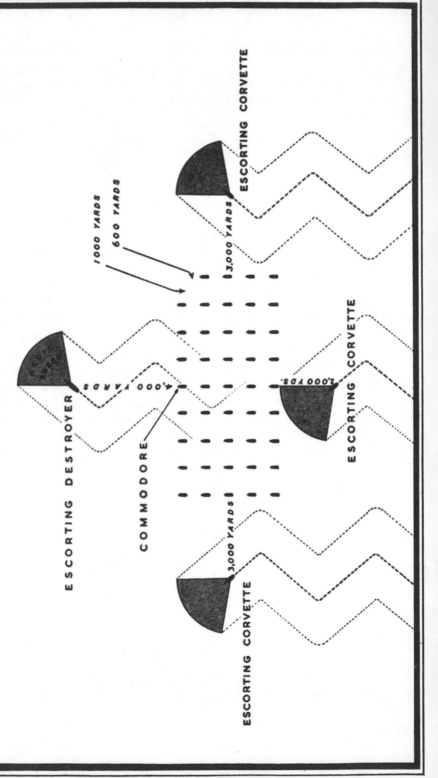

DIAGRAM OF CONVOY AND FOUR ESCORTS

the sea, just missing her; and at the same moment she sighted the U-boat a thousand yards away, making off for the Greenland coast at high speed. *Kenogami* opened fire and gave chase, but almost immediately was recalled. The Commodore's ship at the head of the convoy had sighted another submarine. Ten minutes later two merchantmen made a simultaneous sighting of a third U-boat. Five minutes after that a fourth was seen running down between the columns of the convoy. Then another ship was torpedoed and a minute after that a volcano of flame and debris soared skyward from a third vessel which had been a tanker.

There were at least eight submarines attacking; the escort was outnumbered two to one and forced to divide its attention between the work of rescuing survivors and fighting off the U-boats. Some of the merchant ships stopped to give assistance to men in the water; but for the most part the lumbering columns swept on. Turning out of station and lingering astern made a vessel almost a certain target; every captain had his own ship to consider and hesitated to risk the lives of his own men against the chance of saving others. The corvettes and the destroyer did what they could with scramble-nets and carley floats, only to be called away from rescue work as streams of tracer bullets from the merchant ships indicated new sightings.

Until midnight a high, white moon silhouetted the vessels like so many ducks riding the bands of a shooting gallery. Seven ships with their thousands of tons of steel and grain and fuel oil went hissing through the black fathoms to the bottom; and astern of the convoy *Orillia* was making a desperate effort to salvage the tanker *Tahchee*, torpedoed but still afloat.

A little after midnight a cloudbank moved in from the north-east and covered the moon. The merciful blackness provided an opportunity for the convoy to turn away. The warning for the turn was passed down the columns, but five minutes before the executive order was given there came another spatter of machine gun fire, and tracers whipped out from a merchant ship, aimed at a submarine which was inside the convoy and running up one of the lanes.

Skeena cut into the convoy and raced up the lane after the U-boat. The German, still well ahead, swung at right angles, crossed the line of ships, turned sharply again and ran in the opposite direction down the next lane. *Skeena* and the U-boat passed each other going in opposite directions with a line of merchantmen between them; and a minute later the German's conning tower dipped and slid out of sight in a crash dive.

Almost at that exact moment, with the moon obscured and full blackness on the sea, the convoy executed its turn. *Skeena*, in the midst of it, was trapped among the huge, swinging shapes of the merchantmen. One towered suddenly upon her out of the dark and she put her engines to full astern, sliding away, avoiding the crash by a hair's breadth. Consummate seamanship brought her wriggling her way at last to the outside of the convoy; and the battle again engaged her attention. Another merchantman was hit, sending a geyser of orange flame a hundred feet into the sky. It became a cone of fire and smoke rising to a point, spreading out into a curious downy cushion. "I could sit on it!" one of *Skeena's* watching officers marvelled to himself.

Morning came and the U-boats drew off for a time. Just at noon, however, a torpedo drove into *Thistleglen*. The vessel shuddered, up-ended, and settled slowly, taking a cargo of steel and pig iron to the bottom. This time *Skeena* had sighted a periscope and was already over the spot where it had disappeared. She dropped a pattern of depth charges and came in again, listening on her asdic. The contact was poor and the commanding officer was tempted to break off, when *Alberni* near by got the same or another contact. Then *Kenogami* joined and also got contact. The three ships began a deliberate attack and, after a pattern of depth charges had been dropped, a large bubble of air rose to the surface; then many bubbles; then oil. It was no better than a "probable kill," but the ships could not remain away from the convoy to seek more evidence.

The rest of the day passed with sombre quiet, and there was time to reckon up the losses. *Muneric* was gone; *Empire Springbuck, Baron Pentland, Winterswijk, Stargaard, Sally Maersk, Empire Hudson;* with thousands of tons of fuel oil, grain, phosphate, lumber, ammunition, stores and a fleet of trucks. Many plans afoot in Britain had been deranged that night; many small but much-needed cogs knocked out of the war machine.

With darkness the attacks began again. The escort was smaller than before, as *Orillia* was struggling toward Iceland with the tanker *Tahchee.* The men who had had no sleep the night before and little during the day continued for another ten hours at action stations. The rattle of machine gun fire and the boom of depth charges punctuated the night, spaced periodically as the deeper roar of an exploding torpedo told another tale of loss. This time, however, the fighting was not all in favour of the U-boats.

The order for reinforcements had gone out from the Admiralty, and by nightfall the corvettes *Chambly* and *Moose Jaw* were approaching. The two ships had been carrying out a training cruise south of Greenland, and the opportunity to put their training into practice arrived with unusual promptness.

As they came in from ahead of the convoy, *Chambly's* lookouts sighted two white rockets well down on the horizon. They were the signal indicating that a ship had been torpedoed. *Chambly* increased speed and made for the position from which the rockets had come. *Moose Jaw* was beside her on her starboard beam.

Seventeen minutes after sighting the first rockets two more were seen. One minute later *Chambly* got a submarine contact on her asdic. She followed the echo for two minutes, then let go her depth charges. Just as she was preparing to fire a second pattern the U-boat surfaced about four hundred yards off *Moose Jaw's* port bow and proceeded to run across her course. *Moose Jaw* opened fire, and was bearing down

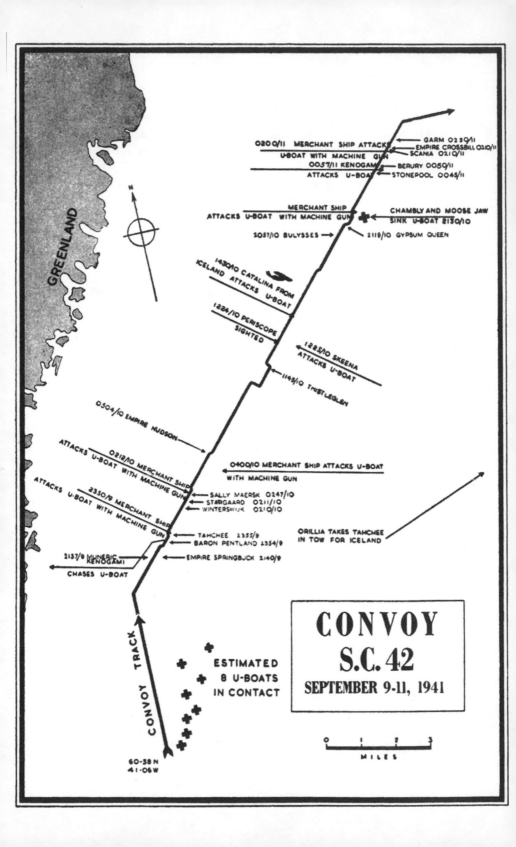

CONVOY
S.C. 42
SEPTEMBER 9-11, 1941

GREENLAND

N

0200/11 MERCHANT SHIP ATTACKS
U-BOAT WITH MACHINE GUN

GARM 0250/11
EMPIRE CROSSBILL 0210/11
SCANIA 0210/11

0057/11 KENOGAMI
ATTACKS U-BOAT

BERURY 0050/11
STONEPOOL 0045/11

MERCHANT SHIP
ATTACKS U-BOAT WITH MACHINE GUN

CHAMBLY AND MOOSE JAW
SINK U-BOAT 2130/10

2057/10 BULYSSES

2119/10 GYPSUM QUEEN

1430/10 CATALINA FROM
ICELAND ATTACKS U-BOAT

1224/10 PERISCOPE
SIGHTED

1225/10 SKEENA
ATTACKS U-BOAT

1143/10 THISTLEGLEN

0504/10 EMPIRE HUDSON

0212/10 MERCHANT SHIP
ATTACKS U-BOAT WITH MACHINE GUN

0400/10 MERCHANT SHIP ATTACKS U-BOAT
WITH MACHINE GUN

2350/9 MERCHANT SHIP
ATTACKS U-BOAT WITH MACHINE GUN

SALLY MAERSK 0247/10
STARGAARD 0211/10
WINTERSWIJK 0210/10

ORILLIA TAKES TAHCHEE
IN TOW FOR ICELAND

TAHCHEE 2355/9
BARON PENTLAND 2354/9

EMPIRE SPRINGBUCK 2140/9

2137/9 MUNERIC
KENOGAMI
CHASES U-BOAT

CONVOY TRACK

ESTIMATED
8 U-BOATS
IN CONTACT

60-38 N
41-06 W

0   1   2   3
MILES

rapidly on the U-boat when the German stopped his engines, abandoning any attempt to escape.

Moose Jaw ran up alongside to find most of the Nazi crew on deck with their hands up. As the corvette closed, the U-boat captain leaped from his own deck to the deck of the corvette, not even wetting his feet in the process. *Moose Jaw* sheered off to prevent any further boarding; and as she did so the U-boat got under way again and attempted to cross her bow. The corvette promptly rammed. Some of the Nazi crew made for their forward gun; but a round or two from *Moose Jaw's* gun discouraged that attempt.

By now *Chambly* had come alongside to put a boarding party onto the U-boat. Lieutenant Edward T. Simmons, the officer in command of the party, ordered the eleven Germans on deck to go below. They refused, even at pistol point, which made it obvious that the submarine had been scuttled; but the boarding party made a brave attempt at salvage. They went down through the conning tower to the interior to discover that all instruments had been smashed; continued a little further to find the lighting system out of action. Then from beneath them came a warning rush of water and they turned back, but not quite soon enough.

If the boat could have been saved, or even some of its secret equipment recovered, it would have been a valuable prize of war. The risk of the investigation was justified; but it was not to be made without cost. With a sudden lurch, the craft began to settle. Most of the boarding party scrambled to safety before it went down, but stoker William I. Brown was sucked into the swirl and drowned. When the effort to rescue Brown was seen to be hopeless, *Chambly* and *Moose Jaw* picked up all but eleven of the U-boat's crew from the water and rejoined the other escorts of the convoy.

The U-boat's captain was a rarity in the German submarine service. He proclaimed that he had given himself up in order to insist that *Moose Jaw* rescue his men, but the explanation did not go down well either with friend or foe. When later he offered his hand to his chief quartermaster it was refused. The submarine, U-501, had come to grief on her first operational cruise; which was fair enough, since most of the men in the two corvettes had never been to sea before.

"Rejoined convoy" is the entry closing the incident in *Chambly's* log. The battle was still flaring and subsiding about SC-42. Two ships had gone down about nine o'clock. Shortly before one, two more were sunk within five minutes of each other. *Kenogami* sighted the U-boat which had fired the torpedoes, drove it under and depth charged heavily without visible result. Her target on this occasion was the U-85, which was sunk more than nine months later by the United States destroyer *Roper;* and papers recovered from the body of one of the U-boat crewmen testified to the effects of *Kenogami's* attack. On this night, however, there was no time for the long vigil necessary in so many U-boat hunts. Two more ships were torpedoed within the half hour; three more before dawn.

There was no way in which the outnumbered escorts could be disposed to screen the convoy completely. Laden with survivors, called constantly from the scene of one sinking to the next, and charged first of all with the duty of attacking U-boats, they divided their efforts as best they could and fought their way on into noon of the next day. At that time a welcome smudge on the horizon to the east proclaimed the arrival of the destroyers of the British local escort. Fifteen ships had been sunk out of the sixty-four which set out and one more was to be lost before the convoy reached its destination.

September in those same Greenland waters also saw the first loss of a Canadian corvette. *Levis* was part of the escort for convoy SC-44, and in the early hours of September 19 a torpedo struck her forward on the port side, ripping the ship open to within about forty feet of the stern and killing seventeen men. *Mayflower* came up in the dark to find *Levis* settling by the head but still upright. A towline was passed and the crippled ship remained afloat for nearly five hours.

Then she listed suddenly and sank. Forty survivors of the torpedoing were taken off by *Mayflower* and *Agassiz*.

Another heavy battle began around Convoy SC-48, four hundred miles south of Iceland on the morning of October 15. The escort, consisting of the Canadian destroyer *Columbia*, and seven corvettes—five Canadian, one British and one Free French—was larger than usual; but when the first torpedo struck, three of the ships were away rounding up stragglers. They were immediately recalled as all signs indicated that a serious attack was developing.

Half an hour before midnight a second merchantman was torpedoed. *Columbia*, the destroyer, fired starshell which burst just in time to illuminate still another torpedoing. *Gladiolus*, the British corvette, set off in the dark to make a counter-attack against the submarine which had fired the torpedo, only to be hit herself and sink with all hands just at dawn.

At one o'clock the next afternoon four American destroyers, one of which was the *U.S.S. Kearney*, arrived; and a little later came the British ships *Broadwater* and *Lobelia*. That night six merchantmen were sunk and *Kearney* received the torpedo which moved the United States a step nearer war. Two more warships, the British destroyer *Veronica* and the Canadian corvette *Pictou* arrived on the scene about midnight; and within an hour *Pictou* gained contact with a U-boat and attacked.

A few minutes after the explosion of *Pictou's* depth charges, the U-boat's wash was seen dead ahead. The boat was surfaced and rapidly drawing away. *Pictou* opened fire and chased the sharply zigzagging German. Two of his torpedoes crossed fifteen feet ahead of her bow, but she gained a little on the U-boat because of its weaving course. Suddenly it made a wide turn to starboard which for the first time presented a good target. *Pictou's* company stood by to ram and the corvette drove in for the German's starboard beam. The U-boat swung to port and *Pictou* followed, the manoeuvreability designed for her by the watcher of whales enabling her to get inside the German's turning circle. She was within a hundred yards of him when he crash-dived; and riding over the bubbling swirl she dropped a mixed pattern of shallow set and deep set charges, hoping to get the enemy above and below.

The explosion of the charges came and then a tremendous, dome-shaped bubble of air, fifteen feet high. Yet the attack, when coldly assessed by the Admiralty, brought *Pictou* only a "probably damaged B." With all the data before them, the anti-submarine experts who knew the toughness of their enemy considered that the charges had been dropped too soon and had exploded too shallowly.

In spite of many similar discouragements as October and November wore away, the escort groups, still insufficiently trained and still lacking much essential equipment, began to see a few signs that their work was having an effect. Germany had five times as many U-boats at sea in September 1941 as she had had in the same month a year before, but the greatly increased force sank 50,000 tons less of merchant shipping. U-boats were attacking convoys with less daring, firing salvoes from a distance rather than coming in to select the most valuable ships. Nor were they getting off so lightly. Asdic technique was being improved and radar was being fitted into the escort ships. The benefits of training and experience were beginning to appear. The time seemed to be coming when it could be said that no attack on a convoy went unpunished. Yet the arithmetic of the situation was still grim enough. One U-boat was being sunk for every ten merchant ships which went down; and two merchant ships were being lost for every one built.

Winter closed in and the convoys, still routed north around the tip of Greenland, made two thirds of their voyage in icy arctic darkness. The monotony and the routine perils of each journey took on a macabre character. A man knew that if his ship were sunk his chance of life was one in a hundred. The freezing cold of that black water washing back along the side would kill him in five minutes. Rescue ships, specially fitted out for taking on survivors and caring for them, were still an unfilled need. Life-saving equipment in all the ships was still inadequate. The magnificent Canadian life jacket, worn like a coat and equipped with lights, flares and a whistle, was a thing of the future.

As the ships ploughed on, sleet and frozen spray sheathed them from stem to stern, coated the guns a foot thick, coated the depth charges, rose in weird caverns about the superstructure. Waves washing over the decks, congealing as they came, formed ice more rapidly than it could be chipped off; sometimes made a vessel unmanageable, occasionally capsized it by sheer weight. Before a group was three days out of St. John's, the ships' bread became a mass of green mould. Along the northward log, around Cape Farewell and on up the Greenland coast, fresh meat and vegetables perished in the primitive refrigerators. Hard tack and pickled beef, with lime juice to prevent scurvy, became the Nelsonian fare of these Canadians of 1941.

Unbathed, unshaven, freezing on their watches above decks, often soaking wet in their reeking quarters below, they drove along through the continual night. Gales battered them and subsided, to be followed by the thunderous swells of the "milestones," which struck the hulls with pile-driving force, hurling men from their bunks and hammocks, breaking up the scanty hours of exhausted sleep. And beyond Greenland lay the long eastern leg to Iceland and the end of the run; "rest" for a few days in bleak, unfriendly Reykjavik or Hvalfjord, where fresh provisions were not to be had, where fuelling, repairs and the landing of survivors took up most of the harbour time, and where—on a rare and gala night—the lissom, blonde, Icelandic girls danced with you, light as a feather, cold as an icicle, silent as the tomb, and left you without a word when the dance was ended.

Always the ships operated on the thin edge where fuel was concerned. It was a major worry of all captains, added to their other plentiful troubles. Time after time, struggling with mighty cross seas and the sudden diversions necessary to take convoys away from U-boat packs, they found themselves nursing their last precious tons of oil. Occasionally, with tanks exhausted, they lay hove-to on the bleak sea waiting for a tow; sitting ducks for a submarine and powerless to fight a storm.

Week after week the battle demanded more and better armament. The ships bulged and bristled, were weighed down and counter-weighted with new guns, new gadgets, new gear. New equipment required more and more of the scanty living space, crowded more and more upon already cramped quarters. Yet new equipment required also more men to operate it; more men to be trained the only way a sailor can finally be trained—in a ship at sea. The ships were always overcrowded, always with a good percentage of desperately seasick lads who spent their hours off watch lying on lockers, in hammocks, at the foot of companionways; wherever they could find six feet of space. They were too sick to move, too sick to care whether they lived or died, but not quite sick enough to quit.

They got no sympathy from their captains. Captains said that it was bad to sympathize with a seasick man. You left him to work out his fate. But they began to tell each other about the boys who went whole voyages with hardly a morsel of solid food, lived on soup and fruit juice, did their work as long as they could stand or hold on to something, kept down their tortured innards and won the doubtful privilege of staying at sea.

The storms of that memorable winter of 1941 hampered the U-boats and attacked the convoys with impartial malignancy. Seven successive convoys, westward bound from the United Kingdom, were dispersed by gales which drove the merchantmen out of touch with each other and with their escorts. The fogs of the Grand Banks added their perils; and among the disasters to ships in convoy was one which resulted in the loss of *Windflower*, first of the Flower class corvettes.

On December 7 the ship was cut down in thick fog by the bow of the freighter *Zypenburg*. One of her boilers blew up and within ten minutes she was sinking. Her starboard lifeboat was thrown overboard by the force of the explosion, dragging along several of the men who had been attempting to launch it. As live steam from the exploded boiler seethed up through the fog the men remaining on board got away the port life boat and one carley float. *Windflower's* stern went under, her fore part rose out of the water and leaned perilously over the men close alongside. Some of those on the float, seeing the looming shape above them, prepared to abandon their refuge for the water, where they would almost certainly have drowned. A Petty Officer, calling upon all his stock of authority and the mighty resources of a naval vocabulary, kept them in their places while the bow leaned off in the other direction and sank slowly from sight. *Nasturtium,* one of the corvettes in company, had mistaken the explosion of *Windflower's* boiler for a torpedoing and had moved away through the fog to search for a submarine. She returned to join with *Zypenburg* in rescuing forty-seven of *Windflower's* company, three of whom died later.

The trials and dangers of the winter weather fell equally upon all ships, and belong to the class which can be better imagined than described. In the same category was the jubilation with which the crew of *Restigouche* viewed the prospect of a Christmas at home. The destroyer, now a salt-scarred veteran and "Rustyguts" to all the navy, was in Hvalfjord early in December when the news reached her that she was to rendezvous with a westbound convoy and escort it to Halifax. On the afternoon of December 12, with five corvettes, she sailed to meet the convoy at a point south of Iceland.

The group came out of harbour into the teeth of a snowstorm driving on a full gale. Hours later when the rendezvous position was reached the merchant ships were not to be found. *Restigouche,* faster than the corvettes, went on ahead to make a search. At dark, having found nothing, she rejoined the other ships, and the group proceeded along what was calculated to be the convoy's mean line of advance.

During the night and the early hours of the following morning the barometer dropped steeply and the gale increased in force, still driving its blinding curtain of sleet before it. The ships struggled on, and about four o'clock in the afternoon a signal from the convoy reached *Restigouche,* giving a position which she estimated to be about thirty miles distant. Before the new rendezvous could be made the gale suddenly rose to hurricane force. Snow and driving spray cut off visibility completely. Mountainous seas roared in over the ships, tearing canvas gun covers to shreds, ripping off splinter mats and carley floats, smashing up fittings on the decks and superstructures. Once again escorts and convoy were driven out of touch with each other.

The corvettes, hidden behind the wall of snow and sleet which churned across the sea, fought their way on for two more days and were eventually forced to heave to. *Restigouche,* heading into the storm, found steering almost impossible; and only kept herself from falling off into the troughs of the sea by using port and starboard propellers alternately to assist the action of the rudder. At five o'clock on the afternoon of the second day there was a thunderous report from above. The ship's foremast had cracked; the upper section above the crow's nest had snapped off and the steel lower section had crashed down to rest across the fore-funnel. With the mast went the ship's wireless; and there was nothing for it but to send a party up in the midst of the storm to rig a jury aerial. Within half an hour men clinging to icy poles thirty feet up from the deck had completed their work and an answer to a testing message had been received from the Admiralty.

Meanwhile the towering seas were playing havoc on the quarterdeck. Depth charges had been torn loose and were charging back and forth with every roll of the ship. Hatch covers had been ripped off and floods of water were washing below deck with every roll. There were already six feet of water in the lower compartments; and a bucket party which went down found calcium flares beneath the surface hissing and fuming and sending out clouds of acrid vapour.

The hatches had to be closed somehow. Sub-Lieutenant S. G. Moore fought his way aft and just managed to get canvas covers over them before a great sea swept him back against one of the depth charge rails, breaking his leg.

Up forward the situation was, if anything, worse. Heavy seas, racking and pounding the ship, had sprung plates and flooded many other compartments. Galley fires had gone out and only a small steam jet rigged by the engineers made it possible to get a rare hot drink to the men. At four in the morning the steering system went out of commission and for an hour the ship had to be manoeuvred entirely by main engines and propellers. There was emergency steering gear, but it was located in the tiller flat in the afterpart of the ship and was already under six feet of water. At five o'clock a mightier blow from the sea knocked the starboard dynamo out of action, the gyro ceased to operate and the battered destroyer was thrown into total darkness, to which the alarm system, set off by the same blow, added a note of pandemonium.

The storm continued without let-up for another day and a half. As it showed signs of abating *Restigouche* received a signal telling her that the convoy she had set out to meet had been ordered to disperse and heave to. She was relieved of her escort responsibilities; but the mere saving of the ship was a grave enough problem. Plates in the bottom had sprung and the forward magazine and shell room were flooded to a depth of seven feet. Although the wind had lessened from its hurricane force, a full gale was still blowing; and in the destroyer's condition there was no longer a possibility of making headway against it. The ship had to be brought about; and if she were caught in a trough of the sea as she turned there would be no hope for her. She came about slowly; rolling sickeningly as the force of the storm struck her broadside-on; but the manoeuvre was safely completed and at last she was running with the wind.

The problem now was to steer the ship with damaged gear and a great following sea battering her from astern.

There was no longer any prospect of making Halifax; nor would it even be safe to heave to. The decision to run for the Clyde was made and signalled during the late afternoon; and for the rest of the day and night the entire ship's company worked on repair and bucket parties.

There was serious danger of running out of fuel as two oil tanks had leaked salt water. A heavy list to port had developed and although sluice valves were opened and every pump and bucket kept on the job continuously the flood level could not be brought down below four feet. Officers and men, some of them wearing diving equipment to protect them from the fumes of calcium flares burning beneath the water of flooded compartments, were still hard at work on the afternoon of December 16 as *Restigouche* crawled slowly in through the harbour gate at Greenock.

Relatives in far-off Halifax and in other homes about Canada would not see these men for Christmas 1941. There was not a stitch of dry clothing on board the ship, nor a man who had had hot food or sleep in the past sixty hours. Nevertheless, from the wrong side of the Atlantic, the commanding officer of *Restigouche* concluded his report of procedings with the comment that: "the decision to proceed to Greenock, as opposed to the long hoped-for Christmas at home in Halifax, was accepted cheerfully; every man regardless of rank, rating or branch, worked ceaselessly day and night for the good of the ship."

The raw Canadian youngsters were coming of age.

CHAPTER FIVE

Two More Oceans and a River

The early morning December 7, 1941, ushered in another and perhaps the greatest climacteric of the war. With the crash of Japanese bombs on Pearl Harbour, huge segments of the world picture, which had been lying about like the pieces of an unsolved jig-saw juzzle, were jolted into place. The shape and scope of the struggle stood clearly forth. For the now united nations, even amid the first shock and dismay, even amid the avalanche of disaster which followed, there must have been a deep, underlying sense of relief. The time for hesitation had been swept away. All doubts were resolved. All tedious fictions of non-belligerence and belligerent neutrality were at an end.

American seamen in the Atlantic had been for nearly two years fighting an undeclared, ill-defined war; with one hand, as it were, tied behind their backs. First there had been the neutrality patrol, in which United States warships warned the ships of belligerent powers away from combat in the waters of the western hemisphere. The warnings, for ships of the Axis, had become sharper and the tendency to disregard them more pronounced as the United States moved closer to the side of Great Britain. The mutual defence pact between the United States and Canada, made in August of 1940, had been followed in September of that year by the exchange of American destroyers for British bases. The Lend Lease Act had been passed in March of 1941; and later in the same month a staff agreement made between the British and American navies had brought about new measures of co-operation in the Atlantic.

Three United States battleships, three cruisers, an aircraft carrier and two squadrons of destroyers had been transferred from the Pacific to the Atlantic fleet by the end of

Two More Oceans and a River

May. In July United States naval and air forces relieved British forces in Iceland. Then in August, at the Atlantic Charter meeting between Roosevelt and Churchill, came portentous new developments. The Atlantic was divided east and west, and the American navy took over the strategic control of operations on the western side. Still not at war, the United States had determined that the trade convoys, already carrying enormous tonnages of American-made war supplies, were going to get through. The United States navy would take over the responsibility for their protection as far as the thirtieth meridian, which ran north and south down the face of the Alantic in the region of Iceland

A large American naval base was already well along toward completion at Argentia in Newfoundland; and authority in the western Atlantic was delegated to the American admiral based there. Canada's Newfoundland Command, as well as her other commands along the eastern seaboard, thus came automatically and abruptly under American control. On September 16, 1941, the first HX convoy sailed from Halifax under the protection of a United States naval task group; and thereafter all HX convoys were to be under American escort as far as a mid-ocean meeting point south of Iceland. SC convoys, originating at Sydney, were to be escorted to the same area by Canadian groups; while British ships were to take over all convoys from the mid-ocean meeting point eastward.

There could have been a measure of friction on the western side over the new arrangements. The staff and the seventy-five ships of Newfoundland Command had been fighting the war for two years, while the United States forces had as yet little experience. The Canadians, with the British and other ships which they controlled, were now placed under an Admiral whose country was not even a belligerent; and were required to operate under his direction in one of the most active theatres of the war. Fortunately, Admiral Bristol at Argentia and Commodore Murray at St. John's were realists and diplomats; and the relations between their

"Iced-up ship"

Landing survivors

staffs were already excellent. Co-operation between the two services was smooth and immediate. Canadian officers set about learning the naval language of the Americans. Staff officers from Argentia arrived one by one in St. John's to master the intricacies of the convoy-and-escort system; and in a minimum of time the combined forces, from admirals to able seamen, were operating as one.

Thus, through October and November, mighty and heartening assistance was coming or preparing to come to the aid of the hard-pressed convoys. United States seamen, sailing in blacked-out ships under all conditions of war, could regard the coming of full belligerence only as the remover of the last harrowing restrictions and the simplifier of many problems. British and Canadian seamen and their superiors ashore, considering the event inevitable, frankly and eagerly looked forward to it.

Yet the blow which fell on December 7 was of such stunning magnitude that for the moment all plans relating to the western war had to be altered to stem a tide of absolute disaster. Before American strength had ever reached the size envisaged in the plan for the Atlantic it had to be diverted to the Pacific; and this at a time when British perils and responsibilities about the world had suddenly and vastly increased. For Great Britain, in the words of the First Sea Lord, "Two great oceans were added at one stroke to the area in which our shipping was menaced by submarine and air attack." The decimation of the United States fleet at Pearl Harbour and the sinking of the *Prince of Wales* and *Repulse* off Malaya two days later, reduced allied naval strength in the Pacific and Indian oceans to temporary insignificance. Singapore was doomed; Australia, India and all the eastern bastions were threatened. The Mediterranean and the Red Sea, always vitally important, became now a channel which, if controlled by the Axis, would permit the linking of Japanese naval strength with German land power in an overwhelming combination. The Royal Navy, whose strength had been diluted since August for the convoys to Murmansk, must be diluted again for the Pacific. United States ships had to be withdrawn from the western Atlantic in such numbers that by February of 1942 only two coastguard cutters remained on escort duty.

The condition reflected no basic change in the plan of global war already determined on by the United States and Great Britain. Germany was the heart of the enemy combination; Germany was the principal enemy and was to be the object of the main attack. Powerful United States task forces were assigned to troop convoys as soon as American soldiers began to move to England. Hundreds of new ships for the protection of trade convoys were to be provided, in time, from building programmes just getting under way. But, at the moment, the long-looked-for accession of a mightly ally meant, for the escort forces of the western Atlantic, an almost fatal draining away of more strength.

Through December of 1941 and January of 1942 the routine nightmare of Atlantic convoy became at times little more than a valiant gesture. Hundreds of ships, unable to keep station amid the incessant gales, were driven apart from the main bodies, far beyond the range of escorts, and left to struggle on alone. Wide alterations of course, made necessary by the weather as often as by the U-boats, added extra days and hundreds of extra miles to the convoy voyages. The escort groups, never built up to the strength envisioned, were under almost unendurable strain.

Ships of the local escort, operating between Halifax, Sydney and St. John's, had a comparatively short distance to cover, but it was through an area of continual fog and foul weather; and the incessant demands upon them reduced harbour time to the vanishing point. The mid-ocean groups, sailing between St. John's and Iceland, had a theoretical twelve days in harbour for twenty-four days at sea; but in practice such a schedule was seldom if ever maintained. Their voyage with convoy was always round-about, and their arrival at the Iceland rendezvous was consequently delayed. When relieved by ships of the British local escort they had still twenty-four hours of steaming to Hvalfjord or Reykjavik for refuelling. Arriving there, frequently with survivors to land or damages to repair, they had to sail again within two days. After another twelve or thirteen days with a westbound convoy they very often arrived off St. John's only to be ordered immediately to Halifax for the fitting of essential equipment not held in St. John's, or simply because the harbour, congested with escorts, merchant ships for convoy and damaged ships which had limped back from other convoys, could not accommodate them. In spite of the four day voyage to and from Halifax they must still be ready to meet their next sailing date with an eastbound convoy.

The result of it all was that the groups operated continually under strength. Men might carry on up to some not yet determined point without sleep or rest, but ships were machines whose limits of endurance were fixed. The number of escorts out of action from enemy damage, weather damage or the simple breakdown of worn out parts was steadily increasing. The entire system of escort in the western Atlantic showed signs of cracking apart.

The situation was being anxiously considered ashore; even while a general reorganization of trade control, consequent upon the entry of the United States into the war, was under way. Decisions made in January affected trade first of all. American authorities would eventually take over supervision of the flow of North American trade, since the greater part of the cargo going to the United Kingdom was of American origin. A long and complicated process was therefore set in motion by which the Canadian trade control mechanism was step by step geared into and expanded with a larger organization embracing the United States, the United Kingdom and Canada.

One function which the Admiralty wished to transfer and which the United States navy was not yet ready to take over was the control of the fast "independents" in the western Atlantic—the liners and merchant ships of over fifteen knots who sailed alone, depending on their speed to avoid submarines. These ships had frequently to be diverted from the original route given them because of the presence of U-boats; and all such diversions up to the end of 1941 had been ordered by the Admiralty. It had by now become apparent that when the ships were in the western Atlantic they could be more efficiently diverted by shore authorities on the western side. The Canadian navy therefore took on responsibility for diversions in an area bounded on the south by the latitude of Bermuda and on the east by the longitude of 40° West.

A Diversion Room was set up in naval headquarters where four experienced officers maintained a round-the-clock watch over the progress of independent ships and the reported positions of submarines. The hour-to-hour position of the ships was plotted and the position of all submarine sightings and intercepted transmissions overlaid on the plot. As a ship was seen to be approaching a suspected submarine area it was signalled an alteration of course; and the educated guesses of the Diversion Room during the next six months were undoubtedly responsible for saving many valuable vessels.

The matter of strategic control in the western Atlantic was also brought into question. With the withdrawal of United States warships, it was beginning to create complications, since most of the ships operating under control of American shore authorities were British or Canadian. For the time being, however, the difficulties were merely noted. A certain amount of tact and deliberation might be employed in ironing out complexities of command, but there could be no further delay in easing the actual physical strain on the ships and men of the escort forces.

The required reorganization came in February 1942. It affected principally the ships of the Canadian navy, which now formed the main strength of the western Atlantic escort forces with thirteen destroyers and seventy corvettes. Of these, the ships running between Halifax and Newfoundland became the Western Local Escort Force; and their journey was extended by setting west ocean meeting point, the point at which their convoys would be taken over by mid-ocean groups, in the longitude of 45° West, some seven hundred miles from Halifax.

The mid-ocean groups of the Newfoundland Escort Force were increased from six to seven by the familiar expedient of reducing the number of ships in each group. Their eastern terminal was also changed. Five hundred miles to the east and south of Iceland lay the port of Londonderry in Northern Ireland. Mid-ocean escorts coming from the west would have a slightly longer lay-over in harbour if, instead of sailing north to Iceland, they continued eastward with their convoys and put into Londonderry.

This new arrangement went into effect with the sailing of Convoy SC 67 early in February. Mid-ocean groups began the famous "Newfie-to-Derry" run on which they were to continue for four years, with the smile of the green Foyle rather than the scowling crags of Iceland greeting them at the end of each voyage.

One of the corvettes on that first Londonderry run was not to see the Foyle. *Spikenard*, senior ship of the escort for SC-67, was lost with heavy casualties on the night of February 10. The voyage had begun in fog and continued with heavy weather but without U-boat attack to a point south of Iceland. Shortly before eleven o'clock on the night of the tenth *Spikenard* was zigzagging on the starboard wing of the convoy when a torpedo drove home in a nearby tanker, *Heina*. Almost simultaneously another torpedo struck *Spikenard*.

The night was very dark, with a high sea running. To the other escorts, disposed about the convoy and separated from *Spikenard* by distances ranging from a mile and a half to seven miles, the explosions came so nearly together that there was doubt as to whether two ships or only one had been torpedoed. *Chilliwack*, one of the corvettes on the port bow of the convoy, was engaged in attacking a contact at the time *Spikenard* was hit. *Dauphin*, astern of the convoy on the starboard side and three miles off, saw one explosion and then what she considered to be a second. She immediately moved toward the position which the blazing *Heina* was now illuminating; and found the tanker settling by the head.

It required two hours of heavy work with scramble-nets, carley floats and boats to get all the living men from *Heina* out of the oily water and on board *Dauphin*. Meanwhile *Shediac* which had observed the explosion from the port quarter astern, several miles away, came alongside and was ordered by *Dauphin* to make a search for a possible second ship torpedoed.

Louisburg had been the ship nearest to *Spikenard*, about a mile and a quarter astern, but a few seconds before the explosion of *Heina* she had seen the wake of a torpedo passing down her own port side. She had immediately turned back along the track, gained a contact and commenced an attack which occupied her for an hour and a half.

Lethbridge was several miles distant, on the port quarter. She heard a heavy explosion and saw a ship, across the width of the convoy and the intervening sea, burst into flames. Her primary responsibility, however, was protection for the port side of the convoy; her orders were to remain in station and she did so. None of the five corvettes could permit either U-boat contacts or search to detain them too long. The convoy was sweeping on and there was every possibility of new attack. Throughout the night, as they regained station, one or other of them endeavoured to get in touch with *Spikenard* by radio telephone; but her silence could very well have been due simply to one of the frequent failures of the equipment. No wireless signal was made because of the fear of homing other U-boats onto the convoy.

Dawn brought no sign of the missing corvette. There was still a possibility, however, that she might be somewhere over the horizon looking for the British local escort which was expected. At about eleven o'clock the British ships joined and the corvette *Gentian* was immediately sent to make a search back along the track of the convoy. After several hours of hunting, *Gentian* came upon a carley float with eight survivors of *Spikenard's* crew; all who were ever found.

None of the rescued men had been on *Spikenard's* bridge at the time of the torpedoing; and no one could say exactly what had happened. It semed possible that *Spikenard* had become aware of the presence of the submarine just before *Heina* was torpedoed. The survivors remembered that action stations had been sounded and speed increased. Then the torpedoes had struck. In *Spikenard* the point of impact had been between bridge and forecastle. Part of the ship's side and part of the deck had been blown away, and fire had broken out immediately, destroying the bridge, the wireless office, and one of the boats.

The flames had reached out to embrace several drums of petrol stowed beside the mast. A wall of fire had climbed to the superstructure and reached down into the bowels of the ship. Men coming up from the mess decks had had to fight their way to the forecastle through a curtain of flame. As they stumbled blindly along, some of them had fallen into the flooded forepart of the ship through a gaping hole blasted in the deckplates. Then *Spikenard* had begun to settle by the head, with her whistle, set off by the explosion, blowing a continual eerie requiem. Five minutes later she went under, and as the sea closed over her another explosion, either from her boilers or from a depth charge, smashed the remaining boat and one of the carley floats.

The ship had completely disappeared before the first corvette, *Dauphin,* reached the position of *Heina.* The light from the flaming tanker had fallen far short of the position where the men of *Spikenard* were struggling in the water. In the black, windy night their shouts were completely lost; and they had had no flares with which to attract attention. Twice they had seen the dim and tossing shape of a corvette in the distance; but in each case the searching ship had passed them by.

The report of this disaster was almost lost in a tide of catastrophe rising nearer home. *Spikenard* and *Heina* had gone down in a battle area which by February 11, 1942 had become one of secondary importance. A new and grimmer phase of the war had opened on January 12 with the torpedoing of the British ship *Cyclops*, just 160 miles south of Halifax. That sinking heralded the coming of a fleet of some twenty U-boats to the waters of the American seaboard.

All along the coast, from south of Newfoundland to Cape Hatteras, the blow fell with stunning force. During the nineteen remaining days of January, thirty-nine ships of nearly 250,000 tons were sunk; and of these sixteen were tankers. Most of the sinkings were close inshore, for the U-boats operated in full scornful awareness of the fact that there were no coastal convoys in American waters. They lay submerged in shallow water by day and surfaced at night to operate in groups against the hundreds of tankers and freighters moving north and south between the great Atlantic ports of the United States. Night after night the dull roar of explosions at sea was heard ashore and the flames of exploding tankers lit up the sky. Sometimes a pall of oily smoke, driven by an onshore wind, hung heavily above cosatal cities and towns; and the noise of gunfire and battle at sea was followed on land by the sight of maimed and exhausted survivors. During the sickening months that were to follow, watchers along the coast from Boston to Key West would see more than two hundred ships go down within ten miles of shore.

The attack was a deadly one, and not only to the United States. The United Kingdom's sources of oil supply were being cut off one by one. The route from the Middle East through the Mediterranean was nearly closed. Borneo and the Dutch East Indies were lost to Japan. Oil from the Persian Gulf, brought through the Indian Ocean and around the Cape, was menaced by Japanese surface raiders and submarines and in any case was an uncertain and insufficient supply. The lubrication of Britain's war machine depended mainly now on tankers sailing up along the American coast from Aruba, Curacao and the Gulfs of Venezuela and Mexico;

and if that stream of shipping were cut off the machine would grind to a stop.

With February the attack not only continued but expanded southward into the Caribbean to strike the oil traffic at its source. Twenty-three more tankers were sunk during the month; and the total shipping losses for January and February amounted to 144 ships of nearly 800,000 tons. The only effective means of reducing these appalling figures was a network of convoys all the way from Panama to Halifax; and the United States did not have the necessary escort ships. Evasive routing was tried with little effect; then sailings had to be curtailed while oil stocks in the United Kingdom, in Canada and in the United States itself fell to a perilous minimum.

March saw the attack swing back north to concentrate along the coast between Charleston and New York; and the hump of Cape Hatteras, jutting out into the Atlantic about midway along this route, became a graveyard where sometimes as many as six ships went down in a single night. The U-boats concentrated grimly and efficiently on unprotected vessels. On passage in the Atlantic or along the Canadian or Newfoundland coast, they practically ignored the escorted convoys. Their instructions were to risk no damage which would put them out of action thousands of miles from base; they were to make every torpedo count and when their torpedoes were exhausted they were to attack with gunfire. They operated in such numbers and with such little risk of interference that they were sometimes reported to be burning orange riding lights for fear of collision among themselves.

The first palliative came in March with the organization of BX and XB convoys between Boston and Halifax. They were to be escorted by Canadian ships withdrawn from the Western Local Escort Force. The vessels assembled in Buzzard's Bay, south of the Cape Cod Canal, proceeded through the Canal and formed up in Cape Cod Bay for the voyage to Halifax. With the sailing of the first BX convoy on

Two More Oceans and a River

March 20 the area between Boston and Halifax was subtracted from the "U-boat's Paradise," but below Boston the heavenly conditions had still several months to run.

Even while the coastal attacks were at their height, a considerable force of U-boats was maintained in the Atlantic. Contacts and sightings were frequent and there were enough sinkings to demand continual vigilance from the escorts. Another worry arose from the continual presence of submarines in Canadian and Newfoundland waters. Even though they were on passage to and from the American coast or the Caribbean, the wide mouth of the St. Lawrence, leading to the heartland of another enemy, gaped invitingly. Ice in the river was beginning to heave restlessly under the fitful warmth of the March sun; navigation would be under way in another month or so; and the opening of the river would mean the opening of another danger area. Amid the distractions of local escort, mid-ocean escort and new commitments in American waters, Canadian naval officers sat down to consider what might be done about the prospect of attack in the St. Lawrence.

The answer was: very little. Mid-ocean and western local escort forces could barely maintain their cycles. The diversion of ships for the Halifax-Boston run had brought the force below what had already been considered an irreducible minimum. Drastic measures must soon be taken to reduce the staggering tanker losses in the Caribbean; and these would in all probability involve the use of more Canadian ships. Valuable as the St. Lawrence traffic was, and even though much of it was destined for ocean convoy, it had to take second place to the defence of the convoys themselves and to the provision of oil.

The St. Lawrence Conference of March 1942 met to review plans made in 1940 for Quebec-Sydney convoys and for the use of Gaspé as a base for a St. Lawrence escort force. It also made preparation against the necessity of overland routing for much cargo which normally went by the river. But the plans remained on paper throughout April and the first ten days of May. Only the coming of the enemy could justify the withdrawal of ships from areas where attacks were actually in progress.

The expected and unwelcome arrival in the St. Lawrence was the submarine U-553, commanded by one Lieutenant-Commander Thurmann. U-553 had set out from her base at St. Nazaire in April and had had a series of frustrating experiences on her voyage across the Atlantic. About midway she had sighted a large merchantman which had escaped her. As she approached North American waters a United States patrol frigate had come almost within torpedo range and then turned suddenly away. U-553 had proceeded down the coast to the neighbourhood of Boston only to find that the new Halifax Boston convoys had cleared the seas of unprotected ships. At this point Lieutenant-Commander Thurmann had decided to turn northward again; and by June 9 he was skirting the southern coast of Newfoundland. Coast watchers in the vicinity of Cape Ray observed him proceeding westward at dawn on the 10th; and later in the same day, when he was about sixty-five miles south of Anticosti, he was attacked by an aircraft which drove him under but did him no damage.

By the night of the 10th he was lying on the surface off Anticosti, enjoying a moonlit calm and speculating about the lights glinting from windows along the hostile shore. At dawn he submerged again and lay on the bottom throughout the day. Surfacing with darkness on the 11th, he moved across the river to take up a position off the south shore a little to the west of Cap des Rosiers. Half an hour before midnight he saw a big freighter bearing down on him. He waited until the ship came into point-blank range and then sent two torpedoes into her. The ship, the British S.S. *Nicoya*, began to sink immediately. Thurmann moved on a little to the northeast, and two hours and forty-five minutes later drove another torpedo into the Dutch freighter *Leto*. Then he headed back down the Gulf, preparing to pass the day on the bottom and commence his journey out of the river with darkness.

Two More Oceans and a River

The glare of the explosions and the flames rising from the two sinking ships had been clearly visible on land. As crowds gathered along the Gaspé coast, exhausted survivors coated with oil and suffering from wounds and shock began to be brought ashore. For the people in the vicinity, and for the whole country as the news spread, the torpedoings were a horrifying blow. The navy was instantly assailed with demands for full information and with queries as to why the disasters had not been prevented. The cry of anger and dismay was perfectly natural; and the only answer which could be given to it was an unpalatable one.

Canada's great waterway was a part of the route by which supplies must reach the United Kingdom; and that route was under sustained attack all along its length. The St. Lawrence had to be viewed in relation to the whole battle, and as yet it was a minor theatre. At the time the first sighting was reported, the entire escort force available for search in the St. Lawrence had consisted of one Bangor minesweeper and two Fairmiles, the gasoline-powered motor launches included in one of the recent building programmes.

These ships had immediately commenced search, and with word of the sinkings were despatched to the Gaspé area. Five more Bangor minesweepers were recalled from duty with the western local escort force to be based on Gaspé. In the meantime, pending the arrival of the Gaspé force and the organization of the Quebec-Sydney convoys, all traffic in the river was brought to a standstill. The arrangements were in accordance with the plan made in March; but none of them could be announced publicly. Still less could it be revealed that ten more corvettes were even now being withdrawn from Canadian forces for service with tanker convoys in the Caribbean.

The only official information given the public was a brief and guarded statement made by the Naval Minister in the House on the afternoon of May 12. It said that a ship had been torpedoed in the Gulf of St. Lawrence; and added that possible future sinkings would not be announced for fear of giving the enemy information of value to him.

Not unnaturally the country, and particularly the part of the country bordering on the river, found the meagre report unsatisfactory. All the people in the neighbourhood of Gaspé knew that not one but two ships had been sunk. They had seen survivors brought ashore and had heard their stories. The identity of the ships was known to them; and the details of the sinkings were common knowledge to hundreds and even thousands of people. It was difficult to understand why the news should be witheld from an anxious country.

The reasons centred about the submarine, still lying somewhere in one of the rocky inlets or under the waters of the Gulf. She had not yet sent any signal to the German admiralty announcing her successes, and if complete, or almost complete, silence could be maintained there was a strong probability that she would do so. German naval practice was very rigid; submarine movements were strictly controlled; and signalled reports of any action were required if the necessary information was not available from other sources. The sparse detail of the official announcement would be of little use to German authorities; but press and radio accounts, harmless as they might seem, could be much more informative under expert dissection. An analysis of one or two accounts which leaked out and were passed by press censors indicated how the piecing together of a few details given in all innocence might enable German authorities to compile vital information.

The time of the torpedoing was given; thereby indicating the best conditions for attack in the area.

The number of ships sunk and the number of explosions was mentioned; revealing the number of torpedoes used by the submarine and possibly the number remaining to her.

The position of the attack was given; enabling German shore authorities to calculate the distance the boat had travelled and therefore its present fuel position.

By mentioning the fact that there was much shipping in the area, German attention had been focussed on it as a zone of future operations.

Weather conditions were described; always valuable information to those directing naval operations.

The names of survivors of the Dutch ship were given; possibly enabling the Gestapo to attack the morale of relatives and friends in occupied countries.

The statement that the merchant ships were unprepared for attack informed the German admiralty that the U-boat had probably sustained no damage.

All this information would have reached Germany in a short time. Its intrinsic value was, in any case, limited. But the reticence of the navy, and the silence which newspapers and broadcasting stations promptly imposed on themselves once they understood the situation, were maintained in the hope that some of this operational information would be signalled by the U-boat. Naval wireless stations on shore were on watch for such a signal transmission. It would almost certainly have been intercepted, its bearing taken from half a dozen widely separated points, and a "fix" made on the position of the enemy. With the position once established, the few ships available could have been sent directly and without loss of time to the most promising area for an attack. None of this happened. For reasons known only to herself, U-553 maintained unbroken radio silence; and for the next ten days was undetected as she worked her way out of the Gulf to safety.

Quebec-Sydney convoys were shortly inaugurated under the protection of a limited escort force based on Gaspé; but the navy held firm against the temptation to divert a larger proportion of its strength than was warranted. The inland attack was humiliating, the dislocation of river traffic and the added strain on railways and the facilities of the Atlantic ports was serious; but the situation elsewhere was becoming desperate. By May 22 the oil shortage both in Halifax and in the United Kingdom had forced the institution of convoys under Canadian escort between Halifax and Trinidad; and a little later between Halifax and Aruba. The convoys were made up entirely of fast tankers, and their progress was charted with even more anxiety than usual because there were times when the sinking of even one of the ships would have meant a temporary paralysis of operations.

The daily average of U-boats operating on the western side of the Atlantic was only about twenty, but they ranged almost at will against the thinly-spread defence forces, pressing home the attack along the American seaboard and in the Caribbean and maintaining a continual threat in mid-ocean. Apart from the sombre evidence of the losses, their confidence, their daring and their ubiquity were testified to by many isolated incidents.

One submarine had lain a mile or so off St. John's, Newfoundland, and driven two torpedoes at the narrow mouth of the harbour. Another, shadowing a westbound convoy, had signalled *Manchester Division,* one of the merchant ships, asking for the vessel's position, course and speed; identifying herself as another merchant vessel with the call sign *Nerk.* No convoy sailed without sightings and threats of attack and a moderate but continual toll of sinkings was exacted. It was obvious that the U-boats were prepared at any moment to return the full weight of their attack to the mid-Atlantic.

Any reduction in the ocean escort forces could have brought disaster; and other factors still loomed large. The men in the warships were becoming more proficient against submarines but they had still much to learn. The merchant seamen, whose unwavering morale was probably the greatest miracle of the Atlantic battle and certainly the basis upon which all success rested, had had no more leisure than the fighting forces to train themselves for the necessities of sea war, and even less opportunity to repair the shortcomings of their ships. Failings in convoy discipline, in spite of all the pleadings of commodores at hundreds of conferences, still occurred and carried a heavy penalty. Many of the old coal-burning ships belched smoke and left a trail above a convoy which attracted U-boats from many miles off. Bilges pumped out during the day left oil-slicks which acted as trails for shadowers, and garbage heaved over the side served the same purpose. Blackouts were even yet not as complete as they should have been. Ships were still blowing their fog whistles too much and burning stern lights oftener than necessary. There were also occasions when, not without reason, a convoy added to its own troubles and the troubles of the escort by an attack of the jitters.

One escort group, consisting of two American ships and the Canadian corvettes *Arvida, Algoma, Shediac,* and *Bittersweet,* had a hard taste of battle and confusion on the nights of May 11 and May 12, the same period during which U-553 was conducting her foray in the St. Lawrence. Their convoy was westbound in mid-ocean, and after dark on the 11th the escorts were disposed about it in a wide screen. About ten o'clock four U-boats which had worked their way in between the warships and the convoy let go salvoes of torpedoes at ranges as low as two hundred yards. Six merchant ships went down and the escorts began the heartbreaking division of work between the rescue of survivors and preparations to meet new attacks.

The shadowing group of submarines was fended off for the rest of the night; but the convoy had been shaken by its ordeal, and anxiety persisted throughout a rainy, misty day. As darkness fell on the night of the 12th the order for an evasive turn at midnight was passed down the columns; but just as the alteration got under way a ship took alarm and fired "snowflake"—the brilliant night illuminant provided for cases where U-boats were known to be present on the surface. Every ship in the convoy immediately followed suit with its own snowflake; the sea was illuminated for miles around, and all benefit of the evasive turn completely lost.

One ship was promptly torpedoed, multiplying the confusion; and *Arvida* was paid what her commanding officer considered "a dubious compliment to our camouflage" when a merchantman fired snowflake directly over her head and then sent a shell whistling past the officers and lookouts on *Arvida's* bridge. Further sinkings in that particular convoy were avoided; but the incident served to emphasize once again the strain under which merchant ships and escorts were carrying on.

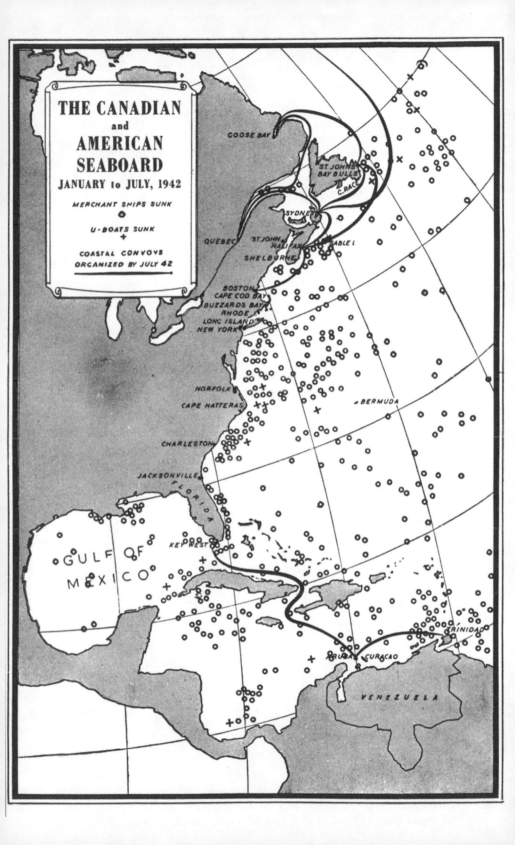

THE CANADIAN
and
AMERICAN
SEABOARD

JANUARY to JULY, 1942

MERCHANT SHIPS SUNK
o

U-BOATS SUNK
+

COASTAL CONVOYS
ORGANIZED BY JULY 42

Survivors from U.S. transport *Chatham* torpedoed in Strait of Belle Isle.

June was worse than May, and one of the worst months of the war. The Halifax-Trinidad-Aruba convoys were operating successfully and without loss. There was no attack on the Quebec-Sydney convoys in the St. Lawrence. The United States Navy had now instituted a partial convoy system between Norfolk, Virginia, and Key West, Florida. But the network was still not complete. Shipping was unprotected to the north between Norfolk and Boston and to the south in the Gulf of Mexico and the Caribbean; and wherever an opening remained the U-boats struck home, bringing losses for the month to a total of 671,000 tons.

From Newfoundland to the Caribbean the grimness of the battle permitted of no mistakes and no second chances. On June 21 a British submarine, P 514, used for training in anti-submarine tactics, was on passage from Argentia to St. John's. She was under the escort of three Canadian corvettes; but in a rough day with poor visibility became separated from her escorts for a few fatal hours. During this interval the Bangor minesweeper *Georgian,* passing down the coast with a small coastal convoy, sighted P 514 and challenged. For some reason never discovered P 514 failed to reply. *Georgian* immediately rammed and the submarine was sunk with all hands. There had been no other course open to the minesweeper; and her commanding officer was completely exonerated for his action. Nevertheless the accident served to darken days which were dark enough in any case.

U-boat operations expanded during June to include the laying of mines in American waters and the landing of parties of saboteurs at Jacksonville, Florida, and on Long Island. Losses by the mines were held down to a total of five ships, and the saboteurs were all rounded up before they could do damage; but it was a sombre fact that German enemies had now actually set foot on the shores of North America. American escort forces were gathering for the defence of their own waters; but the mobilization was still a slow process, continually delayed by the requirements of the Pacific theatre.

Two More Oceans and a River

For Canada, the near approach of the war was again emphasized in the early days of July. Three ships in convoy were torpedoed in the St. Lawrene off Cap Chat on July 6; and another was to go down off Cap de la Madeleine on July 20. The battle was no longer a remote tale echoing back from the dim reaches of the mid-Atlantic. From the U-boat pens of Kiel and Wilhelmshaven and St. Nazaire and Lorient it had advanced to within two hundred miles of Quebec city.

CHAPTER SIX

"The End of the Beginning"

THE Strait of Belle Isle was the next part of the St. Lawrence area to attract German attention. It forms a narrow inland exit from the Gulf, passing between the tip of Newfoundland and the southeastern shoulder of Labrador; and by midsummer of 1942 it had become an important waterway and a potentially dangerous bottleneck. Great quantities of stores and supplies were moving through the Gulf to the northern bases which were now being developed to provide additional air cover over the Atlantic, and also as links in the rapidly expanding ferry service to the United Kingdom. United States bases in Greenland were supplied by convoys under American escort sailing from Sydney through the Strait of Belle Isle; while materials for the Canadian base at Goose Bay in Labrador came down river from Montreal, escorted by Canadian warships, and passed onward by the same route. This flow of valuable traffic was now to be seriously disrupted; mainly by the efforts of a certain Lieutenant-Commander Paul Hartwig who sailed from Kiel in command of the submarine U-517 on August 8, 1942.

Hartwig was an extremely competent submarine officer and a hard drinker, apparently admired by his crew in both capacities. During his stay in the St. Lawrence, however, only the first of his two qualities was in evidence. With orders to attack shipping along the Labrador coast, he crossed the Atlantic at economical speed and made landfall on Belle Isle at the mouth of the Strait during the morning of August 26. From there he worked cautiously down between the island and Cape Bauld; and early on the following morning sighted a Sydney-Greenland convoy under the escort of American coastguard cutters. As the ships came into range Hartwig fired two torpedoes, one of which found its mark in

115

the transport *Chatham,* and sent it to the bottom. Then, evading the counter attacks of the escorts, he doubled back to the north and spent a few hours studying his charts of the Gulf of St. Lawrence. New orders had reached him from Germany giving him wider discretion in his choice of an operational area, and he had made up his mind to push down through the Strait.

During the afternoon of the 27th he sighted a second submarine, U-165; but as the two boats prepared to close each other they were alarmed by the sound of engines overhead. A searching plane, called to the area after the torpedoing of *Chatham,* was bearing down on them and they had to dive. Hartwig made his getaway, circled leisurely around Belle Isle, and about nine-thirty in the evening encountered the same convoy he had attacked before. U-165 was also on hand; and in the second attack each U-boat got one ship.

Escaping undamaged from another series of counter attacks, Hartwig now turned southward down the Strait. By the 29th he was well into the Gulf; and during the afternoon of that day he came in sight of the East Cape of Anticosti. Turning back from there he began to patrol in a northeasterly and southwesterly direction. The sweep continued, monotonous and tense, until the early evening of September 2, when he sighted a northbound convoy under Canadian escort and proceeded to shadow it.

At one-thirty on the following morning, just as an inbound convoy appeared from the north and drew abreast of the outward-bound ships, Hartwig moved in to attack, partially submerged. *Weyburn,* one of the corvettes in escort, caught sight of the glistening wash made by his conning tower, then of the vague hardening upon the darkness which was the U-boat's partial silhouette. She fired rockets, got away two rounds from her four-inch gun and bore down at full speed to ram. Hartwig waited coolly until *Weyburn* was within a thousand yards of him, then altered course, fired a torpedo past the corvette into the merchantman *Donald Stewart* and dived.

Second Campaign in the St. Lawrence

As the flare of the explosion behind her lit up the sky, *Weyburn* crossed the swirl of the U-boat's dive. A full pattern of depth charges had been ordered away, but at the moment of firing the throwers jammed and only two charges went into the water. The explosions were enough to create a disturbance and break off asdic contact, but only great good luck could have made them lethal for the submarine; and it was not *Weyburn's* lucky night. She could not regain contact in the seething water and turned away after half an hour's search to assist the flaming *Donald Stewart*. Hartwig and his men waited beneath the surface in surprised immunity as the two convoys recovered from the confusion caused by the attack and swept away on opposite courses.

Some time during the next day Hartwig, occasionally in company with U-165, took up patrol in the Gaspé passage. Here life was becoming dangerous, and U-517 was continually harried by attacks from aircraft. One plane came screaming down out of a misty sky to drop a bomb squarely on the submarine's deck, almost hard against a ready-use ammunition locker. Hartwig's luck and nerve were still with him, however. The bomb failed to explode; and with the assistance of his engineer officer and two ratings the U-boat captain heaved it overboard.

By the night of September 6 Hartwig had worked his way up the river to within 250 miles of Quebec. Shortly before ten o'clock a Quebec-Sydney convoy hove in sight. Two corvettes, two Fairmiles and the armed yacht *Raccoon* were in escort.

U-517 worked herself into position, and sent a torpedo crashing home in one of the merchantmen. *Arrowhead*, one of the corvettes in escort, pounced on the attacker with depth charges, and this time Hartwig and his men received a severe shaking. Well below the surface, and probably in semi-darkness with his lighting system knocked out of commission, the U-boat commander recollected that he had a new card up his sleeve and decided that now was the time to play it. *Arrowhead*, above, was groping back toward him with the pulsing beam of her asdic searching for a death grip. As the sound of her propeller grew louder in the submarine's hydrophone, U-517 released through a special vent a small, perforated metal cylinder about twice the size of a tomato tin.

It was the *Pillenwerfer,* or submarine bubble target— an ingenious decoy which was to cause trouble in the future. A chemical in the tin, activated by contact with the water, produced a cloud of bubbles which resonated to the frequency of the asdic beam and returned a clear and convincing echo. *Arrowhead's* asdic picked up the false target; the ship altered course and followed a firm, apparently unmistakable contact which suddenly faded and disappeared as the decoy, having done its work, sank to the bottom. *Arrowhead* and the other escorts which had joined in the hunt turned away mystified and disappointed by the vanishing echo, and went to the assistance of survivors from the torpedoed ship.

The rescue work was completed about midnight; and it was then noticed that the yacht *Raccoon* was no longer in company. Shortly after this discovery two heavy explosions were heard from a considerable distance astern. A Fairmile went back to investigate but found no trace of *Raccoon;* and the ship was not seen again. It seems probable that she was sunk by U-165, which was somewhere in the area. She was not torpedoed by Hartwig. The only trace of *Raccoon* ever found was the body of one man washed up several days later on Anticosti Island.

The convoy itself had recovered from its first confusion and was continuing the voyage; but U-517 came upon it again shortly before dawn. Working inside the convoy columns this time, Hartwig fired three torpedoes simultaneously, two from bow tubes and one from astern. Each of the torpedoes found its mark in a ship and the German, although he had several bad moments during a series of attacks carried out amid the turmoil of convoy manoeuvring and rescue, again escaped unscathed.

On September 11, three days later, Hartwig was back in the neighbourhood of Gaspé. The early morning of the

11th was dark with a wreathing mist obscuring the waters of the Gulf. The corvette *Charlottetown,* and the minesweeper, *Clayoquot,* had delivered a convoy to Rimouski and were steaming back toward Gaspé abreast of each other, about a mile apart and zigzagging at nearly maximum speed. Asdic conditions, always peculiarly bad in the Gulf, where the water flows in strata of varying temperatures and returns a multitude of confusing echoes, were rather worse than usual. Neither ship had any indication of U-517's presence until two torpedoes struck *Charlottetown* in quick succession on the starboard quarter.

The corvette began to sink immediately and her company had just three minutes to get overboard before she disappeared. Casualties from the actual torpedoing were light; but as the stern of the ship went under, a depth charge exploded, killing six of the men struggling in the water and injuring several others. There was the usual grim postponment of rescue work while *Clayoquot* searched vainly for the attacking submarine. Then she returned to take on board fifty-five survivors, many of them wounded.

On the afternoon of September 15 and the early morning of September 16, Hartwig, probably again in company with U-165, wrought still more havoc with a Quebec-Sydney convoy, even though the escort on this occasion had been strengthened by a British destroyer temporarily detached from the Western Local Escort Force. In the first attack, working again from inside the convoy columns where detection was most difficult, U-517 sank two ships in as many minutes. In the early morning attack which followed, two more vessels went down, probably sunk by U-165, since Hartwig does not claim them. Escort ships, groping among the disorganized columns of merchantmen while the glare of burning ships fitfully illumined the darkness and the cries of desperate men, choked and blinded by oil, came to them from the pitchy waters, sent their depth charges thundering down on every contact and possible contact, but without visible result. They did, however, manage to give U-517 a fairly severe shaking. Her firing gear was damaged and the capacity of her apparatus for distilling fresh water was reduced from a daily fifty gallons to ten.

The next day found Hartwig down to his last four torpedoes and now cursed with defective firing gear. Most serious of all was the shortage of fresh water, which threatened to deprive his crew of their beloved coffee. Nevertheless the commander announced that he was going to stay in the St. Lawrence until all his torpedoes were gone; and he remained on patrol in the Gaspé passage for another three weeks.

His harvest of shipping, however, had now been completed. One foggy afternoon he passed close alongside a fifty ton sailing vessel, but decided that it was not worth one of his hoarded torpedoes. On the night of October 3 he came upon three fully lighted merchant ships and followed them down the Gulf for a time; but at last decided that they were legitimate neutrals and let them go. They were actually Swedish freighters sailing from Montreal with grain for the relief of Greece. A day or two later Hartwig sighted a convoy of twenty-one ships eastbound through the Gaspé passage; and after following it for two days fired his last salvo at long range. The four torpedoes ran badly because of the damaged gear, and all missed. Weaponless now, and somewhat damped by this final failure, Hartwig nosed out of Cabot Strait on October 5, with a total of 31,101 tons of Allied shipping to his credit. The defensive forces opposing him had been meagre and unsuccessful, but not inactive. The German calculated that he had had twenty-seven bombs and 118 depth charges dropped near enough to cause him discomfort.

Honours awaited him in Lorient; and a generous overestimate of the tonnage he had sunk; but he did not have long to enjoy his Knight's Cross. A month later, on his next outward voyage, he was caught off Cape Ortegal by a seaplane from the British carrier *Victorious;* and within a matter of hours U-517 was on the bottom and her captain, under interrogation by British Intelligence Officers, was yielding

Depth charge away.

ATTACKS
IN THE ST. LAWRENCE
1939 – 1945
WARSHIPS TORPEDOED ▲
MERCHANTMEN TORPEDOED ▢

GOOSE BAY

BELLE ISLE

STR. OF BELLE ISLE

OSTI
LAND

ST. LAWRENCE

OF

CABOT

STRAIT

C.RAY

ST.JOHNS

SYDNEY

ROUTE OF U-517

SABLE IS.

Depth charges exploding

up the story of his St. Lawrence voyage for the benefit of Admiralty records.

This German commander had been an officer of great nerve and skill; and the only Canadian counter attack which achieved any success during his reign of terror in the St. Lawrence was directed at another submarine. On the morning of September 21 the Bangor minesweeper *Georgian* was just nine minutes out of Sydney harbour on her way to join a convoy when she sighted the periscope and part of the conning tower of a U-boat a thousand yards off her port bow. Running in at full speed, *Georgian* dropped one pattern of shallow-set charges directly over the swirl of the dive; then turned quickly back to send ten more gurgling downward. The second series of explosions rumbled in the depths and, as the fountains mushroomed above the water nine hundred yards astern, the U-boat came rocking to the surface.

Georgian bore in to ram; but before she reached the submarine it turned slowly over on its side and sank. Following a wake which widened on the surface for about a minute, *Georgian* sent down charge after charge; and a huge gush of oil welled to the surface, spreading out in wide smear. The minesweeper's crew might well have been pardoned for their exultation over a certain kill; but in actual fact the U-boat, although damaged, made its escape.

U-boats were again in the St. Lawrence during October; and two more merchant ships were sunk. The heaviest blow of all came on October 14 when the passenger vessel *Caribou,* plying between Sydney and Port aux Basques, Newfoundland, was torpedoed and sunk in Cabot Strait with a loss of 136 lives. On the night of November 8 Werner Janowski, a German agent, was landed from a submarine which nosed its way in to shore near New Carlisle. He proved to be a singularly inept specimen who was in the hands of Canadian authorities, lying volubly, within a day of his arrival; but the very fact of his coming rounded out a campaign which had been an almost unmitigated defeat for Canada.

121

"The End of the Beginning"

It was a defeat deliberately and unavoidably accepted, just as the disastrous losses of the campaign along the American seaboard had been accepted. Adequate defence of the St. Lawrence would have meant the recall of many Canadian ships from the Atlantic; and such re-disposition would have been of far more benefit to Germany than all the achievements of Hartwig and his companions. It was in the Atlantic, along the ever-changing lines of the convoy routes, that the pattern of defeat or victory had still to be resolved; and it was there that Canada could best serve her own interests and make her greatest contribution to the allied effort. Sir Percy Noble, Commander-in-Chief, Western Approaches, was to say later that "the Canadian Navy solved the problem of the Atlantic convoys." The resounding tribute had hardly been merited as yet, but it was in process of being earned; and the task demanded both risk and sacrifice.

The St. Lawrence Force, from the opening of the campaign in the spring of 1942 to its close in November, consisted of two corvettes, five Bangor minesweepers and a few Fairmile motor launches; the merest fraction of the navy's strength. Only a comparable fraction was allotted to the Atlantic seaboard; and defences along the Pacific front, lean at best, had to be divided for several months between Canadian waters and the campaign in the Aleutians.

In June the Japanese leap across the Pacific to occupy Attu and Kiska had posed the threat of a serious attack by way of the Northwest. Strong American naval forces had moved into Alaskan waters; and on August 20 the three Canadian armed merchant cruisers, *Prince Robert, Prince Henry* and *Prince David*, together with the corvettes *Dawson* and *Vancouver*, had also sailed from Esquimalt for Kodiak. There, operating under the orders of the United States Navy, they had begun the escort of convoys between Kodiak, Dutch Harbour and intermediate points.

Their tour of duty, which occupied a little over two months, brought no actual contact with Japanese naval forces; but was made memorable by a long series of convoy voyages under excruciatingly foul conditions. The waters were little known, not fully charted and treacherous. There was always the possibility of head-on collision with an overwhelming Japanese task force; and about eighteen enemy submarines were believed to be somewhere among the islands, though they seemed to be handicapped by a shortage of torpedoes. Radar equipment in all the Canadian ships was still in its most rudimentary stage; and without it navigation was a matter of incessant peril. Fog gave place only to gales; and with the passing of the gales fog returned. The curse of curses was the distinctively Aleutian "Williwaw" which roared down the narrow mountain passes from the "storm factory" of the Bering Sea. Men who had had, or were later to have, experience of the worst weather provided by the Atlantic still give evil precedence to their days in the North Pacific.

Meanwhile, in the sunnier waters to the south, Canadian naval strength was becoming more a matter of faith than of fact. In June a Japanese submarine had shelled Estevan Point on Vancouver Island, emphasizing the danger of attacks on coastwise shipping. Nevertheless, before the end of summer the five corvettes which had remained based on Esquimalt after the departure of the Aleutian expedition were sent to the Atlantic. Until the three Prince ships and the two corvettes returned from the north at the end of October, only a force of thirteen Bangor minesweepers could be maintained along the thousands of miles of coastline separating Prince Rupert from Juan de Fuca Strait.

All other Canadian warships — thirteen destroyers, sixty-eight corvettes, twenty Bangors and some sixty smaller craft—were devoted to the defence of the main Atlantic convoy and the tributary convoys which fed into it from as far south as the Caribbean. The circumstances of the war had thrust upon this aggregation of ships, still insignificant by comparison with the great navies of Britain or the United States or Italy or Japan, an importance out of all relation to its size. American warships, with the exception of a few coastguard cutters, had been withdrawn from the trade convoys of the western Atlantic. They were providing the heavy escort now required for troop convoys; and many of the best ships had gone to the Pacific. The leviathans of British naval power—the battleships, the aircraft carriers, the cruisers and the modern destroyers—held the gateways of the North Sea, the Indian Ocean and the South Atlantic; went north with the Russia convoys and warded off a fatal linking of German and Japanese power by way of the Mediterranean.

The war had to be waged and waged without cessation in all these theatres. The Allies could withdraw from none of them and neglect none of them. The powerful ships of the great navies buttressed what remained of the world's old strategic framework and kept the tide of Axis triumphs from becoming a flood which would engulf the earth. Yet all their work—even the great campaign against Japan—was secondary and contributory to the final objective, which was the defeat of Germany by an assault mounted from the British Isles. The conditions and necessities surrounding that long-envisioned and still far-distant objective had not changed. The Atlantic convoy was still the heartbeat of the war.

The Atlantic battle could be fought, ironically enough, with the small ships, the old ships, the secondary ships. Efficient anti-submarine protection required neither heavy gunpower nor great speed. The imposing might of battleships would be largely wasted against U-boats; and with them, as with Fleet aircraft carriers and cruisers, the prospect of disastrous losses far outweighed the value of the work they could do. Even modern destroyers with their increased efficiency and speed would be used wastefully if they were put to jogging along day after day at the side of a slow convoy. The little ships—the older destroyers and the small, slow, lightly-armed corvettes — could do the Atlantic escort work most efficiently and economically; always provided that there were enough of them.

Thus it was that the Canadian contribution had come to assume such vital importance. Canadian shipyards, Canadian recruiting and training bases, all the hastily scraped-together apparatus of naval power, had just managed to keep pace with the widening gap between the resources of the great allied navies and the needs of the war. Canadian ships had prevented the strain from becoming a breakdown, the gap from becoming a breach. They were still doing so; and their efforts were now a very respectable contribution to the total effort. By midsummer of 1942, forty per cent of the escort work about the trade convoys in the North Atlantic was being done by Canadian ships.

Canadian authorities recognized and accepted the role marked out for their navy. Throughout the war their major preoccupation was to be the endless, week-by-week procession of the merchant ships crawling over the stormy seas from North America to Britain. By the end of the summer of 1942, when New York became the main assembly point for ocean convoys in place of Halifax and Sydney, Canadian ships had escorted from Canadian and Newfoundland ports more than sixty-five million tons of cargo. Their weekly and monthly totals were to increase steadily right up to the end of the war in Europe; but the dry statistics told already of the great fact and the great achievement underlying and continuing through all the lost battles and the tragic sinkings, the few spectacular successes and the hearbreaking failures. Canadian ships and their half-trained men, still too few, still scantily equipped, exposed to all varieties of discomfort and danger, were making it possible with every drab, anonymous day's work for sixty thousand tons of war supplies to move toward the United Kingdom.

Although the growth of the navy had been a forced one, proceeding with tumultuous haste from emergency to emergency, there had been a hard substratum of orderly development. The clamour of daily demands had emphasized rather than obscured the need for keeping a wary eye on the future. The naval organization in the summer of 1942 was planning ahead even while present difficulties called for every species of improvization and ingenuity. Personnel of the

"The End of the Beginning"

force, in July, totalled just under 40,000 officers and men. New entries were flowing inward through the twenty-one naval divisions at a rate of over two thousand per month; and recruitment had begun for the Women's Royal Canadian Naval Service.

Training depots and schools could now turn out annually 10,000 general service ratings, 2,000 signalmen, and sizeable quotas of asdic, radar, gunnery, torpedo, electrical and engineering specialists. In addition to the 188 warships in operation there were 46 corvettes of improved design under construction, 16 Bangor minesweepers and many lesser craft. In British shipyards four Tribal destroyers, a class of ship much more powerful than any then in Canadian service, were nearing completion for Canadian account; and the keels of four more Tribals had been laid in Canada. Nineteen Canadian naval bases—eleven on the east coast, four on the west coast, and four in Newfoundland, together with a large Canadian establishment at Londonderry, Northern Ireland, looked after the work of storing, repairing and operating the ships at sea. The building, recruitment, equipment and operation of the navy was now a great national enterprise whose demands affected every phase of the country's life.

At sea the Canadian navy was beginning to assume a peculiar character of its own. Its experience was narrowly channelled into a single aspect of naval war. In July of 1942 scarcely a third of the sixteen thousand men serving at sea were adequately trained by any former naval standard. Three quarters of them were men of the Royal Canadian Naval Volunteer Reserve, who had been rushed into service to man the corvettes, Bangors and smaller craft and fight off the U-boats with what equipment could be scraped together, what training could be disseminated by the small nucleus of the permanent force, and what tactics could be devised or improvised as the need arose.

The tutelage of the Royal Navy was always present in some degree, but could not be too heavily depended upon. British naval resources were as over-strained as our own; and

British ships, too, had had to fill out skeleton crews of experienced men with hosts of newcomers to the sea. Yet the picture had its brighter side in the fact that the work of convoy differed widely from other forms of naval warfare. Many of its problems were entirely new and had to be met with new methods by a single-minded force wholly absorbed in and devoted to the task of keeping the submarines down, sinking as many as possible and in any case driving them away from the precious cargo ships. The Canadian navy, like the portion of the Royal Navy devoted to the Atlantic battle, was becoming such a force.

Its personnel was probably no more disparate in composition than any other of the hastily assembled Allied forces. The fact that every man was a volunteer undoubtedly provided a stiffening and cohesive element. Yet there were possibilities enough of difficulty and dissension. The lower decks, crowded mainly with youngsters whose ages ranged from ninteen to twenty-five, were loudly and assertively democratic. The iron hand of naval discipline fell strangely upon them; and they had had no long training period during which familiarity with "pusser" routine might grow to acceptance.

The gradations of rank, only grudgingly accepted at best, might have bred running sores under the friction of intimate, day-to-day contact. Actually they did not; party because of the very disadvantages with which we entered the war. Youngsters four months out of high school, or fresh from an inland farm or office desk, found themselves suddenly in the midst of convoy battles at sea; and the detested bark of a leading hand or a petty officer or a hard-boiled first lieutenant became the one friendly sound amid the whole vast ocean and the flaming night. The man who knew what to do in those few terrible moments, the man whose voice had training and authority and reassurance behind it, was a man gladly obeyed. He might be cursed again when the moment had passed; but his right to command and instruct was not likely to be questioned. By the same token, his re-

spect for the performance of meadow-green lads in the face
of dangers they had never imagined became the basis for an
unexpressed but very real and valuable sympathy.

There were outlaws in the ranks; and they were tamed
or broken by a system hardened to meet the iron exigencies
of war. But woe to the four-flushers and the wooden-heads
and the brassily rank-conscious among the officers, of whom
there were always some. They were spotted instantly by the
men, tagged and talked about and furtively bedevilled; and
their reward was a lion's share of the misery which rises like
an acrid vapour from the messdecks of an unhappy ship.
There were not many of them, fortunately, among the ship's
companies; and for the most part there flowed beneath the
constant griping which is part of the air breathed by every
fighting formation a thoroughgoing, unsentimental harmony.

In the wardrooms the sleeve lace of the three "brands"
of officers might have seemed, and was frequently proclaimed
to be, an invidious distinction. As the force grew, the straight
stripes of the permanent force, the criss-cross stripes of the
former merchant navy officers and the wavy stripes of the
R.C.N.V.R. began to mingle indiscriminately. The three
groups had come together, each with a pride, a prejudice
and an outlook of its own. There were "the sailors trying to
be gentlemen" and "the gentlemen trying to be sailors," and
no official ruling could have ironed out their inherent differences. Only continuous association and the sharing of hard
experience could do this; was, in fact, doing it. Angelic harmony was neither attained nor greatly desired, but there was
a steadily growing community of respect.

Little by little, in hosts of great and petty emergencies,
the well-rounded training of the permanent force had shown
its value; the remarkable if not always conventional seamanship of the men from the merchant navy had proved itself;
the brash newcomers of the R.C.N.V.R. had shown nerve and
dash and adaptability. The long strain of the great sea battle,
where seconds could mean the difference between success
and failure in attack, between salvation and death in disaster,

made for a grimly impartial sharing of responsibility and a steady oneness of purpose. The force was being hardened and homogenized by seatime and battle. There was a tradition growing up and a certain *élan.*

In Halifax and St. John's and Londonderry there were now the favourite haunts and the specialized gripes; and an established routine of celebration during the precious days of harbour time. Old, walled Derry, with its cobbled, winding streets and leisurely, good-humored populace was a pleasant place to come to down the green and winding twelve-mile inlet of the Foyle. It had learned to accept and even like the Canadians, "who broke less windows than some." St. John's was a hospitable and storied capital where few men lacked a home to go to for a meal. There were friendly hostels, provided, stocked and operated by Canadian service organizations; and there was a hospitality committee staffed by St. John's citizens which could receive and fill without blinking the request of an incoming ship for a hundred girls and a dance "tonight."

Perhaps nowhere in the world was there a garret exactly like the Crow's Nest; fifty-nine steps from street level up the outside of an old store building—officially named the Seagoing Officers' Club and open to officers of the allied fighting ships and the merchant navy. Reminiscences went round the world, and doubtless are still on the wing, of that loud and smoky room where ship's crests and bells and trophies hung thick on every wall and where women were allowed on Tuesday nights only, "provided they do not clutter up the bar."

The ships themselves were becoming entities and close-knit families; each one priding itself on a personality recognized if not applauded by the others; and the various groups of ships were larger families of families. The names of the first five to make their group distinction visible are sometimes debated; but *Saguenay* and *Skeena,* at least, are charter members. The First Lieutenants of the two destroyers, musing over their drinks one evening on the problem of distinctive markings, had decided to paint the funnels in bands of red and white. The name, "Barber Pole," only a thought away, had followed naturally; and the Barber Pole Brigade was now the oldest, proudest, most brassily and bawdily sung-about of all the groups. Nicknames, of course, there had to be in profusion; *Restigouche* was "Rustyguts," *St. Laurent*, "Sally Rand," *Assiniboine*, "Bones;" and others were known with similarly disrespectful affection in many harbours and over many thousand square miles of sea.

Most ships had their "badge" now, which they wore painted on gun shield and bridge wings. It was a fanciful design evolved by the ship's company without reference to formal heraldry but with a large and uninhibited imagination. Among the devices, as a naval publication sedately commented, "humour predominated." *Calgary* displayed the figure of a cowboy astride a bucking corvette, brandishing a six-shooter over a kneeling submarine. *Drumheller* had a flaming devil beating a tattoo on a drum. *Bittersweet*, despairing of making anything of her ladylike name, had adopted Pappy Yokum; while *Trillium*, equally handicapped, had taken Mickey Mouse to sea, equipped him with a fishing net and pictured him in pursuit of a fleeing submarine. *Galt* displayed a grizzled salt spanking a U-boat across his knee; *Moose Jaw* showed a fire-belching moose in pursuit of Hitler; and much circumlocution has been expended in the effort to convey politely the significance of *Wetaskiwin's* crowned lady seated in a pool of water.

There was a character and a spirit growing up in this hastily-assembled, heterogeneous force, these sheep-dog ships and the men who manned them. There was a sense of growing unity and interweaving team work; there was a confidence bred of themselves and of the fact that they had endured and sustained through thirty-five months of war. The new spirit made its small contribution to the changing atmosphere about the world in that midsummer of 1942. Out of it sprang, perhaps, the dash and vigour which met the U-boats as they turned back from the American seaboard to the mid-Atlantic, and the rhythm of the ocean convoys was again punctuated by the muffled thud of torpedo and depth charge, the bark and rattle of gunfire.

St. Croix, one of the former American destroyers, took the first scalp of the period on July 24. She was at sea with a convoy when, late in the afternoon, her masthead lookout sighted a surfaced U-boat several miles away. The destroyer went off in pursuit and in the ensuing race the U-boat dived while still six thousand yards ahead. He had an excellent prospect of escape after having led the destroyer ten miles from the convoy, since he was beyond asdic range, with un-limited choice of depth and course underwater.

Unhappily for the German, *St. Croix* correctly esti-mated his movements, gained an asdic contact and held on grimly. Three times the destroyer sent down a pattern of ten depth charges; and at last some oil and wreckage appeared on the surface. The "evidence" might have been deliberately released through the torpedo tubes, as U-boats under attack were often wont to do. *St. Croix* ran in over the contact again and dropped another pattern. This time the results were defi-nite. Over the place of the explosion, gathering slowly from the depths beneath, was a nasty, oily litter of timber, cloth-ing, pocket books, cigarettes, food packages, and bits of human flesh which immediately attracted the attention of the wheeling gulls. *St. Croix* triumphantly gathered her grisly remnants, which were later found to include a once-filmy brassière labelled, "Triumph, Paris."

Ten days later *Skeena* and *Wetaskiwin* participated in a battle duet of which a rather graphic record has been pre-served. Some seven hundred miles east of Newfoundland on the morning of July 31, *Skeena* was steaming in a diamond-shaped pattern over the area of a doubtful contact, dropping depth charges at each of the angles of the diamond. She was hoping to cause the enemy beneath to reveal himself more clearly by a decided movement; and she signalled the nearby *Wetaskiwin* a request for assistance, adding the reference "Acts 16, Verse 9."

"The End of the Beginning"

Rapid thumbing of *Wetaskiwin's* bible as she steamed toward *Skeena* yielded the following result:

And a vision appeared to Paul in the night; there stood a man of Macedonia and prayed him saying, come over into Macedonia and help us.

Back from *Wetaskiwin's* signal lamp flashed, "Revelations 13, Verse 1;" which revealed itself to *Skeena* as:

And I stood upon the sand of the sea and saw a beast rise up out of the sea having seven heads and ten horns, and upon his horns ten crowns, and upon his head the name of blasphemy.

The horned beast had not yet risen from the sea and was, in fact, never to do so again. The two ships with their black "hunting" pendants at the halyards and their asdics probing the depths, began a deliberate attack, moving across and back with geometrical precision above the area of contact, while the quarry endeavoured to squirm away from them below. The search went on for five hours; and something of its grim relentlessness still breathes from the record of the signals flashed between the hunters:

WETASKIWIN You direct hunt. Give me my station and course.

SKEENA Take station on my port beam; one mile, course 228°.

SKEENA Turn 180° to port together.

SKEENA Course 070°.

SKEENA I am over my last contact. Now start square search from here.

WETASKIWIN Contact bearing 260°, 1900 yards.

WETASKIWIN Contact is firm.

WETASKIWIN Contact bearing 280°, 600 yards.

SKEENA Contact bearing 040°, 800 yards.

SKEENA Contact bearing 070°, 1400 yards.

SKEENA Non sub.

(SKEENA had been led astray by a false echo)

WETASKIWIN Contact bearing 200°, 1300 yards.

WETASKIWIN Attacking.

(WETASKIWIN dropped a pattern of depth charges)

WETASKIWIN   Lost contact at 600 yards.

WETASKIWIN   By my plot you are over sub.

WETASKIWIN   Contact bearing 210°, 1900 yards.

SKEENA   Contact bearing 345°, 1600 yards.

SKEENA   Attacking. Please keep to port.

(SKEENA dropped a pattern of depth charges)

WETASKIWIN   Confirmed right spot.

WETASKIWIN   Contact bearing 300°, 1000 yards.

WETASKIWIN   Attacking.

(WETASKIWIN dropped a pattern of depth charges)

WETASKIWIN   Lost contact.

SKEENA   Echo bearing 120°, 700 yards.

WETASKIWIN   O.K. Let me do an attack now.

SKEENA   Unable to gain contact.

WETASKIWIN   I will try to help you by directing.

SKEENA   Attacking.

(SKEENA dropped a pattern of depth charges)

WETASKIWIN   Excellent.

SKEENA   Did you hear that underwater explosion?

WETASKIWIN   Yes. Definitely.

SKEENA   Your turn.

WETASKIWIN   Plenty of wreckage over this way.

SKEENA   I am lowering a whaler to pick up the guts.

SKEENA   (*General Signal*) U-boat considered sunk by H.M.C.S. WETASKIWIN and H.M.C.S. SKEENA. Floating wreckage and human remains recovered.

Skeena and *Wetaskiwin* entered the ranks of the lucky few among the many ships that slogged on day after day by the side of the crawling convoys, sometimes without any break in the monotony, sometimes pursuing a sighting or an echo with no result, returning again to the merchant ships and slogging on. A convoy or a series of convoys might cross entirely without incident; observed, perhaps, from a distant horizon, but not molested. Then, suddenly, about a succeeding convoy the U-boat packs would gather, heralded through several tense, slow-passing days and nights by a flurry of increased signal traffic, an occasional sighting, a warning message from the Admiralty or Ottawa or Washington.

The present convoy was one of the latter; and the assembling German pack which *Skeena* and *Wetaskiwin* had reduced by one, was still to provide the corvette *Sackville* with a series of hair-raising experiences. Just at dark next evening *Sackville* sighted a U-boat and raced after it into the gathering gloom. Behind her the brilliant white light of "snowflake" flaring above the convoy proclaimed a torpedoing; and she wheeled back. As she did so, the low silhouette of another U-boat appeared between her and the merchant ships, revealed in the glare of illuminants and fires. Before she could reach the second German he was in among the columns of the convoy and out the other side.

Sackville was hardly back in station when the explosion of another merchantman nearby sent a mass of debris spuming upward and lit the sea with an evil glare. In its light the new attacker could be seen, racing away on the surface with the gloomy, fog-ridden night rapidly closing in on him. *Sackville* put up starshell as she turned in pursuit and the light came just in time to show the enemy's bow tilting forward in a crash dive. The corvette rode into the swirl of the dive and her first depth charge brought the U-boat's bow leaping from the water. The glistening, shadowy hull lifted at a sharp angle, revealing nearly sixty feet of its length; then as fountains of water gushed about it from the explosion of other depth charges, it slipped back and disappeared. *Sackville* came in over the spot again and dropped ten more charges. An uprush of oil flooded to the surface, followed by a heavy underwater explosion. The corvette rejoined the convoy with a "probable kill" to her credit.

An hour later she sighted another U-boat just 125 yards to port of her, but lost contact in the gathering fog. Thirty minutes later the sound of submarine propellers was heard again. The enemy was made out two hundred yards ahead crossing the corvette's bows, and *Sackville* went to full speed to ram. Altering course sharply, the German ran straight in until he was so close that the four-inch gun could not be depressed enough to bear on him. He was attempting to keep beneath the gun's bearing and inside the corvette's turning circle.

The two craft ran through the foggy blackness zigzagging almost side by side, *Sackville* attempting to ram, the U-boat weaving and swerving to avoid. They swung apart for an instant; the corvette's gun was brought to bear and a four-inch shell caught the German squarely at the base of the conning tower. Then bursts from *Sackville's* machine guns rattled into the conning tower at point blank range and ricochetted at last from a closed hatch as the German commander left his bridge and the U-boat went under in a crash-dive. It was the end of a busy night's work for *Sackville* and a "possibly damaged" added to her other credit.

Assiniboine's turn came just five days later, on August 6. She was with a convoy some four hundred miles off Newfoundland when, late in the afternoon, a besetting fog lifted momentarily to reveal a U-boat six miles away. The destroyer chased for nearly an hour, holding the quarry in radar contact and occasionally catching a glimpse of him as he wove in and out among the fog patches.

The range began to narrow; and it became evident that the German intended to fight it out on the surface. As *Assiniboine* bore down on him she was met by a hail of incendiary bullets. Then the U-boat ran straight in, making for the charmed circle where the destroyer's guns would not bear and she would be unable to ram. *Assiniboine* swung to counter the manoeuvre, the German countered again, and for thirty-five minutes the two craft ran weaving and dodging together, blasting each other at point-blank range with all available weapons.

Beneath the destroyer's bridge on the starboard side incendiary shells from the German's 40-millimetre cannon set fire to petrol drums stored outside the wheelhouse. A party led by Lieutenant R. L. Hennessy immediately went to work amid the rattling spatter of gunfire to subdue the blaze. Inside the wheelhouse *Assiniboine's* coxswain, Chief Petty Officer Max L. Bernays, saw the flames mounting above his starboard window and ordered his helmsman and telegraphman outside to assist. Then locking himself in the wheelhouse, with the full knowledge that he would never get out alive if the fire was not subdued, and with incendiary shells spattering the bulkheads about him and throwing splinters in his face, he proceeded to carry out faultlessly the 141 helm and engine room orders which were necessary during the wild chase.

The cool determination shown in the wheelhouse and on the blazing starboard side was inspired from the bridge above. With gunfire riddling the woodwork about him as he stood fully exposed on *Assiniboine's* open bridge, Lieutenant-Commander John H. Stubbs watched the German captain in his conning tower bending down to pass wheel orders, and held *Assiniboine* grimly alongside the weaving U-boat. The range was so short that main armament could not be brought to bear on the target, but the small-calibre weapons of the Canadians were sweeping the German's decks and gashing his hull. Every rifle, machine gun and pistol on board the ship was in action. "We threw everything but the potato masher at him," was a later comment. *Assiniboine* was taking her own punishment in return. As the blaze on the starboard side came under control, other fires began to break out about the ship. Several men were wounded, and ordinary seaman Kenneth Watson, the youngest lad on board, was killed as he crossed over the open deck with a shell in his arms.

For an instant the destroyer's 4.7 gun came fully to bear on the U-boat's conning tower and a shell hit dead on, killing the German commanding officer. Some of the Nazi crew were endeavoring to make their way forward to the main gun, but they were literally blasted from the deck by *Assiniboine's* machine-gun fire. Three or four times the

Assiniboine's U-boat. U-210 just before she was rammed.

The
NORTH ATLANTIC

JUNE 1941 to FEBRUARY 1942

AREA OF ATTACKS N
IN NOVEMBER 1

ST. JOHN'S

WESTBOUND ESCORTS
EASTBOUND ESCORTS
WESTERN LOCAL ESCORT FORCE

WE

AREA O
WEST OC
MEETING

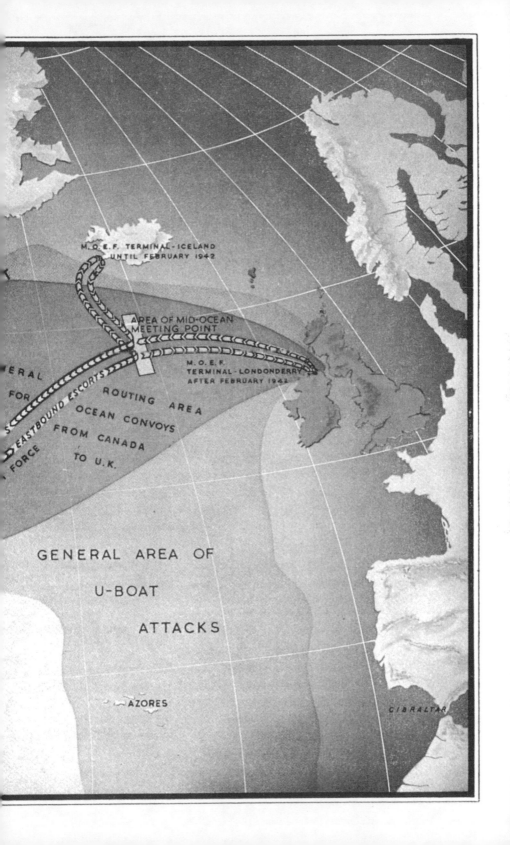

M. O. E. F. TERMINAL - ICELAND
UNTIL FEBRUARY 1942

AREA OF MID-OCEAN
MEETING POINT

M. O. E. F.
TERMINAL - LONDONDERRY
AFTER FEBRUARY 1942

ERAL

FOR

EASTBOUND ESCORTS

ROUTING   AREA

OCEAN CONVOYS

FORCE   FROM CANADA

TO U.K.

GENERAL   AREA   OF

U-BOAT

ATTACKS

AZORES

GIBRALTAR

Cyclone at sea

swerving U-boat had avoided the destroyer's attempts to ram. Now, attempting a crash-dive, she held on a steady course for a few seconds; and in that time, as the U-boat was actually tilting forward and down, *Assiniboine's* bow crashed into her just abaft the conning tower. It was a glancing blow that sent the destroyer swerving away. As she turned back to ram again, the submarine's bow lifted from the water and her stern began to settle. She was heavily damaged but still making about ten knots and still firing. *Assiniboine* rammed again, and as she passed heaved over a pattern of shallow-set depth charges which bounced the German clear of the water. A shell from one of the destroyer's after guns administered the coup de grâce, and the U-boat sank by the head within two minutes. The British corvette, *Dianthus*, which was to get a submarine herself two days later, appeared on the scene just in time for her company to join in "a yell which must have frightened U-boats for about ten miles in the vicinity."

Still the story of summer successes was not complete. In the Caribbean on August 28, *Oakville*, one of the Canadian corvettes on the tanker runs, was with a convoy off Haiti when an American plane spotted a U-boat a mile or so ahead and damaged it with a depth charge. *Oakville* made for the position and her first pattern of depth charges brought the submarine up from its attempted crash-dive. The corvette opened with all her guns, blowing away the enemy's main gun forward and sweeping the gunners from the slippery decks. She bore in and rammed twice; then, for good measure, heaved over a depth charge which exploded while Canadian and German were side by side, and shook both with almost equal violence.

The treatment knocked the fight out of the U-boat's crew; and with their craft lying stopped on the surface they prepared to abandon ship. *Oakville* came alongside; Sub-Lieutenant H. E. T. Lawrence and Petty Officer A. J. Powell leaped down to the enemy decks and found the U-boat rocking soddenly, its conning tower riddled and three or four of the crew lying dead across the hatch. Two Germans, very much alive, emerged from an escape hatch and were ordered below. They not only did not obey but came forward to make a fight of it, and Lawrence and Powell shot them. Another head, which had witnessed the incident from the same hatch, promptly vanished.

Lawrence crawled into the conning tower and bellowed down through the dank darkness of the interior: "Sprechen sie Englisch?"—his entire German vocabulary. There was no reply, but members of the crew began to emerge uneasily and soon twenty were lined up on deck. Going below, the boarding officer found water seeping steadily into the smashed interior. The boat had evidently been scuttled, and a surge of panic among the prisoners as a wave broke over the conning tower suggested that demolition charges had been set. The Canadians ordered their captives overboard to swim for it and then followed, to be picked up by *Oakville's* boats and by the boats of the American destroyer *Lea* which had come to lend a hand.

September brought a heavy loss to balance the successes. Veteran *Ottawa,* one of the six destroyers with which we had entered the war, was torpedoed and sunk on a night which heralded the approach of the autumn storms, the high seas and the long hours of icy darkness which would cost the lives of many men. *Ottawa* was at sea with a convoy on September 13 when, toward midnight, she was hit by a torpedo. It seemed at first to have done her no vital injury and she remained afloat on an even keel. An escort ship closed her and then turned away to assist a sinking merchantman whose crew were already in the water and seemed in more immediate danger. In the interval another torpedo struck the helpless *Ottawa.* She went down quickly and black night closed in about her men as they struggled to keep afloat in the freezing water. By the time rescue finally arrived five officers and 109 men had been lost, including the commanding officer, Lieutenant-Commander C. A. Rutherford, who had given his own life belt to a rating.

Two more convoys were heavily attacked during September with a total loss of seventeen ships; and it was obvious that another winter of discontent was upon us. The Germans were fully aware of the "black pits" still remaining in the Atlantic—the areas where the priceless assistance of air cover could not yet be made available. The radius of the patrolling planes extended some six hundred miles eastward from bases in Canada and Newfoundland, six hundred miles southward from Iceland, and six hundred miles westward from the United Kingdom. Within those zones aircraft had conclusively demonstrated their value, and decisively altered the balance in convoy warfare. They detected U-boats while they were still far off from the merchant ships, drove them under and "blinded" them, homed escort ships to the attack and frequently made successful attacks themselves.

But the wide arcs of air cover did not yet intersect. Through a deep zone of the mid-Atlantic the convoys had to sail with the protection of surface ships alone; and it was in this area that the U-boats were now concentrated. Convoy SC-107, entering one of the "pits" in October with a Canadian escort of one destroyer and four corvettes, was harried by a foretaste of the worst Atlantic winter in thirty years and by attacks which continued without let-up for four days and resulted in a loss of fifteen ships.

During November a seemingly endless series of ferocious gales made it necessary to route convoys on more southerly courses; and southerly routing meant diminution of the air cover from northern bases and more dangers for the convoys over wider areas. Frequently, indeed, the weather made it impossible for planes to fly at all, and the U-boats, which had learned to respect them, extended their lines of patrol with increasing boldness. November weather also brought to an end the active career of *Saguenay*. The destroyer, restored to service after her torpedoing in 1940, collided in fog with the merchant vessel *Azra*, and was so heavily damaged that she was henceforth retained only as a training ship.

December brought still grimmer experiences. Convoy ON-154 westbound, entered the western fringes of the "black pit" area about Christmas day. The convoy consisted of forty-four merchantmen, a rescue ship, and a British special service ship, *Fidelity*, which carried a plane. Several U-boats were spread out in lines of patrol across the vulnerable zone and one of the pack sighted the merchant ships. She began to shadow, and during the next day six or eight more U-boats closed in with her. Meanwhile a furious gale was adding to the convoy's difficulties. Ships were being damaged and driven apart from the main body; and as warning signals and sighting reports began to pour in, the escort, consisting of the destroyer *St. Laurent*, with five corvettes, *Kenogami*, *Battleford*, *Chilliwack*, *Shediac* and *Napanee*, made desperate efforts to round up vessels scattered over miles of sea.

At two o'clock on the morning of the 27th two ships were torpedoed. By four o'clock two others had gone down. The U-boat pack had not completely gathered; the tentative assault was not fully pressed home and ceased with dawn; but there was no abatement of the gale. The corvettes which had steamed hundreds of extra miles in attempts to screen defenseless stragglers, began to run low on fuel. As darkness fell on the evening of the 28th, *Chilliwack* was forced to drop astern of the convoy and attempt the new experiment of fuelling at sea from the tanker *Scottish Heather*. The difficult operation had not progressed very far when *Scottish Heather* was torpedoed; and with her went the escorts' hope of fuel.

Throughout a tense night the full-scale attack still failed to develop. The U-boats nosed about leisurely, probing for weak points in the screen and apparently waiting for still more reinforcement. The situation, in spite of its apparent quiet, was worsening steadily as more U-boats gathered and the escorts' oil stocks fell lower. During the following afternoon *St. Laurent* ordered *Fidelity* to fly off her plane in an attempt to drive some of the shadowing U-boats under. The take-off, in the midst of a half-abated gale, brought new disaster. The plane ran along the water, crashed into a twelve-foot wave and all its landing lights flared with the shock of the impact. For a moment watchers in *St. Laurent* saw plane and occupants tossing in the midst of a great, lighted dome of water. Then the aircraft disappeared, and although the pilot and observer were recovered there was no further hope of air support.

That night the U-boats, with their dispositions made, came in for the kill. *Battleford,* on the starboard beam, got the first radar contact and fired starshell. In the wavering light four U-boats were discovered; steering straight for the convoy in regular line ahead formation, separated by intervals of about a mile. Signal lamps flashed along the German line as *Battleford* opened fire; and the boats turned and made an orderly retreat, drawing the corvette after them. Meanwhile *Kenogami* had reported another contact. *Napanee* spotted a conning tower a moment later; and then attacks broke out from all directions simultaneously. U-boats bored directly in among the columns, firing salvoes of torpedoes from all their tubes. Streams of tracer fire from merchantmen criss-crossed in the night to indicate the many sightings, snowflake flared above torpedoed vessels, and behind the convoy, as it struggled on, the sea was dotted with the wrecks of blazing ships and the multiplying lights of rafts and lifeboats.

Within two hours nine ships had gone down. "At one stage of the attack," reported *Shediac's* commanding officer, "Torpedoes were so numerous in the convoy . . . that the officer of the watch remarked, 'there goes our now, sir,' . . . as if next week's groceries were being delivered. The entire space between the columns seemed filled with the white tracers of the U-boats and the pink tracers of the merchantmen."

As dawn came the attackers drew off to the horizon. Little more than a breathing spell seemed indicated; a pause to rest their men, signal their triumphant battle reports, replenish their tubes. The convoy was still far from air cover or relief; and absolute disaster threatened. *Battleford* and *Shediac* were so low on fuel that they had to leave and try to make the Azores before they were immobilized. *Battleford* had actually to take *Shediac* in tow. With only four escort ships remaining about the convoy there was no possibility of

141

effective defence. The senior officer ordered that vessels of the convoy should make their escape independently if they judged that they had the opportunity to do so.

It was a signal of desperation and an acknowledgment of defeat; and even the miraculous and unexplained withdrawal of the U-boats failed to lessen its sombre significance. The perils to the Atlantic lifeline, in spite of all efforts, had not lessened. They had increased. Submarines were still coming into service faster than they were being sunk. The number of escort ships was still not sufficient; the long-hoped for support groups, the merchant aircraft carriers and the land-based Liberators, had still not materialized, and without them the battle we could look forward to in 1943 would be grimmer than ever.

Yet there was a difference; and an essential one. The shortages of ships and planes were not absolute as they had been in 1940 and 1941. They had, in a sense, been created; by deliberate diversion; by the bold decision to swing over to the offensive in other theatres of the war. Everywhere about the world, and with dramatic synchronization, the initiative had been wrested from the Axis. German armies in Russia had come to an exhausted halt at Stalingrad and were now reeling westward under the Russian hammer. Japan's conquests in the Pacific were ebbing from their high tide; and Rommel had turned his back forever on El Alamein. Fortress Europe itself had been probed; and Dieppe, whatever its toll of loss and disaster, had thrown a long shadow over the gloomy councils of the Reich. The Allied landings in North Africa had been the clearest sign of what was to come; and they had been far more than a sign. The first offensive blow had been struck, powerfully; with strength deliberately gathered, through strain and risk and sacrifice deliberately accepted.

The effort had made its demands on the Canadian navy as on every other allied force. Canadian landing-craft flotillas, some of whose men had already seen service at Dieppe, had ferried British and American troops ashore at Algiers and

Oran. And through the summer and autumn of 1942, at the height of the Atlantic battle, seventeen corvettes had been withdrawn from the meagre escort forces to be armed for the great expedition. Now, while the Atlantic battle still hung precariously in the balance, they were tasting new varieties of warfare in the Mediterranean and on the road from the United Kingdom to Gibraltar.

CHAPTER SEVEN

"Operation Torch"

Of all the mysteriously allusive code names selected for military operations, Torch, the name for the invasion of North Africa, seems the happiest choice. It was indeed the raising of the burning brand; the signal proclaiming to the world that Allied forces were at last prepared to sally out from the defensive. It had been long in preparation; its remote origins went back to the darkest days of the war; and its development had been marked by many expensive gropings toward an offensive strategy.

Even while the threat of invasion still hung heavy over Britain, the earliest moves had begun. They were at first hardly discernible from necessary measures of defence. Light British ships had occasionally shelled the French coast, or attempted to break up the Channel and Biscay convoys which supplied German garrisons. Small British commando parties had descended by night on German-held ports to take prisoners, gain information and do what damage they could. By the end of 1941 these first efforts had lost some of their sporadic quality. Seamen and soldiers had begun to work out specialized landing techniques together, and were assembling into the nucleus of what would eventually become an amphibious raiding force.

This nucleus was at first entirely British; but it soon began to absorb a few of the first Canadians trained in England. Early in 1942, the Canadian contribution was substantially increased. Fifty officers and three hundred ratings who had volunteered for "specially hazardous duty" sailed from Halifax in January. They were shepherded to the United Kingdom by the versatile K. S. Maclachlan who, as a Lieutenant-Colonel in the army, had held the position of Deputy Minister for the Naval Service. Now "dipped" at his own urgent request to the rank of Lieutenant-Commander

144

in the navy, Maclachlan was to have the work of ironing out administrative problems for his charges and was to serve on British combined operations staffs in several theatres.

The newly-arriving Canadians, together with some already in England, were to make up the personnel of six landing craft flotillas. They entered upon their first training at *H.M.S. Tormentor,* the combined operations base which was now established at Northney, east of Southampton. From there they moved on to more advanced flotilla work in conjunction with army personnel at another base, *H.M.S. Quebec,* at Inveraray in Scotland.

Already the combined operations force, now being built up under Lord Louis Mountbatten, was a colourful body. Methods of training were, of necessity, as fluid and unconventional as the situations with which the men would have to deal. Each cross-channel raid—and there were many of them—brought new experience and demands for the revision of tactics, equipment and technique. *"Haven't you heard?—it's all been changed"*—the most familiar greeting in the force—had become a byword and a slogan tacked up in its headquarters even by the time the first Canadian draft arrived.

However unconventional, the standard of discipline and the requirements as to fitness and adaptability were very high. The first Canadian draft, and the drafts which succeeded it, soon began to take on the character of the parent organization. Canadians took part with British commando forces in some of the small, nameless raids, each of which provided its lurid adventures, brought back its quota of information and is now forgotten. There were some of our men in the important raids on Bruneval and St. Nazaire; but even by the time of the Dieppe raid in August 1942 the Canadian naval contribution to combined operations was small.

As the Dieppe operation entered the planning stage, high level discussion was beginning to centre about landings in North Africa. North Africa itself was a preliminary to the great descent upon the coast of France, and Dieppe was the forerunner of both. Experience had to be gained in the large-scale integration of air, sea and ground forces. The enormous difficulties of a landing from sea in the face of heavy shore defences had to be measured in detail. Much could be planned and provided for in advance; but only an actual trial by fire could prove the worth and expose the shortcomings of training, equipment and tactics devised by large staffs through months of study.

The perilous honour of the trial fell mainly to the Canadian army and the British navy, but members of the naval team from Canada had a share. Training was not sufficiently advanced for the Canadians to operate as separate flotillas when the Dieppe expedition sailed from Shoreham and New-haven on the night of August 18; but among the British landing craft fifteen Canadian officers and fifty-five ratings were distributed.

Sub-Lieutenant C. D. Wallace was the first Canadian casualty. He was killed in the dark hours of the morning, when the flotillas on the extreme left flank of the assault made the fatal encounter with a German convoy. Lieutenant J. E. Koyl, a Canadian who was to figure in many happier landings, was boat officer of a flotilla which included thirty-three Canadians. It left its parent ship, *Duke of Wellington*, at 3.34 in the morning. As the craft neared the beach shortly after five, they came under heavy fire from shore. They managed to land their three platoons of the Canadian Black Watch near Puys; but as they were withdrawing the British flotilla officer was seriously wounded and Koyl took charge. Continuing seaward, he transferred the wounded officer to a British destroyer; and about noon, when evacuation of the beach was ordered, led his craft in again through heavy fire from shore and attack from the air. Before he could beach, however, he was ordered to turn back. German weapons were laying down such a curtain of steel that evacuation was an impossibility.

Meanwhile Sub-Lieutenants A. A. Wedd and J. E. Boak, each in command of one of the Landing Craft (Personnel) which had sailed directly from England, came in to shore with their flotilla a little east of Dieppe harbour. Passing through smoke into fire from German weapons of all calibres, they landed their troops and withdrew. They were sent in an hour or so later to Dieppe harbour itself; but were recalled almost immediately and re-routed to one of the beaches near Puys.

As they reached the inner fringe of the smoke shrouding the beach, they came upon a group of Canadian soldiers crouching on a capsized landing craft just off shore, and pinned down by fire. Although the soldiers waved and shouted at them to steer away, the craft ran close alongside, heaved ropes across and managed to rescue three of the men. Then, as the fire from shore blazed up to new intensity, the flotilla was ordered to turn back from the beach. It was not to go in again. Like all the other flotillas, it was to have the memory, most poignant for the Canadians, of having left behind many of the soldiers it had brought ashore.

Unhappy as the immediate results of Dieppe were, the performance of the Canadians in the landing craft had been worthy of their brothers in the army; and some of them remained with the soldiers as prisoners. Lieutenant R. F. McCrae had driven his craft in through a barrage of machine gun and mortar fire, only to have it crippled as it made the beach. Wounded himself, along with several of the men, he gave orders for his crew to disembark and take what cover they could find along with the soldiers. Leading Stoker Robert W. Brown, however, remained behind. He had taken over the wheel when the coxswain was wounded on the run-in; and now he set about helping the injured men and attempting to repair his damaged engines. He remained at the work for several hours, fully exposed to German fire from the cliffs above, and was captured at last along with McCrae and the rest of the crew and the soldiers they had landed.

Out of the many lessons learned at Dieppe emerged the famous naval Force J, which was to figure largely in all the later landings of the war. Assembled first to carry in the soldiers at Dieppe, it was now reconstituted as a permanent force devoted to amphibious operations; and it included, by October 1942, 489 Canadian officers and men, organized into six landing craft flotillas. The force, without any knowledge of what lay ahead, was being groomed and hardened for the North African landings; and in the meantime other preparations were under way far afield.

On August 27, 1942, the First Sea Lord had signalled the Chief of the Naval Staff that an officer would be visiting him in Ottawa "with information." The information proved to be a guarded summary of the projected "Operation Torch," still so secret that only a handful of men in the highest planning circles knew its details. Along with a sketchy outline of the plan, some of its requirements and conditions were made known. Assault convoys and reinforcement convoys moving from the United Kingdom to the Mediterranean were expected to come under heavy attack by submarine and from the air. Escort forces much larger than usual would be required; and it was hoped that Canada could furnish some of her corvettes to assist.

The request, in view of the Atlantic situation and the St. Lawrence situation, was a daunting one. It was also familiar; and familiar expedients were adopted to meet it. The cycle of Atlantic convoys was "opened out." Sailings were rearranged to take place every eight days instead of every seven days. The west ocean meeting point, where ships of the local escort met the ocean escort, was pushed farther out into the Atlantic; so that by longer and less frequent sailings the escort work could be handled by fewer groups. Eleven Canadian corvettes and one British were obtained by this reorganization; and the remainder, to make up a total of seventeen, came by stripping the west coast entirely of the five corvettes based there.

Redisposition and assembly of the ships destined for the Mediterranean began in September, so secretly that even the senior officers under whom they were operating had no idea of the purpose behind the movement. *Louisburg, Woodstock* and *Prescott* sailed from Halifax to the United Kingdom on September 10 and were taken in hand there for fitting out with the heavily increased armament which would be necessary to meet air attacks in the Mediterranean. *Lunenburg* and *Weyburn* sailed on September 16. The remaining twelve, some of which had their additional guns installed at Halifax, made the passage to British ports during October and November, participating in the big autumn convoy battles on the way.

The congested rush of preparation in the ports of the United Kingdom delayed the fitting out of many ships; and only *Louisburg, Prescott, Woodstock, Weyburn, Lunenburg* and the British corvette *Nasturtium* which had also been withdrawn from the Newfoundland Escort Force, were ready to sail with the first of the convoys destined for the assault. The others, *Ville de Québec, Port Arthur, Baddeck, Alberni, Summerside, Regina, Calgary, Kitchener, Camrose, Moose Jaw* and *Algoma*, took the road to Gibraltar with follow-up convoys.

The first objectives of the great armadas which got under way during the late days of October were the ports of Algiers, Oran and Casablanca. The Germans, well aware of the preparations for Torch, were completely misled as to the objectives. Apparently convinced that Dakar was to be the point of landing, they had disposed their large submarine forces well to the south of the actual routes taken by the convoys; and the long processions of allied ships passed to their destinations almost unmolested.

The six flotillas of Canadian landing craft included in the forces which made the landings at Algiers and Oran had an easier time than expected; and their heaviest casualties occurred after all was over, when ships carrying the returning men were torpedoed on the way home. At Algiers, landings began early on the morning of November 8, along six beaches to the west of the town and six to the east. Canadian landing craft ferried in American and British troops almost without incident, although they were occasionally under sporadic fire from French ships and shore batteries. At Oran

"OPERATION TORCH"
THE WESTERN MEDITERRANEAN
NOVEMBER 1942 to FEBRUARY 1943

the story was very much the same; and after the nervous initial stage was over the men were inclined to make a picnic of the work. The assault landings were followed by a week during which reinforcements and supplies had to be ferried ashore. Some of the beaches were blessed with good weather; and the men worked stripped almost to the buff, exulting in the acquisition of a thick Mediterranean tan. The work was by no means all fun. Baie des Andalouses, near Oran, for example, was cursed with shifting sandbars around which landing craft running in from the ships had to navigate under sniping from stubborn French troops. Nevertheless, at the conclusion of landing operations, one of the flotilla officers reported that it had actually been difficult to get his men out of their craft to be relieved.

The first phase of Torch had been completely successful. The sea-borne landings had been made, and all resistance encountered speedily overcome. Now, however, the stubborn German genius for recovery and counter-attack began to make itself felt. Troops by the thousands were ferried into Tunisia from the Italian mainland. German air power gathered over the Mediterranean and German submarines arrived on the scene, late but determined. Allied armies were not going to have a quick success in Tunisia. They were faced with the prospect of a slow, expensive campaign for which enormous quantities of supplies would have to be carried through dangerous waters.

The supply line along which the Canadian corvettes were to operate ran from the United Kingdom to Gibraltar and on into the Mediterranean as far as Bone, which soon became a principal base. Oran, Arzeu, Algiers, Bougie and Philippeville were other ports of call. The conditions of Mediterranean warfare differed in many ways from those of the Atlantic. U-boats did not hunt in packs, but attacked individually; and protection was therefore needed on all bearings. Aircraft attack was always a danger; particularly at dawn, at dusk and on moonlight nights. There were also to be many unpleasant demonstrations of the efficiency with which German planes could home U-boats onto convoys.

"Operation Torch"

It took some time for the Canadian ships to shake down into the routine of the new theatre. The process of dilution, so wearisomely familiar, had filled out their companies with many untrained men, and even some of the captains had sailed only between Halifax and Boston during the quieter periods along that route. Mediterranean conditions were different from those of the Atlantic, and the Canadians were often operating with British ships who had fought a gruelling three-year campaign against the Italian navy. Canadian anti-submarine work was to prove, on the whole, well up to the British standard; but there were some early exceptions. During a convoy *mêlée* one night in December a Canadian corvette, just arrived in the Mediterranean, attempted to ram a torpedo which she had mistaken for a submarine, and came in for some acid congratulations on her "failure."

There had been little time before sailing for instruction in the revised tactics imposed by new conditions; and peremptory rebukes sometimes drew forth plaintive answers. "Very sorry," one Canadian captain signalled to his annoyed senior officer, "but please remember I'm only a poor bloody stockbroker."

A host of minor complications ran down through all the gradations of rank. Canadian ratings, often far less sea-wise than their British counterparts, were better paid. Their mechanical aptitude, on the other hand, was often higher, and they were not reluctant to admit it. They were explosively volatile ashore; and there was a free-and-easy character about their discipline which at first sight caused the raising of some "pusser" eyebrows. The cousinly difficulties were not long in unravelling, however, as increasing familiarity and improving teamwork wove the groups together. Within a month or so, as the convoys ploughed back and forth, air attacks, submarine attacks and every variety of emergency had proved the essential quality both of the veterans and the newcomers and a gusty harmony reigned.

Ville de Québec was the first Canadian ship to provide an actual trophy. Prior to sailing for Operation Torch, her

longest voyage had been between Boston and New York. On
her journey to the United Kingdom experience had come to
her in full measure during a heavy convoy battle, and she had
rescued fifty-four survivors from one torpedoed ship. January 13, 1943, found her in company with a Mediterranean
convoy some ninety miles from Algiers; and during the afternoon she dropped a pattern of depth charges on what seemed
a fairly promising contact.

Simultaneously with the explosion of the charges, a U-
boat careened bow-first to the surface. *Ville de Québec's*
starboard oerlikons opened a barking volley; and two minutes
later her bow crashed into the submarine between the conning tower and the forward gun. The shattering impact
threw a German officer clear out of the opening conning-
tower hatch and into the sea. The U-boat began tilting upward; then the rush of water through her shattered plates
dragged her back and within four minutes she was out of
sight. There was a tremendous underwater explosion and a
few pieces of clothing, insulating material and woodwork
came floating to the surface in the midst of a great pool of
oil. The whole incident, from contact to kill, had taken just
ten minutes.

Less than a week later a Canadian and a British ship
combined to bring the brief career of the Italian submarine
Tritone to an end. *Tritone* sailed from Cagliari on her first
patrol during the early morning of January 17, 1943. She was
to operate off Bougie; and her captain seems to have been a
man whose determination approached the point of foolhardy
obstinacy. During preliminary tests made as the submarine
began her cruise, the engineer officer had reported that
diving gear was not operating properly and that in his opinion the boat should turn back. The captain refused.

Shortly after dawn on January 18 *Tritone* reached her
station off the Tunisian coast; and almost immediately
sighted an Allied convoy proceeding westward. In spite of
the boat's inability to dive properly, the captain closed to
within about 5,000 yards of the convoy at periscope depth.

He was preparing to launch a torpedo when the boat suddenly lost trim and sank out of control to a depth of about sixty feet.

There was a flurry of hasty, rather panic-stricken effort beneath the surface, during which the language of the Italian engineer officer can be imagined by engineer officers the world over. Then the boat was brought back to periscope depth. Her balance was still so precarious that it was impossible to keep her on an even keel for long enough to get torpedoes away; but her captain was fanatically bent upon his mission. He seems to have had no appreciation of the capabilities of asdic and radar; and with a calm sea and good visibilty he continued to work his way in toward the convoy through a screen of escorting ships.

He had already been detected. *Port Arthur,* one of the Canadian escorts, had gained asdic contact at a range of seventeen hundred yards. By the time she had followed her echo to within four hundred yards her hydrophone was also picking up the sound of *Tritone's* propellers. At last realizing his peril, the Italian captain submerged and endeavoured to work away underwater. *Port Arthur's* depth charges came gurgling down to ring him with ten mighty explosions. The boat's main fuses were blown, the electric motors were knocked out of action, most of the pipes of the pressure system were fractured or distorted, and several fuel tanks were holed. *Tritone* went over on her side and sank like a stone to a depth of four hundred feet.

Through some freak, the first and most usual effect of an accurate depth charge attack—failure of the lighting system—did not occur. It is doubtful, however, if the illumination in the smashed interior, revealing the green and panicky faces of the crew, provided much comfort. The obstinate determination of the captain suddenly cracked and he turned to the enginer officer to ask what he should do. The glowering answer was that if he wanted to save their lives he had better use what air remained in the tanks to bring the boat to the surface.

Actually, if *Tritone* had remained below and waited out the attack she might have had better fortune. The explosion of the depth charges had put *Port Arthur's* asdic out of action; and although the British destroyer *Antelope* had joined, she was unable to gain contact immediately in the disturbed water. As it was, *Tritone* came plunging to the surface, a pleasant surprise for *Antelope* seven hundred yards away; and was immediately enveloped in a blaze of gunfire. *Port Arthur* swung about to ram; but had to bear off in order to keep out of *Antelope's* line of fire.

Whatever the abilities of *Tritone's* captain, he had a good share of the courage which flashed out in many of the indivdual actions of the luckless Italian navy. He ordered his guns manned and the firing of all torpedo tubes which would bear on either attacker. His order was never carried out however; partly because the submarine's communications system had broken down and partly because the crew seized on the order as an excuse to make for the conning tower and escape. As the leading escapees emerged from the opened hatch they were just in time to be killed by a direct hit from *Antelope*. *Port Arthur* had now opened fire also; but the intention to surrender was plain and she checked almost immediately. In another few minutes *Tritone* had sunk and her survivors as they emerged from the water were expressing voluble delight at being out of the war. *Port Arthur's* shared triumph was further sweetened by a purse of $1,000.00 which the citizens of her name city had contributed against such an eventuality at the time of the ship's commissioning.

The city of Port Arthur had been a generous foster parent; and in this respect it resembled every other Canadian city and town which gave its name to a ship. Ships which carried the familiar Canadian names out onto the wide waters sailed with many gifts from the communities of their adoption; and men who had never seen Pictou or Saint John or Charlottetown or Shawinigan or Barrie or Collingwood or Lethbridge or Moose Jaw or Brandon or New Westminster or scores of other Canadian towns and cities, swore by the names and cherished warm thoughts of the unknown well-wishers from whom many benefits had come and continued to come. The practice of naming the ships after towns, and the warmhearted response which the commissioning drew forth from the communities concerned, made a heartening link between the citizens on land and the citizens at sea.

During February and March of 1943 very stiff fighting in Tunisia put heavy additional demands on the armies and upon their lines of supply. A number of fast convoys had to be run down from the United Kingdom and on through the Mediterranean in quick succession; and three of the Canadian mid-ocean groups were called in to provide the additional escort necessary. Instead of turning back westward at the end of their Atlantic run; they each made one trip from Londonderry to Gibraltar and onward with ships for Morocco and Tunisia.

The voyages, like most Mediterranean cruises in those days, were crowded with aircraft and submarine incidents; but they were not repeated. Atlantic sinkings had again turned toward one of the peaks of the war; and the ships of the mid-ocean groups were urgently required in the older theatre. It was apparent, even at the beginning of February, that the original seventeen corvettes would soon have to return as well; but before they departed they were to gain another definite success and there were to be two disasters.

On February 6 Convoy KMS-8, bound from Gibraltar for Bone under the escort of six British and nine Canadian corvettes, was about six hours from Oran when three German planes came in out of the low evening sun and dropped bombs near one of the British escorts. The Canadian corvette *Louisburg*, nearby, saw the fountains of water rise about the ship, and then observed one of the returning aircraft driving in for her own masthead. She opened fire, and the plane dropped steeply. For a moment her gunners thought they had scored a hit, but the illusion was quickly dispelled. The plane flattened out, released a torpedo, and swerved away.

Loss of "Louisburg"

The torpedo struck and there was a tremendous explosion in the region of Louisburg's engine room. The ship was immediately sinking and the order to abandon was given. Engine room personnel were almost all casualties but the remainder of the crew proceeded coolly. In the four minutes during which the ship remained afloat, the carley floats were got away and calcium flares were set in the water to assist a nearby British ship in rescue operations.

One of Louisburg's officers, wounded himself, helped a number of injured ratings to get away a carley float and then went over the side wearing a coonskin coat. He was still wearing the coat when fished out of the water; and the remark, "Joe College goes to sea," which came from somewhere out of the gathering darkness, gave a single touch of lightness to a very grim scene. Once again, depth charges, exploding as a ship sank, had added to a long casualty list. Louisburg's commanding officer and thirty-seven of his officers and men were lost.

Six days later Regina avenged her sister ship. She was with a convoy north of Philippeville on the night of February 8; and at about ten minutes after eleven her radar operator reported a slight disturbance on his screen. It seemed at first a most dubious contact, but Regina nosed away through a very dark night to investigate. The image on the radar screen grew steadily more definite and Regina became convinced that she was on the trail of a surfaced submarine. The range closed for a few minutes, still without any visual sighting; then the contact began to move slowly left. Suddenly it disappeared completely. The submarine had become aware of Regina's approach and had dived.

A pattern of depth charges was dropped over the estimated position of the dive; and an anxious ten minutes of waiting followed the explosions. Then, just as Regina was moving in for another attack, she made out the white wake of a submarine surfaced and running away. The boat itself was only the faintest shadow upon the darkness, but Regina opened up with her bridge oerlikons immediately. Answering fire came from the submarine, and the course of the enemy became more clearly distinguishable. *Regina's* machine gun tracers guided her 4-inch gun onto the swerving target, and a shell hit squarely at the base of the conning tower. Fire from the submarine immediately ceased; and the light of a starshell revealed the Italian crew lined up on their decks, making eager gestures of surrender. After sweeping carefully around the victim for fifteen minutes to make sure that there was not another U-boat in company, *Regina* stopped her engines for long enough to put away a boarding party and permit willing Italian prisoners to clamber onto her decks.

Short as the action had been, *Regina's* fire had taken murderous effect. The captain, first lieutenant, navigator and sixteen ratings had been killed or blown overboard. Some of the Italian survivors, as they clambered on board *Regina*, were weeping and hysterical; while one bestowed the traditional double kiss on an unappreciative Canadian rating. Although an attempt was made at salvage, the hit from the 4-inch gun at the base of the conning tower had badly holed the boat; and within half an hour it filled and sank.

An eventful February was to provide yet another major incident, and not a happy one. At eight o'clock on the morning of February 22 *Weyburn* left Gibraltar at full speed to overtake a convoy bound for the United Kingdom. Just as she joined and prepared to take up her screening position, she struck a mine. The explosion came amidships on the port side, opening a large hole, buckling the deck and splitting the funnel for its entire length. Water poured into the engine room, which was already a rocking welter of oil, and throughout the ship there was a continual crash of bursting steam pipes and flying metal parts.

Although the corvette was lying deep in the water, she did not appear to be sinking; and the boilers had not given way. The crew recovered quickly from the effects of the explosion and began to prepare for towing. Primers were removed from all the depth charges except two which had been so jammed by the force of the explosion that it was impossible to work the detonators loose.

Meanwhile the British destroyer *Wivern* had closed *Weyburn* bow to stern and was taking off wounded men. There seemed at first to be little immediate danger but within twenty minutes *Weyburn's* precarious stability vanished. Her bow reared suddenly in the water and she went straight down in a matter of seconds. There followed in close succession two terrific explosions, apparently from the depth charges whose primers had not been removed. The charges had been set at "safe," just as they had been with many other ships in a similar predicament; but the mechanism in use at that time was still not reliable. The results in this case were disastrous for both ships.

The commanding officer and another of the officers on *Weyburn's* bridge were instantly killed, together with a British petty officer who had come across to give aid. A number of men in the water also lost their lives. *Wivern* herself was badly damaged by the double explosion, but her efforts to assist the Canadian seamen were redoubled. Her Medical Officer, Surgeon-Lieutenant P. R. C. Evans, had been thrown from his feet and had both ankles broken. Lying on his back and suffering intensely, he gave directions for the treatment of *Weyburn's* men, and was ably assisted by his sick bay attendant and a number of ratings whom he had instructed in first aid work. He had intended to use *Wivern's* mess decks as a surgery, but they had been wrecked by the later explosions. The wardroom was hastily made ready, and the gravely injured patients were lowered down the ammunition hoist.

The most serious case was Lieutenant W. A. B. Garrard from *Weyburn,* one of whose feet had been frightfully crushed. He refused treatment until all the other men of his ship were cared for, remaining not only conscious but cheerfully talkative through what must have been a half hour of relentless torture. At length, with the other wounded lying about the littered, bloodstained wardroom of the listing ship, he was placed on the table. No general anaesthetic was given. The sick bay attendant took the knife while the Surgeon-Lieutenant, lying on his back with ankles broken and his own face grey with pain, directed the agonizing "cleaning up" of the wound. "Hack away, boys, I'm all in favour of it," were Garrard's words as the operation began.

It was, as *Wivern's* officers pronounced it afterward, "a magnificent example of sheer guts;" and Garrard's name became, with reason, legendary among all who knew of him. Yet the other Canadian survivors, soon to leave the Mediterranean, took with them also the memory of the wounded British doctor; of the sick bay attendant, steady-handed and bathed in clammy sweat; of the British petty officer who had died while helping a wounded Canadian on *Weyburn's* bridge. It was not likely that they would have to be preached to thereafter of the virtues which underlay the peculiarities of the limeys.

By March of 1943 the situation was steadying down in the Mediterranean and the Allies had definitely gained the upper hand. The convoys, still subject to frequent attacks from the air and underwater, were nevertheless getting through with a percentage of loss small enough to justify the detachment of a few escort ships. One by one the Canadian corvettes set off from Gibraltar for the United Kingdom and did not return. They had earned by now many tributes from the Royal Navy and, on both sides, their departure was an occasion for regret. It was necessary, however, and had been delayed to the last possible moment. The North African landings had been successful; and final victory in Tunisia, though it might be delayed, was certain. But during the first months of 1943 it had begun to seem possible that all the fires of hope lighted by Torch might be extinguished again in the gale-ridden wastes of the Atlantic.

Convoy in Bedford Basin, Halifax

THE CLIMAX IN THE ATLANTIC
JANUARY TO SEPTEMBER, 1943

GREEN

C.
FARE

GOOSE BAY

ANTICOSTI

CORNERBROOK

QUEBEC

PORT AUX BASQUES

SAINT JOHN

SYDNEY

ST. JOHNS

WABANA

HALIFAX

SABLE I.

BOSTON

ROYAL CANADIAN AIR FORCE COASTAL SQUADRONS

COMMAND AREA

COMMANDER-IN-CHIEF CANADIAN NORTH WEST ATLANTIC

AREA OF WEST OCEAN MEETING POINT

SC. AND HX CONVOYS TO U.K.

RANGE OF AIR COVER

BY ROYAL CANADIAN AIR FORCE

CONVOYS FOR NORTH AFR

TO ARUBA

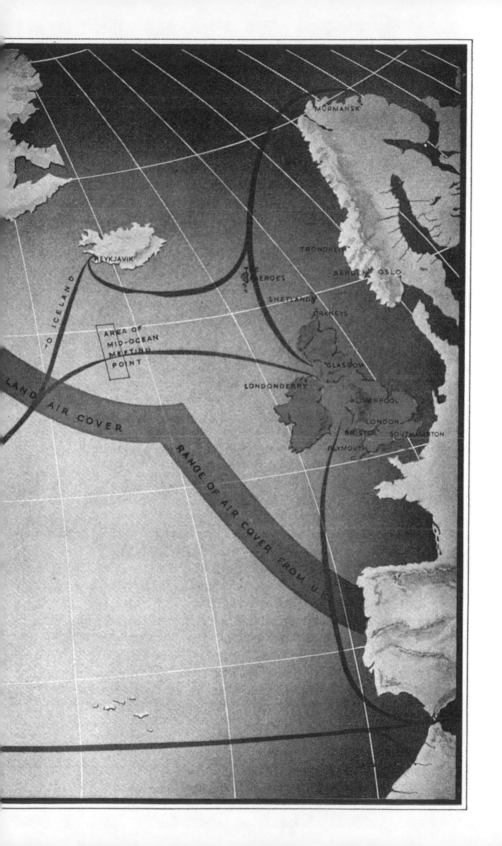

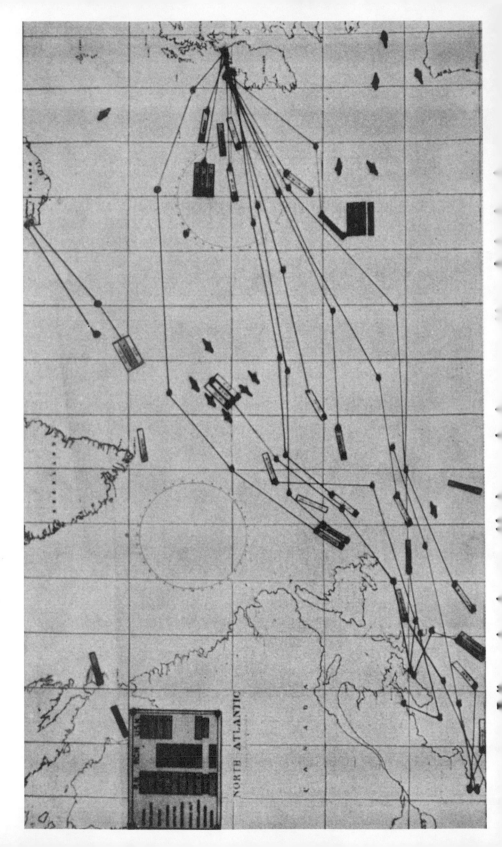

NORTH ATLANTIC

CHAPTER EIGHT

Full Partner

"The U-boat warfare," said Churchill on February 11, 1943, "takes first place in our thoughts." The words were a sobering reminder of the fact that Allied strategy, Allied timing and the use made of available Allied strength had still to be vindicated. We had chosen to throw the weight of British and American power against the Mediterranean frontier of the Axis. Spectacular successes had been achieved and more were immediately in prospect. The conquest of North Africa was assured; Italy seemed little more than a vulnerable bridge-head. While Russia hammered from the east, the arms of the western powers, now muscular and far outflung, were encompassing the writhing enemy in the south. Yet there was on every front the possibility of a fatal drain—of sudden, deadly anaemia. The muscles behind the Russian hammer could be weakened, the encompassing arms in the south could be bled white by the piercing of the slender, sea-borne arteries which fed them.

The weaving and interweaving lines of Atlantic supply ran from North America east by south to Africa, east by north to the United Kingdom, northward again to Russia, and from the United Kingdom southward to Gibraltar. The demands of the North African campaign had multiplied them and doubled their importance, while many of the ships which defended them had been withdrawn. Worse still, serious delay had been imposed on construction, organization, equipment, training; all the new means and methods of convoy defence which, as was fully realized, would be necessary to meet the growing power of the German undersea navy.

How serious the delay would be no man could say, and mighty efforts were being made to reduce it to a minimum. In American and British shipyards the stripped hulls of fast merchantmen were being transformed into flat-topped naval ships. They would be escort carriers armed with a dozen planes, and would form the backbone of support groups free of convoy responsibilities and able to range the seas in search of U-boats. Other merchant ships, still retaining their holds and cargo capacity, were being fitted with flight decks, and would sail in company with convoys as merchant aircraft carriers. Among the ships of the escort groups, training in the all-important and now highly systematized technique of the U-boat hunt had reached a new peak, while detection devices and the weapons of attack were being vastly improved.

Even more impressive than the great plans for seaborne air cover was the shore-based umbrella which was to be extended above the convoys. It was no new thing. British, Canadian, American and other allied pilots had been fighting submarines from the air since the early days of the war. On the eastern side of the Atlantic, Coastal Command, which now included five Canadian squadrons, had taken a great and steadily increasing part in the sea battle. On the western side, United States planes from bases in Iceland, Greenland and Newfoundland, and on the American mainland, together with planes of the Royal Canadian Air Force based in Newfoundland and Canada, had paralleled the efforts of Coastal Command. From both sides intrepid crews operating at extreme range had been pushing out the radius of air cover; and their zones were expanding as larger planes came into service. The day was not far off when the wide arcs of patrol would intersect above the middle Atlantic. The air bases in Greenland and at Goose Bay in Labrador were now completed and almost fully operational. Older bases had been enlarged. Planes of improved type, most importantly the long-range Liberators which would be the final answer to the problem of air cover, were being provided. Improved radar and anti-submarine weapons were being fitted into all of them. Long training and hard experience had already borne fruit, and would soon weave airmen and seamen together into one powerful team of submarine killers.

All this work and equipment, all these plans when completed and combined, would make for a great and probably decisive accession of strength. But diverted and delayed as they had been, the opening months of 1943 found them still largely on the way. The new ships were being rushed toward completion but were not completed; the new groups were forming and training, not formed and trained. Even the shore-based Liberators, though ready and operational at many bases, were still held to comparative impotence by hideous winter weather which for days and weeks on end made patrol flights impossible. Through November and December of 1942, on into January and February of 1943, growing swarms of U-boats were gnawing ever deeper into the close-knit strands of allied trade.

In January of 1943 Doenitz had replaced Raeder as Commander-in-Chief of the German navy. Doenitz was heart and soul a submarine man, with a fanatical belief in the potentialities of the U-boats. All German naval effort was now to be concentrated on the building of more and better submarines and on operating them with even more ruthless efficiency than before. There was, indeed, no alternative for the Reich. In Russia, though she still might stave off utter defeat, she could never attain victory. Invasion of Britain was now unthinkable. The dream of Egypt was gone; the Mediterranean had become a killing-ground from which U-boats had a five per cent chance of returning. If victory, or the stalemate which would now be an acceptable substitute for victory, were ever to be attained, it would be through the disorganization and throttling of the long Allied lines of supply.

It was therefore in the Atlantic, through which the vital lines ran for most of their length, that the U-boats gathered in the opening weeks of 1943. Their numbers increased steadily; and if their energy had a quality of desperation it had also a full measure of the familiar, cold-blooded confidence.

Once again Admiral Winter shouldered aside both combatants for a time. During December, January, February and March the weather was worse than it had been at any period of the war. There were only ten days of those four months when ferocious gales were not raging somewhere over the convoy routes. During January alone, four merchant ships went aground, eight foundered, and forty were heavily damaged by weather. One rescue ship simply turned over and sank with the weight of ice which formed on her decks and superstructure. The Commodore's ship of another convoy split her seams in a gale and went down with no survivors. All these were merely the tangible losses which could be set down and recorded. Beyond them, and adding altogether a far greater toll of loss and delay, was the continual straggling, the complete dissolution of convoys in the face of gales which compelled ships to heave to and ride with the force of wind and sea. Their escorts were in as bad or worse case. Of the 196 Canadian and 35 British ships now under Canadian operational command, less than seventy per cent could be kept in operation at any one time.

The misery of the weather did not by any means spare the U-boats. Not only were the difficulties of attack greatly increased by mountainous seas, sleety gales and impenetrable fogs, but the life of the German crews was an ordeal which it is uncomfortable even to imagine. In the cramped interiors of the steel shells which might well be their tombs, their ears continually assailed by the maddening, inhuman, insistent rhythm of machinery; breathing induced oxygen soiled by fetid humanity, consumed fuel or the acrid vapours rising from the batteries, they spent often as long as three months in the bosom of hostile seas with only an occasional glimpse of stormy sunlight or a breath of night air. There was never an hour during the long war cruises when they were free from danger; never a moment when they could be sure that invisible, unheard fingers were not groping for them, weaving a net which would close for their destruction amid the plunging roar of depth charges.

The fine hope and the fine promise of the earlier years had forsaken them. Their faith in the great Leader was assailed by the news which they received on each return to base, by the letters handed to them, by the sight of ports and harbours bombed to rubble. They were the men of a forlorn hope and they must have known it; yet, though they sometimes showed signs of growing caution, there was never a real weakening. The successes achieved by the allied anti-submarine navies are brought into true perspective when the quality of the men to whom they were opposed is recognized. "Our ideas of heroism may differ," says an Admiralty publication, "but it was not without reason in May, 1945, when all was lost, that Admiral Doenitz paid tribute to his men who were laying down their arms 'after a heroic fight which knows no equal.' "

No calendar division is very accurate in chronicling the winter offensive of 1943. It had been well in progress and, in fact, mounting in intensity during the closing months of 1942. U-boats were coming into service much faster than they were being sunk; and at least a hundred were in the Atlantic during January. They were concentrated mainly on the western side; and although "pestilentially foul" weather and evasive routing of convoys prevented them from operating at full effectiveness there could be no doubt of the menace they presented. What they might accomplish was shown when an oil convoy from the Caribbean, sighted under reasonably good conditions for attack, was cut to pieces, losing seven of its nine priceless tankers.

February, with equally vicious weather, saw the crisis still postponed, and the race between German efforts and Allied defensive preparations becoming a dead heat. The precious and decisive advantage of air cover was delayed as much by weather as by actual shortage of planes. The most valiant efforts could not keep aircraft on patrol for more than a fraction of the time amid the incessant gales and storms. The coming of the merchant aircraft carriers, the escort carriers and the support groups was still delayed; and in the meantime the convoys faced the U-boats and the battering seas, protected only by the usual escort groups, always overworked, always too few.

Full Partner

An indication of the consequences is given by the record of Convoy ON-66. Of sixty-three ships which sailed from Northern Ireland and were almost instantly assailed by a barrage of U-boat transmissions and warning signals from friendly sources, thirteen returned weather-damaged to the United Kingdom, one put in at Iceland, twelve were torpedoed, nine straggled and only twenty-eight reached St. John's in convoy. *Trillium,* one of the corvettes in escort, took on board 160 survivors—nearly twice her own complement—from three torpedoed ships. With exhausted, sick and wounded passengers crowded in above decks and below, short of food and water and low on fuel, she fought three U-boat actions, sailed three more days with the convoy knowing that her life-saving equipment was adequate only for something like a third of those on board; and on arrival in St. John's sailed again for another convoy within forty-eight hours.

Bleak spells of quieter weather began to break the monotony of Atlantic storms in March, and the greatest crisis of the entire battle was upon the allied navies. They faced it with a division of strength and command which had long been considered unbalanced and complex, but which now cried out for adjustment.

The whole of the western Atlantic had been, since late in 1941, under the stategic control of the United States Navy. British and Canadian authorities operated their ships under higher American direction; and for something like eighteen months this had resulted in American control of trade convoys which were largely escorted by British and Canadian ships. As elsewhere in this unusual war, there had been a uniformly good spirit between the three navies, and almost impeccable cooperation. The lack of balance between authority and force was not in any sense a serious bone of contention; but it did make for complexities which sometimes led to contradictions. The Atlantic Convoy Conference, which began to sit in Washington on March 1, 1943, took under consideration as one of its urgent problems the re-organization of the command system.

Re-Organization of Commands

United States naval strength was again building up in the Atlantic; and, as always, strong American task forces provided the escort for troop convoys and for convoys to North Africa. Great numbers of troops were now being carried, however, by fast liners such as the *Queen Mary* and *Queen Elizabeth* which sailed unescorted, and trade convoys to the United Kingdom were escorted almost entirely by British and Canadian ships. The actual division of escort work about United Kingdom trade convoys in the north Atlantic was now fifty per cent British, forty-eight per cent Canadian and two per cent American. So far as the western Atlantic was concerned Canada was now obviously a full partner, and it remained to make her so in form as she was in fact.

The United States Navy withdrew its authority from the Atlantic north of the port of New York. All responsibility for trade convoys and their escorts within an area bounded by a line running eastward from New York and southward from Greenland along the meridian of 47° West was taken over by the Canadian navy; and authority was vested in the Commander-in-Chief, Canadian Northwest Atlantic, Rear-Admiral L. W. Murray, with headquarters at Halifax. South of this area the United States retained control. East of its boundaries authority was to be exercised by the Royal Navy.

Shore-based aircraft of the three nations were to operate to the limit of their range under control of the authorities in whose areas they were based, and without regard to the "chop lines" established on the sea. Support groups, similarly, were to range where the battle took them, always under the control of their base authority.

From the United States Navy, Canada received back the seven corvettes which she had loaned for service in the Caribbean. The Royal Navy arranged for the transfer to her of six over-age Fleet destroyers, five of which were, during the next few months, to be commissioned as His Majesty's Canadian ships, *Kootenay, Saskatchewan, Gatineau, Chaudière* and *Qu'Appelle*. The sixth was to be *Ottawa*, restoring to the Navy List, a name which had disappeared with the original destroyer's sinking in December 1942. With these promised reinforcements, with her seventeen "Torch" corvettes returning from the Mediterranean, and with the new ships contributed by her own building program, Canada entered upon the crisis of the Atlantic battle bearing a large and well-defined share of the responsibility for its success.

Both sides had looked forward to the spring of 1943 as "the crunch of the war." At the beginning of March about seventy U-boats were on station in the northwest Atlantic alone. They were disposed in three great lines of patrol, one across the stretch of northern sea between Labrador and Greenland, another running due south and well to seaward of Newfoundland and Nova Scotia, and a third paralleling the Nova Scotia coastline to a point well below New York. Together, their dispositions boxed in every exit and entry point for the ocean convoys; and extending eastward of the main formations to the fringe of British coastal waters were some forty more U-boats grouped in the likelier areas.

This Atlantic force of 110 U-boats was by no means the total of German resources. Neither the far northern waters nor the Caribbean were neglected. On one day— March 9—five convoys were being simultaneously attacked; two trans-Atlantic convoys, one eastbound and one westbound; a north Russia convoy; a convoy bound from Bahia to Trinidad; and one on passage from the United Kingdom to Gibraltar. The four greatest convoy battles of March involved forces totalling seventy U-boats and thirty-eight allied escort ships; and resulted in the loss of thirty-seven merchant ships.

All the familiar circumstances of other winters were present, aggravated by the increased size of the U-boat concentrations. Escort groups, struggling to keep convoys together in the midst of great gales, arranged themselves vainly in formation after formation. Every variety of tactics was adopted, with little success, to accomplish the impossible task of warding off attackers who came in from many directions at once, often outnumbering the defenders two to one, and sometimes more heavily than that. The escort vessels, the anti-submarine equipment and the training of the groups had all been improved; and the crews of the merchant ships themselves, always gallant, were now experienced warriors skilful in the use of evasive tactics, smoke screens and many other hopeful expedients designed to deceive and confuse the attackers. Yet still the toll of sinking continued to rise.

Convoy SC-121, whose history spanned a few late days of February and the first ten days of March, lost twelve ships amid circumstances which recalled the darkest periods of earlier winters. Escorts joined and detached, forced away by fuel shortages, mechanical defects, or imperative calls for assistance from other quarters. Continuous southwesterly and westerly gales, interspersed with frequent snow and hail squalls, battered the fifty-one merchant ships and drove them far apart, to be rounded up with immense difficulty in conditions of fog and sleet and darkness which sometimes reduced visibility to less than a ship's length.

U-boat sightings and warnings began on the morning of March 6 as the convoy worked its way into the high latitudes west and south of Iceland. By nightfall transmissions from at least ten U-boats had been intercepted. One ship went down before morning, torpedoed and dreadfully alone in the roaring darkness of the gale. *Rosthern*, wallowing through the high seas at daybreak, was the first to learn of the torpedoing when she came upon three half-dead survivors. During the day the gale grew fiercer and the entire two starboard columns lost touch with the convoy and straggled away. Two ships were lost that night; the next night five; and not a ship of the escort was able to claim a successful counter-attack.

Throughout the remainder of March the story was the same or worse for other convoys. Evasive routing was practically useless in view of the great number of U-boats at sea. Every sailing was made with the virtual certainty of encountering a large German concentration; and the losses suffered were outpacing the entire shipbuilding efforts of the United Nations. So many escort vessels were laid up for repair or weather damage in the late and leonine days of March that the group system was in danger of disorganization. Shore-based air cover, too, was largely ineffective because of the weather. It began to seem that the convoy system, after all the years of valiant effort, could not be maintained. Vital imports to the United Kingdom were already scaled to a minimum, and even that minimum was not being met.

The total losses for March were 627,000 tons of merchant shipping. It was not the highest figure of the war; but the terribly ominous fact was that for the first time seventy-five per cent of the losses had been sustained in convoy. The ships had gone down while they were under the best protection which allied resources could, at the moment, provide. The number of the U-boats had increased, and their tactics had improved to a point where they could no longer be warded off by a thin screen of ships closely disposed about a convoy and responsible for every phase of its defence. The forebodings of previous months were darkly confirmed. The forces and dispositions which had successfully defended the Atlantic convoy up to March 1943 would not be adequate for the future. They were being steadily and surely defeated, and if reinforcements did not arrive the defeat would be final.

In the early days of April the U-boats, still increasing in numbers, began to close in upon the western side of the ocean. Several groups, each of ten or twelve boats, formed a patrol arc of some six hundred miles radius from Newfoundland; sweeping across the convoy routes from northeast to southwest of St. John's. They were pressing for a decision, desperately. An atmosphere of crisis hung heavily above the mellowing Atlantic. The great contenders had arrived at one of those periods so familiar in history; long months and years of war had dragged ponderously upward to a pinnacle of time on which one supreme effort would decide all.

The pinnacles are clearer in retrospect than they ever are to contenders in the midst of the event. On neither side could the planners of the Atlantic battle know beforehand the effect of the combining factors which brought the turn in Allied fortunes. Nor could the turn be seen clearly until long after it had actually begun: until its momentum, slowly gathered, had become an inexorable rush. The rare and fickle sunshine of a few March days had shown what the increased resources of shore-based air cover might mean. With improving April weather the great planes flew more patrols; remained longer over the convoys. They had always been a harrassing threat to the U-boat captains. Now they were becoming a deadly menace, and about mid-month other and newer cogs in the allied machine began to move and mesh together.

Five British support groups set sail within a few days of each other. Led by destroyers, they included also new frigates, which were twin-screw ships specially designed for anti-submarine work, larger and faster than corvettes; sloops which were a little smaller than frigates; and the newest and best-equipped corvettes. All the ships of each group were manned by British crews, specially and intensively trained in anti-submarine work; and the ships were hunting ships only. They would seek out known U-boat concentrations, or go to the assistance of immediately threatened convoys. While a convoy was in danger they would provide a far-ranging outer screen of ships to reinforce the close escort. When the danger had subsided they would move off to other areas, without responsibility for actual escort work, always on the hunt.

With the support groups five American escort carriers came into service. The dozen planes which each of them carried were equipped with radar and asdic, guns and depth charges; and they were not long in demonstrating their value. On April 25, three hundred miles southeast of Cape Farewell at the tip of Greenland, a threatened convoy saw the funnels of six friendly warships heave over the horizon. They were one of the support groups; and in the midst of the wide-spread formation was the squat shape of the escort carrier, *Biter*. Within a few hours *Biter's* aircraft, swinging far out over the sea, had located the gathering U-boat pack and pinned down one of the submarines for a surface ship to destroy. Similar events took place elsewhere over the Atlantic at about the same time. Thirty-five merchant ships were sunk during the month and only eight U-boats were destroyed; but of those eight, five were sunk by aircraft alone, and one by aircraft in co-operation with surface ships. It was a sign, indefinite as yet, but promising.

Convoy HX-237 which sailed from New York on May 1 and arrived at its mid-ocean rendezvous on May 5, brought clearer evidence of the changing conditions. The support group which included *Biter* had provided an outer screen for the convoy from May 3, and when there was difficulty in locating the mid-ocean escort at rendezvous point *Biter's* aircraft had found the ships and homed them onto the convoy, saving many hours of weary search.

As the voyage proceeded, with the Canadian corvettes *Morden*, *Drumheller* and *Chambly* as part of the close escort, there were plentiful warnings of U-boats in the vicinity, but no sightings and no attacks. The columns of merchant ships moved on, alert and baffled by the curious serenity of the seas about them. Whenever the intermittent fog cleared, Liberators wheeled above, ranged far ahead and disappeared. The ships of the support group paralleling the convoy's course moved unseen, well below the horizon. There was no evidence for the merchantmen that a battle of consequence was taking place, and that they were the centre of it.

On the morning of the 12th a Liberator, 1200 miles from its base and far out of sight of the merchant ships, attacked and sank a U-boat. Two days later Liberators sank one U-boat and attacked five others. The gathering pack was being broken up before it could come within sight of the convoy. A night later, just before dusk, *Chambly* sighted a U-boat on the horizon and gave chase. The submarine, quite as fast as the corvette, made off, and its escape in the old days might well have been final. The presence of *Biter's* aircraft changed the situation. A plane took up the pursuit, located the U-boat and attacked it with depth charges in the face of heavy anti-aircraft fire. When the submarine dived the plane dropped a marker and circled the area until *Chambly* arrived. A little later came British ships of the support group to take over from *Chambly*. The British ships did not make their attack this time with depth charges. They used a new weapon, just beginning to make its appearance in the Atlantic; and the result of the attack, which came sixteen seconds after its commencement, was a huge explosion and the oily wreckage mixed with bits of clothing and human flesh which were the evidence of a kill.

The new weapon had already appeared, heavily shrouded in tarpaulin, forward of the bridge on some of the Canadian ships more recently arrived in St. John's or Halifax. Inquiries from ship-wise personnel about the dockyards, who instantly spotted the new addition on the cluttered decks, had brought the reply that it was "Anti-Dive-Bombing-Equipment." To anyone present when the tarpaulin was removed, the answer might have seemed credible. The square-set battery of twenty-four spigotted heads pointing forward and skyward at an acute angle might well have had some aerial intention. Actually it had not. The 65-pound bombs on the ends of the spigots were intended on firing to describe a brief arc through the air and enter the water some 230 yards ahead of the ship in an intricate circle pattern about a hundred feet in diameter. Around the circumference of the circle, and at points within its area, the bombs fell spaced twelve feet apart. Each was loaded with thirty pounds of Torpex, an explosive sixty per cent more effective than TNT; and any one of them, dropping straight downward through the water, would explode on contact, with disastrous results for a U-boat.

The new weapon was named "hedgehog;" and it was the answer to the demand for missiles which could be thrown ahead of the ship rather than dropped astern, as in the case of depth charges. In passing over a U-boat and dropping charges astern, there was an unavoidable period during which an attacking ship lost asdic contact. Frequently, after the disturbance caused by the explosions, contact could not be regained and the enemy made his escape. Hedgehog was designed to eliminate this narrow gap between detection by asdic and destruction by high explosive. With hedgehog, the ship, retaining undisturbed asdic contact, threw the charges out ahead while still far enough from the U-boat that an explosion, if it came, would do herself no damage. If the U-boat lay anywhere within the 100-foot area covered by the bombs it would be killed. If not, the charges would sink harmlessly to the bottom while the ship, still retaining her contact, could reload and prepare for another attack.

Hedgehog was not to be the ultimate in ahead-thrown weapons. The contact-fuse principle, exploding the bomb only when it struck the U-boat's hull, was to come into question. More effective ahead-thrown weapons were to be developed later; but in the meantime the still very secret "anti-dive-bombing-equipment" was a valuable addition to the Allied armoury. Asdic had by now been developed to such a point that the ranging of hedgehog onto a good contact was not only efficient, but almost automatic.

Hedgehog again came into action a day or so later; and this time the kill was shared in by the Canadian corvette *Drumheller*. A straggling merchantman had been torpedoed and sunk, far from the same Convoy HX-237, which was proceeding on its way without evidence of battle. *Drumheller* had just picked up fifteen survivors when her lookouts observed a Sunderland about six miles away, circling low over the water. The plane's signal lamp flashed the message that she was over a submarine; and ten minutes later, as *Drumheller* raced for the position, she saw the U-boat. It was running away on the surface; and was putting up a hot barrage against the Sunderland and one of *Biter's* planes, which had joined in the battle. *Drumheller* opened fire as she came within range, and the submarine dived.

Moving over the position, *Drumheller* dropped depth charges; then regained contact in time to guide the British frigate *Lagan* into position for a hedgehog attack. *Lagan's* bombs fell in a neat circle over the target area; there were a few tense seconds of waiting, and then one of the missiles made contact far beneath the surface. The sea's heaving blackness rumbled upward, churning white and green with the explosion. Oil followed, and then a litter of debris amid which there rose a huge bubble of air sixty feet in diameter from the U-boat's shattered pressure tanks. The action report of that German captain, if delivered in Valhalla, might have made mention of the four allied arms responsible for his arrival: shore-based aircraft, carrier-based aircraft, ships of the close escort and ships of the support groups.

Convoy ON-184, which crossed in the latter part of May with generally good weather, provided another demonstration of what the U-boats could now expect. Two British and six Canadian ships were the escort group disposed immediately about the convoy in close support. Shore-based aircraft were overhead almost continually during the early days of the voyage; and when the limits of their range were reached, a support group joined them with the American escort carrier *Bogue*. On the afternoon of May 21 *Bogue's* aircraft attacked two submarines, of which one was possibly sunk. The next day a plane from *Bogue* sighted another U-boat on the surface, and damaged it so severely by depth charges that it was unable to submerge. Then, circling and pelting the German with a vicious hail of gunfire, the plane forced him to surrender and meekly await the coming of *St. Laurent*, which found the boat sinking and the crew in the water.

May was by no means a month of uninterrupted triumphs. Although driven by sheer necessity to cautious tactics, which were often ineffective, the U-boats fought hard. They still took instant advantage of any combination of circumstances which weighed in their favour. When gale conditions prevented effective air support of one convoy, twelve ships out of forty-three were torpedoed. Yet the total of merchant ship sinkings for the month fell to 157,000 tons; and, against that, U-boat losses totalled thirty-seven sunk and thirty-two damaged. At long last, the monthly total of U-boats destroyed or knocked out of action was rising above the total of new craft coming into service.

Through June, July and August, the number of merchant ship sinkings in the Atlantic fell toward insignificance; and the number of U-boat kills rose to heights which would have been incredible a few months before. Defeat on the convoy routes was accompanied by even heavier blows which struck the flotillas as they were setting out from their French bases along the Biscay coast. The air and sea patrols which had always been maintained over the Bay of Biscay were transformed in the spring and summer of 1943 into huge sweeps by forces of aircraft and surface ships; and the support groups, the carrier-based planes and the planes of Coastal Command had a slaughterous field day.

The total of killings dropped to seventeen in June as the U-boats recoiled or were withdrawn under the fury of the attack. It rose again to forty-six in July as the Germans returned with heavier anti-aircraft armament and attempted to fight it out with planes on the surface. By August, when such tactics were proved a failure, there was a general withdrawal of U-boat forces. Only a few remained, hunted and harried guerillas on the convoy routes, or creeping inward and outward through the Bay of Biscay. The total of kills dropped for lack of targets to a lean twenty; and the well-blooded groups searched hungrily over seas empty of the enemy.

Almost every convoy that sailed now included at least one merchant aircraft-carrier. Additional support groups, including a Canadian group, were in operation. Equipment for fuelling at sea from tankers added hundreds of miles to the escorts' radius of action. Reports of convoy commodores still breathe from dusty files a spirit of ecstatic amazement: "I never before had such splendid escort, surface and air;"

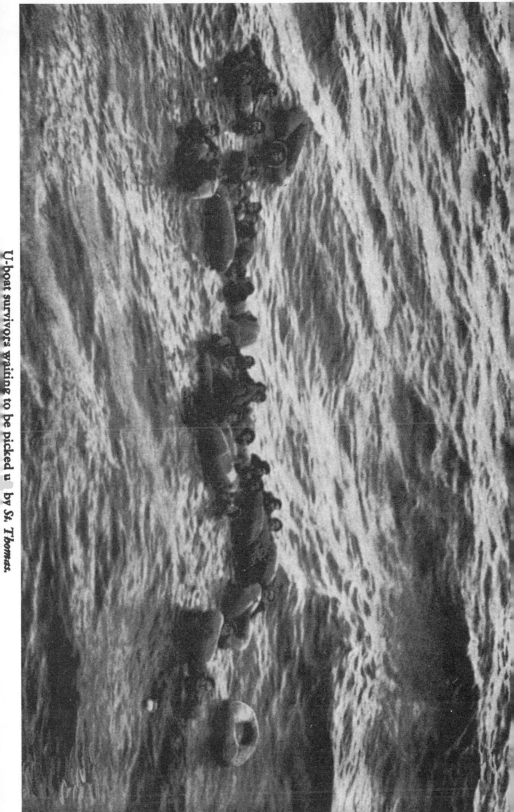

U-boat survivors waiting to be picked up by *St. Thomas.*

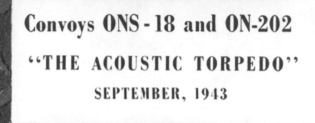

Convoys ONS-18 and ON-202

"THE ACOUSTIC TORPEDO"

SEPTEMBER, 1943

2350
ITCH
TORP

AIR COVER FROM
NEWFOUNDLAND
& LABRADOR

ONS 18

ON 202

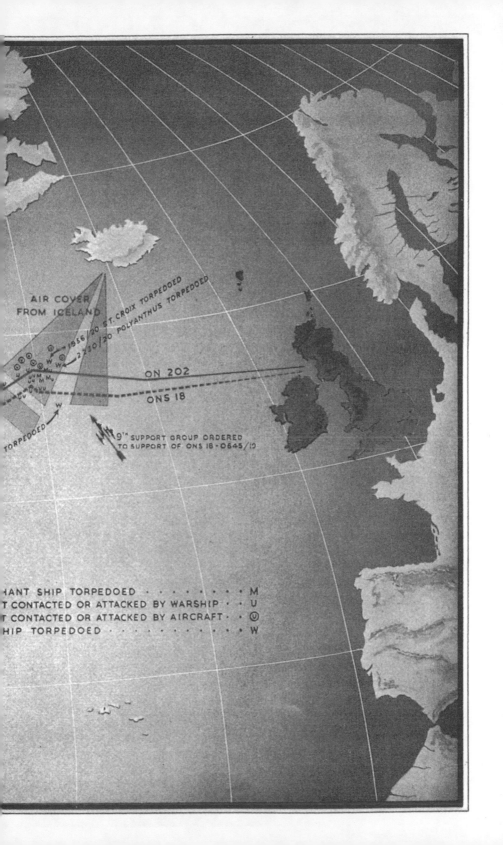

AIR COVER
FROM ICELAND

ST. CROIX TORPEDOED

1956/20
2230/20 POLYANTHUS TORPEDOED

W W

UVM MU
UV M M₂

W
TORPEDOED

ON 202

ONS 18

9ᵀᴴ SUPPORT GROUP ORDERED
TO SUPPORT OF ONS 18 · 0645/19

HANT SHIP TORPEDOED · · · · · · · · M

T CONTACTED OR ATTACKED BY WARSHIP · · U

T CONTACTED OR ATTACKED BY AIRCRAFT · · Ⓤ

HIP TORPEDOED · · · · · · · · · · W

Clayoquot survivors as the rescue boat arrives

"apparently unlimited air cover," "my convoy was tickled to death and felt like a dog with two tails." Evasive routing became unnecessary. Convoys had no longer to be sent on long, delaying, roundabout courses. Cycles could be opened out, permitting longer intervals for the accumulation of larger groups of ships. The bridge between North America and Europe was cleared at last, and cargo was moving over it in tremendous volume.

As usual, when defeat impended in a main theatre, the Germans turned to harrying tactics. Late in May a large mine-laying submarine paid a visit to Halifax waters and ringed the approaches to the port with fifty magnetic mines. They were of a new type, moored for the first time in deep water, and would have posed a nice problem even for thoroughly experienced minesweeping and disposal forces. First evidence of the field was provided by a single mine which had been faultily moored and was sighted on the surface. It was recognized as a new type with which no one in the port was familiar; and a crew of experts immediately made preparations to bring it back "alive" for investigation.

Fog closed down before this could be done, and some time during the following hours a merchant ship, straying from a channel which had already been cleared, ran onto the mine and was sunk. It was a singularly bad piece of luck; for apart from this one stray the Halifax forces established a perfect record. The characteristics of the new mines were very quickly deduced; sweeping operations were undertaken immediately; and within a day or two the field was clear. Another German mine-laying expedition to the waters around St. John's, Newfoundland, was to be as quickly dealt with in October. Canadian minesweepers, still largely inexperienced, gave an indication of qualities which were soon to find employment on a wider stage.

There was to be a sub-phase to the climactic, though not concluding, phase of the Atlantic battle. Naval authorities, through long experience, were accustomed to take a pessimistic view of German withdrawals. Invariably in the past they had been followed by a return to the attack with new devices and methods which posed dismaying problems. This time there was a well-founded suspicion of what the expected return might bring, and expectations were speedily confirmed.

A slow convoy, ONS-18, set out from the United Kingdom on September 12. Three days behind it a faster convoy, ON-202, followed upon its track, escorted by a group which consisted of the Canadian destroyer *Gatineau*, the British destroyer *Icarus*, the British corvette *Polyanthus* and the Canadian corvettes *Drumheller* and *Kamloops*. ON-202 gained steadily on the slower convoy, and by the evening of September 19 was treading on its heels. At about the same time a number of U-boat transmissions began to fill the air. It became evident to the Admiralty that the enforced vacation of the German submarine service was over. The two convoys were signalled to join; and a newly-formed Canadian support group consisting of the British frigate *Itchen* and the Canadian ships *St. Croix*, *St. Francis*, *Chambly*, *Sackville* and *Morden*, was ordered to reinforce the combined escort.

In the early evening of the 20th, while failing daylight merged into a gathering fog, the two convoys approached one another. The junction, which involved careful manoeuvring by large bodies of ships, was difficult, and was long in being made. In the famous description of one escort commander, "the two convoys gyrated majestically about the ocean, never appearing to get much closer, and watched appreciatively by a growing swarm of U-boats." There was undoubtedly an attack impending; and in the meantime a confusing volume of signals between the manoeuvring Allied ships was added to by German signalmen with "constant heckling and often vicious behaviour, to which the escorts replied in kind."

As darkness fell the junction was still not completed. Sixty-three merchant ships were spread out in comparative disorder over miles of sea. The support group ordered to the convoys' assistance was approaching, and the close escort which included a merchant aircraft carrier was heavy. But until the whole body was properly formed the escort could not be organized; and the night-time situation was not promising.

Only one or two minor attacks developed about the convoy itself during the hours of darkness. Astern, however, where the support group was coming up, there had been a series of hot and disquieting actions. The British frigate *Lagan*, one of the ships of the close escort, had swept back from the convoy to make contact with the support group. She had sighted a submarine, pursued it; and while making preparations for an attack had had thirty feet of her stern blown away by a torpedo from another U-boat.

A short time later *St. Croix* was detached from the support group to investigate an aircraft sighting. As she came over the reported position, the Canadian destroyer slowed down to search for a contact and was hit by two torpedoes just as she began to lose way. Fatally wounded, she took on a heavy list, but preparations to abandon were carried out in an orderly fashion. To *Itchen*, a few miles away, she sent the cryptic message, "Am leaving the office." It was the last word from *St. Croix*. Shortly after the signal was dispatched a third torpedo struck the stern of the ship and there was a terrific explosion. Flames vaulted skyward; and within three minutes the destroyer was gone, taking with her the commanding officer and many of the crew.

It was *Itchen's* hard responsibility to search for the enemy before rescuing the remaining men of *St. Croix*. She signalled *Polyanthus* to come to their assistance, and herself disappeared on the hunt. *Polyanthus* never arrived. On the way to the scene she was torpedoed dead astern and sunk with only one survivor who was picked up by *Itchen* next day. *St. Croix's* men were in the water for thirteen freezing hours before *Itchen* finally returned to take eighty-one of them on board.

As the two convoys, now formed into one body, proceeded through the foggy daylight of the 21st there was tense uneasiness in the air. Three escort ships had been torpedoed, and all by torpedoes which struck dead astern, in the region of the propellers. This was unusual, since a ship beam-on naturally offered the better target. There was also reason to believe that in each case the torpedoed ship had been decoyed into position by one U-boat for attack by a second.

The rumour of a new weapon — an acoustic torpedo homed to the ship by the sound of its propellers—had been current for several months. Its principle, in fact, had long been known; but it had been impossible to forecast its exact nature and the tactics which would be employed in using it. These were now becoming evident. *Lagan, St. Croix* and *Polyanthus* had been led by a surfaced U-boat toward the position of an attacker who was lying submerged. The torpedoes which hit them had probably been fired from beam on; but, guided by the sound device, had swung round in a wide arc and homed in on the propeller wash.

There were nine attacks on the convoy during the night of the 21st; and, although they were fought off successfully by the heavy escort, there had been much of the old-time dash and confidence in the U-boats' methods. Although one submarine was rammed and sunk and two more hit by gunfire, there was no abatement of the attacks during the dark hours; and dawn, while it brought a temporary cessation, gave no hint of a withdrawal.

After a foggy day, the night of the 22nd was black but clear, with a low, heavy ceiling. Attacks began at 9.30, but for two hours the enemy was held in check. Then *Morden,* running out ahead of the convoy, sighted and illuminated a surfaced U-boat. A number of escorts converged on the sighting, and there was a confused flurry of gunfire.

Itchen, in the van of the pursuers, switched on the light of her large signal projector and revealed the U-boat three or four hundred yards ahead of her. Other ships nearby heard a burst of fire from her oerlikons; then the light of her projector went out. There was "a tremendous, orange-colored mushroom of flame from the position where *Itchen* had last been seen, and an ear-shocking explosion." *Itchen* vanished from the sea; and of all those on board her only three men were recovered; one the lone survivor from *Polyanthus*, one from *St. Croix*, and one from *Itchen* herself.

The battle continued through the night, overhung by the knowledge that the ships were contending against a new weapon for which they had no adequate defence. It was "the battle of battles," opening what was intended to be a new German offensive in the Atlantic; and already the German radio was trumpeting extravagant claims of the loss inflicted. Altogether, from the torpedoing of *Lagan* until the morning of the 23rd, when Liberators from Newfoundland finally drove off the pack, four escort ships and seven merchantmen were torpedoed.

The reports of the ships arriving from the battle sent a natural flurry of uneasiness through the Allied camp. Yet seventeen days after the first report of the acoustic torpedo, ships were being issued with the "foxer" device to counteract it. This consisted in principle simply of two large metal noise-makers towed on a line a safe distance astern of the ship. The foxers drew the torpedo to themselves and exploded it harmlessly. No one ever came to love foxers or the "cat gear" and other refinements which were introduced later. Yet they proved effective; and the acoustic torpedo remained merely an added nuisance to the end of the war. As a spearhead to introduce a German autumn offensive and a weapon to change the course of the battle, it was an immediate failure.

The tide of Allied power in the Atlantic rose to a flood after the surrender of Italy on September 8. The transformed situation in the Mediterranean released British destroyers for Atlantic service; and within less than a month the ambitious German offensive had again become a shattered rout. In the late days of September six submarines out of fifteen were sunk around one convoy for the loss of one British destroyer and one merchant ship. Through October, November and December the U-boats dashed themselves with steadily weakening power against impregnable defences. Far from the tracks of the convoys they were searched out, found and sunk without even sighting an enemy merchantman.

Air power had been finally and decisively linked with seapower; and, for the time at least, it had beaten the underwater navy to impotence. Planes seemed everywhere above the submarines and above the convoys. Perhaps the final blow came on October 9 when Churchill, giving the House a needed reminder of the treaty which John of Gaunt had concluded with Portugal 570 years before, announced that "Britain's oldest ally" had granted the United Nations permission to establish air and naval bases in the Azores.

The last open segment of the vast Atlantic battleground was now walled in and roofed over by Allied power. A handful of U-boats, scattered here and there along the convoy routes for their nuisance value, compelled unceasing vigilance but accomplished practically nothing. Doenitz himself, prefacing his admission with a far from hollow threat of new measures to come, acknowledged that the Allies had "succeeded in gaining the advantage in submarine defence."

By the end of 1943 the Atlantic lines of communication were firmly held. The primary condition for the invasion of Europe had been established. The final, dramatic surge of achievement had, of course, come mainly from new resources provided by Britain and the United States: the support groups, the multiplied squadrons of shore-based planes, the aircraft carriers. The Canadian navy had contributed the greater part of two support groups, and the planes of the Royal Canadian Air Force had powerfully influenced the battle in the western Atlantic. But the major Canadian contribution in the culminating year, as in all the earlier years, had been the ships of the escort groups. Sailing always with the convoys, herding the slow merchantmen onward through all weather, meeting danger and disaster as it came, their drab days were seldom brightened by the spectacular successes which fell to the lot of the hunting groups. Yet they had been the thin steel chain which had not snapped in the dark days; and they were the coiled mainspring of the offensive in the year of triumph.

The Atlantic campaign of 1943 was decisive; but not final. The victory would be challenged again, and the Canadian navy's part in meeting the challenge would be considerable. Canada was to become, during the spring and summer of 1944, the principal custodian of the trade convoys crossing the Atlantic to the United Kingdom. But she was no longer fighting an entirely single-minded war in an isolated theatre, however vast. Her navy, which now controlled a force of 306 operational warships with a personnel of 71,549 men and 4,453 women, had become something more than a heterogeneous collection of sheepdog ships. From the early years of the war there had been a cautious groping toward the needs of the future. Those needs would lie far afield, and a small proportion of Canadian ships and men had been spared from the Atlantic battle to prepare and learn about them. The proportion of men was no longer so small; and a few Canadian ships, through the eventful months of 1943, had been making a contribution to Allied efforts in other theatres of the war.

CHAPTER NINE

In Other Waters

The Canadian ships and sailors "on loan" with the Royal Navy represented a considerable and rather courageous investment of present resources in the hope of future gain. Few as they were, they could ill be spared while the U-boats ravaged the convoys and the Allies fought like a strong man with a cancer gnawing at his middle. Yet from the beginning all men of good heart, all intelligent planners, had had to base their efforts on the assumption that the Atlantic battle would finally be won; and in its broadest aspects that battle was not defensive. It was a sustained effort to advance the war potential of North America three thousand miles eastward to the beach head of the British Isles. Victory in the Atlantic, all-essential though it might be, was nevertheless only a preliminary. The last and greatest battle would still lie ahead, to be fought on other seas, in narrow waters, on roaring, smoke-shrouded beaches and in the heartlands of the enemy. Short of stalemate and defeat, there was no other prospect before the United Nations; and the final effort would require every ounce of strength which they could summon. Canada again must contribute; a nucleus of Canadian naval strength must be built and trained and ready for the culminating assault.

So it was that many of the Canadians who had gone to England for their training in the first months of the war remained with the Royal Navy. For the same reason many others had followed them, to serve in British ships of all types, from aircraft carriers to motor launches. Canadian naval pilots, from early in 1940, distinguished themselves with the Fleet Air Arm. There were a few Canadians in battleships, cruisers and British ships of nearly every other type, including submarines. In such branches as radar, comparatively new and developing as the war progressed, our men seemed peculiarly apt; and Canadians at one time or another served as radar officers in most of the larger British ships. Canadians served in the Mediterranean and in the Pacific; with the Murmansk convoys and in the Indian Ocean; and at Aden and Port Said, those steaming gateways of the Red Sea.

To a very slight and limited extent their work was compensation for the mighty resources of men, ships, knowledge and equipment, which the British put behind the main Canadian effort in the Atlantic. Far more important, however, and principally motivating Canadian contributions to the Royal Navy, was the fact that the experience of these men on loan was accumulating into a fund upon which Canada could draw in the later years of the war.

The policy, like many plans and policies in war, was never fully implemented. When the climactic days came, and new units and forms of Canadian naval strength began to be assembled, it was found that many officers and men were so widely dispersed or so integrally associated with Royal Navy ships that they could not be withdrawn. Yet in other cases experienced men or groups of men did return from the Royal to the Canadian navy; and their hard-won training became disseminated through its ships, or became the basis upon which other complements and other flotillas were built.

Twenty-three Canadian officers were attached to the Channel Anti-Aircraft Guard when it was first formed in September 1940; and many Canadian ratings joined them a little later. They sailed with the merchant ships of the local convoys which moved from port to port about the coasts of the United Kingdom; and for ten months they helped to fight off aircraft, E-boat and submarine attacks along "bomb alleys" floored with acoustic mines and frequently roofed over by the shells of German long-range guns.

After May 1941, as the coastal routes became safer, most of the officers returned to general service with the Canadian navy; and many of the ratings went into the DEMS crews, which sailed everywhere in the world and added formidable defensive strength to the convoys. The DEMS men (for Defensively Equipped Merchant Ships) were naval gunners or navy-trained merchant seamen who manned the guns of the merchant ships. By the end of the war, fifteen hundred Canadian ratings had seen long service with DEMS, shared to the full every peril of the war at sea, and helped to make the anti-aircraft defence of convoys so powerful that few enemy planes were able to penetrate the area of sky above them.

Many Canadian officers went from their first training at "King Alfred" near Brighton directly to the fast motor torpedo boats and motor gun boats of the Royal Navy, and a few to the Fairmile launches based on the English Channel ports. They were later joined by other officers and ratings trained in Canada, and shared in numerous exploits of the Coastal Forces whose doings figured in so many addenda to naval communiqués. Racing out from Channel bases at night to attack German convoys along the French coast, the self-styled "costly farces" took on at one time or another destroyers, minesweepers, flak ships, submarines and E-boats. Their most ambitious effort, shared in by several Canadian officers, was an attempt to prevent by torpedo attack the passage of *Scharnhorst* and *Gneisenau* through the Channel in February 1942.

From December 1940, Canadian officers began also to filter down to the motor torpedo boat, gunboat and Fairmile flotillas in the Mediterranean, based at Alexandria, Malta and Gibraltar. Canadian officers commanded some boats of the famous 10th Flotilla at Alexandria. They shared in the evacuation of part of the garrison of Tobruk in June 1942, where one of their number was killed. They had a part again in an ill-fated attempt to retake the port by surprise in September.

When Rommel, tensely awaiting Montgomery's assault at El Alamein, was tricked into diverting ten thousand much-needed troops to meet a feigned landing behind his lines, a few Canadian-officered motor torpedo boats formed part of the simulated expedition. When the Eighth Army broke through at Alamein and began the final sweep along the North African coast, the boats of the 10th Flotilla paralleled the advance; attacking German supply convoys, fighting submarines and putting in to shore by night to land parties of commandos behind the enemy lines. They came westward at last to be based at Malta and Gibraltar; joining with British gunboat and Fairmile flotillas in which other Canadians had been fighting battles similar to their own.

The waters of Sicily had become familiar to all the flotillas by the time they were called upon to protect the ships of the Allied invasion armada; and when the conquest of Sicily was complete they operated in the Straits of Messina, the Adriatic and the Aegean. Not all their lurid adventures were concluded nor could all their men be recalled by the time the invasion of Europe got under way and the English Channel became again the principal scene of their activities.

All these far-scattered adventurings, and the individual exploits with which they were thickly interspersed, resulted from the policy of diversion for experience. They involved only a very limited number of men, and the actual results which might stem from them could hardly be calculated. The landing craft flotillas built up in England for combined operations fall into a rather more specific category, and their experience in the Torch landings in North Africa represented a small but definite expansion of Canadian naval operations. An even larger expansion got under way in December of 1942, when the first of the powerful Tribal class destroyers built for Canada in Britain emerged from the shipyards.

The Tribals were ships of the better day; adopted by Canada not for convoy escort but for the time when the Atlantic battle would be won and it would be necessary to drive from the seas the still-considerable remnants of the German surface navy. Although they had been under construction for two years they reached completion at a period which might have seemed from this viewpoint a little ahead of their time. In late 1942 and early 1943, the Atlantic battle was moving toward its climax; Canadian manning and training establishments were just beginning to hit their stride; knowledge and experience, still at a premium, were stridently demanded along the convoy routes. Nevertheless—though all these difficulties complicated the earlier days—the ships, the plans which had brought them into being, and perhaps the difficulties themselves, were to yield rich dividends in the future.

Iroquois, first of the Canadian Tribals, arrived at Scapa Flow for work-up in December 1942. Both the ship and her company were to share fully in the tribulations of the apprentice and the pioneer. *Iroquois* was built to British design at a period when the Royal Navy was tending to make its destroyers almost the equivalent of small cruisers in size and fire power. The design retained, nevertheless, the light destroyer hull, and *Iroquois* was not long in demonstrating— as British tribals had done before her—that additional strength was needed to house her enormous power plant.

Driving through heavy seas at high speed, her thin steel shell was inclined to buckle and distort. After first work-ups in comparatively mild waters, she went on patrol in the winter seas around the Faeroes, only to return with broken plating, twisted frames, rivets sheered off and even her keel bent. This made necessary a weary stay in dock, during which new stiffening was added; and after that came more weeks of exacting trials.

As with every warship built, many changes had intervened between the approval of her design and the hoisting of her commissioning pendant. Three years and more of war had taught many lessons; many marvellous devices had been evolved and were now essential to a modern ship. New metal and new equipment added tons to *Iroquois'* original displacement; compelled new measures of counterbalancing. Guns, asdic, radar, wireless and electrical equipment never planned by the original designers came on board.

The ship emerged at last as a more powerful weapon than the one originally envisaged by the designers. She mounted six 4.7 guns in twin mountings, a pair of 4-inch high angle guns for use against aircraft, six oerlikons, a quadruple two-pounder pompom and four torpedo tubes. Not only did she have double the fire power of earlier destroyers; but her main armament included all the newest features of modern, radar-controlled naval gunnery.

She had entered upon the months of alterations, trials and training—the first anxious, irritating, exacting period of her life—with a Canadian complement of fifteen officers and 239 men, which had almost immediately to be increased. Only a fraction of this company was made up of experienced destroyer men. The majority had been drafted from Canada; from corvettes, Bangor minesweepers and smaller ships, and in many cases direct from training bases.

Even if *Iroquois* had been fully seasoned and shaken down, these new men would have found the stricter discipline and the more exacting requirements of service in a larger ship irksome enough. At it was, the long series of trials, alterations, additions, repairs and new trials gave a continually unsettled atmosphere to their life. Changes in the ship's structure demanded changes in living quarters, while new equipment required new men to operate it. More newcomers from far-off Canada had to be crowded in. Delay, discomfort and frustration were the keynote for December of 1942, and for January, February and March of 1943. It must have seemed that *Iroquois* would never finally get to sea, never train those handsome new guns on an actual enemy. In the meantime, life was a monotony of rigorous routine, storm-battered days in the North Sea on trials or short patrols, interspersed only by a drearier monotony of time ashore at wind-blown, cheerless Scapa, where all seems devised for the welfare of ships and the discomfort of men.

To those long-experienced and wise in the ways of ships, none of this was more than incidental and routine; a process of settling down and shaking in. For *Iroquois'* company it was a dreary nightmare, wearing out the first enthusiasm of green men, and snapping the nerves of the experienced who had to carry most of the load and often do double duty in place of their half-trained charges. When the mechanical problems of the ship began to be ironed out, battle training followed, as harsh and rigorous as the demands of actual warfare—its severity sharpened, it appears, by a captain who drove himself to exhaustion and exhibited more force than tact toward his crew. *Iroquois* was neither a thoroughly worked-up nor a thoroughly happy ship when she went south from Scapa in May to begin operations as a member of the destroyer force based on Plymouth.

Athabaskan, the second Canadian Tribal, was commissioned on February 3, and arrived at Scapa a little later. Although she, too, had her troubles, much had been learned from *Iroquois* both in the matter of the ship and the personnel; and her alterations, work-ups and trials proceeded at a less hectic tempo. After a first operation in June, which took her to the far northern island of Spitzbergen with a British force relieving the garrison there, she went south to team up with *Iroquois* at Plymouth.

There was much action in the waters south from Plymouth; and the Canadians had not long to wait for it. On July 9, *Iroquois* sailed as part of the escort for a troop convoy bound for Gibraltar. The troop carriers were the liners *Duchess of York, California* and *Port Fairy;* and superstitious Canadians who remembered the latter ship's association with the sinking of *Margaree* three years before might have seen an ill omen in her presence. By July 11 the convoy was steaming about three hundred miles off the coast of Portugal in clear, cloudless weather. A Focke-Wulf reconnaissance plane appeared overhead at eight-thirty in the evening, shadowing beyond gun range. Half an hour later two more Focke-Wulfs joined the first, and the three aircraft began wheeling into position for attack.

The tentative, long-range gunfire of the escorts and the liners became a hot barrage as the first plane swept in, coming down sun and down wind for *Duchess of York*. Undeterred, the German roared low over the liner, hitting her with two bombs and setting her furiously ablaze. Four minutes later bombs from the second plane fell on *California;* and the liner began to settle as streamers of smoke and flame rose above her. The third aircraft had selected *Port Fairy* for her target; and was already close overhead. The falling bombs missed by a narrow margin; but by the time the explosions had subsided the first plane was over *Duchess of York* again, trying to finish her off. The two others now singled out *Iroquois*, but the destroyer's gunners had the situation in hand. The barrage from the 4-inch and pompom guns was too much for the first plane and it turned away. The second finished its run-in, but dropped its bombs harmlessly in the water two hundred yards astern.

The failure of the attack on *Iroquois* marked the end of the action; but both *Duchess of York* and *California* were hopelessly ablaze. The undamaged *Port Fairy* was sent on to Casablanca with one of the British escort ships. Two other British ships, *Moyola* and *Douglas,* closed the burning liners and took off troops, while *Iroquois* circled the area on watch for submarines. When she was satisfied that there was no immediate danger from underwater, *Iroquois* closed *Duchess of York* and began to embark survivors. Altogether, she crammed several hundred men into her bunks, messdecks, passages and gangways and loaded the rest, to a total of 628, onto her upper decks. Between the three escorts, all but fifty-seven of the men in the two bombed ships were saved. At 1.35 in the morning, with rescue work completed, the blazing wrecks of the liners were sunk by torpedo. *Iroquois*, in company with the two British escorts, set off for Plymouth; while her crew did what they could for the injured among the multitude of survivors occupying their quarters.

It was, perhaps, unfortunate that on the way back to Plymouth *Iroquois* picked up three survivors, one of them an officer, from a German submarine which had been sunk the day before. The officer's water-soaked jacket was taken, at his request, to be laundered; and when it was returned to him in Plymouth he raised loud complaints over the fact that one of the badges was missing.

He was quite justified. The hand of a souvenir hunter had undoubtedly violated the provisions of the Geneva convention, of which the Germans have an accurate theoretical knowledge. The niceties of war demanded that *Iroquois'* captain should take measures to recover the badge and punish the man who had scalped it. Nor was the matter, perhaps, quite so small as it seemed. The unofficial confiscation or, just as frequently, the unofficial bestowal of prisoners' papers, wallets, photographs and small effects of every kind was a plague not only for ships' officers but for Intelligence officers who knew that material disappeared from which they could glean much useful information.

Nevertheless, the stringency of the measure adopted by the captain of *Iroquois* created a minor but unpleasant incident. To a ship's company which had performed well at sea and in battle, which had gone through an exhausting night of rescue work and a most uncomfortable journey to Plymouth, and which was expecting more action almost immediately, he announced that all leave would be stopped until the missing badge was produced.

Time ashore is precious to a sailor, and the ships' company received the edict with resentment. It was taken as the culmination of a long series of unnecessary severities; and the evidence seems to indicate that the men did have grounds for complaint. On the other hand it might, in fairness, have been remembered that the trials of Scapa, the strain of the air-sea battle off Portugal and all the abrasive worries of taking a new and untried ship into action had fallen most heavily upon the captain. At any rate, after several days of simmering discontent during which no badge made its appearance, all the crew below the rating of leading hand refused duty on the morning of July 19, just as the ship was preparing to sail on a new mission.

The Biscay Sweeps

It was a situation discreditable to everyone concerned; and it was resolved not too happily when the captain, on receipt of the news, collapsed with a heart attack and had to be taken ashore. Nothing in naval law or naval tradition could justify the men's action in time of war; and it might have called down serious consequences upon them. Shore authorities, however, intervened with a considerable measure of the common sense which had not been apparent earlier. The first lieutenant was placed in temporary command; and under him and later under a new commanding officer the crew went about their duties in an exemplary fashion.

The new mission on which the ship sailed that evening with *Athabaskan* and the Polish destroyer *Orkan*, was one of the series of sweeps now in progress against enemy submarines and surface shipping in the Bay of Biscay. The sweeps were contributing mightily to the victory along the Atlantic convoy routes which marked that triumphant summer of 1943; and they were doing much more than that. By attacking the coastal convoys which supplied German garrisons from Bordeaux to Brest they were sealing the enemy's front by sea, forcing his supply traffic back onto the land, making him ever more dependant on the network of French roads and railways, which were to be shattered in their turn by the growing might of Allied air power. Over the Biscay waters by day, Liberators, Halifaxes, Wellingtons, Hampdens, Sunderlands, Beaufighters and Mosquitoes patrolled the air, locating and attacking submarines and surface ships, and fighting off enemy aircraft. By night Catalinas, Wellingtons and other heavy planes, equipped with new and very efficient radar and with powerful searchlights, maintained the watch.

Closely co-operating with the air squadrons were the surface ships, ranging in strong patrols from Ushant to Cape Finisterre. Ships of the support groups were there, as were destroyers from Plymouth; and standing well to seaward of them were cruisers, ready to intervene if the enemy's powerful Narvik and Elbing class destroyers should sally out in strength from the French ports.

The patrol which began on the evening of the 19th for *Athabaskan, Iroquois* and *Orkan* was comparatively uneventful. The ships fought off one attack by Focke-Wulf bombers, recovered survivors from two sunken submarines, and took part in the distasteful but necessary work of driving Spanish fishing craft from the waters of the Bay. It was strongly suspected that the fishermen sometimes acted as eyes for German submarines, and standing orders were that all such craft were to be sunk after the crews had been taken off. At the conclusion of the five-day mission the two Canadian Tribals temporarily parted company; *Iroquois* going to Scapa for service with the Home Fleet while *Athabaskan* remained in Plymouth.

One of the support groups co-operating with the destroyer patrols from Plymouth comprised the British frigates *Nene* and *Tweed,* with three Canadian corvettes, *Edmundston, Calgary* and *Snowberry.* Since June the ships of this group had spent seventy-five per cent of their time at sea, either in the Atlantic or the Bay of Biscay. They were at sea on August 25, carrying out a patrol which had begun three days before off the northwest corner of Spain between Cape Ortegal and Cape Villano. There had been frequent sightings of enemy reconnaissance planes; but no major incident occurred until the early afternoon, when an American Liberator passed overhead making for Gibraltar and flashed the curt message, "Twenty-one enemy planes heading this way." Twelve minutes later fourteen slender-bodied Dorniers and seven JU88 dive bombers flying at a height of four thousand feet appeared ahead of the ships.

The eyes behind the binoculars fixed on the approaching planes may or may not have noted something peculiar about the under-bodies of the Dorniers. In any case, there was no time to speculate as to its nature. The aricraft, splitting up into groups of three, were forming for attack; and the ships prepared for dive-bombing from ahead. Suddenly the Germans altered course and swung far out on the starboard beam of the convoy. The support group re-disposed itself to meet a low-level attack from beam on, but this did not develop either. The JU88's seemed to be acting as escorts, while the Dorniers were behaving in rather an unusual fashion. For a few minutes they ran on a parallel course with the ships. Then they suddenly swung at right angles, bore down toward their targets, and from beneath the fuselage of each plane a small, winged glider shot forward about two hundred feet, leaving a trail of white vapour.

As the barrage from the ships' guns rose to full intensity, the gliders banked over and shot downward at a speed of nearly four hundred miles an hour. It was apparent from the Allied bridges that the uncanny new weapons were controlled by the Dorniers above, and they seemed to be speeding relentlessly for the ships. They were the first of the famous glider bombs—"Chase Me Charlies," as a British yeoman of signals nicknamed them on the day of their appearance.

Participation in the debut of the new weapon was not a pleasant experience; but it had its brighter side in the fact that the German pilots were not yet entirely proficient. All the bombs from the first attack splashed into the water, scoring only two near misses. Gunfire against the missiles had not been particularly effective, as they made very difficult targets; but the ships' evasive action had been both skillful and enthusiastic. At the appearance of the gliders, *Nene*, the senior British ship, had hoisted the signal, "Take individual avoiding action." A little later, weaving and dodging to her utmost capacity, she had queried *Snowberry*, "What is your best speed?"

"Fifteen knots," was the answer; drawing the retort from *Nene*: "Don't give us that; we're doing eighteen and we can't shake you." A later report from *Snowberry's* engineer officer revealed that he had coaxed "ten more revolutions out of the old ice-cream freezer." The reported number of planes had grown to fifty by the time it reached the engine room, and he had considered that a special effort was called for.

Twenty Dorniers returned to the attack on the 27th and had better luck. A little to seaward of the support group on that morning *Athabaskan* was in company with the British frigates *Jed* and *Rother*, and the British sloop *Egret*, which was senior ship. Enemy planes had been shadowing since dawn, and reports of the action of the 25th had put all ships particularly on the alert. At twelve-thirty in the afternoon, while the group was steaming in line abreast, each ship separated from the other by about two miles, a British plane reported enemy aircraft approaching from the north. A few minutes later *Grenville's* radar picked up the planes at a range of twenty-five miles; and as the ships went to action stations the Germans came in sight and in range.

Athabaskan opened fire first, but a group of five Dorniers came in at her through a heavy barrage to release their new bombs. The gliders shot downward at the weaving ship and one, controlled by more skillful hands this time, was dead on line all the way. It struck the destroyer with shattering impact, passed clean through the hull below the bridge, and exploded when it was six feet clear of the side. Less than two minutes later *Egret*, two miles from *Athabaskan*, was squarely hit and disappeared in a great pall of smoke and cordite fumes.

As *Athabaskan* meanwhile coasted to a stop, two more of the original five planes which had run in on her let go their bombs. All missed, but the destroyer was now completely hidden from the other ships by steam and smoke. Her forepart was wrecked, five of her men were killed and twelve wounded. Many large holes had been knocked in her sides. She was heavily afire, and the central control system for her guns had been knocked out. Nevertheless as she lay dead on the water her after guns remained steadily in action. In three or four minutes the forward turrets were also cleared and more gun flashes began to lift above the smoke, providing evidence for the other ships that *Athabaskan* was still afloat.

With the loss of *Egret*, the duties of senior ship passed to *Athabaskan*. As the last of the Dorniers withdrew she signalled to *Grenville*, asking the British destroyer to take over as senior officer, since her own radar and signalling equipment was knocked out and she was in serious danger. *Grenville* stood by to assist while *Athabaskan's* damage control parties fought down the fires; then screened her as she limped away from the area, working up slowly toward a speed of fifteen knots. *Athabaskan's* commanding officer had brought *Saguenay* in from her torpedoing in 1940; and he and his ship's company proved equally determined and resourceful on this occasion. He was given the option of taking the ship either to nearby Gibraltar or to Plymouth; and decided on Plymouth as the port where repairs could be made most quickly. It meant going alone, since no other ships of the group could be spared from patrol of the area to provide a screen.

The four-day voyage was an anxious one, through waters where the German Air Force was still strong and where there was a good chance of encountering enemy destroyers. Apart from the danger of attack, which would almost certainly have been fatal, incessant effort was required merely to keep the ship under way. At noon on the 28th she came to a dead stop just as seven unidentified vessels appeared hull down on the starboard beam. Fortunately they proved to be ships of a small British convoy, and in another hour *Athabaskan* was under way again. Twice more during the next two days and nights the ship came to a stop, but each time her weary engine-room company got her in motion again. On the afternoon of the 30th three British destroyers hove in sight, sent as an escort; and *Athabaskan* made the last six hours of her journey with something of a flourish, working up to a speed of seventeen knots.

The ship was not to see action again until December when, with her damage repaired, she sailed for Scapa. There she found *Iroquois* and two more newly arrived Canadian Tribals, *Huron* and *Haida*. *Iroquois* had already seen much of the northern waters; and the other three were to join her with British forces in sweeps along the Norwegian coast and in escorting convoys to Murmansk. Of all these northern trips, where action against aircraft and submarines was a matter of routine, the most exciting and fruitful came on December 26 when the four Canadian destroyers were part of the screening force for the Russia convoy which lured the German battleship *Scharnhorst* to her death.

The Bay of Biscay continued to be a scene of violent action through the fall and winter of 1943. The U-boats were browbeaten but not subdued. The heavily escorted German convoys fought stubbornly to make their way up and down the French coast. The glider bomb of the *Luftwaffe* was a nasty, harrying weapon against the allied ships. *Prince Robert*, now converted into an anti-aircraft cruiser, operating from Gibraltar in support of fast troop convoys, had several exciting brushes with the new weapon; and in November the British frigate *Nene* and the corvettes *Calgary* and *Snowberry* of a Canadian support group grappled successfully with an older enemy.

On the night of November 21 the ships of the group were about five hundred miles west of Cape Finisterre, moving to the support of a convoy which had been shadowed by U-boats and attacked with glider bombs. *Nene* gained a radar contact which she recognized as a surfaced U-boat, and set off in pursuit through the darkness. *Calgary* joined in and, after a hot chase, starshell revealed the enemy just in range. Both ships opened fire at a distance of two miles and a hit was seen on the U-boat's casing. The German replied with a torpedo which *Nene* avoided, and then he dived.

Calgary and *Nene* attacked for an hour or so without apparent result. When *Snowberry* came up, she gained a good asdic contact, and her depth charges brought an underwater explosion which seemed more promising. Shortly afterward *Nene* gained a perfect echo, ran in on it, and dropped a double pattern of twenty charges. Out of the huge disturbance in the water emerged the conning tower of the submarine, on the starboard bow of *Snowberry*. It dipped beneath the surface for a moment, then rose again, and the full length of the German craft was revealed in the glaring light of starshell.

Under a hail of fire, the boat crawled drunkenly forward at a bare three knots. Hits from 4-inch guns, 2-pounders, oerlikons and Lewis guns crashed into her, opened holes in her conning tower and casing and swept away the men on deck who were trying to reach her gun. In a few minutes she began to drag downward by the stern. Then her crew were seen leaping for the water and the ships checked fire. In a few more minutes the U-boat had disappeared and her bedraggled supermen were being hauled from the water. *Snowberry's* commanding officer reported that his batch of survivors provided "no evidence to make us believe that they were members of the Master Race."

In addition to aircraft and submarines, German destroyers figured largely in many Biscay actions. For the most part they operated in groups of two or three, escorting the more important convoys or carrying out various hit-and-run missions. In the late days of December, however, an effort made in force brought them a drubbing from two British cruisers, one of which was commanded by Captain H. T. W. Grant, the Canadian officer who was later to be Vice-Admiral and Chief of the Naval Staff.

On the morning of December 26, a fast German merchantman, a blockade runner with cargo from Japan, was about five hundred miles west-northwest of Cape Finisterre, inward bound for one of the French Biscay ports. Eleven German destroyers put out from Brest and Bordeaux to escort her in. Five of the destroyers were of the Narvik class, mounting five 5.9-inch guns, faster and more powerful than Tribals. The other six were Elbings, smaller ships with a main armament of four 4.1-inch guns. By the 27th they were well out of the Bay, steaming in two columns for their rendezvous with the blockade runner.

They were not to meet her, and the rendezvous which awaited them was of a different kind. The blockade runner, apparently unknown to the destroyers, was sunk by aircraft

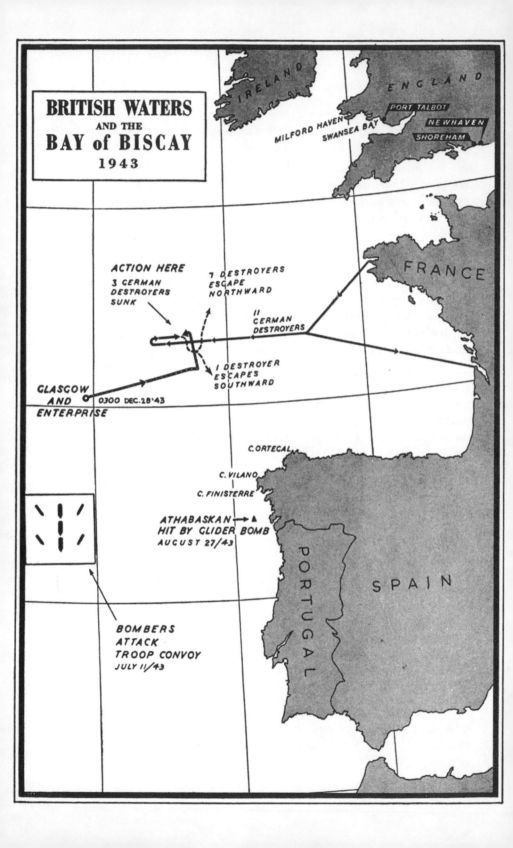

BRITISH WATERS
AND THE
BAY of BISCAY
1943

IRELAND

ENGLAND

PORT TALBOT

MILFORD HAVEN
SWANSEA BAY

NEWHAVEN
SHOREHAM

FRANCE

ACTION HERE
3 GERMAN
DESTROYERS
SUNK

7 DESTROYERS
ESCAPE
NORTHWARD

11 GERMAN
DESTROYERS

1 DESTROYER
ESCAPES
SOUTHWARD

GLASGOW
AND
ENTERPRISE

0300 DEC. 28 '43

C. ORTECAL

C. VILANO

C. FINISTERRE

ATHABASKAN →
HIT BY GLIDER BOMB
AUGUST 27/43

PORTUGAL

SPAIN

BOMBERS
ATTACK
TROOP CONVOY
JULY 11/43

of Coastal Command at around four o'clock on the afternoon of the 27th, while still well to the west of her rendezvous. The German destroyers en route to meet her had been reported by other aircraft, and the Admiralty was determined that as few as possible should get back.

Glasgow and *Enterprise*, the latter ship commanded by Captain Grant, were ordered to rendezvous at a point some three hundred miles northwest of Cape Finisterre, from which position it was hoped that they could cut the Germans off from base. The two cruisers joined at three o'clock on the morning of the 28th, and set off at high speed on an intercepting course designed to bring them between the enemy and the French ports from which he had set out.

Daybreak of the 28th found the Germans still steaming west, ignorant of the fact that their blockade-runner was sunk and that they themselves were now the quarry. They were moving seaward on their westerly course, while the British ships, some forty-five miles to the south of them, were steering almost due east. By a little after nine in the morning the cruisers, now south of the Germans, altered to the northwest in order to place themselves between the enemy and his base.

Although the weather was rough, both German and Allied aircraft were overhead; and one of the enemy planes must have reported the movements of the cruisers. At eleven o'clock, apparently on orders from German Naval Command, the destroyers reversed their course and turned back toward the French coast.

They had waited too long. *Glasgow* and *Enterprise* were now between them and the land; and at thirteen minutes after one the cruisers broke out their battle ensigns. Twenty-five minutes later the first of the German ships appeared, hull down on the western horizon. At 1.46 *Glasgow* opened fire at a range of eighteen thousand yards; and two minutes later, at twenty thousand yards range, the first salvoes from *Enterprise* went arching through the gloomy afternoon.

The German destroyers outweighed the cruisers in total fire power by about five to two, and for a time they seemed determined to make a fight of it. Throwing out a profusion of smoke floats, they came straight on, and as the range closed, the straddling salvoes which splashed about *Glasgow* and *Enterprise* demonstrated the respectable quality of German naval gunnery. The cruisers, for their part, found the large number of targets almost embarrassing, and ranging difficult to maintain on any one ship.

The action developed with the opponents roughly paralleling each other on a southeasterly course. *Glasgow*, the larger of the two cruisers, made the best going of it in the heavy seas, and was drawing ahead. The destroyers were taking punishment, but the heavy smoke about them made it difficult to estimate the damage and their gunfire continued accurate. German planes had also arrived overhead. At twenty-five minutes after two a glider bomb winged down and crashed into the sea near *Glasgow*. Two minutes later *Enterprise* received a light hit from a German shell, and then a second glider bomb sent up a huge explosion in the sea four hundred yards on her port quarter.

The cruisers had little difficulty in fighting off the aircraft, however, and their fire against the destroyers continued unabated. The Germans now altered away and set off northward, while *Enterprise* ran in to head them off. Through the smoke she observed a hit on a destroyer; then she saw the destroyer come to a stop. Drawing nearer she engaged two of the other destroyers and was met with heavy and accurate fire which straddled her consistently; one shell carrying away her aerial. The wreathing clouds of smoke about the Germans, the high seas and the multiplicity of targets were still making it difficult for the cruisers to observe the full effect of their fire except when, as *Enterprise's* gunnery officer mildly describes it, "structural alteration took place; e.g. in the case of the destroyer whose funnel was shot away and went over the side."

In a few more minutes, seven of the destroyers abandoned the action and turned off to the north. Four remained in the area, of which one, heavily hit, was limping away behind a smoke screen. Another was stopped; the third was still in action with *Glasgow;* and *Enterprise* was engaging the fourth. The latter two went down by four o'clock and the ship which had stopped was finished off a little later. With darkness coming on and ammunition running low, the cruisers gave up pursuit of the ship which had made off behind smoke. It was known to be heavily damaged, and among the seven which had made their escape earlier many hits had been scored. The action was the largest effort made by enemy destroyers during the latter part of 1943. It had been largely involuntary, and its results could scarcely have been encouraging to the German High Command.

Biscay operations in their earlier stages had smashed the U-boat flotillas as they set out for the Atlantic, and had put the finishing touches to victory on the convoy routes. More and more, in the later phase, they were concentrated on the destruction of German coastal shipping, closing the seaward fingers of the stranglehold by which enemy garrisons along the west coast of France would eventually be throttled. They were making it necessary to send a large part of the supplies for the German-held Channel ports and the Channel defence areas by the bombed and over-burdened French railways. They were looking toward the still later phase when they would mount an iron guard upon the southerly and westerly entrance to the narrow water across which the fleets of the European invasion must pass.

The armies for that invasion were gathering in England. Many of their divisions were already hardened, trained and ready. Weapons, stores and supplies were accumulating in enormous volume, in incredible variety. Great fleets of Allied bombers were now battering at German industries, cities and strategic centres; at the country's brain, nerve centres and heart. The war seemed to be moving toward its climax, as indeed it was. Yet the grand diversion, the roundabout closing in from the south which had begun with Operation Torch on November 8, 1942, was still in progress; had still to reach the point where it could mesh and move forward as an integral part of the final assault. It had advanced through several phases during the mid-months of 1943, and in some of those phases the landing craft flotillas of the Canadian navy had again played a part.

About the middle of March 1943 several large convoys left British ports for Suez. The end of the North African campaign was coming in sight, and the next step would be the forcing of a passage to the Italian mainland. Sicily lay between North Africa and Italy, separated from the toe of the boot only by the narrow Straits of Messina; and Sicily was chosen by Allied planners as the next step toward Rome.

The convoys, which were to round Africa and come up through the Red Sea to Suez and Port Said at the eastern entrance to the Mediterranean, carried the combined operations flotillas and a portion of the troops for the landings on Sicily; and among them were the 55th and 61st Canadian Flotillas of LCA's—assault landing craft. Later convoys were to carry the 80th and 81st Canadian Flotillas of larger landing craft—LCM's—for the ferrying of vehicles and heavier stores. Together, the Canadian personnel manning these flotillas totalled about 400 men, while another 250 Canadians served in British landing-craft flotillas or in the support ships. They were a microscopic proportion of a force which consisted in all of 2,755 transports, escorts and landing craft of many kinds; yet they were to be an important part of the ferrying forces at the beaches where they were used, and their performance was to be of a high order.

Far from Sicily, as the battle for Tunisia swept on to its conclusion, the men of the landing-craft flotillas trained under the broiling sun of Suez. Large-scale amphibious exercises, as tough and realistic as possible, ironed out difficulties remembered from the Torch landings, tested the men and the craft to their limits, gave rise to excited speculation as to what actual coast resembled the "dummy" beaches against which the exercises were directed.

On July 4 all combined-operations officers were called together for final instructions, and on July 5 the assault convoys sailed from Port Said for a rendezvous position south of Malta. On the 9th the rendezvous was reached, and to the men of the 55th and 61st assault landing-craft flotillas, watching from the decks of the landing ships *Strathnaver* and *Otranto,* it seemed that every horizon was crowded with arriving convoys. At sea in the western Mediterranean and gathering at the rendezvous, were sixteen escorted convoys and two large naval covering forces of battleships, cruisers, aircraft carriers and destroyers.

At the rendezvous position the convoys assembling from the eastern and western Mediterranean divided into two great forces which passed up on either side of Malta. The Western Task Force carried the American Seventh Army which was to land along the southwest coast on a front extending southward from Licata. The Eastern Task Force carried the British Eighth Army, which included the First Canadian Division and the First Canadian Army Tank Brigade. It was to land along a two-corps front extending from the western side of the Pachino Peninsula around northeastward as far as Syracuse. Canadian soldiers and sailors, for this operation, were not to have the satisfaction of working together. The Canadian Division was to drive in on the western side of the Pachino peninsula, carried in British landing craft. The Canadian landing craft flotillas were a part of the subdivision of the Eastern Task Force which was to land British troops on the eastern side of the peninsula, a little to the north of Pachino itself.

Toward evening on the 9th the Eastern Task Force approached the shores of Sicily, and the summit of Mount Aetna loomed through a haze. The weather, which had been reasonably fine in the morning, was worsening steadily. The wind had risen in force, and heavy seas breaking over the wallowing ships gave promise of lashing surf on the beaches. For a time it was thought that the whole operation would have to be postponed, but after darkness it was decided to continue in the hope of better weather with dawn.

Midnight brought the steady thunder of transport planes, passing over to land parachute troops inland. Half an hour later the assault convoy which included *Otranto* and *Strathnaver* arrived at its position seven miles off the coast above Pachino. Rolling in the heavy swell, the landing ships stopped their engines. Troops loaded down with battle equipment came up from the holds and began to climb into the landing craft hanging at the davits, a full platoon to each craft.

One by one, as the platoons settled into their places, the swaying assault craft were lowered forty feet to the water below. Motors began sputtering; the craft moved away from the ships and formed up for the run to shore. It had been planned to have Fairmile motor launches lead each flotilla separately to the assault point; but as only one Fairmile arrived it was necessary for the 55th Flotilla to take station on the 61st which followed directly behind the launch.

At fifteen minutes past one the wavering columns of flat-bottomed craft set off for the beach seven miles away. The night was black and the sea was very rough. It was windy, wet and cold. The soldiers huddling against the gunwales became sea-sick; buckets came freely into use. Even some of the naval stokers, working throttles amid the fumes of their torrid little engine rooms, began to feel the effects. Seas washing over the side called for constant bailing. Coxswains and officers, peering ahead through the darkness, found it difficult to pick out the landmarks which had been shown to them on the charts before the operation began. Navigation of the craft, always difficult, became trebly so in the rough weather, with the southerly set of the water off the coast increased by the force of the wind. A searchlight knifed out from land, swung toward the craft, and illumined every man's face in a white glare. Then it swept on, apparently having revealed nothing to the watchers ashore.

As the flights came nearer in they were unable to locate their beaches. Estimating that they had drifted a bit too far to the south, they turned and ran northward, paralleling the coast. A red flare, apparently dropped by a plane, blazed up; and in its light the exact landing place for the first wave of the flotilla was revealed.

Abreast of each other the craft moved in. As they felt the scrape of sand along their bottoms, the ramps at the front went down and the troops stepped ashore, wet and miserable, crouching in anticipation of a blaze of fire. Only silence greeted them; and they fanned out and made for their objectives. The empty landing craft began to withdraw; and it was not until they were again moving seaward that a single machine gun opened up to spatter the water about them.

The second wave of landing craft found their sector of beach protected by a breakwater which they had to skirt under light fire. As they rounded the breakwater and turned in to shore the fire grew a little heavier; but they grounded without casualties on the rocky beach. The ramps went down; the bark of orders began amid the whistle and spatter of machine gun bullets, and, wet, whey-faced, seasick soldiers, bending under their heavy battle gear, stumbling along decks slimy with sea water, fuel oil and their own vomit, set off unheroically on a historic campaign. Sailors, equally wet, half as miserable, and certainly not envying their "pongo" brothers, made haste to get their craft back to the older element.

Another wave of assault landing-craft was standing off shore with parties of engineers whose work would be to clear mines when the beaches were secured. Some fire from machine-guns and howitzers was falling unpleasantly near; but the main sounds of battle were retreating inland. It seemed clear that the beaches had been gained with little resistance, and the engineers and the landing craft men began to watch impatiently for the Verey light signals from shore which would call them in. The defenders were making things difficult by setting off their own flares of every colour, but at last the authentic signal came and the craft raced in to beach. Fire from shore grew sharper and was unpleasantly accurate, but once again no casualties resulted. By

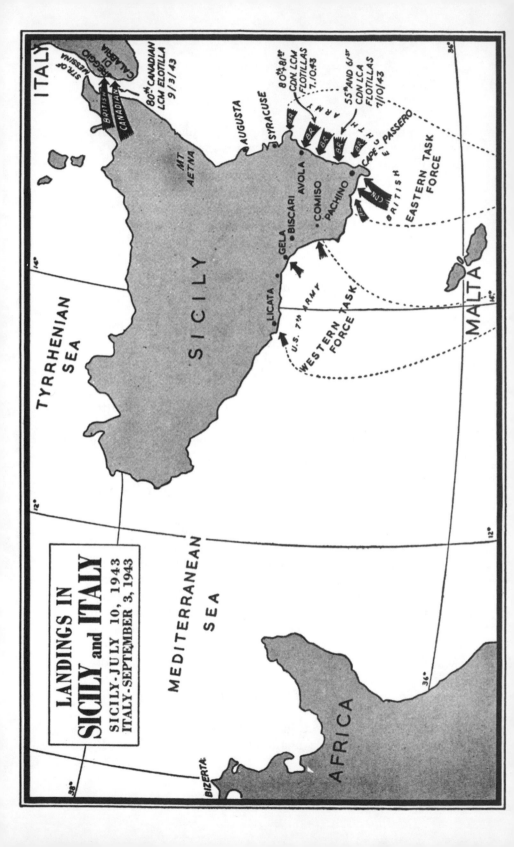

LANDINGS IN
SICILY and **ITALY**
SICILY-JULY 10, 1943
ITALY-SEPTEMBER 3, 1943

ITALY

STR. OF MESSINA

REGGIO DI CALABRIA

CALABRIA

BRITISH

CANADIAN

80ᵗʰ CANADIAN LCM FLOTILLA 9/3/43

MT. AETNA

AUGUSTA

SYRACUSE

80ᵗʰ 8ᵗʰ CDN LCM FLOTILLAS 7.10.43

8ᵗʰ ARMY

BR.

BR.

BISCARI

AVOLA

GELA

COMISO

PACHINO

55ᵗʰ AND 61ˢᵗ CDN LCA FLOTILLAS 7/10/43

8ᵗʰ ARMY

BR.

BR.

CAPE EL PASSERO

BRITISH

CDN.

EASTERN TASK FORCE

BRIT.

LICATA

U.S. 7ᵗʰ ARMY

WESTERN TASK FORCE

MALTA

TYRRHENIAN
SEA

SICILY

MEDITERRANEAN
SEA

AFRICA

BIZERTA

14°

12°

16°

38°

36°

12°

36°

four-thirty in the morning, all the assault landings had been made. The beaches were securely held; mine clearing was in progress. It remained only to ferry the reinforcement troops ashore and empty the transports so that they could move away from the beaches before enemy aircraft arrived.

Sunrise came at three minutes before six, and promptly at six a JU 88 put in an appearance. A little later two Messerschmitts swept down to strafe the ships with cannon fire. They were ineffectual, however, and too late. Reinforcements were streaming shoreward in uninterrupted processions of landing craft, and by two o'clock in the afternoon the assault flotillas had done their work. They were hoisted back aboard the landing ships; and the convoy, much relieved to be out of the area, sailed for Malta. In less than twelve hours the two Canadian flotillas had landed two-thirds of a brigade of British troops with their essential supplies and gear. They had suffered no casualties.

Following the assault convoys and moving into station off the beaches even before the first arrivals withdrew, came ships with the heavier mechanized equipment and supplies for depots to be established inland. Vessels carrying the larger landing craft came with them; and two of these carried the 80th and 81st Canadian LCM Flotillas which were to land near Avola. The LCM's began their work four hours after the LCA's; but instead of finishing in twelve hours they were to be occupied for some ten weeks, first on Sicily and then on the Italian mainland.

The first of the LCM's were lowered from their parent ships at about five-thirty on the morning of the assault, a few minutes before sunrise. Loaded with vehicles and stores, they steered in toward beaches now securely held; deposited their freight, and turned back for more. For the first few hours there was no interruption to the ordered chaos of the build-up. Transports stood off the coast, each with its identification number placarded on its side. Landing craft ran in under their high sides, loaded with feverish haste and put off to unload at the same tempo ashore, satisfying the most urgent of the hand-to-mouth requirements.

At one point gasoline would be required to get vehicles moving inland; at another troops would be running short of ammunition. Headquarters units would require more signalling equipment; troops held up by resistance on the forward fringes might need a howitzer to break through. The landing craft were diverted from ship to ship and from point to point along the beaches to meet each need as it developed. This was the preliminary phase of the work, preceding the stage when shore depots would be established and stored; and it had to be got over with in a hurry before enemy aircraft arrived.

The comparative quiet was broken at nine o'clock in the morning. An enemy bomber came in very fast and dropped a stick of bombs along a stretch of shoreline occupied by two British vessels and by the Canadian landing craft carrying the senior officer of the 80th Flotilla. The smaller British vessel, a tank landing craft, was squarely hit and blown to pieces. The other British ship was heavily damaged, and every man on her bridge was killed. The Canadian craft, well up on the beach with some of her men ashore nearby, had a miraculous escape. The force of the explosions knocked down the men on the beach, and the flotilla officer was blown back into the well deck of his ship; but no one was injured. Considerably dazed, but marvelling at their luck, the men recovered and went to the assistance of the British merchantman, helping to take off her wounded and transfer them to a hospital ship.

Two hours later a series of heavier raids began. Throughout the night and for the next forty-eight hours the attempted blitz rose to a total of twenty-three separate raids, costing the invasion forces five merchantmen and a hospital ship. The decline of the *Luftwaffe's* efforts was rapid, however. Air cover from Malta began to show its murderous effectiveness; and by the third day planes flying from captured Sicilian bases were adding their strength to the Allied umbrella.

During the four weeks that followed, the work of landing stores and reinforcements settled down into a routine for the craft of the 80th and 81st flotillas. It was a grinding routine, and it was never free from danger. Every type of cargo had to come ashore in their craft: sixteen-ton tanks, heavy trucks, tiers of cans of high-octane gasoline, ammunition, army rations, small arms, mortars. Heavy seas often made both the run-ins and the work of loading and unloading very difficult. The huge requirements of the armies put heavy pressure on the ferry system and for the first forty-eight hours of the operation every man remained on the job without rest. Even after that, the best arrangement that could be worked out was a routine of forty-eight hours on for twenty-four hours off.

The Canadian flotillas formed, of course, only a small part of all the flotillas engaged; but wherever they operated the warmly admiring comments of British officers seem to indicate that they were pace-setters. The mechanical aptitude and the loving care which their maintenance parties lavished on the craft gave particular cause to marvel. During eighteen days of continuous work not one craft of the flotilla was out of operation.

The demands of the armies proved higher and the demolitions in Sicilian harbours more inconvenient than had been expected; and landing craft had therefore to be kept longer on the ferry service. This meant a great deal of discomfort for the Canadians, as for all the landing-craft flotillas. The beaches of semi-tropical Sicily in late July and early August were far from being health resorts. Almost every man suffered at one time or another from a variety of disorders which included dysentery, septic scratches, jaundice, sandfly and malarial fever.

The small, amphibious craft were not equipped for life on the beaches. Moreover, their men were now everybody's children and no one's. Their parent landing ships had long since departed. They ferried cargo ashore from every ship that came, but their home was the hot beach, and there their companies had to make what living arrangements they could. Some found accommodation of a sort in an old, disused army camp; and many more had to take shelter in a very dirty and uncomfortable cattle cave. Their food consisted of rations acquired from the army, occasional largesse scrounged from the better-hearted merchant ships, and what they could acquire from an impoverished countryside. The cave-dwelling members of the flotilla had improvised a stove of petrol tins in order to apply some heat to their unsavoury victuals; and one evening the stove blew up. Flames licked back into the cave, igniting another can of petrol and consuming most of the kit bags, hammocks and clothing of the men. About half the personnel of the 80th Flotilla had to get along for the next three months on borrowed gear.

On August 5 operations ceased on the Sicilian beaches; and the two flotillas returned to Malta. After a month of hard work under exceedingly difficult conditions the men were looking forward to a fourteen-day leave which had been promised them, always subject to "exigencies of the service." The news which greeted them on arrival in Malta was, first, that civilian dockworkers were on strike; and secondly, that their craft must be put in condition at once for a landing on the Italian mainland. Twenty-four cranky LCM's, which had been overworked consistently for a month to land 40,959 men, 8,937 vehicles and 40,181 tons of stores, must at once be retuned to concert pitch by the equally over-worked men who had operated them. Complaints were loud, eloquent, sustained and unavailing; but once this routine gesture was over with the Canadians manifested, as always, a peculiar zest for anything mechanical. At the end of two weeks, during which all the fit men of both flotillas worked day and night, they announced to amazed dockyard authorities at Malta that their craft were ready to sail again.

Just before the departure for northern Sicily in preparation for the jump across the Straits of Messina, it was decided that the 81st Flotilla would not be sent. Its craft were not of as recent a type as those of the 80th and would not be as useful in the unfamiliar role of assault landing craft, which was to be the work allotted them. Moreover, a large number of men from the 81st were in hospital with sickness acquired in Sicily. The 80th Flotilla therefore sailed alone from the Great Harbour of Malta on August 27.

On September 1, at one of the assembly points near Messina from which the expedition was to cross, the officers of the flotilla were briefed. Thirty-six hours later they began to embark the Canadians of the Royal 22nd Regiment, the West Nova Scotians, and the Carleton and Yorks. Canadian soldiers and Canadian sailors were operating together at last.

In the early morning darkness of September 3 the loaded craft moved up the strait, close inshore on the Sicilian side, making for their take-off point. Among many ships crowding the narrow waters, *Warspite* and *Valiant* swept by, looming hugely. The wash from the battleships' passing bounced the landing craft like water bugs and sent huge waves over the sides to soak the men. The big ships of the Royal Navy, at that tense, nerve-fraying moment, came in for a heartfelt cursing.

At dawn the armies for the invasion of Italy moved across the six mile strait. *Warspite* and *Valiant* were forgiven their trespass by the men in the landing craft as the navy added to a great barrage put up by artillery firing from Sicily across the strait. Screaming through the half-light overhead, thousands of shells from the artillery of the army and the big naval guns passed above the flotilla. Plumed explosions rose inland as the ramps of the craft went down and the conquerors of Sicily set foot on the Italian mainland. Great transit searchlights from the Sicilian side were cutting through the dim morning to assist navigation; and directing smoke shells were providing some assistance mixed with a good deal of confusion.

For a month after the lightly-opposed Italian landing the 80th Flotilla carried out its familiar routine of ferry work

In Other Waters

The end came with the Italian armistice and a great celebration in which the population of the countryside joined; and after that the word "England" was on every man's lip. The men of the 55th and 61st assault flotillas had long been in the United Kingdom. The 81st was also there. Last of the combined operations units to return to Britain, the men of the 80th Flotilla arrived on October 27.

A little more than two months remained of 1943. In England the men heard cheering news of conditions in the Atlantic and of the war around the world. Good tidings continued to arrive, right up to the destruction of *Scharnhorst* in the closing days of December. Already 1944 was being spoken of as the year of "the invasion," and perhaps the year of decision. The Allied world was girded at last and moving forward in the full tide of its strength and confidence. Yet the bells of the new year ushered in a season of tense foreboding, for the men of Canada as for all men of the warring world. Before the armies now in Italy loomed icy hills fanged with the guns of a desperate and determined enemy. The divisions long trained and ready in England had yet to meet their great and costly test. Canadian airmen knew that the fading *Luftwaffe* had not yet lost its power to sting. The men of the Atlantic escort forces looked forward to a continuance of the weary, four-year-old task, from which the conquest of the U-boats—if it remained a conquest—meant the removal only of the greatest among many perils. For the powerful Tribal destroyers, and the still newer Fleet destroyers which were on the way, there was to be surface combat in the old tradition but with deadlier weapons. And before the men of the landing craft lay other hostile shores.

CHAPTER TEN

Gathering of the Giants

In May of 1945 a Russian war correspondent, entering Berlin and surveying the ruins about him, wrote with something like awe: "It is as if giants with colossal hammers had beaten Hitler's city into the earth." Giants indeed they were; whose strength in the east flowed to them from all of Asia, and in the west from almost every harbour of the world and over almost every sea. There was appalling majesty in the effort called forth to expunge the dream of an Austrian corporal, "that monstrous product of former wrongs and shame."

Operation Overlord was the stately title of the plan which encompassed the share of the western world in the final and total defeat of the *Reich*. Operation Neptune was the seamen's phase of the plan. It embraced, first, the task of landing the armies of liberation on French soil; secondly, the maintenance of their waterborne lines of communication and supply. The direct Canadian contribution of 110 ships and 10,000 men represented approximately four per cent of the total naval strength involved.

The eastward movement and assembly of the fighting vessels began in January of 1944. The flood of cargo moving to the United Kingdom rose also in a long, rhythmic swell through the winter and spring. It rose still higher in June and July, growing with the voracious demands of the armies battling in France; and it did not sensibly decrease until the end of the war.

The cargo moved upon an Atlantic where the allied battle was now truly a defensive one; where the objective had been gained, the bridge established. There remained only the necessity of defending the conquest against an enemy who refused to admit defeat. It was a lesser task than that of earlier years; but it was still not a small one. The sailing of larger convoys at longer intervals had begun late in 1943. Early in 1944 the intervals were opened out again. The number of ships in each convoy continued to increase, until the larger bodies consisted of something like 150 ships which might carry altogether as much as a million tons of supplies.

The walled-in, roofed-over Atlantic was securely held against any threat of a major offensive by the U-boats. Continuous air cover for convoys was now a routine interrupted only by stress of weather. Support groups, although mainly occupied in the waters of Biscay and the near approaches to the British Isles, were available anywhere at short notice. Pending the introduction of some new and startling weapon, the enemy had no longer a chance of throttling the allied lines of supply.

But he might harry them. Guerilla tactics could still impose loss and delay; force the allies to ceaseless vigilance on the convoy routes. A single submarine carrying twenty-one torpedoes was a threat which could not be ignored and which must be met by the provision of many escort ships.

There remained not one but many submarines at sea; and close escort for each convoy was still a necessity. It was equally imperative that the ships for all phases of Operation Neptune should be fitted out and their men trained. From the beginning of 1944, therefore, as many ships withdrew from the convoy routes to the fitting out ports, the remaining ships took on increasing responsibility. Canadian ships as well as British were among the departures; but the proportion of Canadian vessels remaining on escort duty increased steadily. By June of 1944, Canadian ships were providing all the close escort for trade convoys from North America to the United Kingdom and were also furnishing several of the support groups.

The work was routine sentry duty along sea lanes which, in the large view, were now comparatively secure. Yet it was far from being uneventful or free from difficulties. Ships were still lost in the winter and spring of 1944; and men drowned. The large size of the convoys, which might now occupy as much as a hundred square miles of sea, added many difficulties to the work of screening; and although U-Boats came in far smaller packs, or often as lonely outriders, they had still to be dealt with. In each of the months of January, February and April, Canadian ships sank or helped to sink one U-boat. In one week of March they had a large share in the destruction of three. And in May a Canadian warship was sunk by a submarine with heavy loss.

The Canadian corvette *Camrose,* shared credit with the British frigate *Bayntun,* for the January killing; in which heavy depth charge attacks sent a U-boat gurgling to the bottom with no evidence except a vast pool of oil, some bits of wreckage and a uniform cap. On February 24, *Waskesiu,* first of the Canadian frigates, assisted by the British frigate *Nene,* brought a U-boat to the surface after a five-hour hunt and sank it by gunfire. One of the March kills was a combined effort in which the Canadian frigate *Prince Rupert* joined with ships of an American support group, the aircraft carrier *Bogue,* and aircraft of coastal command. Another March attack provided a striking example of the "hunt to exhaustion" which could now be directed against a single U-boat appearing in a comparatively peaceful area.

This marathon hunt—one of the longest of the war for the Canadian navy—occupied thirty-two hours from first contact to kill. Seven ships, five Canadian and two British, were involved; and 291 depth charges carrying a total of 87,300 pounds of high explosive were required to bring a very cagy German to the surface. Fifteen hundred signals passed between the manœuvring ships as they stalked, attacked, waited and attacked again through a day and a night of rough weather.

The involved calculations of depth, bearings, speeds and courses which are inseparable from any U-boat hunt were here at a maximum; and on several occasions the U-boat nearly made its escape. Under the best of conditions, a ship's asdic operator has still to translate and accurately relate the information given him by the beam. The U-boat's course is changing constantly, changing its relation to each of the moving ships. It may alter depth or speed; or it may stop entirely; and in a depth charge attack there is always the anxious interval as the ship approaches and passes over the submarine when asdic contact is lost and the U-boat may defeat all previous calculations by a sudden spurt to change its position. The wilier German captains frequently did this; timing the approach of the attack by the sound of propellers above, and sometimes by the shadow of the ship which they could distinguish through their periscopes from a considerable depth. In the case of this particular attack the usual demands and difficulties were aggravated by rough seas which made for bad asdic conditions. The U-boat remained very deep; and her captain, throughout, showed a full appreciation of the difficulties facing the allied ships, combined with a cool-headed skill in taking advantage of them.

The Canadian destroyer *Gatineau* made first contact with the submerged submarine at about ten o'clock on the morning of March 5, just as she was about to detach from her convoy because of distiller defects. The echo was not particularly good; but *Gatineau* had the courage of her convictions. She signalled *St. Catharines,* the senior ship, that she was onto a good thing. Then she ran in over the position and sent away a pattern of depth charges. The German now proceeded to give first proof of his quality. Moving at a considerable depth, he altered course sharply as the charges were fired, swung round inside the destroyer's turning circle and lost himself under her stern in the disturbance caused by the wake.

St. Catharines, however, had picked up the echo as she approached; and she was closely followed by the corvettes *Chilliwack* and *Fennel,* and the destroyer *Chaudière.* All three ships had detached from the escort group about the convoy. While *Chaudière* and the two corvettes circled the area, carrying out a containing search, *St. Catharines* ran in on her contact and dropped another pattern of charges.

There was no apparent result; nor was an attack by *Chilliwack* half an hour later any more successful. The hopeful preliminaries over with, organization for a sustained "creeping attack" got under way. Through an hour of complicated manœuvering *St. Catharines* jockeyed herself around to a position exactly astern of the U-boat and followed at very slow speed, waiting for him to come onto a reasonably steady course. Then, acting as directing ship, she guided *Gatineau* in. When directly over the U-boat's estimated position *Gatineau* turned herself onto the U-boat's course and dropped a string of 24 single depth charges just ahead of the submarine. *Chilliwack* followed with a similar pattern; but once again the German beneath was too quick for them. He was very deep; the asdic beam reaching out shallowly ahead of the ship lost contact as the range closed, giving the German an opportunity to take avoiding action. With the explosion of the first charge ahead of him he altered sharply to port and put on a brief spurt to get out of the way.

The British destroyer *Icarus* had also been with the convoy; and now, judging that the merchantmen were in no immediate danger, she joined the hunt to relieve *Gatineau*, whose defects compelled her to depart for Londonderry. She had hardly appeared on the scene, however, when the Admiralty signalled that other U-boat transmissions had been heard ahead of the thinly-protected merchant ships. *Icarus* and *Chaudière*, therefore, returned to the convoy, while a British frigate, *Kenilworth Castle*, was detached from a nearby support group to assist the attackers.

Kenilworth Castle joined at about three in the afternoon; and from then until darkness the creeping attacks continued. The sea was rough, asdic conditions were bad, and after each series of explosions there were anxious moments when the elusive echo could not be regained. The enemy was moving very deep, twisting and doubling; taking every advantage of the disturbed water. "Tough league," signalled one corvette ruefully, during the interval following

THE DESTRUCTION OF U-744
MARCH 5-6, 1944

GATINEAU CONTACTS
U-744 1000/5

ST. CATHERINES 1028
CHILLIWACK 1231

GATINEAU
& CHILLIWACK 1236-44
GATINEAU 1305
ICARUS 1357

CHILLIWACK 1231

OPERATION OBSERVANT
GATINEAU, ST. CATHERINES,
CHILLIWACK, CHAUDIERE &
FENNEL

GATINEAU
CHILLIWACK
ST. CATHERINES
FENNEL
ICARUS

CONVOY
HX-280

HX
280

1250/5 KENILWORTH CASTLE JOINS

1400 GATINEAU LEAVES WITH DEFECTS
CHAUDIERE
ICARUS } REJOIN CONVOY

KENILWORTH
CASTLE 1538

GATINEAU 1316
CHILLIWACK 1350
KENILWORTH CASTLE 1458

CHAUDIERE   FENNEL 1642
ST. CATHERINES 1656

KENILWORTH CASTLE 1920
FENNEL   2018
ST. CATHERINES 2029

MIDNIGHT MARCH 5 1944

ST. CATHERINES 0023/6
ST. CATHERINES 0041
FENNEL 0109

0300 ICARUS &
CHAUDIERE
REJOIN

FENNEL 0751
ICARUS 0829

ICARUS 1100
CHAUDIERE 1050
ST. CATHERINES 1013

CHAUDIERE 1004

0730 KENILWORTH CASTLE
LEAVES WITH DEFECTS

N

S

FENNEL   ST. CATHERINES
              CHAUDIERE
CHILLIWACK   ICARUS

1532 U-744 SURFACES

LEGEND

ATTACKS ON U-744

MILES
0 1 2 3 4 5 6 7 8 9 10

an attack, when it seemed that the German had found a gap in the invisible net of the asdic beams.

Contact was regained on each occasion, however. Midnight found the ships manœuvering carefully over a considerable area of sea, burning riding lights to assist in their station keeping. They were now concentrating mainly on keeping in touch with the U-boat. Eventually his batteries and his oxygen would give out and he would be forced to surface. The main thing was not to let him do it at night when he would have a chance of outrunning his pursuers. All ships had streamed the cat gear; a later variant of the foxer device against acoustic torpedoes. Occasionally, when it was suspected that the U-boat might have fired and missed with a "Gnat," a single depth charge was dropped. The idea was to lead the German to think that one of his torpedoes had hit a ship and perhaps bring him up for a look. In such grim manœuvres and guessing games many captains and their crews passed most of the night.

At about five in the morning *Icarus* and *Chaudière*, having seen their convoy out of the danger zone ahead, rejoined the hunt. *Kenilworth Castle*, which had knocked her asdic out of action in one of the depth charge attacks, now left the area and set off to keep an eye on the merchant ships.

Depth charge attacks were resumed in earnest at eight o'clock. The traces on the asdic plots after each attack showed that the U-boat was still dodging slowly beneath, seemingly unhurt and just as determined as ever to get away. About noon one skillful dash into the disturbed area of an attack put him completely out of contact with all the hunters for over half an hour. The anxiety caused by this near getaway called for a new appreciation of the situation, and a change of tactics when he was found again. He was in all probability planning to make his escape on the surface that night. He might very well manage it if the ships above lost contact again. It was decided that no further attacks would be made until four o'clock; and that even then they would be confined to single charges designed to head off possible acoustic torpedoes.

The weary hunters settled down to a long wait. Tedious and dangerous as their side of the battle was, they were at least in better case than the tough U-boat men beneath them. A certain amount of respect was due to a crew which had hung on through thirty-one hours of depth-charging, to men who were now probably gasping in dank, smashed-up darkness as oxygen ran low and the choking chlorine fumes of the batteries seeped ever more insistently through the steel shell which had carried them so far from home and was not likely to carry them back. The hunters above could at least relax a little; and the U-boat captain may have hoped that they would relax too much. At exactly half-past three his conning tower came surging to the surface ahead of *Chilliwack*.

If the German had counted on the effect of surprise he was not very successful. A signalman on *Chilliwack's* bridge was pumping oerlikon shells into the conning tower almost as soon as it broke water. Seconds later the corvette's pom-pom and 4″ gun were in action; and every rating who could lay his hands on a Bren or a rifle was also engaged.

Whether because he had been exhausted by the long pounding from above, or discouraged by the failure of his attempt at a surprise escape, the German's remaining efforts were not very vigorous; and were in any case hopeless. He was enveloped in fire from *Chilliwack*, and from *Fennel* which had now joined in. One set of the U-boat's anti-aircraft guns was ripped from the deck and blown into the sea. The captain, standing in his conning tower, threw up his hands as a shell hit him and slumped forward, dead. The Nazi crew, without attempting to man their gun, began to slide limply into the water.

Chilliwack had borne down on the U-boat at full speed, intending to ram; but it was now apparent that she would not have to smash up her bow for this kill. Her gunfire was ripping open the hull and conning tower in a dozen places and no reply came from the listing enemy. Swerving sharply as she approached the German, closely followed by *St. Catharines*, she stopped engines and both ships put away boats.

Chilliwack's boarding party won the race to the submarine. Their whaler, rocking through the heavy sea, came alongside and bobbed perilously up and down against its hull. The U-boat still had way on and was swinging under starboard helm. Signalman J. R. Starr, who had scored the first hits, had also come with the boarding party and had been as forehanded as most signalmen. Scrambling across to the conning tower, he ran up a white ensign which he had brought with him; and cheers rose from the ships which were now approaching on all sides.

Lieutenants Atherton and Hearn, with Engineroom Artificer Longbottom, crossed the German decks to the conning tower and, with a German rating ahead of them, made their way into the foul blackness of the interior. Choking on gas fumes and in darkness except for the gleam of a flash-flight, they searched the wireless cabin and gathered up a precious haul of code books, signal publications and mechanical equipment. Pushing on into other compartments, they found nothing more of interest that was removable. Water was seeping in, there was every possibility of scuttling charges having been set; and the terrified German guide was convinced that the boat would sink at any moment. The men therefore made their way back toward the open.

The whaler from *St. Catharines* was now alongside the U-boat; but just as *Chilliwack's* boarding party emerged from the conning tower a great sea lifted both boats, flung them against the sides of the German and capsized them. *Fennel* and *Chaudière* had to come to the assistance of Germans and Canadians floundering in the water or marooned on the U-boat's deck; and nearly another hour of strenuous rescue work was required before all were safely recovered. The U-boat was still afloat; but towing her was an impossibility. A torpedo from *Icarus* sent her to the bottom at six-thirty in the evening.

Gathering of the Giants

At about the same time on the same day, far to the north and west, *St. Laurent* was proceeding to rejoin her convoy after a very difficult towing job on a corvette which had damaged its propeller. Veteran *Sally* was now commanded by Lieutenant-Commander G. H. Stephen, a former merchant navy officer who had seen long and hectic service in the Atlantic, and whose record as a good Samaritan to damaged vessels was almost as famous as the *"Follow George"* signal which he hoisted for ships of his group in place of the official sailing pendants. Four years of war had brought him numerous marks of official recognition; but not yet a submarine.

St. Laurent caught up with her convoy and sailed with it for one uneventful day. Then a signal arrived ordering her to the assistance of the Swedish merchantman *San Francisco,* whose cargo of flax was on fire and burning fiercely in her holds. The British senior officer who ordered *St. Laurent* on the rescue mission wrote later, when reviewing his action, that the destroyer's captain, "had had previous experience of a similar nature in which he succeeded beyond all expectations, and although the wind and sea were getting up I felt that the situation would be in good hands. This was proved to be correct."

St. Laurent arrived alongside the burning ship at nine o'clock on the morning of the 8th, with a high wind and a heavy sea running; and began a 48-hour job of fire fighting. The blaze on board *San Francisco* was very nearly out of control. Flames and smoke were pouring from the hatches; decks were buckling in the intense heat; and the ship's pumps could not get up effective pressure. The Swedish crew had fought a hard fight against the blaze; but it was gaining on them. They were tired and inclined to lose heart.

St. Laurent's first move, in view of the weather, was a hazardous gamble. Seeing that there was no hope for the merchantman without more pumps, she decided to transfer a 70-ton pump by boat. A 70-ton pump is so designated because it pumps seventy tons of water in an hour, and not

because it weighs seventy tons. Nevertheless, it is a sufficiently large and unhandy piece of gear to be moved by a whaler across rough water; and a great deal of other equipment had to go with it. Altogether three trips had to be made from the destroyer to the merchantman; and on the third trip the boat capsized, losing all its gear and nearly losing some of its occupants. Essential equipment got across, however. Within two hours the pump was in operation and a salvage party from *St. Laurent* was working shoulder to shoulder with the Swedish crew.

Men, walking cat-footed even in heavy sea boots along the steaming decks, formed a bucket brigade to supplement the streams of water from the pumps. When the blaze in the hold where the fire was worst had been dampened sightly, one of *St. Laurent's* officers went down into it wearing salvus gear, which resembles a diver's helmet and is equipped with an hour's supply of oxygen. A working party from *St. Laurent* followed him; and some of the cargo of blazing flax was got out of the way and overside, so that hoses could be played onto the roots of the fire. Each man could endure the scorching heat and choking fumes only for a few minutes; and the high wind, sucking in through the opened hatches, threatened continually to defeat all their efforts. Spelling each other off, however, and mightily assisted by the efforts of the Swedish first officer and his crew, the men worked on and made some progress.

By four in the afternoon the flames began to come under control; although the flax in one of the holds was still heavily ablaze and fires were smouldering in three others. *San Francisco* got slowly under way and proceeded to rejoin her convoy. *St. Laurent's* entire party remained fighting the fire for eighteen hours; and then was reduced to three officers and fourteen men. These volunteers, side by side with weary, smoke-blackened Swedish sailors, were still attacking the stubborn remnants of the blaze on the morning of the 10th, when they had to be withdrawn hastily to their own ship. A U-boat transmission had been intercepted in

St. Laurent's vicinity; and she would need her entire complement for the hunt.

This was to be *"Sally's"* day. In mid-afternoon a conning tower was sighted far ahead; asdic contact was gained after the U-boat submerged; and although neither depth charge nor hedgehog attacks produced immediate results, a promising hunt was on. The Canadian frigate *Swansea* and the Canadian corvette *Owen Sound* joined toward evening; and about dark the British destroyer *Forester* came up. A series of attacks which were evidently punishing the German continued until thirty-four minutes after ten. Then the U-boat surfaced, fourteen hundred yards ahead of *St. Laurent* and on the starboard bow of *Forester*. The German captain had believed that he was under attack by corvettes; and he had hoped that if the moon were clouded he could outrun them on the surface. His assessment both of weather conditions and of his enemy had been too optimistic. He was under a bright moon; and among his foemen were two destroyers.

Nevertheless, the U-boat made a good run for it. *St. Laurent* had to stream her cat gear before pursuing, to make sure that an acoustic torpedo did not cut her off in the moment of victory. The range opened considerably while the cat was running out and the destroyer was working up to full speed; but *St. Laurent's* guns scored two hits on the conning tower. More hits were observed as the destroyer picked up speed and the bow wave began to boil higher and lash back along her flanks. She was closing the range now and *Swansea* and *Forester*, running flat out, were coming up astern of her on either side.

The U-boat was down by the stern and afire internally. His forward gun, smashed by a shell, was dangling over the side. He was still making a good speed, however; still manoeuvrable and still dangerous. As she overhauled, *St. Laurent* turned in to ram; then thought better of it. Passing up the port side of the German, firing everything from 4.7 guns to pistols, she dropped a pattern of shallow-set depth charges which exploded beneath the submarine and brought it to a broken-backed stop. The destroyer's guns, trained aft as she swept by, gashed out three more holes in the conning tower and hull; and as *Swansea* and *Forester* came abreast of the enemy there was little left to do but pick up prisoners. *St. Laurent's* captain, according to legend, ripped the peak from his battered sea cap in jubilation, as a long career of rescue work was at last crowned with a kill.

Swansea was to have a larger part in another action just about a month later; when she detected a submarine moving in to attack the escort carrier *Biter*. Warning the carrier, which took prompt avoiding action, *Swansea* interrupted the U-boat's manœuvering with a pattern of depth charges. The British sloop *Pelican* joined in; and after a four-hour series of attacks conducted with cold-blooded efficiency the U-boat broke surface to be sunk by gunfire. It had encountered a support group, of which *Swansea*, *Pelican* and *Biter* were a part; and it had sufferd the fate common to most U-boats in such meetings. The training, tactics and equipment of the support groups made the destruction of a U-boat once detected almost a matter of routine. This kill had been a "text book action;" its set movements so coldly and deliberately calculated that *Swansea's* commanding officer had had time to check his position by a leisurely sun sight while the hunt was in progress.

The prisoners taken after the kill showed another aspect of the change which had taken place in the Atlantic war. They were no longer the physical equals of the men who had operated the earlier U-boats. Some of them had defects which would have made them unacceptable for sea duty in the palmy days. Yet there were few signs of a falling-off in their spirit. When the submarine was detected it had been moving into attack *Biter*, the most valuable and most heavily guarded ship of the group. The undersea navy was still a force to be reckoned with; and, although no one doubted the fact, it was re-emphasized in May by the loss of a Canadian ship.

About thirty minutes before midnight on May 6 the Canadian frigate *Valleyfield* was approaching Newfoundland with a mid-ocean group which included two other Canadian frigates and two corvettes. The ships had completed their portion of a run with a convoy from the United Kingdom. Escort duties had been turned over to a local group some hours before; and the men of the mid-ocean ships were already making plans for a first night in St. John's.

There were small icebergs scattered about the area, and radar contacts were many and confused. None of any apparent significance had been obtained, however, as it came time for the watches to change in *Valleyfield*, which was a little astern of the other ships. The officer on the bridge had just sent down word for his relief to be wakened when the instruments gave sudden warning of the presence of a submarine. As the buzz of the Action Stations signal ran through the lower decks, there came the crash of a torpedo ripping into the port side; and then a tremendous explosion. Great chunks of metal lifted skyward, filing the air with flying splinters; there was the roar of escaping steam, the grind of tearing metal and the crash of falling superstructure. The mainmast swung in drunken circles as the wallowing ship, broken nearly in half, staggered and began to settle.

The bow sloped off to starboard and dipped steeply. Within a minute or so the forecastle was lying almost on its side. Men simply stepped off into the water, whose temperature, taken a few minutes before, had registered 32°. As the ship, for a last moment, held precariously together, the settling stern lifted the bow from the sea. It rose threateningly above swimmers choking with thick, nauseous oil which filled their eyes, mouths and noses. Then it leaned away, broke off with a rending crash and sank. The after part tilted forward, upended vertically in its turn and remained for a long moment silhouetted in the moonlight, rudder and screws to the sky.

It went under slowly with a vast moan of escaping air and steam; and then a freezing silence fell over the dark sea. The voices which had made a brave effort to farewell the ship with "For She's a Jolly Good Fellow" were no longer heard;

the shouts of encouragement grew rarer as the icy water tightened its grip on numbing limbs. Other ships of *Valleyfield's* group had been several miles ahead of her at the moment of the torpedoing and had no knowledge of it until some time later. *Giffard* was the first to return to the position but, as always, search for the enemy had to take precedence over rescue work. As the sister frigate passed and merged into the darkness, to be gone perhaps for hours more, some of *Valleyfield's* men gave up, let go their holds on carley floats or wreckage and sank from sight. When *Giffard* returned from an unavailing hunt, 115 officers and rating had been lost. The Atlantic was secure for the passage of invasion supplies, but men had still to die to keep it so.

From January to May, behind the great screen maintained by the escort groups and support groups, the "invasion ships" moved toward the United Kingdom. They were of many nations and of every type; and they approached from far-scattered points about the earth. Their times of assembly varied according to the work they had to do and the work which had to be done to make them ready. Merchant ships remained in service with the convoys up to the time when they had at last to be loaded with supplies for France. Many warships had to be taken in hand early in the year for fitting out with special armament and for special training. Other ships, although earmarked for Neptune, had preliminary duties in other seas.

Two new Canadian acquisitions fell into this latter category. The Fleet destroyers *Algonquin* and *Sioux*, formerly the Royal Navy destroyers *Valentine* and *Vixen*, were commissioned as ships of the Canadian navy about the middle of February. Slightly smaller than the Tribals, and about two knots slower, they mounted four single 4.7 guns as main armament and carried eight torpedo tubes. Their anti-aircraft armament included twin 40-millimetre bofors and several batteries of 20-millimetre oerlikons. Equipped with the latest in radar and asdic, with guns in power mountings, and every form of modern electrical gear, they were ships which would have been almost the equal of a cruiser of the thirties.

Gathering of the Giants

By the end of March the destroyers had concluded work-ups and training at Scapa; and they were absorbed into the heavy British forces operating northward in the waters about the Scandinavian peninsula. *Tirpitz*, sister ship to *Bismarck*, was lying in Alta Fjord, still a source of much anxiety to the Home Fleet. She had been completed during 1943; but a valiant and costly attack by British midget submarines in September of that year had knocked her out for several months. Strenuous efforts had been made to repair her, however; and late in March reconnaisance planes, which maintained a constant watch over the progress of the work, reported that she was in condition to sail from Alta Fjord for a German port. The Admiralty decided that it would be necessary to hit her again.

On March 31 *Algonquin* and *Sioux* joined a force which included four British escort carriers, a British cruiser and four British destroyers; and sailed for Alta Fjord. During the next three days the north-bound armada was joined by other large British ships including the fleet carriers, *Victorious* and *Furious*.

By four o'clock on the morning of April 3rd the force was lying off Alta Fjord within eighty miles of the Norwegian coast. Seafires and Corsairs roared into the air and circled above the ships as fighter cover for the carriers. Then forty Barracuda bombers in two waves, protected by eighty fighters, took off for the narrow inlet where *Tirpitz* lay, protected by sheltering mountains and batteries of heavy anti-aircraft guns. Two of the fighter squadrons heading for the Alta Fjord were commanded by Canadian pilots of the Fleet Air Arm, Lieutenant-Commanders D. B. R. Cosh and G. C. Edwards; and three Canadian pilots, Lieutenant H. P. Wilson, Lieutenant D. J. Sheppard and Sub-Lieutenant B. L. Hayter were at the controls of individual planes in the squadrons. Another Canadian, Lieutenant T. G. Darling, was a section leader of one of the Barracuda bomber squadrons; and two other Canadians, Lieutenants W. Muir and J. Os-

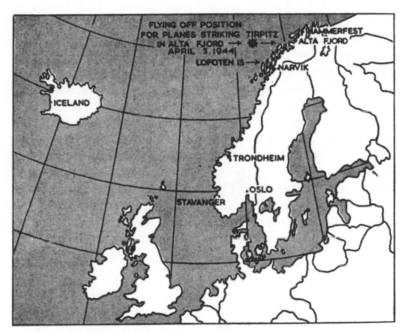

NORTHERN WATERS - 1944

borne, were fighter direction officers in *Victorious* and *Furious*.

To avoid enemy radar detection, the squadrons flew almost at sea level for ten minutes; then rose to 8,000 feet to cross the towering coast. One or two shore batteries and a patrol vessel opened up on them, but no enemy planes appeared. Screened in their approach by the same mountains which hid Tirpitz in her deep anchorage, the bombers swept in over the peaks and peeled off in screaming dives. Twenty-four Barracudas of the first wave attacked at intervals of less than three seconds, using 500-lb., semi-armour-piercing bombs. Tirpitz had been preparing to get under way; and surprise was so complete that the Germans had no time to cover the ship with smoke. The great decks, 792 feet long and 118 feet wide, seemed a huge target to the pilots as they came down in their 3500-foot dives. Nearly every plane of the first strike scored at least one hit.

As the first wave of bombers levelled off and made for the protection of the surrounding mountains the second wave came in. Anti-aircraft fire was heavier and better organized now; some smoke was being made intentionally by the Germans and more by the hits of the first bombers. Once again, however, the attack was pressed home and a good percentage of hits scored. No German plane put in an appearance throughout the raid; only two of the Barracudas were shot down; and among the fighters one pilot ditched near his carrier but was quickly recovered. By seven-thirty all the remaining planes had returned to their ships; and the force retired, leaving *Tirpitz* again out of action for several months.

Algonquin and *Sioux* went deep into northern waters again on April 26, when they formed part of the force screening a Fleet Air Arm strike against German shipping near the Lofoten Islands. There were two more such operations during the first ten days of May. Then came portentous new orders. On May 15, as part of the 26th Destroyer Flotilla, the two ships began an intensive ten-day programme of gunnery training. It was concentrated mainly on the technique of ship-to-shore bombardment; in which the destroyers, cooperating with army observation officers ashore, fired on unseen targets as directed by the observers. The purpose of the training was apparent to all; and few on board the ships had any doubt as to the nature of their next mission when they sailed south for Portsmouth on May 28.

Many other ships wearing the maple leaf on their funnels had now arrived in British assembly ports, or were at sea on pre-invasion duties. Among them was a group of Bangor minesweepers which, after years of dull local escort work on the Canadian side of the Atlantic, were now preparing for a task on which the estimate of casualties was liberal. Early in January, 1944, the Admiralty had calculated the number of minesweepers which would be necessary to sweep the invasion ships in through the minefields to the

French coast. The required number was considerably greater than the Royal Navy could provide; and a request was made for sixteen Canadian Bangors, complete with minesweeping gear.

The ships could be found; but the matter of equipping them was a serious problem for the Canadian navy. Winches and other tackle for minesweeping had long since been removed from many of the Bangors; and in some of them it had never been installed. When Bangors first began to be built in Canada there had been a strong possibility of minelaying in Canadian waters. The threat did not develop to any extent; but Bangors had continued to be built because they were useful escort ships on short runs, and were a known design which shipyards could quickly turn out. Their reversion, at this late date, to a function which few of the ships and men had ever performed, would be a major undertaking. Nevertheless, they were fitted with what gear remained or could be acquired in Canada, supplied with heavier armament, and sailed for the United Kingdom in four groups of four between February 18 and 21.

The completion of their fitting out in the Clyde was difficult for shipyards already burdened with problems enough; but the work was reasonably well along by April. Ten of the first ships to be made ready were formed into a Canadian flotilla which consisted of *Caraquet, Fort William, Wasaga, Blairmore, Malpeque, Cowichan, Minas, Milltown, Bayfield* and *Mulgrave.* The other six, *Canso, Thunder, Georgian, Vegreville, Guysborough* and *Kenora,* were distributed among British flotillas. Training designed to familiarize the crews in the space of a month with all phases of minesweeping work was begun under a large programme titled with sardonic pessimism, "Pious Dream." For the invasion, the minesweepers had before them not only one of the most dangerous but one of the most technically exacting of the tasks which confronted any group of ships. From the seaward fringes of the German minefields they had to sweep and mark a series of channels leading right into the shallow water along the coast. Their navigation would have to be exact; and their sweeping thorough. A channel inaccurately swept or a mine overlooked might bring confusion and catastrophe on a whole column of ships following behind.

The Canadians, almost completely new to minesweeping, had to master their work so thoroughly that none of these disasters could occur. Many sleepless nights and rigorous days went into one of the most intensive training periods ever known among the flotillas of the British Isles; and by late May the prentice sweepers were pronounced ready for actual operations.

Corvettes, also, had begun to disappear from Canadian escort groups at the beginning of 1944. First to go had been the ships in need of refit; and these had retired to Canadian dockyards to be made ready. Ships not requiring such attention were kept on convoy duty until March or April; but by the middle of the latter month the actual assembly in United Kingdom ports was well under way.

There were nineteen corvettes earmarked for invasion duties: *Prescott, Calgary, Mimico, Alberni, Woodstock, Regina, Baddeck, Camrose, Lunenburg, Drumheller, Mayflower, Louisburg, Rimouski, Trentonian, Moose Jaw, Port Arthur, Lindsay, Kitchener,* and *Summerside.* As they arrived in the United Kingdom, their commanding officers and navigation officers were spirited away for a three-day course at the Western Approaches Tactical Unit in Liverpool. There, they got their first inkling of what was in store for them. Intensive training periods followed for all the ships and their companies; and the climax was a seventy-two hour battle exercise off Larne, Northern Ireland.

Here, real battle conditions in all their confusion and complexity were simulated. By day or night "enemy" submarines or aircraft attacked without warning. Launches representing E-boats—the fast German motor torpedo boats —would lash in from various directions towing targets which the corvettes would have to light with starshell and fire at with high explosive. In the midst of this "attack," a plane would fly over towing a drogue target and the anti-aircraft gunners would go into action. While carrying out a mock hedgehog attack a corvette might suddenly have her anti-aircraft gunners called to repel a plane splashing live ammunition around the ship. The training officer supervising the exercise might choose the same moment to let off a thunder-flash fire-cracker, simulating a hit which damage parties would have to get under control. Many corvette men, later in the summer, considered that the battle exercises had been the most exciting part of their invasion.

Woodstock and *Regina* were the first of the Canadian corvettes to commence the preliminary escort work for Neptune. On April 28 *Woodstock* took a miscellanous convoy of tugs and tows to the Thames estuary ports. *Regina* set out on a similar mission the next day. *Prescott, Camrose, Lunenburg, Baddeck* and *Rimouski* soon followed, joining the escort fleet which had to shepherd thousands of ships, craft, tugs and tows, wildly miscellaneous in their character, equipment and cargo, to the main ports of assembly along the south coast.

The vast movement of traffic around the coasts could not be entirely concealed from the enemy. It had been underway to some extent since early in the winter, partially concealed amid the routine movement of coastal convoys. Nevertheless, its increased volume was becoming more apparent all the time; and now the policy was to mislead the Germans. The strength assembling in the southeast would be displayed, pointing a threat directly across the Straits of Dover. Preparations in the south and west, which might have indicated the actual invasion area farther down the French coast, were carefully concealed. Best hidden of all were the assemblages of blockships, barges and breakwaters which were to be used for building the great prefabricated harbours. Had these been noted, the Germans might conceivably have guessed at the most novel and daring feature of the Allied plan.

By the middle of May twelve of the nineteen Canadian corvettes were equipped, trained and engaged on the work of pre-invasion escort. The remaining seven were soon to enter upon the same task. The motley convoys herded through British waters by the corvettes were the strength gathering behind the spearhead of the assault forces; and in those assault forces other Canadian ships were included.

Prince Henry and *Prince David,* now converted from armed merchant cruisers to landing ships, had arrived in the Clyde in February to complete their fitting out. After completion they had gone to Cowes on the Isle of Wight with others of the assembling landing ships. *Prince Henry* was to be senior officer of landing ships in Force J, one of the five assault forces destined for the five sectors of the Normandy beach front. She was responsible from now on for the discipline, navigation, station-keeping and general efficiency of twenty-two converted merchant vessels which she would lead down the swept channels into position off the beaches of Juno sector. *Prince David* was to be senior ship of one of the subdivisions of the same force.

At Cowes on April 21 the two Canadian landing ships were joined by their flotillas of assault landing craft. *Prince Henry* was to carry the eight assault craft of the 528th Canadian Flotilla. *Prince David* would carry the six craft of the 529th Canadian Flotilla. In addition, there arrived within the next few days three Canadian flotillas of the larger infantry landing craft which would make the cross-channel voyage under their own power. They consisted in all of thirty craft, divided into the 260th, 262nd and 264th Flotillas; and their arrival at Cowes had been preceded, as in the case of the assault craft, by an intensive training period. Exercises, in which the Canadian ships and craft combined with many more from the Royal Navy and the United States Navy, now began on a very large scale.

During Fabius, the largest of the exercises, a huge assault force sailed out from the Solent in broad daylight and continued on for twenty-five miles south of the Isle of Wight under a bright moon. It was a dress rehearsal, very probably observed by the enemy; and had he chosen to add realism by attacking the convoys it would have been a welcome gesture. No hostile movement was observed, either from the air, from the seas about, or from the coast of France. The great force, nearly in mid Channel, turned back before dawn and poured its troops ashore under the thunder of supporting guns on the beaches of Bracklesham Bay, some ten miles east of Portsmouth.

Fabius was the final rehearsal. On May 24 the King inspected all the assault ships and craft, now assembled in Southampton Water and the Solent. The commanding officers of *Prince Henry* and *Prince David,* as well as officers of the landing flotillas, were presented; after which the small ships sailed past while His Majesty took the salute. There remained after that only anxious, last-minute preparations and days of waiting.

Meanwhile at Londonderry, eleven Canadian frigates, *Waskesiu, Outremont, Cape Breton, Grou, Teme, Matane, Swansea, Stormont, Port Colborne, St. John* and *Meon,* had been organized into two hunting groups and were preparing to move south to their Neptune base. Two other groups, composed of the destroyers *Ottawa, Kootenay, Chaudière, St. Laurent, Gatineau, Qu'Appelle, Saskatchewan, Skeena* and *Restigouche,* were en route to Plymouth from the north by the end of May. The nineteen corvettes were still moving on passage about the island with last-minute convoys. Eleven of the minesweepers lay at Portland and five at Plymouth.

On land the assault divisions of the armies were moving into the sealed camps. Among the thousands of ships gathered along the west, south and east coasts from Bristol Channel to the Thames, some already held the bound masses of mimeographed papers which were their invasion orders. Others would receive them by special courier at set hours within the next few days. As soon as the orders came on board, the ships, too, were sealed. No man, except on an urgent official mission and with a signed order from his captain, could set foot ashore.

Gathering of the Giants

By the first day of June many ships of Canada were a part of this host separated by barbed wire, bayonets or salt water from all other concerns of men. Others would join within the next day or so; to engage in feverish, last minute preparations or share the tense, weary hours of waiting which still lay ahead. And there were yet other Canadian ships whose work, integrally associated with Operation Neptune, had begun weeks and months before and had still long to continue. On the right flank, where the Channel opened out into the North Sea above the Straits of Dover, and on the left flank, westward through the Channel to the shoulder of Ushant and southward into Biscay waters, much work had been done and much was still to do.

CHAPTER ELEVEN

The Plan and the Preliminaries

The forces of Overlord were to strike the French coast in the region of the Seine estuary, directly across the Channel from Portsmouth, the Solent and Southampton Water. Here, enclosed by a shallow, bowl-shaped indentation known as Baie de la Seine, was the longest stretch of open shore lying within effective range of fighter aircraft based in England. It ran for some sixty miles from the mouth of the River Orne, westward along the southern face and northward up part of the western shoulder of the basin. The waters along this frontage and for a depth of twenty miles seaward to the mouth of the bay would provide anchorage for Neptune shipping. To the east the remaining fifth of the basin would be masked off from the assault area, first by a sector of heavily patrolled water, and then by a large minefield closing in Le Havre and the mouth of the Seine. At the approaches to the bay the great German minebelt, which formed an outer barrier along the coast from Cap de la Hague to Boulogne, would be slitted with lanes through which the assaulting ships could pass.

Three divisions of parachute troops were to be dropped well inland; one on the eastern flank and two on the western. The sea-borne landings were to be made on a five-divisional front; and five naval forces, of which three were British and two American, were to deliver the troops to the beaches. The three British forces were grouped as the Eastern Task Force; the two American, as the Western Task Force. The divisional fronts along the shore—Sword, Juno and Gold in the eastern sector, Omaha and Utah in the western sector—were subdivided into brigade fronts or beaches. These, in turn, were divided into smaller beaches; on each of which naval craft would have to set down the assigned troops and equipment at some exactly appointed day, hour and minute. This appointed time, to which every movement of the operation was related, had been tentatively set for June 5. It remained, however, variable within narrow limits. Known only as H-hour of D-day, it could fall between June 5 and June 7; or it could be postponed with immense difficulty to the period between June 19 and June 21.

June of 1944 was the month prescribed by considerations of grand strategy. The necessary Allied forces would be assembled. Several months of good fighting weather would lie ahead. The time would coincide generally with the reopening of the Russian offensive in the east and with the breaking of the long stalemate in Italy. The entire strength of the United Nations, fully mobilized at last, would strike the enemy simultaneously on every front.

The selected periods in June were dictated by the tactics of the landing. No pre-dawn or moonlight attack against half-subdued defences was to be risked. After a night-long smashing by aircraft, the German strong-points on shore were to be drenched by thirty minutes of naval bombardment in daylight. Then landing craft would run in on a rising half-tide over the mines and beach obstacles which constituted the first line of German defence. Between the 5th and the 7th, or between the 19th and 21st of June, the tide along the beaches of Baie de la Seine would reach the necessary half-flood at the required time after daybreak.

The rocky, gently shelving shoreline of the assault beaches had been charted and studied inch by inch. Thousands of aerial photographs, thousands of intelligence reports, and the lives of many brave men had gone into the compilation of maps which showed every feature of the area, and every battery or minefield or cluster of beach obstacles which could be discovered up to the day of embarkation. Depths and gradients along each foot of the shore were known and planned for. Landing craft were assigned in minute detail to exact beaching positions. By the time of the assault their crews had been so familiarized with the beaches that in some cases the fore-and-aft loading of the craft was

arranged to make the slope of their bottoms correspond to the gradient over which they would ride up on the sand.

The planners of Neptune had little to fear and much to hope from the air. Over the Normandy beaches they would have tenfold superiority in aircraft; opposing 5,900 planes of all types to an estimated German strength of less than 600. Allied fighter planes would provide impenetrable cover for the convoys. Allied bombers, which had already been pulverizing the coast for months, would deliver a numbing, nerve-shattering weight of explosive onto the beaches during the night and early morning preceding the assault.

With the first light of day, before the dust of the aerial bombardment had subsided, the naval bombardment would commence. Seven battleships, twenty-three cruisers and one hundred and four destroyers, together with monitors, gunboats and rocket-firing ships would pour their fire upon the concrete emplacements and the batteries hidden among the dunes or in the innocent-looking farmhouses along the coast. As the bombardment was completed, amphibious tanks, new to warfare, would swim in from the sea on inflated canvas screens. Gun-carrying craft would follow the tanks, with army artillery mounted in them and firing as they came. Other craft, moving still closer to the beaches, would pour a hail of machine-gun and small-arms fire upon selected points. And riding the crest of this storm, preceded by mine and obstacle clearance parties, would come the waves of assault craft carrying the vanguard of the infantry. Seven divisions of Allied soldiers were to be landed within the first twenty-four hours, followed thereafter by reinforcements flowing in at the rate of one and one-third divisions per day with all equipment.

The long heralded blow would fall with a blunt simplicity more baffling to the Germans than the complicated series of operations they had been led to expect. The breach in the Atlantic wall was to be opened almost midway between Le Havre and Cherbourg; and neither of those ports was to be the first objective of the assault. Nor were there to be diversionary landings. A single massive thrust, mounted in the waters about Plymouth, Portland, Portsmouth, Southampton and the Isle of Wight, was to be driven straight southward across the Channel to pour the armies of liberation onto the French shore. There they were to be maintained, supplied, and steadily reinforced with an enormous flood of vehicles, arms, ammunition and stores of every kind. It was hoped that Cherbourg peninsula could be nipped off and the port itself captured within the first few days after the assault, but this was not an essential of the operation. The Allies had prepared themselves to land millions of tons of equipment and more than a million men on an open coast exposed to the pounding surf and the high winds sweeping in from the Channel.

No sea-borne landing even remotely comparable in size had ever been attempted under such conditions. The German general staff was convinced that an operation on the necessary scale would be impossible without the use of at least one great harbour, and in this they were probably correct. What they did not conceive of was the daring and imaginative expedient which had been adopted to meet the necessity. Allied planners intended that the ships of Neptune should bring their own harbours with them to the beaches. Ten thousand men, two hundred tugs, and a group of escort ships which included most of the Canadian corvettes, had been assigned to bring to Normandy an immense congregation of blockships, concrete barges, pontoon piers and floating breakwaters. There, at Arromanches in the British sector and at St. Laurent in the American sector, the barges, piers and breakwaters were to be set in shallow water to form two great artificial harbours, each with a capacity equal to that of Dover. At five other points along the beach front groups of the blockships were to be sunk to form smaller craft shelters.

The six thousand ships involved in Operation Neptune were to rendezvous in an assembly area just south and east of the Isle of Wight. They would pass over the hundred miles of water separating the shores of England from Baie de la Seine on a front only twenty miles broad. On passage through the German mine barrier and along the inner routes to the assault anchorages they would be confined to ten narrow lanes cleared by minesweepers proceeding ahead of them. They would have to move at set times and speeds in rigidly appointed order to exactly defined positions off the coast; and the very immensity of the operation created perils of corresponding magnitude. Any serious disorganization of the precisely planned assault movement might have the most disastrous results. Equally disastrous would be any disruption of the flow of supplies and reinforcements to the armies after they were landed and fighting ashore.

Such was the Neptune plan as it took final shape at the beginning of 1944. Earlier plans had contemplated a landing to be made about May 1 on a front of only three divisions. When further consideration made it appear that five-divisional strength along a wider front was necessary, another month had to be set aside for the massing of additional landing craft and for more widespread and intensive bombing of German defences. The plan for a simultaneous landing in the south of France, which had long been considered an integral feature of Overlord, had also to be postponed. When the Allied armies were securely ashore in Normandy and the drive across northern France had begun, then a secondary drive from the Mediterranean area was to be undertaken. Once the lodgement in the Baie de la Seine area was secure, ships, landing craft, men and matériel could safely be diverted. But until that time every other consideration had to give way before the overriding determination to strike the Normandy coast with irresistible force.

The fear of bad weather was the greatest of many anxieties through the long months of preparation. The thought of high seas and lashing surf which might prevent landing craft from beaching, or of fogs and storms which would ground aircraft and vastly complicate navigation, hung, as Churchill said, "like a vulture poised in the sky over the thoughts of the most sanguine." So far as weather was concerned, however, man could only make his multitude of laborious calculations, judge with what skill was given him and thereafter hope and pray. Against other threats to the success of the operation he could take more positive measures.

While Allied aircraft battered German defences, communications and production centres everywhere in Europe, Allied naval forces attacked the German convoys which plied along the Channel and Biscay coasts. Other ships, or frequently the same ships, fought off the attacks which German E-boats and R-boats sought to deliver against convoys moving along the British coast with invasion matériel. Included in, but occasionally going beyond the scope of these operations, were destroyer patrols whose object was not only to defend our convoys and attack the enemy's, but also to draw out and destroy his remaining fighting ships. During the latter part of 1943 and the early months of 1944, the complicated and continuous pattern of Channel operations was not greatly different from that of previous years. By April, however, it had begun to take on a new intensity. It was directed generally to facilitating and clearing the way for the passage of the invasion ships; and in its latest stages it resolved itself into the business of protecting the long, open, comparatively static flanks which the procession of Neptune shipping would expose to the eastern and western Channel.

The enemy had still available to him, within striking distance of what was to become the cross-Channel highway for Neptune, some 230 surface ships. The force included, in addition to heavily armed trawlers, minesweepers, and lesser craft, about 16 destroyers, 50 E-boats and 60 of the slower but more heavily armed R-boats. Based on his Biscay and Channel ports and on Norway, he had a force of 130 U-boats which might be increased to 200 within a fortnight after D-day.

Small as his naval resources appeared by comparison with the huge aggregation of Allied power, they were by no means insignificant. The narrow, slow-moving, closely timed columns of Neptune would consist for the most part of ships carrying troops and supplies, not equipped to put up a fight against naval vessels, limited in their movements by all the ships about them and confined to narrow swept channels. If enemy surface ships and U-boats, operated with suicidal determination, should break through the covering forces, they might wreak untold havoc. They might throw the assault into confusion, fatally delay some of its operations, or obstruct the all-important reinforcement programme.

While Neptune was in process of organization, allied forces in the Channel must take every step possible to weaken German naval strength. Later, when the assault began, the flanks of the movement would have to be guarded by a complex series of patrols involving ships of many types. To counter the heavier German ships there would be cruisers and the more powerful of the destroyers. Hunting groups, made up of older destroyers or of frigates, would be disposed to intercept and destroy U-boats making for the Channel. And the E-boats and R-boats, which formed an important element of the remaining German sea power, were to be met by their long-time enemies, the motor torpedo boats and gunboats of the coastal forces.

These small, fast craft whose business was the swift night attack had known the Channel as a battleground since the beginning of the war. For them, as for their German opponents, the principal target was the convoy, and the principal weapon surprise. Stalking an enemy in the darkness, dashing in to attack at high speed, letting fly with all guns and torpedoes and making off again, the craft of each side had exacted a considerable toll of enemy shipping. They had fought innumerable sanguinary duels with each other; and neither the German E-boats and R-boats nor the British M.T.B.'s had hesitated to attack larger ships. German E-boats had made trouble for British destroyers in the Channel; and it was just possibly a torpedo from an E-boat which sank the Canadian destroyer *Athabaskan* in April. British M.T.B.'s, among many other exploits, had played a notable part in the attack on *Scharnhorst* and *Gneisenau* during their famous run from Brest. It was obvious that in their coastal craft the Germans had a considerable weapon to use against the huge concentration of shipping which would assemble for Neptune. It was equally obvious that the coastal forces were the weapon which would be principally opposed to them.

On both sides of the Channel coastal force dispositions, made with an eye to Neptune, began to take place during the early spring of 1944. An increasing number of craft assembled under Plymouth Command, looking across to E-boats and R-boats moving into Cherbourg and the Channel Island ports. Portsmouth forces were strengthened, facing new concentrations in Le Havre. Dover Command added to its flotillas to meet the German threat in the eastern Channel area; and five additional flotillas were assigned to sail with the Neptune convoys and patrol the assault anchorage. Among these forces there had now come into being two all-Canadian flotillas: the 65th under Plymouth Command and the 29th under Portsmouth.

The 29th and 65th Canadian Motor Torpedo Boat Flotillas had been organized in March 1944. Most of their officers and men had had a long and lively experience with British coastal forces in the Channel or the North Sea or the Mediterranean. The boats of the 29th Flotilla were of the smaller gunboat or G-type, with a speed of 41 knots, a length of 71' 6", and armament consisting of a power-mounted pom-pom and several smaller-calibre weapons. Normally they carried torpedoes and mounted torpedo tubes, though for some of the Neptune period these were exchanged for depth charges. The boats of the 65th Flotilla were of the D-type; slightly larger and more heavily armed, but not quite so fast. They carried torpedoes and torpedo tubes at all times.

The 29th Flotilla, after an intensive training period, arrived about the middle of May at Ramsgate, the coastal forces base of the Dover Command. The first mission assigned to four of the boats on the night of May 16 was the escort of a hazardous mine-gathering expedition to the coast of France. Samples of the German beach mines were required to facilitate the development of mine-clearance methods; and it had been decided that parties of British engineers would be landed on the French coast to steal the mines from under the noses of the enemy.

Two British M.T.B.'s were assigned to carry the engineer parties; and boats 462, 464, 460, and 465 of the 29th Flotilla sailed with them as escorts. On a calm night, with a phosphorescent sea which seemed to the men in the craft to make their boats stand out like lighthouses, the expedition came within two miles of the coast. Small power dories were put away and the engineer parties steered in for shore. The British carrier boats and the Canadian M.T.B.'s patrolled off the landing place for two hours while mysterious starshell went up from the coast and unsuspecting enemy craft passed them at close quarters. Nothing untoward developed, however. The engineers returned in their dories, were taken on board with their ugly, precious samples; and by dawn the whole party was in Dover, having made a very useful contribution to the success of the invasion.

To nobody's sorrow this particular type of mission was not repeated. Later operations fell into a more congenial pattern. On the night of May 22, boats 459, 464, 465 and 466 put out from Ramsgate in company with four British M.T.B.'s to intercept a strongly escorted German convoy which was known to be moving between Dieppe and Boulogne. By the middle of a very dark night, with a choppy sea and a strong northwesterly wind, the groups were moving along a north-south patrol line twenty-four miles off Boulogne.

After about an hour's patrolling, three of the British boats detached to the southward, while the fourth craft had to withdraw because of engine trouble. Radar contact with the expected convoy was established a few minutes later. The four Canadian boats turned southward in the direction of the echo and drew nearer to the French coast. Starshell and high explosive bursts ahead of them indicated that the three British M.T.B.'s were already in action with the convoy. Then gun flashes lifted from the dark shore, and a few seconds later starshell burst above the Canadians. They had been detected, and shore batteries had them in range.

The boats of the 29th ran out of the starshell glare into the windy darkness of the sea, then into ragged light again as they began to approach the convoy. The British boats were retiring under cover of a smoke-screen. The German force appeared to consist of four shallow-draft, heavily armed flak ships with accompanying E-boats and R-boats; and it was now thoroughly aroused and vigilant. As the M.T.B.'s ran in, the Germans swung their guns away from the retiring British craft and turned their full fire on the newcomers. A dazzling glare of starshell blazed in the eyes of the Canadians; and through it the red, green and yellow streams of tracer fire came arching down.

Replying with starshell of their own, which proved equally disconcerting to the enemy, the Canadians bore in and ran alongside the convoy for five minutes, firing with all guns. At the end of the line of German ships they swung out to sea, laying a smoke-screen behind them. They had suffered no casualties; and they could report no definite losses on the part of the enemy. They had certainly scored many hits; but the brief, slashing action fought under a blaze of starshell gave no opportunity for an assessment of damages.

Farther to the west on the same night the 65th Flotilla was also engaged in its first action. From their base at Brixham near Dartmouth, boats 735, 726, 745 and 727 had sailed into the waters of the Channel Islands on the watch for any E-boat forces which might be assembling. At half-past three in the morning, when they were some eight miles to the northeast of Jersey, they made radar contact with a German convoy 6,600 yards away on the inshore side of them. They disposed themselves immediately in broad quarterline formation, with the boats strung out one astern of another and each well to port of the one ahead; and ran in on the convoy's beam.

BRISTOL CH

FALMOUTH

OPERATION

C.A.

ZONE

ATHABASKAN
SUNK
APRIL 29
1944

HAIDA DRIVES
ELBING ASHORE
APRIL 29
1944

ILE
DE BAS

ILE DE VIERGE

BREST

MORLAIX

LORIE

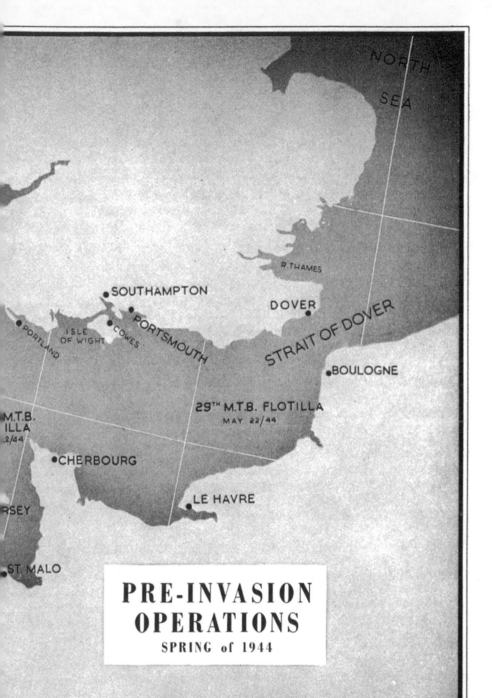

NORTH SEA

R THAMES

SOUTHAMPTON

DOVER

PORTLAND

ISLE OF WIGHT

COWES

PORTSMOUTH

STRAIT OF DOVER

BOULOGNE

29TH M.T.B. FLOTILLA
MAY 22/44

M.T.B.
ILLA
2/44

CHERBOURG

LE HAVRE

RSEY

ST. MALO

PRE-INVASION
OPERATIONS
SPRING of 1944

Boats 735 and 726, the leaders, spotted two German escort ships on the seaward side of the convoy. They attempted to circle astern of them, but were detected, and a hot action developed immediately. The fight lasted just three minutes; but in that time the two Canadian boats poured 2,515 rounds of all calibre shells into the enemy vessels and apparently stopped them.

Meanwhile boats 745 and 727 had passed the escorts and continued straight in for the convoy. Dazzled by the blaze of starshell and tracer fire which met them, they fired their torpedoes by radar and saw no result. Closing the range to less than one hundred yards and opening with gunfire, they then ran along the length of the convoy. As they came racing out from the action, boat 726, mistaking 745 for an enemy E-boat, opened fire on her. Boat 745 switched on her fighting lights, and fire from the other craft was instantly checked; but not before casualties had been suffered. The difficulty of distinguishing friend from enemy in pitch blackness or in the blinding light of starshell had always been and would continue to be an occupational hazard of the coastal forces. The close range, the high speed, and the generally confused nature of the actions, made such tragedies almost unavoidable. Even as the Canadian boats set off for Plymouth with their casualties, they saw behind them two of the German escorts hotly engaging each other.

These nightly patrols and swift, fierce, inconclusive actions were to form the pattern of the work of the M.T.B.'s up to D-day and for several months afterward. Going where destroyers could not go, the small boats ran in over enemy minefields and up to within almost a stone's throw of hostile coasts. A match and more than a match for the E-boats and R-boats, they damaged and disrupted enemy convoys while putting up a very respectable defence for our own. They drove away prowling craft sent to investigate Neptune preparations, headed off an occasional destroyer before it could do damage, and fought it out many times with the heavily armed minesweepers and flak ships which were used for escort. They were eventually to take over the inner zones of the many-layered defence in depth established on both sides of the approach lanes to the Normandy beaches.

A little to the west of the area in which the M.T.B.'s operated, three Canadian destroyers were engaged on more extended operations. *Iroquois*, first of the Canadian Tribals and the longest in service, had been sent to Halifax in February for a refit. *Haida, Athabaskan* and *Huron* remained. They had been attached to Plymouth Command in January as part of the 10th Destroyer Flotilla. By April they had become veteran members of a force whose activities were becoming ever more urgently and directly linked with the preparations for Neptune.

Two methodical, long-range programmes involving almost nightly missions for the destroyers had been carried on under Plymouth Command for many months. The first, known as Operation Tunnel, was a continuous series of patrols directed against German Biscay and Channel convoys. Groups of destroyers, frequently supported by cruisers, placed themselves athwart the well-known routes in the Bay or the western Channel, seeking to destroy both the merchantmen and the strong escort forces which sailed in company.

Operation Hostile, the second of the two programmes, was a minelaying operation in which the destroyers, again frequently with cruisers, served as a covering force. While fast British minelayers went in to mine enemy waters, the covering forces lay to seaward of them, prepared to deal with German ships which might come out to interfere. The mining of enemy convoy routes, and more particularly of the approaches to their harbours along the French coast, was an important feature of the Neptune preparations. As D-day approached, Operation Hostile was stepped up according to a set schedule both in range and intensity. By the time the ships of Neptune sailed, every enemy harbour along the coast was to be ringed with mines of the newest and deadliest type.

By the latter part of April *Haida* had carried out nineteen of the Operation Tunnel or Operation Hostile missions;

Huron had carried out eleven; and *Athabaskan,* nine. Between missions they had fitted in as they could a series of special exercises in night fighting, navigation, and the radar detection and radar-controlled gunnery which were later to prove of deadly effect. Up to the night of April 25, however, none of their sorties had brought them into contact with an enemy force.

On that night another mission under Operation Tunnel was in train; and was to be carried out by the British cruiser, *Black Prince,* the British destroyer, *Ashanti,* and *Haida, Huron* and *Athabaskan.* The force was to sail from Plymouth at nine o'clock on the evening of April 25; and at one-thirty on the morning of the 26th was to arrive in a position seventeen miles east-north-east of Île de Bas, about ten miles off the French coast. From that point it was to patrol in an east-northeasterly direction for two hours. Three German Elbing class destroyers were known to be berthed in St. Malo and were expected to move out early on the morning of the 26th. If they did so, they were to be intercepted. If nothing was seen of them, the British force was to leave its patrol area in time to arrive within twenty miles of the Lizard before dawn.

Black Prince and her destroyers arrived on station punctually and began their patrol. *Haida* and *Athabaskan* were formed up a mile and a half on the cruiser's starboard bow; *Ashanti* and *Huron* had a corresponding station to port of her. Almost at once the force was detected by German radar stations on the French coast; and flashes of gunfire, apparently from shore batteries, appeared in the distance. No salvoes fell near, however, and for a time the patrol continued uneventfully.

Sharp on two o'clock *Black Prince* got a radar echo at 21,000 yards, dead ahead. A moment or so later *Haida* and *Ashanti* confirmed the contact. At that time the force was steaming in a northeasterly direction. The enemy ships were approaching almost head-on; but the radar picture had hardly been analysed when it changed dramatically. The Germans had reversed their course, increased speed from twenty to twenty-four knots and were steaming back for the French coast. The cruiser and her destroyers gave chase at thirty knots, certain now that they were on the track of the three Elbings from St. Malo.

At nineteen minutes after two, with the range reduced to 13,000 yards, *Black Prince* fired starshell over the enemy, while the destroyers raced ahead to engage him. According to the usual plan, *Black Prince* with her superior range would manoeuvre herself into position to provide illumination by starshell while the destroyers carried out the actual attack.

The first starshells from the cruiser burst to the right of the target. *Haida* signalled, "More Left," and the next bursts revealed three destroyers dead ahead at a range now reduced to about five miles. *Haida* and *Athabaskan* opened fire at 2.23; *Ashanti* and *Huron*, at 2.26. The Germans began immediately to make smoke; and soon only wreathing, greyish-white clouds could be distinguished ahead, fitfully illuminated by starshell. Salvoes from the four pursuing destroyers plunged into the murk; and out of it came the return fire of the Germans. The Elbings' gunnery was not particularly good, and they seemed to be concentrating mainly on escape as they zigzagged through the macabre mists of their screen.

Ashanti scored the first hit at thirty-one minutes after two. Five minutes later another bright red flash spumed up through the smoke, indicating a second hit, although it was impossible to tell which destroyer had scored. The chase continued for another fifteen minutes, with the pursuers closing the range to 7,300 yards but still unable to see their enemy. Difficulties increased a few minutes later when one of *Black Prince's* gun turrets jammed and the destroyers were forced to take turns in putting up starshell.

By 3.20 the flying Elbings, occasionally running out of their smoke screen and then ducking back, were hugging the French coastline, heading for St. Malo. They were within twelve miles of shore; and the outlying rocks not only provided inlets where they might hide but were already confusing radar operators with false echoes. *Haida* had noticed that her three radar targets seemed to have decreased to two, indicating that one of the Elbings had fanned out from the others. At about the same time *Black Prince* saw pass down her port side a torpedo which did not appear to have been fired by either of the two ships ahead.

Suddenly at 3.25 *Haida* sighted the Elbing which had broken away. It was two and a half miles distant on her starboard bow and was making off to the south and west after firing the torpedo at *Black Prince*. With *Athabaskan* following her, *Haida* turned at right angles, crossed a British minefield which had been laid in the area, and sent a first salvo crashing into the afterpart of the German ship. Her second and third salvoes struck amidships, starting other fires; and after them more shells came raining down from *Athabaskan*.

In a matter of minutes the Elbing was ablaze from stem to stern, but still firing. He continued his fire when *Ashanti* and *Huron*, having lost their two ships among the rocks of the coast, returned to join in the kill. Each destroyer fired torpedoes, none of which found its mark. Then, circling the blazing enemy at ranges as low as four hundred yards, the ships poured their gunfire into him. Just at the conclusion of the mêlée *Ashanti* and *Huron* collided with each other, doing considerable damage. Gradually the fire from the German vessel slackened. The flames mounted higher about it; then began to be eaten away at their base as the ship settled. At twenty-one minutes after four *Haida* reported to *Black Prince*, "Enemy has sunk."

Three days later, on April 28, *Haida* and *Athabaskan* sailed from Plymouth on an Operation Hostile mission. They were to screen a flotilla of British minelayers whose mission was to sow mines about ten miles east of Ile de Bas, near the mouth of the Morlaix River. By two o'clock on the morning of the 29th they had begun their patrol, and by three o'clock the minelayers had finished their work and were on the way home.

Previous to the departure of the minelayers, however, *Haida* and *Athabaskan* had received a signal from Plymouth, ordering them to steer southwest at full speed. It was a night on which radar conditions were exceptionally good; and radar stations on the English coast had picked up echoes which indicated an enemy force passing in a westerly direction across the entrance to the Morlaix River. At 3.13 Plymouth signalled the destroyers again that the enemy force was nearing them and was expected to pass through a position ten miles north of Ile de Bas. Fifteen minutes later this estimate was altered. The German ships were hugging the coast, and it now seemed that they would pass just one mile north of Ile de Bas.

Haida and *Athabaskan*, steaming southwest for the coast, estimated that they could intercept the enemy after he had passed Ile de Bas and while he was still east of Ile de Vierge. At one minute to four in the morning the first echo came. *Athabaskan* reported a radar contact to port, at a range of fourteen miles. Immediately afterward *Haida* obtained a confirming echo. The first indications were of two ships; but by eleven minutes after four the echoes had increased to three, making it appear that a third smaller vessel had joined the first two.

The range was closing rapidly and by 4.12 it was down to 7,300 yards. *Haida* gave the order, "Ignite", and *Athabaskan* fired starshell. Two destroyers, both Elbings, were revealed in the orange-pink glow of the bursts. Smoke immediately began to form about them as they laid a screen and turned away. *Haida* and *Athabaskan* opened fire; and, as they did so, turned their bows directly toward the enemy so as to present the narrowest possible silhouette for the torpedoes which German destroyers usually fired as they swung round to retreat.

Athabaskan had barely steadied on her new course when a huge sheet of flame shot up from her afterpart into the early morning darkness. She had been hit by a torpedo fired either from one of the two destroyers or from the third smaller vessel, possibly an E-boat, which was never sighted. As the torpedo struck, *Athabaskan* lost way, turned slowly to port and stopped. Probably her propellers or propeller shafts had been smashed and her rudder broken.

Large fires broke out above and below decks, both in the afterpart and amidships. All after guns were knocked out of action immediately, and in a moment or so fire from the forward guns also ceased. As the stern began to settle, the order "Stand by to abandon" was given. Boats were made ready but not lowered; and, as there seemed to be some hope of saving the ship, hands began to prepare cables for towing. The flames began to blaze up more fiercely and were now becoming uncontrollable. A fire party managed to get the ship's seventy-ton pump to the after part where the blaze was worst, and began the work of connecting it. Just as the last connections were falling into place, however, the destroyer's magazine blew up, sending into the sky a column of flame and smoke which was seen by ships thirty miles away.

With the second explosion the destroyer gave a tremendous heave to starboard, swung back slowly onto an even keel, and then listed to port. The men who were still on board and alive and conscious manged to shove a few carley floats overside and follow them into the water. They had a minute or so to push themselves away from the writhing steel sides above them. Then the blazing wreckage of what had been one of the happiest ships in the Canadian navy upended slowly in the water and slid under amid clouds of steam and the doleful roar of escaping air. On the oily, heaving blackness of the sea there remained only a few bobbing lights attached to the life jackets of *Athabaskan's* survivors, who were floating—many of them barely conscious—within five miles of the German-held coast.

For *Haida*, the grim priorities of sea warfare had to be maintained. When the torpedo struck *Athabaskan*, she had swung sharply to port and run across in front of her sister ship to lay a protective smoke screen. Then she had altered away again at full speed and resumed her pursuit of the Elbings, on one of which she had already scored a hit. Destruction of the enemy had still to take precedence over rescue work, and she was now hard on the heels of the Germans.

As usual her gunnery was magnificent, controlled throughout the action mainly by radar, since the Elbings could rarely be made out through their smoke. Just at the moment when *Athabaskan* blew up five miles astern, a salvo from *Haida* landed squarely on the Elbing she had already damaged. It banished all prospect of escape for the German; and he ran in at full speed to ground himself among the off-shore rocks of the coast. He still continued to fire, and *Haida,* coming in as close to the rocks as she dared, poured salvo after salvo into him until he was hopelessly ablaze. Then, with dawn breaking and the other Elbing beyond her reach, she turned back to do what she could for the men of *Athabaskan.*

As she reached their position *Haida* was five miles off the French coast, within range of shore batteries and liable to air attack at any moment. The destroyer stopped and dropped all her boats and floats. Scramble-nets were lowered over the side and word was passed from the bridge that the ship would remain for fifteen minutes. Her own men went down the scramble-nets to drag up dazed and exhausted survivors. Her motor cutter also went over the side, manned by a party of three volunteers in charge of Leading Seaman W. A. MacLure.

Haida remained stopped for fifteen minutes and during this time thirty-eight men were rescued. After that, as day broadened, she was under the absolute necessity of departing. Aircraft might be arriving in force from the German-held coast at any minute; and the first responsibility of *Haida's* commanding officer was to assure the safety of his own ship and her company. Word was passed along that the ship would go ahead in five minutes. The warning was repeated at one-minute intervals to the rescue parties labouring along the side and on the quarter deck. Sixty seconds after the last warning, the order "slow ahead" was given.

The water began to boil back along the destroyer's sides as she moved past clusters of men who raised an occasional faint cheer. Hands clutching at her scramble-nets lost their grip. Two of her own crew who had gone down the nets were washed off by the backrush and remained in the water with the survivors they had not been able to reach. Then, as *Haida* disappeared in the distance, three German mine-sweepers put out from the coast to make prisoners of the men who were left.

MacLure and his men in *Haida's* motor cutter had been cruising about picking up any survivors not on carley floats; and they had now eight in their craft, including their two shipmates who had been washed from the scramble-nets. They were not disposed to accept capture if it could be avoided; and when the mine-sweepers appeared, they set off in the direction of England. One of the German ships chased them briefly, and then for some unaccountable reason turned away. Unpursued, but with a very balky engine, the men in the motor cutter began a cross-channel voyage alone.

They had fuel for thirty hours and some emergency rations, but for a while it seemed that their chances were not good. Three times the motor failed entirely; and even after a leaky feedline had been patched, the best they could get out of their craft was a tedious three knots. In mid-afternoon a flight of bombers passed over them, but failed to observe their Verey lights and hand signalling. A little after four, three planes which they took to be Spitfires came toward them flying very low. Amid a flurry of waving hands the aircraft roared in at a height of about twelve feet, then zoomed upward to give the men in the boat a view of the black crosses of the *Luftwaffe* on the under side of the wings. In the early evening two more planes appeared; and were greeted more circumspectly. This time, however, there was no mistake. The planes were Spitfires; and, as they nosed down for a look, semaphore flags from the cutter spelled out, *"Athabaskan, Canada, Navy."* The Spitfires acknowledged the signal, and remained wheeling overhead until they were relieved by two more Spitfires and a Lancaster. Later in the evening a rescue launch of the Royal Air Force came charging out from the British coast; and by midnight the three men of the cutter's crew, together with the eight passengers, were being protestingly hospitalized "for observation" in Penzance. Their arrival brought the total number of *Athabaskan* survivors to forty-four. The commanding officer and 128 of the ship's company were missing and eighty-three were prisoners of war.

During May *Haida* and *Huron* took part in several other Tunnel and Hostile missions, none of which brought contact with the enemy. Then, toward the latter part of the month, the patrols of the 10th Destroyer Flotilla took on a different character. At Brest, at Cherbourg, and in the Biscay ports, the Germans still had some sixteen destroyers. For a time the all-important work would be to see that these ships did not reach the Neptune area. *Haida* and *Huron*, in company with British destroyers, were allotted to what was called the Hurd Deep patrol, named after a narrow ribbon of deep water, some ninety-five miles in length, lying roughly in mid-channel. The patrol line was to extend for thirty-eight miles parallel to the Deep and about fifteen miles north of it. Here, maintaining an average distance of seventy miles west of the assault lanes, the destroyers would be in a position to intercept any attack against the western flank; and here they were to patrol until the assault ships had entered Baie de la Seine and the troops were landed.

There remained, after all the dispositions against German surface ships had been made, the even more serious matter of protection against U-boats. With a force of two hundred submarines available to him, and with so much at stake, the enemy might be expected to make desperate efforts against invasion shipping. The waters of the Channel were too shallow and restricted, too littered with wrecks and torn by cross-tides, to be favourable U-boat territory. Nevertheless, the Germans had accepted unpleasant conditions before and might do so again. There was a strong suspicion that they had built a number of small submarines with a very high submerged speed which might defeat asdic detection. As it happened, these "Walter" boats, named after the firm of their inventor, never made an appearance. Other improvements were introduced, however, both in tactics and in equipment; and among them "schnorkel" was to prove the most troublesome.

Schnorkel solved to a considerable extent one of the oldest problems of submarine operation, the necessity to surface when charging batteries. U-boats, prior to the introduction of schnorkel, had had to travel on their batteries when under water; and had been forced to surface and run on their diesel engines when it was necessary to re-charge. The new device changed all this. It consisted simply of an air intake and exhaust, about the thickness of a stovepipe and the length of a periscope, which could be raised above the surface while the boat was under way. By means of it the submarine could run beneath the surface on her diesels, charging her batteries at the same time, and thus could remain submerged for an indefinite period. Except for exhaust fumes, which could be seen on the surface in clear weather at a distance of perhaps three miles, there was no indication of the U-boat's presence; and radar picked up only a very slight indication from the small target offered by the schnorkel tube. A few schnorkel-equipped boats had made their appearance late in 1943; and there was a virtual certainty that others would come into operation during the invasion. It was one more of many compelling reasons for the wide-spread system of defence which was being prepared against a submarine offensive in the Channel.

The Home Fleet lay ready to deal with any of the remaining heavy German ships which might venture down from their bases by way of the North Sea. Ample provision was also made against the attempts of U-boats to force the eastern entrance of the Channel by way of the Straits of Dover. The threat from the western Channel mouth, however, was considered the more serious. Here was the wider gateway, opening out into the Atlantic; and it was in this direction that the likeliest German concentrations lay. A number of U-boats could be expected to move inward from Brest, just outside the western lip of the Channel. Larger forces might come up through the Bay of Biscay from the great bases at Bordeaux, La Rochelle, St. Nazaire and Lorient. Still others could be expected, moving down along the coast of Ireland from Norway. Their primary object, when Neptune got under way, would be to attack the lanes of shipping in the central Channel. Prior to the launching of the assault, and for as long as it continued, they would have as a secondary and hardly less important target the innumerable convoys moving Neptune supplies along the coasts.

Their approach routes leading to the Channel mouth would fan out over wide areas, and they should be met as far to seaward as was practicable. The first defence requirement, therefore, was an outer screen of patrols blocking the entrance to the Channel and taking in a large section of the sea outside. For U-boats which might pierce the first screen, there must be other patrols waiting just inside the Channel mouth. Inside of them, again, were still other defences, of which the Tribals on the Hurd Deep patrol formed one and the motor torpedo boats another. The U-boats that penetrated so far, however, would be few; and it was the outer and secondary screens which were expected to have most to do with them.

Operation CA was the cryptic designation of the plan which established the outermost screen. It employed some forty ships assembled into six escort groups, of which two groups were Canadian. Although still retaining the escort title, these forces bore little resemblance to the groups which had sailed with the convoys in the earlier days. They were squadrons of hunting ships, all of them modern frigates equipped with the latest anti-submarine devices; and many of them had taken part in the 1943 offensive which had broken the back of the U-boat warfare in the Atlantic. They were charged now with the defence of a great rectangle of sea, 56,000 square miles in area, extending across the Channel mouth from Ile de Vierge on the French coast to a point in the Atlantic south of Ireland, and from there southward to take in a large section of the Bay of Biscay. Any U-boats attempting to enter the western Channel from the north, west or south would have to pass through this area; and here it was hoped to intercept them.

Waskesiu, Outremont, Cape Breton, Grou and *Teme* were the Canadian frigates comprising Escort Group 6. Escort Group 9, also Canadian, consisted of *Matane, Swansea, Stormont, Port Colborne, St. John* and *Meon*. Both groups were assigned to Operation CA; and on May 31, after a training period, arrived at Moelfre Bay in North Wales, which was to be their operational base. About four days remained before they would sail to take up patrol in the sector of the great rectangle which operation CA assigned to them.

The second zone of defence, immediately within the Channel mouth, was allotted to destroyers; and among these forces two Canadian destroyer groups were included. *Ottawa, Kootenay, Chaudière, St. Laurent* and *Gatineau* had been training at Londonderry as Escort Group 11; and with them had been *Qu'Appelle, Saskatchewan, Skeena* and *Restigouche,* comprising Escort Group 12. They arrived in Plymouth from Londonderry about the end of May; and by June 1 their officers were being briefed on Neptune orders which would send them into two squares of the defence checker-board south and eastward in the Channel from Land's End.

All ships were now moving on a schedule whose days were narrowing to hours. Far in the north the game was already afoot. At nine o'clock on the morning of May 31 five Canadian corvettes, *Trentonian, Mayflower, Drumheller,*

The Plan and the Preliminaries

Rimouski and *Louisburg,* with the British corvette *Nasturtium,* had sailed from Oban, Scotland, escorting the convoys of tows and blockships which were destined for the artificial harbours off the Normandy beaches. They had far to go and many ships would precede them into Baie de la Seine. This was the first movement on the Neptune time-table, however; and following it many other movements were in progress all around the British coast.

The Allies were not yet irrevocably committed. The spearheads had not been launched from the main assembly point, and there were check-points at which the coils of shipping gathering behind them could be stopped. There was to be little delay, however. The ships for the assault arrived at the last degree of readiness by June 3. The convoys moving down the coasts toward the assembly area came steadily on. There was an abortive start on June 4; a recall as the weather worsened, followed by sickening hours of uncertainty. Then, one day later than planned, but still within the prescribed period, the die was cast. The ships of the assault put forth, and far about them the moving walls of their defences swung into position.

At twelve o'clock on the morning of June 5, seven landing craft of the 260th Canadian Flotilla slipped their lines from Southampton docks and proceeded to join a stream of similar craft threading its way down the crowded anchorage of the Solent. Men from the four remaining craft of the flotilla, held back as a reserve, watched them go. Their way through the narrow harbour lanes, winding among more than a thousand ships still at anchor or already manœuvring for position, was difficult; and they had little time to give heed to the cheers which rose about them as they passed. They were heavy in the water and difficult to handle at the slow speed to which exact station-keeping compelled them. On board the seven craft were 250 Canadian and 1,050 British troops, all attached to the 3rd Canadian Division.

By four-thirty the flotilla had passed Spithead Gate at the eastern mouth of the Solent, carried along in a massive stream of shipping which was being joined by other streams from the east and west as the whole converged upon the assembly area. Two hours astern of them in the same stream followed the twelve craft of the 262nd Flotilla, carrying 1,946 Canadian and 148 British troops, also of the 3rd Canadian Division. In another stream, making for the assembly area by way of the western mouth of the Solent, were the seven craft of the 264th Canadian Flotilla, carrying 1,227 troops of the British Northumbrian Division.

The landing ships, larger and faster than the landing craft, were not required to get under way so early. Sailing time for *Prince Henry*, the senior landing ship in Force J, came at 9.10 in the evening. With 362 assault troops of the Canadian Scottish Regiment on board, she weighed anchor and proceeded past Spithead leading nine of her landing ships. *Prince David*, leading another sub-division of five landing ships, and carrying four hundred troops of the Regiment de la Chaudière with two parties of Royal Marines and a detachment of British pioneers, followed half an hour later. *Algonquin*, first of the bombardment destroyers in Force J, had begun her passage from the Solent at 6.15; and *Sioux* followed in her turn at 10.45.

All these and hundreds of other ships were assembling in accordance with the schedule of the Eastern Task Force, bound for Sword, Juno and Gold sectors in the British area. The craft of the 264th Canadian Flotilla were attached to Force G, whose destination was Gold sector. All other Canadian ships were included in Force J which was to land the troops of the Third Canadian Division on *Mike* and *Nan* beaches in Juno sector. Group by group, moving at set speeds and along routes dictated by their allotted stations, the arriving vessels passed into the assembly area and took up their formations. Joining the columns of troop-carrying craft came lines of the heavier and larger tank landing-craft, loaded with the soldiers' vehicles. Troop carriers and vehicle carriers would sail together in double-columned convoys, accepting the difficulties created by their varying sizes and speeds in order that their interdependent cargoes might be delivered to the beaches together.

Warships, transports, and weirdly assorted special craft of every size and kind, were ranging themselves in the order designed to bring them to the required positions off the beaches at the required time. The formed groups began to take on the appearance of individual convoys, each separated by exact intervals from the one behind and the one ahead. Escorts moved into station beside them, and the whole began to feed outward from the assembly area in ten great streams. Leaving behind it a weaving, ordered chaos fed continually by new floods of shipping, it flowed toward the mid-channel positions where dimly lighted buoys marked the entrances to the approach lanes.

Dusk closed down on the Channel at a little after ten. A southwest wind set briskly across the tide and lifted the sea into a choppy swell. By midnight a full moon, rarely seen among patches of ragged, scudding cloud, had lifted from the horizon. Beneath it the dark face of the Channel was combed by twenty lines of white and red lights, winking faintly at one-mile intervals along the port and starboard boundaries of the ten lanes. Between the bordering lights the ribbons of dark water were restless with shadowy movement, churned by an endless series of wakes whose ragged V's pointed steadily southward toward Baie de la Seine.

The columns of ships were speckled with the faint gleams of station-keeping lights; for this massive force, defended by layer upon layer of patrolling planes, had little to fear from the sky. Orders were that no passing aircraft should be fired on since it was almost certain to be friendly. The many engines droning overhead were those of bombers bound for the enemy coast. In an hour or so there would be a deeper, longer-sustained roar as transports and troop-carrying gliders towed in long trains began to pass over with the men of the parachute divisions, bound for the flanks of the beach head.

Across the twenty-mile front of the advance some ships were overtaking others as they moved into their final stations. *Algonquin* had passed up to the head in channel 7, going by *Prince Henry* on her way. *Prince Henry*, in turn, had led her group of landing ships past the twelve craft of the 262nd Flotilla, and then past the three craft which made up the first group of the 260th, all of them tossing and bucketing as they fought to maintain course and station amid the choppy cross sea. In the next lane *Sioux* was moving up astern of *Prince David's* group and would soon pass to take up station toward the head of the line of ships in channel 8. Both had already passed the second group of the 260th Flotilla which was sailing nearly abreast of its sister group in channel 7. Farther astern and to the west in channel 6, the craft of the 264th Flotilla were a part of one of the emerging streams still pouring from the assembly area.

Portsmouth, Southampton and the Solent were emptying now of the assault ships; and convoys were being staged onward around the coast to replenish the flood. The nineteen Canadian corvettes were among the multitude of escorts moving beside their convoys or waiting for the scheduled sailing hour. For most of the corvettes the first convoys would consist of the blockships, concrete barges, towed breakwaters and sections of pontoon piers for the artificial harbours, which were scheduled to arrive off the beaches after the assault was under way. *Trentonian, Mayflower, Drumheller, Rimouski* and *Louisburg* were standing by the blockships they had brought around from Oban to the south coast. *Alberni, Mimico, Lunenburg, Camrose, Baddeck, Prescott* and *Calgary* were at short notice to sail with other tugs and tows for the harbours. *Regina, Summerside* and *Woodstock* were already under way along the south coast with twenty-seven Liberty ships; and *Kitchener* would leave Plymouth in another hour with a convoy of landing craft. *Port Arthur* and *Moose Jaw* had some four hours of waiting before they sailed from Milford Haven on the west coast with a convoy of fourteen motor transport ships; and *Lind-*

say would leave eleven hours behind them with nine merchantmen.

Flung out through the western Channel and on into the Atlantic and the Bay of Biscay, screening the assault lanes and the convoys feeding into them, were the zones of outer defence. Here, too, were Canadian ships in company with many others. Off Point Barfleur, at the western tip of Baie de la Seine, the Motor Torpedo Boats of the 29th Canadian Flotilla were a part of the inmost patrol. On the northern side of the Channel the boats of the 65th Flotilla were stationed along the convoy routes leading across Lyme Bay to the assembly area. In mid-Channel, along the line of the Hurd Deep patrol, *Haida* and *Huron* waited with British ships for German destroyers of whom no movement had yet been reported. Just inside the mouth of the Channel the destroyers of Escort Group 11 and Escort Group 12 swept back and forth along adjoining sectors. Two hundred miles west and north of them in the open Atlantic the frigates of Escort Group 6 and Escort Group 9 had taken up station at the outer limit of the Operation CA zone. Westward of them across the width of the Atlantic, unrecorded yet still deserving a place in any chronicle of Neptune, were the Canadian groups who sailed as guardians of the ocean convoys moving from North America to Britain. And back again in the assault lanes, now within nine miles of the beaches and far ahead of all the approaching ships, sixteen Canadian minesweepers were at work on a task from which not many of their men expected to return.

CHAPTER TWELVE

The Assault

THE lights along the ten lanes of Neptune had been set in place by flotillas of minesweepers, proceeding five miles ahead of the assault ships. Each of the flotillas was responsible for clearing one channel through the outer mine barrier and on into the beaches. As they swept mile by mile inward, they had dropped lighted danbuoys anchored by weights and wires along the borders of each lane.

The 31st Canadian Minesweeping Flotilla was one of those allotted to the assault sweep. With the others it had started out the day before, only to be recalled when worsening weather caused the operation to be postponed. On the morning of June 5, with clearing skies and abating seas in the Channel, the second order for Neptune to go forward had been given; and the 31st had left its Portland anchorage for the assembly area. Among the nine other flotillas, six Canadian ships were included; all of which, like the 31st, were to work in the four western channels leading to the American sector.

The 31st was to sweep channel number 3. On its right, in channel 1, *Canso* would be among the ships of the 16th British Flotilla. *Guysborough, Kenora, Vegreville* and *Georgian* would be with the 14th British Flotilla, sweeping channel 2. Immediately to the left of the 31st, *Thunder* would be one of the ships of the 4th Minesweeping Flotilla in channel 4. Although intervals of departure from the assembly area would be arranged to provide for the varying distances to the points where each lane would be opened, the flotillas would be operating approximately side by side during the progress of the sweep.

The German mine belt which ran up the Channel across the mouth of Baie de la Seine was believed to be some eight miles in depth; with its inner edge about thirty miles from the assault beaches. Starting a little beyond its outer limit, between forty and forty-five miles from the coast, the sweepers were to cut approach channels through the barrier. Inward from that, they were to clear assault channels to an area betwen seven and ten miles off shore where the transports and bombarding ships would anchor. Each flotilla was then to sweep a sector of this transport and bombardment area running all along the beaches. After that they were each to sweep another channel and a series of boat lanes right in to the limit of deep water, clearing the way for the approach of the landing craft.

The schedule of the four flotillas sweeping the Western Task Force area would bring them to the outer edge of the minebelt, in sight of the German shore batteries on Point Barfleur, during the early evening of June 5. Midnight would find them at the end of the approach lanes and in the transport area, nine miles off the beaches. Shortly before dawn, at the limits of the inmost lanes, which were called fire support channels, they would be within a mile and a half of the French coast.

All flotillas were equipped with very new and very secret devices for the jamming of enemy radar reception; and supporting ships would be prepared to assist them if they were heavily engaged. None of this altered the fact that they were almost certain to be detected once their work got under way. Nor could supporting ships do much to protect them from shore batteries which would have them in point-blank range. The sweeping of the lanes was a complex and exacting operation, and the ships would have to sail at all times in rigidly controlled formation, maintaining set courses and speeds. Against fire from shore, or against the torpedoes of a swarm of E-boats, they were hopelessly vulnerable. From one half to one third of the ships in each flotilla sailed as a reserve against expected casualties; and Neptune orders prescribed that the sweep was to be continued without deviation in the face of whatever opposition might be encounterd.

The minebelt was believed to be made up principally of moored mines, suspended on long wires held to the bottom by weights. The Oropesa sweep, which the Canadian Bangor class minesweepers and the other ships of the ten flotillas were equipped to carry out, was designed to cut the mooring wires of the mines and bring them bobbing to the surface. As they emerged, they were not to be exploded or sunk by gunfire as was the usual practice. The danger of explosions which would betray the sweepers' presence to the enemy was considered to be greater than the danger of floating mines, whose mechanism generally rendered them safe upon surfacing. Until the ships had definite knowledge that the Germans were aware of their presence they were to leave all cut mines afloat, to be carried across the other lanes or perhaps out of the area by the cross tide.

The direction of each lane, leading as it did to a certain area off a certain beach, varied slightly from that of all other lanes. Each must conform exactly to the plotted chart which was entrusted to the flotilla's senior officer. He would have every latest navigational device to assist him; but the work, to be done in darkness and across an easterly-setting tide which reversed itself to a westerly set at ten o'clock, was still one of great difficulty and great responsibility. Upon the accurate sweeping and marking of the channels depended the co-ordination of the whole Neptune movement. Assault ships would be entering each lane by the time the sweepers had laid their danbuoys at the fifth mile ahead of them; and there would be no time then for the correction of any man's error.

At 5.35 on the afternoon of June 5 the 31st Canadian Flotilla, with its Neptune orders in effect, proceeded southward from the assembly area off the Isle of Wight. Although some forty miles of open water lay ahead of it before the German minebelt was reached, a sweeping formation was adopted immediately. Mines had been sown liberally between the outer limit of the barrier and the shores of England; and in any case a preparatory sweep would give the ships an opportunity to see that all gear was working properly.

At the head of the sweepers sailed *Caraquet,* in which the senior officer of the flotilla was embarked. It was flanked by three British Fairmile motor launches. Astern of *Caraquet* were the five sweepers, *Fort William, Wasaga, Cowichan, Minas* and *Malpeque,* disposed in G formation to port, an arrangement which put each ship eight hundred yards astern and about two hundred yards to port of the one ahead. *Caraquet* and the other five vessels constituted the actual sweeping formation. A British trawler, *Gunner,* sailed astern of *Fort William* as danlayer on the port side of the lane. *Bayfield,* sailing astern of *Cowichan,* was danlayer for the starboard side. *Milltown, Blairmore* and *Mulgrave* sailed within the formation as reserve ships. At the end of the line was a reserve danlayer, the British trawler, *Green Howard;* and ahead of *Caraquet* a British Fairmile, whose shallow draught rendered it comparatively safe from moored mines, trailed a sweep wire across the bow of the senior ship.

The sweep in G formation had, in principle, some resemblance to the ordinary procedure for mowing a lawn. Down the length of channel 3, and taking in its entire breadth of 1200 yards, overlapping lanes were to be cleared, one by each ship. *Caraquet,* at the starboard boundary of the channel, trailed her long sweep wire astern of her. It was held at the required depth and at the required distance to port by a paravane float. The sweep wire, dragging beneath the surface, was intended to saw through the mooring cables of any German mines which it might encounter and bring them to the surface. Astern of *Caraquet, Fort William* sailed just within the outer limit of the leader's sweep; and was thus in cleared water while her own sweep extended out astern and to port of her, clearing a new lane. The other four ships with their sweeps were staggered similarly in succession behind, their various lanes overlapping each other for safety and extending altogether to the portside border of the channel. In this formation the ships proceeded unhurriedly through the early evening, came in sight of Point Barfleur, and at seven o'clock entered the minebelt.

There was no enemy reaction either from the batteries on Point Barfleur or from the assault beaches which were now within radar range. Apparently unnoticed, the Bangors, which had spent so many drab years with the coastal convoys along the shores of Canada, began the historic operation upon which the dreams and nightmares of the world were centred. The men on board the ships had little opportunity to meditate upon the change in their fortunes, the epic quality of the adventure, or the imminent danger in which they moved. The foot-by-foot exactness of the navigation demanded the utmost vigilance. The long sweep wires, trailed on their floats behind the ships, were a continual source of danger and anxiety. The afterdecks of the danlayers, piled high with buoys, floats, lengths of wire, shackles, weights and miscellaneous gear, were scene of equally tense, nerve-wracking activity. Each danbuoy had to go overside at the correct moment, weighted with two 175-pound blocks shackled to about six hundred feet of wire. It would be a marker eagerly sought by lines of approaching ships and a dan out of place might delay a whole column or throw it into writhing confusion.

The approach channel extended through the width of the minefield for a depth of 8.2 miles, running a little east of due south. Unfired on and apparently unnoticed, the ships of the 31st Flotilla reached the inner end of the lane at ten minutes after ten. It was nearly full dark as they altered a little to the west and began to sweep down the assault channel which would run in toward the beaches for another 18.8 miles. At twenty minutes after midnight this channel, too, was completed. Laboriously maintaining formation, with their sweeps riding around behind them, they altered course again to run along nearly parallel to the shore, sweeping their sector of the transport and bombardment area. They continued on, nearing the coast a little all the time, for a distance of 4.5 miles; and then at five minutes after one turned southward again, directly in toward the beaches, to go down the fire support channel which would take them to within 1.5 miles of shore. They were in this position at three o'clock when the full moon, which had been riding above them lightly obscured by wind-driven clouds, broke through into a patch of clear sky and illuminated the sea for perhaps a minute. As it disappeared, men who had briefly remembered the dangers about them drew breath once more.

The ships altered to seaward and swept back up the fire support channel to the point at which they had begun it, crossed along the breadth of their transport area, then altered formation to line abreast and swept in again to within two miles of shore. The miraculous silence of the enemy continued. Unmolested, the sweepers completed their task at 5.15, returned up the fire support channel as the first of the assault ships began to come down, and anchored inconspicuously in their assault area to await further orders.

The other flotillas, engaged on the same work with only minor variations, took up similar waiting positions when their sweeps were completed. As soon as the movements of the assembling ships permitted, even before the assault itself began, the work would have to be resumed. Channels would have to be broadened and merged; new areas of water would have to be swept and old water re-swept. *Guysborough,* *Kenora, Vegreville* and *Georgian,* with the other ships of the 14th Flotilla, stood by at the inner limit of assault channel 2. The 4th Flotilla, which included *Thunder,* was ordered at six o'clock to commence sweeping between channels 3 and 4, which were to be merged. *Canso* and the other ships of the 16th Flotilla in channel 1 completed their work at 5.16, a minute after their brothers of the 31st, and turned toward their anchorage station under a blaze of anti-aircraft fire directed from shore at some of the bombers arriving overhead.

The assault ships had now been pouring down the channels for some time, elbowing aside the returning sweepers. Dimly outlined in the pre-dawn darkness, the men of the 31st Flotilla made out the shapes of the United States battleships, *Texas* and *Arkansas*. The British cruiser, *Glasgow*, moved by them; and then the French cruiser, *Montcalm*. *Georges Leygues*, another French cruiser following astern, passed so close to *Minas* that she had to go hard to starboard to avoid collision. Neptune was arriving vastly; and to the eastward in the British sector Canadian ships were among the hundreds moving into station.

Force J was ranging itself before the beaches of Juno sector. The landing ships, led by *Prince Henry* and *Prince David*, had now emerged from channels 7 and 8. Reaching their positions seven miles off shore, they swung parallel to the coast and deployed along their sector of the transport area. Times of arrival and deployment from the two channels had varied by only a few minutes; and by 5.35 the nineteen vessels were swinging at anchor in an eerie half-dawn light, each an exact three hundred yards from the next.

Daylight broadened, with a low cloud base breaking up along the horizon. The ten lines of ships were still pouring inward from the north, but those already disgorged from the mouths of the swept channels had spread out eastward and westward along the coast for sixty miles. In front of every sector of the beaches the appointed vessels were swinging at anchor or moving into station at graded distances from shore. The drone of returning bombers was heard overhead; and the dim shoreline glowed and smoked here and there, testifying to the destruction the planes had left behind them. In a few moments there was a dull roar from seaward and the first salvoes of battleships and cruisers began to scream above the long lines of landing ships.

The landing ships themselves were now astir. On board *Prince Henry* and *Prince David* the crews of the assault craft took their stations. In the troopdecks below, the waiting soldiers looked to their gear for the last time; heard the voice, hardened to brassy inexorability by the loud hailer, warning the groups of their approaching times: "Will move in . . . ten . . . minutes" . . . "will move in . . . five . . . minutes" . . . "will move . . . now."

The Assault

First to be lowered into the water from *Prince David* were two Royal Navy craft which she had carried in addition to her own. At seventeen minutes after six, one of the craft, loaded with Royal Marines, went over the side and set off for *Nan* beach, where it was to provide supporting small-arms fire. The second craft went in twenty minutes later, also carrying Royal Marines who were to work waist deep in the water off shore, clearing mines and obstacles ahead of the assault craft.

Then it was the turn of the Canadians. L.C.A. 1375 was lowered from *Prince David*, and L.C.A. 1372 from *Prince Henry*. They were not bound immediately for the beaches, but were to report to the Deputy Senior Officer of their landing-ship groups as general duty craft. Next, while similar preparations stirred all along the lines of landing ships, *Prince Henry's* seven remaining assault craft swung outward on their davits. The soldiers emerged group by group from the troop decks, climbed quietly into their places; and the craft were lowered to the water. From *Prince David* came five more; and the two Canadian flotillas moved out to join the swarm from other landing ships, already assembling into beaching flights, three flotillas to a flight. *Prince Henry's* craft were a part of one of the flights which were to land the assault units of the 7th Brigade of the Third Canadian Division on *Mike Red*, a mile to the east of Courseulles. The flights which included *Prince David's* craft were to land troops of the 8th Brigade on *Nan White*, a mile and a half farther east.

As the flights were formed, each one, led by a motor gunboat, began the seven-mile trip. All along the front of Baie de la Seine, flotillas, flights and forces merged into one vast inward movement, a low disturbance on the water, crawling raggedly toward shore.

H-hour, the touch-down time for the Eastern Task Force, was set for 7.25 in Sword and Gold sectors; and was delayed from twenty to thirty minutes in Juno sector so that the tide could rise higher and cover the off-shore rocks. The L.C.A.'s would be a little over an hour in making the trip from the assault anchorage to the beaches. From behind them came the steady rumble of the bombardment. Passing salvoes screamed incessantly overhead, and before them was obscure confusion marking the preparatory phases to be completed by the time they arrived.

Rough water was interfering with the launching plans for the amphibious tanks; and many of them did not reach shore ahead of the infantry as intended. The rest of the movement was proceeding on most sectors with uncanny precision. Hunt class destroyers and support landing-craft were closely engaging the beach defences. Army artillery, mounted in carrier craft, was moving in, firing as it came. And the Fleet class destroyers of the bombardment force were now in action.

Algonquin and *Sioux* were among the seventy-eight Fleets which opened fire almost simultaneously. *Algonquin's* first target was a battery of two 75-millimetre guns located between some houses just west of St. Aubin sur Mer. As she commenced, the dust from the earlier air bombardment was still floating about her target, making things difficult for her gunnery officers. Her log bears the ungrateful notation, "God damn air force is messing up our target again." Nevertheless, several of her salvoes fell directly on the battery; and with her first target obliterated she transferred to a row of houses sheltering snipers along *Nan Red*.

Sioux's opening target was two large buildings, each sheltering a 75-millimetre gun, a mile and a half to the east of St. Aubin. Within twenty minutes both guns had been silenced; and after briefly shelling another target *Sioux* checked fire. The landing craft were passing inward of the bombardment anchorages; and well ahead of them, now almost at the limit of shallow water, were still other craft.

These were the terrible rocket-firing ships; and their projectiles hurtled inward with a searing roar, blasting lanes of fire through mines, beach obstacles and any defences in their way. Next, threading between the rocket ships, came craft which roared up on the sand unloading the *Avre* tanks of the Royal Engineers, to breach minefields and concrete barriers in the paths of the troops. Still other craft were close behind the *Avre's*, stopping short of the beaches in water five feet deep and spattered by the bullets of German machine guns, to disgorge men who went instantly to work clearing away mines and beach obstructions.

Neither they nor all the gunfire which preceded them could do more than lessen the perils of these man-made reefs lining the beaches for half a mile off shore. Just visible at the half tide mark on Sword and Gold beaches, heavy steel gates, eight feet wide by ten feet high, projected from the bottom. They were designed to canalize the flow of landing craft onto the other obstructions which waited behind them. On Juno beaches, ahead of the Canadians, these gates were not used, apparently because the shore itself was rockier; but on all beaches the second defence to be encountered was line after line of sharp wooden stakes driven into the sand. Behind the stakes were steel-pronged tripods which would rip the bottom out of any vessel passing over them. Many of the tripods were mined; other mines were sown indiscriminately along the shelving bottom; and nearest inshore in the breaking surf were rows of concrete pyramids hung with more mines and with fused shells.

The troop-carrying flights were nearing shore now. Although the Channel had not seemed particularly rough from the decks of the landing ships, it was another thing from the assault craft. Flat-bottomed, difficult to manœuvre, assailed by a brisk wind and a cross tide, they bounced and dipped in the choppy water, drenching everyone on board with spray. Only in the moments when they poised on the crest of a wave could their men get a glimpse of the beaches ahead. From the Canadan assault craft there was a distant, spray-screened blur of smoking shoreline, an occasional suggestion of meadows and woods rolling beyond; but the view along the beach front no longer resembled the clear, neat photographs the men had been made to remember during their briefing sessions. Gunfire from sea had added new wreckage to the debris left by the air bombardment; and every building which might conceal an enemy strongpoint had been ruthlessly smashed.

The assault flights of Force J deployed from line ahead to line abreast, a few hundred yards off *Mike* and *Nan* beaches. Rank by rank behind them the friendly fire from sea rumbled into silence. At twenty-seven minutes after eight the flight which included *Prince Henry's* flotilla charged in through the surf before *Mike Red*, and the awful quiet which had seemed to possess the beaches in contrast to the roar of the bombardment was again broken by mortar and machine-gun fire, the crash of boats tearing out their bottoms on obstacles, and the bursts of exploding mines.

L.C.A. 856 crashed sidewise into one of the concrete pyramids, swerved off and surged on up the beach. L.C.A. 1021, racing in beside a tank landing craft, collided with the larger vessel and was heaved broadside onto shore. The other five craft swept in unharmed to shallow water and began pouring out their troops. Light machine-gun fire and the bullets of snipers whistled overhead and ricochetted from the water about them; but within five minutes the troops from all seven craft were ashore and making for the first row of dunes beyond the beach.

Prince David's L.C.A.'s beached with another flight a mile and a half to the eastward, paying dearly as they charged in over the fangs and mines hidden in the surf beneath them. L.C.A. 1059 reared up, plunged forward, and then sagged down in shallow water with a hole gashed out of her bow by a mine. Another mine had already ripped half the bottom out of craft 1150, and a third explosion sent the nose of 1137 digging into the sand beneath four feet of water. Craft 1138 got safely to shore and had almost finished discharging her troops when a wave lifted her and flung her outward again onto another mine whose explosion synchronized with a burst of German shrapnel directly overhead. Of *Prince David's* five assault craft, 1151 alone made the beach undamaged. Troops from all craft were unloaded, however, with a loss of five killed; and were soon moving inward toward their first objective. Many German gun positions were still unsubdued and the advancing soldiers were meeting with a fairly heavy volume of fire.

It was getting on toward nine o'clock; and all along the beaches the assault craft from the landing ships had delivered the shock troops. With them had come the vehicle-carrying craft to discharge the first requirements of tanks, jeeps, lorries and scores of other strange constructions moving on wheels and caterpillar treads. Craft, vehicles and men had been poured in with deliberate prodigality. There was no easy way through the steel and concrete obstructions and the mines that tossed or floated among them. Fire from sea had churned along the water's edge, clearance parties had laboured, and were still labouring, in surf which splashed about their shoulders, but the deadly teeth gradually disappearing under the rising tide were still innumerable. The assault wave had had to smash its way in over them, reckless of loss. All along the shore, swimming and drowning men, overturned tanks, craft sagging in shallow water or hung at sickening angles on pronged obstructions, were the sights which greeted the approaching waves of the reinforcements.

They were coming in now, carried by the larger landing craft which had crossed the Channel under their own power. Included in separate flights, the two groups of the 260th Canadian Flotilla swung into line abreast before their beaching positions on *Nan Red, Nan White* and *Mike Green.* The three craft of the first group were ordered to hold off; as obstacle clearance parties were still busy in the surf ahead of them. The second group was not delayed. Its four craft came within half a mile of the smoke-shrouded shore, between St. Aubin and Bernières, taking their bearings on the spire of a little church in the distance. They spotted what seemed to be a gap in the rows of obstacles peering through the surf ahead of them, and at 9.10 went in for the beach at full speed.

Craft 298 ground up on the rocky shore undamaged; and her 167 soldiers scrambled ashore under mortar and machine gun fire. Craft 121 had been charging in abreast of 298 when a wave smashed into her bow, tore away her starboard landing ramp, and flung her First Lieutenant overboard ahead of the boat. As he hit the water a strand of wire, ripped free by the wave, looped itself about his neck. He managed to dive under the bow of the craft as it rode over him, free himself of the wire at the same time, and eventually emerge astern to be picked up by another boat. Craft 121 bore on, swerved aside from several obstacles, and then crashed into one which stopped it dead, holed its forward troop space and killed or wounded nine of the soldiers. The remaining troops stepped off into four feet of water and made their way to the beach.

Craft 301, jarring and swerving among several of the concrete blocks, rode up onto the beach without serious damage. Craft 249, with mortar bombs exploding ahead of her, and overturned vehicles blazing on both sides, reached shallowing water before a mine smashed up her port bow and ripped away her landing ramps. Her troops—engineers and demolition squads with much heavy equipment—had to struggle ashore through breast-high water in the face of machine-gun and mortar fire.

Meanwhile, of the 260th Flotilla's first group, boats 177 and 285 were still held off shore and were to remain there till early afternoon. Boat 117 was sent in alone at 9.30. As she ran in side by side with a tank landing-craft, the larger vessel swerved over and gashed a hole in her starboard bow. Listing, she came to a stop in five feet of water. Seamen leaped across her damaged ramps, struggled in to shore with leading lines for the troops to hold onto, and the heavy-burdened soldiers splashed their way toward battle.

The twelve craft of the 262nd Flotilla had made their journey to Baie de la Seine some distance astern of the 260th in channel 7. Shortly after nine they arrived with their flight in the beaching position off *Nan White*, and there they were held until 11.28, circling leisurely in a line one behind the other, while the men on board watched the ambiguous, smoky shore and marvelled at the bewildering assemblage of shipping about them.

At 11.28 the beaching order came. The flotilla unwound its circle, formed abreast, and plunged through the surf in a long east west line. Craft 115 and 125 roared onto the beach with holes gashed in their bottoms by obstacles; 263 stopped a little short, sagging heavily as water poured in through jagged rents in her starboard side. A grazing mine explosion tore away part of 299's hull, and 135 staggered in over another obstacle which gouged out part of her bottom. Next to her, 306 scraped up onto the rocks, the only one of the flotilla to reach shore unhurt.

Craft 270, running in alongside 306, might have had the most serious casualties of all if her commanding officer had not ordered the soldiers out of her forward troop space. He had decided that the men would be safer on deck than down in the bows, even though they would be exposed to the fire of snipers from shore. The troops had hardly emerged from their cramped accommodation when a mine blew in the part of the hull which had sheltered them. Most of them would have been killed had they remained below; and as it was, three of the naval crew were wounded.

Next along the line, 250 had her nose blown off by a mine; 118, her running mate, was also mined; while the tiller flat and the engine room of 262 were blown in by two more explosions. Beyond them, 276 leaped and swerved four times as steel or concrete tore at her hull; and 252 reached the shore line with her starboard propeller knocked out of action by a concrete block, and water pouring in through a hole in her side.

All the vessels, lurching to the rocky sand or fighting their way into water shallow enough for the discharge of the troops, were under mortar and machine-gun fire from still unsubdued strong points. Craft ahead of and all about them thronged the shore, in as bad or worse condition than the Canadians. Landed troops and tanks were milling into formation on the beaches and ahead were the smoke and rattle

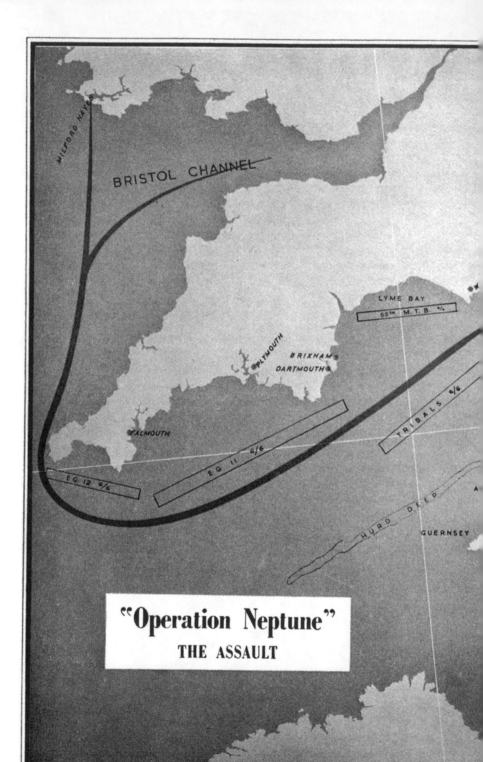

MILFORD HAVEN

BRISTOL CHANNEL

LYME BAY
65ᵀᴴ M. T. B. ⁶⁄₆

PLYMOUTH BRIXHAM
DARTMOUTH

TRIBALS ⁶⁄₆

FALMOUTH

EG II ⁶⁄₆

EG 12 ⁶⁄₆

HURD DEEP

GUERNSEY

"Operation Neptune"
THE ASSAULT

R THAMES

RAMSGATE

DOVER

SOUTHAMPTON   SHOREHAM   NEWHAVEN

CALSHOT   PORTSMOUTH

SPITHEAD   SELSEY BILL

ISLE OF
WIGHT

Z

1.2.34, 5.6.7.8.9.10

POINT
BARFLEUR   CAPE D'ANTIFER

BARFLEUR   102 MILES

WESTERN   EASTERN
TASK FORCE   TASK FORCE

HAGUE   CHERBOURG   FIFTH   TUNNY NORTH
SECTORS   MIXED   LE HAVRE   R SEINE
AREA

OMAHA   TUNNY SOUTH
SECTORS   GOLD   PATROL
SECTORS   JUNO SWORD   AREA

BIG
ST LO   BAYEUX   MIKE   CABOURG
PORT EN BASSIN   JAN
ARROMANCHES   ST AUBIN   OUISTREHAM

CAEN
R ORNE

of fighting. The troops, shaken by the tumultuous last lap of their journey, gathered themselves, stepped over the ramps, and struggled ashore through waist-deep water. All of them were heavily burdened enough, and with most of them came extra gear, adding danger and delay to the work of landing. In many of the L.C.I.'s there were between 150 and 200 bicycles, all to be lifted ashore amid a tumult of shouted orders, the whistle of bullets overhead, and the sound of fiercer fighting inland. In strange contrast, the soaking, sweating men in the landing craft looked up to marvel briefly at the sight of a French farmer emerging from an unscarred stone cottage not two hundred yards away and going placidly with a milk pail toward a meadow where his cow was grazing.

The craft of the 264th Flotilla, coming down channel 6 with Force G, had arrived·off *Jig Red.* two miles east of Arromanches, at 9.40. At 11.50 their beaching order came and at 11.59 they ground up onto the shore in precise formation line abreast, each craft touching down within five seconds of the one beside it. They were the luckiest of all the Canadian flotillas. Though the surf was running more heavily now and piling up dangerously, they made the sand without damage and put their troops ashore twelve feet from high water mark.

Along the miles of beach comprised in the British area the desolation of wrecked craft, the vehicles burning at the waters' edge and the milling masses of men, tanks and guns ashore, had now an appearance of chaos, which was delusive. The landings had gone amazingly well. To the west, in the American area, there was fiercer fighting, but the footholds were being gained and held. Casualties among the troops were lighter than had been expected, and among the naval crews of the landing craft lightest of all. Not one Canadian sailor had been killed and only a handful wounded. Many of the landing craft had been damaged, some of them irreparably; but they were, if necessary, expendable; and the greater number of them were to be recovered. Even now some of them were on their return journey, and men were labouring over others to get them off the beaches and back into the reinforcement pools.

Of *Prince David's* assault flotilla, only one, the duty craft 1175, assigned to the Deputy Senior Officer, was to return to the mother ship, and that not for some time. It had been sent in to the beach behind the first assault waves to pick up wounded and survivors, then on to various ferrying jobs and a hazardous beaching under mortar fire between three burning and exploding tanks. By noon it was ashore waiting to unbeach on the next tide, and in the late evening it returned to the Deputy Senior Officer for new ferrying missions which were to keep it occupied for several days.

The two Royal Navy assault craft which *Prince David* had carried were both sunk close off shore, although their crews were saved. Four of her own craft were hopelessly crippled with their crews high if not dry on the beach. Of the five which had gone in with the assault wave, only one, 1151, had been in condition to make the return journey. The flotilla officer had decided to load all the crews of the other craft into her for the trip back to *Prince David*, and as soon as the tide rose enough to cover most of the beach obstacles, she began her outward journey. She was just in time, however, to be caught by the waves of the reinforcement vessels pouring in. A charging tank carrier forced her over onto an obstacle which tore out her bottom and she sank at once, leaving her men to flounder ashore again. There they waited until one o'clock when an outbound lighter carried them back to *Prince David*.

All of *Prince Henry's* craft, with the exception of 1021, which was mined in coming off the beach, had returned and been hoisted on board by 12.30. Craft 1372, the duty craft, had returned for repairs about noon after having her bow damaged by mortar fire, but was off within an hour on new missions which would hold her in the assault area for several days. By early afternoon both the Canadian landing ships, swinging at anchor with the others of their groups, were the scenes of a different kind of activity. The first of the wounded were now being brought out from the beaches.

Un-Beaching and Return

Prince David took on board fifty-eight men, and *Prince Henry* fifty-six, lowering them on stretchers to the sick bays and the improvised hospitals in the ward rooms. The wounded and the survivors from sunken vessels were an effectual check on any feeling of elation over the progress of the landings. Soaked, dishevelled, and covered with sand from the beaches, some of them were horribly wounded by land mines and shrapnel. Men died as they were being hoisted on board or before they could be laid on an operating table. Others chattered with the feverish cheerfulness of shocked men; while still others, drawing deeply on cigarettes proffered by the watching sailors, were wryly complacent over the blighties which were sending them home. Throughout the afternoon and night the ships' surgeons, sick bay attendants and chaplains cared for the living and administered last rites to those for whom men could do no more.

Meanwhile a limping procession of landing craft was threading its way back toward England through streams of newly-arriving shipping. The two groups of the 260th Flotilla were on their way, with 298 towing 249. L.C.I. 117 and 285 which had beached later and had been forced to wait for the turn of the tide were a little behind them. Of the 262nd Flotilla, craft 306, 125, 250, 252, 118 and 262 in tow of 276, were crawling northward in a long string by early afternoon. Craft 135, shoved into navigable water by bulldozers which scooped a channel ahead of her, was on passage by 4.30. Craft 263, 270, 299 and 115 had been the worst damaged and were still on the beaches with repair parties working furiously over them. They were to be there for the next two days before engineering supervisors on the beaches considerd them to be in a condition even remotely resembling seaworthiness, and during that waiting period some of the Canadian sailors were to find time and room on the beaches for a baseball game. The evening of the 8th was to see them underway for the Solent, shoved into the water by bulldozers and bombed by enemy aircraft which came over just as they set off.

The Assault

Craft 305 and 255 of the 264th Flotilla unbeached and sailed for the Solent in the early afternoon of the 6th. Craft 295, 288, 302 and 311 were retained in the assault area for ferry service, and the men of 310, which was held over till the 7th, took advantage of an afternoon lull to visit the near-by town of Arromanches, returning with several German uniforms and a stock of less warlike souvenirs.

In mid-morning on the 6th the destroyers of the bombardment group resumed fire intermittently. Their visible targets on the beaches had been obliterated and their fire was now controlled by army observation officers ashore. On the sector covered by *Sioux's* guns the fighting was so close and confused that the observer reported himself unable to call down fire without danger to friendly troops; and *Sioux's* guns did not open up again during the day.

Algonquin had better luck. At about ten o'clock her observer located a battery of three 88-millimetre guns two miles inland from Courseulles. The battery was holding up the advance of the Regiment de la Chaudière, part of whose troops had been landed by *Prince Henry's* assault craft. Under the direction of her observer, *Algonquin* moved close inshore and dropped two ranging salvoes around the battery. The third salvo was dead on; and three more were enough to silence the guns. *Algonquin's* gunners learned the result of their work against an unseen target some time later. Thirteen out of fifteen shells had fallen on the battery. The army observer ashore was thoroughly impressed by the performance of "his" ship, and months later was seen cruising the roads of France with *"Algonquin"* painted across the front of his jeep.

Of the minesweepers, the 4th British Flotilla, with *Thunder*, sailed back for Portland on the morning of the 6th to begin sweeping a newly-laid minefield at the head of the approaches. The 16th British Flotilla, with *Canso*, sailed for Plymouth and was to return to the assault area next day. The 14th British Flotilla, with *Guysborough, Kenora, Vegreville* and *Georgian*, had resumed work in Baie de la Seine an hour after the assault; and the 31st Canadian Flotilla was to have begun again at about the same time. Its orders were delayed until two o'clock, however, by the huge volume of signal traffic passing between the ships. At that time it resumed, commencing a series of sweeps through the lanes and anchorages which was to occupy it for some eighteen hours a day until the 13th.

By early afternoon of the 6th the follow-up convoys had begun to arrive off the beaches. At four o'clock *Kitchener* brought in her party of landing craft. Before dawn on the 7th *Alberni* and *Mimico* arrived with barges. *Trentonian*, *Mayflower* and *Drumheller* squeezed their long lines of blockships down the narrow lanes at a little before noon. *Regina*, *Summerside* and *Woodstock* had already arrived with their convoy of Liberty ships; *Prescott* was off the beaches by five in the afternoon. Dawn of the 8th brought *Port Arthur*, *Moose Jaw*, *Camrose* and *Baddeck*. *Rimouski*, *Louisburg* and *Lunenburg* came an hour or so later. *Lindsay* arrived in the forenoon of the 9th after a crossing marked by a sharp battle with E-boats; and *Calgary*, which had been shuttling convoys from the coast to mid-channel, was the last to see the beaches, arriving on the afternoon of the 10th.

Neptune had been undertaken; and in its first phase had succeeded. The armies had been landed and were fighting their way inland. The *Luftwaffe* had been almost impotent; the first crust of the German defences had been weaker than expected. All casualties had been fairly light; naval casualties amazingly so. There remained, however, the overpoweringly urgent matter of reinforcements; the thought of sixty German divisions gathering to throw back into the sea the still comparatively small forces which had been established ashore. The great tide of allied men and material thrusting forward from all the way across the Atlantic must be channelled through the assault lanes and poured onto the coast of France. The game was far from won; and the lanes of Neptune were still vulnerable. By the afternoon of D-day the expected attack on the western flank was preparing.

CHAPTER THIRTEEN

The Screening Forces

At four o'clock on the afternoon of June 6, *Haida* and *Huron*, having spent an uneventful D-day on patrol with British destroyers in the Hurd Deep area, returned to Plymouth for fuel. For the moment no news of their own particular enemies awaited them; and only a cloud of fragmentary but hopeful reports from the Normandy beaches two hundred and fifty miles to the southeast.

Within an hour or so the situation had changed. Three of the powerful German Narvik class destroyers were reported to have left the Gironde Basin and to be heading northward up the Bay of Biscay. At eight-thirty in the evening they were attacked off St. Nazaire by a force of rocket-carrying Beaufighters which included fourteen planes of Canadian Squadron 404; but neither this attack nor a second, delivered a few hours later, diverted them from their northward course. They were evidently heading for the Channel and the Neptune area; probably intending to rendezvous with other German destroyers from Brest.

By nightfall six of the ships from Plymouth had taken up patrol stations just outside the western mouth of the Channel. The British destroyers, *Tartar, Ashanti, Eskimo* and *Javelin*, with the Polish ships, *Blyskawica* and *Piorun*, made up the force. Until eleven o'clock on the night of the 6th they were to patrol along an east-to-west line running some thirty miles south and southwest of the Lizard. Between eleven o'clock on the night of the 6th and five o'clock on the morning of the 7th their patrol was to be moved twenty miles southward. At first light they were to shift back to the original line.

There was no sign of the enemy that night; and at eight o'clock on the morning of the 7th *Haida* and *Huron* sailed from Plymouth to relieve *Piorun* and *Javelin*. The two Canadian ships arrived at the eastern end of the patrol line at ten forty-five in the morning. *Piorun* and *Javelin* departed for Plymouth; and for the rest of the day and the following night the remaining six destroyers continued to patrol without incident.

At 10.55 on the morning of the 8th a signal was received from Plymouth altering the dispositions. *Haida* and *Huron* were to remain where they were. *Eskimo* and *Blyskawica* were to move their patrol station a little to the east; and *Tartar* and *Ashanti* were to return to Plymouth for fuel. If this signal appeared to indicate some lessening of the tension over the Narviks, the impression was dissipated within a few hours. *Tartar* and *Ashanti* were ordered back to the patrol area before they reached Plymouth; and all ships of the 10th Destroyer Flotilla were ordered to concentrate in an area about fifty miles due south of Penzance.

By four-thirty in the afternoon the eight ships had assembled, taken up formation and were steering northeast at twenty-two knots, awaiting further orders. They were disposed in two groups of four; *Tartar* and *Blyskawica*, the leading ships of the subdivisions, abreast of each other and about two miles apart. Two hundred yards astern of *Tartar*, and on her port quarter, was *Ashanti*. *Haida* was on *Tartar's* starboard quarter, twelve hundred yards astern; and *Huron* brought up the rear two thousand yards directly astern of *Tartar*. Ranged in a similar formation behind *Blyskawica* were the ships of her subdivision, *Eskimo, Piorun* and *Javelin*.

The force was now ordered onto a series of courses which threw a wide loop across the southwestern entrance to the Channel. It was first to turn southward and pass through a position twenty-one miles north of Île de Vierge. Altering east and south from there, it was to reach a second point sixteen miles north of Ile de Bas by 9.45 in the evening. From that position it was to turn south-west and sweep back at twenty knots; passing fifteen miles north of Ile de Vierge and continuing westward until four in the morning. Photo-

287

graphic reconnaissance had shown that the three Narviks had arrived in Brest. Awaiting them there was a former Dutch destroyer, the *Tjerk Hiddes*, together with an Elbing. The concentration made it appear that a move against the Neptune flank was imminent; and in all probability it would be made on the night of the 8th by way of the route across which the British ships had been thrown.

By ten o'clock the 10th Destroyer Flotilla had reached its first position north of Ile de Bas. *Blyskawica* and the other three ships of her subdivision were to starboard of *Tartar's* group; and two miles to seaward. The zigzagging, twenty-knot sweep to the southwestward now began.

For several hours nothing developed. The blacked-out ships steamed on with only the rare glint of a signal lamp passing between them. Men, freshly-bathed and wearing clean linen to guard against infection from wounds, sat or stood before brightly-lighted instrument panels in stuffy cabins, their hands busy, their eyes alert. Steel-helmeted gunners waited beside the hatches of the opened magazines; curiously, grimly phantom-like, with the white of anti-flash gloves running up their forearms, and white canvas masks drooping from beneath their helmets to their shoulders, leaving only the eyes and noses visible. Similar phantoms high above them on the bridges spoke in occasional taut murmurs, bent over dials and the mouthpieces of speaking tubes and telephones as the ceaseless flow of orders and information passed back and forth between the nerve centres and the eyes and brains of the ships.

In the sick bays and wardrooms medical officers and attendants cleared extra space, laid out their instruments, drugs and blood plasma. Mess decks and officers' cabins were deserted; hastily abandoned magazines lay open to reveal the columns of unfinished stories; here and there were the pages of a half-completed letter. From the swaying bulkheads flimsily clad pin-ups, or the framed photographs of grey-haired women, or smiling younger women, or groups of a woman and children, looked only on cluttered, steel-enclosed space. Seamen off watch sat or lay or slept beside their action stations, on deck, along dimly-lighted companionways, at the foot of ladders; wherever there was room for a stretched-out or coiled-up body. Deep beneath them the throbbing engines, nursed by the men who would have the least chance of escape from disaster, sent the destroyers weaving onward, twenty degrees to starboard, twenty degrees to port along the mean line of their course. Far ahead of them the questing beams of radar sought out and returned with the numberless impressions which sent the running green ribbon of each operators' dial rising in jagged crests and falling away into troughs like the sea about it.

The weather was overcast with intermittent rain squalls and poor visibility. Banks of low clouds were multiplying and confusing the indistinct radar "blips." Not until one o'clock did the first promising indications begin to come in.

Shortly after midnight a signal from Plymouth had ordered the destroyers to shift the patrol line five miles to seaward in order to avoid British minefields laid off the Brittany coast. A little way along the new line of advance, when the force was about twenty miles west and north of Ile de Bas, images a little less dubious than the earlier ones began to form on the radar screens. First one contact, then another and finally a third and fourth grew more definite. By 1.20 the echoes had been sorted out and analyzed as those of four ships, approaching from the southwest at a speed of twenty-six knots.

The vessels, presumed to be the enemy destroyers, were about six miles distant and on a converging course. The 10th Destroyer Flotilla continued toward them through the squally night; then, as the range closed, *Tartar* ordered a turn to starboard to spread the force across the bearing of the enemy. As the ships turned, the moon broke through the scudding clouds overhead, and the lightly camouflaged sides of the destroyers stood out in the wan light. The straining eyes of their lookouts fastened on the broken silhouettes of the German ships glimmering in the distance. From British,

Canadian and Polish bridges the drone of ranges and bearings began.

It was now probable that the German ships would scatter or retreat, firing torpedoes as they turned. All destroyers of the British force therefore altered to port again, directly toward the enemy, in order to present the narrowest possible target for torpedoes. *Ashanti, Haida* and *Huron* spread out in quarter line to port on *Tartar*. *Blyskawica's* sub-division, some two miles to seaward and a little astern, took up the same formation.

The enemy ships could now be seen altering away to port; distant by about four thousand yards. At 1.27 *Tartar, Ashanti, Haida* and *Huron* opened fire; and a moment later flashes from the guns of *Blyskawica, Eskimo, Piorun* and *Javelin* could be distinguished from seaward. The leading German destroyer turned outward on a northerly course. He would come across the track of *Blyskawica's* sub-division and *Tartar* therefore ignored him. Closing in to point-blank range, but moving warily on account of the danger of torpedoes, she selected the second ship in the German line as her target. *Ashanti* joined in this attack, and almost immediately the salvoes from the two British ships began to register. Haida took on the third enemy ship and *Huron* the fourth. Already a pallid mass of smoke had settled on the sea, spewing out raggedly to the west and north as the projectors of the scattering Germans fed it with new clouds.

For a moment *Tartar* lost her target in the smoke and transferred her fire to *Haida's* opponent. She had hardly done so when the leader of the German ships doubled back from the north and brought heavy fire on her. *Tartar* swung her guns round and scored several hits which temporarily silenced this enemy, but before he ceased fire he inflicted serious injury on the British leader. Three well-placed shells killed four of her men, wounded thirteen others, and set the ship afire. For a few moments *Tartar* managed to keep her guns in action; but fires raging amidships soon became so bad that she had to break off. Reducing her speed to six knots,

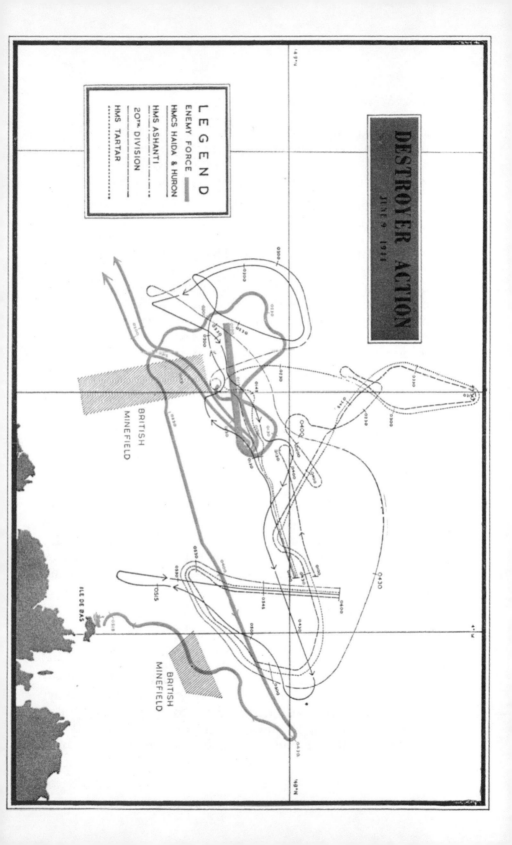

DESTROYER ACTION
JUNE 9 1944

LEGEND

ENEMY FORCE
HMCS HAIDA & HURON
HMS ASHANTI
20ᵀᴴ DIVISION
HMS TARTAR

BRITISH MINEFIELD

BRITISH MINEFIELD

ILE DE BAS

she headed northward, away from the wind which was fanning the flames, while damage control parties fought for the ship's life. Although very vulnerable now, she was left to withdraw unmolested to the fringes of the action.

Meanwhile the remaining contenders were having trouble in making out the course of the battle. Starshell burst above the driving, low-hanging clouds, illuminating them but casting little light on the sea. The smoke-screens about the zigzagging Germans were being continually refreshed, adding not a little to the confusion on both sides. *Ashanti* had continued in pursuit of the second ship, which she and *Tartar* had jointly engaged. Finally losing it in smoke, she swung back to *Tartar's* assistance; but just as she got into action, her former target, which turned out to be the *Tjerk Hiddes,* reappeared on her port bow.

The enemy destroyer was in trouble; stopped or going very slowly. *Ashanti* turned on it with a salvo of four torpedoes, one of which caught it astern while a second blew off a length of its bow. Although mortally hit, the stoutly built ship still showed no inclination to sink. *Ashanti* circled it, pouring in a heavy fire and receiving some fire in return. Flames and smoke wreathing about the vessel were continually hiding it from view. It must have been an inferno from end to end; but one of its guns scored a last hit on *Ashanti.* Then firing ceased; some of the crew could be seen climbing over the sides; and at 2.40, after a brave last hour, *Tjerk Hiddes* blew up with an explosion which lifted a great plume of flame above the evil murk.

Meanwhile, the ships which *Haida* and *Huron* were engaging, had made off very fast to the southwest behind a heavy smoke screen. *Haida's* target drew away from her and she turned her guns onto the destroyer which *Huron* was pursuing. The Canadian ships drew together, each of them scoring hits on the enemy and receiving a steady fire in reply. *Huron* fired torpedoes but failed to score; and a little later the enemy, running southward, suddenly veered east. It was a risky move for him, since it took him squarely across a British minefield; but in the event it was his salvation. The Canadian ships were under orders to skirt the minefield; and the long diversion put them out of touch with their enemy. At 2.15 they abandoned the pursuit and turned back to rejoin the earlier battle.

To the north *Tartar* was out of action, *Tjerk Hiddes* was in her death throes, and *Ashanti* was circling her. *Blyskawica's* subdivision, which had taken little part in the battle so far, had now made contact with *Tartar*. The senior ship had signalled all destroyers of the force to concentrate on her if not actually in contact with the enemy. At the moment *Ashanti* was the only one so engaged. One German vessel had escaped *Haida* to the west; another had outrun *Haida* and *Huron* to the southeast; *Tjerk Hiddes* was sinking and the location of the fourth ship was doubtful.

It was soon to be revealed. As *Haida* and *Huron* drew near to the estimated position of *Tartar*, *Haida* got a radar contact six miles off on her port bow. At first she thought it was the British senior ship. Closing on the contact, *Haida* and *Huron* made out through the darkness the silhouette of a destroyer moving in a northwesterly direction at slow speed. They flashed identification lights and got an unintelligible reply. Bringing their guns to bear, they repeated the challenge. Again the reply was meaningless. By now the ships were within a mile of each other; and *Haida* and *Huron* were still in doubt as to the identity of the other destroyer. There was a strong possibility that it might be *Tartar* with her signalling gear knocked out in addition to her other damage. But, as the Canadian ships crossed warily astern of the stranger, he made a sudden alteration to the south, dropped a smoke float and was off at high speed.

For a short time he disappeared into the dark. *Haida* and *Huron*, with all their doubts resolved, went flat out after him. The ship was a Narvik, more powerful than either of the Tribals; and his gunnery was good. Starshell burst accurately above the Canadians and high explosive lifted straddling splashes in the water about them. The German was

293

making thirty-one knots and opening the range a little. He was bearing generally south and altering gradually to the east, evidently hoping to take refuge in the Channel Islands. *Haida* and *Huron,* east and still astern to the north, were running to head him off.

At 3.11 the enemy altered eastward again; and the new course took him across the same minefield through which the earlier destroyer had escaped. Once again the Canadian ships had to go round; and for a time it seemed that they were in for another disappointment. The range increased to 18,000 yards and finally radar contact was lost entirely.

At four o'clock, *Haida* and *Huron,* having circled the minefield and now echoless, were steering a northeasterly course some twenty miles northeast of Ile de Vierge. They held on for eleven dour minutes with little clue as to the German's whereabouts. Then at 4.12 an echo came. The Narvik was nine miles due east and running northeasterly, evidently for Cherbourg.

The Canadians worked up to thirty-one knots again and set after him. With a considerable start, the Narvik might have made a successful run for Cherbourg. Instead, for some reason not apparent, he altered back to the southwest at 4.32, steering in the general direction of Ile de Bas. The change of course put *Haida* and *Huron* in a position to cut him off. Sharply altering their own course, they steered in across his line of advance, and were waiting for him at five o'clock as he ran out from the fringes of another minefield.

The Narvik found the two Tribals some four miles on his starboard bow; and the final action broke out with the three ships on parallel courses headed directly for the rocky shoreline of Ile de Bas. Salvoes from both Canadian ships plunged onto the target immediately. Splashes of flame began to appear along the German's decks; and his return fire became erratic. He held his course and speed unchanged; and at 5.17 ran in among the rocks of the coast and hard aground. *Haida* and *Huron* followed to within 6,500 yards and maintained a heavy fire on him until he was completely ablaze and helpless. Then, leaving behind them a dense column of smoke against a lightening sky, they turned away. *Haida* reported, "One enemy destroyer beached off Ile de Bas:" and at ten minutes to nine on the morning of June 9 the Tribals entered Plymouth habour with battle ensigns flying at the peak.

Planes over the burning Narvik next day reported that she was listing at an angle of thirty-five degrees, with her bow on the rocks and her stern well down in the water. Beaufighters of a Canadian squadron went over to finish her off with rockets; and on the 12th M.T.B.'s made an attempt to sink her with torpedoes. Neither attack succeeded in driving the ship under water; but it was definitely out of the war.

The destroyer action, comparatively small in scale though it was, broke the back of any serious effort to harry the western flank. Considering the forces they had available, the Germans may not have expected to do much; but now that two of their most powerful ships had been sunk and two more damaged they could do little or nothing. Their capacity to threaten and interfere with allied anti-submarine patrols was also greatly reduced. With the fear of German destroyers largely removed, and with heavy support available to them when needed, Allied escort groups could now carry their sweeps into enemy waters and along the German-held coast under the very mouths of the shore batteries. They could cherish the hope—never to be very fully realized—of a richer harvest than they had known during the first few days of Neptune.

The first submarine movements in the direction of the assault area had come, as expected, from the west and south. On the afternoon of the 6th, seven U-boats were reported heading northward from St. Nazaire and Brest, and five more were already off Ushant moving toward the Channel mouth. The Allied screening forces came a little south to intercept them. Outside the Channel, in the operation CA zone, three of the British frigate groups took up a position west and south of Brest, leaving any boats which might already have entered the Channel to the destroyer groups inside. The Canadian frigate groups, Escort Group 6 and Escort Group 9, remained on their more northerly station throughout the 7th. Then they also were shifted down to positions a little north of Brest. Inside the Lizard the Canadian destroyer groups, Escort Group 11 and Escort Group 12, moved southward to about mid-channel, were drawn back briefly on the 8th to clear the area for the battle then developing between the 10th Destroyer Flotilla and the Narviks, and resumed their station when the German ships were intercepted farther south.

The frigates outside the Channel, like all the ships and planes engaged on Operation CA, were to have an unexpectedly monotonous time of it. The U-boat effort against Neptune was throughout tentative and uncertain. No concentration threatening to force the Channel mouth ever developed. From the 7th to the 10th the Canadian frigates acquired only a rich experience of the difficulties of antisubmarine operations in the outer Channel area. Here, as inside the Channel, there was an average depth of only sixty fathoms. Tides and cross-currents plagued asdic operators with deceptive echoes; and the sunken ships which littered the bottom proved even more troublesome.

Admiralty, well aware of the conditions and expecting the Germans to take advantage of them, had ordered that every contact without exception was to be investigated and attacked. The orders were carried out, with an expenditure of much explosive and a yield mainly of fish. Time after time the ships sent depth charges and hedgehog thundering down on objects which returned a fine echo, but which had eventually to be abandoned as wrecks or "non-sub". The echosounder, as a means of investigating possible submarines on the bottom, came into increasing use. It transmitted vertically downward a sound beam, as opposed to the horizontal supersonic beam of asdic; and its natural function was to register the depth of water on a plot by graphing the time of the returning echo. It was found that by running slowly over a suspicious object on the bottom a trace of its silhouette could be obtained on the plot of the echo sounder. In most cases, so far as Escort Group 6 or Escort Group 9 were concerned, this process had the melancholy result of dispelling all hopes previously roused by the asdic.

During the first few days after the assault, aircraft carriers were used in company with the groups; and on the early morning of June 10th the carrier *Tracker* was in station with Escort Group 6. At about two o'clock, in thick darkness, the Canadian frigate *Teme* got an asdic contact which indicated a possible submarine moving between her and the carrier five thousand yards away. She swung in immediately and attacked, warning the carrier as she did so. In the manoeuvering which followed, the two ships, each moving at a fair rate of speed, got themselves onto collision courses; and *Tracker's* heavy bow crashed into *Teme*, cutting almost through the frigate's lighter hull.

Teme was badly damaged. Her keel was broken through; all generators and both boilers were out of action. Scramble-nets were ordered overside and carley floats made ready; but before the order to abandon ship, *Tracker* worked herself clear and it began to seem possible that the frigate could be saved. Forward compartments and the bulkheads from most of the after holds were still intact. *Teme's* engine room watch had coolly remained at their posts and had done much to minimize the effects of the damage.

The sister-frigate, *Outremont*, came alongside *Teme* and began to assist. In spite of hardy construction and the gallant efforts being made to save her, the ship was still a bad risk, with her back broken and her two halves held together by only eleven feet of undamaged structure. All men on board, with the exception of a working party of fifty, were transferred to *Outremont*. A towing hawser was rigged, while bulkheads were shored up in *Teme*. A telephone wire was strung from the bridge to the tiller flat in the after part of the ship where the emergency steering gear was located. This made it possible to con the ship by hand steering in response to orders telephoned from the bridge. By six in the morning *Outremont* had *Teme* in tow and was struggling away from the scene of the disaster with her labouring, groaning charge. Cardiff, the nearest port, was two hundred miles away; but fine seamanship on the part of both ships' companies brought the damaged vessel to safety. Another Canadian frigate, *New Waterford,* restored the group to strength with its arrival on June 30.

Meanwhile, the destroyers of Escort Group 12 had found action just at the Channel mouth. One U-boat had apparently made a determined effort to pierce the Operation CA screen; and nearly succeeded. *Qu'Appelle, Saskatchewan, Skeena* and *Restigouche* discovered him forty-five miles northwest of Ushant on June 7; and he proved to be one of the toughest and most truculent customers encountered by any Canadian ships throughout the war.

About eight o'clock on the evening of the 7th the group was patrolling line abreast when *Restigouche* got an asdic contact. Almost at the same moment a deep underwater explosion was heard; which was considered to be an acoustic torpedo exploding on the bottom. The U-boat, quite aware of the destroyers' presence, had made an effort to draw first blood.

The four ships immediately streamed their cat gear as protection against more of the same missiles; and proceeded to conduct a square search about the area. Ten minutes of hunting resulted in a contact for *Skeena,* confirmed by *Restigouche.* A first attack with hedgehog produced no results. Asdic conditions were abominable with shoals of fish confusing every echo and producing false echoes of their own. By eight-thirty the destroyers had lost contact. They were again convinced of the U-boat's presence, however, when a column of water eighty feet high lifted astern of *Saskatchewan.* It came from an acoustic torpedo exploding at the end of its run; and eight minutes afterward *Skeena* saw another torpedo swim shallowly past her and sink without an explosion.

At 9.25 *Restigouche* contacted the U-boat again at a range of three hundred yards. Before she could alter for an attack the periscope bobbed up a hundred yards away on her starboard beam. She opened fire; but could not put over depth charges as she was travelling at only seven knots and would have suffered as much as the German from the explosion. *Qu'Appelle* swung round and came in to assist *Restigouche;* but the U-boat dived and contact was again lost. Twenty minutes later *Qu'Appelle* sighted a swirl in the water three hundred yards dead ahead and drove in for the spot with a ten-charge pattern set. Again the periscope emerged from the water, over on her starboard bow and moving away. She swung hard to starboard, let go her depth charges and opened fire with all guns, as the periscope passed down along her side and disappeared. Altering round again, she came in over the location of the dive, when there was a great explosion in the cat gear which *Saskatchewan* was trailing astern of her. It was another torpedo fired at *Qu'-Appelle* by the U-Boat as she went by. The German, apparently unimpressed by the fact that four destroyers were after him, had now favoured each of them with a torpedo.

For the rest of the night he remained sullen and dangerous on the bottom. Wrecks and tide rips and exasperating thousands of herring assisted him by muddling every contact and throwing asdic operators into profane confusion. Then at nine-thirty in the morning, with the ships steaming above him in line abreast, he opened the new day's business with a torpedo which exploded in *Qu'Appelle's* cat gear. Five minutes later a second torpedo, exploding between *Skeena* and *Restigouche,* sent a sheet of water sweeping over *Skeena's* bow. The result of this latest attack, however, was that *Skeena* got the best contact which the ships had yet obtained.

The echo was nine hundred yards distant, moving right. As *Skeena* closed in she saw a pale blue swirl off her starboard bow, apparently from the submarine preparing to surface. She fired hedgehog; and a few seconds after the circle of bombs dropped in the water there came a soul-satisfying explosion followed by a welter of bubbles and oil. Yet once again there was no luck for the attacker. The hedgehog had been exploded on the bottom astern of the U-boat, and only slight damage could be hoped for. A seventh torpedo went lacing across *Skeena's* bows; and three minutes later another explosion between *Qu'Appelle* and *Saskatchewan* gave clear proof that the fight had not been knocked out of the German.

Until noon, the ships clung to a series of good echoes and attacked time and time again. The damage to the U-boat, if any was done, was slight. "Nothing more than a few tons of dead fish", was the senior officer's rueful summation of the morning's work. In the afternoon two ships of a nearby escort group joined in the hunt; but the reinforcements added only to the toll of fish. The U-boat had squirmed his way out of the immediate area. At five in the afternoon an aircraft reported him on the surface eight miles away. *Qu'Appelle* and *Saskatchewan* gave chase, caught a glimpse of him about seven o'clock, then lost him again as he dived. The last sighting and the conclusion to a frustrating, if sufficiently exciting, hunt came at nine o'clock when the faint puffs of a schnorkel exhaust were seen four and a half miles away, disappearing in a rainy dusk. It was the night of June 8th. The Tribals were passing down the Channel to do battle with the approaching Narviks from Brest. The area had to be cleared of other ships and the search abandoned.

It was neither the first nor the last instance of a search being broken off to make way for a larger action in the thronged waters of the Channel. Through its confined spaces hundreds of ships were moving grimly on warlike occasions. The most constant care had to be exercised by the various command headquarters in plotting the movements of groups; and the strain of unremitting vigilance lay heavy upon the ships themselves. On the night of June 15, by which time Escort Group 12 had transferred its patrol southward into the neighbourhood of Ile de Vierge, the ships were moving along the coast when starshell burst suddenly over them. It came from the guns of *Haida* and *Huron* who had been sweeping down from the region of the Channel Islands in search of some of the enemy's remaining Elbings. A few tense seconds followed as the Tribals, hidden in darkness, surveyed the four destroyers standing out in the glare of the illuminants. Identification was made in time, however; and fraternal greetings followed in place of high explosive.

Meanwhile *Ottawa, Gatineau, Kootenay, Chaudière* and *St. Laurent,* of Escort Group 11, had been moved a little nearer in to the invasion lanes. They formed part of a third screen placed to deal with any U-boats which might run the gauntlet of the outer patrols; and during the first week of the invasion they found their territory bare of game. On the night of June 16 a new policy was put into effect. Henceforth during the day the group was to patrol as a unit to the west of the invasion area; but at night the force would split, half of the ships crossing over to the waters of the eastern flank.

On the night of June 26, *Gatineau* and *Chaudière* were the two ships of E.G. 11 assigned to the eastern side of the assault area. About 1.15 they were moving seventeen miles south of Selsey Bill when they observed starshell ten miles off. They made for the disturbance immediately, considering it to be a convoy under E-boat attack; and their assessment proved correct. As they approached, asdic operators reported the sound of fast reciprocating engines. A moment or so later starshell fired over the estimated position revealed three of the German craft two thousand yards away and travelling at high speed. As *Gatineau* and *Chaudière* opened fire the boats broke formation, dropped smoke floats and swung away to the north. Faster than the destroyers, they steadily opened the range; and within eight minutes had outrun their pursuers.

The Germans could not continue northward, however, without risk of being cut off from their base at Le Havre. Half an hour later, attempting to double back, they were detected and engaged again. Out of the invariable smoke screen one of the boats fired a torpedo at *Gatineau,* which she avoided. Then, as the destroyer's gunfire poured into the murk about the enemy, a brilliant flash lifted above the haze. It seemed probable that one of the boats had been hit and blown up, but it was impossible to determine results definitely. Behind their trailing screen the three Germans, or perhaps only the two of them remaining, outran the destroyers again and brought the action to a close.

With it closed the first phase of Neptune operations for Escort Group 11. A week of boiler cleaning in Londonderry was to be next on the agenda. All through the defence zones spread out from the western flank, patrols were being called in. It appeared that there was going to be no concentrated German effort to force an entrance from the outer Channel. Not more than ten U-boats had attempted to penetrate the screens; and of these only two had reached the assault area. Coastal Command, whose planes were constantly over all areas and far to sea, had made the lion's share of the kills since D-day, sinking six and damaging seven. Naval ships had sunk four; and of these, one had fallen to two ships of the 10th Destroyer Flotilla, *Haida* and *Eskimo*.

The Canadian Tribal, with the British ship under her orders, had sailed from Plymouth on the night of the 23rd, assigned to a routine patrol some thirty miles south of Land's End. The two vessels were on station the following afternoon when, at a little before four o'clock, a Czech Liberator was seen dropping depth charges in the distance. When the destroyers came over to investigate, the pilot reported that he had been attacking a submarine which had crash-dived. He had dropped a marker over what he considered to be the point of dive; and *Haida* and *Eskimo* began a series of depth charge attacks on a contact which, throughout the first half of the action, they believed doubtful.

The U-boat, on diving, had gone straight to the bottom and remained there, drifting with the tide on the littered sea-floor, hoping that a multitude of false echoes would eventually discourage his attackers. For over two hours depth-charging brought no result. Asdic contact there certainly was, from some object lying on the bottom in sixty-two fathoms; but there seemed every possibility that it might be a wreck. When *Eskimo's* echo sounder went into operation, however, and revealed on its plot the unmistakeable silhouette of a submarine, attacks were resumed with new determination. At 7.21, just as *Haida* was running in to drop a pattern, the U-boat wearied of the pounding and decided to surface and run for it. The conning tower broke water eight hundred yards ahead of *Haida* and almost on a line between her and *Eskimo*. The British Tribal promptly went full astern to clear the range and then both destroyers opened fire with all guns they could bring to bear.

The German crew went overside in a hurry, and before they were well in the water their riddled boat upended and sank. *Haida* screened *Eskimo* while the British ship took forty-six survivors on board, then pulled the last six Germans from the water herself. When she returned to Plymouth, and this latest piece of news became disseminated among the hungry ships of the escort groups, it seemed a little too much. Other comrades were equally impressed and envious. *Black Prince,* the British cruiser with which *Haida* had sailed on many Tunnel and Hostile forays, signalled, "Narviks, Elbings and submarines all seem to come alike."

By the latter part of June it had become apparent that the outer screens of defence along the flanks of Neptune were too much for the Germans. Closer in, the motor torpedo boats of the coastal forces had presented an equally unyielding defence. Particularly on the western flank, the enemy failed to use his coastal craft against convoys or the invasion lanes to anything like the extent expected. Overwhelming allied air superiority kept his boats in harbour except during the dark hours. The rough weather of the first weeks of the invasion frequently prevented operations by the small craft of either side. In addition, the allied flotillas were so numerous and vigilant, and the watch maintained by ship-based and shore-based radar was so close, that it was almost impossible for enemy craft to sail without being detected and attacked.

The motor torpedo boats of the 65th Flotilla, on the western side, remained until June 11, in approximately the same station they had occupied on the night the ships crossed to France. Their patrol across the mouth of Lyme Bay was designed to protect a part of the convoy route leading along the south coast to the assembly area. After the first few days, however, as it became apparent that no enemy thrust was going to develop in their sector, the boats of the 65th were changed over from defensive to offensive missions. On the night of the 11th, boats 748, 726, 727 and 743 went south and westward across the Channel into the waters of Alderney and Guernsey. They encountered no enemy shipping; but, as they passed along the coast within seven miles of Alderney, twenty explosions heaving up the water within a hundred yards of them, renewed an acquaintance with German shore batteries which was to become more and more extensive.

Several nights of rough weather followed; and patrols of the same area were maintained with difficulty. The seas were so rough and visibility so poor that the small craft had to cruise almost nose to tail to avoid losing touch with one another. Nevertheless, both destroyers and M.T.B.'s combed the waters of the Channel Islands heavily. The Germans had considerable garrisons here which they might endeavour to evacuate by small craft, and the patrols were designed to prevent any such movement. The sorties became more and more the work of M.T.B.'s; as destroyers were hardly so serviceable in the close and narrow waters around the islands and presented better targets for the shore batteries.

The night of June 17 provided a brief interval of better weather and conditions well suited for M.T.B. operations. Boats 748, 745, 726 and 727 of the 65th were scheduled for patrol, and they put out from their Brixham base at 10.25. Crossing the Channel without incident, the four craft passed between Alderney and Guernsey and continued southward five miles to the east of Sark. When they reached a point about four miles west of Cherbourg peninsula they altered north again to cruise along the coast.

They were in this area at two o'clock in the morning when they made radar contact with ships three thousand yards to the west of them. The enemy convoy, as it was presumed to be, was steering south and a little east. The boats of the 65th, steering north betwen the convoy and the coast of the peninsula, were nicely placed to cut it off from Cherbourg. As the flotilla slowed to ten knots and gathered together for the attack, straining eyes began to make out a series of crawling blots on the darkness ahead. It was a German convoy of two merchantmen with several trawlers and gun coasters as escort. A challenge glinted faintly from a distant signal lamp but the M.T.B.'s, moving inward, made no reply.

As a second challenge came the M.T.B.'s opened their throttles and bore down on the convoy. At fifteen hundred yards boat 727 fired two torpedoes. Boat 748 closed to twelve hundred yards and fired two more. Instead of the hoped-for explosions, there came blinding starshell overhead and a heavy burst of gunfire from the Germans. The M.T.B.'s closed to four hundred yards, concentrating the fire of their six-pounders, two-pounders and oerlikons on one of the merchantmen as they passed up the western side of the convoy. A few hundred yards to the north, as darkness succeeded the blaze of starshell, they swung back at high speed, went completely round the German ships and came up again on the west. The manœuvre put them in the lee of Cherbourg peninsula, giving them a darker sea, and they bore in again to run down the enemy line. No major explosion emerged from the glare and clattter of the gunfire to attest a sinking; but as the boats continued northward they left behind them a thoroughly disorganized enemy whose ships were conducting a spirited action among themselves.

A still more eventful night awaited boats 748, 727, 745 and 743 when they returned to Jersey waters on the night of June 22. As they arrived off St. Helier, the capital and principal port of the island, they received orders to proceed to the southwest where four British M.T.B.'s were attacking an enemy convoy. En route to the scene of the action they came upon a returning E-boat, chased it into St. Helier, and spent half an hour sweeping across the rocky, treacherous entrance to the harbour in hopes that the German would venture out again.

When this began to appear unlikely, they altered off to the south, and within fifteen minutes had another contact. It proved to be an enemy convoy, four thousand yards distant; and the M.T.B.'s ran in on it disposed for a torpedo attack. Starshell burst over them; followed by heavy fire. They continued on their course for three minutes and then opened fire, swinging their line around in succession to bring forward, broadside and finally after guns to bear. Midway along the run a German shell, exploding in 745's engine room, forced her to swerve aside and stop.

All boats were now within five hundred yards of the German ships. Boat 745 was temporarily crippled, and 748 circled her, laying a smoke screen. Boats 727 and 743 ran in closer along the German line and made out three minesweepers and an E-boat. Taking on the first minesweeper, 743 raked her at point-blank range with six-pounders and oerlikons. The E-boat closed up to assist the minesweeper and 743 turned her guns on the new enemy, forcing him out of the action with his bow smoking from a direct hit. Boat 727 ran alongside the other two sweepers and then, after a hot exchange, turned back to stand by the damaged 745, while 743 again teamed up with 748.

Boat 748 meanwhile, after laying the smoke screen around 745, had selected a tanker in the convoy, opened fire on it and set it ablaze. Running in to finish off the ship, she had to swing sharply to port to avoid one of the minesweepers which was already sinking. As 743 joined her, both craft were suddenly confronted by two gun coasters which they met with a blaze of fire and silenced. By the time this action was finished 748's original tanker was hopelessly aflame and in need of no further attention. The two boats joined 727 around the damaged 745, whose chief motor mechanic and engine room crew had now got her crawling at a speed of six knots. Screening the injured member, the flotilla set off slowly for Brixham with the flames from the German tanker lighting the sky behind them. It was a not unfitting scene to mark the close of the first phase of their Neptune operations.

For the 29th Flotilla, the primary duty from the afternoon of D-day forward was the close-in protection of the eastern side of the assault lanes and anchorages. The stream of ships was constantly augmenting and renewing itself and hundreds lay at anchor off the beaches. They were principally endangered at night; and, exclusive of all screens, the anchorages presented their own mailed sides to an enemy. Inmost of all the defences was a line of minesweepers anchored at intervals of half a mile to a mile. Outside of them a patrol of four destroyers, called the "Guards Division" was continually in motion along a belt thirteen miles deep to the north of the anchorages. Along the eastern lane, facing Le Havre, was a line of landing craft anchored between four and six hundred yards apart, equipped to give supporting fire against either ships or aircraft. The first screen of patrols lay outside of them, covering the "Tunny" zone, a belt of water which extended to the limits of the minefield closing in Le Havre. Here a number of coastal force flotillas, including the 29th, were to have most of their work during the first phase of Neptune.

There were two troublesome Elbings based on Le Havre, and the city's harbour was also an important base for E-boats and R-boats. The belt of water lying between the assault anchorage and the port had, therefore, to be very closely watched. Radar, as everywhere, was constantly employed; and in the case of the coastal forces the equipment carried by the boats was supplemented not only by shore stations but also by ships. Frigates carrying very efficient radar teams and all the latest equipment, were stationed as control ships to maintain watch and direct, or "vector," M.T.B. flotillas onto any suspicious craft which might enter a particular area. The 29th Flotilla operated under the control of a British frigate, which was anchored each night just inside the defence lines at the north-east corner of the anchorage.

Operations began on the afternoon of D-day. Boats 459, 465, 460 and 466 tied up astern of the control frigate and, since it was too rough to climb on board of her, received their briefing over the side by shouts between commanding officer and commanding officer. The flotilla was to take up patrol in the Tunny South area about thirteen miles southwest of Le Havre.

It was a bad night for coastal craft, with a rough sea and a clear sky which provided too much visibility. At a few minutes after four in the morning, signs of battle appeared to the northward. Running in toward what appeared to be a gun action between British M.T.B.'s and German craft, the boats of the 29th fired starshell over the scene at a range of three thousand yards. The bursts revealed a line of six R-boats moving in the direction of the anchorages. The Canadians opened fire at a range of about seven hundred yards, closed to a range of a hundred and fifty yards in the face of heavy return fire and saw one of the German craft blow up. The others turned away and ran for Le Havre, making smoke. All of them had been hit, some of them repeatedly; and they had now set off on a route which would take them across the British minefield laid in front of Le Havre. The action had already worked in very close to the fringes of the field, and the boats of the 29th had observed two or three surface mines bobbing about them. They therefore turned away, leaving the retreating enemy to pick his way into Le Havre with what luck he could.

Four men had been wounded in the action; and the first task on return to the anchorage in the morning was to find one among all the hundreds of crowded ships who would take the casualties on board. That done, the rest of the day was passed in maximum discomfort, tossing on a rough sea and tugging on lines made fast to a British destroyer. When night fell the boats moved out again to patrol in the same area.

As they had done for some time, they were carrying depth charges in place of the torpedoes which were their favorite weapons. The expected introduction of the small, fast German submarine had caused the Admiralty to make this change in their armament. Had the "Walter" boats come into use, the M.T.B.'s, equipped with depth charges, would have been excellent craft to use against them; but since they did not appear, the result, for a time, was that the M.T.B.'s lacked their principal offensive weapon against surface craft.

They had cause to regret it keenly this night. The two Elbings from Le Havre appeared out of the darkness, nosing their way in toward the anchorage. The M.T.B.'s, hopelessly outgunned and without torpedoes, had no means of attack. All they could do was to let themselves be detected and lead the Elbings away from the assault area on a chase which ended some two miles off Le Havre. Although denied any chance of offensive action, they had at least diverted an attack; and in the morning their disappointment was tempered by personal congratulations from Sir Philip Vian, Naval Commander of the Eastern Task Force.

Boats 459, 465, 460 and 466 returned to Portsmouth for a night's rest on the evening of the 8th. Before they reached harbour the other boats of the flotilla, 461, 462, 463 and 464 had sailed for the operational area. They began their patrol in the central part of Tunny South by chasing some E-boats which outran them to the west. Coming back onto station at a little after two, they stopped engines and began a listening watch by hydrophone. They had been silent and stopped in the dark for a little less than half an hour when, once again, the two Elbings loomed suddenly in front of them, not five hundred yards off. The German destroyers had not sighted the M.T.B.'s, having other preoccupations. They were apparently just getting into position to bombard the assault anchorage. Their first starshells, when they were fired a minute or so later, passed above the heads of the Canadians to burst over the lines of ships before the beaches.

The M.T.B.'s started their engines slowly, hoping to remain unobserved. They were scarcely under way, however, when the German ships turned on them and opened with rapid and accurate salvoes which kept them dodging through a smoke screen for ten minutes. Boat 464, stationed astern and making smoke for the others, took the brunt of the action. One of its men was killed and another seriously injured; but once again a projected attack on the ships at anchor had been broken up.

Still another action of the same kind took place on the night of the 12th, involving boats 461, 463 and 464. The fourth boat of the group was unable to sail, having been damaged, like many other M.T.B.'s, on the underwater obstacles which still abounded in the shallow water of the area. A brighter feature of this night's patrol, as the craft set out, was the fact that 464 now had its torpedoes and tubes back. The probability of the "Walter" boats' appearance was being discounted; and M.T.B.'s were being re-equipped with torpedoes as rapidly as the host of Neptune requirements permitted.

The three boats had been in their waiting station for an hour or so when the two dogged Elbings appeared again. Relying on the torpedoes of 464, the Canadians crept toward the destroyers with heightened hopes. As they approached, however, the advantage of surprise was wrested away from them. Starshell burst overhead from a range of two and a half miles, followed by high explosive shells. Then enemy dive-bombers swooped down on them; following the bombs with machine gun strafing. Undeterred, the boats continued to work into position for a torpedo attack; but, just as the action was taking shape, orders came for them to retire. British destroyers had appeared on the scene; their salvoes went arching over the withdrawing M.T.B.'s, and the Elbings fled with smoke rising from their afterparts.

From then until the 23rd of June the patrols continued without major event. The strain of operating in heavily mined waters and in very rough weather was unceasing. For periods of several days the craft had to take their rest tied up to ships in the assault anchorage, with little sleep and less hot food falling to the lot of their companies. The ordinary discomforts of the period were brought to a peak during the storm which began on June 19; and several of the boats barely managed to ride it out by creeping in toward the beaches and taking what shelter they could find.

Difficulties were, in fact, on the increase, rather than the wane. German mine-laying from the air was steadily becoming more intense, not only in the assault lanes but in the patrol areas about it. German dive bombers were coming over nightly, adding to the perils of each surface action. Nevertheless the patrols were accomplishing their purpose. German probings had not reached through to the anchorages, and there was little sign of any more determined effort to accomplish this. E-boats were still wary and inclined to run. In spite of their daily hardships and nightly perils, the M.T.B.'s seemed, like the ships of the patrolling forces ranked to the westward of them, masters of the situation.

Within its layered defences, the Neptune build-up was going steadily on. Yet in spite of the great number of troops and the enormous volume of supplies poured onto the beaches, no man could say that the Normandy foothold was secure. Many mishaps had occurred; many revisions of detail had inevitably to be made in the plans. Weather had intervened on the 19th with a storm which threatened disastrous consequences; and up to the fall of Cherbourg on June 26 there had never been a day when effort could be relaxed or success confidently claimed.

CHAPTER FOURTEEN

The Build-Up

THE first ships of the assault, returning to England in the twilight of June 7, brought with them little sense of tremendous achievement. Weaving their way across the Channel against new streams of France-bound shipping, they came without fanfare into the familiar waters many of their men had never expected to see again. The ships with casualties on board were directed first to docks where long lines of ambulances stood waiting; many more, fortunately, than were needed. The others, standing off the mouths of harbours so thronged with shipping that there remained only a few narrow, dangerous aisles for entry and exit, waited impatiently for their berthing orders. Flashing their lamps petulantly at port war-signal stations whose attention was demanded everywhere at once, they were greeted with few cheers from passing vessels, and their men were scarcely in a mood to reply to such as were offered. The epic hour had come and gone; and had left in its wake only a numbing lethargy. Nerves tuned through many months to an almost unendurable tension had relaxed. Bodies were bone-weary; minds filled only with an apathetic distaste for the continuing task ahead.

Prince Henry and *Prince David,* leading their groups of landing ships, were among the first to return. Following them at intervals ranging from several hours to several days, came battered processions of landing craft, among whom were many of the 260th, 262nd and 264th Canadian Flotillas. The battle for the beaches was now in full swing. Ships with succeeding waves of troops and matériel were discharging in Baie de la Seine. Others were on the way there. Here in England the returning carriers of the first wave were assembling for the long-range reinforcement programme known as the build-up.

Many anxieties lay ahead. The armies ashore, pushing against the containing walls of their bridgehead, were to come up against a ferocious defence of some of the key points. Weather, continually rough and frequently foul, swung over to the side of the enemy for a time. It interfered with air support, heavily handicapped the builders of the artificial harbours, and immensely complicated the work of supply. At one time, when the storm which began on June 19 raged all along the French shore, tearing huge sections out of the harbour at St. Laurent and heavily damaging the other great shelter at Arromanches, it almost seemed that "the vulture poised in the sky" had struck with fatal malevolence.

The guns of the warships ranged along the beaches had been of vital assistance in blasting an entry for the assault. Their potential fire power was still a strong deterrent to counter attack. But as the fighting moved inland they came more and more rarely into use. For over a month the allied armies were to be held at some points within range of the guns of battleships. *Warspite* was to take a hand in the bombardment which opened the battle for Caen on July 7, but it was not to be so with the destroyers. *Algonquin* and *Sioux*, in common with most of the others, were to move about for many days in heavily mined waters and spend many nights under air attack, without being able to strike more than a few blows in support of the troops ashore.

Algonquin came into action for twenty minutes on June 7, when she was called upon to smash up a row of houses from which German snipers were firing on the beaches. On several of the succeeding nights she was assigned with *Sioux* to the "Guards Division" patrol about the anchorage. She made a fast trip to Portsmouth on the 10th to return with Vice-Admiral Nelles who was now head of the Canadian Naval Mission Overseas; and again on the 18th when she brought General Crerar and his staff to France. In the early morning darkness of the 19th she was called on for fire in support of a dawn attack by a commando of Royal Marines between Ouistreham and Cabourg. Firing into the darkness under the orders of her observer ashore, she let go ten four-gun salvoes at a landing field where a spotting aircraft had been located, and at two concentration points for German reinforcements who were expected to hold up the Marines' attack. Nothing could be seen of the results; but late afternoon brought a gratifying message: "The Commanding Officer and all ranks of the 45th Royal Marine Commando wish to record their appreciation of the excellent support received during the operation at 0445. Its success was due largely to your cooperation."

Sioux, apart from a series of patrols, found rather less employment than *Algonquin*. On the 7th, after a hungry day of waiting, she was given a bombardment target, only to have it taken away in favour of the heavier guns of the cruiser *Belfast*. The occasion, otherwise undistinguished, is recorded as having given rise to one of the worst puns in naval history. An army officer ashore, knowns as Forward Observation Officer or FOO, had been allotted *Sioux* for the shoot. When he and his target were taken over by *Belfast* a mild protest crossed the water from *Sioux's* signal lamp: "Thou shalt not covet thy neighbour's FOO." *Belfast* replied, amid the roar of her opening salvo, "Many are called but FOO are chosen."

On the 23rd *Sioux* bombarded a concentration of enemy troops at a point near the mouth of the River Orne; and later in the same day shelled a nearby battery of field guns. On the 24th she joined *Algonquin* in what was to be their last bombardment mission, a lively half-hour action with a German battery in the Franceville area. Soon after that both ships departed for Scapa. The battle was swaying fiercely and stubbornly inland, beyond the range of destroyers' guns; while before them on the beaches and behind them all the way to England the battle of sea-supply was raging with almost equal intensity.

It might have been hard to convince the men of the landing ships and the landing craft of that fact. The days and weeks which followed their return to England brought them a full measure of the baffling, soul-wearying boredom which is an inseparable part of a great military operation, and one of the heaviest of its trials. Steeled to face the perils of an hour, men found the hour postponed and again postponed. Prepared for the most taxing effort, they spent days and weeks in tense, restless idleness. Where everything should have been orderly haste there appeared to be nothing but spiritless confusion. The cogs in the huge machine were not given to see the direction in which it moved, the obstacles it encountered, the shifting of gears required to overcome them.

Prince Henry led one group of landing ships to Baie de la Seine on June 9, after which she returned to Cowes and remained at anchor for ten days. *Prince David*, after disembarking her casualties at Southampton, went to Cowes on the morning of June 8 and swung on her cables there until June 17. Night after night impatient Canadian sailors saw the great docks and harbour area of Southampton operating at peak capacity under a blaze of floodlights. The urgency of loading cargo outweighed the risk of German air attack; but little of this urgency seemed to apply to the landing ships. *Prince David* made a second voyage to the beaches on the evening of June 17 and *Prince Henry* made a third on the 18th. This was the total of their June missions; and there were to be only three more for *Prince Henry* and two for *Prince David* in July.

Meanwhile the Canadian landing craft flotillas, in common with all the other returning flotillas, had been brought together in one large pool from which groups for cross-channel transport were drawn as required. Many of the badly damaged craft were restored to service in short order by Canadian maintenance parties which worked day and night over the broken-winged birds. Yet for most of the craft, return trips were few and far between; and in the remaining three weeks of June the troops carried by Canadian L.C.I.'s totally only 7,871, as against 4,617 landed on the single day of the assault.

The Build-Up

Neptune was not out of joint, nor was the inward flood to the beaches abating. Nor were any anxieties as yet resolved. In part, the inactivity which plagued many of the vessels was due to the generous surplus of transport provided against loss by enemy action. In greater part it resulted from the deliberate policy of the Allied Naval Commander-in-Chief to keep in hand a large lift-capacity for other landings which might be required. Still other reasons hinged upon the weather, upon the progress of the fighting ashore and upon the German reaction. The planned ratio between the supply of men and the supply of equipment had had to be altered for a time. Enemy defenders had inflicted comparatively light casualties upon troops; but heavy seas pounding in on shore among wrecks, mines and beach obstacles, had caused great loss among vehicles and vehicle-carrying craft. Tanks and transport were therefore in greatest demand; and it was their carriers, rather than the troop-carriers, which had to be forced in through the surf in greatest numbers.

There were other reasons for a momentary holdback in the passage of troops. For a day or so the fall of Cherbourg was awaited. Had its harbour become rapidly available, transports could have landed men dry-shod and in greater volume than was possible across the beaches. By the time it became evident that Cherbourg was going to hold out for a while, German aircraft had so thoroughly re-mined the approaches to Baie de la Seine that much sweeping was necessary before large landing ships could enter with reasonable safety. None of this meant that the reinforcment program could be drastically delayed or altered. Unavoidable risks had to be accepted; thousands of tons of supplies and large numbers of men crossed to France each day; but for the first week or so the lift represented minimum demands rather than maximum capacity. None of these aspects of the developing battle could be, or were, explained to the men of the landing craft. Through tense days and nights many of them were called upon only to carry out the familiar naval manœuvre of waiting, on hourly call and without leave, surveying with mingled wonder and exasperation their taut anchor cables and their empty troop space.

All flotilla distinctions had disappeared as the pool was formed, and the drawing of individual craft, or groups of craft, had inevitably the result that some were worked to exhaustion, while others found assignments rare and harbour time heavy on their hands. Three Canadian craft carried six hundred troops to the beaches on June 8; and from then until the end of the month an average of four Canadian craft per day made the trip in company with others from British and American flotillas. Voyages were made as required to whatever beaches or sectors had need of troops, and the passenger lists included many assorted detachments. The Canadians carried British infantry, marines, pioneers and air force ground detachments, as well as infantrymen, artillerymen and sections of medical and engineering units of the Canadian Army. Their loads also included American medical detachments, parties of nursing sisters, pay corps men, stevedores, refrigeration companies, balloon units, and many others of the myriad pieces of the huge military organization assembling on the other side.

Each voyage was made though heavily mined waters and with the danger of enemy attack both on the surface and from overhead; but for the most part the Canadians got off lightly. L.C.I. 270 had her kedge anchor carried away by an enemy bomb as she lay on the beaches; and L.C.I. 135 had her port engine put out of action by a mine which exploded under her quarter. Craft 277, 271 and 166 had a pre-dawn brush with an enemy plane on the morning of the 14th and a shelling from enemy batteries later in the same day, but emerged unscathed. On the night of the 16th, Craft 276 encountered an R-boat in the darkness of the mid-channel, but the startled enemy made off from the equally startled Canadian without attacking. For all craft, these minor encounters had as their unvarying background the nightly air raids which had to be endured on the beaches.

The ferry work, apart from enemy action, was far from easy. The rough Channel voyage, heavily laden with troops, was always risky. The approach to the beaches was hardly less dangerous than it had been on the D-day run-in. Innumerable mines and beach obstacles still lay uncleared beneath the surf, augmented now by the wrecks of the craft they had trapped and by tanks and trucks which had been overturned and smashed. Bombing and shelling along the fringes of the shore had left great craters, which filled at high tide to make dangerous, hidden pools eight and ten feet deep. Here charging craft, twisting in half out of control, could be smashed; and here men could be drowned.

At dusk on June 10th, L.C.I. 276 beached in the Omaha area on a quickly rising tide. Several yards intervened between the ramps of the craft and the dry shoreline, but it seemed that a quick debarkation could be made in safety through water about shoulder high. Sailors made their way ashore hauling guide-lines; and the first troops began to follow, clinging to the ropes. The leading men found footing on the bottom, but as they struggled through the surf they began to slip among a nest of bogged-down, half-submerged vehicles. The tide was rising, surf was lashing up into the faces of the men and one or two, burdened with heavy gear, became panicky and let go their hold on the guide-lines. The panic flared among others for a few minutes; struggling men floundered off into water out of their depth with the dead weight of their equipment dragging them under; and before help could reach them five were drowned.

On another and happier occasion L.C.I.'s 311 and 288 were tied up together alongside a tank landing-craft anchored some distance offshore. They were disembarking troops from the larger vessel preparatory to ferrying them to the beach; and as one of the soldiers was crossing over he lost his footing and fell into the water. He was directly between the tank landing craft and L.C.I. 311, with tide and wind driving the two vessels together, threatening to crush him. Two of 311's officers immediately dived over the side after him; and at the same time 288 heaved a towline on board 311 and drove her engines at full power to drag the nearer craft back. The manœuvre was successful by a narrow margin; and, just as

318

the two hulls seemed to be closing on them, the soldier and the two sailors were pulled from the water.

During the first two weeks after the landings, the craft retained in the assault area for ship-to-shore ferrying were the hardest worked. Among these were four craft of the 264th Flotilla and two of the 260th, and their men had a strenuous time along the littered beaches. The loading of troops and masses of unwieldy equipment was a precarious business as the small, flat-bottomed vessels heaved up and down by the high sides of merchantmen and transports standing in the rough seas off shore. Once loaded, the forcing of their cargoes in through the surf was still more dangerous. Every craft at one time or another was smashed up sufficiently to call for hours of sleepless work by maintenance parties. Propellers wore sheared off, anchors carried away, and great gashes knocked in the hulls; and the steady process of attrition soon got ahead of the devoted repair men. By the end of the second week it was seen that no amount of patching could keep the craft in operation much longer. They were ordered to England; but before they reached that haven they were to share with some of their sister craft in the rigours of the storm which blew up on the night of June 19.

For three days from that well-remembered Monday, the gale roaring in from the open Channel seemed to threaten the success of the whole Neptune operation. The artificial harbour in the American sector at St. Laurent was almost entirely carried away. The British harbour at Arromanches was battered and broken through in several places, but held sufficiently so that it could later be repaired. The smaller shelters also came in for a merciless pounding; and of all the tossing ships in the crowded anchorages the ones that suffered most were the landing craft.

L.C.I. 305 had come across from England on the evening of the 19th and had anchored at one of the pier-heads inside the harbour of St. Laurent. The usual air raid developed at dark, but was practically ignored in the face of thunderous seas which were already rolling in. About one o'clock in the morning, with the wind still rising and the seas becoming heavier all the time, Craft 305 saw a section of the breakwater tear loose and come riding down toward her. Weighing in haste, she drove in for the beach to anchor, but within an hour her cable broke and she was tossing in the crowded harbour again. A line put across to another landing craft parted almost at once. She dropped a second anchor, only to have a great wave smash into her, broadside on, and snap the cable like a thread. Helpless amid a confusion of struggling ships, she was lifted in toward shore, and it seemed for a moment that she would be blown broadside on the beach and smashed. Fending off desperately, and with her engines going full power, she swerved and bumped her way out through a mass of other vessels to a patch of clear water, where she managed to ride on an emergency anchor for the next eleven hours.

The gale was still rising in fury, and more of the harbour beakwaters gave way during the morning. In mid-afternoon 305's anchor cable parted and she ran out of the harbour into the open Channel, hoping to ride with the wind. The seas were too much for her and she had to claw her way back in. Again, lines and anchor cables parted one after one; the zigzagging craft, terribly beaten by the wind and sea, lurched onto an underwater obstruction which tore a hole in her bottom and then fought her way to the open Channel again. She sheltered through the next night, and during the following day and night, at the little harbour of Port-en-Bessin, with the rest of her lines snapping one after one as the gale renewed itself rather than abated. Finally around noon of the 22nd, with hardly a usable length of wire left on board, she risked the Channel again and started for England. Midnight found her in Calshot, with her men enjoying the first hot food and looking forward to the first dry sleep they had had in eighty-two hours.

Craft 288, 311, 302, 125 and 252 had experiences paralleling those of 305; and for Craft 255 the adventures were carried to melodramatic lengths. She was off Arromanches, already damaged and steering on emergency gear, when the storm broke. Three times she anchored, and three times her anchor cable parted during the day and night of June 20. On the morning of the 21st she dragged her fourth anchor and ran helplessly across the harbour to collide with an ammunition ship. Under the circumstances, she was probably fortunate to get off with nothing worse than a hole in her port quarter above the waterline; but before she had time to assess her damage she was practically under the stern of an unmanned tug which had been lifted from the beaches by a huge sea and was bearing down on her. Collision was avoided by inches and some of 255's men scrambled across to subdue the tug and secure the two vessels together under the lee of a freighter. An hour or so later, when anchor wires parted again, 255 abandoned the dubious security of the harbour and, battered and holed, laboured across the Channel to Southampton.

In spite of similar trials, distributed over all ships in the Channel or at the Normandy anchorages, Neptune weathered the storm. With clearing weather during the latter part of June, the operations of the landing craft began to be stepped up. Craft held in reserve for a landing in the Channel Islands were released to the general pool as the possibility of that landing grew more remote. Canadian craft were to ferry over about thirteen thousand troops in July, and another seven thousand in August, before they were dispersed and their crews returned to general service.

Meanwhile the minesweepers which had led in the assaulting ships on June 6 had resumed their work as soon as, and in some cases before, the first troops were on the beaches. They continued without respite all through the months of the build-up. The enemy's re-mining programme, carried out by aircraft, proved the most harassing of all the defences he put up against Neptune. Throughout the Baie de la Seine area, and all the way across the Channel to the mouths of the English harbours, German planes strewed mines of every variety; some of them, such as the "oyster" or pressure mine, new types against which new methods of sweeping had to be devised.

The Build-Up

Day after day, while new accumulations of shipping demanded new areas of cleared water, lanes already swept had to be gone over again and again. Hundreds of square miles of water were involved. The ten original lanes had to be widened and merged until they formed two large channels, one leading to the American sector and one to the British. All the channels had to be temporarily buoyed as they were widened; and as they grew to their final size they had to be buoyed again in more permanent fashion. Moreover, in addition to the channels, the entire assault area had to be swept yard by yard until it provided full freedom of movement for the manœuvering ships.

The 31st Canadian Flotilla had completed its second D-day sweep at eleven o'clock on the night of June 6, and by a quarter to one in the morning was anchored at Port-en-Bessin. The official time at rest was four hours and thirty-five minutes, since the Flotilla sailed again at 4.30 on the morning of the 7th. It is doubtful, however, if the men in the ships got anything like that allotment of sleep, since all gear had to be repaired and put in working order by first light. The sweep of the 7th was carried out in the American transport area, beginning a seven-day period in which, working an average of eighteen hours per day, the sweepers were to account for seventy-eight mines. A twenty-four hour layover followed; after which work was resumed at a tempo only slightly less hectic.

Guysborough, Kenora, Vegreville and *Georgian*, with the 14th British Flotilla, carried on under the same conditions until June 21. A German sweep-cutting device, which was thickly sown in their area, and which was continually parting their sweep wires, caused them more than usual annoyance and necessitated additional re-sweeping. The 16th British Flotilla, with *Canso*, divided its time between the waters of the assault area and the lanes leading back to England; and on June 16 swept a passage ahead of the cruiser, *Arethusa*, which was carrying the King on his visit to the Normandy beaches. *Thunder*, with the 4th British Flotilla, was engaged for ten days on a newly laid German minefield south of the Isle of Wight; after which she was detached to join a group of American minesweepers being formed in preparation for the coming assault on Cherbourg.

For all the minesweepers the requirements of exact navigation and unceasing vigilance continued unabating. Their work had to be carried out in waters thronged with charging small craft and heavily manœuvering large ships, frequently with bombardments under way or enemy air attacks going on overhead. There was to be no let-up during July; and August was to find the ships, if not the men, about at the end of their tether. Toward the end of this period, *Caraquet*, returning from a sojourn in dock on August 13, signalled *Fort William*, which was still creakingly on duty, that she had "brought a basket to take her back to Plymouth." *Fort William* made suitable reply, limped into Plymouth, and later her commanding officer watched the removal of her old and cranky minesweeping winch, "with mixed feelings. It had been the recipient of so many prayers and curses, and had been in our thoughts so constantly for so many months that we saw it go over with a twinge of regret. Maybe it wasn't such a bad old winch after all."

These mellowing days of August, however, were still in the future when *Thunder* took part with American and British ships in the assault on Cherbourg. The port was an essential for the break-out of the allied armies; and for the tremendously accelerated inpouring of supplies which would be necessary to support a campaign across France. The determined American advance toward the port had met with equally determined resistance. The Germans had contested every foot of ground; and their retreating forces had strongly entrenched themselves about the town itself. By the 24th of June, however, the Americans were in position to launch a final attack from the landward side and ships began to move to their support from the sea.

Thunder was one of the ships which took part in a preliminary and not very successful minesweeping operation on the 24th. Approaching Cherbourg from the direction of the assault area, the sweeping force, escorted by American destroyers, arrived off Point Barfleur in mid-afternoon. Although well in range of the shore batteries, it was given an undisturbed hour to work its way in toward the coast. Then the big guns opened up with fire so accurate and intense that the destroyers wasted no time in deciding on the next move. Snaking around the sweepers and spewing out a smoke screen, they ordered them to cut sweeps and get out of the area at maximum speed. The flotilla withdrew undamaged, but with its respect for German coastal batteries considerably increased.

After this tentative beginning the actual assault by sea and land began next day. *Thunder* returned as one of the flotilla of minesweepers acting with an American task unit. The land attack had already overrun Point Barfleur when the sweepers came into the Cherbourg approaches. Nevertheless shore batteries still in action around the port opened up, and the shelling became so heavy that the battleship *Texas* sent in destroyers to lay a smoke screen. For an hour as the sweepers continued their work, shells whistled around them amid the friendly smoke. One burst close enough to send shrapnel rattling along *Thunder's* quarterdeck, and a destroyer feeding the smoke screen had its funnel carried away by a direct hit.

Farther to the west the British cruiser, *Enterprise*, still in command of Captain H. T. W. Grant, was working in toward the port with a bombardment force which also included her old "chummy ship," *Glasgow*. Ahead of them was another flotilla of minesweepers. It was intended that *Enterprise* and *Glasgow* should take station somewhere between 14,000 and 20,000 yards off shore with the United States cruisers, *Quincy* and *Tuscaloosa*. The American battleship *Nevada* was to bombard from farther out.

Once again, as the sweepers ahead of this force moved into the approaches, shore batteries opened on them with very intense fire. In order to cover them, *Enterprise* brought her guns into action immediately, although she was at her extreme range of 20,000 yards. Continuing in to 17,800 yards and maintaining heavy fire for half an hour, she immediately became a principal target for the shore batteries while every ship in her vicinity began to make smoke for her. Moving at high speed through waters only partially swept, swinging in wide evasive turns and emerging only occasionally from amid the clouds of her screen, she dropped 115 out of 155 shells directly into the target area which was indicated to her by a spotting aircraft.

The target was a four-gun battery in a thick concrete casemate at the western side of the harbour. It made sharp reply; and shrapnel from one of its shells slightly wounded the captain and the executive officer on *Enterprise's* bridge. By the end of half an hour, however, two of the battery's guns were out of action; and since it was now impossible to observe the casemate amid the clouds of smoke rising about it, *Enterprise* transferred her fire to a mobile battery situated on higher ground. After getting away twenty-five rounds against the new target, she re-engaged the old, and silenced its two remaining guns. Shortly after that all ships ceased fire and the final assault swept in upon the port from the landward side.

The fall of Cherbourg brought a new and more confident rhythm to the continuing operations of Neptune. The battered port and its harbour facilities took much time to restore to full efficiency, and the main volume of troops and supplies continued to pour in over the beaches for many weeks. Nevertheless, high priority cargoes were soon being routed through the port, and major anxieties over supply were allayed. Many dangers remained; but the time of doubt had largely passed.

Some of Neptune's immense shipping resources were now diverted to other operations already in train. Landing ships began to be withdrawn for the invasion of southern France, which had waited on the success of Neptune. About the middle of July *Prince Henry* was ordered to dock at Southampton and *Prince David* at Cardiff. The ships were to undergo boiler cleaning and were then to sail for the Mediterranean.

They had carried to Normandy, in all, 5,566 troops; a far smaller number than they had expected. The same was true in greater or less degree of most of the landing ships; and was due both to the prodigal planning and to the generally overwhelming success of the operation. *Prince Henry*, as the senior landing ship in Force J, had had the responsibility for the training, discipline and efficiency of her ships since well before D-day; and on each trip to France had had the nerve-wracking task of leading her vessels through heavily mined waters and down the narrow channels to the beaches. *Prince David*, as the leader of a subdivision, had had only a slightly lesser responsibility. The men of both ships, although some of them might have wished for more excitement and for an opportunity to use the elaborate armament with which they had been fitted, could at least look back on a job to which they had given rather more than the required minimum. The accommodation and food provided for the troops had been, by the standards of war, superlatively good. From commanding officers down, the men of the *Prince* ships were remembered, among far-scattered and diverse units now fighting ashore, for the good-natured helpfulness, the clean billets and the hot meals which had been the soldiers' unvarying portion during the tense voyages to France.

Before the landing ships commenced their dispersal, July brought employment for the R.C.N. Beach Commando, which had been held on the Isle of Wight as a reserve beach party since the week before D-day. On July 6, just when the men had despaired of ever seeing France and were considering leave as an acceptable substitute, they were ordered to the Juno area. They arrived as the battle for Caen was commencing some ten miles away. Salvoes from *Warspite*, standing close offshore, passed above them, a series of aerial dogfights enlivened their first day, and the night was loud with one of the air raids to which they soon became accustomed. During the battle for Caen their beach was a very heavy unloading sector, and like all Canadians allowed to get their hands on mechanical equipment, they established an enviable reputation for their handling of vehicles and craft.

Meanwhile through all the changing phases of Neptune, in spite of mines and weather, E-boats, R-boats and aircraft, the corvettes had brought convoy after convoy to the beaches. The flow of stores had to be, and was, maintained without pause from the beginning. All invasion convoys up to those which arrived at the beaches on the second day after the assault had been pre-loaded before Neptune got under way. As soon as the components for the artificial harbours had been delivered. the Canadian corvettes, with many other escort ships, had turned back to take over these pre-loaded convoys, and after that the other convoys moving down behind them.

From the northern British ports and from across the Atlantic the flood of build-up shipping poured into two great reservoirs: the Bristol Channel ports on the west coast, and the ports of the Thames estuary on the east. Here the invasion convoys formed and moved on around the shoulders of the south coast toward the assembly area. As they came, they were joined by tributary groups from the ports along the route to the Solent; and from there the whole flowed to the British or American task force areas on the beaches.

During June each of the Canadian corvettes made at least six trips to the beaches; and several of them made many more. They came under attack from E-boats on one or two occasions, air attacks were fairly frequent, and the danger of mines was ever present. On the whole, however, the veterans of the Atlantic convoy routes were rather disparaging in their comments on life in the big league. Monotony was with them eternally and excitement was rare.

They were on duty or at short notice continuously. In most of the ships the crews had only two four-hour periods of leave between May 10 and June 22. *Camrose*, the hardest done by, was unable to give any leave at all for forty days. The ships were on call whenever an escort was required, and when the crews were off duty there was little to compensate them. Coming into crowded ports, where ships were already ranked six and eight deep at a jetty, they usually had to berth in the middle of the harbour. This meant that any men who might have been allowed a few hours' leave would have to go in by means of "liberty boats," the small harbour craft which serve as water taxis for leave parties. Since harbour craft invariably had three missions scheduled for every two they could perform, there was seldom a liberty boat available and the men stayed on board.

Each passage in escort was a dismally exacting feat of navigation for captains who had to squeeze unwieldy columns of ships down narrow, mine-bordered lanes of water. Depth charge attacks on asdic contacts were fairly numerous during the convoy voyages; but in almost every case it was found that the echoes came from more of the wrecks which were plaguing the hunting groups farther to the west. The corvettes were called upon to act mainly as herdsmen and policemen, as signal platforms relaying messages between larger ships, and as general duty craft of every kind, even to acting as tugs on one or two occasions. Amid such preoccupations they repelled almost absent-mindedly the few enemy attacks they were called upon to meet during June. *Kitchener* and *Port Arthur* had one voyage enlivened by near misses from glider bombs. *Camrose, Baddeck* and *Louisburg* fought off a series of attacks by E-boats on the nigth of June 13; and early on the morning of the same day *Trentonian* had the most harrowing experience of all when she and the cable ship, *St. Margaret,* were shelled by an American destroyer which mistook them for enemy vessels. *St. Margaret* was hit repeatedly and her commanding officer was fatally wounded. *Trentonian* escaped without casualties although a shell passed through her engine room.

July and the first week of August passed without major incident for the corvettes. The streams of shipping flowed now with an uninterrupted rhythm. Losses were never sufficient to cause more than a minor dislocation of the long, narrow-fronted convoys threading their way to the beaches. Yet losses there continually were. E-boats still came slashing in from time to time; dive-bombing, glider-bombing and strafing aircraft were overhead; mines were ever present, and a few U-boats were creeping along under the shadow of the French shore to operate off the British coast or in the Channel. No man could know when his ship might be the one of all the moving thousands marked out for destruction.

Regina was such a ship. On the evening of August 8, when she was moving with a convoy a few miles off Trevose Head, there came a heavy explosion and one of the merchant ships began to settle. *Regina* came alongside immediately, and the vessel reported that she had been mined. She appeared to be salvageable, and *Regina* ordered an American tank landing craft in the convoy to take off the freighter's crew and a rig a towline. While disembarkation was made and the towline run across, the corvette stood off at a distance of about a hundred yards to superintend.

Just as the towline tightened between the tank carrier and the freighter, *Regina* blew up with a tremendous explosion and sank in a matter of seconds. It had been a torpedo rather than a mine which hit the freighter; and *Regina* was the U-boat's second victim. Sixty-six survivors were recovered, ten of them seriously injured and all of them shocked and coated with oil. The remaining men simply disappeared in a catastrophe which was completed and done with by the time a pillar of smoke and debris had risen a hundred feet in the sky.

Many of *Regina's* men owed their lives to very gallant efforts by the crew of the American tank landing-craft, two of whom dived overboard to assist the Canadians in the water. Others had cause to be grateful for the efforts of the corvette's medical officer, Surgeon-Lieutenant G. A. Gould. Although half-choked with fuel oil, and so painfully wounded that he had to take morphia himself, Gould remained at work throughout the night in the wardroom of the American ship, performing one amputation with only the limited supplies available to him from the vessel's medical chest.

The Build-Up

August brought some diversification of the corvettes' assignments; and also some arrivals and departures. *Port Arthur* and *Mayflower* were stationed alternately as weather reporting ships in the open Atlantic, about six hundred miles west of the Cornish coast. *Algoma* arrived in British waters to relieve *Woodstock*, which was returning to Canada for refit. *Ville de Québec* and *Snowberry* appeared; *Rimouski, Camrose, Prescott, Summerside* and *Lunenburg* departed. Some of the remaining corvettes, as well as some of the newcomers, began to be assigned to anti-submarine patrols; and on one such mission another of their number was lost.

Alberni had distinguished herself on July 26 by shooting down a JU 88 over the Neptune anchorage. Early on the morning of August 21 she was ordered to relieve *Drumheller*, which was on patrol against U-boats in an area a little to the east of the Isle of Wight. At 11.46 in the morning, as she was approaching her station, she was hit by a torpedo and within twenty seconds all but her bow was under water. The ship, as it sank with paralysing speed, turned over on many men who were trying to escape. There was a strong wind with a heavy sea running; and the speed of the disaster allowed no time for the release of the ship's boats and floats. Fortunately for the men who managed to get clear, help arrived quickly. Within forty-five minutes two British motor torpedo boats were on the scene; and their valiant efforts resulted in the rescue of three officers and twenty-eight ratings. Fifty-nine men were lost.

The corvettes, with little opportunity for dramatic action, were still the hardest hit of all Canadian naval forces in Operation Neptune. Their losses totalled ninety men killed and thirty wounded out of the total Canadian casualties of 120 killed and 159 wounded. Nor was their work yet completed. At the end of August many months of danger and sheer montonous hard work still lay ahead of them.

The Channel, however, was now securely won; as the Atlantic had been won before it. Some cargoes, some vessels and some men might not reach France; but the vast majority

of them would. And from there they would go on to the
Rhine and beyond. Neptune had passed the ball to Overlord; and the combined operation was going forward with
enormous impetus and with cold confidence. The naval portion of the great whole had, by the end of August, assumed
secondary prominence, if not secondary importance. The
coastal forces had moved away from Baie de la Seine toward
the shores of the North Sea. The screening forces were ranging farther and farther afield. Many tangled *mêlées* among
the small craft and many sharp encounters of larger ships had
resolved themselves now into a final phase in which the covering forces and the Home Fleet were to reach far beyond
the Neptune lanes to sweep the enemy from every sea on
which he still sailed.

CHAPTER FIFTEEN

"Wherever Wood Can Swim"

"Wherever wood can swim," said Napoleon with imperial petulance, "there I am sure to find this flag of England." His German counterpart, in an age of steel and global war, had landed himself in a worse predicament than the Emperor. Ships flying the ensigns, not of England alone, but of more than twenty nations, had assembled the war power of half the earth and were pouring it through the breach in the Atlantic Wall. By the end of July 1944, the inner defences had given way. Mid-August was to see another breach opened in the Mediterranean front to the south. Along the brittle crust of the remaining wall, wherever Fortress Europe looked upon salt water, its garrisons were to find themselves ringed with Allied ships, riding the horizon, smashing sea communications and battering down the last efforts to contain the inward-flooding power of Neptune.

All this was not to take place in a day. Throughout July the clearing of the flanks, like the cross-channel lift of men and matériel, continued as a strenuous, perilous routine. The screening forces moved warily outward, closed in on the northern French coast, swept along west to Ushant and southward into the Bay of Biscay. Their patrols were almost entirely offensive, but there were still occasions when they were called upon to deal with determined U-boats creeping in toward the Neptune lanes. And in the shallow waters along the inmost fringes of the assault area there was almost nightly thrust and parry between the boats of the coastal forces.

During July and for the first two weeks of August, the motor torpedo boat flotillas which included the Canadian 29th had for their principal territory the stretch of water lying between the eastern flank of Neptune and the approaches to Le Havre. July had hardly begun when one of the innumerable mines infesting the area claimed a Canadian casualty. On the night of the 2nd, boats 460 and 465 were returning from a patrol when 460 suddenly disintegrated. A sheet of flame lifted skyward, followed by a column of water and debris which rose two hundred feet in the air and showered back upon 465 a hundred yards astern. Only six men of the crew were recovered, the commanding officer and nine of his men being lost.

The night of the 4th and early morning of the 5th brought a prolonged engagement with E-boats. Boats 459, 462 and 464 were on their usual protective patrol about the assault anchorage. Shortly before midnight radar indicated the approach of enemy craft from Le Havre. A few minutes of stalking followed; then starshell revealed a line of nine E-boats two thousand yards away, making for the anchorage. As the Canadians opened fire, the German craft broke off into the dark, one of them trailing after the others, heavily hit and ablaze. The rest were overtaken in about half an hour, and the boats of the 29th ripped in through a smoke screen to damage a second craft. Pursuit was complicated by the appearance of a German dive bomber, whose efforts inconvenienced the Canadians but failed to encourage the disorganized E-boats to make a stand. When the chase was finally abandoned at the entrance to Le Havre, one E-boat, lost in smoke, was considered sunk and two others had been badly damaged. The Canadians got off lightly, their only damage being a hit which knocked 459's radar out of action.

An awkward assignment on the night of the 8th brought another mine casualty. Human torpedoes were being launched against the anchorage from the eastern side of the Ouistreham Canal, and the M.T.B.'s were sent close inshore along the area to look for the sites from which the torpedoes came. The boats had to move through shallow water, which had not been swept, since it lay just outside the anchorage along a shore still held by the Germans. At a little after five in the morning, boat 463, after setting off twenty-six small mines without serious damage, struck the twenty-seventh and began to settle. The other boats, closing the position, found 463 too seriously holed to be salvageable, but only four men of her crew were wounded.

The next night brought heavy action for boats 459, 461 and 464. It was clear and calm, and a little after midnight shore batteries detected the craft as they patrolled eleven miles southwest of Cap d'Antifer. For an hour they were forced to zigzag at high speed under starshell and high explosive; and about one o'clock, as the fire from the coastal batteries began to abate, the M.T.B.'s observed new starshell and gunfire to the north. It was rising, evidently, from an engagement of coastal forces close in to shore; and when the Canadians closed to investigate they found two British M.T.B.'s heavily damaged after an attack on a line of ten R-boats which were now lying a mile from land in the lee of the cliffs. Between the R-boats and the two nearest British craft lay a third British boat, crippled and on fire.

Boats 459, 461 and 464 made a run along the enemy line, engaging each R-boat in turn at a range of a hundred yards. As they reversed their course, 461 swerved out of line, ran around the crippled British craft to lay a smoke screen; and then came alongside to assist her crew. The other boats completed their second run; then 464 came over to help with rescue work while 459 circled the area to hide it with more smoke. The R-boats clung to their dark lee shore, making no effort to interfere; and the Canadians departed at last with all but one of the British crew safe on board. They themselves had lost one man killed and four wounded.

The night of July 14 brought an inconclusive engagement for boats 461, 462 and 465, fought out with two enemy minesweepers, eight E-boats, and under the guns of shore batteries. On the next night 459, 466 and 464 took on three E-boats in a fierce five-minute action from which one enemy went limping away heavily afire, while 459 laboured off in the other direction with a hole below the waterline. The Canadian craft was patched up by the following sunset, only to receive a more crippling wound that night.

This time boats 459, 466 and 464 were close in to Le Havre, zigzagging under shellfire from batteries both at Cap de la Hêve to the north of the port and Trouville to the south. About midnight their controlling frigate, lying outside the assault anchorage with its radar team on the alert, vectored them onto some enemy minesweepers which were creeping northward out of Le Havre, close inshore. The three boats made for the position, and as they raced along the coast they were suddenly illuminated by flares dropped from an enemy plane overhead. The flares were followed by bombs. Then came the shells of the shore batteries, screaming down on them at a range of less than four miles. One shell crashed through the light sides of 459 to explode in the engine room, killing two men and wounding another. As wreckage from below spewed up through a hole blown in the deck, the boat began to settle. Another straddling salvo burst in the water and through the descending splashes 466 moved in to take 459 in tow. Boat 464 circled to make smoke while lines were rigged; then followed behind, feeding the screen, as 466 and her tow limped away, still under heavy fire. They reached the anchorage without further damage; and what remained of boat 459 was hoisted onto the beach.

Patrols during the late days of July began to close more and more tightly about the approaches to Le Havre. The enemy was beginning to abandon all his offensive efforts and to think mainly of evacuating his remaining fighting craft and cargo vessels. To do so he must send them creeping northward out of Le Havre along the coast. Well aware of this, Allied commanders stationed nightly patrols of motor torpedo boats off the harbour and all along the escape route.

On the night of July 25, boats 461, 462, 464, 465 and 466—all those of the 29th still in commission—were patrolling a little north of Le Havre between Cap d'Antifer and Cape de la Hêve. The night was calm with low clouds obscuring the moon and providing excellent conditions for M.T.B. operations. The boats kept in as close to shore as they dared in order to have a dark lee from which to attack any shipping they might encounter. A little after midnight radar reports relayed from the control frigate indicated that an enemy convoy was moving up the coast from Le Havre. The M.T.B.'s crawled along in the loom of the shoreline until they made out two minesweepers, two flak trawlers and several R-boats. Then they moved into line abreast formation, opened their throttles and roared out from the shadows.

They were met with sudden and heavy fire from a screen of R-boats which they had failed to observe on the inshore side of the convoy. Plunging through this line they got their torpedoes away and swept past the merchant ships with racketing guns. Behind them a huge explosion lifted above the blaze of starshell and the lurid beads of tracer fire. They had sunk one ship of the convoy at the cost of light damage to their own craft and two men wounded.

August opened with foul weather and with hunting steadily becoming leaner along the eastern border of the assault anchorage. Enemy coastal forces were withdrawing from Baie de la Seine, making their escape as they could, beginning a slow retreat from base to base along the French coast. Dieppe, Boulogne, Calais and Dunkirk would be their first resting places; and British coastal forces were now to follow them. During the second week of August the 29th, with other flotillas, moved to Ramsgate and came again under Dover Command. Coastal force work in defence of Neptune's eastern flank had resolved itself into a long pursuit which would continue to the end of the war, moving eastward and northward stage by stage from the Straits of Dover to the Hook of Holland.

On the western side of the assault lanes, the boats of the 65th Canadian Flotilla had been engaged since late June in the business of search and pursuit rather than of defence. Based at Brixham near Dartmouth, their usual patrol area throughout July lay along the French coast within a few miles of St. Malo. Here they prowled on every night when the weather permitted, in search of enemy convoys, evacuation shipping and whatever else might attempt to sail. The month was to be a poor one for them; but it opened promisingly on July 3.

The boats selected for duty that night, 748, 743, 735 and 736 were off St. Malo when, at about one o'clock, a series of radar echoes led them in toward the coast. Visibility was good and before long an actual sighting confirmed their radar indications. A little inshore and a little ahead of them, an enemy convoy was crawling southwesterly along the coast. Three merchantmen could be made out, with four gun coasters disposed about them.

Unobserved, the four Canadian boats ran along parallel to the enemy's course, drew slightly ahead and then turned to come in at the convoy from the port bow. Closing to within eight hundred yards, they fired torpedoes. Two heavy explosions came from 748's target, the first merchantman in the line. The second ship rocked and slowed suddenly to a crawl as one of 743's torpedoes crashed home; and the third vessel, hit by both 735 and 736, blew up and sank instantly.

Gunfire from the escorts was now coming down heavily on the M.T.B.'s. Boat 743, which appeared to be the principal target, put two more torpedoes into the merchantman already damaged by 748, and the vessel began to sink. While the other two boats maintained their fire on the one surviving merchantman, boat 748 bore in to engage the escorts, and set two of them afire. Then the force withdrew to seaward. Boat 748 had five men wounded and was low in the water with a hole in her bows. Boat 743 had one man wounded and was also slightly damaged; but the tally for the night's work was in favour of the Canadians. Two enemy merchantmen had been sunk, while the third merchantman and two of the escorts had been badly hurt.

Most of July was plagued by such bad weather that the boats had to spend much time in harbour. On the patrols they did make, their mission was now twofold: "for the gathering of intelligence and the destruction of enemy shipping." Their route, taking them down along the coast from the Channel Islands and St. Malo as far as Brest, was along a shoreline still heavily defended. Since the shipping they sought, if it moved at all, moved close in under the protection of coastal guns, the M.T.B.'s had to accustom themselves to 11-inch "bricks" splashing in the water about them from ranges up to fifteen miles.

Between August 9 and 12, as American troops fought their way along the Brittany peninsula, B.B.C. news reports sometimes got a little ahead of them. One such report on the 10th indicated that St. Malo had been taken. M.T.B.'s 735, 726, 736, 727, 743 and 746 were all out that night, and were patrolling in the early hours of the 11th off St. Malo. They had heard that the port had fallen and were quite ready to believe it. A rating on board one of the boats is even reported to have done a good business in tickets for a dance to be held in the Hôtel de Ville at St. Malo on the following evening. A visit to the harbour seemed indicated by the promptings both of duty and curiosity.

The optimism of the flotilla leader became somewhat tempered as the boats drew in past the harbour mouth. There were no welcoming signals. A radar aerial set on high ground beyond the jetties seemed to be training on them, and a large range finder was also twitching in their direction. The wheeling apparatus had an unfriendly aspect; and the order was given for the boats to alter around and retire. They had hardly made their turns when salvoes from the guns of the "captured" port came crashing down all about them, showering the boats and their crews with shrapnel and salt water. They were thoroughly boxed in; and their escape, under smoke screens, at high speed and with every evasive manœuvre they could devise was a minor miracle.

In the early morning of the 12th they again passed St. Malo, and were again shelled. A few nights later they were off Brest; and in the week that followed; the waters of nearby St. Mathieu and the passage between the Sein Islands and the mainland became familiar territory to them. The boats were operating at a considerable distance from their base;

and on one or two foggy days they tried the experiment of lying at sea all day instead of returning to Brixham. On another occasion they spent two days lying at L'Abervrach, an inlet on the French coast near Ile de Vierge, getting their supplies from a British sloop.

This first operation from a foreign mainland was a prelude to other operations still a month or so away, when their base would be at Ostend, on the Belgian coast. In the meantime, their patrols were proving unfruitful so far as enemy shipping was concerned. The process of fanning out from the assault area began again. For the 65th, as for the 29th, it took an easterly direction. The First Canadian Army was now beginning its drive along the Belgian and Dutch coasts; and one arm of the battle for sea supply was paralleling the advance in a long-drawn-out struggle whose goal would be Antwerp. At the end of August the 65th Flotilla crossed over the Neptune lanes and went a stage farther than the 29th, taking up its station at Great Yarmouth, well along the eastern coast, for operations in the North Sea.

Meanwhile, from late June until early August, the destroyer and frigate groups constituting the outer screens were moved back and forth over steadily widening sectors of the western Channel and the Bay of Biscay. Although Cherbourg had fallen, Brest and all the strong German bases along the French Biscay coast were still held. U-boats were arriving and departing from them in considerable numbers; and the Germans were trying desperately to keep the ports supplied and linked together by coastal convoys. The Tribals and the escort groups of destroyers and frigates began to be sent out on missions which were frequently co-ordinated and overlapped to smash up these efforts.

On the night of June 27, *Huron* with her British companion, *Eskimo*, went down through the waters of the Channel Islands and began a sweep along the French coast some twenty miles to the northwest of St. Malo. About one o'clock, radar indicated an enemy convoy approaching. Starshell, fired a few moments later, revealed a minesweeper and two trawlers. The enemy ships immediately made smoke, turned south, and ran along the coast under the protection of shore batteries, which opened up on the destroyers.

Huron's gunfire had already set the minesweeper afire. *Eskimo* followed one of the trawlers, the principal smoke-maker, into the thick of the screen and was soon lost in its swirling clouds. She managed to keep on the track of her target; but, while she was so occupied, the second trawler came close on her port bow and opened fire with three-inch guns, bofors and oerlikons. At close range, and in the midst of thick smoke, this was a damaging attack. A three-inch shell pierced the destroyer's hull and exploded in her engine room, to knock out her steering motor and much of her electrical system. All lights went out, and the power mountings of guns and radar aerials failed. For a few moments, until repairs were made, *Eskimo* was a partially blinded and partially crippled ship. *Huron*, circling the wreathing smoke, was unable to distinguish friend from enemy, until the first trawler was unlucky enough to run out of the smoke screen. Then the destroyer's guns swung onto him at once and after three or four minutes of fire the German blew up. Meanwhile the second trawler, taking advantage of the smoke and the escaping clouds of steam which were rising about the wounded *Eskimo*, made its escape.

Huron went into the same area with the British destroyer, *Tartar* on July 8 and the two ships managed to score a few hits on a pair of German trawlers before shallowing water and the fire of coastal batteries drove them out to sea. *Haida* took over on the night of the 12th when, with *Tartar* and the Polish *Blyskawica*, she went out through the western Channel and down along the Biscay coast to a position off Lorient. Cautiously approaching the important U-boat base which was ringed with some of the Germans' heaviest coastal defences and best radar installations, the destroyers stood off the port until two in the morning, riding a calm sea with no moon above. Echoes at last began to form on the radar screens, indicating that an enemy convoy was leaving Lorient in a northward direction. The destroyers began their stalk, keeping well to seaward for an hour. The German ships worked a little out from the coast, clearing the shallow water and the coastal minefields. Then *Tartar* led her force in under the shore batteries for the kill. Within an hour all the German ships—two merchantmen, a trawler, and a mystifying object later identified as a towed gunnery target—were sunk. The guns on shore, which had been loud but ineffective during the action, sent their shells screaming after the Tribals to a distance of fourteen miles as they turned back for Plymouth.

Meanwhile the destroyers of Escort Group 12 had made up in one action for many weeks of fruitless anti-submarine patrols. On July 5 *Qu'Appelle, Saskatchewan, Skeena* and *Restigouche* were ordered to sail from Plymouth as a striking force to carry out Operation Dredger. By one in the afternoon they had passed the Lizard, and by twenty minutes of midnight were in position south of Ushant. Dredger had been planned after careful and prolonged air observation of U-boat movements. Reconnaissance reports indicated that U-boats on passage inward and outward from Brest were usually met about ten miles south of the port by a force of anywhere from two to five of the heavily armed M-class minesweepers. The rendezvous usually took place about two hours after dark; and on the morning of the 5th both air reconnaissance and a large number of U-boat transmissions indicated that a meeting was scheduled for that night. It was intended that the 12th Escort Group should crash the party.

Shortly before one in the morning, while the Canadian ships were steering in toward Ushant from the sea, a single radar echo indicated movement at nine and a half miles on the port bow. The single echo gradually broke up into three, which were analysed as three enemy ships steering outward from Brest. Escort Group 12, moving on a course which would cut off any return to Brest, followed the echoes until, at 1.37, the range had closed to five and a half miles.

The destroyers were now in a position to attack. They challenged by light; and received no answer. *Qu'Appelle* then ordered illumination by rocket flares; and in the glare which followed, the three expected minesweepers were revealed, together with two submarines which immediately scurried off, unpursued. The escorts were the more important target and had to be dealt with first. Increasing to full speed, the Canadian ships ran in along the German line, *Qu'Appelle* taking the first trawler, *Saskatchewan* the second and *Skeena* and *Restigouche* the third.

Nine minutes later, as the destroyers completed their first run, the leading enemy ship was stopped and smoking. The second was turning off to the southwest with a large fire amidships; and the third was also stopped and afire. Altering round, the group came in for its second run in the face of gunnery which was still accurate and damaging. *Qu'Appelle,* *Restigouche* and *Skeena* bore down to hammer at the leading ship until it blew up. *Saskatchewan* closed to within half a mile of the second and fired a torpedo which missed. Opening with her guns, she blew away the German's bridge structure by a direct hit. A moment later flames rising amidships spread to envelop the whole vessel and all return fire ceased.

The third ship, although stopped, was keeping her guns in action. She was brave, and she was by no means a harmless target. As the destroyers closed to point-blank range they were met by fire which riddled *Qu'Appelle's* funnels, set a depth charge on her quarter-deck afire, and wreaked havoc on her bridge. The commanding officer and several of the men with him on the bridge were seriously wounded, and a moment later the ship's steering gear went out of action, forcing her to disengage. *Saskatchewan* was also heavily spattered by fire and her radar set was knocked out of commission. *Skeena,* ordered to take over as senior ship, led in for a final run past the German ship, and when he was hopelessly ablaze and sinking, began a search for the two U-boats which had made off toward Brest. There was little hope of intercepting them, however, and there were casualties urgently requiring treatment. At dawn the force altered around toward Plymouth.

CHANNEL AND BISCAY
AREA - 1944

1	29th MTB Action	July	4
2	"	July	9
3	"	July	15
4	"	July	16
5	"	July	25
6	65th MTB Action	July	3
7	Huron-ESKIMO Action	June	27
8	Huron-Tartar Action	June	9
9	Haida-Tartar-Błyskawica Action	July	12
10	Qu'appelle, Saskatchewan, Skeena, Restigouche Operation Dredger	July	6
11	Matane hit by glider bomb	July	20
12	Bellona, Tartar, Haida, Ashanti, Iroquois		
12A	Actions	Aug	5/6
13	Qu'appelle, Assiniboine, Skeena, Restigouche Achons	Aug	7
14	Mauritius, Ursa, Iroquois Actions	Aug	14
15	Mauritius, Ursa, Iroquois Action	Aug	22
16	Regina Sunk	Aug	8
17	Alberni sunk	Aug	21

"Wherever Wood Can Swim"

On the same morning, as the scarred ships of Escort Group 12 were coming in sight of the Lizard, two ships of Escort Group 11 were commencing an action in the Channel well to the east of them. *Ottawa* and *Kootenay*, crossing over from the western side of the Neptune lanes, had been ordered to a point about fourteen miles south of Beachy Head, where the British frigate, *Statice*, was in contact with a submarine. They arrived about seven o'clock; and were soon engaged with *Statice* on what was to be a long hunt.

The contact was definite; but there was a strong tide running over the usual cluttered bottom. The submarine was drifting slowly across the current, varying its depth from time to time and otherwise taking full advantage of the difficulties of the ships above. Nevertheless, it was being hurt. By noon an encouraging quantity of Teutonic rubbish was strewing the surface. Boats put away by the ships returned with three bags full of books, clothing and pieces of wooden structure. One of the small, cylindrical bubble decoy targets also appeared, evidently jarred loose from its mooring in the boat by the explosions. Over the whole area there was a large film of oil giving off the distinctive diesel aroma beloved by the U-boat hunter.

A more intense series of attacks was begun in the afternoon. The submarine was now resting on the bottom at a depth of about a hundred and fifty feet; and the comparative shallowness of the water made it possible to adopt a new technique. Attaching a single depth charge to a long wire fitted with a grapnel, *Ottawa* towed it over the German's position. The grapnel hooked the U-boat, drawing close against its hull, and the charge was exploded electrically from above. Other ships repeated the tactics several times; and the cruel battering, followed by hedgehog attacks, brought up more evidence. Air bubbles appeared, then wood. After that came "one tin of German butter, two censor stamps, a tin of white powder and a very worn coat of blue serge with three German buttons attached."

Still the U-boat itself had not been brought to the surface. The search was squarely athwart a main traffic area, and passing convoys were churning the sea and breaking up asdic contact. Darkness was approaching, a heavy rain was falling and *Statice* and *Ottawa* were both low on depth charges. The situation was also somewhat complicated by the fact that in the early evening *Statice* had made contact with what appeared to be another submarine lying on the bottom three thousand yards away from the first. It was unlikely that two U-boats would be found so close together, yet when both contacts were run over with the echo sounder the silhouette of a submarine was obtained in each case.

Ottawa made a dash to Portsmouth for fuel and ammunition during the night, while the British frigate *Redpole* arrived to reinforce the hunters. Attacks directed against both echoes continued. When *Ottawa* returned in the early morning a violent battering of the first contact ended the search. It produced enough additional evidence to convince the Admiralty of a kill, but the second contact was consigned to the limbo of official records as another of the multitudinous "presumed wrecks."

The frigates of the 6th and 9th Canadian escort groups operated throughout July and August in the area of the western Channel mouth, fanning their patrols out northward along the Cornish coast or southward into the Brest approaches. Escort Group 9 was off Brest on the afternoon of July 20 when a heavy explosion was heard astern of the frigate, *Meon*. The first supposition was that the explosion came from an acoustic torpedo, but this was hastily changed when Dorniers were glimpsed overhead through a break in the heavy cloud cover. *Meon* had been missed by a glider bomb; and further attacks were impending.

As the ships took up formation against the planes a Dornier appeared overhead on the starboard quarter of *Matane*, which had been the frigate nearest to *Meon*. One of the winged bombs shot out ahead of the aircraft in a spurt of white smoke, hovered for a moment, then dived straight downward at *Matane*. Coming in at a very steep angle for the frigate's afterpart, it pierced through light upper structure and shot on into the water to explode beside the ship. If its line of flight had been six inches to the right it would have gone down the open ammunition hoist into the magazine; and *Matane* would simply have disappeared from the face of the sea. As it was, the explosion underwater close alongside had done serious damage.

Matane's engine room was flooded, the port engine was knocked out of place and there was a large hole aft on the port side. The engine room bulkheads held, however, and the flood was confined to only one compartment. *Meon* came in through clouds of escaping steam to take *Matane* in tow, while the other ships fought off the planes above. As the attack ended *Meon* got under way with *Stormont* assisting. Through a stormy night and most of the next day the two frigates struggled toward Plymouth with their sister ship, arriving about nine in the evening. Two of *Matane's* men were missing, one man had been killed outright and another died during the journey to Plymouth.

The remaining members of the group had to wait six weeks for their revenge. Long days of monotonous patrol intervened, marked as usual by innumerable contacts which had all eventually to be classed as "non-sub." During the afternoon of September 1, however, *St. John,* patrolling with *Swansea* off Lands End, picked up what seemed to be a promising echo. She lost it for a time; but it was regained in the early evening by *Swansea* and the hunt was on.

As usual, the contact was lost and regained several times; but an echo sounder trace had given too clear an indication of a U-boat for the search to be abandoned. Attacks made throughout the night and on the following morning yielded no result; but at two in the afternoon *St. John* ran in on a particularly good echo and dropped a five-charge pattern. The results were immediate and satisfying. There was a huge gush of oil, followed by a mass of letters and photographs, a certificate commemorating the ten-millionth engine revolution of U-247, log books, shirts, socks, clothing and German charts. It was enough to convince the attacking ships, and later the Admiralty's assessment committee, that U-247's engines would revolve no more.

Both Escort Group 9 and Escort Group 6 had now about completed their Neptune mission. Shortly after the disposal of U-247, the frigates of both groups sailed for the open Atlantic to join an offensive against the last wide-spread effort of the U-boats. A gradual movement of dispersal had already carried other Canadian ships far afield. *Prince Henry* and *Prince David* were in the Mediterranean. The men of the landing craft flotillas had returned their craft to Royal Navy shipyards and had gone back to general service. *Algonquin* and *Sioux* were again with the Home Fleet, operating in Norwegian waters. Most of the corvettes remained in the Channel, however, and the minesweepers had still an arduous year ahead of them. There had been changes among the Tribals and the other destroyers; but their number was as yet unreduced and their last large operation was only now entering its final stages.

The plans for Operation Kinetic had begun to take shape as the outlines of the German policy along the French coast became clear. It grew apparent that the enemy intended to hold Brest and the west coast ports along the Bay of Biscay as long as he could. At the mouth of the Gironde, at La Rochelle, La Pallice, St. Nazaire, Lorient and Brest large German garrisons remained in possession, isolated by land and slenderly fed by sea. They could no longer operate effectively as bases for U-boats, and the underwater flotillas were being withdrawn to Norway. Nevertheless, while the ports held out, the Allies were denied the use of them, and they could impose some limitation on the flow of Allied supplies and Allied freedom of movement. About them the country seethed with the activity of Free French troops. Bodies of intelligently led, well-disciplined Maquis were closing in on each of them, but the French had no arms with which to attack powerful modern defences, and the reduction of any one of the ports would require a sizeable allied assault.

"Wherever Wood Can Swim"

The armies and sea transport needed for such an assault or series of assaults could not immediately be spared; and the bases had to be left for a time in German hands. Measures could be taken, however, to reduce them by a leisurely siege. Since they were fed by sea they could be starved by sea. For a long time allied Biscay operations had seriously inconvenienced them. Operation Kinetic, the last and culminating phase of the Biscay sweeps, was designed to break up their coastal supply links once and for all.

Many small German coasters, withdrawn from the Spanish iron ore trade, had been assembled in Breton ports late in June. Heavily escorted by minesweepers, trawlers and the occasional destroyer, they moved up and down the Biscay coast throughout July, evacuating a few special troops and keeping the garrisons in tolerable health and spirits. Allied naval authorities, well aware of the movement, let it grow to full proportions and settle into the routine so well beloved of the Teuton before they struck.

The time ripened during the last week of July; and on the night of the 31st the first mission under Operation Kinetic went southward from Plymouth. The cruisers *Diadem* and *Bellona* were the heavy ships; and the escort carrier *Striker* sailed to provide fighter support. Screening them were *St. Laurent*, *Chaudière* and *Kootenay;* and the striking force consisted of all the destroyers of the 10th Flotilla, including *Haida* and *Huron.*

"Uneventful" was the weary word which had to be applied to the patrol when the large force returned to Plymouth on the morning of August 3. It had swept down along the coast from Brest to La Rochelle on the night of the 1st, withdrawn to seaward during the following day, and swept in again the next night, but nothing had been encountered. A similar patrol on the 4th found the coastal routes equally bare, and this was to be the last Kinetic and the last Neptune mission for *Huron.* Orders arrived sending her to Canada for refit; and she was replaced with the Plymouth forces by the returning *Iroquois.*

Other redispositions of the force also took place. Fighter protection appeared unnecessary; and *Striker* was therefore dispensed with. *St. Laurent, Chaudière* and *Kootenay*, in place of their screening duties, were sent to establish an independent patrol off Lorient. The force which sailed on August 5 for the next Operation Kinetic mission was a smaller one; consisting of the cruiser *Bellona* and the destroyers *Tartar, Haida, Ashanti* and *Iroquois*.

The third attempt ended Kinetic's short series of unlucky nights. As the force passed down by St. Nazaire and drew abreast of little Ile d'Yeu, very long range radar contacts began to come in. The echoes grew clearer and were identified as those of enemy ships. A convoy was passing Ile d'Yeu, working slowly to seaward of the island.

For two seemingly endless hours the British force stalked the slow merchantmen and their escorts, remaining carefully at a distance until the Germans had worked well out from shore. Then at ten minutes after midnight the four destroyers increased speed to twenty-five knots and, with *Tartar* leading, cut in between the convoy and the land. *Bellona* ran astern of them and to seaward, taking up her position as lamp-lighter and controller.

Battle dispositions were complete at 12.33 and *Bellona's* first starshell burst over the convoy. There were seven German ships; and in less than twelve minutes six of them, including one carrying over eight hundred troops, were afire and sinking. One made its escape. *Iroquois* accounted for two of the vessels; *Tartar* and *Ashanti* between them for three. *Haida* had her first target, an M-class minesweeper, afire and sinking within four minutes of opening fire; and some of her salvoes had landed on one of the other vessels before she suffered the worst mishap of her brilliant career. A shell exploded as it was entering the breach of one of her after guns, wrecking the turret, damaging the after end of the ship, killing two of the gunners, and wounding eight more.

The damage to *Haida* was serious but not crippling, and the night was still young. The force reformed and pro-

ceeded northward along the coast for another two hours. As
the ships passed St. Nazaire, radar indicated another convoy
to the north, approaching inshore of Belle Isle. It was for the
moment almost invulnerable so far as the destroyers were
concerned. Minefields were laid on both sides of the narrow,
rocky channel through which it was moving. Radar-controlled shore batteries had the area everywhere in range.
There was no sea room for the destroyers to manœuvre in
these historic shallows off Quiberon Bay.

There was a considerable chance, however, that the
force had not yet been detected; and the convoy would soon
be moving into more open water. The destroyers retired to
seaward, waited for fifteen minutes and then came in again.
They found the merchant vessels just clear of the shallows
but already alarmed and turning back. Opening with starshell and high explosive, and closing to a range of six
thousand yards, the destroyers saw their hits registering in
jagged red splashes against the sides of the German ships.
Then salvoes from the shore batteries began to come down;
and smoke wreathed up about the scene. The Tribals withdrew, stood a little to seaward silhouetted by the moon, came
in again, and again withdrew. Twice more the same manœuvre was repeated. For forty minutes, alternately drawing
away from the shore batteries and boring in on the ships,
the destroyers harried the convoy as it crawled back toward
the coast. Two of the hardest hit merchantmen had fallen
behind the others; and in spite of approaching dawn and the
risk of air attack, *Bellona* was determined to remain in the
area and finish them off. Plymouth Command had other
ideas, however, and before dawn the order came for the
force to return to base.

On the night of the 7th it became the turn of *Qu'Appelle, Assiniboine, Skeena* and *Restigouche.* Together with
the British destroyer, *Albrighton,* the group was moving a
little south of Brest when an enemy convoy was contacted
at the edge of Audierne Bay. The German vessels were proceeding south and had not yet drawn very far out from land.
Once again the destroyers crawled along in the darkness to

seaward of them, waiting for the moment when the loop could be thrown..

Audierne Bay had figured before in British naval history; and was to figure again. It was the only body of reasonably open water along the route between Brest and Lorient, and enemy ships were well aware of its dangers. The stalk was therefore a long and careful one. First radar contact had been made at shortly before eleven; but the destroyers did not begin to close in from sea until nearly two o'clock.

When they did so they came at high speed. At 2.24 they made out three trawlers vaguely silhouetted by the moon at a range of three miles. Firing rockets to improve the illumination, they closed to 4,600 yards and opened with high explosive. The German ships, confused by their own smoke screen, began firing among themselves. By the time the destroyers had gone past them twice, one of the enemy vessels was listing and on fire and the other two were heading for the shore to beach themselves. A final run sent the third ship reeling in toward the beach, also hopelessly ablaze, and a cottage at the water's edge, hit by a stray shell, added its flames to the scene of destruction.

On the night of the 14th the Kinetic mission was carried out by the British cruiser *Mauritius,* the British destroyer *Ursa,* and *Iroquois.* As the force passed southward off Les Sables d'Olonne, a few miles from La Rochelle, *Iroquois's* radar picked up a contact which, when illuminated, proved to be an armed merchant vessel. Squirming out of the light of starshell the German ship made smoke and ran, but just as *Iroquois* was opening fire on her, an Elbing suddenly appeared amid the smoke screen. *Iroquois* swung her guns onto this more important enemy and followed it in toward the coast. She saw one hit register on the German and wove her way successfully between the tracks of four torpedoes which he fired at her. She fired four of her own but saw no result, and as she closed the coast, shells from the batteries at Les Sables d'Olonne began to come down about her. The Elbing was now well in to shore and there was no point in risking the heavy fire. *Iroquois* withdrew; the force continued southward as far as the mouth of the Gironde, and turned back in the darkness of early morning. The southward sweep had produced, in addition to the slightly damaged Elbing, only one coastal tanker which had been set ablaze and driven ashore. The northward leg was to be more productive.

At 5.40 *Iroquois'* radar, which was a tower of strength through all the actions in which she took part, picked up definite indications of ships to the north at a range of 11,000 yards. Thirty-five minutes later, inshore of the destroyers in water too shallow for the cruiser, three enemy minesweepers were sighted. Fire was opened at a range of 3,200 yards; and in twenty minutes of pursuit two of the ships were driven ashore while the third blew up.

Eight days later, on August 22, Kinetic rose to its climax in Audierne Bay. *Mauritius, Iroquois* and *Ursa,* sweeping down from Plymouth detected a first convoy about midnight. Standing off the mouth of the bay, they gave it time to draw well out from shore, then swept in on the landward side, trapping it. Starshell flared and the rapid salvoes of the destroyers burst among the ships. Three of the vessels drove in for the shoals, ablaze from end to end, and before their keels grated over the rocks, a fourth had blown up.

Two hours later, while the earlier ships were still burning along the coast, another convoy crept into the bay. Followed at long range by *Iroquois'* radar, it was stalked, suddenly illuminated and overwhelmed with fire. Two of the vessels sank; two more, running in to beach themselves, collided and burst into flames. One of them turned over and disappeared. The other rode up high onto the rocks and remained there, lifting jagged tongues of flame into the sky. As the cruiser and the two destroyers reformed and turned toward Plymouth in the early dawn, they left behind them three ships sunk, and five blazing along the beach. The captain of *Iroquois* had been, in September 1941, senior officer of the escort for Convoy SC-42, sixteen of whose ships were sunk in Greenland waters. The whirligig of time had brought in his revenges.

From this night on, the later missions of Operation Kinetic found little shipping to destroy. What vessels remained to the Germans clung to their harbours. The doomed garrisons along the coast could no longer be supplied. Serious attempts to evacuate troops came to an end. Only a few fishing boats, crowded with ragged and hungry soldiers, crawled along at night in the shadow of the coast. By day the Allied destroyers patrolled along the horizon; by night they ran in to the very fringes of the minefields at the harbour mouths. Their work was soon to become a matter of showing the flag for the encouragement of Free French forces ashore, and of landing supplies to assist the Maquis as they closed in about the German bases.

On the afternoon of August 26, four days after the last slaughter at Audierne, *Iroquois* was passing Ile d'Yeu, again in company with *Mauritius* and *Ursa*. There had not been time to restore her paintwork since the night of the action. Her hull was still marked by the scars of shrapnel, her guardrails bent and twisted from the blast of her guns. Lookouts reported a small boat putting off from the direction of the island, apparently making an effort to attract the destroyer's attention. *Iroquois* reduced speed and brought her guns to bear, while binoculars were trained on the approaching craft.

A girl of about twenty-five, clad in slacks, sweater and a beret was standing erect in the boat, waving a handkerchief frantically. Three or four other passengers seated in the thwarts were gesticulating and calling with equal fervour. *Iroquois* came to a stop while *Mauritius* and *Ursa* moved in to screen her. The boat was allowed to come alongside, ropes were tossed over; and the girl, followed by her companions, clambered on board.

She was Mademoiselle Anne-Marie Gaston, a school teacher on Ile d'Yeu, black-eyed, dark-skinned, eager and purposeful. She spoke English, and a great deal of it. The men with her were a deputation of the leading citizens. The German garrison of the island had left the night before. The French Forces of the Interior were now in control. They had information for the Allied ships and they were very short of provisions. Could a party be sent ashore to consult with the French officers and could some provisions be spared?

Signals passed between *Iroquois* and *Mauritius*. Landings by parties from other ships had already been made at points along the coast and valuable information gained. This appeared to be another opportunity to learn something of German dispositions and morale. It was decided to put a party from *Iroquois* ashore. The destroyer would continue the patrol with *Mauritius* and *Ursa* and return for the men next day.

From a volunteer list as long as the ship's roster two officers and three signal ratings were selected. Lieutenant J. S. Saks went in command. Engineer-Lieutenant Richard Scrivener, a French-speaking Montrealer, went as interpreter, and the three signal ratings were Petty Officer Telegraphist R. Mulligan, Telegraphist J. Chevalier, who also spoke French, and Signalman G. A. Sheppard. Signalling gear was loaded into the boat so that communication could be established between the shore party and the ship. Flour, canned meat, canned milk, sugar, chocolate bars and cigarettes followed. The boat, low in the water with its passengers, gear and provisions, put in for shore as *Iroquois* swung seaward and moved away with the other ships.

Mademoiselle Gaston warned the Canadians to be prepared for a welcome. Even so, as they set foot on shore they nearly went down under the deluge of greetings from a cheering, weeping, kissing multitude. They had known Ile d'Yeu only as a series of lines on a chart, an area speckled with minefields, a dangerous site of powerful shore batteries. The modest spire of the lovely old twelfth-century church had been merely an obscure landmark on which the navigating officer occasionally took a bearing. It had probably never occurred to the sailors to think of the people whose

births, marryings and deaths had revolved about it for generations; of the tranquil Breton housewives and the black-
eyed, dark-skinned, smiling men in the wooden sabots, the
berets, the infinitely-patched oilskins and sweaters, whose
occupation it was to gather the sardine, the tuna, the lobster
and the long-legged crab. Most of them had never read or
heard of the small round harbour, crowded like an autumn
forest with the masts and vari-coloured sails of innumerable fishing vessels which for a long time now had been
forbidden the dangerous waters outside their anchorage.
The gabled houses, crowded close together along the steep,
cobbled lanes running up from the waterfront, seemed
strange and other-worldly to these young North Americans,
yet, even without the welcoming crowds, friendly. Ludwig
Bemelmans had been an earlier visitor to this Isle of God;
and he had written of it that it was, "immediately beautiful
and at once familiar."

The men from *Iroquois* were carried shoulder-high to
the town hall. Inside the council room there were more
greetings from the town officials and officers of the French
Forces of the Interior; equally warm but quickly disposed of
in favour of urgent business. Distribution of the provisions
was arranged for. German maps and documents were handed
over. French officers sketched the location, siting and
strength of the German shore batteries in the vicinity. And
now what more could they do?

The shore party asked for a place to set up its signalling apparatus, and was taken first to the church. Mulligan
climbed up inside the tower, and was nearly brained when
some enthusiast below decided to ring the bell. The church
tower was unsuitable. The officials then produced an ancient
car which had not run since the war began. They brought
out a small store of gasoline, filched pint by pint from the
Germans. A demon-driven chauffeur took over; and, tooting
an incessant V for Victory on his horn, rocketed them up the
steep streets of the town to a signal tower standing about
three miles away.

"Wherever Wood Can Swim"

Here in the top loft of the tower the signalmen set up their gear, while the two officers, in the dusty, echoing ground-level compartment, spread out the maps and papers they had been given. The townspeople, who had followed, withdrew to let the Canadians work undisturbed; but toward evening Mademoiselle Gaston reappeared. A small repast had been prepared in the town. Would the Canadians come now and eat? Regretfully the Canadians had to decline. There was much to do and they had not yet reported to their ship. Mademoiselle Gaston departed with their regrets; and the sailors, munching their lean rations of bread and jam, went on working by the flashlights which were the only light they had. About midnight the voice of one of the signalmen boomed down through the dark tower reporting that he had contacted *Iroquois*.

At one o'clock in the morning the drowsing men heard voices outside. They turned their flashlights on a low window, which had been used as an entrance in place of the blocked door, just in time to see Mademoiselle Gaston step over the casement. Behind her, solemnly, one by one and all in their Sunday best, came fifteen ladies and gentlemen of the village. What the men wore is not recalled. But the black silk of the ladies' dresses rustled softly as they stepped over the low window ledge, and standing high and graceful on each head was the exquisite starched lace "coif" of the Breton woman.

Each of the party carried a basket. They had walked the three miles from town with the provisions for the banquet. There were cake and wine and fruits; there were lobsters and sardines. There were the famous crabs of the island, their legs dangling over the sides of the baskets. There were bottles of champagne which had been "requisitioned" from the hotel of a collaborator.

The long table was cleared of papers. The food was spread out. Men gathered wood to make a fire. At first the Canadians were a little bug-eyed and the townsfolk rather solemn. But the stiffness melted away. There was much laughter; and there were valiant attempts at speech-making. There were toasts to Canada, toasts to France, toasts to Ile d'Yeu, toasts to *Iroquois*. And afterward the people spoke with sardonic enjoyment of the departure of their late conquerors.

The Germans had been, in the pleasantly contemptuous French phrase, "pas trop désagréable." But they had become sullen and gloomy as their days began to run out. One had seen them at night listening unhappily to the sound of gunfire rolling in from the sea. Yesterday they had carried out half-hearted demolitions, looted the little post-office of its five thousand francs, stolen a few fishing boats, and set off for the nearest German garrison on the mainland. So, shabbily, the Nazi dream of glory had faded from Ile d'Yeu.

Dinner ended, the townspeople left, and the Canadians worked on in watches through the night. *Iroquois* signalled that a boat would land for them on the seaward side of the island. Early in the morning they prepared to go.

The ancient automobile arrived for them, but with it arrived the head of the local French war veterans' association. There were Allied airmen buried on the island. It was the first Sunday of the liberation and a ceremony was to be held at the graves. Would the Canadians march with the war veterans and the townspeople?

It was a request which could not be refused. The five Canadian sailors fell in with the Fench veterans and over a thousand of the townspeople. At their head was an unusually fine bugle band. They marched first to the graves of the Allied fliers whose bodies had been recovered from the sea. The graves stood in a row, carefully tended, each with a neat headstone. The men came to attention. The bugles rang out in a long, solemn call. There was a minute's silence. Then the march proceeded to the graves of the French war dead and the ceremony was repeated.

The procession moved away from the cemetery and came into the town again. Just before ranks were broken the Commandant insisted that the senior officer of the Canadian party address the crowd. Saks tried to get off with the announcement he had been authorized to make: henceforth the islanders would be permitted to fish during the daylight hours within five miles of shore. The news was greeted with cheers, but still a speech was demanded. Saks made a brave attempt to rise to the occasion with what he could remember of his high school French. "Lord, sir," whispered Chevalier during a pause between the periods, "if you only knew what you're saying!"

Again out of the crowd Mademoiselle Gaston appeared. Her boat was loaded with the Canadians' equipment and was waiting to take them around the island to where the ship's whaler would land. The Canadians followed her to the boat, and were startled to find among their heaped-up gear a huge white cake decorated with the valiantly bilingual inscription: Vive la France, Canada, Britain and America." Baked with some of the flour brought from *Iroquois,* it had been intended to grace the banquet of the previous evening; but since it could not be carried the three miles from town the Canadians must now take it with them.

They put off and came around the island to where the ship's boat was waiting. It was almost invisible under masses of flowers. A crowd of islanders stood about it, cheering the sailors who were making determined efforts to dance with the girls of Ile d'Yeu on the sandy beach. Gear was transferred, farewells were made, and a joyful wave of cheering followed the boat to sea. It was a memory for a man to cherish "in the white winter of his age"; a glimpse of liberation; a foretaste of victory. Weeks later came a tempering foretaste of peace when other ships visiting the island brought word that Mademoiselle Gaston and the group of which she was the quickening spark had come into collision with other groups and had been banished from the island.

On September 20 the assault area in Baie de la Seine reverted to the control of Commander-in-Chief, Plymouth, putting a formal end to Operation Neptune. Among the many ships and powerful squadrons of Britain and the United States, the hundred-odd Canadian ships had settled into the routine which follows victory, or turned toward other seas, or toward their home ports. *Huron* was already in Halifax. *Haida* followed her on September 22. Each ship on its arrival received a welcome such as the old port had never known. *Iroquois* was to be on duty in the Bay and Channel for another month, after which she would go to Scapa for operations against the remnants of German sea power in the north.

The long thrust from the eastern seaboard of North America to the shores of France had been completed. Mightily reinforced by the efforts of his own people, the words of Churchill, spoken to Europe under the shadow of Dunkirk had been fulfilled. Over the long sea road, and "in God's good time, the New World, with all its power and might, had stepped forth to the rescue and liberation of the Old."

CHAPTER SIXTEEN

Far Waters and Near

The dispersion of Neptune ships, begun in July, continued at an accelerating tempo for the next two months. There were still many missions to be carried out on many seas. The U-boats, driven from their Biscay bases, were operating from Germany and Norway; and were reaching out again toward the middle and western Atlantic. The Canadian ships which, during the late spring and summer, had provided all the close escort for the huge trade convoys sailing from North America, began to be reinforced by other ships, British, Canadian and American. Support groups returned in greater number to patrol along the trade routes and in the focal areas. Powerful escort forces had to be assigned to the Russia convoys when they were resumed in August after having been discontinued since March. Many other ships were still required to maintain a firm grip on the Channel, the North Sea and the coastal lanes about the United Kingdom.

All these were defensive measures, expanding and buttressing allied control of the supply routes. Concurrent with them were offensive operations planned to make a direct contribution to the German *débâcle* around the world. They were secondary to Neptune, dependant in large measure on its outcome, and they had got under way as soon as the success of the landings in Normandy seemed assured. By the middle of September the result of the most important of these operations was becoming apparent.

On the southern flank of the German armies, now reeling back across northern France toward the defences of the Siegfried Line, a trickle of doubtful reinforcements began to arrive from below the Loire. Ragged columns of demoralized, bomb-crazed men came streaming northward along the River Saône to join their comrades retreating before the Allied

Southern Forces loading R... April 14, 1966

LOTRE RIVER

RHONE RIVER

MARSEILLES • CANNES •
TOULON • CAP •
ILES D'HYERES
PORT CROS L•

AJA

MINORCA

MAJORCA

GIBRALTAR •
STRAIT OF GIBRALTAR

MEDITERRANEAN SEA

• ORAN   • ALGIERS

The Mediterranean

ADRIATIC SEA
AGOON
NAPLES
BAY OF SALERNO
TARANTO
CORFU
PREVEZA
SALONIKA
AEGEAN SEA
IONIAN SEA
STRAIT OF MESSINA
SICILY
LLARIA
PIRAEUS
ATHENS
GULF OF AEGINA
AEGINA
POROS
KITHERA
MALTA
CRETE
MEDITERRANEAN SEA
TRIPOLI
LIBYA

LCA's from *Davis*—*Hamumering ashore at Biarare, Greece* (turn to the Moon)

drive from Normandy. They were the luckier remnants of the German Nineteenth Army, involved in a disastrous withdrawal from the Mediterranean where another seaborne ram was beating in the walls of Fortress Europe.

Prince Henry and *Prince David* had had a share in the work. On July 24 they had left the United Kingdom for Gibraltar. From there they had been routed onward to Naples in company with ships of the United States, Britain, France, Greece and Poland. In Naples harbour, and in the Bay of Salerno sixty-five miles to the south, a large task force was assembling under American command to carry out Operation Dragoon.

Dragoon was the long contemplated and much debated subsidiary operation designed to bring another army into position on the southern flank of the forces from Normandy and broaden the front for the advance to the Rhine. It was a second and smaller Neptune, directed against the coast of southern France, and many of its difficulties had been reduced by the success of the first operation. The best of the German divisions which might have opposed it had been withdrawn to the north. French Forces of the Interior were now operating as regular military formations south of the Loire and had established control over most of the inland territory. Nevertheless, the ports and coastal areas were still heavily garrisoned by German troops and the allies had prepared to strike them with a powerful blow.

The point of landing was to be a fifteen-mile stretch of shore between Toulon and Cannes. Stong airborne forces were to be dropped behind the coastal defences. Following the paratroopers, the American Seventh Army, carried by a force of some eight hundred ships, including nine aircraft carriers with bombarding cruisers and destroyers, was to thrust in from sea, overrun the ports of Toulon and Marseilles and drive up the valley of the Rhône into the heart of France. There, in the region east of the Loire, the Seventh Army was to make junction with the other Allied armies sweeping from Normandy toward the German border.

Arriving in Naples on July 31, the Canadian ships and their assault craft joined with the assembling forces of Dragoon in a series of landing exercises. On August 6 *Prince Henry* was designated headquarters ship for "Sitka Unit B" one of the subdivisions of the force; and an American naval staff came on board to direct operations. At the same time a British naval staff established itself in *Prince David*, which was to be headquarters ship for another small unit romantically titled "Romeo." Five days later troops were embarked and the ships sailed for Propriano on the west coast of Corsica.

Prince Henry sailed as Flagship to Rear-Admiral T. E. Chandler of the United States Navy, who commanded one of the main divisions of the force under the overall command of Vice-Admiral H. K. Hewitt, U.S.N. In addition to her headquarters staff, the Canadian ship carried 36 officers and 243 men of The First Special Service Force, the famous international assault unit made up of men from both the Canadian and American armies. *Prince David's* troops, totalling 283, were all French commandos. The troops were bivouacked ashore on Corsica for two days while final dispositions of the naval force were made. Re-embarkation began at dawn on the 14th; and about mid-morning Sitka B and Romeo units, constituting the advance guard of Dragoon, began to move off toward the Riviera.

The Sitka B force consisted of *Prince Henry* with four American troop-carrying destroyers, escorted by four American torpedo boats. Romeo unit was made up of *Prince David*, two other landing ships and five torpedo boats. Each of the two small forces comprised advance parties which were to neutralize coastal defences ahead of the main landings. The objectives of Sitka B were batteries and gun positions on the islands of Port Cros and Levant, lying just off the coast and about twenty-two miles east of Toulon. Romeo was to knock out the defences on a nearby coastal headland known as Cap Nègre. The commando landings were to be made at one-thirty on the morning of the 15th, six and a half hours ahead of the general attack.

Shortly after eight o'clock in the evening *Prince David's* unit came into position twelve miles off Cap Nègre. *Prince Henry's* force continued on to take up station three and a half miles south of Levant at about eleven. Times of arrival had been staggered because of the varying distances which the landing parties would have to travel to reach their objectives. Lowering took place without delay and by midnight the assault craft of both forces were on their way toward shore.

The beaches ahead were rough and rocky; but the Mediterranean tide rose and fell scarcely a foot and the sea was calm. Although flares and explosions rose inland from the bombs of attacking planes, there was silence along the coastal fringe. The night was very dark and there was a quality of stealth about these landings which had been absent from the Normandy expedition. Instead of driving in for the beaches with throttles wide open, the landing craft chugged along at slow speed and in comparative silence, acting as miniature tugs. Each one towed behind it six or seven doughnut-shaped boats of inflated rubber, loaded down with hard-bitten commandos. The assault craft themselves were not to beach. As they came within a quarter of a mile of shore they stopped and cast off their towing lines. The versatile commandos in the rubber boats then took up paddles and steered their flabby-looking vessels silently toward the outlying rocks.

An advance party of ninety-five French troops from *Prince David* landed first, while the remainder of the force hovered off shore. No fire greeted the men as they stepped from their boats, and they disappeared silently into the darkness. Half an hour later they sent back word that the enemy gun positions had been silenced. The main body of Romeo unit then came in to beach. About seven hundred strong, the men moved quickly inland, and within an hour or so were established across the main road between Toulon and the Riviera.

All this was accomplished in pre-dawn darkness. Not until daylight, when *Prince David* sent in two heavier vehicle-carrying craft with anti-tank guns and stores, did any fire come down on the beaches; and by that time the main landings had begun and the Romeo assault craft were back on board their mother ships.

Prince Henry's craft, also towing their commandos in rubber boats, made an equally successful landing on Port Cros and Levant. They did not, however, return immediately to their ship. Sharp fighting developed soon after daybreak; and for part of the day the L.C.A.'s were employed in ferrying out casualties and prisoners. This work was completed about three in the afternoon; and by four o'clock *Prince Henry* and *Prince David*, with the other ships of their forces, were on the way back to Corsica.

The main landings had been for the most part lightly opposed; and were completely successful. Marseilles fell on August 23; Toulon, on the 27th. The Germans were already engaged in a nightmare retreat up the valley of the Rhône, decimated by air assault and harried on their flanks by American flying columns and French Forces of the Interior. On September 11 Allied patrols from the south made contact with the armies advancing from Normandy. On the 16th the principal remnant of the German Nineteenth Army was cornered below the Loire and surrendered. On the 21st, one day after the formal termination of Neptune, the American Seventh Army moved into position on the southern flank of the Allied forces and wheeled eastward at Epinal, some forty miles from the German border.

Meanwhile *Prince Henry* and *Prince David* had made two follow-up trips from Corsica to the assault area, completing their Dragoon assignment. The entire operation had been concluded in a little over two weeks, and Allied forces in the Mediterranean were now looking toward Greece. German garrisons here were already withdrawing, concerned merely with the problem of extricating themselves before they were cut off by Russian armies driving across Bulgaria and Jugoslavia in the north. Assault landings were unnecessary, and it was the intention of the Allied command to spare the ravaged country any further fighting. As the Germans moved out, the liberating forces would move in, bringing with them food and supplies and doing what they could to restore order.

Prince Henry's duties in September consisted mainly of ferrying troops and landing craft northward from Messina to ports along the Adriatic coast, where they would be available for landings in Greece and Jugoslavia. *Prince David* came in for one or two rather more exciting missions.

Toward the middle of the month it was reported that the island of Kithera, off the southern toe of the Peleponnessus, had been evacuated by the Germans. The information was considered reliable; but it was possible that holding units had been left behind. It was decided to make a landing on Kithera, sending along a sufficient force to deal with any opposition which might be encountered.

On September 14 *Prince David*, escorted by an aircraft carrier and three destroyers, sailed for the island. Arriving at night she entered the bay of San Nikolo alone, not altogether sure of her reception. She was carrying 35 officers and 495 men of the 9th British Commando, and the first wave carried by the assault craft went in prepared for trouble. They were greeted instead by crowds of rapturous Greeks, who not only warmed the hearts of the liberators with their welcome, but also fell to and assisted in the unloading of the craft. *Prince David* sailed back to Taranto the next morning, leaving the commandos established ashore.

During the next three weeks the men from Kithera, equipped with Royal Navy reconnaissance craft, prowled among the many islands lying along the approaches to Athens, giving an occasional nudge to German garrisons which were slow in departing. By October 8 they had established themselves on Poros in the Gulf of Aegina, and were contemplating an assault on the garrison which still held the nearby island of Aegina.

For this purpose the commandos would require landing craft, and *Prince David* accordingly sailed from Taranto to deliver her flotilla to them. She arrived on the 9th, sent her craft and men ashore, and sailed back to Taranto on the 10th. On the next two nights the commandos reconnoitred Aegina and other islands of the Gulf. Some of the men from *Prince David's* flotilla accompanied them; but most of the Canadians remained ashore, preparing for the assault on Aegina. It was planned for the night of the 13th, but an hour before it got under way word came that the Germans had evacuated the island during the afternoon. They had also abandoned their other positions covering the approaches to Athens, and were moving out of the city, hurried along by Allied parachute troops. The way to the capital was therefore clear.

At Taranto a large force had been assembled for the re-occupation of Greece. Two British brigades were to be landed to harry the northward retreat of the Germans. Immense quantities of food and medical stores were to be carried for the immediate relief of districts where the worst famine conditions prevailed. The expedition was embarked in seven landing ships, of which *Prince Henry* and *Prince David* were the largest. Three minesweeping flotillas were to precede it, and it was to be escorted by four British cruisers, four aircraft carriers, and a large number of smaller craft. For Canada this voyage of liberation was to have particular historical interest, since it was in *Prince David* that M. Papandreou, prime minister of Greece, and members of his government-in-exile were embarked. They came on board on October 14, accompanied by a large and distinguished party, which included Mr. Rex Leeper, the British ambassador to Greece, and senior officers of the expeditionary force. Early on the 15th the ships sailed.

The commandos from Poros and the assault craft from *Prince David* were already in Athens. At one o'clock on the morning of the 14th the Canadian flotilla had set off on the 35-mile journey up the Gulf. Following behind them, in two tank landing-craft, came the British troops and two hundred men of the famous Greek Sacred Battalion. Well ahead, already in the approaches to the capital, a flotilla of British minesweepers was at work.

About dawn the first L.C.A. entered the main harbour of Piræus, the port of Athens. The rest of the craft followed as close astern as they could. The precise naval formation had already become ragged, as cursing, grinning coxswains manœuvred to avoid the scores of caïques, rowboats, and craft of every description, which swarmed out from shore. Every floatable object in the harbour came bearing down, loaded to the swamping point with shouting, waving Greeks. Reckless of nautical precept, the welcomers swept in to hide the flotilla in a swirling naval rout. Boats steered in among the landing craft, collided with them and with each other, backed off and came in again, while men, women and children leaped across gunwales to descend upon the "Ingleesh" with wide-spread arms and hands clutching brilliant masses of flowers.

All this was the merest preliminary. From the shores ahead a wave of cheering billowed out across the water. Harried sailors looked up in wonder as their craft nosed inward through the tumultuous armada which surrounded them. The battered dockside, the harbour area, the streets behind it, and the long road winding up toward Athens, all were black with seething masses of people. As the men stepped onto the jetties the nearest thousands of the Athenians surged down about them. Flowers descended; weeping mothers, pretty girls and bearded men fought to embrace them. They had to struggle to avoid being lifted away bodily into the forest of waving arms. "Ingleesh! Ingleesh! Ingleesh!" rolled deafeningly along the waterfront, mingled with the joyous, staccato syllables of the Greek tongue. And behind this welcoming fringe, far back, it seemed, into the harsh, grey-green hills beyond the city, echoed a mighty thunder of jubilation.

The outburst of joy and gratitude was to continue for many days. Occupation had not dulled the spirit of the Greeks; and their memories were long. British troops had been the first to come and the last to leave Greece in 1940. Some had never left; but had remained to fight on with the guerillas among the hills. And there were thousands in

Greece who had been given at least a chance of life by food sent from Canada during the blackest years of the war. Not for many weeks could a man in British or Canadian uniform walk the streets of Athens without the risk of being swept up onto friendly shoulders and borne to his destination with a cheering crowd behind him.

The first comers in the landing craft had to extricate themselves reluctantly but quickly from their welcomers. Troops and stores had to be landed; a British naval headquarters party had to be set up ashore. Within two days the mine-filled harbour and the miles of battered, semi-demolished docks had to be thoroughly reconnoitred. Safe entrances and docking positions had to be found for the warships and relief vessels which were on the way.

The vanguard of the main expedition from Taranto began to arrive on the 17th. *Prince Henry* came into Piræus with troops. *Prince David,* with the flag of Greece flying at her foremast, stopped off Poros to transfer the Prime Minister and his party to the old Greek cruiser, *Georgios Averoff.* On the 18th the Greek government, no longer in exile, made a formal return to the liberated capital.

During the weeks which followed, the two Canadian ships ferried more men and supplies between Taranto and Athens. Later, as the Germans moved out of northern Greece, they went as part of a large relief expedition to Salonika, through waters so heavily mined that the voyage of three hundred miles from the Piræus to Salonika required five hazardous days behind flotillas of minesweepers. After that there were occasional voyages to outlying islands where relief was required or forlorn enemy detachments remained to be mopped up.

Everywhere they saw the dreadful rigours of famine and wretchedness which the occupation had imposed upon the Greeks. Everywhere their arrival was the signal for a tremendous, heart-warming welcome. But they began to become aware, also, of the sickness which still possessed the country. The despised Italians and the hated Germans were gone, or remained only behind the wire of prison encampments. Liberation could be said to be complete. Yet a desolation of misery and bitterness lay over the nation like debris from a withdrawing flood. By December the soldiers and sailors who had come as friends and been welcomed as demigods were baffled aliens caught in the crossfire of a fratricidal war which they could neither abate nor understand.

They could, occasionally, do something to relieve the worst of its hardships. On December 23 *Prince Henry* was ordered to Preveza on the northwest coast. Fierce civil fighting was going on above the port and thousands of the inhabitants were threatened with annihilation. *Prince Henry* was to take over the duties of Senior Naval Officer in the area and evacuate as many of the people as she could.

At eight-thirty on a raw, blustery Christmas morning the ship arrived in Preveza Roads. She was carrying *Prince David's* assault craft in addition to her own, as the sister ship had been damaged by a mine on December 10. Both flotillas were sent in to shore; and shortly after noon some of the craft began to return, loaded to the gunwales with the first of the evacuees.

The passage from shore to the side of *Prince Henry* was difficult enough, as a strong wind and heavy sea buffeted the tiny vessels. They struggled in under the high sides of the landing ship, and a wailing, shrieking pandemonium ensued as Canadian sailors and Greek soldiers helped and hauled the terrified people of the countryside on board. Women with babies in their arms milled about the decks. Parents who had lost track of their children, and children seeking their parents, screamed at their sweating rescuers in a wild babel of tongues. Famished, freezing and terrified, they clung to pitiful bundles of household gear. Many of them had refused to leave without the goats, sheep, chickens and dogs which were now adding their clamour to the uproar.

A second wave of refugees arrived before the first had been settled below decks. It was followed by another and another. Before the cold, stormy day drew to its close *Prince*

Henry's interior groaned with the accumulated misery of 1,400 hundred homeless, destitute and starving Greeks. They were given what could be scraped together in the way of hot food and drink; and that night the ship sailed through the treacherous, heavily mined channels along the coast to land them at Corfu. She returned on the 27th to take off 1,700 more; and concluded her rescue mission with another load of 1,300 on the 29th.

On December 31 she returned to Taranto. Not many more missions lay ahead. For her, as for *Prince David,* a long wartime career was drawing to a close. If her men had time for reflection as they swabbed out troop decks and cleared away the debris of the Preveza mission, they might have wished for the promise of a more definitive and satisfactory conclusion to their work. They had had a share in many triumphs; and in the Mediterranean at least the power of the enemy had been utterly broken. Nevertheless, it could hardly be said that peace had come.

Elsewhere in the western world the last months of this triumphal year brought sharper disappointments. The hope of an early victory had faded in late September when the gallant attempt to vault the lower Rhine and outflank the Ruhr at Arnhem had ended in failure. Confronted with the unbreached Westwall and the barrier of the great river, the Allies had had to pause and gather strength for powerful new offensives. The supply lines from Normandy were no longer adequate; the great port of Antwerp had to be freed. October and November had seen grim battles along its approaches, and the shedding of much Canadian blood among the canals and causeways of the Scheldt. By December the port was open; but at the year's end the Allies, instead of thrusting forward, were summoning all their power to crush a desperate German counter-offensive which had seemed for a few days to threaten their whole position in France.

At sea the Allied navies controlled every approach to Europe with overwhelming power; yet still they were challenged. In all the familiar waters where the struggle had raged for five long years, the U-boats reappeared. Although they no longer had power to influence the course of the struggle, they seemed determined to make it as costly as possible for their enemies. Among Canadian ships the later months of 1944 were to take as heavy a toll as any of the darkest periods of the war.

Nabob, a British escort carrier commanded and manned by the Canadian navy, was the first casualty of this period. Her brief career as a fighting ship began on August 1 when she arrived at Scapa to join the north-going forces of the Home Fleet. Here, too, a sizeable naval offensive was in progress, aimed at the foundations of German strength in Norway. Shipping which supplied the northern garrisons was a principal target. Even more attractive for the sailors was the prospect of drawing out and destroying the powerful remnants of the German surface fleet. Two pocket battle-ships, eight cruisers and a number of destroyers still remained at full or partial effectiveness in the Baltic or in Norwegian ports. Far up the western coast near Tromso lay the great battleship *Tirpitz*, about which the Admiralty would never be easy until she was on the bottom. Among the powerful forces sent north on a long series of strikes were battleships, fleet carriers, escort carriers, cruisers and destroyers. *Algon-quin* and *Sioux* had been part of the destroyer force since they left the Neptune area in July. *Nabob* was now to be added to the carrier strength.

She was the largest ship operated by the Canadian navy at that time, with a displacement of 15,000 tons, a length of 492 feet and accommodation for twenty planes. Her ship's company of over 1,000 men was mainly Canadian; but, since there was as yet no Canadian naval air arm, her flying per-sonnel was British. As the first ship brought into service by Canada for a new department of naval warfare, she had had her share of teething troubles; but her performance on her first mission gave no cause for complaint.

On August 9, together with *Algonquin* and *Sioux*, she formed part of a large force sent northward from Scapa to

disrupt German shipping in Lepsoyren Channel and Har-
hamsfjord. These waters were part of the "leads" or channels
running along the Norwegian coast above Bergen, sheltered
on their seaward side by cliffs and outlying islands. They
formed a section of the "cursed corridor" through which German shipping could proceed, immune from attack by sea. It
was now the intention to mine these waters by aircraft and
force the German merchantmen outside where they could be
attacked by Mosquitoes and Beaufighters based in northern
Scotland.

The large force which sailed on this mission consisted
of the fleet carrier *Indefatigable,* the escort carriers *Trumpeter* and *Nabob,* the cruisers *Kent* and *Devonshire,* and
eight destroyers including *Algonquin* and *Sioux.* Leaving
Scapa on August 9, the expedition arrived at its flying-off
position near the Norwegian coast at ten o'clock on the morning of the 10th. The planes for the first strike went in for
the leads at one o'clock in the afternoon.

A squadron of twelve Avengers, each carrying a single
mine, took off from *Nabob,* while a similar squadron rose
from *Trumpeter.* Then Seafires and Fireflies soared from the
deck of *Indefatigable* and took up protective formation
above the mine-laying planes. The squadrons bore away
through the grey afternoon; and returned an hour or so later
to report that the operation had been successful. The Germans had been completely surprised; all mines had been laid
and the fighters had swept over Gossen airfield to destroy six
Messerschmitt planes on the ground.

A second strike was scheduled for six in the evening;
and, as expected, the enemy was better prepared. Flak was
accurate and heavy and two planes did not return. An
Avenger from *Trumpeter's* squadron and a Firefly from
among the escorting fighters were shot down. All *Nabob's*
planes returned, and by eight o'clock the force was on its
way back toward Scapa.

Nabob's second and last mission came a week later. On
August 16 she sailed from Scapa as part of a large force which

was intended to put *Tirpitz* out of the war for good. The battleship, which had never seen an action, and which had been temporarily crippled on three or four previous occasions, still lay at Alta Fjord far up the coast of Norway. Scarred and glowering, she posed the threat of a "fleet in being" and was a constant source of worry to the Admiralty. The powerful expedition now sent against her consisted of the battleship *Duke of York*, three fleet carriers, three cruisers, two escort carriers, a group of frigates and thirteen destroyers, including *Algonquin* and *Sioux*.

The force reached its flying-off position north of Tromso and well within the arctic circle on the afternoon of August 20. Rough weather made flying operations impossible and the ships cruised to the westward for two days. When they returned on the 22nd the cloud ceiling was still so low that a part of the operation had to be cancelled. Three squadrons of Barracudas with escorting fighters took off from the fleet carriers; but the Avengers remained on board *Nabob* and *Trumpeter*. They had been scheduled to fly above the bombers and drop mines of a special type about the battleship while the main attack was in progress. Since the heavy clouds prevented proper observation, it was decided not to waste the mines, and the Avengers lost their chance to take part in the strike. *Nabob's* only share in the operation was a protective patrol over the fleet flown by four of her Wildcats.

By late afternoon of the 22nd two strikes against *Tirpitz* had been completed with a loss of eleven planes. The battleship had been heavily hit, escorting fighters had shot down nine Messerschmitts, sunk a number of small ships in the Fjord and strafed enemy gun positions. As the last of the returning planes landed on, the force drew out to sea for the night. Attacks were to be resumed on the 23rd.

Nabob and *Trumpeter* had detached to the westward at about four in the afternoon under orders to fuel three of the destroyers. By five o'clock *Nabob* was in a position some 130 miles north by east of Tromso. Planes had been lowered from her flight deck into the hangar below; and seamen were laying out the lengths of buoyant hose which were to be passed to the destroyers. *Trumpeter* was standing by with some of her planes in the air to provide anti-submarine protection.

At sixteen minutes after five, without any advance warning, a torpedo from an undetected U-boat struck *Nabob* on the starboard side. Eight minutes later a second torpedo struck the destroyer *Bickerton,* a thousand yards away; damaging it so heavily that it had to be sunk about nine o'clock.

For a time the situation in *Nabob* seemed equally serious. All electrical power in the ship failed instantly. Auxiliary machinery and electrically operated ventilating fans came to a stop. The temperature in the engine room soared to an unbearable 150°, making it necessary to shut down main engines and boilers. Through a hole fifty feet long by forty feet deep, water flooded into the after part of the ship, dragging her down at an alarming speed. The stern sank eighteen feet, and a list to starboard developed. Preparations were made to abandon, and boats, rafts and carley floats were put over the side. The destroyer *Kempthorne* came alongside and 214 men, 10 of whom were injured, were transferred from the carrier. By about seven o'clock, however, the situation began to improve.

Damage control parties in the engine room had gone instantly to work closing off the flooded compartments and shoring up bulkheads. The internal structure not already smashed by the explosion seemed to be holding. The engines, shaft and propeller had been surveyed and found undamaged. A diesel generator had been crossed to the main switchboard in the engine room to operate the ventilation fans and auxiliary machinery and this made it possible to start the main engines again. Steam was raised, and at about nine-thirty the ship began to move slowly through the water.

She faced a journey of eleven hundred miles to Scapa, with very little in the way of life-saving equipment on board, since it had been impossible to recover her rafts and floats.

Everything depended on the engine-room bulkheads. They were the walls which now stood alone against the seas battering in through her gashed side. They had been hastily strengthened by men floundering in water along narrow, cramped alleyways, working in stifling heat and in imminent danger. The work was not finished; it would go on without intermission for three days and nights; and it was the skill and daring shown in these noisesome caverns deep in her interior which largely contributed to the saving of the ship.

At two-thirty on the morning of the 23rd a new danger threatened. Four thousand yards away on the starboard quarter, a U-boat was detected by radar, surfaced and moving in for an attack. The crippled ship was dragging through the water at barely ten knots, a sitting target with some eight hundred men on board.

The situation was met by an effort which demanded about equal parts of nerve and skill. Two of the Royal Navy Fleet Air Arm pilots carried by *Nabob* took off in Avengers catapulted from the sloping, buckled deck. Lifting safely into the air with the life of the ship and its company riding their wings, they went back to attack the submarine. It dived and made its escape; but in doing so lost its chance to sink the carrier. The planes kept the U-boat under for three and a half hours while the ship altered away to the west and got safely out of the area. The returning pilots ran even greater risk in landing on than they had in taking off. The first came in safely at four minutes after six. The second, dropping down through a patch of cloud, overshot himself slightly and crashed into the barrier at the end of the deck; but stepped out uninjured.

For the next three days *Nabob* laboured on through steadily worsening weather. Another two hundred men were transferred to *Algonquin* when the destroyer came alongside on the evening of the 23rd. The stern, which had settled down until the quarter-deck was only four feet above water, began to lift slightly as guns, ammunition and heavy gear were jettisoned or moved forward. Ten portable pumps continually at work lightened the ship somewhat. She rode through a full gale on the 24th with the great vault of the hangar below her flight deck giving off a huge, unearthly moaning as air was sucked in and pushed outward again through the vents. At twenty-five minutes after six on the morning of August 27, with the unrecovered bodies of fourteen men tossing in her flooded afterpart, she passed the gate into Scapa Flow. She had lost twenty-one killed and six injured, and she was not to see action again.

The strike in the north against *Tirpitz* had gone on. Sioux had remained as one of the destroyers screening the carriers; and *Algonquin* after transferring the two hundred men of *Nabob's* company to another ship, had returned at full speed to the scene of operations. When the force turned back for Scapa on the 24th, *Tirpitz* was once again thoroughly crippled; but it remained for three Lancasters carrying 12,000-pound bombs to send her to the bottom of Tromso fjord on November 12.

Meanwhile *Algonquin* and *Sioux* remained as the only Canadian ships based at Scapa. On September 11 they formed part of the screening force for another air strike against shipping off Norway. They returned from this mission to sail with a convoy to Murmansk. The blackest days of the Russia convoys were long past; the journey to Kola inlet was made without loss, and only two ships were torpedoed on the way home. Nevertheless, with what forces remained to them, the Germans hacked stubbornly at the Russia supply line. The familiar reconnaissance planes were overhead, torpedo bombers had to be fought off, and no voyage was made without its quota of U-boat sightings and attacks.

During October *Algonquin* and *Sioux* went into Norwegian waters as part of the screening force for three more air strikes. All along the Norwegian coast German convoys and shore installations were battered by the bombs of the carrier planes. The airmen were exacting a toll of northern shipping similar to that of the Biscay sweeps; but it was dull work for the sailors, and they were much cheered when the orders arrived for Operation Counterblast.

NORTHERN
WATERS

HVAL FJORD
●REYKJAVIK
ICELAND

ATLAN

OCEA

THE FAEROES

SHETLAND
ISLANDS

THE HEBRIDES   THE MINCHES   LOCH ERIBOLL   ●SCAPA FLOW

LOCH EWE

INISHTRAHULL   ●OBAN   FIRTH OF CLYDE   EGE
FOYLE   ●ROSYTH
LONDONDERRY   GLASGOW   FIRTH OF
FORTH   NORTH

IRISH
SEA

ST. GEORGE'S CHANN   ●ST. DAVID'S
HEAD

NORTH CAPE

TROMSÖ● ●ALTAFJORD

KOLA INLET
MURMANSK●

LOFOTEN ISL.

●TRONDHEIM

GULF OF BOTHNIA

EN

●OSLO

NGER

STOCKHOLM●

FJORD

RRAK

BALTIC SEA

COPENHAGEN

BURG

●KIEL

EN ELBE R

This was to be a naval strike; and *Sioux*, laid up with a boiler cleaning, was to miss it. On November 12 the British cruisers *Kent* and *Bellona* and the British destroyers *Myngs*, *Verulam* and *Zambesi*, together with *Algonquin*, nosed inward toward the Norwegian coast between Lista Fjord and Egersund. Here there were high cliffs and no fjords along the coast, so that shipping had to stand out to sea. Thick minefields and powerful shore batteries had kept these waters safe from allied naval attack for four years; but this immunity was now at an end.

About eleven o'clock at night *Kent's* radar indicated three or four lines of ships dead ahead at a range of sixteen thousand yards. Travelling at twenty-five knots, the British force drew toward the coast, steering at an angle across the enemy's front. By thirteen minutes after eleven it had passed ahead of the convoy, and starshell from *Bellona* illuminated the merchant ships.

Algonquin opened fire on one of the escorts and hit it with her first salvo. Shells from other destroyers came down on the ship simultaneously and it burst into flames. Jagged splashes of fire began to lift from the rest of the convoy as fire shifted from ship to ship along the lines. The destroyers' orders were to cripple as many as possible, finishing them off later. Within five minutes six of the enemy were ablaze.

As the rest of the convoy turned back for the coast the cruisers and destroyers followed in to within twenty-five hundred yards of shore. They were now fully illumined and salvoes from the shore batteries were plumping down in their midst. *Algonquin* with two other destroyers brought her guns to bear on a second escort ship which blew up and sank. She shifted to a merchantman, sending it to the bottom after a six-minute battering, then swung her guns onto a third escort which disappeared in a huge explosion. *Verulam* fired a spread of eight torpedoes into the midst of the ships that remained. Four of the eight struck home, each in a merchantman. The other four ran in to explode directly under the flashes of a battery firing from shore. *Bellona*, meanwhile, had dropped five salvoes at six-second intervals onto the muzzles of a battery eight miles away to the north. The sea was now empty of targets and the force withdrew. Out of eleven ships in the convoy eight had been sunk and one driven aground.

Sioux rejoined *Algonquin* on November 22 as part of the screening force for another air strike. December 6 found the two destroyers off the Norwegian coast, again escorting carriers with mine-laying planes. On December 30 they sailed with a Murmansk convoy. The passage was almost without incident; and at Murmansk the sailors found time for some exercise ashore under conditions not very different from those of their homeland. A hockey team from *Algonquin* administered a beating to a team from *Sioux*, and was trounced in its turn by representatives of the port of Murmansk. An unadorned but apparently significant footnote records that the final game was played, "with Russian equipment and under Russian rules."

The return from Murmansk was made with a convoy of twenty-nine ships, and terrible arctic weather made a nightmare of the homeward passage. Ferocious gales, sometimes reaching a velocity of eighty-five knots, battered the ships and drove them apart from each other. Crippled merchantmen rode helplessly away in the midst of blinding snowstorms and were located only after days of search. One vessel whose engines had broken down had to be left until rescue tugs could come out for her. *Sioux* and two British destroyers disembarked the merchantman's crew at the height of the storm. Later the Canadian destroyer had to make a great sweep through the wild seas astern of the convoy to locate three damaged stragglers. She found them and brought them into the Faeroes after a seventy-two hour fight, earning the warm commendation of the Vice-Admiral commanding the 10th Cruiser Squadron. No ships of the convoy were sunk but three had to be left in the Faeroes for repairs. The remainder arrived in Loch Ewe after twelve days and nights of unrelenting battle with the elements. The miseries of winter convoy work were as sharp and inalienable on the eve of victory as they had been in the darkest days.

The two destroyers were by no means the only Canadian ships cruising in arctic and sub-arctic waters during this period. The frigates of Escort Group 9 were part of the screen for a Murmansk convoy early in December. The other frigate group, EG 6, spent long periods patrolling east of the Faeroes; and the destroyers of Escort Group 11 ranged beyond them toward Iceland. Southward of these the remainder of a Canadian operational force which now included some 350 ships was spread over an area sufficiently vast. From Reykjavik to the Azores and from the Hook of Holland to the mouth of the Saguenay, the old enemy still waited to strike with his familiar, cold-blooded daring, still fought as if there remained a hope of victory.

Indeed, had the outcome of the war depended only on the struggle at sea the hope might not have been ill-founded. The allies were continually faced with new problems created by the resourceful under-water navy. The laboriously developed methods upon which their successes had been based in the past began to be defeated by new techniques and devices. Larger boats appeared, capable of remaining at sea for months on end. Schnorkel was being steadily improved, permitting long periods of underwater patrol in focal areas. Worst of all, high submerged speeds were being attained which confused and almost defied detection by asdic. Each of the innovations was to give rise to its quota of anxieties and was to exact its toll of men and ships up to the last day of the war.

While Neptune was in progress there had been a period of comparative quiet along the North American seaboard and in mid-Atlantic. Only the occasional lone guerilla or scouting U-boat had put in an appearance during the early and middle summer. The loss or locking up of the Biscay ports now precluded any resumption of a full-scale offensive. There were still many U-boats, but they had been driven back upon German or Norwegian bases. From there the voyage to the open Atlantic was a long and perilous one. They must pass north of the British Isles and work south between Scotland and Iceland, or go farther north and west to come down Denmark

Strait between Iceland and Greenland. Both corridors of this "northern transit area" were closely watched by Allied ships and planes; and the total of kills was large. Nevertheless, some U-boats did get through. They must have been commanded either by the luckiest or the most skillful of the captains; and they carried both their luck and skill far afield.

By the middle of August U-boats were athwart the convoy routes in the Atlantic, in North American coastal waters and in the St. Lawrence. They were few in number and they were met everywhere by strong escorts and by hunting groups. Nevertheless, convoys were attacked; and a merchantman sailing independently between Halifax and St. John's was sunk. In the St. Lawrence there was no score for either side during September; but on October 14 the frigate *Magog* was torpedoed off Pointe des Monts. She was patrolling in company with a hunting group. An acoustic torpedo fired from deep beneath the surface struck her in the stern and blew off nearly sixty feet of the after part of the ship. Other ships of the group got her safely into Quebec; but a long hunt failed to locate the submarine.

Magog's sister-frigate, *Chebogue*, had been crippled ten days earlier in the Atlantic. On October 4 she was about eight hundred miles west of the British Isles with a convoy when her masthead lookout sighted a surfaced U-boat 13,000 yards away. The frigate gave chase and the submarine went under at a range of 10,000 yards. With other ships of her group, *Chebogue* closed the position and began a search which continued without result until ten o'clock in the evening.

At five minutes after ten an acoustic torpedo smashed into *Chebogue's* stern, crippling her. Deep in the water, listing and helpless, the ship began to drift while a full moon overhead revealed her in sharp silhouette. Other ships launched themselves on a newly intensified hunt which failed to locate the U-boat but saved the frigate from further attack. *Arnprior* came alongside to give assistance, while damage control parties went to work in *Chebogue*. By one o'clock on

the following afternoon the ship was in condition for towing
and the veteran corvette *Chambly* began the work.

The 850-mile voyage to Milford Haven filled an arduous
week, during which *Chebogue* was passed from hand to hand
along her route. *Chambly* towed until the evening of the
6th, when she was relieved by a British frigate. At eleven
o'clock on the evening of the 7th the Canadian frigate,
Ribble, took over. On the 9th a rescue tug arrived, and the
last lap of the journey was nearly completed on the afternoon
of the 11th, when a full gale struck the ship at the entrance
to Swansea Bay.

The storm was the worst in years along that part of the
coast, and during the night which followed it seemed that
Chebogue would still be lost. She was deep in the water and
almost unmanageable. About midnight the lines from the tug
broke, the ship swung broadside-on to the wind, and her
stern settled onto the bottom of the bay in twenty-one feet of
water. Her crew was taken off, and for the rest of the night
there was every likelihood that she would founder. With high
tide in the morning, however, her stern lifted slightly off the
bottom and she was eased in to the jetties of Port Talbot. She
would not be numbered among the sombre company of ships
sunk, but her life as a fighting ship was over.

A few days after *Chebogue* staggered to harbour another Canadian frigate, *Annan*, exacted revenge for her in the
northern transit area. With the ships of Escort Group 6, now
far afield from the Neptune waters, she was patrolling west
of the Shetlands on October 16. During the afternoon she
had dropped a pattern of depth charges on what seemed to
be a good contact. Long search, however, had revealed nothing; and as darkness fell she was proceeding in company with
Loch Achanalt to rejoin the other ships.

Before she had quite reached them a radar contact was
reported astern. The frigate swung round and closed in on a
steadily improving echo. It was soon obvious that a surfaced
submarine was moving away, zigzagging sharply. *Annan* followed the U-boat's course until she was within 2,700 yards;

then put up a spread of rockets which revealed the enemy almost beam on.

The German had been damaged by the depth charges dropped in the afternoon; and had been unable to remain submerged. He was still very much in action, however; and as *Annan's* guns opened up he replied with sharp burst of fire. By the time the Canadian ship had closed to within eight hundred yards both her radar and her asdic were knocked out of action and several of her men were wounded. She continued to close, battering the German with 4-inch guns and oerlikons; and eighteen minutes after the action began she ran close alongside him to fire depth charges which bounced off his deck and exploded in the water.

The U-boat began to settle. Her conning tower and escape hatches opened and men were seen jumping over the side. In another two minutes she sank on an even keel. The other ships of *Annan's* group had arrived too late to take much part in the action; but they now lowered boats to recover survivors. By next morning they were in Londonderry with forty-six prisoners.

A week later, far to the west and north, the pendulum swung once more against the Canadians. This time no enemy was involved. The blind gods of the weather intervened to strike a blow which was keenly felt since it involved one of the veteran ships which had been in action since the first day of the war.

Skeena was patrolling south of Iceland on the afternoon of October 24 with the other destroyers of her group. A gale which had been blowing all day rose to such intensity during the late afternoon that the ships were ordered into Reykjavik. By nine-thirty in the evening they were anchored off the harbour near Videy Island. The anchorage gave practically no shelter and the gale mounted steadily. Continual snow squalls reduced visibility almost to zero. Through the driving blizzard only the rarest glimpses could be obtained of the nearby shore, and among the great swells it was difficult to detect any change in position.

Toward midnight the officer of the watch on board *Skeena* caught a fleeting glimpse of Videy Island. It was nearer than it should have been, and he realized that the ship was dragging her anchor. Another anchor was ordered away, and engines were put to full ahead; but before either order could take effect, the ship yawed to a great swell and lifted in, stern first, toward the off-shore rocks. Her propellers locked among jagged granite teeth. Then another sea caught her and *Skeena* swung broadside onto a reef some ninety yards from the mainland of Videy.

As the pounding swell beat in on her, it seemed that she would capsize and sink. Waves were washing the length of the deck. The starboard seaboat was smashed, and the port boat foundered as soon as it touched the water. Only the carley floats, which had been dropped in the lee of the ship as soon as the order to abandon was given, seemed to offer a chance of safety.

The apparent chance proved a tragic illusion. Fifteen men who tried to reach shore in the first three floats were carried past the island and drowned. A few others were swept in to arrive battered and half-conscious on the slippery rocks. Most of these never knew how they got there. Dazed, soaked and freezing, some of them found shelter in caves or abandoned huts. The luckier ones regained consciousness to find themselves wrapped in the blankets and sheepskins of Iceland crofters.

The men remaining on board *Skeena* gave up the attempt to make for shore. At three in the morning two landing craft from Reykjavik, manned by British sailors, made their way out to the ship. In the midst of the storm, however, it was impossible either to land on or to take men off. Neither was it possible to beach the landing craft on the seaward side of Videy facing *Skeena*. Guided by a huge Iceland pilot, the rescue party made its way clear round the island and landed on the leeward side. Then the tireless Icelander led them across the rocky island on foot. By 7.40 in the morning they were down to the shore on the windward side and could signal to *Skeena*. From the ship a coston-gun line was shot to the island. A heavier line followed; and the destroyer's remaining carley floats were attached to it. The Icelander, Einar Sigurdsson, and the British sailors, working neck-deep with him in the icy water, hauled *Skeena's* men to safety.

Later, in Fossaburg cemetery at Reykjavik, the fifteen dead from the ship were buried with full naval honours. "Each man," reports an officer who was there, "rests with a white cross bearing his name and number at his head. The cemetery slopes down to a quiet bay and in the near distance are snowclad mountains which hold Reykjavik in their clasp and blaze like white fire on a sunny day."

November saw U-boats still in the St. Lawrence. A merchantman was torpedoed near Matane on the 2nd. On the 25th the corvette *Shawinigan*, was lost with all hands in Cabot Strait. She had been on an independent patrol maintaining the usual radio silence; and when the torpedo struck she must have gone down too quickly for any message to be sent. A day or so later searching ships came upon fragments of wreckage which were all that remained to indicate what had happened to her.

In December U-boats attacked with even more reckless daring. On the 21st a Liberty ship was torpedoed from a convoy forming up off Halifax. Three days later in the same area the Bangor minesweeper, *Clayoquot*, was sunk with a loss of eight lives. The corvettes *Fennel* and *Transcona*, which were in company with her, each exploded an acoustic torpedo in its cat gear, but made no contact with the submarine.

On the 27th word came that *St. Thomas* and *Edmundston* had sunk a U-boat in mid-Atlantic. It was partial satisfaction, but the wintry close of the year found the men of the escort ships and the hunting groups in no mood of jubilation. Strategists might point out, quite correctly, that the position of the Germans was hopeless. No blow they could strike on sea or land would turn aside the avalanche descending upon the Reich. Yet it seemed that so long as a weapon remained in their hands they would fight with it;

and there were powerful weapons remaining. So far as the U-boat arm was concerned, it was deteriorating only in numbers. In quality it was becoming steadily more dangerous.

Thoughts were turning also to the war against Japan, and the prospect of a weary, savage struggle there. On October 21 the British cruiser *Uganda* had been re-commissioned as a ship of the Canadian navy. On December 30 she sailed from Scapa for Gibraltar on the first leg of a voyage which would take her through the Red Sea and the Indian Ocean to join the British Fleet in the Pacific.

CHAPTER SEVENTEEN

Black Flags and a Setting Sun

Uganda steamed down from northern waters, cut across the trade routes of the middle Atlantic and entered Gibraltar on January 5, 1945. Sailing again the same day, she arrived on January 11 at Alexandria, where her voyage was to be interrupted for a month. She had left Scapa with work-ups and training only partially completed and she now entered upon a series of battle exercises with British cruisers in the eastern Mediterranean. On February 14 "being in all respects ready," she sailed for the Pacific by way of the Suez Canal and the Red Sea.

Behind her, over all the older theatres of battle, hung a sense of approaching finality. As *Uganda* left Port Said, *Prince David* at Malta was preparing to sail for Esquimalt. A month later *Prince Henry* followed her sister ship through Gibraltar, bound for the United Kingdom. The war in the Mediterranean was all but ended. On the northward seas it was passing stormily to its concluding phase.

For the German surface navy a galling record of failure, now almost complete, had continued the unhappy tradition of the first World War. Two pocket battleships, half a dozen cruisers and a number of destroyers remained at fighting effectiveness. They had been held in the north to threaten the Murmansk convoys and as a check on the movements of the Home Fleet. Now they were being withdrawn to the Baltic. Some of them would be used to support German land forces retreating before the Russians. All would be harried from port to port by allied planes; and most would be found at the war's end sunk, capsized or crippled in the harbours of their own inland sea.

It was far from so with the U-boats. From their bases in Norway they still came down the perilous corridors on either side of Iceland. They thronged in the Irish Sea. They moved inward to British coastal waters and outward to the Atlantic and the North American seaboard. Supplemented by E-boats and swarms of the new midget submarines, they threw themselves against the Thames-Antwerp convoy route. They combined with aircraft to hack at the Murmansk supply line; and their loneliest outriders went north to the Barents Sea and south to the waters of Australia and the Indian Ocean. Their numbers were again on the increase rather than the wane; their boats were better and more elusive, and they fought with a vigour unequalled since the days of the wolf packs.

Their grim devotion to a lost cause had its epic quality; but it was useless and worse than useless. All their efforts made hardly a fractional impression on the mighty preponderance of strength now arrayed against them. By the end of March nearly four million Allied soldiers had been delivered to the continent. They were pouring across the Rhine from the west; while from the east the Russian advance was a pillar of cloud by day and of fire by night. Tremendous fleets of Allied bombers ranged over the diminishing area between the two armies, pounding the last strongholds to rubble. Mass raids on the shipyards destroyed in seconds the output of laborious months. In the U-boat bases the debris of barracks, docks, cranes and machine shops lay strewn above the deep steel and concrete shelters from which the sea fighters were controlled.

In spite of it all, nearly a hundred and fifty U-boats were maintained in operation, with more than that number training or under repair. Immense efforts were concentrated on the building of types XXI and XXIII, the new boats with high submerged speed, of which scarcely half a dozen ever saw service. Skillful, resourceful and determined at sea, frantically industrious on land, the underwater navy in the last five months of the war sent half a million tons of Allied shipping to the bottom. Yet the total was less than one per cent of the tonnage moving to Europe; and during the same period Allied shipyards turned out nearly four and a half million tons of new construction. The contrasting figures were an index both to the desperate fanaticism at the core of German resistance and to the criminal futility of prolonging the struggle.

Allied sea communications were no longer vulnerable in any strategic sense. Nor were they subject any longer to delay. The ocean convoys could be forced through to the most convenient ports, defended by overwhelming strength. The roundabout voyage north of Ireland had been eliminated. Long trains of shipping moved directly to the west coast ports, directly up the Channel to Normandy, the Thames or on to Antwerp. Time was being saved, weeks of bloodshed and destruction, yet not without a compensating cost. The main stream of Atlantic supply presented an immense target to guerilla attack. So did the northward stream to Russia. Even more inviting were the two subsidiary networks; the one which fed in at the source along the North American seaboard and the one which carried out final distribution through British and European waters. Nowhere along this multitude of seaways could strategic invulnerability mean complete immunity. Loss must be accepted; and, fractional though it might be, the fraction represented ships and the lives of men.

Everywhere naval forces vastly out of proportion to those of the Germans had to be employed. The general movements of Allied shipping were well known; while the enemy could disperse or concentrate against it at will. Hunting forces had to counter his movements, anticipate them if possible. Every convoy that sailed had to be given protection, though perhaps only one in ten might be attacked. The mobility, range, secrecy and endurance of the U-boats had to be countered by large numbers, long patrols and vigilance everywhere.

For the Canadian navy this meant, as always, the employment of its main force in support of the Atlantic convoy. The mid-ocean groups and the western local groups which had borne the full burden of close escort about the trade convoys during the spectacular days of Neptune, had long been reinforced by returning British and United States ships. Their own numbers had continued to grow up to the end of 1944. Sixty Canadian frigates and corvettes were now operating on the mid-ocean run between St. John's and Londonderry. Another forty-five, organized as the Western Escort Force, brought the convoys to and from the western terminal of the mid-ocean run. Behind them another force, numerically larger but composed for the most part of older and smaller ships, made the "Triangle Run" between New York, Boston and Halifax, or shepherded the feeder convoys moving between Canadian and Newfoundland ports. There remained, in addition, a considerable force in British waters. Seventeen corvettes and fourteen Bangor minesweepers were serving in the Channel and along both coasts. The 29th and 65th Canadian Motor Torpedo Boat Flotillas were operating along the Thames-Antwerp convoy route. Over and above all these were eight Canadian destroyers and forty-five frigates, formed into support groups operating as required in Canadian waters, British waters, the Arctic or the main Atlantic.

The first blows of the year fell upon shipping at the extremities of the supply chain. On January 4 two ships out of the three making up a small coastal convoy were torpedoed twenty miles off Halifax. A few days later, just as a convoy from Boston was forming up to enter Halifax harbour, two more vessels were sunk in quick succession. In neither case did the escorting ships gain any sure contact with the submarine. The month's results on the eastern side of the Atlantic were equally unsatisfactory for the Allies. In the Irish Sea and the Channel four merchant ships went down and two more were damaged without a balancing success. Altogether, out of some fifty attacks and counter-attacks the score was eight ships to zero in favour of the Germans. The comparatively quiet mid-Atlantic yielded the only kill of the month when the explosives of an American task group brought fragments of a U-boat drifting to the surface north of the Azores.

Black Flags and a Setting Sun

In February there seemed to be a withdrawal from the Canadian and American coast and a stepping up of activity in mid-Atlantic. The main effort, however, was directed against British waters. Here, from Brest to the Faeroes, the U-boats drove in; to be met by concentrated forces of ships and planes. Eleven submarines were sunk during the month; but five Allied naval ships, of which one was Canadian, also went down.

Trentonian was the Canadian casualty. On February 22 during the early afternoon she was steering eastward with a Channel convoy a few miles off Falmouth. At twenty minutes after one, with no previous warning, a torpedo struck the second ship in the port column. *Trentonian*, which had been out in front of the convoy, immediately altered back and commenced search. The merchant ship had reported herself torpedoed on the starboard side; and as *Trentonian* was then on the port side of the convoy she steered in through the lanes of ships to cross over.

Just as she cleared the starboard side a torpedo struck her, slewing her around in the water and gashing open the afterpart of the ship. Within four minutes the engine room was flooded and the stern was settling rapidly. The order to abandon was given; and the last man had hardly got over the side when the corvette upended slowly and sank. Six men had been killed by the explosion and eleven wounded; and although search of the area was begun immediately by a heavy force of ships no contact with the U-boat could be gained.

The loss of *Trentonian* had been preceded by a tragic accident which wiped out nearly the whole of the 29th Canadian Motor Torpedo Boat Flotilla. In company with the 65th and with British flotillas, the 29th had moved from the Neptune area to bases along the British east coast, following the retreat of the E-boats. More recently the two Canadian flotillas had been transferred with other coastal forces to Ostend on the Belgian coast. Here they were now operating in support of the Thames-Antwerp convoys; fighting off the

390

nightly forays of E-boats and midget submarines and making frequent forays of their own against the Dutch harbours on which the enemy forces were based. As always with coastal craft, the dark hours were for work and the day for sleep.

On the afternoon of Februay 14, several of the flotillas, including the 29th, were berthed inside Ostend harbour in a narrow passage known as The Crique. A patrol was scheduled for that night; and men not on watch had been given a "make-and-mend," or afternoon off. Many of them were sleeping below decks. Others had taken advantage of the opportunity to go ashore. Suddenly a sheet of fire was seen running along the water toward the jetties. Defuelling had been carried on earlier in the day; and in some way the highly volatile gasoline discharged onto the surface had become ignited.

Before an alarm could be given the flames had licked in about the close-ranked boats and many of them were infernoes above and below decks, shrouded in oily smoke and surrounded by blazing gasoline. Some men on the decks dived overboard into the fiery waters and swam beneath the surface to safety. Others never got up from below. Still others were killed by flying debris as they emerged from the hatches. Explosions began to rip craft after craft wide open, showering the flaming wreckage farther along the line. A pall of smoke towered along the waterfront; and out of it for two terrible hours came the roar of bursting fuel tanks, the missiles of exploding ammunition and the cries of men.

Three boats of the 29th were saved by men who fought down the flames in one, brought their craft alongside two more and towed them out of the harbour. The Medical Officer of the flotilla, Surgeon Lieutenant William L. Leslie, was returning from the hospital in town with a truckful of medical supplies when he saw the fire break out. Driving straight onto the nearest jetty with his two sick bay attendants, he worked over casualties throughout the afternoon, and was joined among the clouds of smoke and flying fragments by the flotilla's chaplain and by soldiers, sailors, marines and nurses from an evacuation train nearby.

Black Flags and a Setting Sun

At the end of the day the 29th Flotilla had ceased to exist. Five of its eight boats had been destroyed. Seven British boats had been lost and many more were damaged. Twenty-six Canadian and thirty-five British sailors had been killed. The disaster was a stunning blow to men of the small craft everywhere; and only the 65th Canadian Flotilla now remained to carry on to the end of the war with what was perhaps the most colorful, the most closely knit and the most thoroughly "allied" of all the forces in which men of British, Canadian, French and many other nationalities worked together.

During March, a few more U-boats appeared to be arriving in Canadian waters; but they accomplished nothing and were heavily attacked. The mid-ocean area was also comparatively quiet. In British waters, however, there was a resurgence of German strength which was met once again by a redoubling of allied sea and air power. Out of ten submarines sunk during the month for a loss of two naval vessels, the first Canadian kill came on the morning of March 7, in St. George's Channel.

The frigates, *Strathadam, La Hulloise* and *Thetford Mines,* gained an asdic contact in the early hours of March 6. They followed it, attacking without apparent result, until the following midnight. Shortly after midnight the asdic echo was lost; but *La Hulloise* gained a small radar contact. Guessing that the U-boat might have surfaced, *La Hulloise* moved in and illuminated her target. It proved to be the Schnorkel tube and periscope of a submarine, and as the boat dived the three frigates were upon it. A series of depth charge and hedgehog attacks began to bring diesel oil to the surface. The submarine was going to its maximum depth, and the attacking ships followed it with deeper-set charges. Unmistakable evidence of destruction began to appear. German ration kits rose to the surface; then shoes, clothing, shattered pieces of engine room equipment, snapshots and a harmonica. Finally, in the midst of an oil slick which now covered eight square miles of sea, there appeared log books and confidential naval publications which revealed the victim as U-1302.

Ten days later *Guysborough,* one of the Neptune minesweepers, went down with many of her men. She had been sent to Canada for refit; and on March 17 was returning to the United Kingdom, en route between Horta and Plymouth. At ten minutes to seven in the evening an acoustic torpedo struck her dead astern. The ship sagged heavily and took a list to port; but the damage did not appear to be fatal. The crew was mustered, ordered into warm clothing and told to remain on the upper deck. Guns were manned, and damage control parties went to work. No one had been injured by the explosion, and for forty-five minutes the Bangor appeared to have a good fighting chance. Then the U-boat, which had neither surfaced nor been contacted by asdic, drove home a second torpedo, finishing off the ship. The order to abandon was given; and thirty-five minutes later *Guysborough* sank.

The ship's sea boat had been destroyed by the second explosion and several men had been injured. Nevertheless five carley floats had been put over the side, all men had got away from the ship, and in spite of a moderately heavy swell the situation did not seem too threatening. Yet it was a case of men at the mercy of the sea, and this time the sea was not to prove merciful. Four of the carley floats with about twelve men on each were carried well away from the ship before other men swimming in the water could reach them. Onto the fifth, which remained near alongside, forty-two men, some of them injured, had to be crowded.

The men on the first four floats were unable to get back to relieve the congestion on the fifth. Soon the contrary seas had separated each party by two or three miles; and none was sure of the others' location. Men who had already been injured by the explosion of the second torpedo were dying. Shock and exposure began to leave others numb and helpless. Along the sides of the crowded float, as darkness closed down, exhausted men let go their holds and disappeared. Twice the buffeting seas turned the float itself completely over; and each time some ten men less remained. Thirty-six of this party were dead or missing by the time a British ship arrived on the scene at two o'clock the following afternoon. From among the others fifteen more had been lost, making a total of fifty-one deaths out of a ship's company of ninety.

Before *Guysborough's* survivors reached Plymouth other Canadian ships were in action far to the north. Two Canadian frigate groups, based on Londonderry, formed part of the forces patrolling the northern corridor. One of the groups, Escort Group 26, consisting of *New Glasgow, Beacon Hill, Jonquiere, Ribble,* and *Sussexvale,* had sailed from Londonderry on the night of March 20 and was just clearing Lough Foyle when *New Glasgow* sighted a schnorkel broad on her bow. She bore in at high speed, swept over the partially submerged periscope, and lifted from the water with a grinding crash as her bottom made contact with the U-boat's hull.

Swinging back, with little apparent damage from the collision, *New Glasgow* began a series of depth charge and hedgehog attacks. The other frigates of her group joined in. *Strathadam, Thetford Mines* and *La Hulloise* of Escort Group 25 came out from Londonderry to assist. For two days it seemed that in spite of the very promising beginning the hunt was not to yield evidence of a kill. *New Glasgow,* finding her underwater damage more serious than it had first appeared, was forced to retire to harbour. The other ships carried on with steadily lessening hopes.

On March 23, however, as the hunt reached out over a wider area, *Strathadam* and *Thetford Mines* came upon an unhappy group of Germans riding life rafts sixteen miles off Inishtrahuill. They were survivors of U-1003, *New Glasgow's* victim. The submarine had bottomed after the ramming and had remained on the sea floor for forty-eight hours, hearing the explosions of depth charges about her but suffering no damage from them. *New Glasgow's* blow, however, had done enough. The boat's schnorkel and periscopes were out of action. She was flooding heavily and pumps were fighting a losing battle against the in-rushing water. She could operate only on her electric motors; and when their batteries gave out she would be unable to surface. At midnight on the 22nd, as the hopelessness of the situation became apparent, the crew had abandoned.

New Glasgow was laid up only briefly with her honourable scars; but before the end of the month another Canadian frigate was knocked out of the war. On March 29 *Teme*, in company with *New Waterford*, was sweeping astern of a convoy in the Channel. She gained an asdic contact which seemed after twenty minutes of investigation to be only another of the myriad false echoes plaguing ships in the area. Just as she was altering back toward the convoy, however, asdic operators picked up a new disturbance in the water. It proved to be a torpedo, too far on its way to be avoided. There was a great explosion and nearly sixty feet of the ship's stern disappeared. With three men dead and one dying she was towed into nearby Falmouth.

April brought the last large-scale combined operation of the European war. As the Allied armies swept across France and on over the Rhine into Germany, they had left unsubdued behind them several of the former U-boat citadels on the Biscay coast. St. Nazaire and Lorient remained, impotent and practically ignored, until the general German surrender. Two other garrisons, however, astride the mouth of the Gironde at Royan on the north bank and Pointe de Grave on the south, were of more importance since they prevented the use of Bordeaux. On April 15 a combined land, sea and air attack was launched against them, with a strong French naval force headed by the battleship, *Lorraine*, providing the seapower. Proceeding well ahead of *Lorraine* were the minesweepers of the 31st Canadian Flotilla, assigned to duties strongly reminiscent of their Neptune adventure.

Black Flags and a Setting Sun

The ships of the flotilla, which now consisted of *Thunder, Kenora, Canso, Vegreville, Caraquet, Minas* and *Bayfield,* sailed from Plymouth for the mouth of the Gironde at ten o'clock on the night of April 12. *Wasaga,* the remaining member, had been slightly damaged in a collision the day before; and the British danlayer *Sursay* took her place. By six o'clock on the evening of the 14th the ships were in position off the estuary and ready to commence operations.

They were to go in under the shore batteries, sweeping lanes of approach and bombardment areas as they had done on D-Day. A flotilla of French minesweepers was to follow behind them to clear up magnetic and acoustic mines. The sweep got under way at 7.32, closed in to the coast and continued for five hours. Once again not a gun on shore opened up. By one o'clock in the morning, with their primary duties completed, the ships of the 31st Flotilla had begun an anti-submarine patrol about the bombardment area. At dawn as squadrons of Allied bombers roared overhead and French assault troops began their attack from the landward side, *Lorraine* and her supporting cruisers appeared on the horizon. At 7.45 the 14-inch guns of the battleship and the smaller guns of the cruisers opened fire.

From then until noon of the 16th the minesweepers continued their patrol about the bombardment area. By that time Royan had been taken, Pointe de Grave was falling, and the naval force was preparing to retire. The 31st Flotilla set course for Plymouth; and, an hour after leaving, stopped and boarded a German armed trawler. The trawler had been sent out from Point de Grave to round up other vessels which had bolted during the French bombardment. *Thunder* took off the German crew, put a Canadian party on board and the trawler arrived in Plymouth with the flotilla, wearing the white ensign.

Meanwhile the charts in the operational headquarters on both sides of the Atlantic had grown black with symbols of the month's attacks and sinkings. Perhaps because there was no longer any thought of maintaining a reserve, the

Germans were throwing still heavier forces against the shipping lanes. E-boats and midget submarines made nightly forays against the Antwerp route; and the motor torpedo boats from Ostend sailed nightly to meet them. The E-boats, wary but dogged, were depending more on mines than torpedoes. The midgets used both. Blundering, vulnerable and sunk in shoals, they still came on by tens and dozens to account for at least three Allied ships during the month. In the Channel the Canadian frigate *Loch Alvie* had already joined with the British destroyer *Watchman* to sink a submarine whose captain had made a determined attack on a convoy escorted by three frigates and a destroyer. The German had sunk one large merchantman and was still working in on the others when he was sent to the bottom himself. Other captains, equally doomed, equally daring, ranged in growing numbers over all the familiar areas of battle.

In the Irish Sea, the Channel and along the eastern, western and northern approaches to the British Isles, twelve merchant ships and two naval vessels were mined or torpedoed. Allied ships and planes accounted for nineteen U-boats and midget submarines. In the Atlantic two ships went down near Ushant. An American destroyer was sunk south of Flemish Cap, and the attacking U-boat was destroyed in return. Another five U-boats were sunk in mid-Atlantic during the month, still seeking to penetrate the screen about the ocean convoys. In waters nearer home, U-boats were sighted and attacked south of Halifax, in the approaches to Sydney and off Sable Island. A United States patrol vessel was torpedoed off the Maine coast; two merchantmen went down off Cape Hatteras and another near Norfolk. The last Canadian casualty of the war came on April 16, when the Bangor minesweeper, *Esquimalt*, was sunk in the Halifax approaches.

The ship was on patrol only a few miles out from the coast. A torpedo struck her on the starboard side, killing many men with its explosion; and tons of sea water flooded in through a great hole to drag the Bangor down with sickening speed. The seaboat was under water and flooded

397

on its davits before it could be released. Four carley floats got away and the survivors of the explosion swam and floundered through the water to take refuge on them. Through six hours of waiting, icy waves washed over the shocked and exhausted men. By the time *Sarnia,* a sister ship, arrived on the scene, thirty-nine were dead or missing out of a crew of sixty-five.

April wore to its close with no apparent reduction either in the numbers or morale of the U-boats at sea. There came, instead, reports of small packs forming to the north of the Azores and to the south of Ireland. The many captains sailing alone were still as active, still as dangerous as ever. There was something aimless and convulsive about the vigour they displayed, as well there might be. Doenitz, now wearing the ragged mantle of the Fuehrer, no longer thought and planned for them. The Americans had met the Russians at Torgau on the Elbe, isolating the Baltic and the North Sea fringe on which their bases lay. The bases themselves, if not bombed out of existence, were within days of being overwhelmed by British armies rushing north from Bremen. From the remaining control centres, at Flensburg on the Danish border and at Bergen in Norway, the orders reaching them began to be garbled and fragmentary as transmission broke down. Disintegration was far advanced and darkness was closing upon the underwater navy, yet the great sea beast displayed a terrible vitality. Its far-reaching tentacles, almost severed now from the battered head, still writhed and struck.

Step by step with the naval war in the Atlantic region, the battle in the Arctic and sub-Arctic moved toward its conclusion. The convoys to Murmansk were being fought through with none of the staggering losses of earlier days, yet still against dogged opposition from underwater and from the air. Cruisers, carriers and destroyers based on Scapa were going into Norwegian waters in a steady procession of strikes designed to cut off supplies to German garrisons and make the evacuation of troops as costly as possible. In these waters and on some of these tasks, *Algonquin* and *Sioux* completed their war service.

Algonquin's time in the north was running out when she returned with *Sioux* from a Murmansk voyage late in January. The two ships took part in one more air strike before the end of the month. On February 1 they made a last voyage together when they went to the Minches to meet the new escort carrier *Puncher*, a sister ship to *Nabob*, and, like her, British-owned but Canadian-manned. A final operation in which *Algonquin* was scheduled to take part was cancelled because of bad weather; and on February 5, with annual refit considerably overdue, the destroyer sailed for Halifax.

Puncher began her first northern operation on February 11, when her squadron of Wildcats flown by British pilots formed part of the fighter escort for carrier planes laying mines in the Skatestraum, well up along the west coast of Norway. A second and similar mission followed ten days later, directed this time against the Salhusstraum, near Stavanger. The object of these mine-laying expeditions, as of earlier ones, was to forbid German ships the use of the coastal channels and force them out into the open sea where they could be attacked by planes of Coastal Command. The second of the two missions also included a protective sweep by *Puncher's* planes over a flotilla of British minesweepers which had been brought along with the force to clear up a German minefield near the coast.

Sioux, meanwhile, was en route to Murmansk with a convoy which had to fight its way north through foul weather and a series of attacks by German torpedo bombers. After several days of shadowing by reconnaissance planes, a flight of Junkers 88's came in out of a snowy sky on the afternoon of February 10. One plane swept down to launch a torpedo on a very accurate course for *Sioux*. The destroyer had to take drastic avoiding action; but as she swerved aside she saw her anti-aircraft fire registering on the German. He disappeared, smoking heavily and dropping toward the water; and twenty minutes later another flight of twelve Junkers came in amid squall and sleet. Once again hits from the destroyer blossomed in red splotches on the under side of a plane; but once again it was over the horizon before a confirming splash could reward the gunners.

The convoy arrived at Kola Inlet on February 13, with the loss of only one frigate which was mined in the approaches. Here a new mission awaited *Sioux*. Soroya Island, at the far northern fringes of the Scandinavian peninsula, had recently been evacuated by the Germans; and word had come that its five hundred inhabitants were in desperate straits. *Sioux* and two British destroyers, *Zambesi* and *Zest*, were ordered there as a relief expedition.

Sailing on February 14, laden down with blankets and food, and carrying a small party of Norwegian soldiers to garrison the island, the ships arrived off Soroya on the afternoon of the 15th. In three and a half hours all inhabitants were taken off, the Norwegian garrison and its supplies were landed, and the destroyers were racing back for Kola Inlet at full speed. At Kola the islanders were transferred to merchant ships of the convoy forming for return to the United Kingdom the next day.

Once again it was to be a voyage marked by some of the last heavy attacks of the torpedo bombers. U-boats also gathered in force for the first few days of the passage, sinking a British sloop and a British corvette for the loss of one of their number. As the U-boats fell behind a ferocious gale set in and there was a spell of weary work in rounding up stragglers. Then came the planes; and *Sioux* found herself in the thick of another action. A group of eleven Junkers, driving in for the merchant ships, was turned away by her gunfire; and as it broke off, one plane, thoroughly riddled, dived into the sea. Fighters from the escorting carriers shot down another five planes; and none of the merchant ships was hit. The next day, however, seventeen bombers swarmed down on a lone straggler far behind the convoy and sent it to the bottom.

Diagram 17 Opposed. Smoke and explosions from burning MTB's

H.108, renamed . . . the R.C.N. and utilizes under the white ensigns for Bay Bulls, Newfoundland.

Sioux arrived at Scapa on February 27, and departed again for Murmansk on March 12. After a quiet passage to the very mouth of Kola Inlet, the convoy was met by a force of U-boats which sank two merchantmen and a British sloop. The return journey was enlivened only by an occasional distant glimpse of a scouting plane; and with her arrival at Scapa, *Sioux* had completed her northern duties. On April 6 she sailed for Canada.

Haida and *Iroquois* had now arrived to take the place of the Fleet destroyers. *Huron* was also an occasional visitor, although her duties consisted mainly of escort work between Scapa and the Clyde. The first mission for *Haida* and *Iroquois* came on March 19, when they went north as part of the screening force for a mine-laying strike in the Gravesund. On the 24th they went again with a larger force, which included *Puncher*, for a blow at the Trondheim leads. *Iroquois* took part in a small gun action which damaged three German merchant ships on April 3; and later on the same day *Puncher* started north with another air strike which had to be abandoned because of the weather. On April 16, *Haida*, *Huron* and *Iroquois* sailed together with a Murmansk convoy which was to be their last.

The voyage north was made without loss; and while berthed at Ekaterinberg in Kola Inlet the Canadian crews had an opportunity to take part in a memorable celebration of the Russian entry into Berlin. Next day, in return for hospitality extended, *Huron* invited over a hundred Russian naval ratings on board the ship for dinner. Victory was in the air as the convoy formed up for the return journey on April 29.

Outside the approaches, however, conditions seemed remarkably unchanged. Amid the rattle of gunfire and the roar of exploding depth charges a British frigate went down, followed shortly by the U-boat which had fired the torpedo. Another torpedo laced through the water narrowly missing *Haida*; and *Iroquois* had a close shave an hour or so later. Fighting off and outrunning the U-boats, the convoy began to sight the familiar scouting planes wheeling overhead. On two occasions a day or so later, bomber formations appeared in the distance; but this time the weather was ahead of the enemy. A full gale swept down, driving the planes to their landing fields, and battering the convoy onward to its destination. The Tribals arrived at Scapa with the other ships of the escort force on May 6.

Rumours and counter rumours of general German surrender were going around the world. For the worn men in from the north, it must have been hard to believe them. It must have been hard for the men on many seas. On May 5 an American freighter was torpedoed off Rhode Island. On the 6th an American destroyer, called to the position, was bringing the familiar litter of German naval papers and submarine debris to the surface. On the 7th a U-boat was attacked in the approaches to New York harbour, and later in the same day two merchant vessels and a minesweeper were torpedoed in the Irish Sea. On the morning of May 8 a cargo vessel was sunk off Ostend; and at twenty-one minutes after eight that night a British escort group began an attack on a U-boat off St. David's Head, a little to the north of Bristol Channel. An hour and forty minutes later, while wreckage from this attack was streaming to the surface in the midst of a great lake of oil, the sea war officially ended.

At one minute after ten on the night of May 8, the German High Command broadcast at Allied dictation an order to all its U-boats at sea. The order contained the following instructions:

A. Surface and remain surfaced.
B. Report your position and number to the nearest British, United States, Canadian or Soviet wireless station.
C. Fly black or blue flag by day and burn navigation lights by night.
D. Jettison ammunition; render torpedoes and mines safe.

E. Make all signals in plain language.

F. Refrain from scuttling or in any way damaging your U-boat.

G. Report your position, course and speed every eight hours.

H. Proceed by the prescribed route to the prescribed Allied port.

The signal was repeated two hours later; and again at the next two-hour interval, and the next. It was to circle the globe with monotonous reiteration for the next three weeks, followed at last by warning messages to the boats not accounted for. Of some the exact fate would never be known. Two at least were scuttled at sea. Many more were scuttled in their harbours. Several which remained submerged after May 8, whether recalcitrant or because they did not receive the signal, were attacked and probably sunk. Up to the last week of May, Allied ships were reporting contacts and attacks, none of which was certainly verified.

One by one, most units of the underwater navy rose to the surface. At 6.39 on the morning of the 9th, Canadian naval wireless stations intercepted the position report of U-805 in mid Atlantic. Twenty-five minutes later an unidentified boat reported herself to the west of Land's End, and a minute after that U-1105 spoke from northwest of Ireland. At intervals through the day followed seven more reports: from the western Atlantic, from the Channel mouth, from northeast and northwest of the Shetlands, and from north of Scotland. Eight boats reported on the 10th; six, on the 11th; and from that time on, the welcome messages dwindled to a trickle of two or three daily.

The behaviour of the surrendering boats was in most cases correct. Certain misconceptions, however, were revealed by the captain of U-532, who signalled to Doenitz from northwest of the Faeroes on May 11, asking to be informed if last-minute sinkings could be credited and if promotions would follow in the usual course. From Bergen, a methodical German Control, apparently with Allied permission, replied on the 15th that due to the termination of hostilities there would be no further promotions. U-532 by that time was lying beside a jetty in Loch Eriboll with her wireless sealed.

At six o'clock on the evening of May 10 an American Liberator sighted U-889; two hundred and fifty miles southeast of Cape Race, proceeding on the surface and flying a black flag. The Canadian frigates, *Dunvegan* and *Rockcliffe*, arrived on the scene, took station on either side of the U-boat and gave her a course for Shelburne, Nova Scotia. After making only part of the journey they were relieved by the frigates, *Buckingham* and *Inch Arran;* and returned to the convoy they had left. Shortly after noon on the 13th the two latter frigates, with the black-flagged enemy riding between them, arrived off Shelburne. Fairmiles carrying a boarding party came out from the harbour to meet them; and at three o'clock formal surrender was made. The U-boat crew filed off their decks for the last time; a Canadian crew took over, hoisted the white ensign and the boat was sailed into Shelburne harbour.

Another boat, U-190, was already on her way toward Bay Bulls, Newfoundland, under the escort of *Victoriaville* and *Thorlock*. She had reported her position on the evening of the 11th; and the Canadian ships had arrived shortly before midnight to find her surfaced and burning navigation lights. A boarding party had crossed over; and at two o'clock in the morning the U-boat captain had put his signature to a three-line declaration typed on a letterhead of the Department of National Defence: "I hereby unconditionally surrender German Submarine U-190 to the Royal Canadian Navy through the Flag Officer, Newfoundland."

U-190 proved to be the submarine which had sunk *Esquimalt.* After firing the torpedo she had gone to the bottom and remained there, undamaged by the depth charges of *Sarnia.* As the attacks subsided she had moved out to sea; and during the next three weeks had made several unsuccessful attacks on ships which she knew only as "frigates." The last distinct signal from Bergen had reached her on April 12. Her captain stated that the first order to surrender had been received only in fragmentary form, too garbled to understand. He had tried to obtain further information by signal but had been unable to make contact with Control.

On the other side of the Atlantic, *Thetford Mines*, in company with British, American and French ships, arrived in Lough Foyle on the 14th, escorting eight U-boats from sea. On the 16th *Loch Alvie, Monnow, Nene, St. Pierre* and *Matane* were detached from a Murmansk convoy, still proceeding under heavy escort, to meet fourteen U-boats coming down from arctic waters under the guns of the Norwegian destroyer, *Stord*. Taking up their stations about the long, black-flagged convoy, the Canadian ships brought it into Loch Eriboll on the 19th. By the end of May ninety U-boats had arrived at ports in the United Kingdom; five were in United States harbours, one in Newfoundland and one in Canada. Forty-seven seaworthy boats had been taken over in German or Norwegian ports and over fifty more had been found scuttled.

The tally was not yet complete, but it was realized that it never could be. By May 28 it was considered that the delay and navigational risk of sailing in convoy now outweighed the danger from enemy attack. At midnight on that day a signal went out discontinuing convoys in the north and south Atlantic, the Caribbean, the Gulf of Mexico, the Arctic Ocean, the North Sea, the Baltic, the Black Sea, the Red Sea and the Mediterranean. One by one, hesitantly as the signal reached the merchant ships, points of red, green and white began to twinkle among them. Then came full illumination. The convoys stood out like brilliant cities tossing on the dark seas; and men who had long sailed amid a hostile blackness found it hard to adjust themselves to the lights of peace.

On the afternoon of May 11, *Iroquois* sailed from Rosyth with a force of British and Norwegian ships, to carry out Operation Kingdom. On board the British minelayer

Apollo, was Crown Prince Olaf of Norway, returning from exile. Decked with many flags, the ships put into Oslo on the afternoon of the 13th; where a royal welcome greeted the Prince and the sailors were not forgotten. More sombre was the mission of a few days later, when *Iroquois,* in company with the cruisers *Dido* and *Devonshire* and the destroyer *Savage* sailed to escort the German cruisers, *Prinz Eugen* and *Nurnberg* from Copenhagen to Kiel.

Meanwhile *Huron* and *Haida* had left Scapa in company with the British cruiser *Berwick,* carrying relief supplies to Trondheim. In the days that followed their arrival the ships called at some of the fjords along the coast, landing relief supplies and greeting thousands of the liberated people who came on board. Probably the most hectic and enjoyable event of the week for *Haida* was a memorable party at which she entertained some fifteen hundred Norwegian children. On the 24th the two destroyers returned to Greenock, where *Iroquois* joined them on the 30th. On June 4 all three left Greenock together for Halifax.

Other Canadian ships, and some men now without ships, were homeward bound. The 65th Canadian Flotilla, whose motor torpedo boats were British owned, had returned from Ostend to Great Yarmouth for paying off. The frigates and destroyers of the support groups were coming into port on both sides of the Atlantic. The corvettes in the Channel had begun to disperse. *Mayflower* and *Snowberry,* Canadian manned but British owned, were returned to the Royal Navy on May 21. *Baddeck* sailed for Canada on the 24th. By the 15th of June all the other corvettes were on the way home. The minesweepers remained, with over a year's work ahead of them before European waters could be pronounced safe again.

"Make Noise" was the signal of the British commodore commanding at Londonderry as one of the last of the Canadian mid-ocean groups departed under a lowering dawn sky. Readily complying, the ships let loose with guns pointed at the clouds and sirens blowing until the last ounce of steam died down. As they wound their way seaward along the twelve-mile passage of the Foyle, the sun broke through upon the general pandemonium; and the lush rolling fields bordering the narrow inlet shone with all the green of Ireland.

Many of the men were already having a last look at the crops and browsing cattle, the white-washed cottages and the crumbling, green-grown ruins of the old castle, but there was a general rush to the side as the order, "All hands to port for Boom Hall," went out over the loud hailers. Boom Hall had been the wartime home of British and Canadian Wrens who did much of the administrative work at Londonderry. It was well within the sound of sirens from the Foyle, and the spectacle of waving girls lined along the river bank had become as familiar as the sight of ships coming and going. Now the erstwhile "parties" of many a man at many a dance appeared again in an early morning rush; wearing, apparently, what had lain nearest to hand; bell-bottom trousers, raincoats over pyjamas, and, as an officer records in a neat classical reference but not too gallantly, "with curlers recently withdrawn. A gathering of proud but sorrowful Dido's, watching their collective Aeneas disappear from sight."

On down the Foyle the ships passed long lines of U-boats sombrely at anchor; waved to an incoming Canadian group back from a last Gibraltar convoy. The bronzed men passing inward from the south grinned with envious amazement at the sight and sounds of feminine passengers on board the outgoing ships. Eight Canadian Wrens from Londonderry had been granted passage to Greenock as a victory gift. One of them was in her husband's ship and one in the ship commanded by her fiancé. All were in a state of rapturous excitement toward which, as the naval recorder continues: "A kindly tolerance was displayed by the salty veterans. Headquarters-types crowded the bridges, borrowed binoculars and ate the ships' food. Nor did amenities stop there. *Glace Bay* fired eight rockets, four of which worked, and two depth charges to provide thrills for the guests. *Bowmanville* fired some more. The visitors were roasted in the boiler room and boiled in the engine room, as long-suffering engineer officers explained what made the wheels go round. This was the navy at play."

Welcomings in Canada were even warmer than the farewells abroad; but all were short-lived and hastily thrust aside. There remained the other war; and plans already under way for two years were being rushed to completion. Following in the wake of *Uganda*, a navy much different in composition from the one which had fought in the European war was to be sent to the Pacific. In the western ocean anti-submarine warfare played a minor part. Distances were too great for the employment of short-range corvettes. Some frigates could be used for convoy work; the fleet destroyers could be employed as screening units for fast carrier task forces; and the Tribals would perform the same service for cruiser groups which did not operate so far from base. *Prince Robert*, probably the most travelled ship in the Canadian navy, was to serve as an anti-aircraft ship. Two light fleet aircraft carriers to be manned by the Canadian navy were building at Belfast, and were expected to be in commission toward the end of the year. Already a second cruiser, *Ontario*, was in commission. The complete force planned by the Canadian navy for the Pacific was to consist of some sixty ships manned by about 13,500 men. Actually *Uganda* was the only ship to take part in any of the fighting, and that part was a small one.

The cruiser arrived to join the British Pacific Fleet at Sydney, Australia, on March 9, 1945. From there she moved up to the advance base at Leyte in the Philippines. On April 6 she sailed north from Leyte to join British Task Force 57 which was taking part in the widespread naval operations centering about the struggle for Okinawa.

Operation Iceberg, the highly incongruous designation for the Okinawa campaign, involved some new and exceptional hazards for the ships. Particularly was this so in the case of the huge forces assembled by the United States Navy. For days and weeks on end, battleships, carriers, cruisers and many other ships were forced to stand off the island lending the support of their guns and planes to troops fighting ashore.

Comparatively immobile, and with their presence fully known to the Japanese, they had to sustain the full fury of Japanese air attacks. Up to the time of Okinawa the suicide planes—the Kamikaze, or "Divine Wind"— had been something of a rarity. During the long and bitter fight for the island, however, they came on in great numbers, driving in to crash themselves, pilot and all, against the largest battleships and carriers.

Task Force 57, which operated under the command of the United States Fifth Fleet, consisted of the battleships *King George V* and *Howe;* the fleet carriers *Indomitable, Victorious, Illustrious* and *Indefatigable;* five cruisers, of which *Uganda* was one; and twelve destroyers; with many tankers and smaller units. Its task was to prevent the Japanese from supporting their troops on Okinawa by planes flown either from the Sakishima group of islands, to the south of Okinawa, or from Formosa. Operating in the area between the Sakishimas and Okinawa, the force was certain to draw upon itself some of the attacks which would have been directed against the American ships; and this also was part of the plan.

By the time *Uganda* joined Task Force 57 off the Sakishimas, Operation Iceberg was in full progress and many air strikes had already been flown off against airfields in the British target area. Japanese efforts to stage planes onward toward Okinawa had been seriously impeded; and the enemy had not been slow to react. *Illustrious* was already scarred from the blow of a Kamikaze plane which had killed fourteen of her men and wounded sixteen others.

Uganda's work during the first period of the operation was as dull as that of the other cruisers. In the absence of Japanese ships, Iceberg was almost entirely an air show. Several times each day planes rose from the decks of the carriers and bore away toward the Sakishimas or Formosa, returning an hour or so later, frequently with some of their numbers missing, to report air strips pitted, hangars destroyed and planes shot down. The cruisers, stationed about the fleet on arcs at a twelve-mile radius from its centre, had only the

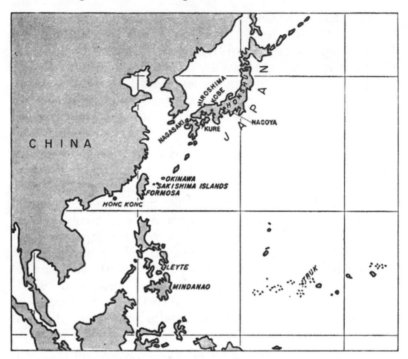

UGANDA IN THE PACIFIC

duty of maintaining radar watch against approaching enemy planes. The monotony of the work was broken for *Uganda* on May 4, when she sailed to take part in a naval bombardment of Sukuma Airfield on Miyako Jima. Next day she returned to the task force for another spell of picket duty, which remained uneventful until May 9.

On that day there came a strong gust of the "Divine Wind." A large force of Kamikazes hurled themselves down through a tremendous anti-aircraft barrage to centre their attack first on *Victorious*. One plane, followed half a minute later by a second, drove straight into the carrier's bridge and ricochetted off into the sea. As smoke and flames rose about *Victorious*, hiding her completely from sight, another plane was seen driving in for the battleship *Howe*, some thirty-five hundred yards from *Uganda*. In this case, however, the massive shield of gunfire thrown up by the battleship and her supporting cruisers was too much. The plane disintegrated in mid-air, showering the sea for hundreds of yards about it with fragments of the explosion.

Eight minutes later *Formidable* was hit by another Kamikaze, and the after part of her flight deck was completely hidden in towering clouds of flame and smoke. Out of the smoke came a steady rattle of gunfire; and a second plane was spun off its course and sent blazing into the water just as it was about to strike the ship. In spite of casualties and superficial damage, both carriers withstood the shock of the attack. Within half an hour the report came from *Victorious*, "Fighting efficiency unimpaired"; and from *Formidable*, "Fires extinguished. Ready for any speed and course."

On June 12, after the conclusion of Operation Iceberg, *Uganda* sailed with a force of British cruisers and the carrier *Implacable* for a strike against Truk. Coming within range of the once-impregnable base on the 14th, a series of air sorties was flown off during the day. At 6.45 the next morning the force commander transferred his flag from *Implacable* to *Uganda* and led his cruisers in for a naval bombardment. For an hour landing fields, shore installations and a seaplane base on Dublin Island were heavily pounded. Then the ships withdrew to rendezvous again with the carrier and screen another series of air strikes which continued though the next day.

By the first week of July the naval war had moved into the very home waters of Japan and the way was being prepared for invasion. "We intend," said Admiral Nimitz, "to deny the enemy the use of the waters surrounding him, even down to the detail of hampering his efforts to get fish out of them." On July 16 *Uganda* sailed with the British Pacific Fleet to rendezvous with the United States Third Fleet; and the combined force bore in through the coastal waters of Japan to attack Honshu. For two days wave after wave of planes went in from the carriers to batter the naval base. It was expected that some of the remaining Japanese ships would be there; but none appeared and although ground defences were still formidable only sporadic air opposition was encountered. The combined fleets turned back down the west coast, moving in full sight of land, brazenly entered the sacred inland sea, and threw their planes against Kure, Kobe and Nagoya. On the 26th, with the operation concluded, the British fleet withdrew toward its fuelling area.

Everywhere the Allied ships sailed almost unopposed. The enemy's few serviceable warships were in hiding. What planes remained to him he seemed to be husbanding as a reserve against invasion. Japan was doomed, the rising sun was sloping westward, but there was still a powerful and fanatically devoted army to be reckoned with. The prospect before the Allies seemed now to be one of organization for great naval landings, and of fierce, prolonged and terribly costly fighting ashore.

At the moment, with tremendous naval force available and with the sweep to the enemy's shores almost completed, individual ships could well be spared. *Uganda* had reached the Pacific before Canadian war policy for the new theatre had finally been determined. Her men were legally entitled to re-volunteer or not, as they chose; and those who did elect to continue were entitled to receive thirty days "Pacific Leave." Not at all unnaturally, they wished to exercise their rights in common with other men in the service; and now was the appropriate time. *Uganda* was ordered to proceed to Esquimalt, re-man the ship with volunteers who had already had their leave, and return to the Pacific.

On July 27, therefore, the cruiser sailed for Eniwetok and from there to Pearl Harbor for onward routing. The plans for a speedy return were, of course, never carried out. All men had seen the long shadow gathering over Japan; but only a few had known how dark and terrible that shadow was. *Uganda* left Pearl Harbor on the evening of August 4, and on August 10 passed through Esquimalt Gate to secure at Ammunition Wharf. For the Canadian navy the second of two wars had now ended; and what remained was aftermath. *Ontario* was in the Red Sea en route to join the British Pacific Fleet, and *Prince Robert* was in Sydney, Australia. Both ships were diverted to Hong Kong at the conclusion of hostilities; and a landing party from *Prince Robert* was the first to enter Sham Shui prison camp, where 370 Canadians were among the 1,500 men awaiting liberation.

On the other side of the world *Puncher* and a few destroyers were ferrying personnel from the United Kingdom. Other destroyers were in harbour or in refit. Many of the frigates had been returned to the Royal Navy or were awaiting disposal. A gallant but melancholy fleet of corvettes lay at Sorel in the St. Lawrence, destined to be scrapped or sold. Only the Bangors continued at a warlike task; clearing the waters of Europe of the mines that infested them by the tens of thousands. The atomic bombs had fallen on Hiroshima and Nagasaki; and the world had fought its way through years of savage darkness into vistas of clouded promise and appalling portent.

CHAPTER EIGHTEEN

"Goodbye, Brothers!

*You were as good a crowd as ever gave back
yell for yell to a westerly gale.*" —CONRAD.

O n August 9, the day before *Uganda* reached Esquimalt on her return journey from the Pacific, a powerful
British task force swept up along the west coast of Japan toward Honshu. Only six days remained of the war; but the
battering of Japanese ships, ports and naval bases was to
continue until the cease-fire. By mid-morning the force had
reached its flying-off position. Planes began taking to the air;
and among the flights circling into position above the carrier
Formidable was one led by a Canadian pilot, Lieutenant
Robert Hampton Gray of Nelson, British Columbia.

Gray was one of some two hundred Canadians serving
with the Royal Navy's air arm as pilots or observers. There
were among that number men who had known longer service
over wider areas than he; and of those now with him in the
Pacific several had already given their lives. Lieutenant D.
W. Baker and Lieutenant C. R. Thurston had been killed in
April during Operation Iceberg; Lieutenant William B. As-
bridge, also flying a plane from *Formidable*, had been shot
down in flames only two days before. Among the veterans of
other theatres, Lieutenant-Commander Digby Cosh, killed a
few months before in a training accident, had commanded
fighter squadrons on many Arctic strikes, had been one of
the first men to lead a squadron of night fighters from the
deck of an escort carrier, and had fought many successful
battles with German aircraft about Atlantic and Murmansk
convoys. Lieutenant-Commander G. C. Edwards had led
another squadron of fighters in the Arctic and the Atlantic;
and had twice received the not altogether welcome "Order
of the Goldfish," signifying that he had crashed in northern
waters. Lieutenant Edmond Jess, then in the Pacific with

Illustrious, had memories going back to the Mediterranean and the worst days of the Malta convoys. Lieutenant Richard Bartlett had emerged only a few months before from a German prison camp where he had spent five years after having been shot down over Norway in 1940; and there were many others who had sailed and flown wherever British naval air-power spread its wings.

Gray was more or less typical of them all. He was twenty-seven years old and war was the only profession he had ever known. Leaving the University of British Columbia when he was twenty-one, he had joined the navy as a rating and had begun his training in England as a candidate for the air arm. Completing his course, and receiving his commission as sub-lieutenant in December 1940, he had returned to Kingston, Ontario, for six months' advanced training. His operational career had taken him first to Kenya in East Africa and later to the fleet carrier *Illustrious.*

In August 1944, he joined *Formidable.* He was by that time a seasoned flier; though five years of war do not seem to have aged him unduly. "Deceptively youthful in appearance," is a comment which appears in one of the reports following him from appointment to appointment. "Might assert himself more," is another. Less official are the comments of his brother officers: "He had to be good to do the things he did and live as long as he did," and, "He was a rare hand in a crap game." Not one of the reports fails to mention in some way the engaging personality which made him a welcome addition to any squadron and to any ship.

During August of 1944, *Formidable* had been operating northward from Scapa against *Tirpitz.* On August 24 and again on August 29 Gray had led his section of fighters in to strafe heavy anti-aircraft positions guarding the Alta Fjord where the battleship was lying. He had pressed his attacks to the hilt both against the batteries and against three Narviks lying at anchor. During the *mêlée* on the 29th his plane had been heavily hit and he had brought it back to *Formidable* with most of its rudder shot away. Before the ship could manœuvre into position for him to land on, he had had to circle for forty-five minutes, in imminent danger of a crash. Nevertheless, when finally waved in he had come down to a neat landing with all the cool-headed competence which seems to have been native to him. He had been mentioned in dispatches reporting on the two actions, "for undaunted courage, skill and determination."

A month or so later *Formidable* went to the Pacific; and her airmen were in the thick of fighting which ranged northward from the Java Sea to the shores of Japan. On July 18, 1945, Gray had led a flight of planes which strafed airfields in the Tokyo area. On the 24th and again on the 28th he had led strikes against the bases along the inland sea, sinking a destroyer in the course of the second mission. A day or so later he had been recommended for the Distinguished Service Cross, and the award was actually to be gazetted on August 18. On the morning of the 9th, however, as his section wheeled away from *Formidable* and bore in toward Onagawa Bay, he had no knowledge either of the recommendation or of the forthcoming award.

The flights approached Onagawa, and as the naval base and harbour came in sight five warships were seen lying at anchor. From them and from the powerful batteries ringing the bay a curtain of anti-aircraft fire, steadily increasing in intensity, began to envelop the planes. Fliers astern of Gray saw him go into a run aimed at one of the destroyers. As his plane swung onto an attacking course a cone of fire from ships and shore batteries centred upon it. A first hit registered; then a second. A moment later streamers of flame began to bleed out astern of the aircraft.

It still held steadily to its course. Weaving and ablaze, it bore down to within fifty yards of the destroyer before its bombs were seen to fall. One struck directly amidships; a second fell on or near alongside the target. The ship sank almost immediately; but before it disappeared Gray's riddled plane had dived into the waters of the bay.

Robert Hampton Gray, V.C., D.S.C., R.C.N.

H.M. Jervois and Her sister ship the New Zealand on the beach

Robert Hampton Gray

The attack had been delivered with the cold precision of an instructor at a training school. It had been made with the skill born of five years' experience; and with complete understanding of the risks involved. It had been made by a man who considered both himself and his plane expendable; who was prepared to trade both for the chance of inflicting greater damage on the enemy; or, to put it another way, who was prepared to offer everything he had for the advancement of the cause he fought for.

In recommending Robert Hampton Gray for the posthumous award of the Victoria Cross, Vice-Admiral Sir Philip Vian, Commander of the Task Force, said:

> I have in mind firstly his brilliant fighting spirit and inspired leadership; an unforgettable example of selfless and sustained devotion to duty without regard to safety of life and limb. The award of this highly prized and highly regarded recognition of valor may fittingly be conferred on a native of Canada, which Dominion has played so great a part in the training of our airmen.

Gray was the one man in the Canadian navy to receive the award of the Victoria Cross during the Second World War. It is perhaps not unfitting that, among a force which acquired 1,677 British and 64 foreign decorations, this highest recognition should have gone to one of the many Canadians who spent much or all of the war apart from the main body of the service. Altogether, some four thousand men served for varying periods "on loan" to the Royal Navy; some of them engaged from time to time on bizarre missions which must have been remote indeed from any conceptions they had formed when they first entered an R.C.N.V.R. division to sign their attestation papers. There was little leave at home for any of them; comradeship, however warm, must have lacked the rich support of a shared background; and the record of their work, merged and lost in that of the greater service, remains only in their own memories or in the occasional curt paragraph of an official report, set down in the dry phrase of war.

Before the end of 1939 three hundred Canadians were training with the Royal Navy in England. By 1940 the number had risen to eight hundred. It increased to a peak of about twenty-four hundred during 1943, and declined again to some fourteen hundred as men on loan rejoined the Canadian service to bring their diversified experience to the larger ships and expanded activities of their own navy. From the first, the role of these men was an active and varied one.

Two hundred of the earliest Canadian arrivals in England served as anti-aircraft gun crews in the merchant ships of the Channel convoys during 1940 and 1941. These were the days when German planes, U-boats and surface craft made a nightmare of the "bomb alleys" along the coast; and the Canadians and the merchant navy gunners fought them off with what scanty weapons were at hand. They were the forerunners of another body of Canadian sailors, fifteen hundred strong, who sailed on all the seas of the world as the DEMS men: naval gunners in defensively equipped merchant ships.

As the coastal routes about the British isles became reasonably secure some of these first Canadians on loan went into British motor torpedo boats, gunboats, and Fairmiles. Some others had preceded them and many more were to follow. By the end of 1941 there were about a hundred Canadians in coastal craft in British waters and another twenty-five in the Mediterranean. Operating both from Alexandria and from Gibraltar they shared considerably in the excursions of those desperate days. On September 15, 1942, a Canadian officer commanding a motor torpedo boat, Lieutenant S. C. Lane, was killed in an abortive sea expedition against Tobruk. Another Canadian, Lieutenant P. Douglas, commanded a Fairmile during the second British evacuation of Tobruk; and lost his life when his ship, one of the last to leave the harbour, came under the fire of advancing German tanks.

Canadians in motor torpedo boats and motor gunboats were in operation off Tunisia, Pantelleria and Sicily during 1943. They operated along the coast of Italy during 1944; and some of their most famous captains—Burke, Fuller, Ladner, Maitland among others—continued in action in the Adriatic, the Ionian and the Aegean Seas up to the time the last spark of German resistance was extinguished.

Canadians on Loan

British Fairmiles commanded by Canadians formed part of the coastal forces at Malta in 1942; and during 1943 Fairmiles commanded by Lieutenant G. W. Stead and Lieutenant A. M. Brodie served with a mine-sweeping flotilla which cleared over four hundred magnetic mines from North African, Sicilian and Italian waters, and was the first to enter the harbours of Catania, Tripoli and Sfax. Other Canadians in Fairmiles took part in the "underground" ferry service which landed stores and agents on several of the Greek islands during the period of German occupation.

The work of another Canadian, Lieutenant-Commander George Douglas Cook of Toronto, who served as bomb-disposal officer at Haifa during 1941 and 1942, is perhaps indicated by the citation which accompanies the award of a bar to the George Medal which he had already won:

A mine was dropped on shore at Haifa and Lieutenant Cook took charge of the disposal of it. He identified it as a type that has a series of devices meant to explode if it is not fully immersed as a mine. Since it had not exploded he suspected that some defect had developed which might rectify itself of its own accord or through incautious interference. Therefore he decided not to risk moving it but to strip it on the spot. The area was ordered to be cleared next day. Some 14,000 people were affected and the site was sandbagged and a tent put up over the mine. The complicated operation of stripping the mine took Lieutenant Cook three and a half hours of patient work, part of it done in total darkness, since this type of mine has an explosive device sensitive to light, with the knowledge that if he made one mistake he would have no warning and no chance of escape.

Work of equal danger and even more macabre in character was done by Commander James Leslie Harries. He was one of the "frog men" called upon to meet the menace of German mines laid in harbours and in shallow waters along the beach fronts. Garbed in diving suits of special type, fitted with long rubber fins on the feet, he and those who worked with him spent hundreds of hours walking and swimming in underwater blackness, groping for mines. Frequently the mines located proved to be of new types whose exact properties were unknown; and when they were considered too dangerous to move the frogmen stripped them underwater, relying only on their sense of touch. Harries had over a year of this grim and secret toil along the beaches of Normandy and in the harbours of northwest Europe.

419

"Goodbye, Brothers!"

Twenty Canadians served in submarines of the Royal Navy; and one of them, Lieutenant-Commander F. H. Sherwood, commanded the submarine *Spiteful* which did good service in the Pacific. Nearly fifty Canadian medical officers were on loan to British ships, some of them during the time of the evacuation from Greece and Crete. In addition to the pilots and observers, a number of Canadians served as fighter direction officers in British carriers. Of the hundreds who served with the Royal Navy on combined operations perhaps the one with the most unusual story to tell was a red-haired, scrawny, fever-ridden spectre who staggered out of a Malayan jungle on August 23, 1945. He was identified as Lieutenant Ian Alcock, missing since June 8, and the supposed source of mysterious signals which had been emanating from the interior fastnesses of the Malayan underground.

Alcock had been a member of one of the British combined operations teams known by the inoffensive name of "pilotage patrols." Highly trained and fantastically equipped, the men of these teams went in by night to reconnoitre Japanese beaches on which Allied landings were later to be made. Submarines brought them within range of the coast. Leaving the submarines in small canoes, each carrying two or three men, they made their way inshore to chart beach gradients, locate under-water obstructions and establish the positions of batteries and strong points. Alcock's experience had included several of these eerie voyages; and the mission of June 8 had been a similar reconnaissance of positions south of Morib on the Malayan coast.

The party had left the submarine in four canoes, one of which included Alcock and his paddler, a British sailor by the name of Turner. As usual, the canoes had gone close inshore; and the reconnaissance men, swimming to shore and prowling along the beaches, had made their observations under the noses of the Japanese sentries. All went according to plan except that the work took about an hour longer than expected. When Alcock returned to his canoe he and Turner realized that it would be impossible to get out to the submarine before daybreak and that they were certain to be detected by Japanese air or surface patrols if they made the attempt.

They decided to beach and hide the canoe, make off into the jungle and try to contact the anti-Japanese underground forces. This they did, heading into thick jungle in the midst of a drenching rain and passing so close to the Japanese camp that they could look through the barracks windows to see soldiers asleep. A trek of forty-eight hours, without sleep and with a minimum of food and water from their emergency ration kits, brought them at last to a post of the underground; and here they found two more of their party already arrived. In this country of jungles, swamps and paddy fields, where Chinese and natives carried on a secret, unremitting struggle with the Japanese, spies abounded and were given terribly short shrift. The four strangers in green-daubed battle dress who claimed to be sailors were received with the greatest suspicion; and their urgent requests to be taken to a post from which they could send out a wireless signal only added to the doubts already held about them.

For two weeks the men were passed on through miles of jungle to post after post. Finally brought to the well-concealed headquarters of a senior Chinese officer, Alcock underwent a long grilling which seemed to convince the officer of his genuineness. He was given permission to write out a signal and was assured that it would be sent. At the same time a rather overpowering proposition was made to him. The Chinese officer controlled a force of some ten thousand natives, trained in the use of small arms but possessing only about a hundred rifles in all. If Alcock would send another signal to Southeast Asia Command, arranging for the dropping of arms and ammunition by aircraft, the officer would carry out any orders transmitted by headquarters through Alcock; and he was certain that he could clear the Japanese out of most of Malaya.

The signal was sent after long discussion between Alcock and the members of his party, all of whom were uneasily aware that they were not in Malaya to form armies.

"Goodbye, Brothers!"

Later some of the arms requested were actually dropped. During the interval of waiting, however, Japanese patrols threatened the jungle hideout and the sailors had to get on the move once more. Weeks of marching and hiding exhausted them. All but Alcock came down with fever or with the agonizing jungle sores which ate away the flesh to the bone. Sick or crippled, they had each to be left behind at one of the posts, where rescue parties were to find them many days later. Meanwhile Alcock, going on by circuitous jungle routes which never seemed to bring him any nearer the promised headquarters, and constantly making long detours to avoid Japanese patrols, began to entertain a thorough distrust for the various guides that were assigned to him. When he came down with fever himself he began to lose what little hope had remained.

He had, however, mistaken the apparent casualness and evasiveness of the underground fighters. One day toward the end of July, as he and his latest guide were resting in an improvised hut, a blank-faced native with no English appeared from a jungle trail and handed him a slip of paper. It proved to be a message from a British detachment already established in Malaya. Alcock's signals had got through to Southeast Asia Command and he was directed to make for Negri Sembilan on the west coast.

Another nightmare journey of more than three weeks, still by way of the underground network through counter networks of Japanese patrols, brought him at last to the sight of salt water and a waiting British ship. Through the haze of a semi-delirium he learned that the last unyielding detachments of Japanese were being mopped up and that the war had been officially over for more than a week.

Along more orthodox lines, a most important contribution made to the Royal Navy by Canadians as a group was in the field of radar. Here civilian scientists in Canadian universities worked step by step with those in England; and Canadian research and training were of very great importance. Before the war was three months old, men were being recruited and trained in Canada for the Royal Navy. A group of nineteen Canadians went to the United Kingdom in May of 1940. Within a month all but six of them were at sea, although at that time only seven British ships were fitted with complete radar sets.

Other drafts from Canada followed the first; and Canadians were for a time actually a majority of the sea-going radar component of the Royal Navy. Thirty out of forty radar officers who completed their training with the Admiralty in 1940 were Canadians. Throughout the war there were about a hundred and twenty-five Canadians serving in some of the largest ships and most responsible radar appointments.

Their service began and continued in the hottest theatres of the war. In October 1940, Sub-Lieutenant G. H. K. Strathey, radar officer in the famous cruiser *Ajax* was killed in an action with three Italian destroyers near Crete. Sub-Lieutenant D. H. Robb and Lieutenant W. F. Page were lost in the Mediterranean during 1941 when cruisers in which they were serving went down. Lieutenant J. W. Loaring was a survivor of the sinking of the cruiser *Fiji*, and lived to become a Lieutenant-Commander and senior instructor for radar officers at Portsmouth. Canadian radar officers served and some of them died with the Malta convoys, in the Indian Ocean and in the Java Sea. Lieutenant Stuart Padden, another Canadian, sailed with the battleship *Prince of Wales*, in charge of the most complicated radar equipment of his day, and was a survivor when the ship was sunk off Malaya.

During the early days of the war in the Mediterranean the famous carrier *Ark Royal*, sailing in escort of convoys, was not equipped with radar. Lieutenant-Commander D. B. Armstrong, a Canadian radar officer in the cruiser *Hermione*, made a distinguished success of controlling "the Ark's" fighters from his own ship. He went on from *Hermione* to the battleship *Anson;* and during the Neptune period became adviser on radar matters to the Allied Naval Commander, Expeditionary Force.

"Goodbye, Brothers!"

Lieutenant-Commander J. C. Maynard, serving in the carrier *Illustrious,* worked out a technique for determining the height of enemy planes which was later adopted by the Admiralty. Lieutenant-Commander H. G. Burchell held the post of Fleet Radar Officer to the Commander-in-Chief of the Eastern Mediterranean Fleet, and later became staff radar officer to the Commander-in-Chief, Mediterranean. Two Canadians, Lieutenant H. Teekman and Lieutenant J. L. Fraser, were attached to the coastal force base at Dover in September 1941 and between then and October of 1943 were reputed to have gone out on every motor torpedo boat mission emanating from that lively command. Scientists as well as adventurers, their journeyings resulted in important improvements to the radar equipment of the small craft.

Canadian radar men were present at almost every action in which the big ships of the Royal Navy took part. At Matapan the guns of the flagship *Valiant* were the first to open fire in the dark on the Italian fleet; and they were laid on from the radar reports of Lieutenant E. J. Apps. There were Canadian radar officers in four of the British ships which took part in the sinking of *Scharnhorst,* and another Canadian, Lieutenant D. Baillie, spent several weeks of the Tunisian campaign driving a wheeled radar "circus" up and down the hills of the North African coast on watch for enemy targets at sea. At least sixteen battleships, twenty-three fleet and escort carriers and thirty-seven cruisers had Canadian radar officers at one time or another during the war.

Such were a few of the offshoots branching out from the main work of the Canadian navy. The story of the parent force has already been sketched; in terms of ships rather than of men, and not without a pang at the omission of gallant and rememberable names. Yet it has seemed more justly told in this way, both for the reader and the seaman. The ship, an empty, echoing steel machine as the commissioning pendant rises above it, takes on, with the passage of time overhead and salt water beneath, a personality of its own, representing and comprehending the many changing companies who have served in it. Bridge and quarterdeck, ward-

424

room and messdecks, echo with remembered voices and remembered storms and perils. Not a voice, not a hand, of all those hands and voices, but has played some part in the long, scrawled history mounting in the log; is worthy of remembrance and is in some way remembered. The story of all, therefore, merges equally into the story of the ships they cursed and loved and boasted of, into whose keeping they gave their lives and for whose preservation their lives were ready forfeit. And, again, the stories of many individual ships melt namelessly into the general pattern of the navy's work.

Canada's naval achievement was a large one for a nation of twelve million people, and many of its aspects were not without brilliance. Yet it derives its principal significance from dogged effort applied in a critical theatre of the war. The pre-war thinking of the layman, and perhaps of the professional, had envisaged the Canadian navy as a small, separate force employed for the protection of Canadian coasts and coastal waters. That conception had to go by the board almost from the first day of the war. The nation's economic life was a portion of the great body of world trade, flung out, living and vulnerable, over every sea. If that body died or became the slave of hostile powers, the Canadian economy, too, would die or be enslaved. So would every other aspect of Canadian life. Trade was a mighty living whole, contributing to the livelihood and well-being of every Canadian. It was the base and nourishment of the civilization we wished to preserve. Its bulwark for generations had been the might of the Royal Navy; and more recently that of the United States. When those tremendous powers were shaken, the possibilities of catastrophe became limitless, and undreamed-of efforts were required to meet the danger. They were forthcoming from Canada in a degree which rivalled the contribution of any other power.

Our naval effort, like the efforts of the other services and in many varied fields, was a revelation of the latent powers of the nation. A force of two thousand men was expanded to nearly ninety thousand, and included in addition six thousand women whose wildest pre-war dreams could never have pictured them in naval uniform. The six ships of 1939 grew to a force of nearly four hundred, with other hundreds of auxiliary craft and with bases, shore establishments and an organization to supply, serve and operate them. Shipyards and training schools sprang up; factories and laboratories, newly created or expanded out of all recognition, turned the products of mines, farms and forests to the needs of the sea war. Brawn and brains combined with limitless energy and confident determination to forge a powerful weapon.

The weapon was much and widely used, often before it was thoroughly tempered. First, as a part of pooled and all too scanty forces, Canadian ships sailed wherever they could best be used to meet immediate needs; from the coastal waters of Canada to the coastal waters of the British Isles when invasion or strangulation threatened; to the Atlantic as the attacks upon the convoys moved westward; to the Mediterranean when a few could be spared and the tide of allied disaster had begun to turn. As strength increased, as the Allied navies found an opportunity to draw breath and organize for a climactic effort, Canadian forces were concentrated again: the navy assumed responsibility for the northwest Atlantic where its strength could best be exercised. That responsibility, assumed in March of 1943, continued to the end of the war and was expanded during the pre-invasion period when all trade convoys crossing the north Atlantic moved under Canadian escort. By that time, too, there was a large surplus of strength over and above the needs of Atlantic convoy; and this was devoted to the huge requirements of the Neptune operation. Here the Canadian contribution ranked next to, though far behind, the contributions of the United Kingdom and the United States, and was more than equal to that of all the other Allied powers combined.

The campaign against the U-boats was won by a precariously narrow margin. During the first four years, when all hopes for the successful outcome of the war centred upon the Atlantic convoy, the lack of a hundred destroyers and corvettes might have defeated those hopes. No man can say and few care to think what might have happened if convoy sailings had been interrupted for a long period, if the flow of fuel and war supplies to the United Kingdom had been cut off, if paralysis and disorganization had settled down upon the Atlantic. They never did. Before the hunting groups came on the scene, before air power reached its full effectiveness, a margin of superiority was maintained just sufficent to stave off the greatest efforts of the U-boats. That marginal force, that very narrow surplus, might and probably would have been scraped up by Britain or the United States, through other efforts and by the acceptance of other consequences which we cannot now measure. In the event, however, it came from Canada.

The six pre-war destroyers all became part of the Atlantic force. Immense effort concentrated upon ship-building began to bear fruit and the corvettes came down the slipways. Ruefully adopted with all their limitations, only acceptable because they could be quickly built and there was nothing else to be had, the little ships still proved capable of performing their sheepdog function about the convoys. The citizen-sailors, fifty per cent of whom came from inland provinces where they had never smelt salt water, were rushed to sea to learn as they fought. The line of the Atlantic was held somehow; until, out of a gallant chaos of early effort, there emerged a force of ships and seamen capable of holding up its head in any naval company.

The development was not based merely on good will and gallantry, however. A hard and saving core of experience had been built up in the pre-war years. The thousand-odd men who came to the navy from the merchant ships were pearls beyond price. The men of the permanent force were the nucleus upon which everything grew and from which everything stemmed. Parcelled out meagrely among many green crews as they took to sea were a few officers and ratings whose long training was invaluable and whose lot was not to be envied. They were the men who had to carry on where their fellows in the bases had left off, supply the

"Goodbye, Brothers!"

vast deficiencies of knowledge remaining after a lad had been hurried through a course of ten or twelve weeks ashore. They had to meet normal seafaring emergencies; they had to train their men and most of their officers to meet them. They had to build confidence and team spirit; and they had to prepare themselves with the others to face the myriad new perils of a changing war. Still others of the permanent force, many of them the men who were most senior and who would have been most valuable at sea, had to spend months and years ashore, providing the direction which no one without their experience could supply.

Around its core of professional experience the bulk of the force had grown, channelled to the sea through twenty-one divisions of the Royal Canadian Naval Volunteer Reserve. The volunteer force, organized in 1922 along the lines of an earlier prototype, had been in a sense a product of desperation. The lean naval budgets of the twenties and thirties permitted neither the acquisition of new ships nor the full operation of the old. The maintenance of any standing force, even remotely adequate, was out of the question. Ruefully, therefore, the navy had transformed itself and its few ships into a training organization. Royal Canadian Naval Volunteer Reserve divisions were opened in the larger cities across the country. Lads in high school or at work or in the universities were prevailed upon to give up week-day evenings to nautical lectures and seemingly futile training periods in barracks echoingly void of equipment. Slender "training pay" was an inducement of sorts, and more potent was the prospect of an annual cruise ranging from two weeks to three months in naval ships.

How much a man learned under such conditions was a proposition for the philosophers; and there must have been scepticism as to the usefulness of such a body in September of 1939. Yet by the time war was declared every division had mustered at full strength. Within a matter of months the advance guard of the "Wavy Navy" was in action; and behind those first men, flowing inward through the divisions, followed eighty thousand more. Few of them, probably, were ever fully trained by exacting naval standards; and certainly in the beginning they were ill-equipped to contend with the vast difficulties and terrifying novelties of modern war. Yet, in the event, necessity had mothered a navy which was, perhaps, more soundly based on the breadth of the whole country than if it had been confined to a class set apart and segregated in the ships and seaports.

The influence of the Royal Navy permeated every fibre of the younger service; strengthening it in the bad times, giving it always the onward, confident thrust of growth. British personnel was available, somehow, when the Canadians had for the moment reached the end of their resources. It was a Royal Navy officer, later transferred to the Canadian Navy, who directed and inspired from the beginning to the end of the war the immense Trade and Convoy organization. Three British "Captain's D" at Newfoundland will be long and gratefully remembered; as will the many men who served from time to time as senior officers of escort groups. Less in the limelight but no less valuable were the specialist officers and ratings supplied to Canadian ships and establishents; men of the engineering branch, signals experts, specialists in asdic, gunnery, torpedo work and in the intricacies of naval administration. Canada, in effect, was given a blank cheque on the Royal Navy. Wherever and whenever help was required for the swift process of expansion, that help was forthcoming.

Another blank cheque given Canada by the Admiralty in September 1939 proved of almost incalculable value. Many retired officers and men of the Royal Navy were living in this country when the war began. Instead of recalling them, the Admiralty informed the Canadian navy that it was free to make use of their services; and the result was a priceless accession of knowledge and experience exactly at a time when those treasures were most needed. Retired captains and commanders, still in vigorous middle age but with memories going back to Jutland and before, got into uniform again and reported to Ottawa. Petty Officers and Leading Seamen, long out of service but still weather-worn, tough and knowledgeable, appeared in the training divisions. All, of course, applied every resource of eloquence, mendacity and persistence to get to sea; but those unable to achieve that dearest goal released younger Canadians from responsible positions ashore.

The ratings formed the backbone of many training and technical establishments; the retired British officers held, during the early days of expansion, a good proportion of the key posts in the higher echelons of command. In the work of ship-building and training, in the organization of the convoys, in the development of anti-submarine techniques, in the arming of merchant ships and to the general building and gearing of the war machine they brought a fund of desperately needed sea lore. Their experience was invaluable, their energy inexhaustible, their good humour almost limitless, and their confidence in the outcome of the war as tranquilly British as that of their grandfathers in the days of Palmerston. It would be hard to over-estimate or acknowledge too generously their contribution to the growth and success of the Canadian navy.

Canadian ships, alone or in company with other ships and planes, sank a total of twenty-seven U-boats during the war. They sank, captured or destroyed forty-two enemy surface ships. The statistics of battle are not unfavourable; yet they are the highlights struck off from a great and moving body and they are dwarfed by the main achievment. During 2,060 days of war, 25,343 merchant ship voyages carried 181,643,180 tons of cargo from North American ports to the United Kingdom under Canadian escort. Over the bridge which the navy helped to build and maintain some 90,000 tons of war supplies passed daily toward the battlefields of Europe.

There was a price to be paid in ships and men. *Fraser,* sunk off the mouth of the Gironde in 1940, was a victim of the days of ruin and disaster for the Allied cause. *Athabaskan* went down during the grim and confident sweeps along Neptune's western flank. *Regina, Alberni* and *Trentonian* were sacrificed during the long and grinding process of supplying the armies in Normandy. *Louisburg* and *Weyburn* were a part of the cost of Torch in the Mediterranean. Eight ships, *Bras D'Or, Otter, Raccoon, Charlottetown, Chedabucto, Shawinigan, Clayoquot* and *Esquimalt*, were sunk in the defence of our own coastal waters, and the six-year battle along the convoy routes of the North Atlantic claimed *Margaree, Levis, Windflower, Spikenard, Ottawa, St. Croix, Valleyfield, Skeena* and *Guysborough*. In these ships and in others, and in actions ranging over most of the world's seas, 1,797 Canadians lost their lives, 319 were wounded and 95 became prisoners of war.

With demobilization the navy was re-built as a peacetime force of less than ten thousand. It was still four times as large as the old permanent force, and there was a heavy emphasis on personnel with high technical qualifications. Obsolete ships were scrapped or sold. A light fleet aircraft carrier, two cruisers, some of the most modern destroyers and a few frigates and auxiliary craft made up the new navy: a nucleus and a mothering ground for seamen whose concerns extend now to the sea floor and the stratosphere.

The men in only for the duration, who made up ninety per cent of the navy of the Second World War, went back to their homes as eagerly as they had come to sea. There was the hard business of earning a living to be faced; they were anxious to make up for the lost years; many who had come from the classroom to the quarterdeck had still to face the hazards of a first job. In the moment of parting, as they lined up before rehabilitation officers and scrawled down pencilled estimates of their gratuities, they were scarcely concerned with the tradition they had bequeathed to the continuing navy. Yet it can hardly be doubted that they look back now with a certain nostalgia and a certain satisfaction.

They shared in an achievement which would have been flatly dismissed as impossible before the war. They contributed to the rescue of a civilization which, however imperfect, is still better than the barbaric darkness with which it was threatened. They were a part, consciously or not, of the mighty drawing-together of the nation; saw on their own bridges, quarterdecks and forecastles its differences of race and outlook melt away in the solvent of common danger. The motivations which brought them to sea were as diverse as most men's, and their ideology was probably no less vague. Certainly they made little high talk in the messdecks and wardrooms of the blacked-out ships. Yet they did, in the fumbling, groping manner of democracies, know their own minds. They fought with a clear conscience, and no men anywhere fought better.

Few of the skills they brought back with them from six years of war could be turned to account in the market-places of peace. There were horrific naval vocabularies to be forgotten and tales whose pungent saltiness required dilution for the benefit of parents and admiring friends. There was much to be changed, much to be learned and done in order to catch up and fit in with a life which had gone on in their absence. There was the essence and the reality of things past and things endured which could never be conveyed to anyone who had not known them. And out of it all there came, one would like to think, an intangible, abiding reward. Perhaps Angus L. MacDonald did not speak too optimistically of the men whose fortunes he had directed for nearly six years when he "ventured to say" in parliament toward the close of his term as naval minister, "that so long as memory lasts the recollection of those great days will be with them and . . . they will carry in their hearts forever the image of a gallant ship and the spell of the great sea."

Appendices

CANADIAN WARSHIPS
SECOND WORLD WAR

ANTI AIRCRAFT CRUISER

LANDING SHIP

ESCORT CARRIER

FAIRMILE

M.T.B. "G"

M.T.B. "D"

L.C.A.

L.C.M.

L.C.I. (L)

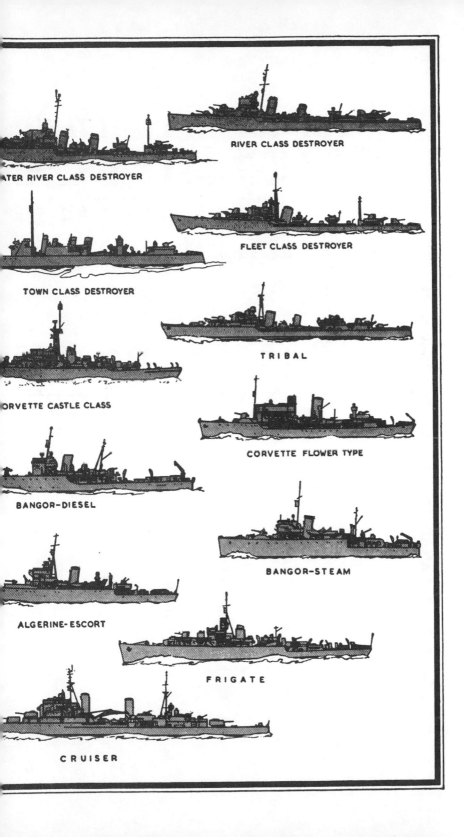

RIVER CLASS DESTROYER

ATER RIVER CLASS DESTROYER

FLEET CLASS DESTROYER

TOWN CLASS DESTROYER

TRIBAL

ORVETTE CASTLE CLASS

CORVETTE FLOWER TYPE

BANGOR-DIESEL

BANGOR-STEAM

ALGERINE-ESCORT

FRIGATE

CRUISER

APPENDIX I

ROYAL CANADIAN NAVAL VOLUNTEER RESERVE

DIVISIONS 1939-1945

Division	Ship	Commanding Officer	From	To
Calgary, Alta.	HMCS TECUMSEH	Lt. R. Jackson, R.C.N.V.R.	1 Sept., 1939	31 Mch., 1940
		Lt. R. D. deWinton, R.C.N.V.R.	1 Apl., 1940	31 Dec., 1941
		Lt. H. D. Bulmer, R.C.N.V.R.	1 Jan., 1942	29 June, 1943
		A/Lt. Cdr. D. R. Dattels, R.C.N.V.R.	30 June, 1943	30 Aug., 1945
Charlottetown, P.E.I.	HMCS QUEEN CHARLOTTE	Lt. Cdr. J. J. Connolly, R.C.N.V.R.	1 Sept., 1939	3 Sept., 1940
		Lt. K. Birtwistle, R.C.N.V.R.	4 Sept., 1940	28 Jan., 1942
		A/Lt. Cdr. E. S. Cope, R.C.N.V.R.	29 Jan., 1942	22 Mch., 1942
		Lt M. G. McCarthy, R.C.N.V.R.	23 Mch., 1942	14 May, 1943
		Lt. C. P. MacKenzie, R.C.N.V.R.	1 May, 1943	12 Apl., 1946
Edmonton, Alta.	HMCS NONSUCH	Lt. Cdr. E. P. Shaver, R.C.N.R.	1 Sept., 1939	11 Apl., 1941
		Lt. C. S. Glassco, R.C.N.V.R.	12 Apl., 1941	30 May, 1942
		Lt. G. L. Crawford, R.C.N.V.R.	1 June, 1942	9 Jan., 1943
		Lt. J. A. Dawson, R.C.N.V.R.	10 Jan., 1943	30 June, 1945
Esquimalt, B.C.	HMCS MALAHAT	Lt. D. S. Scott, R.C.N.V.R.	15 Jan., 1944	15 Jan., 1946
Halifax, N.S.	HMCS HALIGONIAN	Cdr. J. P. Connolly, M.C., R.C.N.V.R.	5 Sept., 1939	1 Dec., 1939
		Lt. W. E. Flavelle, R.C.N.V.R.	1 Oct., 1943	1 Mch., 1944
		Lt. C. S. Boucher, R.C.N.V.R.	1 Mch., 1944	30 Nov., 1944
		A/Lt. Cdr. H. S. C. Wilson, R.C.N.V.R.	1 Dec., 1944	19 Apl., 1945
		Lt. Cdr. J. C. Mackintosh, R.C.N.V.R.	20 Apl., 1945	16 Jan., 1946
Hamilton, Ont.	HMCS STAR	Lt. J. C. Hart, R.C.N.V.R.	1 Sept., 1939	9 June, 1940
		Lt. W. R. Morrison, R.C.N.V.R.	10 June, 1940	11 Nov., 1940
		Lt. F. F. Waterman, R.C.N.V.R.	12 Nov., 1940	14 Feb., 1941
		Lt. W. H. B. Thomson, R.C.N.V.R.	15 Feb., 1941	30 Apl., 1941
		Lt. J. McFetrick, R.C.N.V.R.	1 May, 1941	19 Feb., 1944
		Lt. Cdr. R. Jackson, R.C.N.V.R.	20 Feb., 1944	28 Mch., 1945
		A/Lt. Cdr. C. S. Glassco, R.C.N.V.R	29 Mch., 1945	17 Jan., 1946

			From	To
Kingston, Ont.	HMCS CATTARAQUI	Lt. W. C. Rigney, R.C.N.V.R.	20 Sept., 1939	2 July, 1940
		Lt. W. H. B. Thomson, R.C.N.V.R.	3 July, 1940	7 Feb., 1941
		Lt. S. T. Hill, R.C.N.V.R.	8 Feb., 1941	14 Apl., 1943
		Lt. G. E. Kernohan, R.C.N.V.R.	15 Apl., 1943	9 Mch., 1944
		A/Lt. Cdr. H. J. Plaxton, R.C.N.V.R.	10 Mch., 1944	5 Dec., 1944
		A/Lt. Cdr. W. C. Rigney, R.C.N.V.R.	6 Dec., 1944	2 Aug., 1945
London, Ont.	HMCS PREVOST	Lt. E. E. Hart, R.C.N.V.R.	1 Sept., 1939	9 June, 1940
		Lt. J. R. Hunter, R.C.N.V.R.	10 June, 1940	1 Jan., 1944
		Lt. F. N. Carmichael, R.C.N.V.R.	2 Jan., 1944	24 Mch., 1946
Montreal, Que.	HMCS CARTIER	Lt. P. S. Major, R.C.N.V.R.	1 Sept., 1939	15 Jan., 1941
		A/Lt. Cdr. M. R. Campbell, R.C.N.V.R.	1 Apl., 1942	6 Sept., 1944
		A/Cdr. J. McFetrick, R.C.N.V.R.	7 Sept., 1944	15 Sept., 1945
Montreal, Que.	HMCS DONNACONA	Cdr. E. R. Brock, R.C.N.V.R.	1 Sept., 1939	30 Sept., 1940
		Lt. Cdr. P. W. Earl, R.C.N.V.R.	1 Oct., 1940	31 Mch., 1942
		A/Lt. Cdr. M. R. Campbell, R.C.N.V.R.	1 Apl., 1942	15 Nov., 1942
		Lt. A. R. Webster, R.C.N.V.R.	16 Nov., 1942	26 Dec., 1942
		A/Lt. Cdr. M. R. Campbell, R.C.N.V.R.	27 Dec., 1942	6 Sept., 1944
		A/Cdr. J. McFetrick, R.C.N.V.R.	7 Sept., 1944	15 Sept., 1945
Ottawa, Ont.	HMCS CARLETON	Lt. F. H. Sherwood, R.C.N.V.R.	15 Sept., 1939	9 June, 1940
		Lt. T. D. McGee, R.C.N.V.R.	10 June, 1940	24 July, 1940
		Lt. Cdr. W. J. F. Hose, R.C.N.V.R.	25 July, 1940	30 Apl., 1941
		Lt. C. A. E. White, R.C.N.V.R.	1 May, 1941	3 May, 1942
		Cdr. W. G. Shedden, R.C.N.V.R.	4 May, 1942	21 May, 1942
		Lt. D. C. Mackintosh, R.C.N.V.R.	23 Nov., 1942	30 Nov., 1942
		Lt. J. G. Fraser, R.C.N.V.R.	1 Dec., 1942	29 Jan., 1943
		Lt. H. C. McGowan, R.C.N.V.R.	30 Jan., 1943	16 Feb., 1943
		Lt. S. P. A. Redgrave, R.C.N.V.R.	10 Apl., 1943	8 Aug., 1943
		Lt. A. A. Hargraft, R.C.N.V.R.	9 Aug., 1943	14 Oct., 1944
		Lt. G. L. Bott, R.C.N.V.R.	15 Oct., 1944	18 Apl., 1946
Port Arthur, Ont.	HMCS GRIFFON	Lt. J. M. Hughes, R.C.N.V.R.	1 Sept., 1939	30 Apl., 1941
		Lt. F. A. Bryan, R.C.N.V.R.	1 May, 1941	30 Aug., 1943
		Lt. H. S. C. Wilson, R.C.M.V.R.	1 Sept., 1943	28 Sept., 1944
		A/Lt. Cdr. W. Johnson, R.C.N.V.R.	1 Nov., 1944	14 Sept., 1945
Prince Rupert, B.C.	HMCS CHATHAM	Lt. O. G. Stuart, R.C.N.V.R.	1 Sept., 1939	14 June, 1940

ROYAL CANADIAN NAVAL VOLUNTEER RESERVE DIVISIONS 1939-1945—*Continued*

Division	Ship	Commanding Officer	From	To
Quebec, P.Q.	*HMCS MONTCALM*	Lt. Cdr. F. A. Price, R.C.N.V.R.	1 Sept., 1939	9 Aug., 1940
		Lt. K. L. Johnson, R.C.N.V.R.	10 Aug., 1940	30 Sept., 1942
		Lt. R. M. S. St. Laurent, R.CN.V.R.	1 Oct., 1942	29 June, 1943
		A/Lt. Cdr. E. F. Noel, R.C.N.V.R.	30 June, 1943	30 Mch., 1946
Regina, Sask.	*HMCS QUEEN*	Lt. Cdr. D. A. Grant, R.C.N.V.R.	1 Sept., 1939	30 Sept., 1940
		Lt. Cdr. A. C. Ellison, R.C.N.V.R.	1 Oct., 1940	2 Jan., 1943
		Lt. Cdr. N. L. Pickersgill,R.C.N.V.R.	3 Jan., 1943	11 Dec., 1943
		A/Lt. Cdr. F. C. Aggett, R.C.N.V.R.	12 Dec., 1943	15 June, 1945
		A/Cdr. N. E. Whitmore, R.C.N.V.R.	18 June, 1945	10 Apl., 1946
Saint John, N.B.	*HMCS BRUNSWICKER*	Lt. F. Brock, R.C.N.V.R.	1 Sept., 1939	15 May, 1940
		Cdr. P. B. Cross, R.C.N.V.R.	16 May, 1940	7 Mch., 1941
		Lt. Cdr. F. P. Coombs, R.C.N.V.R.	8 Mch., 1941	15 Sept., 1942
		Lt. G. A. Brown, R.C.N.V.R.	16 Sept., 1942	6 June, 1944
		A/Lt. Cdr. F. R. K. Naftel, R.C.N.V.R.	7 June, 1944	29 Sept., 1944
		A/Lt. Cdr. G. M. Butler, R.C.N.V.R.	30 Sept., 1944	4 Oct., 1945
Saskatoon, Sask.	*HMCS UNICORN*	Lt. Cdr. H. W. Balfour, R.C.N.V.R.	1 Sept., 1939	9 June, 1940
		Lt. C. F. R. Wentz, R.C.N.V.R.	10 June, 1940	31 Dec., 1941
		Lt. R. M. Wallace, R.C.N.V.R.	1 Jan., 1942	7 May, 1942
		Lt. Cdr. C. A. E. White, R.C.N.V.R.	7 May, 1942	15 July, 1945
Toronto, Ont.	*HMCS YORK*	Lt. Cdr. W. G. Shedden, R.C.N.V.R.	1 Sept., 1939	14 Oct., 1940
		Lt. Cdr. A. C. Turner, R.C.N.V.R.	15 Oct., 1940	14 June, 1942
		A/Lt. Cdr. G. C. Bernard, R.C.N.V.R.	15 June, 1942	15 Feb., 1943
		Capt. E. R. Brock, R.C.N.V.R.	1 Dec., 1942	1 Nov., 1945
		(Commanding Officer Reserve Divisions)		
Vancouver, B.C.	*HMCS DISCOVERY*	Lt. J. V. Brock, R.C.N.V.R.	1 Sept., 1939	10 Nov., 1939
		Lt. Cdr. H. R. Wade, R.C.N.V.R.	11 Nov., 1939	12 Feb., 1941
		Cdr. N. C. S. Gooch, R.C.N. (Temp.)	13 Feb., 1941	30 Apl., 1941
		Lt. W. H. Richardson, R.C.N.V.R.	1 May, 1941	31 May, 1942
		Lt. C. S. Glassco, R.C.N.V.R.	1 June, 1942	29 June, 1943
		A/Lt. Cdr. K. C. McRae, R.C.N.V.R.	30 June, 1943	16 Aug., 1947

			Appointed	Relieved
Windsor, Ont.	*HMCS HUNTER*	Lt. J. H. Marshall, R.C.M.V.R.	21 Dec., 1939	30 Sept., 1940
		Lt. G. N. Bruce, R.C.N.V.R.	1 Oct., 1940	5 Sept., 1942
		Lt. R. K. Baker, R.C.N.V.R.	6 Sept., 1942	24 Sept., 1942
		Lt. G. N. Bruce, R.C.N.V.R.	25 Sept., 1942	31 Dec., 1942
		Lt. A. R. Webster, R.C.N.V.R.	1 Jan., 1943	17 Dec., 1945
Winnipeg, Man.	*HMCS CHIPPAWA*	Lt. Cdr. C. R. Frayer, R.C.N.V.R.	1 Sept., 1939	5 Apl., 1940
		Cdr. H. G. Nares, R.C.N.V.R.	6 Apl., 1940	14 Mch., 1941
		A/Cdr. E. T. C. Orde, R.C.N.V.R.	15 Mch., 1941	15 Feb., 1943
		A/Lt. Cdr. G. F. McCrimmon, R.C.N.V.R.	1 Apl., 1943	13 Mch., 1944
		A/Lt. Cdr. G. E. Kernohar, R.C.N.V.R.	14 Mch., 1944	14 July, 1945

Royal Canadian Navy

PRINCIPAL COMMANDS AND APPOINTMENTS

SEPTEMBER 1939

THE NAVAL STAFF

Chief of the Naval Staff............Rear-Admiral Percy W. Nelles

Deputy Chief of the Naval Staff.....Captain Leonard W. Murray

Director of Naval Intelligence.......Commander Eric S. Brand, R.N.

Director of Personnel.............Commander Cuthbert R. H. Taylor

Director of Plans.................Commander Frank L. Houghton

Director of Operations............Commander Joseph W. R. Roy

Director of Mercantile Movements...Commander Donald W. Farmer

Director of Naval Engineering......Engineer Captain Angus D. M. Curry

Naval Secretary..................Paymaster Captain Marie J. R. O. Cossette

Director of Naval Stores...........Edward Lisle, Esq.

PRINCIPAL BASES AND ESTABLISHMENTS

Commanding Officer, Atlantic Coast
HMCS Stadacona..............Captain H. E. Reid, R.C.N.

Commanding Officer, Pacific Coast
HMCS Naden.................Captain V. G. Brodeur, R.C.N.

Naval Officer-in-Charge, Saint John, N.B.
HMCS Captor................Commander J. E. W. Oland, D.S.C., R.C.N.

Naval Officer-in-Charge, Sydney, C.B.
HMCS Protector.............Commander M. Goolden, D.S.C., R.C.N.

Naval Officer-in-Charge, Quebec, P.Q.
HMCS Chaleur...............Commander R. L. Jermain, R.C.N.

Naval Officer-in-Charge, Vancouver, B.C.
HMCS Burrard..............Commander B. L. Johnson, D.S.O., R.C.N.

DECEMBER 1940

Naval Minister

Honourable Angus L. MacDonald

THE NAVAL STAFF

Chief of the Naval Staff .... Rear-Admiral Percy W. Nelles

Deputy Chief of the Naval Staff ..... Captain Howard E. Reid

Director of Naval Intelligence .... Commander Eric S. Brand, R.N.

Director of Personnel .... Captain Harold T. W. Grant

Director of Naval Ordnance .... Commander Rupert W. Wood

Director of Plans .... Commander Frank L. Houghton

Director of Operations .... Commander Roger E. S. Bidwell

Director of Mercantile Movements ... Commander Donald W. Farmer, R.C.N.

Engineer-in-Chief .... Engineer Captain Angus D. M. Curry

Director of Technical Division ...... Engineer Commander John F. Bell

Naval Secretary .... Paymaster Captain Marie J. R. O. Cossette

Director of Naval Stores .... Edward Lisle, Esq.

Acting Director of Naval Stores ..... Allan B. Coulter, Esq.

PRINCIPAL BASES AND ESTABLISHMENTS

Commanding Officer, Atlantic Coast
HMCS *Stadacona* .... Commodore 1st Cl. G. C. Jones, R.C.N.

Commanding Officer, Pacific Coast
HMCS *Naden* .... Commodore 1st Cl. W. J. R. Beech, R.C.N.

Naval Officer-in-Charge, Saint John, N.B.
HMCS *Captor* .... Commander J. E. W. Oland, D.S.C., R.C.N.

Naval Officer-in-Charge, Sydney, N.S.
HMCS *Protector* .... Captain M. Goolden, D.S.C., R.C.N.

Naval Officer-in-Charge, Quebec, P.Q.
HMCS *Chaleur* .... Captain R. L. Jermain, R.C.N.

Naval Officer-in-Charge, Montreal, P.Q.
HMCS *Hochelaga* .... Commander C. J. Stuart, O.B.E., R.C.N.R.

Naval Officer-in-Charge, Prince Rupert
HMCS *Chatham* .... Commander G. Borrie, R.C.N.R.

Naval Officer-in-Charge, Vancouver
HMCS *Burrard* .... Commander B. L. Johnson, D.S.O., R.C.N.

Canadian Naval Attaché,
Washington, D.C. .... Commodore 1st Cl. V. G. Brodeur, R.C.N.

DECEMBER 1941

Naval Minister

Honourable Angus L. MacDonald

THE NAVAL STAFF

Chief of the Naval Staff............Vice-Admiral Percy W. Nelles

Deputy Chief of the Naval Staff.....Commodore Howard E. Reid

Director of Personnel..............Captain Harold T. W. Grant

*Director of Naval Intelligence
and Trade*.....................Captain Eric S. Brand, R.C.N.

Director of the Technical Division...Commander Godfrey M. Hibbard

Director of Naval Ordnance.........Commander Rupert W. Wood

Director of Plans and Signals.......Commander Frank L. Houghton

Director of Operations.............Commander Horatio N. Lay

Engineer-in-Chief.................Engineer Captain George L. Stephens

Naval Secretary..................Paymaster Captain Marie J. R. O. Cossette

Director of Naval Stores...........Edward Lisle, Esq.

Acting Director of Naval Stores.....Allan B. Coulter, Esq.

PRINCIPAL BASES AND ESTABLISHMENTS

*Commanding Officer, Atlantic Coast
HMCS Stadacona*..............Commodore 1st Cl. G. C. Jones, R.C.N.

*Commodore Commanding Newfoundland Force
HMCS Avalon*................Commodore 1st Cl. L. W. Murray, R.C.N.

*Captain Commanding Canadian Ships and Establishments in United Kingdom
HMCS Niobe*.................Captain C. R. H. Taylor, R.C.N.

*Commanding Officer, Pacific Coast
HMCS Naden*.................Commodore 1st Cl. W. J. R. Beech, R.C.N.

*Naval Officer-in-Charge, Saint John, N.B.
HMCS Captor*................Captain J. E. W. Oland, D.S.C., R.C.N.

*Naval Officer-in-Charge, Sydney, N.S.
HMCS Protector*.............Captain M. Goolden, D.S.C., R.C.N.

*Naval Officer-in-Charge, Quebec, P.Q.
HMCS Chaleur*...............Commander L. J. M. Gauvreau, R.C.N.

*Naval Officer-in-Charge, Montreal, P.Q.
HMCS Hochelaga*............Commander C. J. Stuart, O.B.E., R.D., R.C.N.R.

*Naval Officer-in-Charge, Gaspe, P.Q.
HMCS Fort Ramsay*..........Commander H. G. Nares, R.C.N.V.R.

442

Depot Ship, Esquimalt, B.C.
  HMCS Givenchy..............Commander J. McCulloch, R.C.N.

Naval Officer-in-Charge, Shelburne, N.S.
  HMCS Shelburne.............Commander V. P. Alleyne, R.C.N.

Signal School, St. Hyacinthe, P.Q.
  HMCS St. Hyacinthe..........Commander A. P. Musgrave, R.C.N.

Royal Canadian Naval College, Victoria, B.C.
  HMCS Royal Roads...........Commander J. M. Grant, R.C.N.

Depot Ship, Ottawa, Ont.
  HMCS Bytown...............Commander H. N. Lay, R.C.N.

Depot Ship, Halifax, N.S.
  HMCS Venture..............Captain W. B. Creery, R.C.N.

Chief Examination Officer, Mulgrave, N.S.
  HMCS Mulgrave ....Lieut.-Commander G. A. Burton, R.C.N.R.

Depot Ship, Destroyers and Escort Vessels, Halifax, N.S.
  HMCS Sambro...............Commander G. R. Miles, R.C.N.

Officers' Training Establishment, Halifax, N.S.
  HMCS Kings................Commander A. M. Hope, R.C.N.

Canadian Naval Attaché,
  Washington, D.C............Commodore 1st Cl. V. G. Brodeur, R.C.N.

DECEMBER 1942

Naval Minister

Honourable Angus L. MacDonald

THE NAVAL BOARD

First Naval Member and
  Chief of the Naval Staff..........Vice-Admiral Percy W. Nelles, C.B.

Second Naval Member and
  Vice-Chief of the Naval Staff......Rear-Admiral George C. Jones

Third Naval Member and
  Chief of Naval Personnel........Captain Edmond R. Mainguy, O.B.E.

Fourth Naval Member and Chief of
  Naval Equipment and Supply.....Captain Godfrey M. Hibbard

Fifth Naval Member and
Chief of Naval Engineering and
  Construction...................Engineer Captain George L. Stephens, C.B.E.

Deputy Minister for Naval Services..W. Gordon Mills, Esq.

Secretary to the Naval Board........Paymaster Lieutenant-Commander
                                    Robert Pennington, R.C.N.V.R.

443

THE NAVAL STAFF

Chief of the Naval Staff............Vice-Admiral Percy W. Nelles, C.B.

Vice-Chief of the Naval Staff.......Rear-Admiral George C. Jones

Director of Naval Intelligence......Lieut. Charles H. Little, R.C.N.V.R.

Director of Plans.................Commander Henry G. DeWolf

Director of Trade.................Captain Eric S. Brand, R.N.

Director of Operations............Commander Horatio N. Lay, O.B.E.

Director of Signals...............Commander George A. Worth

PRINCIPAL BASES AND ESTABLISHMENTS

Commanding Officer, Atlantic Coast
  HMCS STADACONA.......Rear-Admiral L. W. Murray, R.C.N.

Flag Officer, Newfoundland Force
  HMCS Avalon...............Commodore H. E. Reid, R.C.N.

Captain Commanding Canadian Ships and Establishments in United Kingdom
  HMCS Niobe...............Captain R. I. Agnew, O.B.E., R.C.N.

Commanding Officer, Pacific Coast
  HMCS Burrard..............Commodore W. J. R. Beach, R.C.N.

Naval Officer-in-Charge, Saint John, N.B.
  HMCS Captor...............Captain C. J. Stuart, O.B.E., R.C.N.R.

Naval Officer-in-Charge, Sydney, N.S.
  HMCS Protector............Captain C. M. R. Schwerdt, C.V.O., R.N.

Naval Officer-in-Charge, Quebec, P.Q.
  HMCS Chaleur..............Captain L. J. M. Gauvreau, R.C.N.

Naval Officer-in-Charge, Montreal, P.Q.
  HMCS Hochelaga...........Captain J. E. W. Oland, D.S.C., R.C.N.

Naval Officer-in-Charge, Prince Rupert, B.C.
  HMCS Chatham.............Commander A. H. Reed, R.C.N.R.

Naval Officer-in-Charge, Gaspe, P.Q.
  HMCS Fort Ramsay..........Commander P. B. German, R.C.N.

Naval Officer-in-Charge, Esquimalt, B.C.
  HMCS Givenchy.............Captain M. Goolden, R.C.N.

Naval Officer-in-Charge, Shelburne, N.S.
  HMCS Shelburne............Commander C. D. Donald, R.C.N.

Training Establishment, Cornwallis, N.S.
  HMCS Cornwallis...........Commander G. McClintock, R.C.N.

Signal School, St. Hyacinthe, P.Q.
  HMCS St. Hyacinthe.........Commander A. P. Musgrave, R.C.N.

Royal Canadian Naval College, Victoria, B.C.
  HMCS Royal Roads..........Commander J. M. Grant, R.C.N.

R.C.N. Barracks, Esquimalt, B.C.
HMCS Naden................Captain F. G. Hart, R.C.N.

Depot Ship, Ottawa, Ont.
HMCS Bytown..............Lieut.-Commander E. S. Cope, R.C.N.V.R.

Officers' Training Establishment, Halifax, N.S.
HMCS Kings...............Commander A. M. Hope, R.C.N.

Naval Member Canadian Joint Staff
Washington, D.C..............Rear-Admiral V. G. Brodeur, R.C.N.

Canadian Naval Attaché
Washington, D.C..............Commander H. G. Nares, R.C.N.V.R.

W.R.C.N.S. Establishment, Galt, Ont.
HMCS Conestoga.............Chief Officer D. Isherwood, W.R.C.N.S.

DECEMBER 1943

Naval Minister

Honourable Angus L. MacDonald

THE NAVAL BOARD

First Naval Member and
Chief of the Naval Staff..........Vice-Admiral Percy W. Nelles, C.B.

Second Naval Member and
Vice-Chief of the Naval Staff......Read-Admiral George C. Jones, C.B.

Third Naval Member and
Chief of Naval Personnel........Captain Edmond R. Mainguy, O.B.E.

Fourth Naval Member and Chief of
Naval Equipment and Supply.....Commander Edmund Johnstone, O.B.E.

Fifth Naval Member and
Chief of Naval Engineering
and Construction...............Engineer Rear-Admiral George L. Stephens, C.B.E.

Financial and Civil Member
and Deputy Minister for
Naval Services.................W. Gordon Mills, C.M.G., Esq.

Secretary to the Naval Board.......Paymaster Commander Joseph Jeffrey, R.C.N.V.R.

THE NAVAL STAFF

Chief of the Naval Staff............Vice-Admiral Percy W. Nelles, C.B.

Vice-Chief of the Naval Staff.......Rear-Admiral George C. Jones, C.B.

Assistant Chief of the Naval Staff...Captain Wallace B. Creery

Director of Operations............Commander George H. Griffiths, O.B.E.

Director of Plans................Captain George R. Miles, O.B.E.

Director of Warfare and Training...Captain K. F. Adams

Director of Trade Division.........Captain Eric S. Brand, O.B.E.

Director of Signals Division.......Commander George A. Worth

Director of Naval Intelligence.......Lieut.-Commander (S.B.) Charles H. Little,
R.C.N.V.R.

Hydrographer....................Captain Donald W. Farmer, F.R.G.S.

PRINCIPAL BASES AND ESTABLISHMENTS

Commander-in-Chief, Canadian North West Atlantic
  HMCS Stadacona.............Rear-Admiral L. W. Murray, C.B.E., R.C.N.

Flag Officer, Newfoundland Force
  HMCS Avalon...............Commodore 1st Cl. C. R. H. Taylor, R.C.N.

Senior Canadian Naval Officer, London
  HMCS Niobe................Captain F. L. Houghton, R.C.N.

Commanding Officer, Pacific Coast
  HMCS Burrard..............Rear-Admiral V. G. Brodeur, C.B.E., R.C.N.

Naval Officer-in-Charge, Saint John, N.B.
  HMCS Captor...............Captain C. J. Stuart, O.B.E., R.D., R.C.N.R.

Naval Officer-in-Charge, Sydney, N.S.
  HMCS Protector............Captain C. M. R. Schwerdt, C.V.O., C.B.E., R.N.

Naval Officer-in-Charge, Quebec, P.Q.
  HMCS Chaleur..............Captain L. J. M. Gauvreau, R.C.N.

Naval Officer-in-Charge, Montreal, P.Q.
  HMCS Hochelaga............Captain J. E. W. Oland, D.S.C., R.C.N.

Naval Officer-in-Charge, Prince Rupert, B.C.
  HMCS Chatham..............Commander C. M. Cree, R.C.N.

Naval Officer-in-Charge, Gaspe, P.Q.
  HMCS Fort Ramsay..........Lieut.-Commander G. C. Bernard, R.C.N.V.R.

Naval Officer-in-Charge, Esquimalt, B.C.
  HMCS Givenchy.............Captain M. Goolden, D.S.C., R.C.N.

Naval Officer-in-Charge, Shelburne, N.S.
  HMCS Shelburne............Captain C. D. Donald, R.C.N.

Training Establishment, Cornwallis, N.S.
  HMCS Cornwallis...........Captain J. C. I. Edwards, R.C.N.

Signal School, St. Hyacinthe, P.Q.
  HMCS St. Hyacinthe.........Captain A. P. Musgrave, R.C.N.

Royal Canadian Naval College, Victoria, B.C.
  HMCS Royal Roads..........Captain J. M. Grant, C.B.E., R.C.N.

R.C.N. Barracks, Esquimalt, B.C.
    HMCS Naden................Commander R. Jackson, R.C.N.R.

Depot Ship, Ottawa, Ont.
    HMCS Bytown...............Lieut.-Commander J. H. Rooney, R.C.N.V.R.

Officers' Training Establishment, Halifax, N.S.
    HMCS Kings................Commander C. H. Bonnycastle, R.C.N.V.R.

Depot Ship, Halifax, N.S.
    HMCS Venture..............Captain J. A. Heenan, R.D., R.C.N.R.

Naval Member Canadian Joint Staff
    Washington, D.C............Rear-Admiral H. E. Reid, C.B., R.C.N.

Canadian Naval Attaché,
    Washington, D.C...............Captain E. C. Sherwood, R.C.N.

W.R.C.N.S. Establishment, Galt, Ont.
    HMCS Conestoga............Lieut.-Commander I. J. Macneill, W.R.C.N.S.

W.R.C.N.S. Training Course, Ottawa, Ont.
    Ottawa.....................Lieutenant A. E. Graham, W.R.C.N.S.

DECEMBER 1944

Naval Minister

Honourable Angus L. MacDonald

THE NAVAL BOARD

Deputy Minister of National
    Defence for Naval Services.......W. Gordon Mills, C.M.G., Esq.

Chief of the Naval Staff............Vice-Admiral George C. Jones, C.B.

Chief of Naval Personnel..........Commander Humphrey McMaster

Chief of Naval Equipment
    and Supply....................Commander Geoffrey B. Hope, O.B.E.

Chief of Naval Engineering
    and Construction................Engineer Rear-Admiral George L. Stephens, C.B.E.

Chief Staff Officer Reserves........Captain Paul B. Cross, V.D., R.C.N.V.R.

Secretary to the Naval Board.......Paymaster Commander Joseph Jeffrey, R.C.N.V.R.

THE NAVAL STAFF

Chief of the Naval Staff............Vice-Admiral George C. Jones, C.B.

Assistant Chief of the Naval Staff...Captain Henry G. DeWolf, D.S.O., D.S.C.

Director of Operations............Commander David K. Laidlaw

Director of Plans.................Commander Herbert S. Rayner, D.S.C.

447

Director of Warfare and Training...Lieutenant-Commander Duncan L. Raymond

Director of Trade Division.........Captain Eric S. Brand, O.B.E.

Director of Signals Division.......Commander George A. Worth

Director of Naval Intelligence......Commander (S.B.) C. H. Little, R.C.N.V.R.,

Hydrographer....................Captain Donald W. Farmer, F.R.G.S.

Operational Intelligence Centre......Commander John M. B. P. deMarbois, O.B.E., R.D.

Director of Naval Air Division......Lieutenant-Commander John S. Stead

Director of Operational Research....Electrical Commander John H. L. Johnstone, O.B.E., R.C.N.V.R.

PRINCIPAL BASES AND ESTABLISHMENTS

Commander-in-Chief Canadian North West Atlantic
  HMCS Stadacona.............Rear-Admiral L. W. Murray, C.B., C.B.E., R.C.N.

Flag Officer, Newfoundland Force
  HMCS Avalon...............Commodore 1st Cl. C. R. H. Taylor, C.B.E., R.C.N.

Head of the Canadian Naval Mission Overseas
  HMCS Niobe...............Vice-Admiral P. W. Nelles, C.B., R.C.N.

Commanding Officer, Pacific Coast
  HMCS Burrard...............Rear-Admiral V. G. Brodeur, C.B.E., R.C.N.

Naval Officer-in-Charge, Saint John, N.B.
  HMCS Captor...............Captain C. J. Stuart, O.B.E., R.D., R.C.N.R.

Naval Officer-in-Charge, Sydney, N.S.
  HMCS Protector.............Captain C. M. R. Schwerdt, C.V.O., C.B.E., R.N.

Naval Officer-in-Charge, Quebec, P.Q.
  HMCS Chaleur...............Captain L. J. M. Gauvreau, R.C.N.

Naval Officer-in-Charge, Montreal, P.Q.
  HMCS Hochelaga............Captain P. W. Earl, R.C.N.V.R.

Naval Officer-in-Charge, Prince Rupert, B.C.
  HMCS Chatham...............Commander M. A. Wood, R.C.N.

Naval Officer-in-Charge, Gaspe, P.Q.
  HMCS Fort Ramsay..........Commander G. C. Bernard, R.C.N.V.R.

Naval Officer-in-Charge, Esquimalt, B.C.
  HMCS Givenchy.............Captain P. B. German, R.C.N.

Naval Officer-in-Charge, Shelburne, N.S.
  HMCS Shelburne.............Captain C. D. Donald, R.C.N.

Training Establishment, Cornwallis, N.S.
  HMCS Cornwallis............Captain J. C. I. Edwards, R.C.N.

Signal School, St. Hyacinthe, P.Q.
  HMCS St. Hyacinthe.........Captain A. P. Musgrave, O.B.E., R.C.N.

Royal Canadian Naval College, Victoria, B.C.
  HMCS Royal Roads..........Captain J. M. Grant, C.B.E., R.C.N.

R.C.N. Barracks, Esquimalt, B.C.
  HMCS Naden...............Commander G. F. McCrimmon, R.C.N.V.R.

Depot Ship, Ottawa, Ont.
  HMCS Bytown..............Commander J. H. Rooney, R.C.N.V.R.

Commodore Superintendent, Halifax and East Coast
  HMCS Scotian..............Commodore 2nd Cl. G. M. Hibbard, R.C.N.

Officers' Training Establishment, Halifax, N.S.
  HMCS Kings...............Lieut.-Commander B.G. Sivertz, O.B.E., R.C.N.R.

R.C.N. Training Base, Bermuda
  HMCS Somers Isles..........Captain K. F. Adams, R.C.N.

Depot Ship, Halifax, N.S.
  HMCS Venture.............Commander T. D. Denny, R.C.N.V.R.

Drafting Depot, Halifax, N.S.
  HMCS Peregrine............Captain C. R. Frayer, V.D., R.C.N.V.R.

Naval Member Canadian Joint Staff
  Washington, D.C..............Rear-Admiral H. E. Reid, C.B., R.C.N.

Canadian Naval Attaché
  Washington, D.C.............Captain E. C. Sherwood, R.C.N.

W.R.C.N.S. Establishment, Galt, Ont.
  HMCS Conestoga............Commander I. J. Macneill, O.B.E., W.R.C.N.S.

W.R.C.N.S. Training Course, Ottawa, Ont.
  Ottawa......................Lieut.-Commander K. M. Fensom, W.R.C.N.S.

JULY 1945

Naval Minister

Honourable Douglas C. Abbott

THE NAVAL BOARD

Deputy Minister of National
  Defence for Naval Services........W. Gordon Mills, C.M.G., Esq.

Chief of the Naval Staff............Vice-Admiral George C. Jones, C.B.

Chief of Naval Personnel...........Captain Adrian M. Hope

Chief of Naval Equipment
  and Supply...................Commander Geoffrey B. Hope, O.B.E.

Chief of Naval Engineering
  and Construction................Engineer Rear-Admiral George L. Stephens, C.B.E.

Chief Staff Officer Reserves.........Captain Paul W. Earl, R.C.N.V.R.

Secretary to the Naval Board.......Paymaster Commander Joseph Jeffrey, R.C.N.V.R

THE NAVAL STAFF

Chief of the Naval Staff.............Vice-Admiral George C. Jones, C.B.

Assistant Chief of the Naval Staff...Captain Henry G. DeWolf, D.S.O., D.S.C.

Director of Operations.............Commander David K. Laidlaw

Director of Plans.................Commander Herbert S. Rayner, D.S.C.

Director of Warfare and Training...Lieutenant-Commander Duncan L. Raymond

Director of Signals Division........Commander George A. Worth

Director of Naval Intelligence
   and Trade......................Captain Eric S. Brand, O.B.E.

Hydrographer....................Captain Donald W. Farmer, F.R.G.S.

Operational Intelligence Centre......Commander John M.B.P. DeMarbois,
   O.B.E., R.D.

Director of Naval Air Division......Lieutenant-Commander (A) John H. Arbick,
   R.C.N.V.R.

Director of Operational Research....Electrical Commander John H. L. Johnstone,
   O.B.E., R.C.N.V.R.

PRINCIPAL BASES AND ESTABLISHMENTS

Commander-in-Chief Canadian North West Atlantic
   HMCS Stadacona.............Rear-Admiral L. W. Murray, C.B., C.B.E., R.C.N.

Flag Officer, Newfoundland Force
   HMCS Avalon...............Commodore 1st Cl. C. R. H. Taylor, C.B.E., R.C.N.

Head of the Canadian Naval Mission Overseas
   HMCS Niobe................Captain F. L. Houghton, C.B.E., R.C.N.

Commanding Officer, Pacific Coast
   HMCS Burrard..............Rear-Admiral V. G. Brodeur, C.B.E., R.C.N.

Naval Officer-in-Charge, Saint John, N.B.
   HMCS Captor...............Captain J. A. Heenan, O.B.E., R.D., R.C.N.R.

Naval Officer-in-Charge, Sydney, N.S.
   HMCS Protector.............Captain P. B. German, R.C.N.

Naval Officer-in-Charge, Quebec, P.Q.
   HMCS Chaleur..............Commander F. B. Latchmore, R.C.N.R.

Naval Officer-in-Charge, Montreal, P.Q.
   HMCS Hochelaga............Captain T. D. Kelly, R.C.N.R.

Naval Officer-in-Charge, Prince Rupert, B.C.
HMCS Chatham...............Commander M. A. Wood, R.C.N.

Naval Officer-in-Charge, Gaspe, P.Q.
HMCS Fort Ramsay...........Commander G. C. Bernard, R.C.N.V.R.

Naval Officer-in-Charge, Esquimalt, B.C.
HMCS Givenchy...............Captain C. D. Donald, R.C.N.

Naval Officer-in-Charge, Shelburne, N.S.
HMCS Shelburne.............Captain F. G. Hart, R.C.N.

Training Establishment, Cornwallis, N.S.
HMCS Cornwallis............Captain J. C. I. Edwards, R.C.N.

Signal School, St. Hyacinthe, P.Q.
HMCS St. Hyacinthe.........Captain A. P. Musgrave, O.B.E., R.C.N.

Royal Canadian Naval College, Victoria, B.C.
HMCS Royal Roads...........Captain J. M. Grant, C.B.E., R.C.N.

R.C.N. Barracks, Esquimalt, B.C.
HMCS Naden................Commander T. G. Fuller, D.S.C., R.C.N.V.R.

Depot Ship, Ottawa, Ont.
HMCS Bytown...............Commander J. H. Rooney, R.C.N.V.R.

Commodore Superintendent Halifax and East Coast
HMCS Scotian...............Commodore 2nd Cl. G. M. Hibbard, R.C.N.

R.C.N. Training Base, Bermuda
HMCS Somers Isles..........Captain J. D. Prentice, D.S.O., D.S.C., R.C.N.

Depot Ship, Halifax, N.S.
HMCS Venture..............Commander T. G. Denny, R.C.N.V.R.

Drafting Depot, Halifax, N.S.
HMCS Peregrine.............Captain C. R. Frayer, V.D., R.C.N.V.R.

Naval Member Canadian Joint Staff
Washington, D.C...............Rear-Admiral H. E. Reid, C.B., R.C.N.

Canadian Naval Attaché
Washington, D.C...............Commander F. J. D. Pemberton, R.C.N.V.R.

APPENDIX III

PRINCIPAL SHIPS OF THE ROYAL CANADIAN NAVY

1939-1945

PREPARED BY DIRECTORATE OF MANNING AND PERSONNEL STATISTICS

SHIP	CLASS	COMMANDING OFFICER	FROM	TO
AGASSIZ	*Corvette*	Lt. B. D. D. Johnson, R.C.N.R.	23 Jan., 1941	14 Mch., 1943
		Lt. Cdr. E. M. Moore, R.C.N.R.	15 Mch., 1943	13 May, 1944
		Lt. F. E. Burrows, R.C.N.V.R.	14 May, 1944	5 May, 1945
		Lt. G. C. Thomas, R.C.N.V.R.	6 May, 1945	12 June, 1945
ALBERNI	*Corvette*	Lt. Cdr. G. O. Baugh, O.B.E., R.C.N.R.	6 Jan., 1941	11 Oct., 1942
		Lt. I. H. Bell, R.C.N.V.R.	12 Oct., 1942	21 Aug., 1944
ALGOMA	*Corvette*	Lt. J. Harding, R.C.N.R.	26 May, 1941	14 Oct., 1943
		Lt. E. R. Hyman, R.C.N.V.R.	15 Oct., 1943	4 Apl., 1944
		Lt. S. B. Kelly, R.C.N.V.R.	5 Apl., 1944	5 Apl., 1944
		Lt. L. F. Moore, R.C.N.R.	6 Apl., 1944	24 Aug., 1944
		Lt. J. N. Finlayson, R.C.N.R.	25 Aug., 1944	2 July, 1945
ALGONQUIN	*Destroyer*	Lt. Cdr. D. W. Piers, R.C.N.	22 Dec., 1943	19 Apl., 1945
		Lt. Cdr. P. E. Haddon, R.C.N.	20 Apl., 1945	2 Sept., 1945
AMHERST	*Corvette*	Lt. Cdr. A. K. Young, R.C.N.R.	6 Feb., 1941	20 Nov., 1941
		Lt. H. G. Denyer, R.C.N.R.	21 Nov., 1941	19 Sept., 1942
		Lt. L. C. Audette, R.C.N.V.R.	20 Sept., 1942	24 May, 1944
		Lt. D. M. Fraser, R.C.N.V.R.	25 May, 1944	16 Dec., 1944
		Lt. K. W. Winsby, R.C.N.V.R.	17 Dec., 1944	11 July, 1945
ANNAPOLIS	*Destroyer*	Lt. Cdr. F. C. Smith, R.C.N.R.	29 Mch., 1941	1 July, 1942
		Lt. Cdr. G. H. Davidson, R.C.N.	2 July, 1942	3 Dec., 1942
		Lt. Cdr. A. G. Boulton, R.C.N.V.R.	4 Dec., 1942	2 Mch., 1944
		Lt. Cdr. H. C. Walmesley, R.C.N.R.	3 Mch., 1944	24 Aug., 1944
ANNAN	*Frigate*	Lt. Cdr. C. P. Balfry, R.C.N.R.	11 Mch., 1944	10 May, 1944
		Lt. J. H. Corbett, R.C.N.V.R.	11 May, 1944	21 June, 1945

Ship	Type	Commanding Officer	From	To
ANTIGONISH	*Frigate*	Lt. Cdr. R. D. Barrett, R.C.N.R.	15 Jan., 1944	4 May, 1945
		Lt. Cdr. J. A. Dunn, R.C.N.V.R.	5 May, 1945	2 Sept., 1945
ARNPRIOR	*Corvette*	Lt. S. D. Thom, R.C.N.V.R.	8 June, 1944	2 Sept., 1945
ARROWHEAD	*Corvette*	Lt. V. Torraville, R.C.N.	21 Nov., 1940	17 Jan., 1941
		Lt. Cdr. E. G. Skinner, R.C.N.R.	18 Jan., 1941	25 Mch., 1942
		Skpr. Lt. L. A. Hickey, R.C.N.R.	26 Mch., 1942	21 Oct., 1944
		Lt. R. H. Sylvester, R.C.N.V.R.	22 Oct., 1944	27 June, 1945
ARVIDA	*Corvette*	Lt. A. I. MacKay, R.C.N.R.	1 Nov., 1940	6 Aug., 1942
		Lt. D. G. King, R.C.N.V.R.	7 Aug., 1942	25 Nov., 1943
		Lt. J. C. P. Desrochers, R.C.N.V.R.	26 Nov., 1943	15 Mch., 1944
		Lt. D. W. G. Storey, R.C.N.V.R.	16 Mch., 1944	10 June, 1945
ASSINIBOINE	*Destroyer*	Cdr. E. R. Mainguy, R.C.N.	10 Sept., 1939	2 Apl., 1940
		Commodore G. C. Jones, R.C.N.	3 Apl., 1940	14 Sept., 1940
		Capt. C. R. Taylor, R.C.N.	15 Sept., 1940	29 Oct., 1940
		Commodore L. W. Murray, R.C.N.	30 Oct., 1940	11 Feb., 1941
		Lt. Cdr. J. H. Stubbs, R.C.N.	12 Feb., 1941	1 Oct., 1942
		Lt. R. Hennessy, D.S.C., R.C.N.	2 Oct., 1942	1 Dec., 1942
		Lt. Cdr. E. P. Tisdall, R.C.N.	2 Dec., 1942	10 Feb., 1943
		Cdr. K. F. Adams, R.C.N.	11 Feb., 1943	30 Sept., 1943
		Lt. Cdr. R. P. Welland, D.S.C., R.C.N.	1 Oct., 1943	8 Nov., 1944
		Lt. Cdr. R. Hennessy, D.S.C., R.C.N.	9 Nov., 1944	21 Feb., 1945
		Capt. E. L. Armstrong, R.C.N.	22 Feb., 1945	8 Aug., 1945
ATHABASKAN	*Destroyer*	Capt. G. R. Miles, O.B.E., R.C.N.	2 Feb., 1943	22 Oct., 1943
		Lt. Cdr. J. H. Stubbs, D.S.O., R.C.N.	23 Oct., 1943	29 Apl., 1944
ATHOLL	*Corvette*	Lt. W. D. H. Gardiner, R.C.N.V.R.	14 Oct., 1943	12 July, 1945
ASBESTOS	*Corvette*	Lt. J. Cuthbert, R.C.N.R.	24 Apl., 1944	4 July, 1945
BADDECK	*Corvette*	Lt. A. H. Easton, R.C.N.R.	18 May, 1941	5 Apl., 1942
		Lt. F. W. Thompson, R.C.N.V.R.	6 Apl., 1942	20 Apl., 1942
		Lt. L. G. Cumming, R.C.N.V.R.	21 Apl., 1942	5 Oct., 1942
		Lt. J. Brock, R.C.N.V.R.	6 Oct., 1942	17 Aug., 1943
		Lt. D. H. Fozer, R.C.N.V.R.	18 Aug., 1943	17 Oct., 1943
		Lt. G. C. Brown, R.C.N.V.R.	18 Oct., 1943	15 June, 1944
		Lt. C. R. Campbell, R.C.N.V.R.	16 June, 1944	19 June, 1944
		Lt. Cdr. F. G. Hutchings, R.C.N.R.	20 June, 1944	29 June, 1945

PRINCIPAL SHIPS OF THE ROYAL CANADIAN NAVY 1939-1945—*Continued*

Ship	Class	Commanding Officer	From	To
BARRIE	*Corvette*	Lt. R. M. Mosher, R.C.N.R.	12 May, 1941	9 Jan., 1942
		Ch. Skpr. G. N. Downey, R.C.N.R.	10 Jan., 1942	28 Mch., 1942
		Lt. R. M. Mosher, R.C.N.R.	29 Mch., 1942	13 Mch., 1943
		Lt. H. O. Magill, R.C.N.V.R.	14 Mch., 1943	8 Oct., 1943
		Lt. D. R. Watson, R.C.N.R.	9 Oct., 1943	15 June, 1944
		Lt. W. D. Stokvis, R.C.N.V.R.	16 June, 1944	22 June, 1945
BATTLEFORD	*Corvette*	Lt. R. J. Roberts, R.C.N.R.	31 July, 1941	31 Aug., 1942
		Lt. F. A. Beck, R.C.N.V.R.	1 Sept., 1942	25 June, 1943
		Lt. H. H. Turnbull, R.C.N.V.R.	26 June, 1943	19 June, 1944
		Lt. P. A. F. Lanlois, R.C.N.V.R.	20 June, 1944	12 May, 1945
BAYFIELD	*Minesweeper*	Lt. D. W. Main, R.C.N.R.	26 Feb., 1942	3 Nov., 1942
		Lt. A. H. Gosse, R.C.N.R.	4 Nov., 1942	31 Dec., 1942
		Lt. D. W. Main, R.C.N.R.	1 Jan., 1943	6 Aug., 1943
		Lt. F. A. Cunningham, R.C.N.V.R.	7 Aug., 1943	19 Jan., 1944
		Lt. S. Pierce, R.C.N.R.	20 Jan., 1944	15 Oct., 1944
		Lt. J. C. K. McNaught, R.C.N.V.R.	16 Oct., 1944	26 Sept., 1945
BEACON-HILL	*Frigate*	Lt. Cdr. E. T. Simmons, D.S.O., R.C.N.V.R.	14 Apl., 1944	2 Sept., 1945
BEAUHARNOIS	*Corvette*	Lt. E. C. Smith, R.C.N.V.R.	1 Aug., 1944	20 May, 1945
		Lt. J. M. Pretty, R.C.N.V.R.	21 May, 1945	6 July, 1945
BEAVER	*Patrol Craft Special Duties*	Skpr. E. L. Thompson, R.C.N.R.	17 Sept., 1940	27 Feb., 1941
		Lt. J. Nolan, R.C.N.R.	28 Feb., 1941	16 Mch., 1941
		Lt. Cdr. G. H. Griffiths, R.C.N.	17 Mch., 1941	31 July, 1941
		Lt. Cdr. R. I. Swansburg, R.C.N.	1 Aug., 1941	15 Oct., 1942
		Lt. J. F Watson, R.C.N.R.	16 Oct., 1942	19 Sept., 1943
		Lt. Cdr. H. C. Walmesley, R.C.N.R.	20 Sept., 1943	5 Mch., 1944
		Lt. Cdr. C. G. Williams, R.C.N.R.	6 Mch., 1944	13 Mch., 1945
		Skpr. Lt. I. E. Abbot, R.C.N.R.	14 Mch., 1945	1 Oct., 1945
BELLECHASSE	*Minesweeper*	Lt. H. H. Rankin, R.C.N.R.	6 Dec., 1941	5 Jan., 1944
		Lt. Cdr. W. Redford, R.C.N.R.	6 Jan., 1944	17 Apl., 1945
		Lt. J. M. MacRae, R.C.N.V.R.	18 Apl., 1945	23 Oct., 1945

Ship	Type	Commanding Officer	From	To
BELLEVILLE	*Corvette*	Lt. J. E. Korning, R.C.N.V.R.	18 Oct., 1944	6 May, 1945
		Lt. Cdr. R. M. Powell, R.C.N.V.R.	7 May, 1945	30 June, 1945
BITTERSWEET	*Corvette*	Lt. Cdr. J. A. Woods, R.C.N.R.	1 Nov., 1940	30 Nov., 1942
		Lt. F. B. Brooks-Hill, R.C.N.V.R.	1 Dec., 1942	9 July, 1944
		Lt. F. W. Bogardus, R.C.N.V.R.	10 July, 1944	7 Dec., 1944
		Lt. B. Sangster, R.C.N.V.R.	8 Dec., 1944	16 Dec., 1944
		Skpr. Lt. F. C. Smith, R.C.N.R.	17 Dec., 1944	22 June, 1945
BLAIRMORE	*Minesweeper*	Lt. W. J. Kingsmill, R.C.N.V.R.	17 Nov., 1942	24 Oct., 1943
		Lt. J. C. Marston, R.C.N.V.R.	25 Oct., 1943	22 Apl., 1945
		Lt. J. C. MacMillan, R.C.N.V.R.	23 Apl., 1945	16 Oct., 1945
BORDER CITIES	*Algerine*	Lt. B. P. Young, R.C.N.R.	20 Mch., 1944	2 Sept., 1945
BOWMANVILLE	*Corvette*	Lt. Cdr. M. S. Duffin, R.C.N.V.R.	28 Sept., 1944	2 Sept., 1945
BRANDON	*Corvette*	Lt. J. C. Littler, R.C.N.R.	22 July, 1941	24 Nov., 1942
		Lt. H. E. McArthur, R.C.N.V.R.	25 Nov., 1942	25 Apl., 1944
		Lt. J. F. Evans, R.C.N.V.R.	26 Apl., 1944	26 Apl., 1945
		Lt. P. J. Lawrence, R.C.N.R.	27 Apl., 1945	20 June, 1945
BRANTFORD	*Corvette*	Lt. W. D. F. Johnston, R.C.N.R.	15 May, 1942	26 Apl., 1943
		Lt. J. A. R. Allan, R.C.N.V.R.	27 Apl., 1943	17 Aug., 1943
		Lt. R. C. Eaton, R.C.N.V.R.	18 Aug., 1943	28 Sept., 1944
		Lt. J. P. Kieran, R.C.N.R.	29 Sept., 1944	27 Apl., 1945
		Lt. R. M. Smillie, R.C.N.V.R.	28 Apl., 1945	17 Aug., 1945
BRAS D'OR	*Minesweeper*	Lt. A. K. Young, R.C.N.R.	9 Oct., 1939	30 June, 1940
		Lt. C. A. Hornsby, R.C.N.R.	1 July, 1940	19 Oct., 1940
BROCKVILLE	*Minesweeper*	Lt. C. Peterson, R.C.N.R.	19 Sept., 1942	13 Mch., 1943
		Lt. B. P. Young, R.C.N.R.	14 Mch., 1943	17 Sept., 1943
		Lt. F. K. Elles, R.C.N.V.R.	18 Sept., 1943	19 May, 1944
		Lt. J. R. Bell, R.C.N.V.R.	20 May, 1944	30 July, 1944
		Lt. M. G. McCarthy, R.C.N.V.R.	31 July, 1944	7 Feb., 1945
		Lt. J. O. L. Lake, R.C.N.R.	8 Feb., 1945	24 Aug., 1945
BUCKINGHAM	*Frigate*	Lt. Cdr. M. H. Wallace, R.C.N.R.	2 Nov., 1944	2 Sept., 1945

PRINCIPAL SHIPS OF THE ROYAL CANADIAN NAVY 1939-1945—*Continued*

Ship	Class	Commanding Officer	From	To
BURLINGTON	*Minesweeper*	Lt. Cdr. W. J. Fricher, R.C.N.	....	2 May, 1942
		Lt. M. Russell, R.C.N.R.	2 May, 1942	16 May, 1944
		Lt. G. F. Bayne, R.C.N.V.R.	17 May, 1944	22 Nov., 1944
		Lt. J. M. Richardson, R.C.N.V.R.	23 Nov., 1944	2 Jan., 1945
		Lt. K. G. Clark, R.C.N.V.R.	3 Jan., 1945	4 Feb., 1945
		Lt. P. P. Jeffries, R.C.N.V.R.	5 Feb., 1945	2 Sept., 1945
BUCTOUCHE	*Corvette*	Lt. W. W. Mackney, R.C.N.R.	5 June, 1941	6 May, 1942
		Skpr. Lt. G. N. Downey, R.C.N.R.	7 May, 1942	4 Aug., 1943
		Skpr. Lt. H. E. Young, R.C.N.R.	5 Aug., 1943	4 Dec., 1944
		Skpr. Lt. E. S. N. Pleasance, R.C.N.R.	5 Dec., 1944	4 Feb., 1945
		Skpr. Lt. E. L. Ritchie, R.C.N.R.	5 Feb., 1945	12 June, 1945
CALGARY	*Corvette*	Lt. G. Lancaster, R.C.N.R.	15 Dec., 1941	19 June, 1942
		Lt. H. K. Hill, R.C.N.V.R.	20 June, 1942	21 June, 1943
		Lt. G. M. Orr, R.C.N.V.R.	22 June, 1943	12 Aug., 1943
		Lt. R. B. Bush, R.C.N.V.R.	13 Aug., 1943	17 Mch., 1944
		Lt. A. A. R. Dykes, R.C.N.R.	18 Mch., 1944	15 Sept., 1944
		Lt. L. D. M. Saunders, R.C.N.V.R.	16 Sept., 1944	12 June, 1945
CAMROSE	*Corvette*	Lt. L. R. Pavillard, R.C.N.R.	30 June, 1941	24 Nov., 1944
		Lt. J. B. Lamb, R.C.N.V.R.	25 Nov., 1944	18 July, 1945
CANSO	*Minesweeper*	Lt. H. S. MacFarlane, R.C.N.R.	5 Mch., 1942	3 Feb., 1943
		Lt. J. Kincaid, R.C.N.R.	4 Feb., 1943	4 Oct., 1944
		Lt. J. M. Gracey, R.C.N.V.R.	5 Oct., 1944	26 Sept., 1945
CAP-DE-LA-MADELEINE	*Frigate*	Lt. Cdr. R. A. Judges, R.C.N.V.R.	30 Sept., 1944	2 Sept., 1945
CAPE BRETON	*Frigate*	Lt. Cdr. A. M. McLarnon, R.C.N.R.	25 Oct., 1943	4 Jan., 1945
		Lt. Cdr. J. C. L. Annesley, R.C.N.	5 Jan., 1945	2 Sept., 1945
CAPILANO	*Frigate*	Lt. Cdr. H. E. McArthur, R.C.N.V.R.	25 Aug., 1944	2 Sept., 1945
CARAQUET	*Minesweeper*	Lt. A. A. R. Dykes, R.C.N.R.	31 Mch., 1942	3 Nov., 1943
		Lt. Cdr. A. H. G. Storrs, R.C.N.R.	4 Nov., 1943	12 Nov., 1944
		Lt. G. W. Leckie, R.C.N.V.R.	13 Nov., 1944	26 Sept., 1945

			8 Nov., 1944	2 Sept., 1945
CARLTON PLACE	Frigate	Lt. Cdr. C. E. Wright, R.C.N.V.R.	8 Nov., 1944	2 Sept., 1945
CHAMBLY	Corvette	Lt. E. T. Simmons, R.C.N.V.R.	3 Dec., 1940	17 Dec., 1940
		Lt. Cdr. F. C. Smith, R.C.N.R.	18 Dec., 1940	25 Mch., 1941
		Cdr. J. D. Prentice, R.C.N.	26 Mch., 1941	5 Sept., 1942
		Lt. A. F. Pickard, R.C.N.R.	6 Sept., 1942	26 Jan., 1944
		Lt. S. D. Taylor, R.C.N.R.	27 Jan., 1944	22 June, 1944
		Lt. H. A. Ovenden, R.C.N.R.	23 June, 1944	28 Apl., 1945
		Lt. Cdr. J. B. B. Shaw, R.C.N.	29 Apl., 1945	15 June, 1945
CHARLOTTETOWN	Corvette	Lt. J. W. Bonner, R.C.N.R.	12 Dec., 1941	11 Sept., 1942
CHARLOTTETOWN	Frigate	Lt. Cdr. J. Harding, R.C.N.R.	28 Apl., 1944	23 Apl., 1945
		Cdr. W. C. Halliday, R.C.N.R.	24 Apl., 1945	2 Sept., 1945
CHAUDIERE	Destroyer	Lt. Cdr. C. P. Nixon, R.C.N.	16 Oct., 1943	27 Mch., 1945
		Lt. Cdr. W. Davenport, R.C.N.R.	28 Mch., 1945	1 May, 1945
		Lt. J. W. C. Raymond, R.C.N.R.	2 May, 1945	17 Aug., 1945
CHEBOGUE	Frigate	Lt. Cdr. T. MacDuff, R.C.N.R.	22 Feb., 1944	23 July, 1944
		Lt. Cdr. M. F. Oliver, R.C.N.R.	24 July, 1944	21 Jan., 1945
		Lt. D. F. McElgunn, R.C.N.V.R.	22 Jan., 1945	25 Sept., 1945
CHEDABUCTO	Minesweeper	Lt. J. H. B. Davies, R.C.N.R.	27 Sept., 1941	31 Oct., 1943
CHICOUTIMI	Corvette	Lt. William Black, R.C.N.R.	10 Apl., 1941	10 May, 1942
		Lt. H. G. Dupont, R.C.N.R.	11 May, 1942	8 Jan., 1943
		Lt. Cdr. J. F. Stairs, R.C.N.V.R.	9 Jan., 1943	8 Aug., 1943
		Lt. F. Cross, R.C.N.R.	9 Aug., 1943	3 Sept., 1944
		Lt. A. F. Giffin, R.C.N.V.R.	4 Sept., 1944	14 June, 1945
CHIGNECTO	Minesweeper	Lt. L. F. McQuarrie, R.C.N.R.	21 Oct., 1941	28 June, 1944
		Skpr. Lt. G. F. Cassidy, R.C.N.R.	29 June, 1944	1 Mch., 1945
		Lt. R. C. Eaton, R.C.N.V.R.	2 Mch., 1945	2 Sept., 1945
CHILLIWACK	Corvette	Lt. L. F. Foxall, R.C.N.R.	8 Apl., 1941	25 May, 1943
		Lt. Cdr. C. R. Coughlin, R.C.N.V.R.	26 May, 1943	11 Apl., 1944
		Lt. D. R. Watson, M.B.E., R.C.N.R.	12 Apl., 1944	9 July, 1945

PRINCIPAL SHIPS OF THE ROYAL CANADIAN NAVY 1939-1945—*Continued*

Ship	Class	Commanding Officer	From	To
CLAYOQUOT	*Minesweeper*	Lt. Cdr. G. A. Thomson, R.C.N.	20 June, 1941	18 Nov., 1941
		Lt. Cdr. R. B. Campbell, R.C.N.	19 Nov., 1941	13 Apl., 1942
		Lt. H. E. Lade, R.C.N.R.	14 Apl., 1942	7 Apl., 1943
		Lt. C. L. Campbell, R.C.N.V.R.	8 Apl., 1943	18 Apl., 1943
		Lt. J. W. Fitzpatrick, R.C.N.V.R.	19 Apl., 1943	28 July, 1944
		Lt. Cdr. A. C. Campbell, R.C.N.V.R.	29 July, 1944	3 Aug., 1944
		Lt. P. W. Finlay, R.C.N.V.R.	4 Aug., 1944	24 Dec., 1944
COATICOOK	*Frigate*	Lt. Cdr. L. C. Audette, R.C.N.V.R.	25 July, 1944	2 Sept., 1945
COBALT	*Corvette*	Lt. Cdr. R. B. Campbell, R.C.N.	10 Sept., 1940	19 May, 1941
		Lt. C. J. Angus, R.C.N.R.	20 May, 1941	5 May, 1943
		Lt. R. A. Judges, R.C.N.V.R.	6 May, 1943	30 Mch., 1944
		Lt. A. W. Bett, G.M., R.C.N.R.	31 Mch., 1944	25 June, 1944
		Lt. Cdr. R. M. Wallace, R.C.N.V.R.	26 June, 1944	15 June, 1945
COBOURG	*Corvette*	Lt. G. H. Johnson, R.C.N.V.R.	20 Mch., 1944	10 June, 1945
COLLINGWOOD	*Corvette*	Lt. N. G. Bennett, R.C.N.R.	10 Sept., 1940	16 Apl., 1941
		Lt. W. Woods, R.C.N.R.	17 Apl., 1941	9 Dec., 1942
		Lt. D. W. Groos, R.C.N.	10 Dec., 1942	16 May, 1943
		Lt. Cdr. R. J. C. Pringle, R.C.N.V.R.	17 May, 1943	2 Jan., 1944
		Lt. H. R. Knight, R.C.N.R.	3 Jan., 1944	2 May, 1945
		Lt. Cdr. E. B. Pearce, R.C.N.V.R.	3 May, 1945	19 July, 1945
COMOX	*Minesweeper*	Cdr. R. S. Agnew, R.C.N	10 Sept., 1939	27 July, 1940
		A/Cdr. S. H. Saulsbry, R.C.N.	28 July, 1940	9 Oct., 1940
		Lt. R. R. Kenny, R.C.N.R.	10 Oct., 1940	3 Nov., 1940
		Mate. J. R. Biggs, R.C.N.R.	4 Nov., 1940	25 Mch., 1942
		Mate. F. G. Hutchings, R.C.N.R.	26 Mch., 1942	26 Mch., 1942
		Ch. Skpr. J. E. N. Vezina, R.C.N.R.	27 Mch., 1942	3 Aug., 1942
		Lt. J. P. A. Duggan, R.C.N.R.	4 Aug., 1942	23 July, 1945
COPPERCLIFF	*Corvette*	Lt. A. D. Ritchie, R.C.N.V.R.	19 Apl., 1944	25 July, 1944
		Lt. Cdr. F. G. Hutchings, R.C.N.R.	26 July, 1944	2 Sept., 1945
COQUITLAM	*Minesweeper*	Lt. G. J. McNamara, R.C.N.V.R.	8 July, 1944	2 Sept., 1945

Ship	Type	Commanding Officer		
COLUMBIA	Destroyer	Lt. Cdr. S. W. Davis, R.C.N.	20 Sept, 1940	13 May, 1942
		Lt. Cdr. G. H. Stephen, R.C.N.R.	14 May, 1942	17 Mch., 1943
		Lt. Cdr. B. D. L. Johnson, R.C.N.R.	18 Mch., 1943	23 Nov., 1943
		Lt. Cdr. R. A. S. MacNeil, O.B.E., R.C.N.R.	24 Nov., 1943	26 Nov., 1943
		Lt. T. A. G. Staunton, R.C.N.V.R.	26 Nov., 1943	28 Nov., 1943
		Lt. M. L. Devaney, R.C.N.V.R.	29 Nov., 1943	22 July, 1944
		Lt. J. C. Hughes, R.C.N.R.	23 July, 1944	12 June, 1945
COUGAR	Patrol Craft	Lt. W. R. Kirkland, R.C.N.R.	1 June, 1940	19 Aug, 1940
		Lt. T. M. W. Golby, R.C.N.R.	20 Aug, 1940	1 Jan., 1941
		Lt. H. G. Denyer, R.C.N.R.	2 Jan., 1941	11 May, 1941
		Ch. Skpr. G. F. Cassidy, R.C.N.R.	12 May, 1941	....
		Ch. Skpr. R. W. Sparks, R.G.N.R.	........, 1943	23 Nov., 1943
		Skpr. D. J. Smith, R.C.N.R.	24 Nov., 1943	12 Jan., 1944
		Skpr. Lt. G. F. Cassidy, R.C.N.R.	13 Jan., 1944	22 June, 1944
		Skpr. Lt. K. Bennett, R.C.N.R.	23 June, 1944	15 May, 1945
		Skpr. Lt. W. R. Chaster, R.C.N.R.	16 May, 1945	2 Sept., 1945
COURTENAY	Minesweeper	Lt. A. R. Ascah, R.C.N.R.	2 Mch, 1942	22 Mch, 1944
		Lt. W. H. Black, R.C.N.V.R.	23 Mch., 1944	2 Sept., 1945
COWICHAN	Minesweeper	Lt. R. Jackson, R.C.N.R.	13 June, 1941	30 June, 1941
		Lt. J. R. Kidston, R.C.N.V.R.	1 July, 1941	6 Feb., 1942
		Skpr. Lt. H. W. Stone, R.C.N.R.	7 Feb., 1942	25 Oct., 1942
		Skpr. Lt. K. N. W. Hall, R.C.N.R.	26 Oct., 1942	9 Oct., 1945
CRANEBROOK	Minesweeper	Lt. C. G. Trotter, R.C.N.V.R.	11 Apl, 1944	6 Oct., 1944
		Lt. R. Stark, R.C.N.V.R.	7 Oct., 1944	2 Sept., 1945
DAERWOOD	Minesweeper	Lt. Cdr. E. S. McGowan, R.C.N.V.R.	23 Apl., 1944	19 Nov., 1944
		Lt. T. S. A. Mulhern, R.C.N.V.R.	20 Nov., 1944	14 Feb., 1945
		Skpr. Lt. W. E. Eccles, R.C.N.R.	15 Feb., 1945	2 Sept. 1945
DAUPHIN	Corvette	Lt. R. A. S. McNeil, R.C.N.R., O.B.E.	12 Apl., 1941	17 Jan., 1943
		Lt. M. H. Wallace, R.C.N.R.	18 Jan., 1943	10 Oct., 1944
		Lt. E. R. O'Kelly, R.C.N.V.R.	11 Oct., 1944	6 May, 1945
		Lt. G. R. Brassard, R.C.N.V.R.	7 May, 1945	16 June, 1945
DAWSON	Corvette	Lt. A. H. G. Storrs, R.C.N.R.	6 Oct., 1941	7 June, 1943
		Lt. Cdr. T. S. P. Ryan, O.B.E., R.C.N.R.	8 June, 1943	30 Mch., 1944
		Skpr. Lt. J. B. Cooper, R.C.N.R.	31 Mch., 1944	15 June, 1945

SHIP	CLASS	COMMANDING OFFICER	FROM	To
DIGBY	*Minesweeper*	Lt. S. W. Howell, R.C.N.R. Skpr. Lt. J. W. Sharpe, R.C.N.R. Lt. E. O. Ormsby, R.C.N.V.R.	26 July, 1942 10 July, 1943 19 Mch., 1944	9 July, 1943 18 Mch., 1944 31 July, 1945
DRUMHELLER	*Corvette*	Lt. Cdr. G. H. Griffiths, R.C.N. Lt. L. P. Denny, R.C.N.R. Lt. Cdr. A. H. G. Storrs, R.C.N.R. Lt. H. R. Beck, R.C.N.R.	13 Sept., 1941 16 Oct., 1942 21 Aug., 1943 28 Dec., 1943	15 Oct., 1942 20 Aug., 1943 27 Dec., 1943 5 July, 1945
DRUMMONDVILLE	*Minesweeper*	Lt. J. P. Fraser, R.C.N.R. Lt. H. C. Hatch, R.C.N.V.R. Skpr. Lt. F. W. M. Drew, R.C.N.R. Lt. G. E. Cross, R.C.N.V.R.	30 Oct., 1941 10 May, 1943 6 Aug., 1943 10 Apl., 1945	9 May, 1943 5 Aug., 1943 9 Apl., 1945 28 Oct., 1945
DUNDAS	*Corvette*	Lt. R. W. Draney, R.C.N.R. Lt. R. W. Hart, R.C.N.V.R. Lt. R. B. Taylor, R.C.N.V.R. Lt. D. E. Howard, R.C.N.V.R.	13 Mch., 1942 18 May, 1943 2 Mch., 1944 18 Feb., 1945	17 May, 1943 1 Mch., 1944 17 Feb., 1945 13 May, 1945
DUNVEGAN	*Corvette*	Lt. J. C. Pratt, R.C.N.V.R. Lt. J. A. Tullis, R.C.N.R. Lt. S. A. Burris, R.C.N.R. Lt. J. A. Rankin, R.C.N.R. Lt. Cdr. R. L. B. Hunter, R.C.N.V.R.	10 May, 1941 23 May, 1941 26 Jan., 1943 6 July, 1944 12 Mch., 1945	22 May, 1941 25 Jan., 1943 5 July, 1944 11 Mch., 1945 28 June, 1945
DUNVER	*Frigate*	Lt. Cdr. W. Woods, O.B.E., R.C.N.R. Lt. W. Davenport, R.C.N.R. Cdr. St. C. Balfour, R.C.N.V.R. Lt. Cdr. C. P. Balfry, D.S.C., R.C.N.R.	11 Sept., 1943 25 Aug., 1944 27 Mch., 1945 27 May, 1945	24 Aug., 1944 26 Mch., 1945 26 May, 1945 2 Sept., 1945
EASTVIEW	*Frigate*	Lt. A. M. Kirkpatrick, R.C.N.V.R. Lt. W. D. M. Gardiner, R.C.N.V.R. Lt. R. C. G. Merriam, R.C.N.V.R.	10 Apl., 1944 17 Sept., 1944 8 Dec., 1944	16 Sept., 1944 7 Dec., 1944 2 Sept., 1945
EDMUNDSTON	*Corvette*	Lt. R. D. Barrett, R.C.N.R. Lt. J. Leky, R.C.N.V.R.	21 Oct., 1941 22 May, 1944	21 May, 1944 12 June, 1945

Ship	Type	Commanding Officer	Appointed	Left
ELK	*Armed Yacht*	Lt. Cdr. N. V. Clark, R.C.N.R.	20 June, 1940	10 June, 1941
		Ch. Skpr. W. K. S. Hines, R.C.N.R.	11 June, 1941	13 July, 1941
		Lt. R. Hocken, R.C.N.R.	14 July, 1941	17 Aug., 1941
		Lt. T. Gilmour, R.C.N.R.	18 Aug., 1941	31 Oct., 1941
		Lt. T. B. Edwards, R.C.N.R.	1 Nov., 1941	30 Nov., 1941
		Lt. J. A. Dunn, R.C.N.V.R.	1 Dec., 1942	4 Aug., 1945
ESQUIMALT	*Minesweeper*	Lt. F. J. N. Davies, R.C.N.R.	26 Oct., 1942	20 Jan., 1943
		Lt. P. O. Taylor, R.C.N.V.R.	21 Jan., 1943	12 Mch., 1944
		Lt. J. M. S. Clark, R.C.N.V.R.	13 Mch., 1944	14 Dec., 1944
		Lt. J. C. Tyrer, R.C.N.V.R.	15 Dec., 1944	28 Jan., 1945
		Lt. R. C. MacMillan, D.S.C., R.C.N.V.R.	29 Jan., 1945	16 Apl., 1945
ETRICK	*Frigate*	Lt. C. G. McIntosh, R.C.N.R.	29 Jan., 1944	15 Mch., 1944
		Lt. Cdr. E. M. Moore, R.C.N.R.	16 Mch., 1944	30 May, 1945
EYEBRIGHT	*Corvette*	Lt. E. Randell, R.C.N.R.	1 Nov., 1940	25 Nov., 1940
		Lt. H. C. R. Davis, R.C.N.R.	26 Nov., 1940	27 Dec., 1942
		Lt. H. L. Quinn, R.C.N.V.R.	28 Dec., 1942	1 Sept., 1944
		Lt. R. J. Margesson, R.C.N.V.R.	2 Sept., 1944	9 Jan., 1945
		S/Lt. P. A. Lefroy, R.C.N.V.R.	10 Jan., 1945	17 June, 1945
FENNEL	*Corvette*	Lt. Cdr. J. N. Smith, R.C.N.R.	1 Nov., 1940	31 Oct., 1941
		Lt. J. M. Gillison, R.C.N.R.	1 Nov., 1941	26 May, 1942
		Lt. R. B. Warwick, R.C.N.V.R.	27 May, 1942	5 Sept., 1943
		Lt. Cdr. W. P. Moffat, R.C.N.	6 Sept., 1943	15 May, 1944
		Lt. Cdr. K. L. Johnson, R.C.N.V.R.	16 May, 1944	12 June, 1945
FERGUS	*Corvette*	Lt. H. F. Farncomb, R.C.N.V.R.	24 Oct., 1944	9 July, 1945
FORT ERIE	*Frigate*	Lt. Cdr. A. W. Ford, R.C.N.R.	25 Sept., 1944	20 Feb., 1945
		Lt. Cdr. E. F. Pyper, R.C.N.V.R.	21 Feb., 1945	2 Sept., 1945
FORT FRANCIS	*Algerine*	Lt. D. E. Ryerson, R.C.N.V.R.	4 Oct., 1944	2 Sept., 1945
FORT WILLIAM	*Minesweeper*	Lt. H. Campbell, R.C.N.R.	25 Apl., 1942	13 Sept., 1942
		Lt. G. E. Kelly, R.C.N.R., D.S.C.	14 Sept., 1942	4 Oct., 1943
		Lt. Cdr. H. Campbell, R.C.N.R., D.S.C.	5 Oct., 1943	23 Oct., 1945
FOREST HILL	*Corvette*	Lt. E. J. Jones, R.C.N.R.	1 Dec., 1943	5 July, 1945

PRINCIPAL SHIPS OF THE ROYAL CANADIAN NAVY 1939-1945—*Continued*

Ship	Class	Commanding Officer	From	To
FRASER	*Destroyer*	Cdr. W. B. Creery, R.C.N.	10 Sept., 1939	25 June, 1940
FREDERICTON	*Corvette*	Lt. Cdr. J. H. S. MacDonald, R.C.N.R.	15 Nov., 1941	17 Feb., 1942
		Lt. J. E. Harrington, R.C.N.V.R.	18 Feb., 1942	20 July, 1944
		Lt. J. C. Smyth, R.C.N.R.	21 July, 1944	9 July, 1945
FRENCH	*A/S Patrol Craft*	Lt. J. W. Bonner, R.C.N.R.	18 Sept., 1939	19 Jan., 1940
		Ch. Skpr. K. W. N. Hall, R.C.N.R.	20 Jan., 1940	26 Feb., 1941
		Lt. D. W. Main, R.C.N.R.	27 Feb., 1941	22 Oct., 1942
		Ch. Skpr. W. G. Kent, R.C.N.R.	23 Oct., 1942	2 Sept., 1945
FRONTENAC	*Corvette*	Lt. E. T. F. Wennberg, R.C.N.V.R.	26 Oct., 1943	15 Mch., 1945
		Lt. D. R. Baker, R.C.N.V.R.	16 Mch., 1945	17 July, 1945
FUNDY	*Minesweeper*	Lt. Cdr. W. P. Robertson, R.C.N.R.	10 Sept., 1939	23 Feb., 1940
		Lt. Cdr. A. G. Stanley, R.C.N.R.	24 Feb., 1940	26 Oct., 1941
		Mate. J. B. Raine, R.C.N.R.	27 Oct., 1941	9 Mch., 1942
		Ch. Skpr. F. A. Heckman, R.C.N.R.	10 Mch., 1942	23 July, 1945
GANANOQUE	*Minesweeper*	Lt. E. M. Moore, R.C.N.R.	8 Nov., 1941	28 Mch., 1943
		Skpr. Lt. E. S. N. Pleasance, R.C.N.R.	29 Mch., 1943	24 May, 1944
		Lt. Cdr. A. P. Duke, R.C.N.V.R.	25 May, 1944	13 Oct., 1945
GASPE	*Minesweeper*	Lt. H. D. Mackay, R.C.N.R.	3 Sept., 1939	11 Apl., 1941
		Lt. R. T. Ingram, R.C.N.R.	12 Apl., 1941	2 Aug., 1941
		Lt. T. Gilmour, R.C.N.R.	3 Aug., 1941	22 Sept., 1941
		Ch. Skpr. G. A. Myra, R.C.N.R.	23 Sept., 1941	2 Aug., 1942
		Lt. W. S. Bryant, R.C.N.R.	3 Aug., 1942	7 May, 1943
		Skpr. Lt. A. J. Burke, R.C.N.R.	8 May, 1943	7 Jan., 1945
		Skpr. Lt. R. A. Doucette, R.C.N.R.	8 Jan., 1945	23 July, 1945
GATINEAU	*Destroyer*	Lt. Cdr. H. V. W. Groos, R.C.N.	23 Nov., 1943	9 Nov., 1944
		Lt. Cdr. G. H. Davidson, R.C.N.	10 Nov., 1944	2 Sept., 1945
GEORGIAN	*Minesweeper*	Lt. Cdr. A. G. Stanley, R.C.N.R.	23 Sept., 1941	2 Sept., 1942
		Lt. A. Grant, R.C.N.V.R.	3 Sept., 1942	25 Sept., 1942
		Lt. P. M. Crawford, R.C.N.R.	26 Sept., 1942	25 Jan., 1943

Ship	Type	Commanding Officer	Appointed	Left
GIFFARD	Corvette	Lt. Cdr. A. Boucher, R.C.N.V.R.	26 Jan., 1943	20 June, 1944
		Lt. Cdr. D. W. Main, R.C.N.R.	21 June, 1944	23 Mch., 1945
		Lt. T. C. McLaughlin, R.C.N.R.	24 Mch., 1945	23 Oct., 1945
GLACE BAY	Frigate	Lt. Cdr. C. Peterson, R.C.N.R.	30 Oct., 1943	9 May, 1944
		Lt. G. H. Matheson, R.C.N.R.	10 May, 1944	30 June, 1945
GODERICH	Minesweeper	Cdr. J. N. S. MacDonald, R.C.N.R.	2 Sept., 1944	23 Feb., 1945
		Lt. Cdr. F. W. Bogardus, R.C.N.V.R.	24 Feb., 1945	2 Sept., 1945
GRANBY	Minesweeper	Lt. R. R. Kenny, R.C.N.R.	4 Oct., 1941	1 Apl., 1943
		Lt. J. S. C. Pratt, R.C.N.V.R.	2 Apl., 1943	21 Mch., 1944
		Lt. J. E. Taylor, R.C.N.V.R.	22 Mch., 1944	2 Sept., 1945
GRANDMERE	Minesweeper	Mate J. R. Biggs, R.C.N.R.	30 Mch., 1942	10 Oct., 1943
		Lt. G. E. K. Holder, R.C.N.V.R.	11 Oct., 1943	9 May, 1944
		Lt. D. A. P. Davidson, R.C.N.V.R.	10 May, 1944	30 July, 1944
		Lt. Arnold M. Brodie, R.C.N.V.R.	31 July, 1944	31 Jan., 1945
		Lt. E. S. Turnhill, R.C.N.V.R.	1 Feb., 1945	31 July, 1945
	Minesweeper	Lt. J. Cuthbert, R.C.N.R.	26 Nov., 1941	9 Oct., 1942
		Lt. J. O. Rose, R.C.N.V.R.	10 Oct., 1942	20 Apl., 1944
		Lt. N. W. Winters, R.C.N.V.R.	21 Apl., 1944	23 Oct., 1945
GROU	Frigate	Lt. Cdr. H. G. Dupont, R.C.N.R.	8 Nov., 1943	2 Sept., 1945
GUELPH	Corvette	Lt. G. H. Hayes, D.S.C., R.C.N.R.	13 Mch., 1944	14 May, 1945
		Lt. F. D. Wicket, R.C.N.V.R.	15 May, 1945	23 June, 1945
GUYSBOROUGH	Minesweeper	Lt. B. T. R. Russell, R.C.N.R.	8 Apl., 1942	17 Mch., 1945
GALT	Corvette	Lt. A. D. Landles, R.C.N.R.	10 Apl., 1941	9 Mch., 1942
		Lt. A. M. Kirkpatrick, R.C.N.V.R.	10 Mch., 1942	9 Aug., 1943
		Lt. E. P. Taylor, R.C.N.V.R.	10 Aug., 1943	24 Apl., 1945
		Lt. J. C. Lorriman, R.C.N.V.R.	25 Apl., 1945	19 June, 1945
HAIDA	Destroyer	Cdr. H. G. DeWolf, R.C.N.	30 Aug., 1943	18 Dec., 1944
		Lt. Cdr. R. P. Welland, D.S.C., R.C.N.	19 Dec., 1944	2 Sept., 1945

SHIP	CLASS	COMMANDING OFFICER	FROM	TO
HALIFAX	Corvette	Lt. Cdr. Copeland, O.B.E., R.C.N.R.	15 Nov., 1941	6 Feb., 1943
		Lt. M. F Oliver, R.C.N.R.	7 Feb., 1943	21 June, 1944
		Lt. Cdr. R. M. Hanbury, R.C.N.V.R.	22 June, 1944	3 Sept., 1944
		Lt. L. E. Horne, R.C.N.V.R.	4 Sept., 1944	10 July, 1945
HALLOWELL	Frigate	Lt. L. D. Canon, R.C.N.V.R.	21 June, 1944	21 June, 1944
		Skpr. Lt. E. S. N. Pleasance, R.C.N.R.	21 June, 1944	18 Oct., 1944
		Lt. Cdr. R. H. Angus, R.C.N.V.R.	19 Oct., 1944	2 Sept., 1945
HAMILTON	Destroyer	Lt. Cdr. N. V. Clark, R.C.N.R.	25 June, 1941	19 July, 1943
		Lt. Cdr. D. G. Jeffrey, R.C.N.R.	20 July, 1943	18 Jan., 1944
		Cdr. F. Poole, R.C.N.R.	19 Jan., 1944	23 Nov., 1944
		Skpr. Lt. J. D. Burnham, R.C.N.R.	24 Nov., 1944	8 June, 1945
HAWKESBURY	Corvette	Lt. W. G. Curry, R.C.N.V.R.	20 Mch., 1944	7 July, 1945
HEPATICA	Corvette	Lt. C. Copelin, R.C.N.R.	27 Aug., 1940	31 Oct., 1941
		Lt. T. Gilmour, R.C.N.R.	1 Nov., 1941	11 Apl., 1943
		Lt. H. E. Lade, R.C.N.R.	12 Apl., 1943	5 Sept., 1943
		Lt. J. A. Ferguson, R.C.N.R.	6 Sept., 1943	4 Nov., 1944
		Lt. E. M. Lutes, R.C.N.V.R.	5 Nov., 1944	27 June, 1945
HESPELER	Corvette	Lt. Cdr. N. S. C. Dickson, R.C.N.V.R.	28 Feb., 1944	13 Nov., 1944
		Lt. G. F. Manning, R.C.N.V.R.	14 Nov., 1944	2 Sept., 1945
HUMBERSTONE	Corvette	Lt. Cdr. A. Boucher, R.C.N.V.R.		5 Sept., 1944
		Lt. G. C. MacDonald, R.C.N.V.R.	6 Sept., 1944	2 Sept., 1945
HUNTSVILLE	Corvette	Lt. C. B. Hermann, R.C.N.V.R.	10 Apl., 1944	
HURON	Destroyer	Lt. Cdr. H. S. Rayner, R.C.N., D.S.C.	19 July, 1943	22 Sept., 1944
		Lt. Cdr. H. V. W. Groos, R.C.N.	23 Sept., 1944	
HUSKY	Armed Yacht	Lt. J. E. Harrington, R.C.N.V.R.	5 June, 1940	10 July, 1940
		Lt. H. Freeland, R.C.N.R.	11 July, 1940	5 Sept., 1941
		Lt. W. E. Harrison, R.C.N.R.	6 Sept., 1941	18 Oct., 1941
		Lt. A. H. Rankin, R.C.N.R.	19 Oct., 1941	30 Apl., 1942

	Type	Commanding Officer		
INGONISH	*Minesweeper*	Lt. J. P. Kieran, R.C.N.R.	1 May, 1942	29 Sept., 1944
		Lt. W. E. Jolliffe, R.C.N.V.R.	30 Sept., 1944	12 Nov., 1944
		Lt. E. B. Pearce, R.C.N.V.R.	13 Nov., 1944	30 Apl., 1945
		Lt. R. C. Hayden, R.C.N.V.R.	1 May, 1945	......
		Lt. Cdr. T. P. Ryan, O.B.E., R.C.N.R.	29 Apl., 1942	2 May, 1943
		Lt. F. E. Burrow, R.C.N.V.R.	3 May, 1943	4 Apl., 1944
		Lt. R. C. B. Merriam, R.C.N.V.R.	5 Apl., 1944	15 Sept., 1944
		Lt. H. V. Shaw, R.C.N.R.	16 Sept., 1944	26 Mch., 1945
		Lt. C. D. Chivers, R.C.N.V.R.	27 Mch., 1945	......
INCH ARRAN	*Frigate*	Lt. J. W. E. Hastings, R.C.N.R.	12 Oct., 1944	......
IROQUOIS	*Destroyer*	Capt. W. B. L. Holms, R.C.N.	1 Oct., 1942	29 July, 1943
		Cdr. J. C. Hibbard, D.S.C., R.C.N.	30 July, 1943	7 Feb., 1945
		Cdr. K. F. Adams, R.C.N.	8 Feb., 1945	......
JOLIETTE	*Frigate*	Lt. Cdr. G. N. Downey, R.C.N.R.	12 May, 1944	2 Feb., 1945
		Lt. Cdr. W. E. Harrison, R.C.N.R.	3 Feb., 1945	......
JONQUIERE	*Frigate*	Lt. Cdr. A. Marcil, R.C.N.V.R.	20 Mch., 1944	23 Mch., 1944
		Lt. Cdr. J. R. Kidston, R.C.N.V.R.	24 Mch., 1944	24 Mch., 1944
		Lt. D. C. Lennox, R.C.N.V.R.	25 Mch., 1944	......
KALAMAIKA	*Minesweeper*	Lt. C. J. Henrickson, R.C.N.V.R.	25 Aug., 1944	......
KAMLOOPS	*Corvette*	Lt. J. M. Gillison, R.C.N.R.	17 Mch., 1941	31 Oct., 1941
		Lt. P. J. B. Watts, R.C.N.R.	1 Nov., 1941	4 Feb., 1942
		Lt. I. W. McTavish, R.C.N.R.	5 Feb., 1942	1 Mch., 1942
		Lt. D. M. Stewart, R.C.N.R.	2 Mch., 1942	27 Mch., 1942
		Lt. Cdr. J. H. Marshall, R.C.N.V.R.	28 Mch., 1942	22 Aug., 1942
		Lt. N. S. C. Dickinson, R.C.N.V.R.	23 Aug., 1942	28 Sept., 1942
		Lt. P. R. Gillis, R.C.N.V.R.	29 Sept., 1942	......
KAMSACK	*Corvette*	Lt. E. Randall, R.C.N.R.	4 Oct., 1941	1 Mch., 1943
		Lt. D. M. Stewart, R.C.N.R.	2 Mch., 1943	17 Mch., 1943
		Lt. Cdr. W. C. Halliday, R.C.N.R.	18 Mch., 1943	4 May, 1945
		Lt. Cdr. R. F. Wilson, R.C.N.V.R.	5 May, 1945	......
KAPUSKASING	*Algerine*	Lt. Cdr. A. N. Rankin, O.B.E., R.C.N.V.R.	17 Aug., 1944	2 Sept., 1945

PRINCIPAL SHIPS OF THE ROYAL CANADIAN NAVY 1939-1945—*Continued*

Ship	Class	Commanding Officer	From	To
KELOWNA	*Minesweeper*	Lt. W. Davenport, R.C.N.R.	5 Feb., 1942	11 Jan., 1944
		Skpr. Lt. E. W. Suffield, R.C.N.R.	12 Jan., 1944	27 Oct., 1945
KENOGAMI	*Corvette*	Lt. Cdr. R. Jackson, R.C.N.V.R.	8 May, 1941	2 Aug., 1942
		Lt. R. G. McKenzie, R.C.N.V.R.	3 Aug., 1942	21 Nov., 1942
		Lt. J. L. Percy, R.C.N.V.R.	22 Nov., 1942	5 July, 1945
KENORA	*Minesweeper*	Lt. F. R. F. Naftel, R.C.N.V.R.	6 Aug., 1942	14 Sept., 1943
		Lt. D. W. Lowe, R.C.N.V.R.	15 Sept., 1943	. . . .
KENTVILLE	*Minesweeper*	Lt. J. G. Hughes, R.C.N.R.	15 Sept., 1942	21 July, 1944
		Lt. F. G. Rainsford, R.C.N.V.R.	22 July, 1944	28 Oct., 1945
KINCARDINE	*Corvette*	Lt. R. P. Brown, R.C.N.V.R.	19 June, 1944	. . . .
KIRKLAND LAKE	*Frigate*	Lt. J. A. Tullis, R.C.N.R.	21 Aug., 1944	13 Nov., 1944
		Cdr. N. V. Clark, O.B.E., R.D., R.C.N.R.	14 Nov., 1944	2 Sept., 1945
KITCHENER	*Corvette*	Lt. W. Evans, R.C.N.V.R.	28 June, 1942	16 Jan., 1944
		Lt. J. E. Moles, R.C.N.V.R.	17 Jan., 1944	5 July, 1945
KOKANEE	*Frigate*	Lt. Cdr. J. H. Marshall, R.C.N.V.R.	10 May, 1944	14 Dec., 1944
		Lt. Cdr. F. W. Lucas, R.C.N.V.R.	15 Dec., 1944	31 Jan., 1945
		Lt. Cdr. W. J. Kingsmill, R.C.N.V.R.	1 Feb., 1945	2 Sept., 1945
KOOTENAY	*Destroyer*	Lt. Cdr. K. L. Dyer, D.S.C., R.C.N.	12 Apl., 1943	28 Apl., 1944
		Lt. Cdr. W. H. Willson, D.S.C., R.C.N.	29 Apl., 1944	26 Oct., 1945
LACHINE	*Minesweeper*	Lt. B. P. Young, R.C.N.R.	9 June, 1942	15 Feb., 1943
		Lt. F. R. Spindler, R.C.N.V.R.	16 Feb., 1943	8 May, 1943
		Lt. L. F. Moore, R.C.N.R.	9 May, 1943	21 Mch., 1945
		Lt. F. M. Travers, R.C.N.V.R.	22 Mch., 1945	23 Apl., 1945
		Lt. G. F. Pipe, R.C.N.V.R.	24 Apl., 1945	31 July, 1945
LACHUTE	*Corvette*	Lt. R. G. Hatrick, R.C.N.V.R.	25 Sept., 1944	6 July, 1945

Ship	Type	Commanding Officer		
LA HULLOISE	*Frigate*	Lt. J. Brock, R.C.N.V.R.	10 Apl., 1944	2 Sept., 1945
LA MALBAIE	*Frigate*	Lt. Ian W. McTavish, R.C.N.R.	5 Feb., 1942	11 Feb., 1943
		Lt. James S. Davis, R.C.N.V.R.	12 Feb., 1943	7 June, 1944
		Lt. Ernest F. Piper, R.C.N.V.R.	8 June, 1944	21 Feb., 1945
		Lt. Timothy H. Dunn, R.C.N.V.R.	22 Feb., 1945	2 July, 1945
LANARK	*Frigate*	Lt. Cdr. John F. Stairs, R.C.N.V.R.	6 July, 1944	5 Apl., 1945
		Cdr. B. D. L. Johnson, O.B.E., R.C.N.R.	6 Apl., 1945	8 Aug., 1945
LASALLE	*Frigate*	Lt. Cdr. F. A. Beck, R.C.N.V.R.	8 May, 1944	2 July, 1945
		Lt. Cdr. R. D. Barrett, R.C.N.R.	3 July, 1945	2 Sept., 1945
LAUZON	*Frigate*	Lt. Cdr. W. Woods, O.B.E., R.C.N.R.	22 June, 1944	10 Apl., 1945
		Lt. Cdr. J. B. Graham, R.C.N.V.R.	11 Apl., 1945	2 Sept., 1945
LAVALLEE	*Minesweeper*	Skpr. Lt. J. R. Smith, R.C.N.R.	21 Mch., 1945	3 May, 1945
		Lt. Cdr. C. P. Trotter, R.C.N.V.R.	4 May, 1945	2 Sept., 1945
LEASIDE	*Corvette*	Lt. G. G. K. Holder, R.C.N.V.R.	3 July, 1944	15 June, 1945
		Lt. H. Brynjolfson, R.C.N.V.R.	16 June, 1945	....
LETHBRIDGE	*Corvette*	Lt. W. Mahan, R.C.N.R.	11 May, 1941	24 June, 1941
		Lt. H. Freeland, R.C.N.R.	25 June, 1941	20 Oct., 1942
		Lt. Cdr. R. S. Kelly, R.C.N.R.	21 Oct., 1942	21 Apl., 1943
		Lt. Cdr. W. Woods, R.C.N.R.	22 Apl., 1943	22 Apl., 1943
		Lt. J. Roberts, R.C.N.V.R.	22 Apl., 1943	15 June, 1943
		Lt. Cdr. St. C. Balfour, R.C.N.V.R.	16 June, 1943	14 Mch., 1944
		Lt. F. H. Finfold, R.C.N.V.R.	15 Mch., 1944	17 Mch., 1944
		Lt. J. W. Bessey, R.C.N.V.R.	18 Mch., 1944	7 May, 1945
		Lt. J. Holland, R.C.N.V.R.	8 May, 1945	18 July, 1945
LEVIS	*Frigate*	Lt. P. T. Molson, R.C.N.V.R.	5 June, 1944	5 June, 1944
		Lt. Cdr. P. C. Evans, R.C.N.R.	5 June, 1944	2 Sept., 1945
LEVIS	*Corvette*	Cdr. J. D. Prentice, R.C.N.	18 Nov., 1940	9 Mch., 1941
		Lt. C. W. Gilding, R.C.N.R.	10 Mch., 1941	19 Sept., 1941
LINDSAY	*Corvette*	Lt. G. A. V. Thomson, R.C.N.V.R.	15 Nov., 1943	14 July, 1945
LLEWELLYN	*Minesweeper*	Mate J. A. MacKinnon, R.C.N.R.	24 Aug., 1942	16 May, 1943
		Lt. F. W. Anderson, R.C.N.V.R.	17 May, 1943	2 Sept., 1945

PRINCIPAL SHIPS OF THE ROYAL CANADIAN NAVY 1939-1945—*Continued*

Ship	Class	Commanding Officer	From	To
LLOYD GEORGE	*Minesweeper*	Ch. Skpr. W. H. Crocker, R.C.N.R.	24 Aug., 1942	15 Sept., 1942
		S/Lt. K. R. MacLeod, R.C.N.V.R.	16 Sept., 1942	14 Feb., 1945
		Lt. J. F. Stevens, R.C.N.V.R.	15 Feb., 1945	8 May, 1945
		Skpr. Lt. C. C. Darrach, M.B.E., R.C.N.R.	9 May, 1945	2 Sept., 1945
LOCH ACHANALT	*Frigate*	Lt. R. W. Hart, R.C.N.V.R.	8 May, 1944	24 Mch., 1945
		Lt. R. J. Belt, R.C.N.V.R.	25 Mch., 1945	20 June, 1945
LAURIER	*Patrol Craft*	Lt. R. A. S. MacNeil, R.C.N.R.	12 Apl., 1940	10 Apl., 1941
		Ch. Skpr. D. E. Freeman, R.C.N.R.	11 Apl., 1941	2 Sept., 1945
LOCH ALVIE	*Frigate*	Lt. Cdr. E. G. Old, R.C.N.R.	8 May, 1944	11 June, 1945
LOCH MORLOCH	*Frigate*	Lt. Cdr. L. L. Foxall, R.C.N.R.	6 Mch., 1944	18 Dec., 1944
		Lt. G. F. Crosby, R.C.N.V.R.	19 Dec., 1944	20 June, 1945
LOCKEPORT	*Minesweeper*	Lt. D. Trail, R.C.N.R.	27 May, 1942	21 Aug., 1943
		Lt. R. M. Wallace, R.C.N.V.R.	22 Aug., 1943	23 June, 1944
		Lt. C. A. Nicol, R.C.N.R.	24 June, 1944	2 July, 1945
LONGBRANCH	*Corvette*	Lt. Cdr. W. J. Kingsmill, R.C.N.V.R.	5 Jan., 1944	16 Apl., 1944
		Lt. Cdr. R. J. G. Johnson, R.C.N.V.R.	17 Apl., 1944	7 Oct., 1944
		Lt. Cdr. J. B. O'Brien, R.C.N.V.R.	8 Oct., 1944	21 Feb., 1945
		Lt. Cdr. K. B. Culley, R.C.N.V.R.	22 Feb., 1945	14 June, 1945
LONGUEUIL	*Frigate*	Lt. Cdr. M. J. Woods, R.C.N.V.R.	10 Apl., 1944	2 Sept., 1945
LOUISBURG	*Corvette*	Lt. Cdr. W. F. Campbell, R.C.N.V.R.	19 July, 1941	6 Feb., 1943
LOUISBURG	*Corvette*	Lt. J. B. Elmsley, R.C.N.V.R.	12 Dec., 1943	10 Feb., 1945
		Lt. M. W. Knowles, R.C.N.V.R.	11 Feb., 1945	21 June, 1945
LUNENBURG	*Corvette*	Lt. W. E. Harrison, R.C.N.R.	4 Dec., 1941	10 Oct., 1942
		Lt. D. L. Miller, D.S.C., R.C.N.V.R.	11 Oct., 1942	22 Dec., 1944
		Lt. W. S. Thomson, R.C.N.R.	23 Dec., 1944	18 July, 1945
MAGOG	*Frigate*	Lt. L. D. Quick, R.C.N.R.	20 Mch., 1944	20 Dec., 1944

Ship	Type	Commanding Officer	From	To
MAHONE	*Minesweeper*	Lt. D. M. Stewart, R.C.N.R.	29 Sept., 1941	31 May, 1942
		Lt. K. D. Heath, R.C.N.R.	1 June, 1942	3 Dec., 1942
		Lt. W. J. Gilmour, R.C.N.V.R.	4 Dec., 1942	29 Nov., 1943
		Lt. J. C. Tyrer, R.C.N.V.R.	30 Nov., 1943	9 Jan., 1944
		Lt. W. Turner, R.C.N.V.R.	10 Jan., 1944	4 June, 1944
		Lt. L. R. Hoar, R.C.N.V.R.	5 June, 1944	25 Mch., 1945
		Lt. N. R. Chappel, R.C.N.V.R.	26 Mch., 1945	6 Nov., 1945
MALPEQUE	*Minesweeper*	Lt. W. R. Stacey, R.C.N.R.	4 Aug., 1941	27 Apl., 1943
		Lt. O. R. Archibal, R.C.N.V.R.	28 Apl., 1943	22 Aug., 1943
		Lt. D. Davis, R.C.N.V.R.	23 Aug., 1943	9 Oct., 1945
MARGAREE	*Destroyer*	Cdr. J. W. R. Roy, R.C.N.	6 Sept., 1940	23 Oct., 1940
MATANE	*Frigate*	Lt. Cdr. A. H. Easton, D.S.C., R.C.N.R.	22 Oct., 1943	22 Oct., 1943
		Lt. J. J. Coates, R.C.N.V.R.	23 Oct., 1943	21 Jan., 1944
		Cdr. A. F. C. Layard, D.S.O., R.N.	22 Jan., 1944	28 Mch., 1945
		Lt. Cdr. F. J. Jones, R.C.N.V.R.	29 Mch., 1945	....
MATAPEDIA	*Corvette*	Lt. R. J. Herman, R.C.N.R.	9 May, 1941	26 Apl., 1943
		Lt. J. D. Frewer, R.C.N.V.R.	27 Apl., 1943	12 May, 1944
		Lt. C. F. Usher, R.C.N.V.R.	13 May, 1945	14 June, 1945
MAYFLOWER	*Corvette*	Lt. Cdr. G. H. Stephen, R.C.N.R.	9 Nov., 1940	12 May, 1942
		Lt. V. Browne, R.C.N.V.R.	13 May, 1942	2 Mch., 1944
		Lt. D. S. Martin, R.C.N.R.	3 Mch., 1944	31 May, 1945
MEDICINE HAT	*Minesweeper*	Lt. J. Bevan, R.C.N.R.	4 Dec., 1941	1 May, 1943
		Lt. J. E. Howard, R.C.N.V.R.	2 May, 1943	28 Aug., 1944
		Lt. R. J. Keelan, R.C.N.V.R.	29 Aug., 1944	7 May, 1945
		Lt. K. C. Clark, R.C.N.V.R.	8 May, 1945	2 Sept., 1945
MELVILLE	*Minesweeper*	Lt. R. T. Ingram, R.C.N.R.	4 Dec., 1941	19 June, 1942
		Lt. E. R. Shaw, R.C.N.R.	20 June, 1942	16 May, 1943
		Lt. D. B. Harding, R.C.N.V.R.	17 May, 1943	11 Oct., 1943
		Lt. D. A. C. Newton, R.C.N.V.R.	12 Oct., 1943	7 Nov., 1943
		Skpr. Lt. J. B. Cooper, R.C.N.R.	8 Nov., 1944	19 May, 1944
		Lt. J. S. Foster, R.C.N.R.	20 May, 1944	16 July, 1945
MEON	*Frigate*	Lt. Cdr. S. C. Balfour, R.C.N.V.R.	2 Feb., 1944	3 Jan., 1945
		Lt. N. W. Adams, R.C.N.V.R.	4 Jan., 1945	22 Apl., 1945

PRINCIPAL SHIPS OF THE ROYAL CANADIAN NAVY 1939-1945—*Continued*

Ship	Class	Commanding Officer	From	To
MERRITTONIA	*Corvette*	Lt. F. K. Ellis, R.C.N.V.R.	10 Nov., 1944	5 Apl., 1945
		Lt. Cdr. J. F. Stairs, R.C.N.V.R.	6 Apl., 1945	6 May, 1945
		Lt. R. J. Keelan, R.C.N.V.R.	7 May, 1945	5 July, 1945
MIDDLESEX	*Algerine*	Lt. W. J. Piercey, R.C.N.R.	8 June, 1944	2 Sept., 1945
MIDLAND	*Corvette*	Lt. A. B. Taylor, R.C.N.R.	8 Nov., 1941	31 Oct., 1943
		Lt. W. O. Barbour, R.C.N.R.	1 Nov., 1943	11 July, 1945
MILLTOWN	*Minesweeper*	Lt. Cdr. J. H. Marshall, R.C.N.V.R.	18 Sept., 1942	14 Apl., 1943
		Lt. E. H. Maguire, R.C.N.V.R.	15 Apl., 1943	18 Sept., 1944
		Cdr. A. H. G. Storrs, R.C.N.R.	19 Sept., 1944	2 Sept., 1945
MIMICO	*Corvette*	Lt. F. J. Jones, R.C.N.V.R.	8 Feb., 1944	14 Feb., 1945
		Lt. Cdr. J. B. Elmsley, R.C.N.V.R.	15 Feb., 1945	13 May, 1945
MINAS	*Minesweeper*	Lt. J. C. Barbour, R.C.N.R.	2 Aug., 1941	3 Jan., 1942
		Lt. J. G. Kingsmill, R.C.N.V.R.	4 Jan., 1942	13 Sept., 1942
		Lt. W. F. Wood, R.C.N.R.	14 Sept., 1942	17 June, 1943
		Lt. J. B. Lamb, R.C.N.V.R.	18 June, 1943	2 Sept., 1945
MIRAMICHI	*Minesweeper*	Lt. W. G. Johnstone, R.C.N.R.	26 Nov., 1941	28 Feb., 1943
		Lt. G. H. Matheson, R.C.N.R.	1 Mch., 1943	23 Jan., 1944
		Lt. R. J. Williams, R.C.N.V.R.	24 Jan., 1944	2 Sept., 1945
MONCTON	*Corvette*	Lt. A. W. Ford, R.C.N.R.	12 Oct., 1942	3 Feb., 1944
		Lt. Cdr. A. T. Morrell, R.C.N.R.	4 Feb., 1944	3 Apl., 1944
		Lt. Cdr. R. J. Roberts, R.C.N.R.	4 Apl., 1944	20 June, 1944
		Lt. O. H. M. Wright, R.C.N.V.R.	21 June, 1944	26 Jan., 1945
		Lt. W. McCombe, R.C.N.R.	27 Jan., 1945	2 Sept., 1945
MONNOW	*Frigate*	Cdr. E. G. Skinner, D.S.C., R.D., R.C.N.R.	3 Feb., 1944	11 June, 1945
MONTREAL	*Frigate*	Lt. R. J. Herman, R.C.N.R., O.B.E.	12 Nov., 1943	4 July, 1944
		Lt. Cdr. S. W. Howell, R.C.N.R.	5 July, 1944	26 Nov., 1944
		Lt. Cdr. C. L. Campbell, R.C.N.V.R.	27 Nov., 1944	4 Oct., 1945

Ship	Type	Commanding Officer	From	To
MOOSEJAW	*Corvette*	Lt. F. E. Grubb, R.C.N.	19 June, 1941	13 Feb., 1942
		Lt. L. D. Quick, R.C.N.R.	14 Feb., 1942	10 Aug., 1943
		Lt. A. Harvey, R.C.N.R.	11 Aug., 1943	13 Mch., 1944
		Lt. H. Brynjolfson, R.C.N.V.R.	14 Mch., 1944	3 July, 1945
MORDEN	*Corvette*	Lt. J. J. Hodgkinson, R.C.N.R.	6 Sept., 1941	2 June, 1943
		Lt. E. C. Smith, R.C.N.V.R.	3 June, 1943	14 Oct., 1943
		Lt. W. Turner, R.C.N.R.	15 Oct., 1943	21 May, 1944
		Lt. K. B. Culley, R.C.N.V.R.	22 May, 1944	18 Feb., 1945
		Lt. F. D. Spindler, R.C.N.V.R.	19 Feb., 1945	25 June, 1945
MULGRAVE	*Minesweeper*	Lt. D. T. English, R.C.N.R.	4 Nov., 1942	10 Oct., 1943
		Lt. R. M. Meredith, R.C.N.R.	11 Oct., 1943	7 June, 1945
NABOB	*Escort Carrier*	Capt. H. N. Lay, O.B.E.	15 Oct., 1943	10 Oct., 1944
NANAIMO	*Corvette*	Lt. Cdr. H. C. C. Daubeny, R.C.N.R.	26 Apl., 1941	7 Oct., 1941
		Lt. T. J. Bellas,	8 Oct., 1941	20 Aug., 1942
		Lt. (N) E. U. Jones, R.C.N.R.	21 Aug., 1942	10 Oct., 1943
		Lt. J. E. Hastings, R.C.N.R.	11 Oct., 1943	9 Oct., 1944
		Lt. R. C Eaton, R.C.N.V.R.	10 Oct., 1944	22 Mch., 1945
		Lt. Cdr. W. Redford, R.C.N.R.	23 Mch., 1945	28 Aug., 1945
NANOOSE ex-NOOTKA	*Minesweeper*	Lt. Cdr. A. T. Morrell, R.C.N.R.	10 Sept., 1939	15 Mch., 1942
		Ch. Skpr. G. F. Burgess, R.C.N.R.	16 Mch., 1942	13 Sept., 1943
		Skpr. Lt. G. C. Burnham, R.C.N.R.	14 Sept., 1943	23 July, 1945
NAPANEE	*Corvette*	Lt. Cdr. A. H. Hobson, R.C.N.R.	12 May, 1941	5 Dec., 1941
		Lt. S. Henderson, R.C.N.R.	6 Dec., 1941	10 June, 1943
		Lt. Cdr. G. A. Powell, R.C.N.V.R.	11 June, 1943	6 July, 1945
NENE	*Frigate*	Lt. Cdr. E. R. Shaw, R.C.N.R.	6 Apl., 1944	11 June, 1945
NEW GLASGOW	*Frigate*	Lt. Cdr. G. S. Hall, R.C.N.R.	23 Dec., 1943	29 Aug., 1944
		Lt. Cdr. R. M. Hanbury, R.C.N.V.R.	30 Aug., 1944	28 Mch., 1945
		Lt. Cdr. E. T. P. Wennberg, R.C.N.V.R.	29 Mch., 1945	5 Nov., 1945
NEW LISKEARD	*Algerine*	Lt. W. M. Grand, R.C.N.V.R.	21 Nov., 1944	2 Sept., 1945
NEW WATERFORD	*Frigate*	Lt. Cdr. E. R. Shaw, R.C.N.R.	21 Jan., 1944	23 Mch., 1944
		Cdr. W. E. S. Briggs, R.C.N.R. D.S.C.	24 Mch., 1944	11 Nov., 1945
		Lt. Cdr. J. M. Leming, R.C.N.V.R.	12 Nov., 1944	12 Nov., 1945

SHIP	CLASS	COMMANDING OFFICER	FROM	TO
NEW WESTMINSTER	Corvette	Lt. Cdr. R. G. McKenzie, R.C.N.R.	31 Jan., 1942	19 June, 1945
NIAGARA	Destroyer.	Lt. Cdr. E. L. Armstrong, R.C.N.	24 Sept., 1940	2 July, 1941
		Lt. Cdr. T. P. Ryan, O.B.E., R.C.N.	3 July, 1941	23 Feb., 1942
		Lt. Cdr. R. F. Harris, D.S.C., R.C.N.	24 Feb., 1942	9 Sept., 1943
		Lt. Cdr. W. H. Willson, R.C.N.	10 Sept., 1943	22 June, 1944
		Cdr. R. B. Mitchell, R.C.N.R.	23 June, 1944	15 Sept., 1945
NIPIGON	Minesweeper	Lt. Cdr. A. T. Morrell,	12 Aug., 1941	14 Feb., 1942
		Lt. Cdr. C. A. King, R.C.N.R.	15 Feb., 1942	11 May, 1942
		Lt. J. Brock, R.C.N.V.R.	12 May, 1942	4 Oct., 1942
		Lt. W. J. Piercey, R.C.N.V.R.	5 Oct., 1942	11 Apl., 1944
		Lt. D. R. Baker, R.C.N.V.R.	12 Apl., 1944	4 Feb., 1945
		Lt. J. R. Brown, R.C.N.V.R.	5 Feb., 1945	13 Oct., 1945
NORANDA	Minesweeper	Lt. W. R. Nunn, R.C.N.R.	15 May, 1942	10 Jan., 1943
		Lt. J. E. Francois, R.C.N.R.	11 Jan., 1943	17 Oct., 1944
		Lt. R. A. Wright, R.C.N.V.R.	18 Oct., 1944	7 Nov., 1944
		Lt. G. E. Gilbride, R.C.N.V.R.	8 Nov., 1944	28 Aug., 1945
NORSYD	Corvette	Lt. J. R. Biggs, R.C.N.R.	22 Dec., 1943	20 Oct., 1944
		Lt. W. P. Wickett, R.C.N.V.R.	21 Oct., 1944	21 June, 1945
NORTH BAY	Corvette	Lt. Cdr. B. Hynes, R.C.N.V.R.	25 Oct., 1943	23 Jan., 1945
		Lt. J. W. Radford, R.C.N.R.	24 Jan., 1945	18 Feb., 1945
		Lt. Cdr. A. C. Campbell, R.C.N.V.R.	19 Feb., 1945	26 June, 1945
OAKVILLE	Corvette	Lt. A. C. Jones, R.C.N.R.	18 Nov., 1941	11 May, 1942
		Lt. Cdr. C. A. King, D.S.C., R.C.N.R.	12 May, 1942	21 Apl., 1943
		Lt. H. F. Farncomb, R.C.N.V.R.	22 Apl., 1943	22 Oct., 1944
		Lt. M. A. Griffiths, R.C.N.V.R.	23 Oct., 1944	16 July, 1945
ONTARIO	Cruiser	Capt. H. T. W. Grant, R.C.N. D.S.O.	26 Apl., 1945	2 Sept., 1945
		Cdr. E. P. Tisdall, R.C.N.	....	2 Sept., 1945
ORANGEVILLE	Corvette	Lt. Cdr. F. R. Pike, R.C.N.V.R.	24 Apl., 1944	2 Sept., 1945

Ship	Type	Commanding Officer	From	To
ORILLIA	*Corvette*	Lt. Cdr. W. E. S. Briggs, R.C.N.R.	25 Nov., 1940	4 Sept., 1942
		Lt. H. Y. W. Gross, R.C.N.R.	5 Sept., 1942	13 Feb., 1943
		Lt. Cdr. R. Jackson, R.C.N.R.	14 Feb., 1943	16 Apl., 1943
		Lt. Cdr. J. E. Mitchell, R.C.N.V.R.	17 Apl., 1943	7 May, 1944
		Skpr. Lt. J. W. Sharpe, R.C.N.R.	8 May, 1944	27 June, 1945
ORKNEY	*Frigate*	Cdr. V. Browne, R.C.N.V.R.	18 Apl., 1944	28 Mch., 1945
		Cdr. J. M. Rowland, D.S.C. & Bar, R.N.	29 Mch., 1945	....
		Lt. N. J. Castonguay, R.C.N.V.R.	....	2 Sept., 1945
OSHAWA	*Algerine*	Lt. Cdr. J. C. Pratt, R.C.N.V.R.	6 July, 1944	27 May, 1945
		Lt. Cdr. R. S. Williams, R.C.N.V.R.	28 May, 1945	2 Sept., 1945
OTTAWA	*Destroyer*	Capt. G. C. Jones, R.C.N.	10 Sept., 1939	1 Apl., 1940
		Capt. E. R. Mainguy, R.C.N.	2 Apl., 1940	20 July, 1941
		Lt. Cdr. A. G. Boulton, R.C.N.V.R.	21 July, 1941	....
		Cdr. H. F. Pullen, R.C.N.	....	13 Nov., 1941
		Cdr. C. D. Donald,	14 Nov., 1941	4 July, 1942
		Lt. Cdr. C. A. Rutherford,	5 July, 1942	13 Sept., 1942
OTTAWA	*Destroyer*	Cdr. H. F. Pullen, O.B.E., R.C.N.	20 Mch., 1943	18 May, 1944
		Cdr. J. S. D. Prentice, D.S.O., R.C.N.	19 May, 1944	11 Oct., 1944
		Lt. N. Cogdon, R.C.N.	12 Oct., 1944	4 Feb., 1945
		Lt. Cdr. P. D. Budge, D.S.C., R.C.N.	5 Feb., 1945	12 Oct., 1945
OTTER	*Patrol Vessel*	Lt. D. S. Mossman,	31 May, 1940	26 Mch., 1941
OUTARDE	*Minesweeper*	Lt. H. M. Kennedy,	4 Dec., 1941	18 May, 1942
		Lt. R. Jackson,	19 May, 1942	5 Feb., 1943
		Lt. Cdr. J. A. MacDonnell,	6 Feb., 1943	9 Apl., 1944
		Lt. A. C. Jones, R.C.N.R.	10 Apl., 1944	23 Aug., 1944
		Lt. H. B. Tindale, R.C.N.V.R.	24 Aug., 1944	24 Nov., 1945
OUTREMONT	*Frigate*	Cdr. H. Freeland, R.C.N.R. D.S.O.	27 Nov., 1943	11 Aug., 1944
		Lt. Cdr. F. O. Gerity, R.C.N.R.	12 Aug., 1944	5 Nov., 1945
OWEN SOUND	*Corvette*	Lt. Cdr. J. M. Watson, R.C.N.R.	17 Nov., 1943	13 Apl., 1945
		Lt. F. H. Pinfold, R.C.N.R.	14 Apl., 1945	14 July, 1945
PARRY SOUND	*Corvette*	Lt. Cdr. W. J. Gilmore, R.C.N.V.R.	30 Aug., 1944	7 July, 1945

PRINCIPAL SHIPS OF THE ROYAL CANADIAN NAVY 1939-1945—*Continued*

Ship	Class	Commanding Officer	From	To
PENETANG	*Frigate*	Lt. Cdr. A. R. Hicks, R.C.N.V.R.	19 Oct., 1944	10 Nov., 1945
PETERBOROUGH	*Corvette*	Lt. J. B. Raine, R.C.N.R.	1 June, 1944	14 July, 1945
PETROLIA	*Corvette*	Lt. P. W. Spragge, R.C.N.V.R.	29 June, 1944	10 Nov., 1945
PICTOU	*Corvette*	Lt. A. G. S. Griffin,	29 Apl., 1941	14 Mch., 1943
		Lt. P. T. Byers,	15 Mch., 1943	19 Nov., 1943
		Lt. Cdr. G. K. Fox, R.C.N.V.R.	20 Nov., 1943	1 Oct., 1944
		Lt. F. Cross, R.C.N.R.	2 Oct., 1944	29 June, 1945
PORTAGE	*Algerine*	Lt. B. P. Young, R.C.N.R.	22 Oct., 1943	9 Jan., 1944
		Lt. Cdr. G. M. Kaizer, R.C.N.R.	10 Jan., 1944	2 Sept., 1945
PORT ARTHUR	*Corvette*	Lt. E. T. Simmons, D.S.C.	26 May, 1942	8 July, 1943
		Lt. Cdr. K. T. Chisholm, R.C.N.V.R.	9 July, 1943	11 July, 1945
PORT COLBORNE	*Frigate*	Lt. Cdr. C. J. Angus, R.C.N.R.	15 Nov., 1943	2 Apl., 1945
		Lt. Cdr. M. F. Oliver, R.C.N.R.	3 Apl., 1945	7 Nov., 1945
PORT HOPE	*Minesweeper*	Lt. W. Turner,	30 July, 1942	1 Dec., 1942
		Lt. A. H. Rankin,	2 Dec., 1942	8 Apl., 1943
		Lt. R. K. Lester, R.C.N.V.R.	9 Apl., 1943	17 Mch., 1944
		Lt. R. M. Montague, R.C.N.V.R.	18 Mch., 1944	13 Oct., 1945
POUNDMAKER	*Frigate*	Lt. Cdr. H. S. Maxwell, R.C.N.V.R.	17 Sept., 1944	14 Apl., 1945
		Lt. Cdr. J. T. Baind, R.C.N.V.R.	15 Apl., 1945	19 Apl., 1945
		Lt. Cdr. W. R. Moffat, R.C.N.V.R.	20 Apl., 1945	25 Nov., 1945
PRESCOTT	*Corvette*	Lt. H. A. Russell,	26 June, 1941	11 Sept., 1942
		Lt. Cdr. W. McIsaac, R.C.N.V.R.	12 Sept., 1942	28 Dec., 1944
		Lt. G. J. Mathewson, R.C.N.V.R.	29 Dec., 1944	17 July, 1945
PRESERVER	*Depot Ship*	Capt. B. L. Johnson, D.S.O.,	11 July, 1942	16 Dec., 1943
		Cdr. G. Borrie, R.C.N.R.	17 Dec., 1943	17 Apl., 1945
		Lt. Cdr. H. C. Walmesly, R.C.N.R.	18 Apl., 1945	18 Oct., 1945

PRESTONIAN	*Frigate*	Lt. Cdr. I. Angus, R.C.N.V.R.	13 Sept., 1944	1 Apl., 1945
		Lt. Cdr. G. N. Downey, R.C.N.R.	2 Apl., 1945	9 Nov., 1945
PRINCE DAVID	*Armed Merchant Cruiser (converted to) Landing Ship Infantry*	Cdr. W. B. Armit, R.C.N.R.	28 Dec., 1940	24 Mch., 1941
		Cdr. K. F. Adams, R.C.N.	25 Mch., 1941	1 Dec., 1941
		Capt. V. S. Godfrey, R.C.N.	2 Dec., 1941	2 Dec., 1943
		Capt. T. D. Kelly, R.C.N.R.	3 Dec., 1943	21 Mch., 1945
PRINCE HENRY	*Armed Merchant Cruiser (converted to) Landing Ship Infantry*	Capt. R. I. Agnew, O.B.E., R.C.N.	4 Dec., 1940	19 Dec., 1941
		Capt. J. E. C. Edwards, R.C.N.	20 Dec., 1941	31 Dec., 1942
		Capt. F. L. Houghton, R.C.N.	1 Jan., 1943	18 Mch., 1943
		Ltd. Cdr. E. W. Finch-Noyes, R.C.N.	19 Mch., 1943	22 Mch., 1943
		Lt. Cdr. T. K. Young, R.C.N.R.	23 Mch., 1943	23 May, 1943
		Cdr. T. D. Kelly, R.C.N.R.	24 May, 1943	29 Nov., 1943
		Cdr. K. F. Adams, R.C.N.	30 Nov., 1943	11 Dec., 1943
		Capt. V. S. Godfrey, R.C.N.	12 Dec., 1943	6 Apl., 1945
PRINCE ROBERT	*Armed Merchant Cruiser (converted to) Auxiliary A/A Ship*	Cdr. F. G. Hart, R.C.N.R.	31 July, 1940	21 June, 1942
		Capt. F. L. Houghton, R.C.N.	22 June, 1942	31 Dec., 1942
		Cdr. O. C. S. Robertson, R.C.N.	1 Jan., 1943	5 June, 1943
		Capt. A. M. Hope, R.C.N.	6 June, 1943	7 Dec., 1944
		Capt. W. B. Creery, R.C.N.	8 Dec., 1944	2 Sept., 1945
PRINCE RUPERT	*Frigate*	Lt. Cdr. R. W. Draney, R.C.N.R., D.S.C.	30 Aug., 1943	2 Sept., 1945
PROVIDER	*Depot Ship*	Capt. J. A. Heenan, R.C.N.	1 Dec., 1942	4 May, 1943
		Lt. Cdr. W. H. Koughan, R.C.N.R.	5 May, 1943	3 July, 1943
		Cdr. E. G. Skinner, D.S.C.	4 July, 1943	17 Nov., 1943
		Cdr. T. Gilmour, R.C.N.R.	18 Nov., 1943	14 Feb., 1945
		Capt. L. J. M. Gauvreau, R.C.N.	15 Feb., 1945	2 Sept., 1945
PUNCHER	*Escort Carrier*	Capt. R. E. S. Bidwell,	10 Apl., 1944	16 Jan., 1946
QU'APPELLE	*Destroyer*	Cdr. D. C. Wallace, D.S.C., R.C.N.R.	8 Feb., 1944	4 Dec., 1944
		Cdr. E. L. Armstrong, R.C.N.	5 Dec., 1944	2 Apl., 1945
		Lt. Cdr. I. Angus, R.C.N.V.R.	3 Apl., 1945	21 June, 1945
		Lt. Cdr. W. Davenport, R.C.N.R.	22 June, 1945	2 Sept., 1945

PRINCIPAL SHIPS OF THE ROYAL CANADIAN NAVY 1939-1945—*Continued*

SHIP	CLASS	COMMANDING OFFICER	FROM	TO
QUATSINO	*Minesweeper*	Lt. S. Douglas,	3 Nov., 1941	14 Dec., 1941
		Lt. Cdr. T. MacDuff,	15 Dec., 1941	27 May, 1942
		Lt. A. E. Gough,	28 May, 1942	5 Oct., 1942
		Lt. J. H. Lincoln,	6 Oct., 1942	2 Apl., 1943
		Lt. A. H. Gosse, R.C.N.R.	3 Apl., 1943	29 Sept., 1943
		Lt. H. H. Rankin,	30 Sept., 1943	22 Oct., 1943
		Lt. A. H. Gosse, R.C.N.R.	23 Oct., 1943	2 Jan., 1945
		Lt. Cdr. B. C. Cook, R.C.N.V.R.	3 Jan., 1945	26 Nov., 1945
QUESNEL	*Corvette*	Lt. J. A. Gow,	23 May, 1941	16 Nov., 1942
		Lt. M. Smith, R.C.N.R.	17 Nov., 1942	11 Apl., 1943
		Lt. J. M. Laing, R.C.N.R.	12 Apl., 1943	28 June, 1945
QUINTE	*Minesweeper*	Lt. C. A. Nicol, R.C.N.R.	30 Aug., 1941	26 Nov., 1944
		Skpr. Lt. C. C. Clattenburg, R.C.N.R.	27 Nov., 1944	30 Nov., 1944
		Lt. D. C. MacPherson, R.C.N.V.R.	1 Dec., 1944	2 Sept., 1945
RACCOON	*Armed Yacht*	Lt. Cdr. J. L. Diver, R.C.N.R.	18 May, 1940	17 Oct., 1940
		Lt. F. Roberts,	18 Oct., 1940	16 Apl., 1941
		Lt. N. G. Bennett,	17 Apl., 1941	22 July, 1941
		Lt. D. W. Main,	23 July, 1941	16 Nov., 1941
		Lt. A. H. Cassivi,	17 Nov., 1941	4 Dec., 1941
		Lt. Cdr. J. N. Smith,	5 Dec., 1941	7 Sept., 1942
RED DEER	*Minesweeper*	Lt. A. Moorhouse, R.C.N.R.	24 Nov., 1941	2 Feb., 1943
		Lt. J. A. Mitchell, R.C.N.R.	3 Feb., 1943	5 June, 1944
		Lt. D. B. D. Ross, R.C.N.V.R.	6 June, 1944	30 Oct., 1945
REINDEER	*Armed Yacht*	Lt. Cdr. E. G. Skinner,	11 July, 1940	17 Jan., 1941
		Lt. Cdr. F. A. Price,	18 Jan., 1941	16 May, 1941
		Lt. L. C. Cumming,	17 May, 1941	30 Apl., 1942
		Lt. F. J. G. Johnson,	1 May, 1942	23 Nov., 1942
		Lt. D. M. Coolican,	24 Nov., 1942	8 Feb., 1943
		Lt. R. G. James, R.C.N.V.R.	9 Feb., 1943	19 May, 1944
		Lt. J. H. Ewart, R.C.N.V.R.	20 May, 1944	7 Oct., 1944
		Lt. W. C. Hawkins, R.C.N.V.R.	8 Oct., 1944	20 July, 1945

Ship	Type	Commander	From	To
RESTIGOUCHE	*Destroyer*	Cdr. W. B. L. Holms, R.C.N.	10 Sept., 1939	25 Dec., 1939
		Cdr. H. N. Lay, R.C.N.	26 Dec., 1939	29 June, 1941
		Lt. Cdr. D. W. Piers, R.C.N.	30 June, 1941	5 Dec., 1943
		Lt. Cdr. D. W. Groos, R.C.N.	6 June, 1943	3 Dec., 1944
		Lt. Cdr. P. E. Haddon, R.C.N.	4 Dec., 1944	15 Apl., 1945
		Lt. Cdr. R. J. Herman, R.C.N.R., O.B.E.	16 Apl., 1945	4 Sept., 1945
REVELSTOKE	*Minesweeper*	Skpr. Lt. J. E. Moore, R.C.N.R.	15 Sept., 1944	24 Apl., 1945
		Lt. A. B. Plummer, R.C.N.V.R.	25 Apl., 1945	2 Sept., 1945
RIBBLE	*Frigate*	Lt. Cdr. A. B. Taylor, R.C.N.R.	24 July, 1944	20 Nov., 1944
		Lt. Cdr. A. A. R. Dykes, R.C.N.R.	21 Nov., 1944	11 June, 1945
RIMOUSKI	*Corvette*	Lt. J. W. Bonner, R.C.N.V.R.	27 Apl., 1941	11 Nov., 1941
		Lt. Cdr. A. G. Boulton, R.C.N.V.R.	12 Nov., 1941	1 Dec., 1942
		Lt. R. J. Pickford, R.C.N.V.R.	2 Dec., 1942	13 Apl., 1943
		Lt. C. D. Chivers, R.C.N.V.R.	14 Apl., 1943	17 Dec., 1944
		Lt. Cdr. D. M. MacDonald, R.C.N.V.R.	18 Dec., 1944	19 July, 1945
RIVIERE DU LOUP	*Corvette*	Lt. R. N. Smillie, R.C.N.V.R.	21 Nov., 1943	22 Jan., 1945
		Lt. R. D. Weldon, R.C.N.V.R.	23 Jan., 1945	27 June, 1945
ROCKCLIFFE	*Algerine*	Lt. J. E. Heward, R.C.N.R.	30 Sept., 1944	14 Sept., 1945
ROSSLAND	*Minesweeper*	Skpr. Lt. E. E. Kinney, R.C.N.R.	15 July, 1944	2 Sept., 1945
REGINA	*Corvette*	Lt. Cdr. R. F. Harris,	22 Jan., 1942	23 Feb., 1942
		Lt. R. S. Kelly,	24 Feb., 1942	20 Oct., 1942
		Lt. Cdr. H. Freeland,	21 Oct., 1942	3 Sept., 1943
		Lt. J. W. Radford, R.C.N.R.	4 Sept., 1943	9 Aug., 1944
ROSTHERN	*Corvette*	Lt. W. Russell,	17 June, 1941	20 Nov., 1941
		Cdr. P. B. Cross,	21 Nov., 1941	24 Nov., 1942
		Lt. Cdr. R. J. G. Johnson, R.C.N.V.R.	25 Nov., 1942	1 Feb., 1943
		Lt. S. R. P. Annett, R.C.N.V.R.	2 Feb., 1943	3 Nov., 1944
		Lt. Cdr. R. F. Wilson, R.C.N.V.R.	4 Nov., 1944	6 Apl., 1945
		Lt. D. R. Smythies, R.C.N.V.R.	7 Apl., 1945	16 July, 1945
ROYAL MOUNT	*Frigate*	Lt. Cdr. J. S. Davis, R.C.N.V.R.	25 Aug., 1944	30 Mch., 1945
		Lt. J. H. Dunne, R.C.N.V.R.	31 Mch., 1945	17 Nov., 1945

PRINCIPAL SHIPS OF THE ROYAL CANADIAN NAVY 1939-1945—Continued

Ship	Class	Commanding Officer	From	To
RUNNYMEDE	Frigate	Lt. Cdr. R. C. Chenoweth, R.C.N.V.R.	14 June, 1944	9 Feb., 1945
		Cdr. A. M. McLarnon, R.C.N.R.	10 Feb., 1945	22 Mch., 1945
		Lt. Cdr. R. C. Chenoweth, R.C.N.V.R.	23 Mch., 1945	8 June, 1945
		Cdr. C. A. King, D.S.O., D.S.C. & Bar., R.C.N.R.	9 June, 1945	22 Oct., 1945
SAGUENAY	Destroyer	Cdr. G. R. Miles, R.C.N.	10 Sept., 1939	16 Apl., 1940
		Lt. F. H. Davidson,	17 Apl., 1940	7 Apl., 1942
		Lt. Cdr. D. C. Wallace,	8 Apl., 1942	14 Jan., 1943
		Lt. J. W. McDowall,	15 Jan., 1943	23 Aug., 1943
		Lt. J. H. Ewart, R.C.N.V.R.	24 Aug., 1943	28 Dec., 1943
		Lt. W. E. Hughson, R.C.N.V.R.	29 Dec., 1943	15 Apl., 1945
		Lt. K. P. Blanche, R.C.N.V.R.	16 Apl., 1945	30 July, 1945
SAINT JOHN	Frigate	Lt. Cdr. R. M. Mosher, R.C.N.R.	12 Dec., 1943	20 Feb., 1944
		Lt. Cdr. W. R. Stacey, R.C.N.R.	21 Feb., 1944	8 Oct., 1945
SANS PEUR	Armed Yacht	Lt. Cdr. W. C. Halliday, R.C.N.	23 Oct., 1939	31 Jan., 1940
		Lt. Cdr. W. C. Halliday, R.C.N.	1 Feb., 1940	3 June, 1942
		Lt. Cdr. T. MacDuff	4 June, 1942	14 May, 1943
		Lt. Cdr. W. Redford, R.C.N.V.R.	15 May, 1943	9 Jan., 1944
		Lt. Cdr. H. S. MacFarlane, R.C.N.R.	10 Jan., 1944	2 Sept., 1945
SARNIA	Minesweeper	Lt. C. A. Mott, R.C.N.R.	13 Aug., 1942	17 July, 1943
		Lt. R. C. Chenoweth, R.C.N.V.R.	18 July, 1943	12 Mch., 1944
		Lt. H. A. Plow, R.C.N.V.R.	13 Mch., 1944	9 Oct., 1944
		Lt. R. P. J. Douty, R.C.N.V.R.	10 Oct., 1944	28 Oct., 1945
SASKATCHEWAN	Destroyer	Cdr. R. C. Medley, R.N., D.S.C.	31 May, 1943	5 Apl., 1944
		Lt. Cdr. A. H. Easton, D.S.C., R.C.N.R.	6 Apl., 1944	24 Aug., 1944
		Lt. Cdr. T. G. Pullen, R.C.N.	25 Aug., 1944	14 Oct., 1945
SASKATOON	Corvette	Lt. F. J. Jones,	9 June, 1941	4 Feb., 1942
		Lt. Cdr. C. A. King, D.S.C., R.C.N.R.	5 Feb., 1942	14 Feb., 1942
		Lt. J. S. Scott,	15 Feb., 1942	
		Lt. J. F. Evans,		9 July, 1943
		Lt. Cdr. T. MacDuff, R.C.N.R.	10 July, 1943	14 Mch., 1944
		Lt. Cdr. R. S. Williams, R.C.N.V.R.	15 Mch., 1944	25 June, 1945

Ship	Type	Commander	Appointed	Left
SAULT STE MARIE	Algerine	Lt. Cdr. R. Jackson,	24 June, 1943	11 Feb., 1944
		Lt. Cdr. A. Moorhouse, R.C.N.R.	12 Feb., 1944	2 Sept., 1945
ST. BONIFACE	Algerine	Lt. Cdr. J. J. Hodgkinson, R.C.N.R.	10 Sept., 1943	12 May, 1944
		Lt. Cdr. J. D. Frewer, R.C.N.V.R.	13 May, 1944	14 Apl., 1945
		Lt. Cdr. J. M. Watson, R.C.N.R.	15 Apl., 1945	19 Aug., 1945
		Lt. Cdr. R. N. Smillie, R.C.N.V.R.	20 Aug., 1945	2 Sept., 1945
ST. CATHARINES	Frigate	Lt. Cdr. H. C. R. Davis,	31 July, 1943	14 Mch., 1944
		Lt. Cdr. A. F. Pickard, O.B.E., R.C.N.R.	15 Mch., 1944	13 Dec., 1944
		Lt. Cdr. J. P. Fraser, R.C.N.R.	14 Dec., 1944	24 May, 1945
		Lt. A. B. Swain, R.C.N.V.R.	25 May, 1945	18 Nov., 1945
ST. CROIX	Destroyer	Lt. M. A. Medland, R.C.N.	25 Sept., 1940	10 Oct., 1940
		Cdr. H. Kingsley,	11 Oct., 1940	20 Apl., 1941
		Lt. C. J. Smith,	21 Apl., 1941	5 Jan., 1942
		Lt. Cdr. A. H. Dobson, D.S.C.,	6 Jan., 1942	20 Sept., 1943
ST. FRANCIS	Destroyer	Lt. Cdr. H. F. Pullen, R.C.N.	24 Sept., 1940	25 Aug., 1941
		Lt. C. A. Rutherford,	26 Aug., 1941	3 July, 1942
		Lt. Cdr. F. C. Smith,	4 July, 1942	17 Feb., 1943
		Lt. Cdr. H. V. W. Groos, R.C.N.	18 Feb., 1943	2 June, 1943
		Lt. G. L. MacKay, R.C.N.	3 June, 1943	16 Jan., 1944
		Lt. Cdr. J. E. Watson, R.C.N.R.	17 Jan., 1944	11 Oct., 1944
		Skpr. Lt. C. C. Clattenburg, R.C.N.R.	12 Oct., 1944	12 Nov., 1944
		Lt. Cdr. J. F. Watson, R.C.N.R.	13 Nov., 1944	6 July, 1945
ST. JOSEPH	Minesweeper	Lt. A. B. Plummer, R.C.N.V.R.	24 May, 1944	23 Apl., 1945
		Skpr. Lt. J. Craig, R.C.N.R.	24 Apl., 1945	8 Nov., 1945
SACKVILLE	Corvette	Lt. W. R. Kirkland,	30 Dec., 1941	5 Apl., 1942
		Lt. A. H. Easton, D.S.C.,	6 Apl., 1942	9 Apl., 1943
		Lt. Cdr. A. H. Rankin, R.C.N.V.R.	10 Apl., 1943	17 May, 1944
		Lt. A. R. Hicks, R.C.N.V.R.	18 May, 1944	17 Sept., 1944
		Lt. C. C. Love, R.C.N.V.R.	18 Sept., 1944	5 Nov., 1944
		Lt. J. A. McKenna, R.C.N.R.	6 Nov., 1944	2 Sept., 1945
ST. LAMBERT	Corvette	Lt. R. C. Hayden, R.C.N.V.R.	27 July, 1944	27 Oct., 1944
		Lt. Cdr. W. D. H. Gardiner, R.C.N.V.R.	27 Oct., 1944	16 July, 1945

PRINCIPAL SHIPS OF THE ROYAL CANADIAN NAVY 1939-1945—*Continued*

SHIP	CLASS	COMMANDING OFFICER	FROM	TO
ST. LAURENT	*Destroyer*	Lt. Cdr. A. M. Hope, R.C.N.	10 Sept., 1939	5 Oct., 1939
		Lt. Cdr. H. G. DeWolf, R.C.N.	6 Oct., 1939	13 July, 1940
		Lt. Cdr. H. S. Rayner, D.S.C., R.C.N.	14 July, 1940	18 Feb., 1942
		Cdr. E. L. Armstrong, R.C.N.	19 Feb., 1942	13 Nov., 1942
		Lt. Cdr. G. S. Windeyer,	14 Nov., 1942	19 Jan., 1943
		Cdr. H. F. Pullen, R.C.N.	20 Jan., 1943	12 Mch., 1943
		Lt. Cdr. G. H. Stephen, D.S.C. & Bar, O.B.E., R.C.N.R.	13 Mch., 1943	7 Nov., 1944
ST. PIERRE	*Frigate*	Lt. Cdr. M. G. Stirling, R.C.N.	8 Nov., 1944	7 Apl., 1945
		Cdr. G. H. Stephen, D.S.C. & Bar, O.B.E. R.D., R.C.N.R.	8 Apl., 1945	10 Oct., 1945
ST. STEPHEN	*Frigate*	Lt. Cdr. N. V. Clark, O.B.E., R.C.N.R.	22 Aug., 1944	5 Dec., 1944
		Lt. Cdr. J. A. Tullis, R.C.N.R.	6 Dec., 1944	9 Aug., 1945
		Skpr. Lt. E. L. Ritchie, R.C.N R.	10 Aug., 1945	22 Nov., 1945
ST. THERESE	*Frigate*	Lt. Cdr. C. Peterson, R.C.N.R.	28 July, 1944	22 Jan., 1945
		Lt. Cdr. R. C. Chenoweth, R.C.N.V.R.	23 Jan., 1945	22 Mch., 1945
		Lt. Cdr. N. S. C. Dickinson, R.C.N.V.R.	23 Mch., 1945	17 Sept., 1945
ST. THOMAS	*Corvette*	Cdr. J. E. Mitchell, R.C.N.V.R.	28 May, 1944	22 Aug., 1945
		Lt. B. J. Jackson, R.C.N.V.R.	23 Aug., 1945	22 Nov., 1945
SEACLIFFE	*Frigate*	Lt. Cdr. L. P. Denny, R.C.N.R.	4 May, 1944	26 Jan., 1945
		Lt. Cdr. B. Hynes, R.C.N.	27 Jan., 1945	20 June, 1945
		Lt. J. B. K. Stewart, R.C.N.V.R.	21 June, 1945	22 Nov., 1945
		Lt. Cdr. J. E. Harrington, R.C.N.V.R.	26 Sept., 1944	25 Sept., 1944
SHAWINIGAN	*Corvette*	Lt. Cdr. C. P. Balfry,	19 Sept., 1941	4 Jan., 1944
		Lt. R. S. Williams, R.C.N.V.R.	5 Jan., 1944	14 Mch., 1944
		Lt. W. E. Callan, R.C.N.V.R.	15 Mch., 1944	4 June, 1944
		Lt. W. J. Jones, R.C.N.R.	5 June, 1944	24 Nov., 1944
SHEDIAC	*Corvette*	Lt. John E. Clayton, R.C.N.R.	8 July, 1941	22 Mch., 1943
		Lt. Cdr. A. Moorhouse,	23 Mch., 1943	9 Feb., 1944

Ship	Type	Commander	From	To
SHERBROOKE	Corvette	Skpr. Lt. J. B. Cooper, R.C.N.R.	10 Feb., 1944	30 Mch., 1944
		Lt. Cdr. T. P. Ryan, O.B.E., R.C.N.R.	31 Mch., 1944	31 July, 1944
		Lt. Cdr. P. D. Taylor,	1 Aug., 1944	28 Aug., 1945
SIOUX	Destroyer	Lt. Cdr. E. E. G. Boak, R.C.N.	21 Feb., 1944	29 June, 1945
		Lt. Cdr. R. A. Webber, D.S.C., R.C.N.	30 June, 1945	8 Nov., 1945
SPIKENARD	Corvette	Lt. Cdr. H. G. Shadforth,	7 Apl., 1941	10 Feb., 1942
SKEENA	Destroyer	Cdr. H. T. W. Grant, R.C.N.	10 Sept., 1939	1 Apl., 1940
		Lt. Cdr. J. Hibbard, R.C.N.	2 Apl., 1940	10 Dec., 1941
		Cdr. H. Kingsley,	11 Dec., 1941	19 May, 1942
		Lt. Cdr. K. L. Dyer, D.S.C., R.C.N.	20 May, 1942	28 Feb., 1943
		Lt. E. E. G. Boak, R.C.N.	1 Mch., 1943	20 Nov., 1943
		Lt. Cdr. P. F. Russell, R.C.N.	21 Nov., 1943	25 Oct., 1944
SMITH FALLS	Corvette	Lt. Cdr. P. T. Byers, R.C.N.R.	28 Nov., 1944	4 July, 1945
SNOWBERRY	Corvette	Lt. R. S. Kelley,	30 Nov., 1940	5 Feb., 1942
		Lt. Cdr. P. J. B. Watts,	6 Feb., 1942	9 May, 1943
		Lt. J. B. O'Brien,	10 May, 1943	9 Nov., 1943
		Lt. Cdr. J. A. Dunn, R.C.N.V.R.	10 Nov., 1943	30 Apl., 1945
		Lt. B. T. R. Russell, R.C.N.R.	1 May, 1945	8 June, 1945
SOREL	Corvette	Lt. J. W. Dowling,	19 Aug., 1941	22 Dec., 1941
		Lt. D. M. Cameron,	23 Dec., 1941	7 June, 1942
		Lt. M. H. Wallace,	8 June, 1942	14 Jan., 1943
		Lt. Cdr. P. D. Budge, R.C.N.	15 Jan., 1943	19 Feb., 1943
		Lt. Cdr. R. A. S. MacNeil, O.B.E., R.C.N.R.	20 Feb., 1943	11 June, 1943
		Lt. W. P. Wickett,	12 June, 1943	13 Mch., 1944
		Lt. J. A. M. Levesque, R.C.N.R.	14 Mch., 1944	24 Jan., 1945
		Lt C. W. King, R.C.N.V.R.	25 Jan., 1945	20 June, 1945
SPRINGHILL	Frigate	Cdr. W. C. Halliday, R.C.N.R.	21 Mch., 1944	23 Apl., 1945
		Lt. Cdr. J. Harding, R.C.N.V.R.	24 Apl., 1945	12 Sept., 1945

481

PRINCIPAL SHIPS OF THE ROYAL CANADIAN NAVY 1939-1945—*Continued*

Ship	Class	Commanding Officer	From	To
STAR XVI	*Minesweeper*	Lt. Cdr. T. S. H. Beament, Lt. J. M. Gracey, R.C.N.V.R. Lt. C. J. Metcalfe, R.C.N.V.R.	31 Mch., 1941 20 Jan., 1942 2 Oct., 1944	19 Jan., 1942 1 Oct., 1944 31 July, 1945
STELLARTON	*Corvette*	Lt. R. A. Jarvis, R.C.N.V.R. Lt. Cdr. M. G. McCarthy, R.C.N.V.R.	29 Sept., 1944 20 Dec., 1944	19 Dec., 1944 26 June, 1945
STETTLER	*Frigate*	Lt. Cdr. D. G. King,	7 May, 1944	9 Nov., 1945
STONETOWN	*Frigate*	Lt. Cdr. W. P. Moffat, R.C.N.V.R. Lt. Cdr. J. T. Band, R.C.N.V.R.	21 July, 1944 21 Apl., 1945	20 Apl., 1945 2 Sept., 1945
STORMONT	*Frigate*	Lt. Cdr. G. A. Myra, R.C.N.	27 Nov., 1943	2 Sept., 1945
STRATFORD	*Minesweeper*	Lt. R. M. Meredith, Lt. R. J. C. Pringle, Lt. D. W. G. Storey, Lt. H. A. Ovenden, R.C.N.R. Lt. R. G. Magnossen, R.C.N.V.R. Lt. J. P. Charbonneau, R.C.N.V.R. Lt. J. M. S. Clark, R.C.N.V.R.	29 Aug., 1942 31 Oct., 1942 5 Aug., 1943 21 Dec., 1943 22 June, 1944 2 Apl., 1945 26 Apl., 1945	30 Oct., 1942 4 Aug., 1943 20 Dec., 1943 21 June, 1944 1 Apl., 1945 25 Apl., 1945 4 Oct., 1945
STRATHADAM	*Frigate*	Lt. Cdr. H. L. Quinn, D.S.C., R.C.N.V.R.	29 Sept., 1944	7 Nov., 1945
STRATHROY	*Corvette*	Lt. Cdr. W. F. Wood, R.C.N.R. Lt. H. D. Pepper, R.C.N.V.R. Lt. J. D. Moore, R.C.N.V.R.	20 Nov., 1944 28 Dec., 1944 1 Feb., 1945	27 Dec., 1944 31 Jan., 1945 6 July, 1945
SUDBURY	*Corvette*	Lt. Cdr. A. M. McLarnon, Lt. D. S. Martin, Lt. G. L. Mackay, R.C.N.R. Lt. Cdr. J. W. Golby, R.C.N.V.R., D.S.C.	15 Oct., 1941 4 May, 1943 28 Dec., 1943 20 Mch., 1944	3 May, 1943 27 Dec., 1943 19 Mch., 1944 28 Aug., 1945
SUDEROY IV	*Minesweeper*	Mate C. A. Mott, R.C.N.R. Lt. R. J. C. Pringle, Lt. C. A. Mott, R.C.N.R. Lt. Cuthbert, F. R. Dalton,	7 May, 1941 3 Apl., 1942 10 June, 1942	2 Apl., 1942 .... 9 June, 1942 25 Sept., 1942

Ship	Type	Commanding Officer	From	To
SUDEROY V	*Minesweeper*	Lt. L. D. Clarke,	26 Sept., 1942	28 Feb., 1943
		Lt. W. Russell,	1 Mch., 1943	16 Apl., 1943
		Lt. D. J. Van Bommel, R.C.N.V.R.	17 Apl., 1943	31 July, 1945
SUDEROY VI	*Minesweeper*	Mate R. M. Meredith, R.C.N.R.	2 June, 1941	11 June, 1942
		Lt. M. W. Knowles,	12 June, 1942	2 Aug., 1942
		Lt. D. E. Francis, R.C.N.V.R.	3 Aug., 1942	31 July, 1945
	Minesweeper	Lt. R. J. C. Pringle,	19 Mch., 1941	15 Mch., 1942
		Lt. W. Russell,	16 Mch., 1942	24 Dec., 1942
		Lt. P. M. MacCallum,	25 Dec., 1942	29 Jan., 1943
		Lt. R. Stark,	30 Jan., 1943	24 Nov., 1943
		Lt. J. C. Smith, R.C.N.R.	25 Nov., 1943	23 Feb., 1944
		Lt. D. I. McGill, R.C.N.V.R.	24 Feb., 1944	9 Apl., 1944
		Lt. J. S. Barrick, R.C.N.V.R.	10 Apl., 1944	31 July, 1945
SUMMERSIDE	*Corvette*	Lt. Cdr. F. O. Gerity,	11 Sept., 1941	21 Apl., 1943
		Lt. G. E. Cross, R.C.N.V.R.	22 Apl., 1943	31 Aug., 1943
		Lt. G. S. Mongenais, R.C.N.V.R.	1 Sept., 1943	9 Oct., 1944
		Lt. H. S. Hardy, R.C.N.V.R.	10 Oct., 1944	17 Dec., 1944
		Lt. F. O. Plant, R.C.N.V.R.	18 Dec., 1944	2 July, 1945
SWANSEA	*Frigate*	Cdr. C. A. King, D.S.O., D.S.C., R.C.N.R.	4 Oct., 1943	4 Nov., 1944
		Lt. Cdr. J. T. Band, R.C.N.V.R.	5 Nov., 1944	15 Apl., 1945
		Lt. Cdr. G. A. Larue, R.C.N.V.R.	16 Apl., 1945	2 Sept., 1945
SWIFT CURRENT	*Minesweeper*	Lt. Cdr. A. G. King,	11 Nov., 1941	18 Apl., 1942
		Lt. I. H. Bell,	19 Apl., 1942	27 Sept., 1942
		Lt. J. Evelyn, R.C.N.R.	28 Sept., 1942	7 Apl., 1944
		Lt. K. D. Heath, R.C.N.V.R.	8 Apl., 1944	13 May, 1945
		Lt. J. N. Fraser, R.C.N.V.R.	14 May, 1945	23 Oct., 1945
SUSSEXVALE	*Frigate*	Lt. Cdr. L. R. Pavillard, R.C.N.R. D.S.C.	29 Nov., 1944	2 Sept., 1945
ST. CLAIR	*Destroyer*	Lt. Cdr. D. C. Wallace, R.C.N.R.	24 Sept., 1940	5 Apl., 1942
		Lt. Cdr. G. O. Baugh,	6 Apl., 1942	26 Dec., 1943
		Lt. W. D. Boulton, R.C.N.V.R.	27 Dec., 1943	7 Mch., 1944
		Lt. J. E. Burnett, R.C.N.V.R.	8 Mch., 1944	2 Sept., 1945
TEME	*Frigate*	Lt. Cdr. D. G. Jeffrey, D.S.O., R.C.N.R.	28 Feb., 1944	20 Feb., 1945
		Lt. D. P. Harvey, R.C.N.V.R.	21 Feb., 1945	3 May, 1945

Ship	Class	Commanding Officer	From	To
THE PAS	Corvette	Lt. Cdr. E. G. Old, Lt. R. H. Sylvester, R.C.N.V.R. Lt. J. H. Ewart, R.C.N.V.R.	29 Oct., 1941 15 Apl., 1944 10 Oct., 1944	14 Apl., 1944 9 Oct., 1944 19 July, 1945
THETFORD MINES	Frigate	Lt. Cdr. J. A. R. Allan, R.C.N.V.R. D.S.C.	24 May, 1944	2 Sept., 1945
THORLOCK	Corvette	Lt. J. E. Francois, R.C.N.R.	13 Nov., 1944	10 July, 1945
THUNDER	Minesweeper	Cdr. H. D. Mackay, R.C.N.R.	14 Oct., 1941	6 Oct., 1945
TILLSONBURG	Corvette	Lt. Cdr. W. Evans, R.C.N.V.R.	29 June, 1944	26 Nov., 1945
TIMMINS	Corvette	Lt. J. A. Brown, Lt. J. M. Gillison, Lt. N. S. C. Dickinson, Lt. Cdr. J. H. S. MacDonald, Lt. Cdr. H. S. Maxwell, R.C.N.V.R. Lt. R. G. James, R.C.N.V.R. Lt. J. Kincaid, R.C.N.R.	10 Feb., 1942 31 Aug., 1942 12 Jan., 1943 20 Mch., 1942 19 Apl., 1943 2 Sept., 1944 16 Dec., 1944	30 Aug., 1942 11 Jan., 1943 19 Mch., 1943 18 Apl., 1943 1 Sept., 1944 15 Dec., 1944 10 July, 1945
TORONTO	Frigate	Lt. Cdr. H. K. Hill, R.C.N.V.R. Lt. Cdr. A. G. S. Griffin, R.C.N.V.R.	6 May, 1944 12 Mch., 1945	11 Mch., 1945 2 Sept., 1945
TRAIL	Corvette	Lt. Cdr. G. S. Hall, Lt. G. M. Hope, R.C.N.V.R. Lt. D. J. Lawson, R.C.N.V.R.	30 Apl., 1941 9 Oct., 1943 10 Oct., 1944	8 Oct., 1943 9 Oct., 1944 12 July, 1945
TRANSCONA	Minesweeper	Lt. H. B. Tindale, R.C.N.V.R. Lt. A. E. Gough, R.C.N.R. Skpr. Lt. H. V. Mossman, R.C.N.R.	25 Nov., 1942 18 Jan., 1944 19 May, 1945	17 Jan., 1944 18 May, 1945 31 July, 1945
TRENTONIAN	Corvette	Lt. W. E. Harrison, R.C.N.R. Lt. C. S. Glassco, R.C.N.V.R.	1 Dec., 1943 31 Jan., 1945	30 Jan., 1945 22 Feb., 1945
TRILLIUM	Corvette	Lt. Cdr. R. F. Harris, Lt. H. D. Campsie,	22 Oct., 1940 15 Nov., 1941	14 Nov., 1941 8 Dec., 1941

Ship	Type	Commanding Officer		
		Skpr. Lt. G. E. Gaudreau, R.C.N.R.	9 Dec., 1941	25 Feb., 1942
		Lt. P. E. Evans, R.C.N.R.	26 Feb., 1942	21 May, 1944
		Lt. K. E. Meredith, R.C.N.V.R.	22 May, 1944	27 June, 1945
TROIS RIVIERES	*Minesweeper*	Lt. G. M. Kaizer, R.C.N.R.	12 Aug., 1942	15 Nov., 1943
		Lt. W. G. Garden, R.C.N.V.R.	16 Nov., 1943	12 Sept., 1944
		Lt. R. C. G. Merriam, R.C.N.V.R.	13 Sept., 1944	....
		Lt. J. M. S. Clark, R.C.N.V.R.	....	23 Apl., 1945
		Lt. M. Gagnon, R.C.N.V.R.	24 Apl., 1945	31 July, 1945
TRURO	*Minesweeper*	Skpr. Lt. G. O. Myra, R.C.N.R.	27 Aug., 1942	1 Aug., 1943
		Lt. G. D. Campbell, R.C.N.V.R.	2 Aug., 1943	19 Aug., 1943
		Lt. E. E. MacInnis, R.C.N.R.	20 Aug., 1943	31 July, 1945
UGANDA	*Cruiser*	Capt. E. R. Mainguy, O.B.E., R.C.N.	21 Oct., 1944	2 Sept., 1945
UNGAVA	*Minesweeper*	Lt. C. Winterbottom, R.C.N.R.	5 Sept., 1941	19 Jan., 1942
		Lt. F. E. Scoates, R.C.N.R.	20 Jan., 1942	8 Feb., 1943
		Lt. D. M. Coolican, R.C.N.V.R.	9 Feb., 1943	12 Mch., 1944
		Lt. J. M. Home, R.C.N.V.R.	13 Mch., 1944	17 Dec., 1944
		Lt. J. W. Radford, R.C.N.R.	18 Dec., 1944	30 Jan., 1945
		Lt. S. Henderson, R.C.N.R.	31 Jan., 1945	9 Apl., 1945
		Lt. F. K. Ellis, B.C.N.V.R.	10 Apl., 1945	2 Sept., 1945
VALLEYFIELD	*Frigate*	Lt. Cdr. D. T. English, R.C.N.R.	7 Dec., 1943	7 May, 1944
VANCOUVER	*Corvette*	Lt. P. F. M. DeFreitas, R.C.N.R.	20 Mch., 1942	7 June, 1943
		Lt. Cdr. A. T. Morrell, R.C.N.R.	8 June, 1943	4 Feb., 1944
		Lt. Cdr. A. W. Ford, R.C.N.R.	5 Feb., 1944	9 Oct., 1944
		Lt. G. C. Campbell, R.C.N.V.R.	10 Oct., 1944	22 June, 1945
VEGREVILLE	*Minesweeper*	Cdr. F. A. Price.	10 Dec., 1941	19 Jan., 1942
		Lt. Cdr. T. H. Beament,	20 Jan., 1942	30 Sept., 1942
		Lt. T. B. Edwards, R.C.N.R.	1 Oct., 1942	6 Nov., 1944
		Lt. J. W. Ross, R.C.N.V.R.	7 Nov., 1944	6 June, 1945
VICTORIAVILLE	*Frigate*	Lt. Cdr. L. A. Hickey, M.B.E., R.C.N.R.	11 Nov., 1944	2 Sept., 1945

PRINCIPAL SHIPS OF THE ROYAL CANADIAN NAVY 1939-1945—*Continued*

SHIP	CLASS	COMMANDING OFFICER	FROM	TO
VILLE DE QUEBEC	*Corvette*	Lt. Cdr. D. G. Jeffrey,	24 May, 1942	29 Sept., 1942
		Lt. I. H. Bell,	30 Sept., 1942	11 Oct., 1942
		Lt. Cdr. A. R. E. Coleman,	12 Oct., 1942	12 June, 1943
		Lt. J. L. Carter, R.C.N.V.R.	13 June, 1943	12 Mch., 1944
		Lt. C. S. Glassco, R.C.N.V.R.	13 Mch., 1944	1 May, 1944
		Lt. Cdr. H. C. Hatch, R.C.N.V.R.	2 May, 1944	3 July, 1945
VISON	*Armed Yacht*	Lt. Cdr. R. I. Swansburg,	8 July, 1940	31 July, 1941
		Lt. Cdr. F. A. Price,	1 Aug., 1941	21 Nov., 1941
		Cdr. W. G. Sheddon, R.C.N.R.	22 Nov., 1941	
		Lt. J. Evelyn,		5 Apl., 1942
		Lt. W. E. Nicholson, R.C.N.R.	6 Apl., 1942	4 Aug., 1945
WALLACEBURG	*Algerine*	Lt. Cdr. F. R. K. Naftel, R.C.N.V.R.	18 Nov., 1943	2 May, 1944
		Lt. Cdr. R. A. S. MacNeil, R.C.N.R.	3 May, 1944	9 Jan., 1945
		Lt. Cdr. F. E. Burrows, R.C.N.V.R.	10 Jan., 1945	21 May, 1945
		Lt. Cdr. J. H. G. Bovey, R.C.N.V.R.	22 May, 1945	2 Sept., 1945
WASAGA	*Minesweeper*	Lt. Cdr. W. Redford,	1 July, 1941	9 Mch., 1942
		Lt. J. B. Raine, R.C.N.R.	10 Mch., 1942	23 Dec., 1943
		Lt. J. H. Green, R.C.N.R.	24 Dec., 1943	6 Oct., 1945
WASKESIU	*Frigate*	Lt. Cdr. J. H. S. MacDonald, R.C.N.R.	16 June, 1943	4 Feb., 1944
		Lt. Cdr. J. P. Fraser, R.C.N.R.	5 Feb., 1944	13 Dec., 1944
		Lt. Cdr. L. D. Quick, R.C.N.R.	14 Dec., 1944	2 Sept., 1945
WENTWORTH	*Frigate*	Lt. Cdr. S. W. Howell, R.C.N.R.	8 Dec., 1943	4 July, 1944
		Lt. Cdr. R. J. C. Pringle, R.C.N.V.R.	5 July, 1944	15 Jan., 1945
		Lt. J. B. Graham, R.C.N.R.	16 Jan., 1945	10 Oct., 1945
WESTMOUNT	*Minesweeper*	Lt. F. G. Hutchings, R.C.N.V.R.	15 Sept., 1942	16 Mch., 1944
		Lt. R. L. B. Hunter, R.C.N.V.R.	17 Mch., 1944	25 Mch., 1945
		Lt. R. P. Jackson, R.C.N.R.	26 Mch., 1945	5 Sept., 1945
WESTYORK	*Corvette*	Lt. M. Smith, R.C.N.R.	6 Oct., 1944	29 Dec., 1944
		Lt. Cdr. W. F. Wood, R.C.N.R.	30 Dec., 1944	6 July, 1945

Ship	Type	Commanding Officer		
WETASKIWIN	*Corvette*	Lt. Cdr. G. Windeyer, R.C.N.	17 Dec., 1940	4 Nov., 1942
		Lt. J. R. Kidston, R.C.N.V.R.	5 Nov., 1942	21 Mch., 1944
		Lt. A. Walton, R.C.N.R.	22 Mch., 1944	16 June, 1945
WEYBURN	*Corvette*	Lt. Cdr. T. M. W. Golby, R.C.N.R.	26 Nov., 1941	22 Feb., 1943
WHITBY	*Corvette*	Lt. Cdr. R. K. Lester, R.C.N.V.R.	6 June, 1944	12 July, 1945
WINDFLOWER	*Corvette*	Lt. Cdr. J. H. S. MacDonald,	4 Feb., 1941	13 Oct., 1941
		Lt. J. Price,	14 Oct., 1941	7 Dec., 1941
WINNIPEG	*Algerine*	Lt. Cdr. W. D. F. Johnston, R.C.N.R.	29 July, 1943	4 Apl., 1944
		Lt. Cdr. R. A. Judges, R.C.N.V.R.	5 Apl., 1944	3 Oct., 1944
		Lt. Cdr. G. K. Fox, R.C.N.V.R.	4 Oct., 1944	10 Sept., 1945
WOLF	*Patrol Craft*	Lt. J. A. Gow, R.C.N.R.	9 Sept., 1940	21 Apl., 1941
		Ch. Skpr. J. M. Richardson, R.C.N.R.	22 Apl., 1941	18 Sept., 1941
		Ch. Skpr. A. W. Ogden, R.C.N.R.	19 Sept., 1941	20 Nov., 1941
		Skpr. Lt. W. R. Chaster, R.C.N.R.	21 Nov., 1941	16 May, 1945
WOODSTOCK	*Corvette*	Lt. L. P. Denny,	1 May, 1942	18 Oct., 1942
		Cdr. G. H. Griffiths,	19 Oct., 1942	19 Jan., 1943
		Skpr. Lt. J. M. Watson, R.C.N.R.	20 Jan., 1943	16 Aug., 1943
		Lt. C. E. Wright, R.C.N.V.R.	17 Aug., 1943	5 Oct., 1944
		Lt. W. McCombe, R.C.N.R.	6 Oct., 1944	18 Apl., 1945
		Lt. Cdr. J. S. Cunningham, R.C.N.V.R.	19 Apl., 1945	11 Mch., 1946

PRINCIPAL SHIPS OF THE ROYAL CANADIAN NAVY 1939-1945—*Continued*

FAIRMILES	COMMANDING OFFICER	FROM	TO
M.L. 050	Sub/Lt. D. R. Grierson, R.C.N.V.R.	4 Jan., 1942	8 June, 1942
	Sub/Lt. T. H. Crone, R.C.N.V.R.	8 June, 1942	25 Aug., 1942
	Lt. J. T. Sharp, R.C.N.V.R.	26 Aug., 1942	24 July, 1943
	Sub/Lt. J. M. Duck, R.C.N.V.R.	25 July, 1943	9 Jan., 1944
	Lt. A. C. Beardmore, R.C.N.V.R.	10 Jan., 1944	20 Apl., 1945
	Lt. J. J. McLaughlin, R.C.N.V.R.	21 Apl., 1945	......
M.L. 051	Lt. T. C. Sewell, R.C.N.V.R.	1 Apl., 1942	1 Apl., 1942
	Lt. J. W. Tait, R.C.N.V.R.	1 Apl., 1942	13 Dec., 1942
	Lt. W. H. B. Thomson, R.C.N.V.R.	14 Dec., 1942	16 Dec., 1943
	Lt. R. Dikinson, R.C.N.V.R.	17 Dec., 1943	8 Feb., 1944
	Lt. R. A. Wyllie, R.C.N.V.R.	9 Feb., 1944	2 Mch., 1944
	Lt. Cdr. W. H. B. Thomson, R.C.N.V.R.	3 Mch., 1944	14 Jan., 1945
	Lt. D. S. Marlow, R.C.N.V.R.	15 Jan., 1945	......
M.L. 052	Sub/Lt. S. C. Robinson, R.C.N.V.R.	19 Apl., 1942	......
M.L. 053	Sub/Lt. S. E. C. Garlick, R.C.N.V.R.	11 Mch., 1942	30 Apl., 1942
	Lt. R. P. Baldwin, R.C.N.V.R.	1 May, 1942	26 Apl., 1943
	Lt. G. M. Schuthe, R.C.N.V.R.	27 Apl., 1943	25 Jan., 1944
	Lt. W. P. Munsie, R.C.N.V.R.	26 Jan., 1944	......
M.L. 054	Lt. D. G. King, R.C.N.V.R.	19 Apl., 1942	11 June, 1942
	Lt. W. C. Rigney, R.C.N.V.R.	12 June, 1942	21 July, 1943
	Lt. H. F. Bartram, R.C.N.V.R.	22 July, 1943	13 Apl., 1944
	Lt. C. N. Blagrave, R.C.N.V.R.	14 Apl., 1944	......
M.L. 055	Lt. F. N. Greener, R.C.N.V.R.	19 Apl., 1942	4 June, 1942
	Lt. R. W. Rankin, R.C.N.V.R.	5 June, 1942	14 Jan., 1944
	Lt. J. E. White, R.C.N.V.R.	15 Jan., 1944	24 Apl., 1945
	Lt. R. G. Spence, R.C.N.V.R.	25 Apl., 1945	......
M.L. 056	Lt. G. P. Manning, R.C.N.V.R.	11 Mch., 1942	26 Aug., 1942
	Sub/Lt. G. D. Patterson, R.C.N.V.R.	27 Aug., 1942	7 Oct., 1943
	Lt. R. A. F. Raney, R.C.N.V.R.	8 Oct., 1943	2 May, 1945
	Lt. J. R. Jenner, R.C.N.V.R.	3 May, 1945	......

M.L.	Officer		
M.L. 057	Sub/Lt. J. F. Gallagher, R.C.N.V.R.	6 May, 1942	8 June, 1943
	Lt. R. C. Denny, R.C.N.V.R.	9 June, 1943	10 Sept., 1943
	Sub/Lt. J. A. Davis, R.C.N.V.R.	11 Sept., 1943	15 Nov., 1943
	Sub/Lt. K. F. Hurst, R.C.N.V.R.	16 Nov., 1943	26 Sept., 1944
	Lt. C. D. Gillis, R.C.N.V.R.	27 Sept., 1944	1 May, 1945
	Lt. J. S. Gardiner, R.C.N.V.R.	2 May, 1945	......
M.L. 058	Lt. H. K. Hill, R.C.N.V.R.	1 Apl., 1942	19 June, 1942
	Sub/Lt. S. E. C. Garlick, R.C.N.V.R.	20 June, 1942	14 Feb., 1943
	Lt. G. E. Rising, R.C.N.V.R.	15 Feb., 1943	25 Jan., 1944
	Lt. R. Synette, R.C.N.V.R.	26 Jan., 1944	26 May, 1944
	Lt. J. G. Chance, R.C.N.V.R.	27 May, 1944	......
M.L. 059	Sub/Lt. H. A. Batey, R.C.N.V.R.	21 Apl., 1942	17 Nov., 1943
	Sub/Lt. D. B. Drummond, R.C.N.V.R.	18 Nov., 1943	18 Aug., 1944
	Lt. W. B. McTavish, R.C.N.V.R.	19 Aug., 1944	8 Nov., 1945
	Lt. K. M. Ross, R.C.N.V.R.	9 Nov., 1945	......
M.L. 060	Lt. J. S. Davis, R.C.N.V.R.	18 Apl., 1942	30 Apl., 1943
	Sub/Lt. A. M. Byers, R.C.N.V.R.	1 May, 1943	10 Oct., 1943
	Lt. R. J. M. Allan, R.C.N.V.R.	11 Oct., 1943	29 Jan., 1945
	Lt. J. W. MacKenzie, R.C.N.V.R.	30 Jan., 1945	17 Apl., 1945
	Lt. G. A. Sweenney, R.C.N.V.R.	18 Apl., 1945	10 Oct., 1945
	Lt. R. J. M. Allan, R.C.N.V.R.	11 Oct., 1945	......
M.L. 061	Sub/Lt. H. M. Gordon, R.C.N.V.R.	2 Mch., 1942	30 Apl., 1942
	Sub/Lt. G. W. Leckie, R.C.N.V.R.	1 May, 1942	29 Jan., 1943
	Lt. S. B. Marshall, R.C.N.V.R.	30 Jan., 1943	10 Oct., 1943
	Sub/Lt. E. V. Anderson, R.C.N.V.R.	11 Oct., 1943	25 Aug., 1944
	Lt. C. A. Balfry, R.C.N.V.R.	26 Aug., 1944	17 Jan., 1945
	Lt. J. A. Barrett, R.C.N.V.R.	18 Jan., 1945	......
M.L. 062	Lt. W. L. Moore, R.C.N.V.R.	1 Apl., 1942	1 Apl., 1942
	Lt. H. D. Pepper, R.C.N.V.R.	1 Apl., 1942	......
M.L. 063	Sub/Lt. N. M. Simpson, R.C.N.V.R.	1 Apl., 1942	......
M.L. 064	Sub/Lt. N. L. Williams, R.C.N.V.R.	1 May, 1942	11 Oct., 1943
	Sub/Lt. C. R. Godbehere, R.C.N.V.R.	12 Oct., 1943	4 Feb., 1944
	Sub/Lt. W. J. Langston, R.C.N.V.R.	5 Feb., 1944	5 Mch., 1944
	Lt. E. G. Jarvis, R.C.N.V.R.	6 Mch., 1944	1 Jan., 1945
	Lt. R. A. F. Raney, R.C.N.V.R.	2 Jan., 1945	......

PRINCIPAL SHIPS OF THE ROYAL CANADIAN NAVY 1939-1945—*Continued*

FAIRMILES	COMMANDING OFFICER	FROM	TO
M.L. 065	Sub/Lt. J. J. McLaughlin, R.C.N.V.R.	1 May, 1942	8 May, 1942
	Lt. F. H. B. Dewdney, R.C.N.V.R.	9 May, 1942	11 Nov., 1943
	Sub/Lt. C. P. Martin, R.C.N.V.R.	12 Nov., 1943	25 Jan., 1944
	Lt. J. H. Beeman, R.C.N.V.R.	26 Jan., 1944	1 Aug., 1944
	Lt. G. E. McCabe, R.C.N.V.R.	2 Aug., 1944	6 Aug., 1944
	Lt. J. J. Caya, R.C.N.V.R.	7 Aug., 1944	8 Mch., 1945
	Lt. W. B. McTavish, R.C.N.V.R.	9 Mch., 1945	....
M.L. 066	Lt. C. F. Draney, R.C.N.V.R.	6 Mch., 1942	23 Nov., 1942
	Lt. W. E. W. Snaith, R.C.N.V.R.	24 Nov., 1942	31 Mch., 1943
	Lt. W. A. Smith, R.C.N.V.R.	1 Apl., 1943	12 June, 1943
	Skpr. Lt. L. S. W. Pussey, R.C.N.R.	13 June, 1943	3 July, 1943
	Lt. R. R. Maitland, R.C.N.V.R.	4 July, 1943	12 Jan., 1944
	Lt. J. W. Shaw, R.C.N.V.R.	13 Jan., 1944	....
M.L. 067	Sub/Lt. C. C. T. McNair, R.C.N.V.R.	27 Mch., 1942	15 June, 1943
	Lt. J. F. Beveridge, R.C.N.V.R.	16 June, 1943	6 Apl., 1944
	Lt. E. S. Blanchet, R.C.N.V.R.	7 Apl., 1944	14 July, 1944
	Lt. J. M. Ferris, R.C.N.V.R.	15 July, 1944	3 Nov., 1944
	Lt. H. W. Patterson, R.C.N.V.R.	4 Nov., 1944	....
M.L. 068	Ch. Skpr. H. E. Young, R.C.N.R.	7 Mch., 1942	7 Feb., 1943
	Lt. E. P. Ashe, R.C.N.V.R.	8 Feb., 1943	8 Sept., 1943
	Lt. R. D. Linton, R.C.N.V.R.	9 Sept., 1943	....
M.L. 069	Ch. Skpr. F. W. M. Drew, R.C.N.R.	28 Mch., 1942	10 May, 1943
	Lt. R. M. Francis, R.C.N.V.R.	11 May, 1943	3 Sept., 1943
	Lt. J. E. Kendrick, R.C.N.V.R.	4 Sept., 1943	25 Oct., 1943
	Lt. H. W. Patterson, R.C.N.V.R.	26 Oct., 1943	21 July, 1944
	Lt. D. A. Smith, R.C.N.V.R.	22 July, 1944	20 Sept., 1944
	Lt. E. U. Anderson, R.C.N.V.R.	20 Sept., 1944	....
M.L. 070	Sub/Lt. J. O. L. Lake, R.C.N.V.R.	13 Mch., 1942	18 Nov., 1942
	Ch. Skpr. G. B. McCandless, R.C.N.R.	19 Nov., 1942	17 Jan., 1943
	Lt. D. F. G. Fladgate, R.C.N.V.R.	18 Jan., 1943	22 Oct., 1943
	Lt. F. G. Mitchell, R.C.N.V.R.	23 Oct., 1943	21 Nov., 1944
	Lt. R. Muir. R.C.N.V.R.	22 Nov.. 1944	....

M.L.	Officer		
M.L. 071	Ch. Skpr. L. S. W. Pussey, R.C.N.R.	10 Apl., 1942	6 Feb., 1943
	Lt. J. E. E. Richardson, R.C.N.V.R.	7 Feb., 1943	3 Mch., 1944
	Lt. D. J. Morrison, R.C.N.V.R.	4 Mch., 1944	17 Apl., 1945
	Lt. E. N. Pottinger, R.C.N.V.R.	18 Apl., 1945	....
M.L. 072	Lt. C. L. Campbell, R.C.N.V.R.	10 Mch., 1942	31 Mch., 1942
	Lt. D. S. Howard, R.C.N.V.R.	1 Apl., 1942	13 Dec., 1943
	Lt. J. A. Davis, R.C.N.V.R.	14 Dec., 1943	23 Apl., 1944
	Lt. F. Amyot, R.C.N.V.R.	24 Apl., 1944	16 Mch., 1945
	Lt. A. M. C. Kenning, R.C.N.V.R.	17 Mch., 1945	....
M.L. 073	Lt. S. O. Greening, R.C.N.V.R.	1 Apl., 1942	1 Apl., 1942
	Lt. J. H. Stevenson, R.C.N.V.R.	1 Apl., 1942	19 Feb., 1944
	Lt. R. D. Hayes, R.C.N.V.R.	20 Feb., 1944	....
M.L. 074	Lt. T. G. Denny, R.C.N.V.R.	21 Apl., 1942	20 Jan., 1943
	Lt. V. J. Wilgress, R.C.N.V.R.	21 Jan., 1943	28 Oct., 1943
	Lt. E. Leyland, R.C.N.V.R.	29 Oct., 1943	....
M.L. 075	Lt. J. G. Humphrey, R.C.N.V.R.	28 Apl., 1942	31 May, 1943
	Lt. J. M. Todd, R.C.N.V.R.	1 June, 1943	11 Oct., 1944
	Lt. J. D. Lineham, R.C.N.V.R.	12 Oct., 1944	29 Jan., 1945
	Sub/Lt. H. O. MacFarlane, R.C.N.V.R.	30 Jan., 1945	....
M.L. 076	Lt. W. H. Pinchin, R.C.N.V.R.	28 Apl., 1942	12 July, 1942
	Sub/Lt. J. Leitch, R.C.N.V.R.	13 July, 1942	21 Mch., 1943
	Sub/Lt. K. F. Hurst, R.C.N.V.R.	22 Mch., 1943	7 Nov., 1943
	Sub/Lt. E. A. Annear, R.C.N.V.R.	8 Nov., 1943	23 Feb., 1944
	Lt. W. E. W. Snaith, R.C.N.V.R.	24 Feb., 1944	20 July, 1944
	Lt. F. B. Pugh, R.C.N.V.R.	21 July, 1944	....
M.L. 077	Lt. J. W. Braidwood, R.C.N.V.R.	21 Apl., 1942	29 Aug., 1943
	Lt. C. H. Adair, R.C.N.V.R.	30 Aug., 1943	2 Oct., 1943
	Sub/Lt. P. Thomas, R.C.N.V.R.	3 Oct., 1943	7 Oct., 1943
	Sub/Lt. R. Paddon, R.C.N.V.R.	8 Oct., 1943	10 Dec., 1943
	Lt. P. B. C. Samsone, R.C.N.V.R.	11 Dec., 1943	24 Apl., 1945
	Lt. D. R. Lester, R.C.N.V.R.	25 Apl., 1945	....

PRINCIPAL SHIPS OF THE ROYAL CANADIAN NAVY 1939-1945—*Continued*

FAIRMILES	COMMANDING OFFICER	FROM	TO
M.L. 078	Sub/Lt. J. N. Finlayson, R.C.N.V.R.	21 Apl., 1942	21 Apl., 1943
	Lt. D. G. Creba, R.C.N.V.R.	22 Apl., 1943	7 Oct., 1943
	Sub/Lt. L. O. Stonehouse, R.C.N.V.R.	8 Oct., 1943	16 Sept., 1944
	Lt. S. C. Kilbank, R.C.N.V.R.	17 Sept., 1944	5 Feb., 1945
	Lt. C. R. Godbehere, R.C.N.V.R.	6 Feb., 1945	21 Mch., 1945
	Lt. J. L. Gourlay, R.C.N.V.R.	22 Mch., 1945	....
M.L. 079	Lt. S. B. Fraser, R.C.N.V.R.	21 Apl., 1942	3 July, 1942
	Sub/Lt. H. R. Cruise, R.C.N.V.R.	4 July, 1942	13 Aug., 1943
	Lt. C. J. Holloway, R.C.N.V.R.	14 Aug., 1943	15 Aug., 1943
	Lt. J. B. LeMaistre, R.C.N.V.R.	16 Aug., 1943	4 Nov., 1943
	Sub/Lt. C. A. Balfry, R.C.N.V.R.	5 Nov., 1943	22 Apl., 1945
	Lt. F. J. Johnson, R.C.N.V.R.	23 Apl., 1945	30 Apl., 1945
	Sub/Lt. B. J. G. Davies, R.C.N.V.R.	1 May, 1945	....
M.L. 080	Sub/Lt. J. W. Collins, R.C.N.V.R.	21 Apl., 1942	31 May, 1942
	Sub/Lt. G. E. Burrell, R.C.N.V.R.	1 June, 1942	6 Oct., 1943
	Lt. J. E. M. Jones, R.C.N.V.R.	7 Oct., 1943	12 May, 1944
	Lt. G. E. McCabe, R.C.N.V.R.	13 May, 1944	22 Apl., 1945
	Lt. J. J. Caya, R.C.N.V.R.	23 Apl., 1945	....
M.L. 081	Lt. F. K. Ellis, R.C.N.V.R.	21 Apl., 1942	23 Nov., 1942
	Lt. J. M. Todd, R.C.N.V.R.	24 Nov., 1942	10 Oct., 1943
	Sub/Lt. G. C. Brain, R.C.N.V.R.	11 Oct., 1943	20 Apl., 1944
	Lt. A. D. Stairs, R.C.N.V.R.	21 Apl., 1944	26 Nov., 1944
	Lt. W. J. King, R.C.N.V.R.	27 Nov., 1944	4 Apl., 1945
	Lt. R. G. Cannell, R.C.N.V.R.	5 Apl., 1945	22 Apl., 1945
	Lt. A. D. Stairs, R.C.N.V.R.	23 Apl., 1945	....
M.L. 082	Lt. A. B. Strange, R.C.N.V.R.	21 Apl., 1942	25 Jan., 1944
	Lt. J. F. Stevens, R.C.N.V.R.	26 Jan., 1944	....
M.L. 083	Lt. W. M. Grant, R.C.N.V.R.	9 May, 1942	10 May, 1943
	Lt. M. C. Knox, R.C.N.V.R.	11 May, 1943	7 Oct., 1943
	Lt. J. R. Akin, R.C.N.V.R.	8 Oct., 1943	4 Nov., 1943
	Lt. G. A. Sweeney, R.C.N.V.R.	5 Nov., 1943	11 Sept., 1944

M.L. No.	Officer	From	To
M.L. 084	Sub/Lt. W. W. McIlveen, R.C.N.V.R.	12 Sept., 1944	22 Apl., 1945
	Lt. R. J. M. Allan, R.C.N.V.R.	23 Apl., 1945	......
M.L. 085	Sub/Lt. R. N. McDairmid, R.C.N.V.R.	9 May, 1942	3 June, 1942
	Lt. G. E. Cross, R.C.N.V.R.	4 June, 1942	12 Oct., 1943
	Lt. J. M. Duck, R.C.N.V.R.	13 Oct., 1943	3 Apl., 1944
	Lt. V. W. Marples, R.C.N.V.R.	4 Apl., 1944	22 Apl., 1945
	Lt. J. C. Mackey, R.C.N.V.R.	23 Apl., 1945	......
M.L. 086	Sub/Lt. W. E. D. Atkinson, R.C.N.V.R.	21 Apl., 1942	21 Oct., 1942
	Sub/Lt. G. C. Clark, R.C.N.V.R.	22 Oct., 1942	4 Apl., 1944
	Lt. R. M. Greene, R.C.N.V.R.	5 Apl., 1944	30 Apl., 1945
	Lt. H. J. Dow, R.C.N.V.R.	1 May, 1945	......
M.L. 087	Lt. T. G. Sewell, R.C.N.V.R.	25 Oct., 1942	27 Oct., 1942
	Lt. J. R. Sare, R.C.N.V.R.	28 Oct., 1942	21 Mch., 1943
	Lt. G. L. James, R.C.N.V.R.	22 Mch., 1943	16 Nov., 1943
	Sub/Lt. P. Husoy, R.C.N.V.R.	17 Nov., 1943	3 Dec., 1944
	Lt. V. B. Chew, R.C.N.V.R.	4 Dec., 1944	......
M.L. 088	Lt. A. D. Stairs, R.C.N.V.R.	11 Nov., 1942	9 Jan., 1944
	Lt. W. G. Finlay, R.C.N.V.R.	10 Jan., 1944	6 Feb., 1945
	Lt. V. B. Chew, R.C.N.V.R.	7 Feb., 1945	6 Mch., 1945
	Lt. J. C. Austin, R.C.N.V.R.	7 Mch., 1945	......
M.L. 089	Lt. Cdr. W. L. Moore, R.C.N.V.R.	10 May, 1943	11 Oct., 1943
	Sub/Lt. R. S. Graves, R.C.N.V.R.	12 Oct., 1943	24 Nov., 1943
	Lt. W. G. Cunningham, R.C.N.V.R.	25 Nov., 1943	16 Aug., 1944
	Lt. T. M. Kirkwood, R.C.N.V.R.	17 Aug., 1944	......
M.L. 090	Sub/Lt. A. G. Beardmore, R.C.N.V.R.	26 Sept., 1942	9 Jan., 1944
	Lt. J. H. Curtis, R.C.N.V.R.	10 Jan., 1944	16 Mch., 1945
	Lt J. A. D. Alguire, R.C.N.V.R.	17 Mch., 1945	......
	Lt. Cdr. A. C. Campbell, R.C.N.V.R.	11 Nov., 1942	22 Nov., 1943
	Lt. C. A. L. Maase, R.C.N.V.R.	23 Nov., 1943	24 Jan., 1945
	Lt. D. A. Dobson, R.C.N.V.R.	25 Jan., 1945	......

PRINCIPAL SHIPS OF THE ROYAL CANADIAN NAVY 1939-1945—*Continued*

Fairmiles	Commanding Officer	From	To
M.L. 091	Lt. S. C. Robinson, R.C.N.V.R.	17 May, 1943	8 Oct., 1943
	Sub/Lt. J. G. McClelland, R.C.N.V.R.	9 Oct., 1943	23 Nov., 1943
	Lt. F. H. B. Dewdney, R.C.N.V.R.	24 Nov., 1943	23 Mch., 1944
	Lt. R. A. Wyllie, R.C.N.V.R.	24 Mch., 1944	22 May, 1944
	Lt. E. B. Kendall, R.C.N.V.R.	23 May, 1944	....
M.L. 092	Lt. H. J. Browne, R.C.N.V.R.	28 Sept., 1942	8 Oct., 1943
	Lt. E. Leyland, R.C.N.V.R.	9 Oct., 1943	28 Oct., 1943
	Lt. G. L. Parker, R.C.N.V.R.	29 Oct., 1943	1 Feb., 1944
	Lt. R. Dickinson, R.C.N.V.R.	2 Feb., 1944	....
M.L. 093	Lt. D. M. Fraser, R.C.N.V.R.	2 Nov., 1942	27 Dec., 1942
	Lt. R. Carfrae, R.C.N.V.R.	28 Dec., 1942	1 Nov., 1943
	Lt. A. W. Murray, R.C.N.V.R.	2 Nov., 1943	18 Apl., 1944
	Lt. E. G. Arthurs, R.C.N.V.R.	19 Apl., 1944	21 Jan., 1945
	Lt. J. C. Austin, R.C.N.V.R.	22 Jan., 1945	....
M.L. 094	Lt. G. Marcil, R.C.N.V.R.	29 Nov., 1942	4 Mch., 1943
	Lt. A. P. Morrow, R.C.N.V.R.	5 Mch., 1943	21 Mch., 1943
	Sub/Lt. C. J. VanTighen, R.C.N.V.R.	22 Mch., 1943	8 Mch., 1944
	Lt. C. Carras, R.C.N.V.R.	9 Mch., 1944	....
M.L. 095	Lt. N. L. Williams, R.C.N.V.R.	21 Feb., 1944	....
M.L. 096	Lt. J. M. Lewis, R.C.N.V.R.	....	15 Apl., 1943
	Lt. T. H. Browne, R.C.N.V.R.	16 Apl., 1943	11 Aug., 1943
	Sub/Lt. A. M. Harper, R.C.N.V.R.	12 Aug., 1943	27 Aug., 1943
	Sub/Lt. R. W. Kettlewell, R.C.N.V.R.	28 Aug., 1943	26 Sept., 1944
	Lt. J. H. Morrison, R.C.N.V.R.	27 Sept., 1944	....
M.L. 097	Lt. E. P. Jones, R.C.N.V.R.	5 Jan., 1944	15 Sept., 1944
	Lt. J. H. Bailey, R.C.N.V.R.	16 Sept., 1944	....
M.L. 098	Sub/Lt. T. A. Welch, R.C.N.V.R.	7 Nov., 1942	18 Nov., 1945
	Lt. E. G. Jarvis, R.C.N.V.R.	19 Nov., 1943	18 Apl., 1944
	Lt. E. Desrosiers, R.C.N.V.R.	19 Apl., 1944	3 Dec., 1944

M.L. No.	Officer		
	Sub/Lt. D. R. DeLaporte, R.C.N.V.R.	4 Dec., 1944	16 Mch., 1945
	Sub/Lt. M. L. M. DeMartigny, R.C.N.V.R.	17 Mch., 1945	....
M.L. 099	Sub/Lt. G. G. D. Armour, R.C.N.V.R.	7 Mch., 1942	6 Nov., 1942
	Lt. G. M. Moors, R.C.N.V.R.	7 Nov., 1942	7 Oct., 1943
	Sub/Lt. P. G. D. Armour, R.C.N.V.R.	8 Oct., 1943	7 Jan., 1945
	Lt. J. B. LeMaistre, R.C.N.V.R.	8 Jan., 1945	....
M.L. 100	Lt. E. G. Scott, R.C.N.V.R.	8 Nov., 1942	16 Nov., 1943
	Lt. D. A. Dobson, R.C.N.V.R.	17 Nov., 1943	6 Jan., 1945
	Lt. J. R. Jenner, R.C.N.V.R.	7 Jan., 1945	7 Apl., 1945
	Lt. D. A. Dobson, R.C.N.V.R.	8 Apl., 1945	....
M.L. 101	Lt. A. A. MacLeod, R.C.N.V.R.	20 Oct., 1942	6 Nov., 1942
	Lt. P. B. C. Samson, R.C.N.V.R.	7 Nov., 1942	7 Nov., 1943
	Lt. P. B. Paine, R.C.N.V.R.	8 Nov., 1943	16 Nov., 1943
	Lt. G. L. James, R.C.N.V.R.	17 Nov., 1943	24 Jan., 1945
	Lt. F. H. B. Dewdney, R.C.N.V.R.	25 Jan., 1945	....
M.L. 102	Lt. B. C. Heintzman, R.C.N.V.R.	8 Oct., 1942	13 Nov., 1942
	Sub/Lt. H. M. Gordon, R.C.N.V.R.	14 Nov., 1942	24 Oct., 1943
	Lt. J. K. MacDonald, R.C.N.V.R.	25 Oct., 1943	....
M.L. 103	Lt. H. A. Agar, R.C.N.V.R.	18 Nov., 1942	21 June, 1943
	Lt. F. H. Galway, R.C.N.V.R.	22 June, 1943	6 Jan., 1945
	Lt. W. G. Lumsden, R.C.N.V.R.	7 Jan., 1945	26 Apl., 1945
	Lt. J. B. Barbeau, R.C.N.V.R.	27 Apl., 1945	....
M.L. 104	Lt. J. R. Culley, R.C.N.V.R.	8 Oct., 1943	3 Apl., 1944
	Lt. Cdr. J. W. Braidwood, R.C.N.V.R.	4 Apl., 1944	18 Feb., 1945
	Lt. F. H. Galway, R.C.N.V.R.	19 Feb., 1945	....
M.L. 105	Lt. J. D. Addison, R.C.N.V.R.	5 Sept., 1943	29 Aug., 1944
	Lt. W. P. T. McGhee, R.C.N.V.R.	30 Aug., 1944	....
M.L. 106	Sub/Lt. F. B. Pugh, R.C.N.V.R.	28 Aug., 1943	3 Jan., 1944
	Lt. C. F. W. Cooper, R.C.N.V.R.	4 Jan., 1944	17 Jan., 1945
	Lt. C. N. Blagrave, R.C.N.V.R.	18 Jan., 1945	....
M.L. 107	Lt. H. P. R. Brown, R.C.N.V.R.	25 Oct., 1943	....

PRINCIPAL SHIPS OF THE ROYAL CANADIAN NAVY 1939-1945—*Continued*

FAIRMILES	COMMANDING OFFICER	FROM	TO
M.L. 108	Lt. I. L. Campbell, R.C.N.V.R.	14 Aug., 1943	5 Apl., 1944
	Lt. K. M. Ross, R.C.N.V.R.	6 Apl., 1944	4 Feb., 1945
	Lt. P. C. Simpson, R.C.N.V.R.	5 Feb., 1945	....
M.L. 109	Lt. J. G. W. MacKenzie, R.C.N.V.R.	23 Aug., 1943	10 Oct., 1943
	Lt. J. S. Stephen, R.C.N.V.R.	11 Oct., 1943	....
M.L. 110	Lt. R. Dickinson, R.C.N.V.R.	......, 1943	10 Oct., 1943
	Lt. W. B. Bailey, R.C.N.V.R.	11 Oct., 1943	18 Oct., 1943
	Lt. H. A. Batey, R.C.N.V.R.	19 Oct., 1943	23 Jan., 1944
	Lt. J. U. MacFall, R.C.N.V.R.	24 Jan., 1944	6 Feb., 1945
	Lt. W. B. Bailey, R.C.N.V.R.	7 Feb., 1945	4 Apl., 1945
	Sub/Lt. R. R. Peirson, R.C.N.V.R.	5 Apl., 1945	....
M.L. 111	Lt. A. M. Harper, R.C.N.V.R.	30 Aug., 1943	5 Apl., 1944
	Lt. S. L. Burke, R.C.N.V.R.	6 Apl., 1944	6 Feb., 1945
	Lt. P. B. Paine, R.C.N.V.R.	7 Feb., 1945	....
M.L. 112	Lt. R. C. Denny, R.C.N.V.R.	25 Oct., 1943	18 Apl., 1944
	Lt. G. R. Brassard, R.C.N.V.R.	19 Apl., 1944	28 Apl., 1944
	Lt. W. R. Duggan, R.C.N.V.R.	29 Apl., 1944	....
M.L. 113	Lt. C. J. Holloway, R.C.N.V.R.	8 Nov., 1943	15 Sept., 1944
	Lt. E. R. Whitehouse, R.C.N.V.R.	16 Sept., 1944	20 Mch., 1945
	Lt. J. E. M. Jones, R.C.N.V.R.	21 Mch., 1945	....
M.L. 114	Lt. R. Synnette, R.C.N.V.R.	5 Nov., 1943	22 Oct., 1944
	Cdr. W. L. Moore, R.C.N.V.R.	23 Oct., 1944	28 Jan., 1945
	Lt. G. E. Rising, R.C.N.V.R.	29 Jan., 1945	13 Feb., 1945
	Lt. J. H. Osler, R.C.N.V.R.	14 Feb., 1945	....
M.L. 115	Lt. R. W. Kettlewell, R.C.N.V.R.	8 Nov., 1943	7 Feb., 1944
	Lt. C. R. Godbehere, R.C.N.V.R.	8 Feb., 1944	....
M.L. 116	Lt. E. P. Jones, R.C.N.V.R.	10 Apl., 1944	8 Sept., 1944
	Lt. J. D. Addison, R.C.N.V.R.	9 Sept., 1944	25 Mch., 1945

M.L.	Officer		
M.L. 117	Lt. J. D. Addison, R.C.N.V.R.	26 Mch., 1945	1 Apl., 1945
	Lt. W. A. Jay, R.C.N.V.R.	2 Apl., 1945	......
M.L. 118	Sub/Lt. E. H. Gudewill, R.C.N.V.R.	17 Dec., 1943	25 Jan., 1944
	Lt. G. E. Rising, R.C.N.V.R.	26 Jan., 1944	8 July, 1944
	Lt. J. G. Menzies, R.C.N.V.R.	9 July, 1944	......
M.L. 119	Sub/Lt. D. M. Collison, R.C.N.V.R.	2 Nov., 1943	19 Nov., 1943
	Lt. V. L. Wilgress, R.C.N.V.R.	20 Nov., 1943	19 Apl., 1944
	Lt. J. H. Osler, R.C.N.V.R.	20 Apl., 1944	10 Apl., 1945
	Lt. W. J. King, R.C.N.V.R.	11 Apl., 1945	......
M.L. 120	Lt. J. J. McLaughlin, R.C.N.V.R.	16 Oct., 1943	7 Mch., 1944
	Lt. F. H. B. Dewdney, R.C.N.V.R.	8 Mch., 1944	18 Mch., 1945
	Lt. W. G. Dale, R.C.N.V.R.	19 Mch., 1945	......
	Sub/Lt. H. K. Ralston, R.C.N.V.R.	10 Jan., 1944	21 Jan., 1944
	Lt. J. M. Todd, R.C.N.V.R.	22 Jan., 1944	19 Feb., 1944
	Lt. J. H. Stevenson, R.C.N.V.R.	20 Feb., 1944	21 Sept., 1944
	Lt. W. J. King, R.C.N.V.R.	22 Sept., 1944	29 Oct., 1944
	Lt. J. H. Stevenson, R.C.N.V.R.	30 Oct., 1944	21 Jan., 1945
	Sub/Lt. J. H. Joyce, R.C.N.V.R.	22 Jan., 1945	......
M.L. 121	Lt. R. N. McDiarmid, R.C.N.V.R.	17 Apl., 1944	16 Apl., 1945
	Lt. J. G. W. MacKenzie, R.C.N.V.R.	17 Apl., 1945	26 July, 1945
	Lt. Cdr. J. M. Todd, R.C.N.V.R.	27 July, 1945	......
M.L. 122	Lt. R. T. McKean, R.C.N.V.R.	10 Oct., 1944	......
M.L. 123	Lt. J. W. Shaw, R.C.N.V.R.	5 June, 1944	......
M.L. 124	Lt. E. S. Blanchet, R.C.N.V.R.	30 June, 1944	......
M.L. 125	Lt. J. E. Kendrick, R.C.N.V.R.	2 June, 1944	8 June, 1944
	Lt. F. J. Fiander, R.C.N.V.R.	9 June, 1944	......
M.L. 126	Lt. R. C. Denny, R.C.N.V.R.	29 July, 1944	24 Aug., 1944
	Lt. W. H. Davidson, R.C.N.V.R.	25 Aug., 1944	......
M.L. 127	Lt. J. M. Lewis, R.C.N.V.R.	25 Sept., 1944	17 Nov., 1944
	Lt. C. K. D. Smith, R.C.N.V.R.	18 Nov., 1944	......

FAIRMILES	COMMANDING OFFICER	FROM	TO
M.L. 128	Lt. R. K. Baker, R.C.N.V.R.	4 July, 1944	28 July, 1944
	Lt. E. S. Ray, R.C.N.V.R.	29 July, 1944	11 Jan., 1945
	Lt. G. E. Devlin, R.C.N.V.R.	12 Jan., 1945	10 June, 1945
	Lt. B. J. Arnet, R.C.N.V.R.	11 June, 1945	......
M.L. 129	Lt. G. L. James, R.C.N.V.R.	25 Sept., 1944	30 May, 1945
	Lt. E. L. MacDonald, R.C.N.V.R.	31 May, 1945	......
M.T.B. 459	Lt. C. A. Law, R.C.N.V.R.	26 Jan., 1944	11 Sept., 1944
	Lt. J. H. Shand, R.C.N.V.R.	12 Sept., 1944	......
M.T.B. 460	Lt. D. Killam, D.S.C., R.C.N.V.R.	25 Feb., 1944	......
M.T.B. 461	Lt. C. A. Burk, D.S.C., R.C.N.V.R.	28 Feb., 1944	17 Sept., 1944
	Lt. T. K. Scobie, R.C.N.V.R.	18 Sept., 1944	8 Feb., 1945
	Lt. J. R. Cunningham, R.C.N.V.R.	9 Feb., 1945	......
M.T.B. 462	Lt. R. J. Moyse, R.C.N.V.R.	1 Mch., 1944	9 Oct., 1944
	Lt. R. P. B. Graham, R.C.N.V.R.	10 Oct., 1944	23 Jan., 1945
	Lt. R. Paddon, R.C.N.V.R.	24 Jan., 1945	......
M.T.B. 463	Lt. D. G. Creba, R.C.N.V.R.	16 Mch., 1944	......
M.T.B. 464	Lt. L. C. Bishop, R.C.N.V.R. D.S.C.	26 Mch., 1944	24 Feb., 1945
	Lt. C. V. Barlow, R.C.N.V.R.	25 Feb., 1945	......
M.T.B. 465	Lt. C. D. Chaffey, R.C.N.V.R.	27 Mch., 1944	8 Feb., 1945
	Sub/Lt. J. F. Howard, R.C.N.V.R.	9 Feb., 1945	......
M.T.B. 466	Lt. G. E. Bampton, R.C.N.V.R.	18 Apl., 1944	7 Jan., 1945
	Lt. S. B. Marshall, R.C.N.V.R.	29 Mch., 1944	17 Apl., 1944
	Lt. J. M. Adams, R.C.N.V.R.	8 Jan., 1945	......
M.T.B. 485	Lt. D. G. Creba, R.C.N.V.R.	31 July, 1944	......
M.T.B. 486	Lt. Cdr. C. A. Law, R.C.N.V.R.	5 Aug., 1944	24 Feb., 1945
	Lt. C. D. Chaffey, R.C.N.V.R.	25 Feb., 1945	

M.T.B. 491	Lt. C. A. Burk, R.C.N.V.R. D.S.C. Lt. R. J. Moyse, R.C.N.V.R.	4 Oct., 1944 27 Jan., 1945	26 Jan., 1945 ....
M.T.B. 726	Lt. A. P. Morrow, R.C.N.V.R.	1 Feb., 1944	....
M.T.B. 727	Lt. L. R. McLernon, R.C.N.V.R. D.S.C. Lt. G. D. Pattison, R.C.N.V.R.	7 Jan., 1944 5 Apl., 1945	4 Apl., 1945 ....
M.T.B. 735	Lt. J. W. Collins, R.C.N.V.R. Lt. J. E. Davidson, R.C.N.V.R. Lt. J. R. Culley, R.C.N.V.R.	14 Feb., 1944 .... 3 Oct., 1944	.... 2 Oct., 1944 ....
M.T.B. 736	Lt. S. O. Greening, R.C.N.V.R. Lt. J. R. Tale, R.C.N.V.R. Lt. A. M. Byers, R.C.N.V.R.	29 Mch., 1944 10 Apl., 1944 23 Oct., 1944	9 Apl., 1944 22 Oct., 1944 ....
M.T.B. 743	Lt. M. C. Knox, R.C.N.V.R.	27 Mch., 1944	....
M.T.B. 744	Lt. G. M. Moors, R.C.N.V.R.	14 Feb., 1944	....
M.T.B. 745	Lt. O. B. Mabee, R.C.N.V.R.	15 Jan., 1944	....
M.T.B. 746	Lt. J. W. Collins, R.C.N.V.R.	11 Dec., 1944	....
M.T.B. 748	Lt. D. B. Wilson, R.C.N.V.R. Lt. Cdr. J. R. H. Kirkpatrick, R.C.N.V.R. Lt. R. C. Smith, R.C.N.V.R.	10 Jan., 1944 26 Jan., 1944 20 Mch., 1945	25 Jan., 1944 19 Mch., 1945 ....
M.T.B. 797	Lt. R. C. Smith, R.C.N.V.R. Lt. J. G. McClelland, R.C.N.V.R.	11 Oct., 1943 10 Dec., 1944	9 Dec., 1944 ....

APPENDIX IV

Canadian Landing Craft in Operation Neptune

528th Canadian L.C.A. Flotilla—(Carried in PRINCE HENRY)

L.C.A. 856............Lt. J. C. Davie, R.C.N.V.R., *Flotilla Officer*

1372............Lt. G. E. Nuttal, R.C.N.V.R.

736............Lt. G. W. Hendry, R.C.N.V.R.

1033............Sub.-Lt. J. A. Flynn, R.C.N.V.R.

850............L/Smn. P. Duchnicky, R.C.N.V.R.

1021............L/Smn. D. Townson, R.C.N.V.R.

925............L/Smn. Moody, R.C.N.V.R.

1371............A/B Mellway, R.C.N.V.R.

529th Canadian L.C.A. Flotilla—(Carried in PRINCE DAVID)

L.C.A. 1150............Lt. R. G. Buckingham, R.C.N.V.R., *Flotilla Officer*

1375............Lt. G. E. Allin, R.C.N.V.R.

1059............Lt. J. McBeath, R.C.N.V.R.

1151............Lt. D. Graham, R.C.N.V.R.

1138............Lt. J. Beveridge, R.C.N.V.R.

1137............L/Smn. Le Vergne, R.C.N.

260th Canadian L.C.I. Flotilla (Landing Craft, Infantry—Large)

Flotilla Officer...........Lt.-Cdr. H. Doheny, R.C.N.V.R.

L.C.I. 117............Lt. R. L. Gordon, R.C.N.V.R.

121............Lt. D. H. Botly, R.C.N.V.R.

166............Lt. G. M. Oliver, R.C.N.V.R.

177............Lt. W. C. Gardner, R.C.N.V.R.

249............Lt. J. E. O'Rourke, R.C.N.V.R.

266............Lt. J. G. Wenman, R.C.N.V.R.

271............Lt. W. R. Sinclair, R.C.N.V.R.

277............Lt. W. H. M. Ballantyne, R.C.N.R.

285............Lt. H. S. Square, R.C.N.V.R.

298............Lt. J. S. Monteith, R.C.N.V.R.

301............Lt. R. M. Smith, R.C.N.V.R.

262nd Canadian L.C.I. Flotilla (Landing Craft, Infantry—Large)

Flotilla Officer..........Lt.-Cdr. H. T. Huston, R.C.N.V.R.

L.C.I. *115*.............Lt. V. D. Ramsay, R.C.N.V.R.

118.............Lt. C. R. Bond, R.C.N.V.R.

125.............Lt. C. R. Parker, D.S.C., R.C.N.V.R.

135.............Lt. J. D. Kell, R.C.N.V.R.

250.............Lt. H. M. Harrison, R.C.N.V.R.

252.............Lt. R. E. St. J. Wakefield, R.C.N.V.R.

262.............Lt. P. R. Hinton, R.C.N.V.R.

263.............Lt. J. B. B. Shaw, R.C.N.V.R.

270.............Lt. A. C. Clark, R.C.N.V.R.

276.............Lt. A. A. Wedd, D.S.C., R.C.N.V.R.

299.............Lt. W. B. McGregor, R.C.N.V.R.

306.............Lt. A. K. Stephens, R.C.N.V.R.

264th Canadian L.C.I. Flotilla (Landing Craft, Infantry—Large)

Flotilla Officer..........Lt.-Cdr. L. S. Kyle, R.C.N.V.R.

L.C.I. *255*.............Lt. H. E. Trenholme, R.C.N.V.R.

288.............Lt. W. E. Charron, R.C.N.V.R.

295.............Lt. P. G. R. Campbell, R.C.N.V.R.

302.............Lt. J. M. Ruttan, D.S.C., R.C.N.V.R.

305.............Lt. C. B. MacKay, R.C.N.V.R.

310.............Lt. L. Williams, R.C.N.V.R.

311.............Lt. D. J. Lewis, R.C.N.V.R.

R.C.N. Beach Commando "W"—in Operation Neptune

Principal Beach Master..........Lt.Cdr. D. J. O'Hagan, G.M. and Bar, R.C.N.V.R.

Deputy Principal Beach Master......................A/Lt.-Cdr. R. J. Johnstone, R.C.N.V.R.

Beach Master W.1.............Lt. D. M. Sutherland, R.C.N.V.R.

Beach Master W. 2.............Lt. A. D. Rayburn, R.C.N.V.R.

Beach Master W. 3.............Lt. F. Angus, R'C.N.V.R.

GENERAL INDEX

INDEX OF SHIPS

511

INDEX OF SHIPS

INDEX OF SHIPS